D1318913

The Practice of
Collective Bargaining

THE IRWIN SERIES IN ECONOMICS

Consulting Editor
LLOYD G. REYNOLDS
Yale University

The Practice of Collective Bargaining

EDWIN F. BEAL
Professor of Management
University of Oregon

EDWARD D. WICKERSHAM
Late of the University of Detroit

PHILIP KIENAST
Assistant Professor
Department of Management and Organization
University of Washington

FOURTH EDITION • 1972

Richard D. Irwin, Inc. *Homewood, Illinois 60430*
IRWIN-DORSEY LIMITED *Georgetown, Ontario*

© RICHARD D. IRWIN, INC., 1959, 1963, 1967, and 1972

All rights reserved. No part of this publication may be reproduced, stored in a retrieval system, or transmitted, in any form or by any means, electronic, mechanical, photocopying, recording, or otherwise, without the prior written permission of the publisher.

First Printing, April 1972

Library of Congress Catalog Card No. 70–141398

Printed in the United States of America

To EDWARD DEAN WICKERSHAM
1927–1966

PREFACE

The fourth edition of this book goes to press at the outset of what President Nixon calls Phase II of his economic program. The aim, he says, is to halt or, at any rate, slow down inflation. The method is, in part, to limit the wage raises unions might otherwise seek, and management grant.

In a reversal of previous policy and pronouncements, the President opened Phase I on August 15, 1971, by freezing wages and prices for 90 days. Phase II rescinds the outright freeze but sets up machinery for controlling prices and wages. A Pay Board representing labor, management, and the public is to pass on proposed wage increases and make sure they conform to policy guidelines the administration lays down.

This is not the first time in the 20th century that the government has taken a hand in shaping decisions that ordinarily come out of collective bargaining. In both world wars, and in the Korean war, agencies set up by government and acting with government authority have regulated wages. Perhaps more surprising than the imposition of controls, despite the drama of the August 15th announcement, is that they took so long in coming, for the war in Indochina has become the longest war in U.S. history. As this book goes to press, the end is not in sight; neither are the end results of the anti-inflationary measures, including wage controls.

In spite of controls, and regardless of what may happen to wage levels, organized workers and their employers will continue to bargain and negotiate, for, as this book makes clear, money wages and salaries are by no means all they bargain about. Labor and management over the years have not only failed to find a better way of regulating their relations with each other, but nothing as good; and while the institutional arrangements are not perfect and the results not always what the public—or, for that matter, the bargainers—want, unions and employers continue to gain experience and improve procedures. Those critics and commentators who from time to time have pronounced unions obsolete and collective bargaining outworn have once again proved wrong. The contrary is true: Collective bargaining is alive and well.

Since the preceding, third edition of this book was published, government employees who had hitherto been slow to unionize have turned by the millions to the collective bargaining way of regulating work relations with their public sector employers—federal, state, and local. Teachers, and even college professors, bargain collectively with school boards, boards of regents, and university administrations. Agricultural workers, too, though specifically excluded from the protection of federal labor law, have taken up the traditional union weapons of strike and boycott to win bargaining rights on the big farms, orchards, and vineyards—the "factories in the fields"—of the southwest. At this writing, the only sizable segment of the nation's work force that is not already decisively unionized is the white collar workers in the private sector. And who knows?—perhaps Phase II and the example of white collar workers in the public sector may bring them to collective bargaining too.

Through its three previous editions, this book has kept pace with developments in American labor-management relations. Changes in this fourth edition, over the third, aim at making the book shorter, clearer, and more relevant to the needs and interests of students of labor-management relations in the decade of the 1970s. Two chapters have been dropped, two added, and four extensively rewritten and revised. There are fewer cases, but those retained have proved to be most useful, and those added have been chosen for greater variety and applicability to the present day. They include cases from the public sector.

One chapter that appeared in the third but has been dropped from the fourth edition dealt with collective bargaining in other countries. Reports from the field showed that very little use was made of this chapter. Another omission is last edition's "crystal ball" chapter on the future of collective bargaining. It was written when automation was the big question-mark in labor-management relations, and it hazarded some predictions on how management and the unions would adjust through collective bargaining to acute technological change.

Events were kind to the chapter. Most of its predictions came true; but the issue is largely disposed of today, and well understood. It belongs to the past now, not the immediate future. The substitute chapters, entirely new to this edition, look through no crystal ball, but deal with an aspect of collective bargaining that is new, active today, and likely to show increasing activity in the future. That is public employee bargaining and negotiations. Law and custom differ in the public sector, but union and employer aims are similar, and both look to the experience in private sector bargaining for guidelines to their own activities.

Although much more work still needs to be done before the intricacies of collective bargaining can be adequately explained, this book attempts to analyze the practice of collective bargaining in two "model" situations: (1) handicraft industry and craft unionism; (2) mass production industry and industrial unionism. Variants upon these models are noted among professional associations and in the public sector. The viewpoint of this book is set in perspective against developments in the theory of collective bargaining, the ongoing research of behavioral scientists, and the onward march of economic and social progress. The probable effects of recent and anticipated changes in the structure of employment in the United States on collective bargaining are analyzed.

The conclusions set forth in these pages came out of the experience of the authors as teachers, consultants, arbitrators, and representatives in collective bargaining situations in the United States and Europe. Some of this experience dates back as far as the mid-thirties when the CIO was making its first sweep through American industry. Most of the material presented here has been used by the authors in the college classroom and special refresher courses for management and union representatives. Teachers and students who have used this material have been most helpful in suggesting ways of clarifying the issues and improving the presentation of materials.

Some of the explanations and interpretations given by the authors may be found, like other writings in this far-from-settled field, to be controversial. The authors take full responsibility for all such statements of position and for errors or omissions that have eluded them in preparing the material for the press.

The authors are grateful to many people for their constructive criticism and helpful suggestions. Their greatest debt is to Professor Lloyd G. Reynolds of Yale University for reading the first edition manuscript and for his valuable and helpful comments then, and since. Professor Dale S. Beach of Rensselaer Polytechnic Institute provided constructive criticism and valuable suggestions that were incorporated in the revised edition. Professor Thomas W. Gavett, West Virginia University, Professor Dalton E. McFarland, Michigan State University, Professor Thomas H. Patten, Jr., University of Detroit, and Professor Dell Bush Johannesen, University of North Carolina, provided valuable comments that are incorporated in the third and fourth editions.

Many publishers generously granted permission to reproduce copyrighted material. Special thanks are due to the Bureau of National Affairs, Inc., for the use of cases in Part V[1] of the book. Thanks are also due to: the American Arbitration Association; the American Management Association; the Bureau of National Affairs, Inc.; Commerce Clearing House; the Committee for Economic Development; the Economic Research Department of the Chamber of Commerce of the United States; the Foundation on Employee Health, Medical Care and Welfare, Inc.; *Harvard Business Review;* Division of Research, Graduate School of Business Administration, Harvard University; *Industrial and Labor Relations Review; Industrial Management Review;* Industrial Relations Counselors, Inc.; New York State School of Industrial and Labor Relations at Cornell University; National Industrial Conference Board; Prentice-Hall, Inc.; Public Affairs Press; Professor George Strauss; and

---

[1] The Bureau of National Affairs, Inc., publisher of *Labor Arbitration Reports,* provided the material used in Cases 6 and 7, 9–13, and 15–35. Credit to the arbitrator of these and other cases is given in the introduction to the cases themselves.

John Wiley & Sons, Inc. As in the case of noncopyrighted AFL–CIO and governmental sources, appropriate credit is shown at the places where this material is used.

March 1972   EDWIN F. BEAL
                                                 PHILIP KIENAST

CONTENTS

PART I

Organizing for Collective Bargaining

Part I of this book explores the nature of the collective bargaining system in the United States and the parties who have a vital interest in the operation of the system. It deals primarily with formal organizations designed to represent the interests of employers, workers, and the general public, and presents historical background on the unions and collective bargaining.

Chapter 1

THE COLLECTIVE BARGAINING SYSTEM

Collective bargaining centers in the enterprise, where workers and managers meet. From there, it has to look outward and upward into the international unions and union federations, the employer organizations, the government agencies concerned with labor relations. It also has to look inward and downward to the departments that make up the enterprise, the work groups in the departments, the cliques and factions in the local union. The point of view remains that of the enterprise; for the enterprise—not the industry, not the state or nation—is the highest autonomous unit of economic activity in capitalist society. The enterprise and the local union: these are what take up the foreground of the field of view in the study of collective bargaining; and collective bargaining is the only study that takes them both in and concentrates on their relationship.

It is quite true, as later chapters in this book will show, that there is a trend toward carrying the practice of collective bargaining to higher levels, above the individual enterprise. Many of today's labor agreements are reached by unions and associations of employers rather than, in the first instance, between a local union and its enterprise. That does not take collective bargaining out of the enterprise. The rules laid down in the master agreement reach into the enterprise. They almost always have to leave important questions to be settled specifically and in detail at enterprise level. Local agreements supplement the master agreements and apply their terms to the local situation. Furthermore, administering and enforcing agreement terms is always an enterprise responsibility: management's and the local union's. One field of enormous present importance deals almost exclusively with enterprise incidents and issues: that is industrial arbitration.

This book makes no apologies for centering the study of collective bargaining in the enterprise, and on the relations between its management and the members and officers of the local union. It is from this vantage point that the entire system can best be seen in meaningful perspective. But enterprises differ from each other. So do unions; and so, consequently, do the relations between them. No single enterprise is more than a unit—

3

often an inconsiderable one—of the total economy whose markets bind together the whole system of production and exchange of goods and services. In the same way, collective bargaining, which is specific and particular in the enterprise, goes on there as a part and extension of an entire system, the industrial relations system. This is a subsystem of the general social system, and collective bargaining is one of the forms it takes.

The concept of the industrial relations system as a subsystem of the enveloping social system comes from the work of John T. Dunlop, one of the scholars who have attempted to explain collective bargaining in a theoretical setting in the present day.

Dunlop is a prolific writer on economics and on many specific issues of collective bargaining. He brought together some of his ideas on collective bargaining theory, considering the matter as a whole, in a single book, *Industrial Relations Systems,* published in 1958. The introductory first chapter of this book states Dunlop's position in summary form.

It is hard to still further compress ideas already stated in concentrated form, but the main points can be outlined. The writers of this book accept the general framework Dunlop laid down, borrow from it, and acknowledge their debt to him, but do not follow him exactly. What follows is a paraphrase and not a reproduction of Dunlop's thoughts; it rearranges the order of his presentation, but it sticks to the line of argument he laid down and builds upon the base he laid.

THE INDUSTRIAL RELATIONS SYSTEM

Dunlop sees the industrial relations system as a set of relationships between people in society which take place under particular conditions. This can be studied—abstracted—in exactly the way economists study market relations, and political scientists, power relations. The industrial relations system, like the economic system and the political system, is a subsystem of the general social system. All three of these subsystems overlap in part and interact with the others. The industrial relations system, Dunlop says, may be studied in terms of what he calls three contexts. These are the market context, the context of technology at the workplace, and the context of power relations of the enveloping society, as reflected in the workplace.

The Three Contexts

Every enterprise or organization lives and grows (or withers and dies) by satisfying (or failing to satisfy) some human need and effective market demand, whether this be for cigarette lighters or for child welfare services. This is true for the private enterprise, and it is just as true for the governmental agency or nonprofit private organization, where the "market" consists of the budgetary limitations within which the agency must operate. No enterprise can, in the long run, put more into its operation than it gets out of the market. Thus in any given period the market context limits the possibilities open to any given enterprise. The market therefore has a hand in determining the technology of the workplace, which is the second limiting context of the industrial relations system. For example, the mass market for cars at prices buyers are willing to pay practically dictates the technology of mass production and pushes the manufacturers toward automation. Relations between workers and managers in a Detroit factory today take shape in these contexts.

In turn, the technology of the workplace (or work flow, and the kind of jobs created at individual stations along the work flow) determines the kind of people brought into the production process in any given enterprise, and their relations with each other. The sizable remnant of handicraft technology upon which the construction industry still depends brings into that industry the skilled building trades worker who has served a trade apprenticeship and mastered his craft. Mass-production industry, on the other hand, calls mainly for semiskilled workers who get their training on the job. Such jobs consist of simple and usually repetitive tasks, easily learned and leading to no comprehensive mastery of a complex set of skills. In this way both the qualifications of the individual employees and their relations to the work, to those who manage and direct their efforts, and to each other grow out of the technology of the workplace, and work flows.

It may be worthwhile at this point to make clear the concept of workplace technology, as seen by the authors of this book. There are, as they see it, three technologies: handicraft, mass production, and automation.

In *handicraft* production, the goods produced or services rendered and sold by the employer are turned out directly by the labor of skilled craftsmen, working with their hands and with hand tools. These skilled men may have nonskilled helpers, but it is what the skilled men do that transforms the raw materials into the finished product. Thus there may be those who haul bricks and mortar to a construction site, but each brick is placed in the wall, by hand, by a bricklayer who has spent years learning his trade. Neither the contractor nor the construction foreman needs to tell this man *how* to do his job—he knows that; all they need to tell him is *what* they want him to do.

In *mass-production* manufacturing the employer's product is turned out directly by nonskilled operators, working with their hands or with machines, assisted by a few skilled workers. In an automobile assembly plant, for example, the employee working at any station along the line does only a simple, small part of what it takes to put a car together. This employee comes on the job without knowing either what he is to do or how to do it. Management trains him on the job, may even rigidly prescribe the exact bodily motions he has to make to complete his operation cycle. The movement of the conveyor paces the speed at which he works.

He is a semiskilled worker. Others more skilled than he may help him, by making the tools and dies, the jigs and fixtures that he uses, or they may set up or repair and maintain his machines; but it is he and his counterparts, the semiskilled, who turn out the product. There is a wide range of semiskills, from almost completely unskilled work to tasks requiring the highest degree of expertise. The difference between expertise and skill in this context is that the expert is a specialist, the skilled worker a generalist in his trade. Later chapters in this book will deal with the question more fully.

Under the technology of *automation*, the product is literally turned out by machines without direct human labor, skilled or nonskilled. Technicians program the work, which the machines perform otherwise unaided. Skilled craftsmen maintain and repair the machines. Semiskilled workers "supervise" the machines; that is, they see that the machines are kept supplied, that nothing occurs that might cause a malfunction, and they turn the machines on and off as necessary or when directed.

These are the three technologies, in their historical order. Mass production displaced handicraft technology in manufacturing wherever there was a mass market. It proved capable of bringing products into common use, like airplanes and refrigerators, that were beyond the practical reach of handicraft technology. It did not exterminate the handicrafts: they flourish today in local and luxury or specialty markets. Automation now seems to be displacing mass production in many areas, but not in all. Automation depends to an even greater degree on mass markets. It cannot completely drive out either mass production or the handicrafts. The three technologies will serve different sectors of the market, different consumer needs.

The three technologies show most clearly in manufacturing, but have their application in the extractive, distributive, and service industries. This will be examined in later chapters. Also, the three general technologies described in principle above take on reality and concrete form in application to various industries, and, within an industry, to an enterprise. Each workplace may be said to have its own technology. This consists of the application of one or more of the three basic technologies, objectified in actual machines and equipment arranged in a specific layout of work stations, designed to carry out the processes of the particular enterprise.

The third of Dunlop's contexts is that of the power relations of the enveloping social system, as reflected in the enterprise. This is probably the hardest to grasp and to explain. It means the influence, authority, prestige, or power managers and workers have outside the shop, that follows them into the shop and affects their relations toward each other. Thus in a country where workers have the right to vote, they stand in a quite different relation to their employer—a fellow citizen—than do workers in a country governed by a feudal or dictatorial regime. The authors of this book consider that collective bargaining is part of the power context in the industrial relations system. When employees organize in an "outside" union, they alter the power context inside the enterprise. The act of organizing is itself a reflection of the power relations of the enveloping social system, which must be such as to tolerate or encourage union organization.

The Contexts Are Dynamic

It should be noted at this point, and never forgotten, that the three contexts are not static elements but dynamic forces. They change; they interact. A context stands as given only for a single period, or point of time, in a particular analysis, not for eternity.

In a given market context, for instance, changes in technology can generate forces that change the market which, in turn, encourages the spread of that technology. Thus at the time of the Industrial Revolution, a growing, but still only potential, mass market welcomed the developing technology of mass production, initially of textiles but subsequently of other factory-made goods. The availability of cheap, high-quality factory products in turn strengthened the market and swept competing handicraft products off the counter.

The United States provides another example drawn from the early years of this century. An existing demand for means of local transportation was met through the local manufacture, by handicraft methods, of horse-drawn buggies and wagons. The earliest automobiles were also custom built by handicraft methods and sold in a luxury market—rich people to whom the mechanical buggies were a new toy and a visible symbol of their wealth. Then Henry Ford adapted the technology of mass production to the new product and began the serialized manufacture of a cheap and practical car, the famous Model T. The Model T welded the scattered local markets of the carriage makers into a national mass market for gas-powered vehicles. Anyone wanting now to serve this market had to compete with Henry Ford and had to adopt mass-production technology.

It ought not to be necessary to multiply examples to underscore the interdependence and interaction of the contexts.

These three contexts make up one of the theoretical concepts Dunlop offers. Another constitutes his identification of what he calls the actors. Who are the actors?

The Actors

Dunlop uses the word "actors" to refer to the participants or parties to industrial relations activity. There seems to be no good reason not to follow his terminology. There are three actors: (1) managers and their hierarchy both within the enterprise and in employer associations at levels above the enterprise; (2) workers and their hierarchy of organized representatives within the enterprise and above or beyond it; and (3) agents of government who play specific roles in the industrial relations system, plus nongovernmental agents and agencies (such as, for example, arbitrators) called into being by the other actors.

The actors, as identified by Dunlop, are groups of individuals or organizations. It would be well at the outset to consider what brings individuals into the following groupings: (1) the worker and the enterprise, (2) the worker and the local union, and (3) the local union with other union organizations. In a free society, each of these relationships must be based on a degree of mutual consent—a mutually beneficial exchange.

The potential work force of a modern enterprise consists of individuals who are free to contract for their own labor. Of their own free will they may decline a particular offer of employment; but they are driven by individual needs to accept *some* offer, for without a job most people cannot live except on charity. The needs of the individual and the needs of the enterprise are reciprocal. Every individual needs to find a job, and to hold a job or jobs, and to earn a decent living at acceptable levels of effort. The reciprocal needs of the enterprise are to find suitable employees, to hold an appropriate work force, and to get competitive productivity from that work force. The relationship of the worker to the enterprise is explored in greater detail in Chapter 3.

A worker joins and remains a member of a union either because he considers it to be to his advantage or because he believes that the disadvantages of nonmembership outweigh the disadvantages of membership. He may want to belong to a union because he believes that this membership will raise his wages, or give him status, or provide an opportunity for pleasant social contacts, or he may accept union membership only because he feels that this is less onerous than losing his job or enduring social ostracism from his fellow workers.

Union affiliation usually goes beyond simple membership in an autonomous local union. Union associations beyond the individual and autonomous enterprises of the local unions are, in part, a rational recognition of market and political forces beyond the enterprise, which if not met in a unified way may seriously impede the effectiveness of the autonomous units. Thus it is reasonable to expect that individual and autonomous unions of Chrysler, Ford, and General Motors workers would have certain market interests in common and would form a supralocal union to deal with these problems. On the political scene, a federation of 15 million members would be a more influential spokesman than 75,000 autonomous but unconnected locals representing the same membership.

Managers.   Managers are the most important actors because they establish the enterprise, set its goals, exercise initiative in choosing the technology to be employed, and ultimately are accountable for the success or failure of the enterprise. Managers create and control the institution which provides employment opportunities. Chapter 3 discusses the problems confronting managers in creating an organization for effective employee relations. The discussion in Chapter 3 will deal with such matters as the relationship between the output of an enterprise, its size, geographic location, and ownership, and the nature of its organizational structure for effective employee relations.

Employee Organizations. This book argues that there are two "model" types of employee representative organizations, craft unions and industrial unions, and a third that combines some of the attributes of both, amalgamated unions. Since references to the models will occur throughout the book, it would be well to introduce them now. Chapter 4 compares the models in the course of a discussion of union organizational structure and examines their applicability to professional associations that engage in collective bargaining.

The Craft Union Model. Handicraft technology is the technological context in which craft unions appear. The building construction industry is the most prominent example of handicraft technology in modern American industry. Handicraft industry consists of enterprises in which the employer sells a product or service which is turned out directly by the hands of craftsmen. These craftsmen are workers who have served an apprenticeship or have learned by long experience an entire recognized trade, such as plumbing, carpentry, sheet metal work, or electricity.

Skilled labor here is a *direct* factor of production. Without the skilled labor of trained tradesmen, working with hand or power tools, the employer would have no product or service to sell. If he could not find skilled workers, he could not run his business, for it takes time to train skilled workers; indeed, it takes years. If he lost his skilled workers, production would stop, for there is no substitute for their skill.

The construction industry depends upon and uses to this day the handicraft method of production. Its product market is local. Construction work is carried out on the spot by skilled workers, who bring their efforts to bear on the building as it grows in place. Nonskilled workers may haul bricks to a construction site, but the brick is laid in the wall by qualified bricklayers who have served trade apprenticeships and are skilled tradesmen.

Job content in any given area of skill is the same; one carpenter performs the same kind of work as another carpenter; one roofer does the same job as another. Every skilled worker must at various times perform each of a range of tasks associated with the trade. In any given craft the worker qualifications are the same. Each worker must command a certain range of knowledge and of manual skills, common and traditional to the craft. The consequence is that in the handicrafts, for any given craft, labor is homogeneous. It is not entirely surprising, then, to find workers organized according to their particular skills into separate craft unions.

"One skill, one union" might well be the slogan of craft unions. The local craft union takes in all the craftsmen of its trade in any particular locality, and no others. (This may include, however, helpers and ap-prentices.) When these skilled men go on the job the employer does not have to tell them or show them *how* to do the work. They know how. He only needs to tell them *what* they are to do. They take it from there.

While it may not be surprising to find craft unions organized along lines of skill, it is still necessary to explain why they do actually so organize. A general contractor employs not only carpenters but masons, bricklayers, plumbers, plasterers—an entire array of skills. Why should not all of these be organized in a single union to bargain for them all with their common employer? Again the context of technology supplies the answer.

Erecting a building calls for the use of skills *in sequence.* At one time the only work performed at a building site is clearing the land and excava-tion. This is work for pick and shovel men, who are unskilled laborers, or for the semiskilled cat and bulldozer operators who have replaced them. Next, there is the rough carpentry work in the construction of forms for pouring concrete foundations; and work for masons, eventually for brick-layers, perhaps for ironworkers, certainly for carpenters. The plasterers, the painters, the sheet metal workers, the roofers, and many other crafts do not come on the job until later. By the time the electrician has wired the building, for instance, there is usually no further need for masonry workers.

Thus the personnel, the skills involved, and the actual crews employed are seldom the same from one week to the next. There is much overlap; but any given construction project, if surveyed at different points in time, will show a different composition of the work force.

The labor market reflects this technological need of the construction industry. For efficient operation it is necessary to have pools of all the various skills, from which any given construction project may draw at just the time such skills are needed on the job. It is also necessary that those employed when their skills are needed should be released when the need is over, so that they may go on to another project at a different stage of development. The employer needs to have the skills held separate, and administered separately, so that he may get the men he wants when he needs them and let them go when he is through with them. No contractor could afford to keep a crew of painters on his payroll from the time he broke ground just to paint the finished structure, nor to retain the opera-tors of the ground-moving equipment after the foundations had been laid.

The result of these necessary conditions, established by the context of the product market and the context of technology, is to bring into being as an actor, opposite the enterpriser, an entire galaxy of local unions organized by skills: craft unions. The fact of unionization introduces a new element in the context of power relations which influence the work-place rules and give rise to craft union practices.

At heart, craft unions are conservative. They guard and hoard an ancient skill and tradition that goes back to the medieval guilds. Though not direct descendants of the guilds, craft unions are their counterparts in today's changed situation and perform for our society the handicraft services the guilds performed for theirs. They are fraternities, entered by initiation and apprenticeship, practicing—as the guilds did—a "mystery," the secrets of the trade.

They make their bargains over wages by a strategy of bidding a restricted supply against what they conceive to be a fixed or relatively fixed demand. The essentially economic nature of their activity gives them a "lump of work" mentality that is hard to alter.

Scarcity of work, scarcity of skills, scarcity of product (always, of course, in relative terms) are the concepts in which craft unions deal in a scarcity sector—the handicraft sector—of the economy. They more often resist than welcome innovation; they more often resist than gladly adopt devices (such as skill-saving machinery) that would change the ways and habits of the craft.

A society moving restlessly and relentlessly forward into the abundance and the potentially limitless production made possible by factory methods puts craft unions on the defensive. The defensive position is a strong one wherever handicraft methods still prevail. Well-entrenched craft unions have even held their own in places where technology has conquered some of the problems of their craft. Craft unions and craft-union bargaining will be with us for a long time.

The Industrial Union Model. Mass-production technology carries even further the *division of labor* by the breakdown of a set of what were formerly skilled operations into a series of simple tasks. No individual is the craftsman of the product turned out by a factory. Instead, the entire factory becomes a composite, or collective, craftsman. Its few skilled workers do not turn out the production; all they do is help the other workers, by preparing work for them, repairing, or setting up their machines. The bulk of the employees are nonskilled. They have come to be called *semiskilled* workers.

Unlike the craftsman, the semiskilled operator has not spent years of apprenticeship or mastered a recognized trade. He learns on the job, while working. He comes to the job without any knowledge of its tasks. The training he gets does not take long. The jobs are easily learned, and each of the workers specializes in a very minor part of the total process. This specialization may in some cases reach the point of a very high degree of *expertise*. It differs from the skill of a craftsman in that it is specialized rather than general, and often not applicable to anything but the particular processes of the workplace where it is exercised.

At this point it would be desirable to draw the distinction carefully between skill and expertise. In common parlance, the work "skill" is very loosely used. For the purposes of this exposition, it needs a tighter definition. What is meant here by *skill* is the range of knowledge, ability, manual dexterity, and performance capability that is mastered through an apprenticeship in one of the recognized trades.[1]

What is meant by *expertise* is expertness, deftness, ability, or knowledge of some specialized task or group of tasks, such as can be acquired only through experience at that task, or on the job which groups those tasks. Perhaps an illustration of each of these terms will make them clearer.

Driving an automobile is often loosely called a skill. A persons starts out very timidly and clumsily, learns by instruction and experience, and gradually gets better at driving, the more hours he spends behind the wheel. Under the definition used in this chapter, that would be expertise. This expertise may become further specialized. The driver of a heavy truck gets to be expert at rolling his big rig uphill and down, swinging it around right-angle corners, and backing it into crowded warehouse docks. The background knowledge of driving and the sensorimotor responses do not much differ from those required for driving a passenger car, but they have become more specialized. The passenger-car driver could not take the wheel of the truck, but the truck driver can handle either vehicle.

Even the truck driver does not have skill; what he has is expertise. The skilled work connected with the use of automobiles is that of the auto mechanic. The auto mechanic may be a less competent driver than the owner of the vehicle, but in the shop, if the car breaks down, the auto mechanic can diagnose the trouble and repair the truck. Diagnosing the trouble and repairing the truck are not mere expertise; they are the practice of a skill.

In mass production many jobs are said to call for skill when what they require is a high degree of expertise. Only confusion would result from failure to distinguish between skill and expertise.

Job content, under mass-production technology, consists of a variety of semiskills, up to the highest degree of expertise. Worker qualifications to meet this job content are, initially, simple aptitudes. With training and experience, aptitude turns into ability to perform one particular task or a small group of related semiskills—into expertise.

While there is labor turnover in the factory, and movement in and out

---

[1] Some readers may appropriately comment that the authors are putting too great emphasis on a formal apprenticeship and that many journeymen members of craft union locals have not served a formal apprenticeship. Such a criticism is sound and based on solid facts. The authors would respond to this criticism only by arguing that the existence of a formal apprenticeship program does establish the content of a trade and that the apprenticeship program is recognized as the best method of receiving the training necessary to master the trade. Those journeymen who have acquired membership in the union without serving the apprenticeship typically have very long experience working in most if not all of the specialized segments of the trade.

of the work force, the factory is a stable organization. That is, it replaces individuals from time to time, but there is not much displacement of jobs. The shoe factory must always and simulaneously have people who cut out soles, who stitch uppers, who sew or glue liners, who pack the finished pairs. The automobile assembly plants needs men at every station along the line, all the time, each doing different tasks which are co-ordinated by the production plans and layout to build the car. The result of this is that the appropriate organization for employees cannot be based on any given skill, for these are not skilled jobs. Organization has to be based on the entire coordinated process in the workplace; workplace unionism or industrial unionism.

The slogan of the industrial union might well be "one shop, one union." In the industrial union all the employees working for a given enterprise at a given workplace belong to the same local union without regard for what they do in the plant. The industrial union local takes in not only the semiskilled who directly turn out the product but such skilled workers also as may play an auxiliary part in the production process. It takes in, too, the completely unskilled, such as janitors or a yard gang—if there be any in the plant.

In his workplace the factory employee must accept direction, super-vision, discipline, that inevitably looks upon him as a "replaceable part." He is a unit in an integrated whole, highly differentiated in its parts, sub-divided into specialties and group of specialties, variable in magnitude up to the factory employing tens of thousands. It is necessary for him, as a worker in this vast complex, to be at his machine or station at the minute when all the others are at theirs, to work while they work, at a set pace, and to quit when they quit work for the day. He moves in crowds as he enters and leaves the gate, and at the noon-hour break.

He never sees the shareholders who own the factory; he rarely sees the man who runs it. Management, to him, is a foreman who is a hired hand like himself, and has a boss who has a boss in an upward chain of command reaching to a shining but far-distant pinnacle. The three simple upward steps in status from apprentice to journeyman to master that stand clear before the craftsman have given way to a dizzy stairway of many steps that leads up out of sight. There is no longer any personal warmth or friendly contact between master and man. Orders come down from on high, to be obeyed; no visible means exists for sending comment and questions back up the line.

The worker who makes his living in a factory has lost the status that skill gives the craftsman. He has lost independence and become depen-dent. He never learned the craftsman's satisfaction in work as a creative act. What has he gained?

He has gained money wages that outdistance what he could earn elsewhere as an unskilled laborer. He has begun to earn without serving an apprenticeship, and his real wage is such that he has enough to live on. As he gains practice in his specialty he may, under an incentive system, take home pay that compares favorably with the craftsman's earnings.

His union does not fight the technology of the factory, does not object to new machines, new processes. Instead, it seeks to master them. Above all, it strives to secure for its own members, through seniority rights and the right to retraining, the new opportunities technology creates.

Internally, it practices democracy and suffers from ills that beset democratic institutions with a heterogeneous citizenry: the pulling and hauling of special interest groups; the seesaw of ins and outs, and controversy over policy and tactics; membership indifference and inaction when there are no pressing issues in the air. Today, the threat of mass displacement as a result of technological change puts the industrial union under a strain. Fewer and fewer of the overriding issues can be settled in the shop; only a rear-guard action can be fought there against mass displacement. The interests of threatened members can be furthered only by such broad social action as government can take. At the same time, concrete adjustment to the new technology has to be made where it appears: on the shop floor.

Industrial union leadership, with a generation of experience behind it now, is wary, and conscious of the dangers facing it. It is ready to cooperate, but ready still, if necessary, to fight.

The Amalgamated Union Model. This variant combines certain features of both basic models. It is not common, but important where it occurs. The garment industries provide an example.

The skill of the tailor turns cloth, thread, and other materials into a completed garment made to the customer's measure. Tailors have plied their craft since man began to wear clothes. The factory system with its division of labor broke down the process into a set of subskills, resulting in a product that is not a perfect fit but a nearfit: ready-made clothes in standard sizes that with minor alterations can be made to fit most normal wearers. For various reasons, however, the economics and technology of the industry did not jump from the single craftsman sitting cross-legged on his bench to the full-scale factory. The putting-out, or homework system, a stage of the early Industrial Revolution, persisted longer than in other manufactures, and turned into a system of subcontracting. This brought into being many small, independent entrepreneurs, each of whose workshops carried the garment one stage further toward completion and sale. A workshop tended to employ people who had acquired one or another of the subskills of the tailors' trade. When they unionized, they formed what might be considered truncated craft unions of the various subcrafts. In structure and behavior they followed the craft union model.

Eventually, large-scale factory production evolved, particularly in men's clothing, where changes in style are comparatively slow. Big companies like Hart, Schaffner & Marx and Hickey-Freeman, reassembled, as it were, the complete range of tailoring skills under a single roof and management. The separate craft unions now found it desirable to amalgamate, and deal with their factory employer as if they were an industrial union. Through a joint board, with representatives of all the crafts, they negotiate a single agreement for the factory work force. At the same time, they retain their autonomy, because subcontracting still prevails in the industry and is likely to continue. Changes in style, especially in the women's garment industry, often favor—at least temporarily—the producer whose investment is minimal.

The amalgamated union thus meets a dual challenge: the necessity of dealing with the industry's giants in the factory, where the industrial union model applies, and the need for dealing with the small shops where the craft model is appropriate. Amalgamated unions are thus both models in one, depending on the employer with whom they deal. Chapter 4 will show that teachers organize in a way reminiscent of the amalgamated union model, and in their relationships with educational administrations behave (like the amalgamated union in the factory) in accordance with the industrial union model.

Government. The third actor in the collective bargaining system is mainly the government. The role of government in American collective bargaining is largely permissive. Nevertheless, the state is the ultimate source of power and order in any economic system. In other countries, the state plays a more important role in setting the conditions of employment than is true in the United States. In some countries the state itself carries out activities which are performed by unions in the United States. The rules for rule making which the United States government establishes are of vital interest to the general public and to the two main actors in the collective bargaining system.

Employer and union organizations designed to influence the formulation of rules for rule making are discussed in Chapters 3 and 4. Chapter 5 is devoted to a discussion of the public interest in collective bargaining and the current status of the rules for rule making in the United States. Other important legislative and judicial matters are dealt with elsewhere in the book.

The result of the interaction of the actors, according to Dunlop, is the establishment in a given industrial relations system of rules, and rules for rule making. The word "rules," in the sense intended here, must be given a very broad interpretation. The rules cover a wide range of regulatory arrangements, from a national labor relations law (a rule for rule making) down to something as detailed and specific as, for example, an agreed vacation schedule in a labor-management agreement. As used in this book "rules for rule making" generally mean laws, and all lesser manifestations of regulatory power are referred to as "rules."

The Rules

The authors of this book believe that the study of collective bargaining should begin with a study of the rules. It does not end with the rules, but it must rest upon them in the same way that a study of government does not end with laws and constitutions but lacks meaning without reference to them.

The Rules under Nonunion Conditions. Every free employment relationship centers on the wage and effort bargain. It is an exchange of the worker's ability and time for compensation provided by the employer. This exchange requires a consideration of: (1) pay for time worked, (2) the effort bargain (production standards), (3) premium pay, (4) pay for time not worked, e.g., paid holidays, vacations, and (5) contingent benefits, e.g., Blue Cross and Blue Shield, and pensions. Nonunion employers, regardless of size or industry attachment, must consider these five elements in establishing the conditions of employment. Nonunion workers weigh the value of various employers' "packages" against other employment opportunities or the value of leisure. The wage and effort bargain also provides the base for all collective bargaining agreements.

The larger the scale of an enterprise, the more complex its employee relations problems. Perhaps out of fear of unionization, some medium- and large-scale enterprises have established what under collective bargaining would be called individual security measures. Individual security measures must meet: (1) the individual workers' relative claim to available work and (2) the worker's claim to fair treatment on the job, or the establishment of a system of due process. A relative claim to available work raises such questions as: (1) Who gets laid off? (2) Who gets recalled from layoff when work becomes available? (3) Who gets promoted? and (4) Who get overtime work and overtime pay when it is available? Due process deals with such questions as the fairness of disciplinary rules and the right of an employee to his day in court on disciplinary actions.[2]

Under nonunion conditions, the employer unilaterally establishes the rules on the wage and effort bargain and, perhaps, individual security measures. If he can find workers who will accept these unilaterally established rules, he operates his enterprise without interference, except the veto power always available to a free worker of quitting his employment, or the ability of his employees to force him to change the conditions of employment by restriction of output.

---

[2] The existence of individual security measures in such diverse organizations as the Roman Catholic clergy, the military establishment, and the civil service must be noted as evidence that the need for a system of individual security is more basic than an employer fear of unionization. On the other hand, individual security measures which are unilaterally established and not subject to an impartial outside interpretation can hardly be considered to have the potency of identical measures which have been negotiated by collective bargaining. Cf. William G. Scott, *The Management of Conflict: Appeal Systems in Organizations* (Homewood, Ill.: Richard D. Irwin, Inc., and the Dorsey Press, 1965).

The Rules under Collective Bargaining. Typically the rules under collective bargaining are explicit and written, while under nonunion conditions the rules may be largely implicit. Once a union has won recognition, when the rules must be established bilaterally by negotiation, the substance of the specific rules changes and the coverage of the rules is significantly broadened. The written *labor-management agreement* is the basic rule under a collective bargaining relationship.

The labor agreement performs four functions. It establishes rules for: (1) union security and management rights, (2) the wage and effort bargain, (3) individual security, and (4) administration. The two functions of union security and management rights, and administration, are unique to collective bargaining. Union security and management rights may be summarized as four questions to be answered in the agreement: (1) Who speaks for whom? (2) With what authority? (3) For how long? and (4) Except in what conditions? Administration deals with problems of making the written agreement an operational document in day-to-day activities. It provides a system of on-the-job representation for workers and establishes the procedures by which persons not employed by the enterprise will act if they are called in as neutrals to interpret the collective bargaining agreement. Chapter 9 discusses problems in agreement administration in some detail. The authors of this book would argue that individual security is also unique to the collective bargaining agreement on the assumpton that no unilateral system of individual security would be genuinely binding on the employer who created it.

Figure 1–1 provides a preliminary summary of the rules under collective bargaining. Chapter 8 provides a more comprehensive tool for the analysis of labor agreements and contrasts the practices of craft unions, industrial unions, and professional associations in establishing the basic rules of employment. Chapters 10–14 treat the rules in America in some detail.

Levels of Application of the Rules. The object of the rules in the long run is to regulate relations at work, in the workplace during the working day, between the two main actors, managers and workers. Every workplace evolves or adopts a body of substantive rules. When the workers are organized in a union, these rules result from collective bargaining; but even without bargaining and without a union, there are always rules, no matter how one-sided. These substantive rules emerge out of procedures, or policies, or customs, or laws that may be called the rules for rule making.

This book distinguishes three levels at which rules and rules for rule making appear. They are the national level, the enterprise level, and various points between, which may be lumped together as an "intermediate" level.

National Level. Governmental action through laws, decrees, administrative and judicial decisions normally provides rules for rule making.

During a national emergency, as in wartime, the government may intervene directly in the affairs of individual enterprises; but ordinarily it acts in a general and not a specific way. The rules for rule making that are laid down by government cut across industry lines and regional and state boundaries. They affect the entire industrial relations system. Of this nature, for instance, is labor relations law, such as the Taft-Hartley Act.

Enterprise Level. Here is where the substantive rules are made by the

FIGURE 1–1. The Rules under Collective Bargaining

Rule	Scope
Union Security and Management Rights	Who speaks for whom? With what authority? For how long? Except in what conditions?
The Wage and Effort Bargain	Pay for time worked The effort bargain (Standards) Premium pay Pay for time not worked Contingent benefits
Individual Security	Relative claim to available work Absolute claim to fair treatment
Administration	On-the-job representation Arbitration

This presentation is taken from an article by Edwin F. Beal which appeared in the September/October 1962, issue of *Personnel,* journal of the American Management Association, by permission of the copyright owner. This presentation is expanded upon in Chapter 8 and Figure 8–1.

actors under rules for rule making that come down from higher levels or that are elaborated on the spot—"ground rules"—by these same direct actors. The substantive rules cover, at a minimum, the wage and effort bargain (money for work) that is the root of the employment relationship. Under collective bargaining conditions they almost always deal with other issues in addition. This book will have a great deal more to say about the substantive rules.

Intermediate Level. Above the level of the enterprise but below the national level, interaction between the actors on industrial relations problems takes many forms designated here as "intermediate." Perhaps the commonest intermediate form in the craft unions is bargaining at regional level and in the industrial unions, at the industry level. A greater proportion of the activity is private and voluntary (rather than government sponsored) at intermediate levels.

Collective bargaining characteristically starts at enterprise level, but the trend seems to be toward progression and expansion, by agreement of the actors, to regional or industry level. A common example of regional bargaining is the building trades union's agreement with an employer association for an entire metropolitan area, or a county, or a whole state. A striking example of the industry trend comes from the steel mills whose managers negotiate an industry agreement with the steelworkers' union.

SUMMARY

This book takes for the center of its field of view the practice of collective bargaining in the enterprise. It looks outward from time to time to the macroeconomic scene, backward into history, forward to the march of technological and social progress, and inward to the psychological and social aspects of the work group in the enterprise and the local union. Chiefly it concerns itself, however, with the enterprise as a whole in its dealings with the union that speaks for the employees there. None of the established disciplines of the social or behavioral sciences has taken, or can take, quite this point of view.

The approach to the practice of collective bargaining will be descriptive, analytical, and theoretical. The main theoretical concept is of collective bargaining as an aspect of the industrial relations system, a subsystem of the social system, linked with and overlapping the economic and political subsystems of the same social system.

The industrial relations system, both at enterprise level and above the level of the enterprise, takes shape in three *contexts.* They are the market context, or budgetary limitations; the technology context, as applied in the workplace; the power relations context of the enveloping social system, as reflected in the workplace.

Within these contexts, the industrial relations system evolves by interaction of the *actors.* They are managers and their hierarchy inside and above the enterprise; workers and their hierarchy of representatives; agents of government, or private agents activated by the other two actors.

The result of the interaction of the actors in the industrial relations system is a body of *rules.* They include rules for rule making, and substantive rules.

These rules take force at various *levels.* These may be classified as: national level, enterprise level, and intermediate level.

QUESTIONS FOR DISCUSSION

1. American law does not require nonprofit hospitals to engage in collective bargaining. Why might a hospital administrator find it worthwhile to study collective bargaining?

2. Show how Dunlop's concept of the *Industrial Relations System* requires an interdisciplinary approach to the study of collective bargaining.
3. An hourly wage certainly is an important "rule." Show how this rule might be applied at the national level, the enterprise level, and the intermediate level.
4. How does the prevailing technology of a society influence power relations in that society?
5. Can individual security, as discussed in this chapter, exist without unionism? Besides unionism, what institutions might provide security?

Chapter 2

AN INTERPRETATION OF AMERICAN UNION HISTORY

This chapter is a departure from the discussion of the contemporary practice of collective bargaining in America. It looks backward into history and documents the historical events which have caused the authors of this book to conclude that there are two model systems of collective bargaining: (1) handicraft industry and craft unionism and (2) mass-production industry and industrial unionism; and their analogues and counterparts.

QUESTIONS OF IMPORTANCE TO AN INTERPRETATION OF UNION BEHAVIOR

Writing in 1948,[1] John T. Dunlop posed four basic questions which would be of importance to an interpretation of union behavior or the development of a theory which could *predict* union behavior. Here are Dunlop's four questions, somewhat abbreviated, with italics added:

1. How is one to account for the *origin or emergence* of labor organizations?
2. What explains the patterns of *growth and development* of labor organizations?
3. What are the *ultimate goals* of the labor movement?
4. Why do *individual workers join* labor organizations?

Relatively few scholars have given serious thought to the questions raised by Dunlop, or to related questions. The most comprehensive treatment of the subject in America to date, Mark Perlman's *Labor Union Theories in America*, published in 1958, mentions fewer than 20 scholars who dealt with these questions; and Perlman made an exhaustive study.

Before outlining the present authors' interpretation of history, it is desirable to review the work of the most prominent labor union theorists.

---

[1] John T. Dunlop, in Richard A. Lester and Joseph Shister (eds.), *Insights into Labor Issues*, "The Development of Labor Organizations: A Theoretical Framework," (New York: Macmillan Co., 1948).

Here are the names of the important theorists, with the dates of their most significant contributions:

In England

Sidney and Beatrice Webb, 1897

In America

Robert Hoxie, 1917
John R. Commons, 1919
Frank Tannenbaum, 1921, 1951
Selig Perlman, 1928

International Schools of Thought

The Marxists, an entire group of writers whose ideas derive from the doctrines first put forth by Karl Marx and Friedrich Engels, beginning in 1847
The Catholics, who expound the social justice doctrines contained in three papal encyclicals, *Rerum Novarum* (Leo XIII, 1891), *Quadragessimo Anno* (Pius XI, 1931), and *Mater et Magistra* (John XXIII, 1961)

An orderly approach would be to see what answers the theorists named in the list have given to these questions, what predictions they have made (if any) and how their answers have stood the test of time.

Origin or Emergence

Sidney and Beatrice Webb regarded unions as the workingman's attempt to regulate and control competition for work opportunities. Unless unionized, every worker faced the competition of every other worker seeking a job. Employers would thus be able to bid down the price of labor, and would, in fact, have to do so in self-defense against the most unscrupulous employer—the one who would drive the meanest bargain—in order to stay in business. The organized worker's answer to this threat took the form, according to the Webbs, of two Devices, which they called the Device of the Common Rule and the Device of the Restriction of Numbers.

The Common Rule was to standardize wages and conditions of work. This was the defense against that most unscrupulous employer. It also aimed to prevent any one employer from setting his workers in competition with each other to work harder or faster than any of their fellows.

The Restriction of Numbers denied entrance to the trade except to candidates who had passed through an apprenticeship over which the union exercised some control. This had the long-run effect of regulating the total supply of qualified workers to the total demand, so that the bargains made collectively would provide favorable wages and include the Common Rule.

As a background to these two fundamental Devices, the Webbs identified what they called Doctrines guiding the activities of unions. There were three such Doctrines: Vested Rights, Supply and Demand, and the Living Wage.

Under the Vested Rights doctrine unions opposed innovations and technological changes that would reduce work opportunities for the existing group of qualified workers. Supply and Demand, as the words imply, aimed to restrict the number of qualified workers to the amount of work available. The Living Wage doctrine had to do with the wage level and the amount of work performed for the wage.

The Webb analysis explains craft-union aims and activity. The Webbs saw unions of their day as a regulator of a fundamental economic relationship: the supply of labor of a given quality against the demand for it. Unions were, in short, an economic institution.

Robert Hoxie did not show much interest in the reasons for the origin of unions. He found them on the scene and took them somewhat for granted. To the extent that he gave thought to their emergence, he ascribed it to the psychology of the workingman caught up in an industrial society, without delving very profoundly into the psychological phenomena.

What interested Hoxie was the diversity of unions, their different forms and manifestations. He is the only one of the theorists to stress diversity, rather than to look for similarities. In this he was unique and prophetic even though students who came later have questioned the value of his classifications. Hoxie's awareness of difference takes on significance today because of the emergence of a type of unionism—industrial unionism in mass-production manufacturing—quite different from the craft unions with which his contemporaries were concerned, and beyond which they seem not to have looked.

The work of *John R. Commons* covers a wider span than the one key date ascribed to him in the list. He was a historian of the labor movement and an active social investigator and reformer as well as a theorist. He saw unions as an economic institution that arose as a result of the separation of the traditional threefold function of the craftsman.

The master craftsman of handicraft industry days had been at one and the same time and in his own person a buyer (of materials), a manufacturer, and a seller (of finished goods). The growth and development of markets divided these functions between the merchant and the manufacturer, and reduced the worker to the status of employee of the manufacturer, who now bought and combined labor and materials and sold finished goods to the wholesale merchant, who resold them. Competition in the market squeezed the manufacturer, who squeezed the worker. Unions were the worker's answer to loss of control over the product market, where he had formerly been able to offer the products of his labor at prices that would bring a fair return. He could counter now only by organizing the labor market, and by raising wage demands seek to assure a fair and sufficient return for his labor. Like the Webbs, therefore, Commons saw the unions as an economic institution, called into being by economic pressure on the workers.

Selig Perlman believed that unionism had its roots in the "scarcity consciousness" of the worker: scarcity of job opportunity. By organizing, the worker could turn these scarce employment opportunities into "job property" through the adoption of rules that gave workers control over the jobs and the conditions of work.

Perlman expressed his views in a somewhat polemic tone. He showed little patience with the programs or the theories of intellectuals (he signaled his scorn for "intellectuals" by always putting the word between quotation marks) but he derived his theory from the actions of the unions themselves. He found these actions sprang from what he called the "job consciousness" of the working man—a kind of practical pragmatism that led the unions, as if by instinct, to do what was necessary to secure and maintain job control: a sort of ownership of the jobs.

Frank Tannenbaum depicted unions as the workingman's answer to the machine and to the role of dependence in which the machine put him. Organized in unions, the worker sought to regain some control over the decisions that affected his living and daily existence.

Tannenbaum published two books on the subject, one in 1921, the other in 1951; but in a sense they are really the same book. The basic analysis is similar; only the conclusions drawn from the analysis differ, and they are poles apart. In 1921 Tannenbaum saw the unions as a revolutionary force, leading toward a reorganization of the industrial system under the control of the workers. In 1951 he saw the unions as a counterrevolutionary force, seeking to give the worker a kind of security reminiscent of the static society of the middle ages, when workers had a fixed, secure status, along with other classes of society.

There is no point here in passing judgment on the conclusions. In either case Tannenbaum's analysis does not picture unions as economic institutions so much as power groups rising out of the worker's psychological response to the insecurity of industrial society.

The Marxists regard unions as only one aspect—and a minor one at that—of the class struggle inherent in the conflict between capital and labor. This struggle, rooted in the contradiction between social production and private ownership of the means of production, is a political struggle to be led by the political party of the working class, whose aim is revolution. Any reform, such as higher wages or better working conditions, can be only temporary and insecure, short of the revolutionary overthrow of the capitalist class: therefore, unions can make no lasting contribution. They do, however, rally the masses for the larger struggle, and so are to be created by the revolutionary party as a training ground and reserve for the political conquest of power.

The Catholic writers regard unions as the workingman's answer to abuses and injustices which are not inherent in the capitalist system, or universally practiced, but which the system makes possible. Unions arise out of the moral need for social justice, and help hold the abuse of power in check.

Patterns of Growth and Development

The fundamental nature of the preceding first question on origins made it desirable to list the explanations of all the theorists in sequence. Needless to say, they have been compressed extremely. The student seriously interested in theory should consult the works themselves, which will be found listed in the bibliography.

Turn now to the second question on growth and development. Here some had nothing to say. Others gave it only minor attention.

The one who had most to say was Hoxie. He found great diversity in the *forms* and in the *functions* (practices) of unions.

Forms. He distinguished the forms by *levels:* local (enterprise), state, and national. He also distinguished by type of industry in which the union occurred, and nature of the attachment: craft, trade (multi-craft), industrial, and labor (multi-industrial). He carried this classification down into even greater detail: compound craft, quasi-industrial, and so on.

Practices. Hoxie observed the ways in which various unions carried out their regular functions, and made an elaborate classification based on this behavior. For a detailed treatment of this and other aspects of his classification, it would be best to consult his own work.

The authors of this book respect Hoxie for recognizing the diversity of forms and functions which unions are capable of assuming. They do not accept his classification system, which to them seems based on fortuitous factors, not rooted in the environment. Use of the Dunlop framework from Chapter 1 of this book, plus application of behavioral science findings, are likely to give results of more lasting value than Hoxie's pioneer classifications; but he is to be honored for seeing the fact and the possibilities.

Hoxie was alone in stressing this point. The others comment upon it, in a sense, only by their silence. That is, they imply that unions are homogeneous organizations and thus deny the prospect of differentiation and change. Comment on the reasons for this, and its significance for use of their theoretical contributions, will appear below after the four questions have been canvassed.

Ultimate Goals

It is on the ultimate goals of organized workers that the Marxists have the most, and all other theorists the least, to say. The Marxists, however, do not see the appropriate organization of workers to be unions, but a revolutionary political party. The unions are the auxiliary troops to be drawn into the revolutionary battles. Industry, by employing them and concentrating them in the workplace, has itself brought about the preliminary organization of workers; on this concentration the revolution is to build its forces around a vanguard of the elite party of the workers.

In the socialist state that is to result from the revolution, again unions are to have a subsidiary role. They are to be the party's auxiliary in maintaining discipline and productivity at the workplace.

Perlman had something to say about ultimate goals, though he was anti-Marxist and condemned all who try to hold ultimate goals before the working man. In the last chapter of his book on theory, Perlman discusses the ideas of a German writer named Carl Zwing, who proposed a plan for the control of industry by joint labor-management councils. This would not actually create a new society, but represents a goal toward which unions might work to insure fair distribution of the fruits of industry. A pale reflection of Zwing's ideas (first put forth in the early 1920s) took shape in German industry after 1946. It is called codetermination—much too complicated to discuss at this point, and not sufficiently significant.

Philip Taft, an associate of Commons and of Perlman, had this to say about the ultimate goals of unions:

> American unionism has a philosophy of simple pragmatism. Such a philosophy is not as ostentatious and lacks the architectonic grandeur of philosophical systems such as Marxism. This perhaps makes American trade unionism less attractive to those who enjoy the aesthetic experience of beholding a beautiful intellectual system. However, the absence of these qualities helps to make the American movement more democratic, tolerant, and flexible. Trade unionism in the United States is a means of protecting the individual against arbitrary rule and raising his standard of living. While it may not rank high for philosophy, it deserves high score on the latter count.[2]

Why Individuals Join

This question seems at first glance like a variation on Question 1: Origin and emergence. The individual might be thought of as responding to the forces, or perceiving the rationale, set forth in the analysis of the various theorists.

The cynic may even be heard to say, in answer to that question today, he joins because he is forced to: union shop. Antiunion elements make this the basis of their "right-to-work" laws, on the presumption that if workers did not have to join unions, they wouldn't. If workers join unions purely for individual psychological reasons, or through coercion, this would effectively dispose of all general theory. If not, then one must look for other reasons why unions emerge: economic and political rea-

---

[2] Philip Taft, "Theories of the Labor Movement," *Interpreting the Labor Movement* (Industrial Relations Research Association, 1952), p. 38.

sons. Theory cannot be disposed of merely by denying that there could be a theory.

But the interaction of the individual with his organization, his enterprise, and his fellow workers is a highly important subject for investigation. It has become the field of the psychologist, the sociologist, the anthropologist, the political scientist, as well as the investigators who originally claimed it, the economists.

In the same book in which Dunlop propounded his four questions, two sociologists also asked some questions. They were Frederick H. Harbison and Robert Dubin. Here are the questions they asked:

There are two categories of extremely pressing, yet for the most part unanswered, questions. First, there are problems relating to the implications of large power concentrations in the hands of private groups. Can large-scale unionization operate within the framework of the present private enterprise system, or must it bring about some modifications in this system? Will the modifications be in the nature of joint economic planning of basic industries? Will concentrations of power in big unions, which parallel similar concentrations of power in big business, inevitably result in some form of bilateral monopoly? Are there automatic or natural limits, inherent in our present economic and political organization, to the exercise of power by large unions and large employers? What social controls through governmental action, if any, should be placed on the accumulation and exercise of such power by either side?

Another set of questions involves the balance of power between individual unions and managements and the resultant kind of union-management relationship which develops. These questions have to do with issues centering in the plant, whose resolution leads to conflict or cooperation, and stability or instability. Under what circumstances do cooperative relationships develop between employers and unions? What changes in human relations accompany the working out of harmonious union-management relations? What social skills are necessary to make such relationships work? What are the limiting factors on union-management collaboration, and, if collaboration is achieved, how stable is it likely to be? Where conflict rather than cooperation prevails, is there an effective basis for mutual survival in labor-management relations?[3]

The questions in this set call for the research methods of the behavioral scientists. Like Dunlop's questions, they are not theory but a call to theoretical work, and a suggested framework for it.

Critique of the Older Theory

The works of the theorists cited represents a sizable body of work by careful observers.

The work they did was adequately descriptive. It took the measure of existing labor organizations, though no one writer covered the entire spectrum. The Webbs dealt almost exclusively with craft unions. So did

---

[3] Lester and Shister (eds.), *Insight into Labor Issues.*

Perlman, though he devoted some attention to the garment unions, built on the craft pattern but on their way toward developing into industrial unions by amalgamation of the crafts. Hoxie described many types, but based his descriptions on their superficial features without finding the key to their differentiation. Tannenbaum, having himself once been a casual laborer, seems to have been greatly influenced by the plight and mentality of the rootless laborer. This is an unusual kind of worker, and the labor organization he developed—the IWW—was unusual too.

The major phenomenon of our times—industrial unionism—is absent from the descriptions. That is because they were written when industrial unionism was no more than the slogan of the radical left and could be found in practice in only one industry: mining. Mining is not manufacturing. Also, no law required that union agreements be reduced to writing, and in fact a great many were verbal. Craft unions regulate by their own rules many things that are written out between the parties in the industrial union agreement; thus it appeared that the "common rule" of the craft was an essential part of collective bargaining. Writers searching the documentary evidence then available—union constitutions and bylaws, union publications—did not have access to actual labor-management agreements to the extent now possible.

A test of any explanation is to predict behavior and compare what actually happens with the prediction.

One prediction emerges either explicitly or implicitly from all the theories which see unions as an attempt to reduce competition between workers in the face of a scarcity of job opportunities. It is that unions will grow and become strong during periods of prosperity and will decline during periods of depression. Perlman, for one, points out that the AFL was the first national union federation ever to survive a major depression.

The history of craft unionism throughout the 19th and early 20th centuries bore out this analysis. The figures proving this, and therefore the statistical justification of the prediction, were assembled by Leo Wolman in his book, *The Ebb and Flow in Trade Unionism*, published in 1936. The facts of industrial unionism in the Great Depression of the 1930s directly contradict the thesis.

The first world war made mass-production industry the major form of production institution and source of national wealth. The 1920s were a period of rising prosperity. During that decade membership in the American Federation of Labor, a federation of craft unions, declined.

The depression brought, as predicted, a still further decline in numbers and bargaining influence of the AFL craft unions; but it also released the greatest organizing drive of all time in America in the mass-production factories.

It might be said of industrial unions that they tend to organize more actively in periods of depression, and to decline—not in absolute numbers or strength, but by deceleration of growth—during periods of prosperity.

That has been the history of the CIO and of the industrial-union components of the AFL-CIO since 1935.

Thus the prediction based on past theory that prosperity stimulates union growth and depression destroys it remains true only for one sector—the craft unions, and mainly in their stronghold, the building trades. It fails to account for the phenomenon of industrial unionism.

Implicit in the older theory, also, is the prediction that doctrines and devices useful to the existing unions would continue to be applied. Any theory based on the premise that unionism is a homogeneous thing implies that future growth will be a quantitative addition to the present, on the same pattern as the past.

As surely as mass-production technology destroyed handicraft production in much of the national product market, the rise of industrial unionism in mass production broke the craft pattern.

A general criticism of the older theory may therefore be that the theorists concentrated too closely on unions and failed to take note of the context of technology, which sets the conditions of interaction between the union, one actor, and management and government, the other actors in the system.

The older theory thus tends to break down when applied to industrial unionism. Various attempts to comprehend the new phenomena of industrial unionism have come to grief by using the older theory without critical reevaluation. Addition of industrial unionism has also changed the context of power relations, so that older theory may have to be further limited.

This deficiency of older theory is not the result of any failure in observation or scholarship of the theorists. They wrote before industrial unionism came on the scene. Even then at least one of them, Hoxie, foresaw changes which would affect unionism in mass production. They did not have access to a huge body of data that has accumulated since their day, in written form and so available to the scholar. That is the labor agreements themselves.

AN EXCURSION INTO THEORY

The Premises

This excursion into collective bargaining theory starts from the following premises:

1. That collective bargaining, since it is carried on by conscious human beings, is a rational process. This does not imply that emotionalism may not enter into the behavior of the participants. It simply presumes that the parties do have rational ends in view, and that they pursue these ends by means which reason tells them will lead to the desired aim; not in haphazard, random, or irrational fashion.

2. That what unions ask for in collective bargaining indicates what they want.
3. That what unions get from management in labor management agreements represents, on the average and over time, a rational accommodation of what they want with what management in its circumstances and pursuing its aims can and will give them. That is, union agreements register limits and boundaries. Each actor has certain ends in view. Each pursues these ends by rational means. Their bargain or agreement represents an accommodation of their separately held aims, whether or not these are antagonistic (requiring compromise), or complementary (requiring only definition).

What this boils down to then is that unionism is a search for security on the part of those dependent on a wage or salary for their living. The industrial relations systems based upon bond labor were long on security, short on individual freedom. The capitalist economic system and democratic political system are long on freedom and short on individual security.

Labor unions emerge when individuals become dependent upon a wage or salary for their living, and are without assurance as individuals of continued employment. Union organization and collective bargaining provide this assurance. It is the rational and effective means of reconciling the needs of employers and of individual workers in an area of reciprocal and not incompatible interests. The employer needs a work force. The employee needs work. The employer's need for workers creates the job opportunities, but it is a matter of indifference to him what individuals occupy these jobs so long as his work gets done. To the worker on the job it is a matter of supreme importance to hold the job. He does not expect work when there is no work available, but as long as he is performing in a satisfactory manner in a given job, he considers it only fair that he be continued in that job. The employer wants "a body." The worker wants to make sure that it is *his* body. They are able to accommodate each other's needs, and do so in the labor agreement.

An individual gets relative security if he possesses characteristics or attributes scarce and desired by society. True skill is a scarce factor of production and gives its possessor relative security compared with the nonskilled worker. Consequently, unions of skilled workers bend their policy to preserve the relative scarcity of their skill. Counterparts of skill in the craft sense, raised to a higher level, may be found in some of the professions. These professions are entered by something that compares with an apprenticeship.

Collective bargaining in the union pattern tends to emerge in answer to felt threats or overt attacks upon individual security, when management fails to provide job rights or observe due process, including effective appeal to impartial review of decisions. Collective bargaining also seeks to influence the terms of the wage and effort bargain.

Union demands on management, and the agreements that result from collective bargaining, reveal that unions are primarily a device for bringing a measure of individual security into the employment relationship and regulating the terms of the work contract—the wage and effort bargain—between the employer and each individual in the bargaining unit. They have no ultimate aims consciously in view. They accept the existing economic system; they accept the existing political system; they seek only to play a regulatory part in the industrial relations system as one actor influencing the rules.

While adjustment by collective bargaining practices will not become universal, it will be the adjustments so arrived at that will set the pattern for the others. The solutions will be, as today and in the past, pragmatic solutions. Because unions will take part in reaching them, they will consider the social welfare. Collective bargaining may somewhat retard the rate of technological progress, or make it more expensive, but will not obstruct it.

The rest of this chapter offers an interpretation of the history of collective bargaining in America. An interpretation differs from a chronicle in that it tries to point out the significance of events rather than just their sequence. Because this chapter is an interpretation, a chronology of events in collective bargaining history, for reference, follows the chapter. The chronology aims to provide detailed factual support of the narrative; the narrative to give meaning and significance to the sequence of bare facts.

THE TWO HISTORIES OF COLLECTIVE BARGAINING IN AMERICA

Collective bargaining between managers of handicraft enterprises and representatives of craft unions has been going on in the United States almost since the nation won its independence, or for nearly two centuries. It still goes on, for the same ends and in much the same form, in the restricted sector of the economy where handicraft methods prevail. The outstanding example today is the construction industry, with its building-trades unions of skilled craftsmen.

Collective bargaining between industrial unions and the managers of mass-production manufacturing plants, and kindred enterprises mainly employing nonskilled labor, is much newer. It has been going on for less than half a century, although factory methods and mass production began to replace handicraft shops at least a century ago.

Not until after the year 1933 did unions succeed in establishing permanent organizations of factory workers, except in the garment trades which were by no means solidly organized. The only sizable industrial union was not in manufacturing but in the coal mines, and seemed then to be struggling against disintegration. The CIO drive to organize the unorganized, which began to gather headway in 1935, built up the weak existing unions to a commanding position in their industries and created new unions where none had been before, as in the automobile and steel industries.

The story of collective bargaining thus becomes, in reality, two stories: a long and consistent, but somewhat discontinuous, tale of craft unions bargaining with handicraft employers in a relatively diminishing sector of the economy; and a brief, spectacular drama of industrial-union bargaining in mass-production industry, whose enterprises make up the vital and decisive elements of the economy today.

Industrial unionism burst on the modern scene suddenly; but nothing as powerful, substantial, and enduring as it has proved to be materializes out of nothing. Three quarters of a century of history lay behind the dramatic appearance.

This chapter aims to outline the developments that led to the CIO sweep through the mass-production manufacturing plants in the late 1930s. The first sign of the emerging pattern comes to light about the time of the Civil War, when craft-union bargaining was an established practice. The craft and industrial strands of the pattern do not lie parallel. They sometimes intertwine, and sometimes spread apart. One of the strands— craft-union bargaining—runs consistently, though intermittently, with very little wavering. The other—industrial unionism, laboring to be born —traces a jagged path.

Three main stages in the quest for industrial unionism preceded the answers found in practical bargaining today. They may be called: (1) industrial unionism *in embryo;* (2) preindustrial unionism *of the left;* and (3) preindustrial unionism *of the right.* Explanations in this chapter will make the three terms clear.

Craft unionism and craft bargaining emerged before the first of the three stages. This chapter starts with the craft-bargaining story and keeps craft-union growth in the field of view as attention focuses on the development of the forces that brought industrial-union bargaining to birth.

At the end of the chapter there is a bibliography containing references that will supplement the brief notes of the chronology and provide a basis of critique and analysis for the interpretation of events.

CRAFT-UNION PREHISTORY IN COLONIAL AMERICA

At the beginning of the colonial period there was no industry; by the end of the period there was still very little. Agriculture, plus a growing trade and commerce, dominated the economy. Manufacturing was in the handicraft stage and largely done at home.

Skilled craftsmen began early to establish a few small shops in the seaboard cities. As their "front room" enterprises grew they took apprentices, and some eventually began to employ wandering journeymen. Their trade was strictly local: village blacksmiths, shoemakers, and menders; tailors, carpenters, printers, tanners.

Not all workers were free laborers; some were slaves, indentured servants, or bound apprentices. Qualifications tended to cluster at the two extremes: a man was either skilled in a trade that had to be learned by serving an apprenticeship, or, whether free or bond, he was an unskilled field hand or common laborer.

There could be no question of union organization of bond laborers. The free laborers worked only singly, or if they were skilled, in small "family" groups, often actually living in the master workman's house and supping at his table.

Wages were high by the standards of those days. From the beginning of settlement in North America there was a chronic shortage of labor, and its price reflected the excess of demand over supply. Attempts to set maximum wages by law all failed, because the need for labor—skilled or unskilled—was so great that the employers themselves broke the law in bidding for labor. Individual, face-to-face bargaining, was the rule.

The Labor Market

Labor is not a commodity in the usual sense, but the price of labor, like commodity prices, may be subject to the fluctuations of supply and demand in the *labor market*. This was particularly true under the conditions that prevailed in the colonies in the early days. Communities were practically isolated from each other, except by water. The main influx of new workers was by ships that came from Europe, and the frontier drained a steady outflow to the west. Thus there would be a certain number of jobs and potential job openings at any given time, and a certain number of workers. A worker on foot could canvass and personally interview all his prospective employers.

The Unskilled Worker. Wages paid for unskilled labor might vary slightly with the physical fitness or the willingness or persuasiveness of the individual, but tended to reach a general level at some point between two extremes: (*a*) In good times, employers seeking labor when it was scarce, bid wages up to the limit of what they could afford to pay and still make a profit. (*b*) In bad times, workers seeking jobs when jobs were scarce bid wages down to the limit of what they could afford to accept and still keep body and soul together—gain their subsistence.

Normally in the colonies there were more jobs or potential jobs than workers, and wages were nearer the upper than the lower limit. As time went on, after the colonial period, steady streams of immigration changed this picture, and the closing of the frontier finally reversed it. There came to be many more people than jobs, and wages dropped to near the lower limit.

Skilled Labor. Just as there was a limit to the number of common laborers available for hire, and free to hire themselves out, there was an absolute limit at a given time to the number who possessed a skill—any particular skill. The same forces that acted on wage levels for common labor in the labor market acted upon wage levels in the smaller labor markets for each skill. Skilled labor was in special demand. A journeyman who had served his time as an apprentice could not "name his own price," but he could bargain within the limits described above, and do it face to face with the man who wanted to employ him. Being free to quit his job, he could get a raise when times were good by further bargaining with his employer.

When individual bargaining worked as well as has been outlined here—and this was the condition in the colonies through a good part of the 18th century—there was little need for collective bargaining; besides, the number of workers employed by one employer was usually small. Many economic and psychological factors also worked against the combination of working men into unions. Land was cheap and easy to get if a man wanted it, and in the growing towns it was easy to make a living and get ahead. Class distinctions, left behind in Europe, had not jelled again too firmly. Society was fluid; most young men expected to rise in the world. So far as the records show, there were no unions, but as time went on there came to be certain kinds of worker organizations.

Worker Organizations

In some of the seaboard cities workers of the same skill or craft founded social clubs, like the clubs of merchants and professional men. Also like the associations of their colonial "betters," these clubs gave status to their members, who were several steps above the immigrant common laborers, bondmen, and slaves. Life insurance was unavailable in those days and there were no workmen's compensation laws, so it is not surprising that some of these clubs turned to establishing mutual funds out of which they paid death benefits to widows and orphans of deceased members, and gave relief to the sick or injured.

Embryo Unions. Members of craftsmen's clubs and mutual benefit societies would not have been human if they had not indulged in "shop talk," and part of shop talk is wages, hours, and working conditions. Members were unwilling to have their wages and conditions undermined by competition from itinerant workers, or "half-baked" craftsmen who would depreciate the standards of workmanship and water down their skill. They found three ways of handling the problem:

The Closed Shop. One method of reducing potential competition was to subsidize itinerant brothers of the craft until they found a job or moved on. This was often done by boarding them around in the homes of members. Another way, more drastic, was to refuse to work with "foreigners," particularly if they had not served their time and mastered the trade. An employer faced with a "turnout" of dependable local workmen would find hiring a floater or an ill-trained man expensive. The result was the informal beginnings of the "closed shop"—the shop that was closed to anyone not a member of the union.

Apprenticeship. In those days youths were bound out for periods of from four to seven years to master workmen, who were the employers. The youngsters learned the tricks of the trade from their employer and other old hands in the shop.

The employers as a group could have relieved the scarcity of skill in the labor market if they had been able to train enough apprentices, but each apprentice during his learning years was a drain on the individual employer, and besides, the already skilled workers did not favor training so many replacements that they would create potential competition for themselves. Since the employers needed the cooperation of the skilled hands to train the replacements, the result was usually a compromise in which the skilled men, as a group, got a voice in setting the number of apprentices. This gave them a large measure of control over the right of access to the trade, and kept their skill scarce in the labor market.

Wages and Output. Finally, there was the question of the speed, or tempo, of the work. Since the craftsman performed this with his own hands, he could control it, but the employer was naturally anxious to encourage the man who worked the fastest, and to hold the others up to his standard. To avoid this, organized members of local groups agreed upon shop rules, either among themselves or with the employers. Once a standard of daily output had been established, it was logical to insist upon a standard daily wage, and this the group negotiated with the employers through spokesmen.

A Craft-Union Program. All this adds up to a full-fledged program of craft unionism, valid and practiced (with some additions) to this day. Little of it shows in the records and documents that have come down, for most of it was done by word of mouth, but it can be fairly inferred from what there is in print.

The basic strategy behind it was to control a scarce and vital element of production—skill. Keeping it scarce by limiting the number who possessed it and regulating the terms on which they offered it kept its price up in the labor market.

Any organization with fortunes tied so closely to the labor and product market is bound to suffer with the fluctuations of the economy. Craft unions flourished in a boom, languished when the bust came; appeared, disappeared, reappeared. The story of craft unions up to the Civil War, and after, is one of ebb and flow; it need not be followed in detail.

If cats have nine lives, craft unions were like cats. Tied in a sack and drowned during a depression, they came scratching at the employer's door again as soon as times improved. They are still around.

INDUSTRIAL UNIONISM IN EMBRYO: RISE AND DECLINE OF THE KNIGHTS OF LABOR

The independence of the young republic had made possible expansion and activity that colonial status discouraged. Trade with Europe increased, particularly after the Napoleonic wars which ended in 1815. The government encouraged native industry and manufacture, which grew in importance to the economy, though methods of production remained primitive and did not change radically at first. Roads and canals, and, later, railroads linked the cities and connected them with the hinterland. The market for goods ceased to be local and became national. Shoes and guns and yard goods made in New England sold in Michigan and Missouri. The labor market, too, ceased to be narrowly local (though it is never as "national" as the market for wheat or automobiles). Immigration increased greatly. Cities grew in size. Bankers extended their financial operations, and with the increased interdependence of the national economy, national panics and depressions made their periodic appearances.

Rise of the Factory System

England's Industrial Revolution took a generation to cross the Atlantic. American industry felt its influence after about 1840. It brought the factory system. Craft unions continued to grow, because the economy was growing, and handicrafts with it, but factory production began to displace handicraft manufacturing and spread to new areas of enterprise.

The Civil War, 1861–65, gave the factory system an enormous boost. The government, with armies in the field, became an insatiable cash customer for products in quantities such as only mass-production methods could supply. After the war there was a long depression, which brought about the usual eclipse of craft unions and shut down factories; but the factories had come to stay. With the return of prosperity the factories reopened. Craft unions revived in the handicraft shops and occupations that were still active, but the craft unions never succeeded in organizing the factories.

In 1869 a small group of custom tailors in Philadelphia formed a craft union which they called the Knights of Labor. Unlike other organizations of handicraft workers, it did not confine its membership to workers in a single trade, but spread, first as a multicraft federation, then as a general order of working men. By 1878 it had become a national organization. Unknowingly, it contained the embryo of industrial unionism. Though it did not reach the stage of collective bargaining in the factories, it did succeed temporarily on the railways, and it laid the foundations for an industrial union of miners.

What made the factory such a hard nut to crack?

Difficulties of Organizing. The traditional basis of organization was lacking in the factory. Unions could not control entrance to the "trade" because semiskilled work was not a trade and required no apprenticeship. Even apprenticeship for the regular trades slipped from union control in the factory, for factories were big enough to train their own apprentices for replacements. They did not need and did not ask for union help.

Skill itself was no longer vital. Skilled workers made up only a small minority of total factory payroll. The factory easily hired the small number of skilled workers it needed away from union control because it could offer union pay and conditions, or better, plus the inducement of steady work. A 10 percent raise for the toolmakers or maintenance men might not increase the total wage bill by as much as 1 percent; thus a factory could pamper its few skilled men. If pampering did not work and the skilled men responded to a union call, the factory could get along without them, for a while at least, because the factory did not depend upon their output as a *direct* element of production. They made tools and dies for the production workers, or repaired machines; they did not turn out the factory's product. That was the job of the majority, the semi-skilled.

The Semiskilled Worker. The semiskilled worker, trained in a few days or weeks in the factory, was dependent on his job in the factory that trained him. His alternate employment opportunities were at best restricted. Often the work he did was unique to the factory where he worked. If he wanted a job anywhere else, he would have to start as an unskilled trainee. Furthermore, he was easily replaceable—another raw hand could with the same few days or weeks of training that he got easily take his place.

Lack of Union Tradition. The semiskilled worker ordinarily had had no contact with or experience of unionism. He may have come from the farm, or from a peasant holding in a foreign country. He could hardly feel any solidarity with the skilled man who held himself above the common herd. Semiskilled workers came from every country in Europe, from the rural areas and from the towns, in all ages, shapes, and colors, in both sexes. Often they could not, literally, speak the same language.

A Living Wage. The semiskilled worker did not make as much money as the skilled worker, but he made good money in relation to the learning time invested. The skilled worker must have put in four or more years of practically unpaid labor learning his trade. The semiskilled worker showed up on the job with no training at all, learned it in a matter of days or weeks, and got paid in the process. It was always enough to live on. (Except in certain depressed industries, like textiles, or during times of depression, as in the early 1930s, the factory in America has always paid a living wage.) If he came from any European country, he had a higher standard of living at the lowest wage he could earn in America than the majority of his compatriots in the Old Country. What is more, he could sometimes increase his earnings by hard work under a piecework plan, or qualify for higher graded jobs with higher pay. He was not tied, as the skilled worker is, to a single hourly rate for the life of a contract. All these things made it hard to organize him.

Employer Opposition. Factory employers were more powerful than their handicraft counterparts had been. The factory represents a larger concentration of capital and economic power than the handicraft shop, and the factory employer was richer and more influential, individually and as a group, than the employer of a previous day. He controlled more job openings, exercised greater community leadership, and had more money to spend on lobbying or campaigning for political favors than his predecessors. Many of the early employers smothered potential opposition with kindness, through "paternalism"—providing special benefits and care to their workers. Sometimes, however, this was resented rather than appreciated, but it attracted the loyalty of a part at least of the working force.

The Knights of Labor

The Knights of Labor never squarely met the factory challenge, never fully comprehended it. They did not gain their victories in manufacturing, but they brought factory organization and collective bargaining into the workingman's ken and made them part of his aims. The Knights established the first truly national union movement in America. They wrote a picturesque and honorable page of American labor history.

The Structure of the Knights of Labor. At the height of their development, the Knights showed an organizational structure of three levels and had three kinds of local assemblies.

Levels of Organization. The basic unit of the Knights was the local assembly. A dozen or more local assemblies, geographically close to each other, made up a district assembly. All the district assemblies, taken together, made up the national assembly, headed by a Grand Master Workman and an executive board.

Kinds of Local Assemblies. The Knights recognized two kinds of local assembly. It is possible today to recognize three.

1. Craft Assembly. The first local assembly of the Knights was composed exclusively of journeymen tailors; the second, of ship carpenters. In the course of time many other local assemblies composed entirely of skilled practitioners of a single craft received charters.
2. Mixed Assembly. The Knights differed from previous labor organizations in accepting for membership any and all who worked for a

living, regardless of their skill or lack of it. (In fact, they excluded only tavern keepers, professional gamblers, persons of ill repute, and lawyers. They did not exclude employers, though it does not appear that many big employers joined the Knights.) The advance of the factory system produced a category of nonskilled worker called semi-skilled. The craft unions had always kept such people out; the Knights took them in. A community with only one local assembly of the Knights would have a mixed assembly. After enough craftsmen "swarmed" to found new craft assemblies, those who remained would still constitute a mixed assembly.

3. Industrial Assembly. In any locality where there was only one employer, what the Knights called a mixed assembly would turn out to be what now may be called an industrial assembly. This condition occurred in such places as textile towns with a single large mill, and in the coal "patches," and by chance in other places here and there. Such assemblies were mixed in the sense that they showed a mixture of various skills and degrees of skill, but they were homogeneous in terms of the industry from which the members came and the identity of their common employer. They were an embryo form of the industrial union local whose slogan is: One shop, one union.

Activities of Local Assemblies. The craft assemblies of the Knights engaged in collective bargaining exactly as the preceding—and succeeding—craft unions did, and with the same results, depending on the condition of the labor market and the scarcity of skill.

The industrial assemblies provided local and sporadic examples of collective bargaining, notably in railroad strikes in 1885. Local assemblies of miners also won some battles, but in manufacturing there is no record of success either in conducting strikes or collective bargaining.

The mixed assemblies probably could not do much collective bargaining (the record is blank on this) because it is hard to represent *all* employees in a locality with *all* employers.

Decline of the Knights. The program of the Knights was more ambitious than it lay within their power to attain. They multiplied the number of craft assemblies, but brought nothing new to craft unionism. Eventually they lost their craft assemblies to a rival federation of craft unions willing to concentrate on craft problems and let the semiskilled and unskilled workers go by the board.

Neither did the Knights succeed in working out a consistent program of industrial unionism. For one thing, they did not recognize the problem in their "mixed" assemblies, and for another, change was too rapid and factories were growing too lustily to be unionized.

The very grandeur of the Knights' conception of uniting all labor under a single banner helped seal the doom of the Order. It raised too many hopes, roused too many fears. Quite to its own surprise, the Order found itself fighting too many wars on too many fronts. In the first Wabash strike, it won a victory far in advance of the times. This was the first collective bargaining agreement of the industrial-union type. It provided for recognition of local committees and the adjustment of grievances. But when exuberant members tried to repeat and spread the victory, they lost, just one year later, all they had gained, and more. (See the chronology in the appendix to this chapter for details.)

An organization that was content with partial gains, on behalf of only part of the working population, in a part of the economy—and a shrinking part at that—took over where the Knights had nobly failed. That organization was the American Federation of Labor. The AFL fully succeeded, in a humdrum way, in carrying out part of what had been the grandiose total program of the "Noble and Holy Order of the Knights of Labor."

LABOR'S RETREAT, INDUSTRY'S ADVANCE: THE RISE OF THE AMERICAN FEDERATION OF LABOR

The AFL represented what may be called the "production model" of craft unionism, the result of a century of unconscious experimentation in union forms and activities. It discarded the excess weight of the unskilled and semiskilled, and by concentration on the skilled worker, adopted the features of unions that—up to that time—worked. They still work today, but in a relatively declining sector of the national economy.

The craft-union tradition was almost as old as the nation, but the history was broken, discontinuous, and regional. That is, craft unions had sprung up, died, and sprung up again. They were confined before 1860 largely to the eastern seaboard cities. Even though some of them had united in national federations, they had few locals west of the Alleghenies. It was from one of these craft federations, the Cigar Makers' International Union, that Samuel Gompers came to lead the AFL.

The Knights of Labor gave *craft unionism* a tremendous boost in numbers by organizing *craft assemblies* throughout the land, all the way to the Pacific coast. Still, the older national craft unions retained their identity and held on to their Locals, because craft unionism worked regardless of the label, and there was no room in the structure of the Knights for anything but local assemblies. In other words, the Knights did the *new* organizing in the field, the federations held on to the old.

The Craft-Union Strategy

In relation to the Knights, Gompers seems to have had two leading ideas: (1) to keep the already organized craft federations from losing their identity in the vague, mixed structure of the Knights, and (2) to capture the new membership represented in the craft assemblies of the

Knights. He and his associates succeeded in both aims. Gompers brought off the coup with two brilliant strokes.

The Strike for the Eight-Hour Day.   In 1881 a number of national craft unions came together in the National Federation of Organized Trades and Labor Unions, with Gompers as president. The member unions stuck to winning craft gains while the Knights stood forth as the champions of all labor; yet craft gains attracted the craft assemblies of the Knights.

In 1886 Gompers sent out a call for a nationwide strike on May 1 in favor of a popular demand: the eight-hour day in the building trades. He publicly sought the endorsement of Terence V. Powderly, Grand Master Workman of the Knights, but Powderly declined. He was wary of strikes in general after the spectacular defeat of the "second Wabash" strike earlier in 1886, which had damaged his organization; and he was wary in particular of Samuel Gompers and his craft unions.

But craft assemblies in the Knights wanted the eight-hour day as ardently as any of Gompers' National Federation men, and joined the strike. Then Powderly had a stroke of bad luck.

During a meeting at Chicago's Haymarket Square called by the Knights to protest violence against strikers, someone (possibly anarchists, possibly police provocateurs) exploded a bomb which killed several people. The Knights of Labor, who had sponsored the meeting, illogically and unjustly were blamed for the bombing, because anarchists charged with the crime were found to have been members of the Knights.

This incident accelerated the disintegration of the Knights. It gave Gompers a further opportunity.

The Breakaway of the Craft Assemblies.   The trades and labor unions federation now proposed that the craft assemblies of the Knights affiliate with their appropriate national craft unions, and that the Federation then affiliate with the Knights in a body. This proposal would have taken the skilled men in the craft assemblies away from their direct affiliation with the Knights and concentrated them, with their brethren of the Organized Trades and Labor Unions, in a virtually independent separate division. To this craft division the Knights might lend their celebrated name, but they could hardly expect to exercise much control over it. Powderly refused, but the craft assemblies proved more receptive to the invitation. It was by now commonly felt that the Knights were on the decline. As one after another of the craft assemblies went over to the Federation's national craft affiliates, the Order began to lose ground. The skilled men had been a cohesive force in the Knights. For them, collective bargaining worked and brought results; without them, the nonskilled industrial workers failed to maintain the Order and it gradually fell apart.

Gompers picked up the pieces. Not all the pieces; just the pieces he wanted—the craft assemblies. He put them together in a pattern that has lasted to the present day.

Those left out of the new Federation, which reorganized in 1886 as the AFL, found the factory and mass-production industry an even stronger fortress against the assault of unionism, as a result of developments that call for attention at this point.

Scientific Management

The movement that came to be known as "scientific management" dates from the same decade that saw the almost simultaneous dissolution of the Knights of Labor and establishment of the AFL. Scientific management accompanied, and must be regarded as part of and an adjustment to, a series of technological achievements so advanced that they have been called by some a "new" and essentially "American" industrial revolution. It was marked by new inventions and the application of new sources of power: the telephone, the electric light, the internal-combustion engine, the electric motor, and many others. It also brought new methods of production. Henry Ford carried to its ultimate, logical development the serialized production of a complex mechanical product, the automobile, built out of interchangeable parts.

Aided by scientific management, the American industrial revolution brought sweeping changes in society and in the work relationship between employer and employee. The factory became the dominant unit of production in the economy, and in the factory the engineers had all but licked the problems of shortage of skill and shortage of unskilled labor. They created instead the place of the semiskilled worker, and in so doing:

a)   They cut the ground from under craft unionism in the factory.
b)   They nullified, in manufacturing, the labor-market basis of bargaining for skill as a scarce and vital element of production.
c)   They increased productivity, built living standards, and made it possible for the untrained worker to come in and earn a living wage, after a few days' factory training.
d)   They made the jobs so simple that the worker was just as much an interchangeable and replaceable part as the product he worked on.

All these developments made the factory impregnable to unionism of the old kind. If factories were going to be organized, new ways would have to be found.

It was no use looking to the AFL for the new ways. At the very time when the factory system quickened its advance on a broad technological and managerial front, the AFL beat its historic retreat into the handicrafts, not to move out again for nearly 50 years.

If it could be established that Gompers and his AFL colleagues foresaw, however dimly, what that half century would bring, the retreat might deserve to be called "strategic." The evidence available does not justify using the term in its full conscious implications, but students of the labor movement see in it today at least the strategy of elementary survival: He who simply runs away will live to fight another day.

PREINDUSTRIAL UNIONISM OF THE LEFT

The tangible assets left behind by the Knights of Labor—the craft assemblies—went to the AFL. The spiritual heritage passed to the radicals in and around the labor movement: the political socialists and the nonpolitical syndicalists. The syndicalists, in particular, who in 1905 founded the Industrial Workers of the World (IWW) built on the grand conception of the Knights, which was a single, all-embracing Order of those who worked for a living. The "Wobblies" (IWW) reached out to organize those working men and women to whom the AFL was closed, because they had no skill—the industrial workers. The Wobblies preached their gospel with a fervor that had not been felt since the great days of the Knights.

The Industrial Workers of the World (IWW)

In 1912 there was a spontaneous walkout of textile workers in some big factories in Lawrence and Lowell, Massachusetts, in protest against wage cuts and unadjusted grievances. The Wobblies, who had members in the mills, assumed the leadership of the strike and led the workers to victory: restoration of the wage cuts, adjustment of grievances. In the face of considerable provocation, they avoided violence, though an attempt was made to blame them for an explosion in the mills that was later discovered to have been set off by one of the factory managers.

This victory was as electrifying for its day as the Knights' victory in the first Wabash strike, but the success was short-lived. The following year the IWW lost an equally important strike in the silk mills of Paterson and Passaic, N.J. Taught by the experience of their Massachusetts brethren, the New Jersey mill owners did not wait for a pretext for violent action against the strikers, but turned unremitting violence against them at the plant gate from the very start.

Even if the IWW had won both strikes, there is a question whether they could have built a permanent organization or achieved settled collective bargaining. Their radical ideology opposed the very thought of making "peace with the exploiters." They did not know how to establish a permanent living relationship with management. To be fair, it ought probably to be said that management was no more reconciled than the IWW to the idea of peace and collective bargaining. Industrial workers *had* to strike to get a hearing. The Wobblies showed that such strikes could be won.

Lessons of the IWW Strikes

The IWW experiences in the textile mills showed that the factory was a single, unified, coordinated organism. It had to be organized totally, and all at once; it could not be organized piecemeal. The individual was too easy to replace. The entire force had to walk out to stop production.

This called for a *mass movement* of the workers. Mass movements were possible only under unusual conditions, when all the workers were stirred up at once. Spontaneous walkouts against wage cuts or widespread grievances provided the union's best opportunity of organizing.

Once workers were on strike, it became necessary for the union to control *physical access to the plant*. This was for the purpose of keeping not only outside replacements but wavering union members from going to work.

Any strike brings economic pressure to bear on the strikers. Craft unions, which rarely had more than a fraction of their members out on strike at one time, could ease the pressure by paying direct strike benefits. An industrial union that tried to pay benefits to keep strikers from going back would simply go broke, and even if it were possible, that would not keep the employer from hiring outside replacements. Thus the strategy of industrial unionism depended upon control of the plant gate. As long as moral persuasion or appeals to solidarity kept the gate closed, well and good. If these should fail, militants on the picket line had to keep out the timid by threats or violence. Violence on one side evokes it on the other.

Failure of Radical Industrial Unionism

Early industrial unionists had little experience to go on. To many their theories seemed impractical. Industrial unionism had, indeed, existed in the mines since the 1890s, but mining is not manufacturing and has problems that are peculiar to the industry. Radical leadership of industrial unionism failed for several reasons.

It clashed with AFL vested interests. The AFL craft unions claimed jurisdiction over all members of their crafts, including those who worked in factories, even though they were unable to organize the factory craftsmen. They also opposed "dual unionism." Thus they opposed any attempt to organize dual factory unions that would deprive them of their jurisdictional rights.

Radical sponsorship was a liability. The socialists, syndicalists, anarchists, and others who had a program for organizing the factories also had things in their programs that many workers would not swallow. The Wobblies for instance, who were syndicalists, drew a large proportion of their members from itinerant workers—hoboes—whose mentality and view of life differed sharply from that of the stay-at-home factory worker with a roof over his head. The anarchists preached and practiced violence.

The IWW experiment in preindustrial unionism was not the last attempt carried out by leftist elements. After the First World War the newly founded Communist Party led some strikes, all of which were lost. The communists in the AFL formed a "Trade Union Education League" to propagandize for industrial unionism, but were rebuffed and expelled, whereupon they changed the name of their organization to Trade Union Unity League and organized "dual" industrial unions. None of these made any headway toward collective bargaining.

PREINDUSTRIAL UNIONISM OF THE RIGHT

Although there were some further, ineffectual efforts from the left to form industrial unions after the war, the war year, 1917, may be taken as the year of its defeat. The same year marked the start of a new development that evolved into industrial unionism "of the right."

The First World War, 1914–18

Factory production expanded tremendously, mostly in the metal-working industries, under stimulus of the war. For the first time since the appearance of large-scale factory production in America there was an *absolute* shortage of labor in all categories. A foreman could no longer keep a worker in line by pointing to the crowd of job applicants at the gate. There wasn't anybody at the gate any more.

Old ways of doing things had to be discarded. Many supervisors were hastily promoted workmen unaccustomed to the ways of supervision. Foremen who had formerly, for instance, done the hiring of new employees could not spare the time to do it any more. Centralized hiring, centralized training, centralized handling of wages and raises, under newly established personnel departments, became the rule.

Wages skyrocketed as employers bid against each other for the available labor supply. Turnover became a major problem of management as workers shopped around for higher wages. The government had to resort to wage-freeze and job-freeze methods.

The Unions and the War. Gompers and the AFL stoutly supported the war effort. They gave a no-strike pledge for the duration and volunteered their services in war bond drives and other win-the-war activities. As has been seen, they did not have many members in the factories, where the bulk of war production was going on, but now there began to be an AFL influx to the factories.

Boom times are the traditional times of craft-union expansion, for the labor-market situation favors their bargaining power. Union men got jobs in factories, and skilled men in the factories joined unions. Employers had to bargain with the AFL unions in order to keep their men. This did not solve all the employer's problems. He had problems with *all* his men, and dealing with craft unions could, at best, only solve part of his problems.

Though an employer might be willing to deal with a craft union on day-to-day problems, as a temporizing measure, he did not relish the idea of permanent *recognition* of an organization—or cluster of organizations—that could not solve his problems.

The National War Labor Board. When in the First World War (as in the Second), the government froze wages and jobs it had to provide a substitute for the mechanisms of the market that had been abandoned. Labor relations and the regulation of labor resources became emergency problems. The government put these problems in the hands of a National War Labor Board, which had authority to determine questions of wages and representation on a plant-by-plant basis, as trouble developed or threatened.

A device the NWLB tried out to solve labor relations problems in war industry factories was the "works council." This was a plan that permitted employees to select representatives, by departments, and required employers to meet and deal with these representatives on grievances and matters of wages, hours, and working conditions. The program worked so well that it was applied to factory after factory, not only where trouble had broken out, but even in cases where trouble merely threatened. The works councils gave management and employees a way of settling current emergency problems, while side-stepping two issues considered important by management and by the AFL unions, respectively:

Recognition. Management did not have to recognize the unions, but only the elected representatives of their own employees.

Jurisdiction. The works councils, which were not membership organizations, did not challenge the jurisdictional claims of the established unions.

Postwar Industry

The war created larger factories and more of them. The labor shortage vanished when peace returned. This was the result of the loss of war orders, and it was augmented as time went on by reconversion cutbacks and widespread rationalization of plant and equipment.

Experience with Labor Relations. A number of factory managements got their first taste of dealing with employee representatives during wartime. Their experience seems to have taught them that craft unionism provided no constructive answer to the problems involved in running a factory in which craftsmen are a minority, semiskilled workers the majority. The experience with works councils was favorable, or at least neutral. At their best, the works councils helped solve grievances and problems of upward communication, and they gave workers a sense of participation in the effort for production that the entire factory was making.

The Works Councils. When the NWLB disbanded at the end of the war, the legal and official sanctions that had sustained the works councils expired. This left it up to each individual employer to choose whether to continue them under his own sponsorship.

Some employers dissolved their works councils, but a good many continued them. They did so because they had proved to be a good device for grievance adjustment and for securing employee cooperation, and were a hedge against unions, since they performed certain union functions without having either a membership base or outside affiliations.

As time went on, the works-council idea spread in the form of "Employee Representation Plans" or ERP's. This was partly the result of favorable experience of individual employers with the ERP's and partly on recommendation of employer organizations which made studies of them.

It is noteworthy that the ERP's, while not actually unions, had two important characteristics that go along with industrial unionism. "One shop, one ERP" might be a companion slogan to the industrial union slogan, "One shop, one union." Representation was by department, not by skill or status.

The committees set up by the plans closely correspond to industrial union shop-steward systems.

The Employee Representation Plan Committees. During the years from 1920–30 Employee Representation Plans increased from a total of 196 to 869, and the number of workers covered from 403,765 to 1,547,766.

During the same period AFL membership declined from 4,124,200 to 3,479,800.

The AFL called these plans "company unionism," and condemned them one and all. Looking ahead for a moment to the decade of the 1930s, it might be noted here that several of the CIO unions (steel and autos) got a good part of their start by capturing these company unions. They were, in fact, industrial unionism "of the right," created by management. They needed only to build their management-sponsored representation into a membership base, and gain a union affiliation, to emerge as full-fledged industrial unions.

This brings to an end the prehistory of industrial unionism and industrial-union bargaining in America. Labor gained experience in the ways and workings of the factory; management found that worker consent to factory conditions made for productive operations. The point implicitly at issue between labor and management was not whether there should be factory organizations of workers but whether these organizations should "belong" to management or to the unions.

The answer came in 1933.

THE TRIUMPH OF INDUSTRIAL UNIONISM

The Great Depression of the 1930s was the backdrop for the drama of the rise of industrial unionism. Never before had unions succeeded in establishing themselves in the factories; never since have they been driven out or lost appreciable ground.

The Great Depression, 1929–40

The tremendous number of persons thrown out of work or into part-time employment by the depression (estimated at up to one third of the working force, with others on reduced pay) had never been equaled, but this is only one measure of the impact of the event. It was a blow to management prestige and confidence. Herbert Hoover had been elected President in 1928 as a "great engineer." With the deepening of the depression, the prestige that had surrounded engineers and managers in the prosperous 1920s disappeared. Not only did the worker lose confidence in the ability of management to solve the problems of depression, but managers lost confidence in themselves. An appreciable number broke with traditional attitudes of independence to ask for help from the government.

The depression brought a growth of radicalism. As has been true whenever economic hardships threatened the worker's subsistence, he turned to radical political solutions. Demonstrations of the unemployed, "bonus marches," "hunger marches," armed skirmishes of farmers against tax sales, and similar instances of direct action took place. The Democratic victory in 1932 was largely a negative anti-Hoover vote. The New Deal program channeled the discontent into positive support for thorough-going measures of reform.

As has been brought out, company unions and Employee Representation Plans (ERP's) followed the wartime works councils into the factories. Management-sponsored and controlled, these organizations performed grievance-handling functions and were a medium of communication with the working force. Raises and benefits that had accompanied prosperity were passed on to employees through the ERP's. When wage cuts took the place of raises, workers lost faith in the efficacy of management-sponsored ERP's.

Effect on the AFL.   The AFL, which had been shrinking in numbers through the preceding decade of prosperity, further lost members and influence as the depression advanced. The industries on which it depended, such as construction, went into stagnation. The AFL leaders turned to political lobbying for public works, and for such measures as the Davis-Bacon Act requiring payment of "prevailing wages" on government work. Prevailing wages, where the unions had any strength at all, meant the union scale.

NRA and the Unions.   The NRA came at a time when the AFL was at its lowest ebb, and did not immediately help it recover. (The NRA, in fact, did not bring actual recovery, though it gave that illusion; genuine recovery came only when the war in Europe began to stimulate American industry with orders.) NRA developments affected the international unions making up the AFL in different ways:

The Craft Unions. Construction work, the mainstay of the craft unions, was slow to recover. Union men found part-time employment on public works, where they drew (under Bacon-Davis Act provisions) union wages for each hour worked, but shared the hours to spread employment. Craft-union activity waned in the private sector of the economy to concentrate on "pressure-group" tactics with the big employer of the day, the government. Full-scale recovery, when it came, put them back in the business of negotiating with private employers, but this was simply a return to what they had been doing before; depression did not change them.

The Mine Workers. The only true industrial union in the AFL was John L. Lewis's United Mine Workers. This union came to vigorous life, out of a slump, under the influence of the NRA. It rapidly completed the organization of the independently owned mines, but failed to make headways in the "captive" mines owned by the steel companies. Company unions had employer recognition in the captive mines. These included some of the largest and most productive, and the steel companies were constantly extending their mine holdings. Unless he could sign up the workers in the captive mines, Lewis's hold on the independents was threatened. This constituted pressure—pressure from the right—to organize the steel mills. The Homestead strike of 1892 had taught the lesson that the steel mills could only be organized industrially.

The Garment Unions. Two sizable "quasi-industrial" unions operated in the twin fields of men's and women's clothing: the Amalgamated Clothing Workers (ACW) and the International Ladies' Garment Workers (ILGWU). Each was a collection of craft unions amalgamated or fused into a single top-level organization, with joint boards at membership level to knit the locals together for united action. Under the NRA these garment unions made strides in organizing the many small shops that make up the production units of their industry, the bulk of which was centered in New York. They looked around for other fields to conquer. A special problem for them was the "runaway shops" that moved out of New York to escape the union. In addition, a large proportion of the members were foreign-born, from eastern European and Mediterranean countries. In this group a small but influential core of communists, surrounded by their sympathizers, strove to take away the leadership of the unions from the conservative socialists who headed them. Thus for ideological reasons—pressure from the left—the garment unions pressed for industrial organization of the factories throughout the land. This was a long-standing goal of the radical left in the labor movement.

Conflict of Interests and Personalities. It is in the interest of craft unionists to organize all who practice their craft, and no one who does not. To take in others, not qualified, is to water down their greatest asset.

skill. Looking at the factories, craft-union leaders saw a minority of skilled workers whom they could accept as members, surrounded by a majority whom they would not. The easiest thing to do—and the most practical— was to let the factories alone, but if someone did organize the factories, the craft unions wanted these skilled men. They wanted them for the job opportunities they represented, and to extend their control over the right to learn the trade. That demand ran counter to a fundamental tenet of industrial unionism: One shop, one union; and only industrial unions could organize the factories.

Tradition also plays a part in any organization, and the tradition of the AFL was to stay out of the factories. Gompers taught them not to dilute their crafts but to concentrate on the skilled trades. They got their fingers burned every time they touched the factories.

Personalities. Human passions and ambition play their part in history. John L. Lewis was an able and ambitious man, with bitter enemies as well as powerful support in the top councils of the labor movement. Sidney Hillman was a dedicated man, a "reasonable" and practical labor diplomat and strategist, but nonetheless an old Socialist. Young men were on the way up in the labor movement, too, impatient for power and unwilling to wait for the entrenched old guard labor leaders (who, like old soldiers, never die), to move out and make room for them. No vested interests, no sentimental memories, no hallowed traditions held them to the AFL; they stood to gain more by striking out on their own. Personal factors like this helped bring the CIO into being.

The Factory Workers. Leaders do not entirely determine the direction of events; the "masses"—people, public opinion, in this case, workers —have a share. Most of the new members who flocked spontaneously into the NRA unions were semiskilled workers with no previous experience of unionism. Their working lives had been spent in a factory environment; they thought in terms of "the shop," not any particular skill. They saw no place for their kind in the old-style craft union, and they resented craft-union attempts to split their ranks by taking out the members they prized the most—their own collection of skilled men. (In Akron, for example, after federal locals were organized in the rubber factories, the AFL tried to put maintenance men from the shops into their corresponding building-trades locals. The answer was open revolt, and the rubber workers joined the CIO. The skilled factory workers themselves showed that their first loyalty was not to their craft, but with the shop.) Wherever the NRA called new unions into life, the pressure of the rank and file was practically unanimous for the industrial form of organization.

The Rise of the CIO

The moves and countermoves in labor's civil war are listed in the chronology, and the conflicting interests and motives of the contestants have been noted above. Here it is proposed to concentrate on the direction taken by the rebel branch of the labor movement, and the results achieved.

A brief reminder of the lessons taught by the IWW strikes in the textile mills is first in order. That experience showed that there were two essential conditions for success in organizing the mass-production factories: (1) organization must be total and simultaneous; and (2) the union must be able to control physical access to the plant.

Ideally, all of the workers of the factory must join the union at the same time. Practically, a good majority (or even, on occasion, a determined minority, provided they had the sympathy of the rest) would be enough, and they would have to join not at the same instant but in a very short time—a few days at most. That was to prevent the factory from hiring replacements, as could easily be done if organization were piecemeal and stretched over time.

Once organized, the union must be able to shut the plant gate by means of a picket line, and keep the plant gate closed. It might not have to do so, but that was the ultimate test of its ability to survive. Again, this was to prevent replacement.

The CIO organizing drive went through three phases, the first of which directly confirms the conditions set forth above. The two later phases do not contradict them, but reflect the modification of the situation that resulted from the Supreme Court's upholding of the Wagner Act.

The Phase of Mass Organization. From the inception of the NRA to the defeat of the bitter strikes in Little Steel, workers literally poured into the new factory unions. It was a mass movement, like water flooding out of a broken dam. It took place during the period when the validity of the Wagner Act was still in doubt and while employer challenges against it were still pending before the Supreme Court which had declared the NRA unconstitutional. Some of the mass movement manifestations were the following:

Spontaneous Organization of "NRA Unions." Some of these unions died as quickly as they were born. Others, as noted, found places in the internationals such as the mine workers' and the garment workers' unions, that were ready to receive them. Still others, as in autos and rubber, made a nucleus around which new internationals were formed. Few of these latter unions came into being as the result of any concerted outside organizing drive; they were real instances of "spontaneous generation."

Capture of Company Unions. At least two of today's mightiest industrial unions, the Steelworkers and the Autoworkers, got their start by capturing the councils management had set up in the factories to give employees representation. The members of these ERP councils had been elected by their fellow workers; they were the natural leaders. Depression experiences had shown many of them the futility of trying to get important results for their constituents when they were dependent upon management. Now, by going over in a body to the CIO, a General Motors or United States Steel ERP council could quickly convert its electorate into *a membership*. Membership support made a council independent of management. The issuance of a CIO charter, furthermore, ended the isolation of the individual plants and linked their workers up with others in the industry. The auto locals had to fight to keep their independence. In big steel, the companies signed up without a fight. In either case, there was a mass shift from company-union status to the CIO.

The Sit-down Strikes.   Control of the plant gate is all very well, but when you control physical access to the very machine you work at, only physical violence can get you out to make room for a replacement. There is something hysterical and primitive about this notion, but the sit-downs were not festivals of pure reason: they were direct, emotional reactions to the mass movement of the day. They worked, though even their most ardent advocates knew they would not work forever. Either the emotional outburst that lay behind them would die down, or would develop into the most destructive violence in labor history. To the eternal credit of Governor Murphy of Michigan, the most critical of the sit-down strikes were settled without violence.

The Wagner Act Phase.   The Wagner Act (Wagner-Connery Act) modified the situation in several important ways. The issue in the early CIO clashes with industrial management was recognition: Recognition always has to be the first issue in labor-management relations. The Wagner Act provided legal ways of getting recognition, and required employers to bargain "in good faith" with the unions that had recognition. It was no longer necessary to shut the shop gate; only to win a majority in a Labor Board election.

Union Jurisdiction and the "Appropriate Unit."   The Wagner Act ignored the traditional AFL claim to determine "jurisdiction," with its corollary of "no dual unionism." Regardless of craft claims or industrial ideologies, the Labor Board had the power to determine the appropriate unit. To clinch this even further, the Board gave the union winning recognition an absolute right—a kind of monopoly—to bargain for that unit for a reasonable period of time, without disturbance from rival labor unions. In practice, the Board made the factory the appropriate unit in cases where factory organization was at issue. This was not done just to please the industrial unionists. Management preferred dealing with one union to having the headaches, well known in the building trades, of jurisdictional disputes, rivalry, and strikes between fractional or competing unions.

At first the AFL contested this arrangement, but the Board paid no attention to craft claims unless the contesting craft unions could show a previous history of collective bargaining with the company for the craftsmen in the plant. This, of course, they could not do, for the craft unions had never cracked the factories. Later the Board modified its position (the

"Globe doctrine") and permitted small craft units to be carved out of the factories, provided the workers in the smaller unit desired it. This neither harmed the industrial unions very greatly nor very much benefited the craft unions. The AFL did not succeed in stopping the CIO steamroller until the AFL Internationals decided to reverse their tactics. Old craft unions like the International Association of Machinists and the International Brotherhood of Electrical Workers copied the CIO and started organizing unskilled and semiskilled, as well as skilled men, in the factories. Only when they began to do this was the decline of the AFL checked. A dose of industrial unionism was the medicine that brought recovery.

A Law with Teeth in It. Section 7a of the National Industrial Recovery Act had given workers the right to organize and warned employers not to interfere with the exercise of that right, but there were no "teeth" in the law. Company unions flourished alongside the affiliated unions under the NRA. The Wagner Act had teeth. It outlawed company unions and effectively prevented employers from discriminating against workers for joining or being active in a union.

This would seem to make the first of the essential conditions mentioned above—simultaneous and total unionization of the factory—no longer essential. Piecemeal organization now seemed possible. The difficulty for the union lay in proving that when a company fired a union man it was on account of his union activity. At first the unions won many cases, because employer habits were strong and methods direct, but as managers refined their tactics it became harder to get the evidence. (At the same time, real management conformity to the law increased.) An unfair labor-practice charge, at best, was not enough to organize a factory, and brought efforts in that direction to a standstill while the case was pending. If the Board's verdict went against the union, previous gains could easily be lost. Workers had never known the kind of protection the act guaranteed. They had to see results before they trusted it.

The company unions also proved harder to deal with than had been expected. Where management gave its support openly, the case was easily proved and the company union disestablished and dissolved. Where the support was secret, or subtly given, it was harder to draw the line between a company union and a genuine independent. It was the experience of most CIO organizers that the company union, except in its most obvious form, was their hardest nut to crack; harder by far than the AFL, until the AFL took up industrial-union tactics.

The Wagner Act phase was by no means a setback for the CIO but it was a period of slower going in organization. The mass movement days were over. A union had to make its way now by winning an election. It had to convince the worker that he ought to vote for the union when he stepped into the polling place and cast his secret ballot.

The Collective Bargaining Phase. The third phase of CIO growth overlapped the second phase in time, but shifted the emphasis from organizing to collective bargaining. Organizing still went on, but it was based on reaching the individual worker by "doorbell-ringing" methods of individual approach, either at home or in his department in the factory. Mass media—handbills, shopgate meetings, loudspeaker appeals—became a supplement to, and not the mainstay of, organizing techniques. Reaching the individual worker, in his tens of thousands, called for inner-union organization. This naturally took the form of departmentalization, after the pattern of the departments in the shop, since it is in his department that the worker meets his fellows and knows them best.

Parallel with this development came grievance handling by the union as a service to its members. Local unions set up grievance machinery in the newly negotiated contracts, and set about gaining experience in settling grievances by contact with their equally inexperienced managements. The departmental organization was a natural for that, too. The inner-union organization that is active in the shop during the working day is the shop-steward system. It would seem that in the steward system, or shop committee, unions in mass-production manufacturing have found the organ that enables them to operate effectively in the factories. In doing so they have solved, quite incidentally, some of management's problems in the field of grievance handling and communications. They have given workers a vital feeling of participation. The stewards make up a complete and flexible on-the-job medium for mutual accommodation and understanding between union and company. How well this medium works for both depends upon their attitudes, their trust in each other, their training and skill in dealing with each other, and the stresses and strains their over-all relationship exposes them to. If stewards were to disappear tomorrow from the factories, management would probably have to call them back in some form.

Subsequent Developments

The situation has not basically changed since the CIO unions reached the third phase of development described above. The process has continued; the parties have matured. It is necessary merely to mention four big incidents in this development:

The Second World War. The demands of national unity in the face of the emergency brought management and labor together for practical cooperation under the sponsorship of government. The two branches of the labor movement also dropped their rivalry for the duration. Both gave a "no-strike" pledge, and in return were given the means of adjusting grievances and disputes with management by representation on the tripartite National War Labor Board. In contrast to the First World War, the labor members now had a membership base, and agreements in the plants whose problems reached the Board. The unions could help with implementing, as well as making, Board decisions. They did much to "sell" the idea of unrestricted output to the war workers in the shops. These workers found that being in a union meant representation on the body that had power over their wages, hours, and working conditions. Union growth, as a consequence, continued and accelerated during the war.

The Strikes of 1946 and the Taft-Hartley Law.   Just as the reconversion to peacetime production brought a wave of strikes in 1919, in the course of which management shook off the hold the unions had briefly gotten in the plants, a wave of strikes took place in 1946 after the Second World War. This time the unions were industrial unions, and they held their place. While wages, with prices, had been frozen, labor and management had to make their mutual accommodations during wartime mostly at the fringe. After the war, now, pensions and fringe benefits came to the fore along with the traditional issue of wages.

Public reaction against the magnitude of the postwar strike wave created an atmosphere favorable to the passage in 1947 of a law Senator Robert A. Taft had been pushing for some time. Technically an amendment to the Wagner Act, the Taft-Hartley law reaffirmed its basic principles, but with some changes. It aimed at restoring balance by weighting the management side of the scale which, Taft contended, had been empty in contrast to the heavy concessions to labor. It is here enough to say that the new law worked out not so badly as labor leaders predicted nor so well as management people hoped.

The AFL-CIO Merger.   It has been shown above that the issue of principle between the craft and industrial unionists, so bitterly contested in labor's civil war, ceased to separate the practice of the parties after the AFL adopted industrial-union forms in addition to its old craft forms. To bring this about it had been necessary to split the labor movement. Once the principle was accepted, there was no reason for the split to continue.

Still, the two labor federations did not come together very quickly. Reasons for their reluctance were various. The left-wing unions in the CIO feared any move that would put them under the domination of the outspokenly anti-Communist AFL. That problem the CIO solved by expelling the left-wing unions and issuing new charters to absorb their former members. Personal rivalries, particularly after the death of Phillip Murray, president of the CIO, also played a part. But logic, and the Taft-Hartley law, inevitably pushed the AFL and the CIO toward a reconciliation.

Why it came exactly when it did, and in the form it did, is a matter for detailed study, but it was bound to come someway, sometime. It finally took place in 1955. The two organizations merged first at the top. The merger worked its way slowly down through state organizations to regional and city councils.

It did not bring about much realignment of international union jurisdictions. While it cut down on interunion rivalry and raiding within its ranks, it did not solve the problems of dual unionism, for some important unions failed to join and others left the ranks. "A rope of sand" was John L. Lewis's characterization of the newly formed federation. The two separate but intertwining strands of labor organization, craft and industrial, seemed again to be untwisting, as they had throughout the history of labor in the United States.

The Alliance for Labor Action. Today, nearly two decades later, the AFL-CIO remains stable and united despite serious defections and the rise of some large new independent unions. In 1957 the federation expelled the Teamsters Union which, with 1.6 million members, was (and is) the largest American union on grounds of alleged racketeering associations. Its president, James Hoffa, went to prison on charges of jury tampering, but the union continued to flourish. In 1968 Walter Reuther led his million-member UAW out of the federation and the following year joined with the independent Teamsters to form the Alliance for Labor Action (ALA), which was later joined by some smaller unions.

Superficially, this seems to repeat the history of the CIO breakaway from the AFL, but events so far have not borne this out. The dissidents made no attempt to raid or weaken existing AFL-CIO unions; inter-union rivalry, on the whole, somewhat declined. Thus when President Nixon set up machinery to implement his Phase II economic program, first launched with the wage-price freeze of August 1970, Fitzsimmons of the Teamsters (who followed Hoffa as president) and Woodcock of the Auto Workers (who followed Reuther) sat with Meany, long-term president of the AFL-CIO, on the national wage board and cooperated with him and the other labor members on national wage policy issues.

Public Employee Bargaining

Without any doubt, the most significant development in collective bargaining today is the emergence of large-scale, vigorous unionization of public employees: federal, state, and local. Some have organized in craft unions or craftlike professional associations. The bulk of them belong to organizations of the industrial union type.

This extension of collective bargaining to government agencies and jurisdictions employing some nine million people would be a big event in terms of numbers alone. Besides that, it raises new issues with far-reaching implications. For example, government employees almost without exception are forbidden by law to strike—yet they do strike, or have begun to do so recently. A strike of public employees takes effect in direct proportion to the essentiality of the services the strike denies. When 200,000 postal workers walked out for about a week in early 1970, they gave lawmakers and executive branch administrators some problems to solve that went far beyond the simple restoration of postal services or rise in postal rates. How do you deal with massive disobedience to law, particularly when the illegal act—the strike—would be legal if the employer were not the government? What follows if you deal with the leaders of the employees who are taking the illegal action? What follows if you *don't* deal with them?

The right of public employees to strike is a troublesome issue, but only one of many raised by unionization of this hitherto inactive group. Since government workers have shown they *can* strike even though they *may* not, is there a substitute for the strike over substantive issues? And if one can be found—thus far none has—will the substitute also apply in the private sector, where labor and management are at present free to resort to the strike or the lockout?

Unionized public employees thus seem to have chosen to follow the collective bargaining path towards altering and defining their relations with public employers. Because of the importance of this development, the authors of this book defer discussion at this point. Instead, they devote two later chapters to the subject, Chapters 15 and 16, which make up Part IV; and have included several cases on public employee bargaining in Part V.

SUMMARY

Collective bargaining in America takes two forms: craft-union bargaining in handicraft industry, and industrial-union bargaining in mass-production industry.

Craft-union bargaining took shape early. It survives today, in the restricted sector of the economy still ruled by handicraft methods, not much changed from its original form.

Industrial-union bargaining did not become a practical reality until long after the rise of the factory system and the development of mass-production methods, which created the conditions for its eventual emergence. The history of the past century is therefore the story of a quest; a search —groping and tentative at first, confident and sure at last—for answers to the social and organizational problems raised by mass-production industry.

It is the story of the industrial worker's fight for something that would give him the kind of say in determining his conditions that craft unions give their members, as he struggled to create organizations that would win him the right to engage in collective bargaining with his employer.

It is also the story of the industrial employer's fight to stay clear of the restraints of collective bargaining in the exercise of his function as enterpriser in a growing economy. Factory methods and machinery freed him from the craft union's control in the first place, and he easily defeated every attempt at forcing him to bargain craft-union style. Industrial unionism in its embryo form posed a stronger challenge, but he defeated that, too, though it sometimes took bloody battles at the plant gate.

But the growth of enterprises, first in mere size, then in the increasing complexity of their internal organization and interdependence in a changing world, created needs—management needs—that in the end only industrial unionism and collective bargaining could answer.

The answers found to date are not final, but as this book has tried to show, they work. They raise new questions, but their study points, perhaps, to solutions that may serve society even better in the future.

QUESTIONS FOR DISCUSSION

1. Craft unions came early on the scene; industrial unions, late. Why did the industrial form not make the craft form obsolete and drive it out of existence? What has, in fact, made many craft unions obsolete? What keeps others alive?

2. How do you account for the success of the Knights of Labor? For its eventual failure?

3. Both the radical Industrial Workers of the World and the conservative Employee Representation Plans were, in contrast to the AFL, oriented towards factory conditions at a time when factory production had become dominant in the economy. How do you account for the fact that the craft-oriented AFL outlived them both?

4. What historical conditions favored the rise and ultimate success of the CIO? How did these differ from the conditions favoring the establishment of the AFL?

5. What made it possible for the AFL and CIO to drop their rivalry and merge in the AFL-CIO? Why did the merger not come a decade sooner? A decade later?

APPENDIX: CHRONOLOGY OF EVENTS IN THE HISTORY OF COLLECTIVE BARGAINING IN THE UNITED STATES, 1786–1960.

1786   First recorded strike, called by Philadelphia Journeymen Printers, against a wage cut.

1799   First recorded attempt at collective bargaining by Philadelphia Journeymen Cordwainers (shoemakers) was answered by the employers with a lockout and followed by a negotiated settlement between the union and the employer association.

1806   First criminal conspiracy case against Cordwainers in Philadelphia. Defendants found guilty of a combination to raise wages.

1820   A depression year. Unions died out or became inactive.

1824   With return of prosperity unions became active again. Numerous strikes in the larger cities.

1825   Boston House Carpenters struck for the 10-hour day; lost.

1827   Building-trades workers, striking in Philadelphia for the 10-hour day, formed the first City Central organization of local unions, the Mechanics' Union of Trade Associations. (This in turn established the first political party of labor, the Working Men's Party, which, like other labor parties of the 19th century, suffered defeat but left an imprint on the established political parties by causing them to woo the workingman with planks in the platform such as: free and compulsory public education, abolition of imprisonment for debt, and other reforms demanded by the labor parties.)

1831　　New England Association of Farmers, Mechanics and Other Working Men formed in Providence, R.I., spread throughout New England. Seen by some as the first industrial union, but was more a political than a union movement. Agitated for the 10-hour day in textile mills and factories. Died out after 1834.

1833–37　During these years the workingmen's benevolent societies turned into genuine unions of craftsmen. City centrals were established in many cities; there were many strikes for wage demands. Some specific developments during this period were as follows:

1834　　First attempt at forming a national organization of Labor: a federation of City Centrals called the National Trades' Union. Disappeared in 1837.

1835　　In the Geneva Cordwainers case, and a similar case involving Tailors in 1836, New York courts upheld a law based on the conspiracy doctrine, making concerted activity to get a raise in wages illegal.

1836　　Employer Association activity became marked in response to union activity. Fought closed-shop demands by attempting to refuse to employ union members. Turned with greater frequency to court action against unions under the conspiracy doctrine and existing legal precedent.

First national federation of local unions of a single craft was organized: the National Cooperative Association of Journeymen Cordwainers. Printers also federated, and other crafts followed in succeeding years

1837　　Depression year. Dropoff of union activity.

1842　　In the case of *Commonwealth* v. *Hunt* the very influential Massachusetts Supreme Court overturned the conspiracy doctrine and declared unions not illegal.

1840–60　Gradual (though intermittent) increase in volume of union activity along lines already followed: Local union bargaining with local employer associations, activity of City Centrals, formation and growth of national federations of the various crafts.

Industrial Revolution influence increasingly felt: Bessemer process for steelmaking introduced to U.S.; greater mechanization; intensification of factory methods and invasion of many handicraft fields by the factories. Unions find little success in penetrating factories.

1861–65　The Civil War intensified the trends mentioned above.

1866　　National Labor Union, a federation of national craft federations, established under leadership of William H. Sylvis, head of the Iron Moulders' Union. Lasted until 1872.

1869　　Knights of Labor founded in Philadelphia by a group of journeymen tailors. Began as a secret society and spread slowly at first among skilled-worker groups; but under the influence of Uriah H. Stephens, a member who had started out to become a Baptist minister, it opened its ranks to all who belonged to the "Brotherhood of Toil."

1873   Financial panic, followed by a long depression.

1877   Strikes against pay cuts on the railways broke out on lines east of the Mississippi, with violent clashes between strikers and federal troops in Baltimore and Pittsburgh. More than 100 killed. Troops finally put down the strikes.

1878   Knights of Labor organized nationally. Stephens, first Grand Master Workman, succeeded by Terence V. Powderly.
Period of recovery from depression began.

1881   Delegates of craft unions met in Pittsburgh to form the Federation of Organized Trades and Labor Unions (the forerunner of the AFL).

1882   After negotiations between Powderly and Cardinal Gibbons of Baltimore, the Knights of Labor renounced secrecy and revised its ritual, and the Roman Catholic church withdrew its ban on membership in the Knights.
Strike of railway workers on the West Coast against wage cuts, led by members of the Knights of Labor, resulted in rescinding of cuts.

1883   Depression year.

1885   Railway workers on the "Southwest System" controlled by Jay Gould, New York financier, struck against wage cuts. Organized into the Knights of Labor after the strike broke out spontaneously, the workers kept the trains from moving until Gould met and signed an agreement in New York with Powderly: first "Wabash strike."
Frederick W. Taylor started experiments at the Midvale and Bethlehem steel plants that led to the discoveries of "scientific management."

1886   A "big year" in labor history.
A strike which started as a "wildcat" on the Gould-controlled MKT line was decisively defeated. The Knights lost prestige and members as a result. (Second "Wabash strike.")
The Federation of Organized Trades and Labor Unions, led by Gompers, called a nationwide strike for the eight-hour day, to start May 1. Powderly refused to give the move the official support of the Knights, but many Local Assemblies of the Knights answered the strike call. Chicago police killed four strikers at the McCormick Reaper works. At a meeting in Haymarket Square called to protest these killings, a bomb was thrown that killed several policemen. The Knights of Labor became unjustly associated in the public mind with violence. This caused further loss of prestige and shrinking of membership.
Later in the year the Federation of Organized Trades and Labor Unions (craft unions) proposed a merger with the Knights which would give them control in the affairs of the Craft Assemblies of the Knights. Powderly turned down the merger offer. The Federation then sent out its own call for a convention and met in Columbus, Ohio, late that year to form the American Federation of Labor.
The American Federation of Labor elected Samuel Gompers presi-

dent. As the Knights of Labor began to disintegrate, the AFL picked up most of its Craft Assemblies.

1892   Homestead Steel strike, led by AFL Amalgamated Association of Iron, Steel, and Tin Workers, led to violence between strikers and armed Pinkerton men. The strikers defeated the Pinkertons but were subdued by troops. After the strike only about 800 out of some 4,000 workers were taken back, all others being replaced by nonstrikers from outside.

1894   Pullman strike, put down by federal troops, Eugene V. Debs, Socialist and railway union leader, emerged to national prominence.

Frederick W. Taylor read a paper entitled "A Piece Work System" to the American Society of Mechanical Engineers: his first appearance before them, followed by others which gave him great influence. National Association of Manufacturers organized.

1905   Industrial Workers of the World (IWW) organized in Chicago. "Big Bill" Hayward one of its leaders.

1908   Section 10 of the Erdman Act applying to railroad employees, whereby the "yellow dog" contract was outlawed and an employee was forbidden to discharge a worker for union membership, was declared unconstitutional (*U.S.* v. *Adair*).

A boycott by the United Hatters of Danbury, Conn., against D. E. Loewe and Co. was held to be in restraint of trade under the Sherman Anti-Trust Act of 1890. The individual union members were held responsible for the union's acts and assessed damages and costs totaling $252,000.

1911   A congressional committee conducting hearings on legislation for government-operated arsenals and navy yards heard testimony from Taylor and his associates. At these hearings Louis Brandeis, later to become a Supreme Court Justice, coined the term "scientific management," and helped publicize the achievements of the Taylor group, but Congress outlawed the use of the stopwatch and "efficiency" methods in arsenals and navy yards.

1912   Strikes against wage cut and "stretchout" in textile mills in Lawrence and Lowell, Mass., broke out spontaneously and striking workers were quickly organized by the IWW. The industrial form of organization, the well-conducted relief activities, and the nonviolent tactics the IWW employed in this strike resulted in a victory for the strikers, who got wage increases, revision of the stretchout program, and adjustment of grievances.

1913   Strikes in the silk mills of Paterson and Passaic, N.J., led by the IWW, were met by stern police measures, and failed.

1914   Clayton Act approved. It exempted unions from the provisions of the Sherman Act, limited the use of injunctions in labor disputes, and provided that picketing and other union activities were not to be considered unlawful. (Later judicial interpretation reversed the apparent prolabor provisions.)

1914–19 A war-boom period, characterized by labor shortages, rapid expansion of factory production, shifts in the labor force. The AFL under

Gompers supported the Allied war effort and pledged cooperation with employers to win the war. AFL membership increased in the factories, but employers were reluctant to recognize unions, while unions were jealous of jurisdictional lines. To resolve these difficulties the National War Labor Board, created by Congress as an emergency measure, ordered the establishment in many factories of "works councils" consisting of elected representatives of workers in the various departments. These councils side-stepped the question of recognition and of jurisdiction, and carried on collective bargaining and grievance-adjusting activities with factory managements.

1917   The Suprem Court upheld the "yellow dog" contract and declared that union efforts to organize workers subject to such contracts were unlawful (*Hitchman Coal and Coke Company* v. *Mitchell*).

1919   Strike wave in steel and other industries, as industry reconverted and employers withdrew such recognition as they had accorded unions during wartime. Unions of the AFL lost their foothold in the factories. Legislation creating the National War Labor Board lapsed and works councils created by NWLB lost specific legal sanction, but many companies retained the councils as consultative bodies and for grievance adjustments.

National Industrial Conference Board started a series of studies of the works councils, and Employee Representation Plans that developed from them, and ended by recommending the idea to manufacturing employers.

1920–29   General trends: craft unions were ousted from the factories where they had gained a foothold during the war—"open shop" prevailed in manufacturing with many large companies establishing employee-representation plans; widespread adoption of the lessons of the scientific management movement; mounting prosperity up to the crash of 1929.

1926   Railway Labor Act. Established collective bargaining for the railways to guard against stoppages in vital national transportation system. Outlawed "company unions," provided grievance procedure and arbitration machinery.

1929   Stock-market crash signaled the beginning of depression and large-scale unemployment.

1932   Norris-La Guardia Act. Outlawed the yellow dog contract and made the use of the injunction in labor disputes difficult.

1933   A turning-point year for industrial unionism.

Inauguration of Franklin D. Roosevelt as President ushers in the "New Deal" administration.

NRA. Section 7a of the National Industrial Recovery Act gives workers the "right to bargain collectively through representatives of their own choosing without interference, coercion or restraint on the part of the employer."

Unions receive big impetus from Section 7a. This includes company unions as well as the AFL.

AFL Convention votes to hold a Conference to devise ways of organizing industrial workers.

1934   AFL Conference advocates federal locals for the factories; sidesteps question of craft-union jurisdiction over workers in these locals. "Labor's Civil War" begins at AFL San Francisco convention between craft and industrial unionists; first result a compromise.

1935   Supreme Court declares NRA unconstitutional.
Congress reenacts the substance of Section 7a in the form of the Wagner Act; outlaws company unions; establishes the National Labor Relations Board.
Clash at AFL Atlantic City convention ends with victory of craft unionists. Industrial-union advocates meet in November to form the "Committee for Industrial Organization," CIO.

1936   AFL Executive Council calls on AFL-affiliated unions to sever connection with CIO; few comply.
Sit-down strikes in auto factories in December.

1937   AFL expels unions connected with the CIO.
Auto Workers (UAW-CIO) sign contract with General Motors in February, Chrysler in April; Steelworkers (SWOC) sign with Carnegie-Illinois, U.S. Steel, Jones & Laughlin.
Strikes in "Little Steel" result in union defeats.
Supreme Court upholds constitutionality of Wagner Act.

1938   CIO organizes on permanent basis as "Congress of Industrial Organizations," with John L. Lewis as its first president.

1940   Lewis resigns as president of CIO; Phillip Murray elected in his place.

1941   United States declares war on the Axis powers; gets a "no-strike" pledge from labor; sets up tripartite (labor-management-public) National War Labor Board to deal with wartime disputes.
Ford Motor Co. Signs first contract with UAW-CIO.

1946   Postwar strike wave, most extensive to date in U.S. history. As after World War I, recognition at stake in some of the strikes. Unions succeed in winning new agreements.

1947   Taft-Hartley law.

1955   AFL-CIO merger.

1957   Teamsters Union expelled from AFL-CIO on grounds of alleged racketeering associations.

1959   Landrum-Griffin Act.

1962   Civil rights campaign starts in southern states with boycott of segregated buses in Montgomery, Alabama, led by Rev. Martin Luther King.

1962   President John F. Kennedy issues Executive Order 10988 authorizing collective bargaining in the federal services.

1968   UAW withdraws from AFL-CIO, forms an "alliance" with Teamsters, later formalized (1969) as Alliance for Labor Action (ALA) joined by a few other AFL-CIO and independent unions.
Strikes of teachers, sanitation workers, other public employees in New York, Baltimore, other cities and school districts.
Martin Luther King assassinated while leading support activities for striking sanitation workers in Memphis, Tennessee.
Senator Robert F. Kennedy, campaigning for Democratic presidential nomination, assassinated in Los Angeles, where he appeared with Cesar

Chavez, agricultural labor leader, in support of efforts to organize grape pickers.

1969   Strikes in transportation: railways and airlines. Merger of four large Railway Brotherhoods into United Transportation Union, with 270,000 members.

Civil rights militants demand jobs for blacks in construction industry; hold "Black Mondays" demonstrations in Pittsburgh, Chicago, and elsewhere. U.S. government offers "Philadelphia Plan" to open apprenticeship to minority workers; AFL-CIO opposes it.

President Nixon supersedes Executive Order 10988 with Executive Order 11491, mainly confirming and clarifying the previous order.

1970   Wildcat strike of postal workers spreads throughout U.S. Postmaster calls for troops to handle mail, but negotiates settlement with strikers.

Walter Reuther dies in plane crash; Leonard Woodcock succeeds him in presidency of UAW, directs negotiations with auto companies for new agreement.

SELECTED ANNOTATED BIBLIOGRAPHY

This bibliography consists of two parts: (1) the theory of union behavior and (2) history of labor relations.

1. THE THEORY OF UNION BEHAVIOR

BROOKS, GEORGE W.; DERBER, MILTON; McCABE, DAVID A.; and TAFT, PHILIP (eds.). *Interpreting the Labor Movement.* Madison, Wis.: Industrial Relations Research Association, 1952.

Special attention is invited to: "Theories of the Labor Movement," by PHILIP TAFT; "The Union Role in Industry. Its Extent and Limits," by L. REED TRIPP; "Union Policies As to the Area of Collective Bargaining," by DAVID A. McCABE; and "Union Attitudes toward Economic and Social Roles of the Modern State," by Rev. GEORGE C. HIGGINS.

CHALMERS, W. ELLISON; CHANDLER, MARGARET K.; McQUITTY, LOUIS L.; STAGNER, ROSS; WRAY, DONALD E.; and DERBER, MILTON. *Labor-Management Relations in Illini City.* Champaign: University of Illinois Institute of Labor and Industrial Relations, 1953. Vol. I: The Case Studies; Vol. II: Explorations in Comparative Analysis.

An interdisciplinary study of labor-management relations. Vol I deals with case studies at the enterprise and the local community. Volume II attempts quantitative analysis.

CHAMBERLAIN, NEIL W. *The Union Challenge to Management Control.* New York: Harper & Bros., 1948.

A study of the impact of the union on the authority of management in the large corporation.

DERBER, MILTON; CHALMERS, W. ELLISON; and STAGNER; ROSS, with the cooperation of MILTON EDELMAN. *The Local Union-Management Relationship.* Urbana: Institute of Labor and Industrial Relations, University of Illinois, 1960.

In 1953–54, the University of Illinois Institute of Labor and Industrial

Relations published a two volume report, *Labor-Management Relations in Illini City,* which attempted to lay the foundation for a systematic approach to the study of the process of accommodation between organized labor and organized management at the local establishment level. The *Illini City* project was a study in depth and thereby limited to eight establishments in a single community.

The *Local Union-Management Relationship* study extends the *Illini City* approach to 41 establishments in 3 communities. The present study is based on a survey technique involving detailed interviews with only a few top leaders of the management and the union in each establishment. For the most part, data are the *perceptions* of the men and women who were mainly responsible for and best informed about the formulation and general administration of the basic rules by which the day-to-day life of the establishment was guided. As in *Illini City* studies, a further attempt is made at quantitative analysis.

DUNLOP, JOHN THOMAS. *Industrial Relations Systems.* New York: Holt, Rinehart & Winston, Inc., 1958.

Develops an analytical framework for the general study of industrial relations in different countries. Includes a comparative study of work rules in bituminous coal mining in eight nations and in the building industry of nine nations.

———. "Structural Changes in the American Labor Movement and Industrial Relations System," *Proceedings of the Ninth Annual Meeting of the Industrial Relations Research Association,* pp. 12–32. Madison, Wis.: The Association, 1957.

Discusses the impact of the government and the AFL-CIO merger on the structure of the American labor movement.

HOXIE, ROBERT FRANKLIN. *Scientific Management and Labor.* New York: D. Appleton and Co., 1920.

Based on an investigation of scientific management in its relations to labor made for the United States Commission on Industrial Relations. An attempt to compare Taylor's claims for scientific management with the operation of the system in shops.

———. *Trade Unionism in the United States.* New York: D. Appleton and Co., 1917, 1923.

An intensive investigation of the goals and nature of American labor unions. Appendix II, Students' Report on the Trade Union Program, outlines the methods used by Professor Hoxie and his students in their investigations.

KERR, CLARK; DUNLOP, JOHN T.; HARBISON, FREDRICK; and MYERS, CHARLES A. *Industrialism and Industrial Man.* Cambridge, Mass.: Harvard University Press, 1960.

The character of any industrial relations system is theorized to be dependent on the type of "elite" introducing the industrialization process into a country. Based on field studies of the organization of different economies.

LESTER, RICHARD A., and SHISTER, JOSEPH (eds.). *Insights into Labor Issues.* New York: The Macmillan Co., 1948.

Special attention is directed to: "Toward a Theory of Labor-Management

Relations," by FREDERICK H. HARBISON, ROBERT K. BURNS, and ROBERT DUBIN; and "The Development of Labor Organization; a Theoretical Framework" by JOHN T. DUNLOP.

LOZOVSKY, A. *Marx and the Trade Unions.* New York: International Publishers, 1935.

Cited by Philip Taft in his discussion on Marxism in *Interpreting the Labor Movement.*

PERLMAN, MARK. *Labor Union Theories in America: Background and Development.* Evanston, Ill.: Row, Peterson & Co., 1958.

Summarizes and assesses literature on American labor unionism. Classifies theories or "basic interpretations" into five groups: unionism as a moral institution, as a revolutionary institution, as a psychological reaction, as a welfare institution, and as a part of the democratic process.

PERLMAN, SELIG. *A Theory of the Labor Movement.* New York: The Macmillan Co., 1928.

A classic study of the factors responsible for the economic conservatism and limited political involvement of American trade unions. Stresses the job security psychology of the workingman and the adaptation of unions to American conditions. Compares American, British, pre-Nazi German, and Russian experience.

Rerum Novarum, Quadragesimo Anno, and *Mater et Magistra.*

Pope Leo XIII, Pope Pius XI, and Pope John XXIII discuss Roman Catholic views on the conditions of labor and the right of working people to association in encyclical letters in 1891, 1931, and 1961.

SOMERS, GERALD G. (ed.). *Essays in Industrial Relations Theory.* Ames, Iowa: The Iowa University Press, 1969.

A broad sample of theoretical notes by leading analysts of American industrial relations. The trend in the essays discloses a greater use of the behavioral sciences to explain union-management relations. The essays include:

HENEMAN, HERBERT G., JR. "Toward a General Conceptual System of Industrial Relations: How Do We Get There?"

DUNLOP, JOHN T. "Industrial Relations Systems at Work."

SOMERS, GERALD G. "Bargaining Power and Industrial Relations Theory."

JOSEPH, MYRON L. "Approaches to Collective Bargaining in Industrial Relations Theory."

GOMBERG, WILLIAM. "Collective Bargaining and the New Industrial Engineering."

FILLEY, ALAN C. "New Directions in Organization Theory."

WHYTE, WILLIAM FOOTE. "Building Better Organizational Models."

SAYLES, LEONARD. "Industrial Relations and Organization Behavior: Parent and Child?"

MOORE, DAVID G. "Toward More Comprehensive Human Relations in Industry."

BARBASH, JACK. "Rationalization in the American Union."

EDELMAN, MURRY. "The Conservative Political Consequences of Labor Conflict."

DERBER, MILTON. " 'Industrial Democracy' as an Organizing Concept for a Theory of Industrial Relations."

TANNENBAUM, FRANK. *The Labor Movement, Its Conservative Functions and Consequences.* New York: Alfred A. Knopf, Inc., 1921.

An analysis of the aims and consequences of labor organization, tinged with the casual worker mentality.

————. *A Philosophy of Labor.* New York: Alfred A. Knopf, Inc., 1951.

Argues that labor unions are a counterrevolutionary force seeking to establish a community of secure relationships analogous to the status system of the Middle Ages.

WEBB, SIDNEY, and WEBB, BEATRICE. *Industrial Democracy.* London: Longmans, Green; First pub. 1897, latest ed., 1920.

A classic study of the internal structure, method of government, regulations, and policies of British trade unions. Part IV presents a theory of the effect of trade unions "on the production and distribution of wealth and the development of personal characters."

2. HISTORY OF LABOR RELATIONS

BOK, DEREK C., and DUNLOP, JOHN T. *Labor and the American Community.* New York: Simon & Schuster, 1970.

A comprehensive contemporary look at the American industrial relations system. Includes a discussion of the social, political, and economic impact of trade unionism and the reciprocal effect of American institutions on the policy and practices of trade unions.

BROOKS, GEORGE. *The Sources of Vitality in the American Labor Movement.* Ithaca, N.Y.: New York State School of Industrial and Labor Relations Bulletin No. 41, 1960.

An eloquent defense of American trade unionism in the wake of the McClellan Committee investigations which led to the passage of the Landrum-Griffin Bill in 1959. Written by the former education director of the International Brotherhood of Pulp, Sulfite and Paper Mill Workers.

CHAMBERLAIN, NEIL W.; PIERSON, FRANK C., and WOLFSON, THERESA (eds.). *A Decade of Industrial Relations Research, 1946–1956.* New York: Harper & Bros., 1958.

A volume published by the Industrial Relations Research Association. Special attention is invited to: "Collective Bargaining," by JOSEPH SHISTER; "The Economic Effects of Unionism," by GEORGE H. HILDEBRAND; and "Employee Benefit Plans," by ROBERT TILOVE.

CHRISTIE, ROBERT. *Empire in Wood: A History of the Carpenters Union.* Ithaca, New York: New York State School of Industrial and Labor Relations, 1956.

A well-done analysis of the conflict between the ideologies of social reform and pure and simple unionism as illustrated by the early growth and development of the carpenters union. Christie notes the emergence of the role of the business agent as the key event which led to the demise of the reform-oriented segment of the union led by the international union's founding father, Peter J. McGuire.

COMMONS, JOHN R., and ASSOCIATES. *History of Labour in the United States, 1896–1932.* 4 vols. New York: The Macmillan Co., 6th printing, 1951.

The classic University of Wisconsin study of American labor history, comprising:

Volumes I and II, by John R. Commons, David J. Saposs, Helen L. Sumner, E. B. Mittelman, H. E. Hoaglund, John B. Andrews, and Selig Perlman.

Volume III, *Labor Movements*, by Selig Perlman and Philip Taft.

Volume IV, *Working Conditions and Labor Legislation* by Don D. Lescohier and Elizabeth Brandeis.

Duborsky, Melvin. *We Shall Be All*. Chicago: Quadrangle Books, 1969.

A thorough treatment, from a sympathetic point of view, of the IWW. Captures some of the spirit and mentality of the Wobblies, their day and generation.

Filipetti, George. *Industrial Management in Transition*. Rev. ed. Homewood, Ill.: Richard D. Irwin, Inc., 1953.

Analyzes the mainstream of management thinking and practice in industrial enterprises. Discusses the emergence of an international scientific management movement.

Galenson, Walter. *The CIO Challenge to the AFL: A History of the American Labor Movement, 1935–1941*. Wertheim Publications in Industrial Relations. Cambridge, Mass.: Harvard University Press, 1960.

A descriptive history of labor developments in the steel, auto, coal mining, electrical, rubber, clothing, textile, meat, lumber, petroleum, and maritime industries, as well as those affected by the teamster, machinist, building trades, printing and publishing, and railroad unions. Author relies heavily on hitherto unavailable AFL Executive Council and CIO Executive Board minutes.

Hardman, J. B. S. (ed.). *American Labor Dynamics*. New York: Harcourt, Brace & Co., 1928.

Thirty-two labor men, teachers, editors, and technicians discuss the problems of organized labor during the bleak 1920s. Readers will find here a realistic statement of the problems of organizing the unorganized as they existed in the pre-New Deal era.

Landsberger, Henry A. *Hawthorne Revisited*. Ithaca, N.Y.: Cornell University, 1958.

A critical appraisal of the Hawthorne Experiments and developments in human relations in industry.

Litwack, Leon. *The American Labor Movement*. Englewood Cliffs, N.J.: Prentice-Hall, 1962.

A stimulating collection of documents placed in historical sequence that gives the reader a richer experience of the development of American labor. Documents ranging from the preamble of the IWW constitution to the eloquent defense by Clarence S. Darrow of the union shop.

MacDonald, Robert M. "Collective Bargaining in the Postwar Period," *Industrial and Labor Relations Review*, Vol. 20 (1968).

An excellent brief account of the changing structure and issues of collective bargaining since the end of World War II. Relates these changes to developments both in the external environment and the attitudes and beliefs of the parties themselves.

Millis, Harry A., Research Director. *How Collective Bargaining Works*. New York: Twentieth Century Fund, 1942.

This volume is a comprehensive statement of collective bargaining processes in 16 industries with notes on 13 more industries up to 1940. The contents are:

TAFT, PHILIP. "Organized Labor and the New Deal."
BURNS, ROBERT K. "Daily Newspapers."
BROWN, EMILY CLARK. "Book and Job Printing."
HABER, WILLIAM. "Building Construction."
FISHER, WALDO E. "Bituminous Coal."
———. "Anthracite."
WOLF, HARRY D. "Railroads."
MYERS, ROBERT J., and BLOCH, JOSEPH W. "Men's Clothing."
TAYLOR, GEORGE W. "Hosiery."
HARBISON, FREDERICK H. "Steel."
McPHERSON, W. H. "Automobiles."
ANTHONY, DONALD. "Rubber Products."
DERBER, MILTON. "Glass."
———. "Electrical Products."
CHRISTENSON, C. LAURENCE. "Chicago Service Trades."
TAFT, PHILIP. "Collective Bargaining Before the New Deal."
———. "Brief Review of Other Industries."

PELLING, HENRY. *American Labor.* Chicago: University of Chicago Press, 1960.

An excellent short history of the American labor movement.

PERLMAN, SELIG. *A History of Trade Unionism in the United States.* New York: The Macmillan Co., 1922.

Part I is a summary of the first two volumes of the *History of Labor in the United States* by J. R. Commons and associates. Part II carries the history down to 1923. In Part III the author begins to develop his own theory of the American labor movement, stressing that the attempt to improve the bargaining position ("job control") of the worker and not the desire for a revolutionary transformation of society "is the key to the conduct of organized labor in America."

PIERSON, FRANK C. *Unions in Postwar America: An Economic Assessment.* New York: Random House, 1967.

A brief but comprehensive view of the relation of union policy and practices to the American economic system.

RASKIN, A. H. "The Labor Movement Must Start Moving," *Harvard Business Review,* Vol. 48 (Jan.–Feb. 1970).

An assessment of the institutional hardening of the arteries that is currently troubling the American labor movement, by the labor editor of the *New York Times.*

SLICHTER, SUMNER H. *Union Policies and Industrial Management.* Washington, D.C.: Brookings Institution, 1941.

The pioneer study of the impact of the union on the management of industrial enterprises and the economic effect of union policies. Most of the research for this volume was completed before the union organization of mass-production industry.

SLICHTER, SUMNER H.; HEALY, JAMES J.; and LIVERNASH, E. ROBERT. *The Impact of Collective Bargaining on Management*. Washington, D.C.: Brookings Institution, 1960.

A comprehensive treatment of contemporary American collective bargaining practices ranging from such specific topics as control of evaluated rate structures, hiring, and concepts of seniority to such general questions as the importance of line and staff cooperation. Authors resist developing an explicit theory of collective bargaining, but do provide some generalizations regarding the emerging characteristics of collective bargaining. In part, an updating of Slichter's *Union Policies and Industrial Management*.

TAYLOR, FREDERICK WINSLOW. *Scientific Management, Comprising Shop Management, The Principles of Scientific Management, Testimony before the Special House Committee*. New York: Harper & Bros., 1947.

The father of Scientific Management explains its principles to the American Society of Mechanical Engineers in 1903, the general public, and a special committee of the House of Representatives in the winter of 1911–12.

WEBB, SIDNEY, and WEBB, BEATRICE. *The History of Trade Unionism*. New York: Longmans, Green & Co.; First published, 1894, latest ed., 1920.

A classic history of trade unions in Great Britain. After rejecting the guild theory of the origin of unions and suggesting that unions arose only after "the great bulk of workers ceased to be independent producers," it traces the development of British trade unions from the latter part of the seventeenth century through the first two decades of the twentieth.

WITTE, EDWIN E. *The Evolution of Managerial Ideas in Industrial Relations*. Ithaca, N.Y.: New York State School of Industrial and Labor Relations Bulletin No. 27, 1954.

A leading authority on industrial relations traces the changes in American management's view of industrial relations in the 20th century.

Chapter 3

ENTERPRISE ORGANIZATION FOR EMPLOYEE RELATIONS

This chapter aims to set forth the alternatives available to employers in establishing enterprise organizations for the purpose of achieving effective employee relations. It also seeks to describe some of the major characteristics of the structure of American enterprises. Much of what is said in this chapter will apply equally to unionized and nonunionized enterprises. The next chapter, dealing with worker organizations, emphasizing how the union influences enterprise organization for employee relations.

CHANGING EMPLOYER-EMPLOYEE RELATIONS

The "employer" of antiquity (and the not too distant past) held his "employees" in a bond relation as slaves. Slaves were the personal property of the slaveowner. If he was wise and self-controlled he treated them well and got good work from them by the standards of those days, but he did not have to take their wishes into account and could compel them by force to do his will.

Today's employer cannot compel his workers by any kind of force. He cannot fine them. The most severe disciplinary penalty that he can impose is to dismiss them—terminate the employment contract—so that they cease to be employees. His way of drawing workers to him, keeping them in his service, and motivating them to be productive is to make them want to do the work. Older systems bound one party to the relation and benefited the other. The free labor system binds both parties but binds them only to their mutual benefit. The contract that so binds them lasts only as long as both receive benefit from it. It rests upon consent, and it confers reciprocal advantage.

THE GENERAL OBJECTIVES OF AN ENTERPRISE

Just as a man needs objectives for his life to be meaningful, every enterprise and every human organization needs objectives in order to behave rationally. Management scholars and executives agree that objectives are the starting point of management philosophy and the practice of management.

What should the objectives of an enterprise be? That is, the objectives of the organization as distinct from the aims of those who may happen to own it. Their objectives may stop at profit; but the organization does not make profits in the abstract. It must first produce some good or service that gives satisfaction to the members of the enterprise directly, or to others. This sets its *operating* objectives. The operating objectives of most enterprises are so obvious that they are frequently taken for granted. A few dogmatic statements may serve as a reminder of the importance of operating objectives in several types of enterprise:

The operating objective of an army *must be* to win a battle or a war.
The operating objective of a school *must be* to provide educational opportunities.
The operating objective of a shoe store *must be* to sell shoes.
The operating objective of a coal mine *must be* to mine coal and to sell it.
The operating objective of an automobile manufacturer *must be* to make and sell cars.

The operating objective of an enterprise is a very important determinant of the behavior of the enterprise. It takes different kinds of human and material resources to run a school, sell shoes, or mine coal, and the resources that are needed are deployed in different ways to achieve these different objectives. Operating objectives of the sort discussed here transcend such various considerations as the ownership of an enterprise, the personal aspirations of its members, or the very important profit motive.

The profit objective certainly is important in most business enterprises, yet even in the most aggressive business the quest for profit is frequently moderated by self-restraint and a feeling of responsibility to customers, employees, and other individuals or groups associated with the enterprise.

One might suppose that owner-managers would encounter little difficulty in setting objectives for their enterprises, where it would appear impossible for any conflict to develop between personal and enterprise objectives. In practice, however, the operating objectives of owner-manager enterprises are not always subject to control and are frequently set by persons other than the owner alone. This situation creates the possibility of conflict between personal objectives and enterprise objectives.

Possible conflicts of this sort, between ownership and operations, are more strikingly illustrated, however, in the corporate form of business organization. A particular stockholder and true part-owner of a corporation may be solely interested in maximum profit while the officers might run the corporation with the objective of growth or even for their personal gain. It must be emphasized that conflicts between personal objectives and enterprise objectives are not limited to corporate business enterprise; many readers of this book will be able to think of situations where a given college professor's personal objective of supplemental income or professional status conflicted with his college's objective of providing educational service.

The objectives of the enterprise, including the profit motive, are influenced by personal objectives of the members of the enterprise as well as by many external circumstances. The general enterprise objectives which emerge set the framework for the personnel management objectives. These are derivative of the enterprise operating objectives.

PERSONNEL MANAGEMENT OBJECTIVES OF THE ENTERPRISE

The personnel management objectives of any enterprise can be simply stated as: (1) to find suitable employees, (2) to maintain an adequate work force, and (3) to get competitive productivity from that work force. The achievement of these objectives is far from simple and the methods used for their achievement are diverse.

What are *suitable employees* and how can they be found? The answer to this question is provided in part by how management designs jobs. In mass-production industry, management has designed jobs in such a way that the bulk of suitable potential employees need little special prior experience or training, but even in mass-production industry there is a need for some employees possessing substantial experience or training, and these are sometimes in very short supply. In this situation the employer has to search for people possessing the needed skills or take the sometimes more difficult and costly route of training present employees to the skill level needed.

What is an *appropriate work force* and how can it be held? An appropriate work force is the number and kind of employees that management needs at the time that management needs them. Just as management needs enough workers, it also needs to be able to get rid of unneeded workers. Holding an appropriate work force boils down to making employment at a particular enterprise attractive to the kind of employees needed and insuring sufficient management flexibility to escape having unneeded or redundant employees.

The measure of *competitive productivity* is unit labor costs. Low wages give an enterprise a competitive edge only when those low wages are accompanied by output that equals that of higher wage competitors. In the same vein, high wages may mean a competitive advantage over a lower wage competitor if the high-wage firm achieves higher man-hour productivity.

In order to achieve objectives, the work to be done must be assigned to individuals who will perform it. This division of work, with the concomitant delegation of authority and assignment of responsibility, is the task of formal organization.

THE ORGANIZATION OF AN ENTERPRISE

Organization cannot take place without a system of authority. The dictionary defines authority as "legal or rightful power"—which rather unhelpfully turns the question, *What is authority?* into the question, *What is power?* The literature of management, and of the social sciences as well, abounds with controversy over the nature and source of power, the meaning of authority. It is tempting—but would be distracting—to join the fray and try to define once and for all these abstract words which stand for a very real and dynamic thing: the thing that seems to make the enterprise go. The authors of this book prefer to sidestep the full philosophic implications of the question and instead to say that authority is "something." It is the something that many management writers say flows downward in an enterprise (whether or not the downward flow starts with the owners or with top management); it is a right to make decisions affecting others, to commit resources, to require compliance. It is something that other writers say becomes effective only by acceptance upward, from employees at the bottom and at each successively higher level.

To avoid future confusion, the word "authority" in this book may always be understood as something that flows downward through an organization; but the reader must remember that there must always be a corresponding upward flow of acceptance. This upward flow will be noted only when it ceases—that is, when nonacceptance of authority (as, for instance, in a work stoppage or strike) stops the downward flow. Otherwise, the downward flow prevails.

Because authority flows downward, it is more concentrated at the top and diminishes at successively lower levels as it branches out and divides by delegation from above. Thus, the higher a persons stands in an organization, the greater his authority. The President of the United States possesses greater authority than any other member of the United States federal service. A plant superintendent possesses greater authority than any production worker or foreman in his plant.

For purposes of discussion here, there are four important points to keep in mind about formal authority in the enterprise: (1) organizational authority flows from the top of the hierarchy down, (2) the flow of organizational authority is limited by the willingness of subordinates to accept it, (3) organizational authority is confirmed by employee acceptance in a free employment relationship, and (4) organizational authority exists even in nonprofit-seeking enterprises such as the government, a school, a church, or a union. An individual in the enterprise is a manager if he possesses organizational authority over subordinates. He is not a manager if he does not possess organizational authority over subordinates.

One of the major tasks of the man at the top of any organization is designing the formal organization structure. Formal organization structure increases in complexity with the number of employees in the enterprise. The two major components of a complex organizational structure are: the line organization and staff organizations.

The Line Organization

The first step in the development of a complex organization comes when the volume of business done by the enterprise reaches a magnitude that calls for departmentalization. That is, the work increases beyond the power to perform of a single group of workers bossed by a single person. The additional workers hired make up one or more additional gangs or departments.

The principle that the top executive follows in dividing up his labor force by departments depends upon the nature of his operations, but the effect of this division on his relation toward his workers is always the same. One enterprise may simply seek to keep the gangs small enough to be manageable or to divide forces to disperse in space, even though all perform essentially the same work, as a company of infantrymen breaks down into platoons and platoons into squads. Another may form its groups around specialized functions so that each department handles a different process. In either case, creating the new department puts the workers in it under a gang boss or foreman and moves the top men a step away from his employees, with the foreman in between. The foreman now exercises management authority over his work group. He gives the men their orders and assignments and makes, or interprets and applies, enterprise rules or policy that affects them.

Management now consists of two levels, the top executive and his foreman. Ultimate authority still rests in the top manager's hands. His is the last word—and usually the first as well—in general policy decisions, but he delegates to his foreman supervisory authority over the workers, and may also delegate certain policy-making authority. The top manager determines, for instance, what products to manufacture, and in what quantity, for as chief executive he must also be concerned with selling whatever is made. The foreman's job is to see to it that his work group or department turns out its allotted share of production or its expected quota of sales.

Now this is the simplest line organization, a top manager and his foreman. In larger enterprises, the management structure remains a line organization as long as each foreman or subordinate manager has full authority and responsibility for all the activities in his department or group of departments. The line organization is the essential means of getting the work of the enterprise done. It has proved capable of setting large masses of men into motion, directing and controlling them, bringing their combined efforts to bear upon attainment of a common objective determined by or known to the top man or men in the organization. Figure 3–1 illustrates the operation of a pure line organization in a business organization.

The larger an enterprise grows and the more numerous the levels of management authority, the more apparent become some of the drawbacks and inadequacies of the straight-line form of organization. The man who during the last decade of the 19th century and the first decade of the 20th did most to call attention to the inadequacies of the straight-line organization for manufacturing, and who accomplished the most toward improving it, was Frederick W. Taylor.

Taylor came from a well-to-do Philadelphia family. He made the unusual choice, for a young man in his circumstances, of a career in manufacturing industry and prepared himself by serving an apprenticeship as a machinist. He did this because he intended to work his way up through the ranks and knew that a manufacturing foreman, under the then-prevailing line form of organization, had to be proficient in the technology of the work he was to supervise.

Contemporary practice was to hand the department foreman an order for a certain quantity of items to meet stated specifications and expect him to carry on from there. It was up to the foreman to plan the operations necessary to manufacture the part or product, to order materials, to design tools and fixtures, to lay out the sequence of tasks, to train and assign workers and keep them under discipline so that they produced the volume of work required, to inspect their output and maintain quality, to keep the machines in good working order, and at the expected time to deliver the completed order. With all these responsibilities to answer for, the line supervisor had broad authority over the group through which he accomplished the tasks. He had the power to hire and fire, to set hourly rates or piece rates, to grant or withhold pay raises, to punish or reward his workers.

Taylor recognized that so wide a range of duties called for a degree of versatility and ability not often found in any one man. A foreman who was ingenious in solving technical problems might lack understanding in how to get along with his men; while another foreman, effective as a leader, might be weak on the technical side. Taylor's proposed solution was to divide up the foreman's functions between eight specialists, four specialists in the department to boss the workers at their tasks and four in the front office to plan the work. Although the "pure functional" organization form advocated by Taylor is a relic in the history of organization theory, his two basic ideas of assigning several specialists to complex jobs and divorcing plannng from operations exerted a mighty influence on most modern-day manufacturing organizations. These two ideas find expression in the development of staff organizations.

FIGURE 3–1. Straight Line Organization

A. Single Plant
   1. President reserves to himself finance and product decisions.
   2. Sales effort organized geographically. Sales personnel decisions delegated to vice president–sales and district sales managers.
   3. Production organized by·process. Production personnel decisions delegated to vice president–production and department foremen.

B. Multiplant
   1. President reserves to himself finance and product decisions.
   2. Sales effort organized geographically. Sales personnel decisions delegated to vice president–sales and district sales managers.
   3. Production organized by location and process. Production personnel decisions delegated to vice president–production, plant managers, and department foremen.

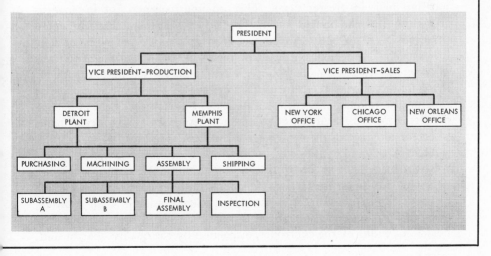

Staff Organizations

The purpose of staff organizations is to advise and counsel line management, to serve the line organization, and to carry out management controls over line operations in specified functional areas. Colonel Lyndall F. Urwick makes a useful distinction between three kinds of staff: personal staff, special staff, and general staff.[1]

Personal staff consists of people who provide personal services which relieve the pressure on a manager's time. The secretary who takes oral dictation and types out letters the manager would otherwise have to write himself is an example of personal staff. Another example is the "Assistant to" the manager. The contribution of these employees is direct personal services to a particular manager at any level in the organization.

Special staff consists of people who possess special knowledge or other qualifications which the manager whom they serve may be presumed not to have himself. The legal adviser, the engineer, the staff psychologist are special staff people. They give advice, which the manager weighs in making decisions to which the advice is pertinent. Thus, unless he were himelf a lawyer, he would not know the legal alternatives available to him in deciding whether to defend, or settle, or make countersuit in a legal process directed against the company. Even though he might be an electrical engineer, he still might need advice on product or process from a chemical engineer or other specialist. The special staff contribution is expert advice and takes the form of *recommendations*, or the analysis of alternatives.

General staff consists of people who do part of the manager's own job but do it in greater detail. The top line manager, for instance, is responsible for the budget, but the controller (a general staff manager) must make sure the figures are correct down to the last decimal point. The line manager's judgment on the components of the budget ought to be as good or better than the controller's. The line manager is quite capable of sizing up the value of the controller's work (as he would not be capable of judging the validity of a chemist's formula) but he needs help in getting detailed proposals in order, coordinating them with all the departments affected, and putting them together in final form.

General staff also provides services, this time not to a specific individual manager but to his entire line organization (example: recruiting personnel for an entire factory, a general staff service of the personnel manager) and counsel to any manager who may ask for it. In addition, general staff carry out routine managerial controls in their various staff fields: i.e., audits by the controller, inspection by the quality control staff,

---

[1] Colonel Lyndall F. Urwick, *Organization in Business: An Address Given at the University of Virginia Graduate School of Business Administration, April 2, 1957* (Occasional Papers on Business Management, No. 2) (Charlottesville: University of Virginia Graduate School of Business Administration, 1958).

job analysis and evaluation by the personnel staff, and so on. In carrying out services and control, general staff act with organizational authority. They get this, just as any line manager does, by delegation from higher management. They use it on behalf of the whole organization or a division thereof under a particular line manager, but strictly within the bounds of their field of responsibility.

In an enterprise employing more than 10,000 persons, the organization of the industrial relations department (a general staff department) may pose a major organizational problem. These large industrial relations departments are important to this discussion because they are found in a relatively few very large corporations and because it is likely that much of the most progressive management thinking on industrial relations problems develops in these large depositories of money and brains.

Figure 3–2, which is a greatly abbreviated sketch of the corporate industrial relations staff of an enterprise employing well over 100,000 persons, provides only a hint of the problems inherent in the organization of the industrial relations department of a giant corporation. Note that this company has three industrial relations specialists bearing the title vice president and six directors of industrial relations subspecialties. As is the case in many large corporations, Figure 3–2 shows a divorce of functions for hourly and salaried personnel, the vice president–labor relations having major responsibility in the area of hourly personnel while the vice president–personnel and organization is primarily concerned with salaried personnel problems. Typically, hourly rated employees are represented by a union while salaried employees frequently are nonunion. The divorce of hourly and salaried personnel activities is significant in at least two respects: (1) the necessity for careful coordination of compensation and benefits lest the salaried people feel left out and retaliate by unionization and (2) the rapidly increasing costs of providing tandem adjustments for salaried people as their number increases. Twenty years ago it was not uncommon for the salaried employee head count to represent less than 20 percent of corporate employment. Under these conditions, it was relatively inexpensive to discourage salaried unionism by giving salaried employees a little something extra above and beyond what the union was able to negotiate for hourly rated employees. Today in many large corporations salaried employee head counts equal or surpass hourly employee head counts. Under these present-day conditions it is vastly more expensive to discourage salaried employee unionism by providing extra generous benefits. The problem is further complicated by the fact that any benefits granted to salaried employees this year will certainly be demanded by the union for hourly employees the next time negotiations roll around.[2]

---

[2] Some of the problems of "tandem" adjustments for unionized and nununion employees in a large corporation are discussed in Case No. 8, pp. 563–66 of this book.

FIGURE 3–2. Partial Organization Structure of Corporate Industrial Relations Staff Department: Multi-Industry, Multinational, Multiplant, Corporation

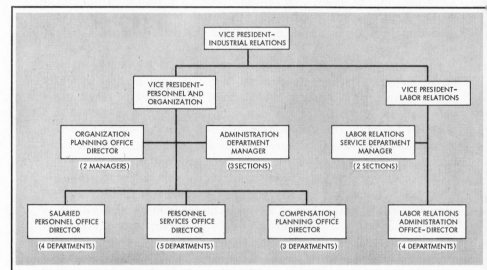

Examples of Advisory Service and Functional Authority Provided by Central Staff Organizations

1. In the personnel administration field, the director, salaried personnel office, provides *advisory-service* such as:
    recommending recruitment, selection, and placement policies applicable to salaried personnel,
    recommending training and management development programs applicable to salaried personnel.
    exercises *functional authority* such as
    coordinating company-wide recruitment of college graduate trainees.
    conducting attitude surveys of salaried employees.
2. In the labor relations field, the director, labor relations administration office, provides *advisory service* such as:
    advising on local agreement negotiations,
    advising on content of labor relations training sessions for foremen,
    advising on grievances at steps below umpire appeal level.
    exercises *functional authority* such as:
    negotiating company-wide master agreements with international unions,
    researching present and future issues in collective bargaining,
    presenting grievance cases at the umpire appeal level.

A full discussion of the organization of the industrial relations department in mammoth enterprises is beyond the scope of this chapter. In an investigation of the employee relations function in large-scale enterprises, Professor Dalton E. McFarland has identified four basic structures of employee relations department organization: the integrated department, the extended department, the split-function department, and the staff-coordinated department. Readers who are concerned with both the structural problems inherent in the organization of the industrial relations department and the attitudes generated by line and staff conflict in industrial relations are referred to his *Cooperation and Conflict in Personnel Administration.*[3]

Formal organization consists of dividing up the work to be done in such ways as to achieve enterprise objectives economically. Organization for personnel administration is the assignment of personnel activities to line and staff organizations so that they will be efficiently performed to achieve enterprise objectives.

The principle of division of functions between line and staff is fairly simple. The line manager is responsible for operations—that is, for results—in the particular unit of the organization which he heads. Everything that concerns the relationship of his people to their tasks, at the workplace, during working hours, is of immediate and vital concern to him. He, in turn, links his own unit with those grouped under the higher manager who is his line superior. The personnel manager is responsible for those matters that have been specifically assigned to him that concern all the employees, at any level, and in any unit, in their relationship with the enterprise as a whole; and with those matters which link the enterprise or any part of it with the body of its employees. An example will make this clear.

A line foreman in a production department has to be the one to say just when a newly trained worker may be put in charge of a delicate or expensive piece of equipment, because the foreman is to blame if an ill-trained worker ruins equipment. Once the foreman has qualified the employee and put him to work on the machine, a staff personnel manager may—if he has been authorized to do so—determine the classification of the newly qualified employee under the rules of a company-wide job evaluation program; and so indirectly designate his pay range. Running the machine is a production department responsibility and working on the machine takes place, in time and space, in the line department. Determining pay ranges under job evaluation may be a company-wide project which has to cut across departmental lines.

The principle of division between line and general staff is clear, but application of the principle is sometimes difficult. It is not more so, however, than inner-organizational relations even between line departments where delegations of authority touch or clash. The production department, under a line manager, may get into a fight with the sales department, also under a line manager, and if the two fail to agree their only recourse is to higher authority. Clear definition of functions helps prevent, but does not eliminate, such clashes.

---

[3] Dalton E. McFarland, *Cooperation and Conflict in Personnel Administration* (New York: American Foundation for Management Research, 1962).

Assigning Personnel Management Activities within the Enterprise

The general function of manpower management is to insure the efficient procurement, development, and utilization of manpower resources in employment. This general function consists of a host of activities which must be performed in every enterprise, large or small, public or private, profit seeking or nonprofit seeking. These activities are usually performed within the enterprise by line or staff organizations, but some of these activities may be contracted out of the enterprise, either to consultant organizations or to formal employer associations, which may advise the enterprise or act as its agent. In some exceptional cases, to be discussed later, it appears that management has contracted some personnel activities out to the union. The question of who performs these activities is the essence of enterprise organization for personnel management. The methods by which these activities are performed is the reality of personnel management activity and, one might argue, even the essence of management.

One outline of personnel activities[4] lists 110 personnel activities under 14 major classifications—and this list devotes most of its attention to the work of a staff personnel department. Such a comprehensive outline would be most helpful in very large-scale enterprises such as the "Big Three" automobile producers, the Department of Defense, or the New York City Board of Education. An enterprise must employ more than 500 persons to justify elaborate organizations. It seems unlikely that as many as 10,000 United States enterprises employ as many as 500 people. Nevertheless, such a comprehensive outline does provide an insight on the breadth and complexity of personnel management activities.

A simple outline of personnel management activities is provided in Figure 3–3, Alternative Methods of Performing Personnel Management Activities. With the possible exception of labor law compliance and legislative liaison, the activities listed in Figure 3–3 are closely parallel to the table of contents of most personnel management texts. All of the activities shown in Figure 3–3 could be performed by a pure-line organization. It seems reasonable to say that in most enterprises with less than 100 employees all of the activities shown in Figure 3–3 either are performed by pure-line organization or are neglected or are contracted out. In most cases, an enterprise will not establish a personnel department before its employment reaches or exceeds 100 persons. As will be shown later in the discussion of the structure of American enterprise, it is very important that the reader remember that the problem of sharing personnel management activities between line and staff organizations is a problem of large-scale organizations.

---

[4] H. H. Carey, "An Outline of Personnel Activities," *Personnel* (May 1947), pp. 348–87, reproduced in William Grant Ireson and Eugene L. Grant (eds.), *Handbook of Industrial Engineering and Management* (Englewood Cliffs, N.J.: Prentice-Hall, Inc., 1955), pp. 183–85.

Most large-scale organizations seem to be plagued with conflict between line and staff organizations. This conflict is the subject of much of management literature. The problem appears to be particularly touchy in the personnel management area because the management of men is certainly the very heart of the line manager's job.

The erosion of the old-time authority of the foreman has resulted from the centralization of personnel management activities. The authors of this book believe that five forces are largely responsible for this centralization of personnel management activities: (1) the steadily advancing growth in the size of employing enterprises, (2) recurring acute labor shortages, (3) increasing governmental regulation of the employment relation, (4) collective bargaining, and (5) a movement toward what has been called the professionalization of the personnel administration field. Perhaps there are other equally important forces, but these five merit at least brief discussion.

Between 1945 and 1956, the number of United States firms employing over 100 workers grew from 31,600 to 38,700 while the number of firms employing over 500 workers grew from 6,000 to 6,400.[5] It seems reasonable to assume that as an enterprise grows in size, the complexity of the employment relationship increases and thus accelerates the movement toward centralization of personnel management.

Acute labor shortages, such as those occasioned by World Wars I and II, cause a centralization of personnel management activities within the enterprise. In such periods of labor shortage, millions of new, inexperienced workers must be hired, trained, and introduced to new situations. Such mass activities can be handled only by a central organization. In these times, foremen, too, are hard to find. Thousands of them are newly promoted workers, technically qualified bench and machine hands, but lacking in experience as supervisors. As a class, the quality of foremanship declines in a period of acute labor shortage.

The Wagner Act of 1935 probably was the most smashing single blow to the authority of the American foreman in the 20th century. Its provisions, which required management to bargain with unions and prohibited discrimination against union members, had the effect of reducing the foreman's authority to hire and fire. Although the provisions of the act did not single out the foreman for regulation, management tended to centralize authority, either to be sure of compliance with the law or to develop the shrewdest methods of evading its letter and intent. The 1964 Civil Rights law's prohibitions on racial discrimination in employment probably will also result in further centralization of personnel management activities.

Collective bargaining greatly reduces the autonomy of the foreman. The grievance procedure and the steward system, which are discussed in

---

[5] *1962 Statistical Abstract of the United States*, p. 490.

FIGURE 3–3. Alternative Methods of Performing Personnel Management Activities

Personnel Activities	In a Large Enterprise, How Activities Might be Shared Between:		In Smaller Enterprises, How Activities Might be "Contracted Out"
	Line Organization	Staff Personnel Department	
Job Description and Analysis	Design of work flows.	Writing job descriptions. Determining transferability of employees between departments of plants.	If contracted out, consultant would perform same functions as assigned to personnel department.
Recruitment	Identify need for new employees.	Develop sources of prospective employees. Conduct search for new employees. Identify candidates for promotion from within.	Search could be contracted out to consultant or employment agency, public or private. Search could be contracted out to union through a hiring hall arrangement.
Selection	Makes final selection from candidates referred by personnel department.	Interview applicants. Aptitude Testing. Psychological testing. Reference checks. Verification of claimed experience. Physical examinations.	Entire process except final selection could be contracted out to consultant.
Training	Identifying training needs.	Run a vestibule school. Provide trainers. Advise on training methods.	Consultant could perform all functions except determining training needs.
Performance Appraisal	Since only line management is in day-to-day contact with employees, it must retain the responsibility for the actual appraisal of individual employees.	Propose a system for performance appraisal. Train supervisors in interviewing techniques. Maintain records on employee performance and development.	Should not be contracted out.
Discipline	Identify needs for rules. Administer the rules.	Advise on rule formulation, drawing on experience from outside the enterprise. Keep records.	Should not be contracted out.

Function	Line/Management Decision	Staff Function	Contracting Out
Wage and Salary Administration	Make final decision on system to be used. Identify changes in job content. Determine wage and salary budget.	Propose alternative systems of job evaluation. Evaluate jobs according to accepted system. Conduct internal and external wage and salary surveys.	Consultant could perform same functions as personnel department.
Employee Benefits and Services	Determine benefits and services to be given, approve system of administration. Identify potentially eligible employees.	Expert advice on sources and costs of benefits. Verify employee eligibility. Keep records.	Consultant could perform same functions as personnel department.
Union Relations	Final decision on contents of agreement. Administering the agreement day by day.	Advise on agreement contents. Negotiating expertise. Surveys of competitive practice. Preparation and presentation of arbitration cases.	Negotiations could be contracted out to attorney or consultant. Negotiations could be contracted out to employers' association. Arbitration cases could be contracted out to attorney or consultant. Liaison could be contracted out, but policy formulation and implementation should not be contracted out.
Labor Law Compliance	Final decision on formulation of company policies, implementing compliance. Application of policy.	Expert advice on interpretation of statutory and administrative law. Education of the line organization on methods of compliance. Expert liaison with enforcement agencies. Record administration needed for compliance.	
Legislative Liaison	Company stand on proposed legislation should be determined by top line officers. Line officers might serve as enterprise representatives at hearings on proposed legislation.	Expert advice to line officers on probable impact of proposed legislation. Employee education on proposed legislation. Expert testimony on enterprise standpoint. Liaison with industry representative or Chamber of Commerce or National Association of Manufacturers.	Could be contracted out to professional lobbyists. Could be contracted out to industry association. Could be contracted out to organization like Chamber of Commerce or National Association of Manufacturers.

the next chapter, are the mechanisms which check the foreman's freedom of action.

Personnel administration is a growing field of employment, and the practitioners of the function are jealous of their status. There is no question that personnel administration is important and that its practitioners are dedicated to improving the quality of work in the field. However, every step of progress toward the professionalization of personnel administration results in further diminishing the influence of the foreman in the management of his men.

The Foreman's Critical Role in Employee Relations in the Large-Scale Enterprise

It is the foreman who must take the plans of the specialists in the production control department and translate them into units of product by the use of people. In doing so he must exactly conform to the personnel policies and rules laid down in the labor agreement and interpreted by the specialists in the personnel department. His leeway for personal initiative and decision in both the technical and personnel aspects of his job has thus been narrowed; his authority has shrunk with his reduced responsibility, yet he remains management's living link with the human element of production. He is also management's living link with the union in action, for he faces a shop steward not once a year in negotiations nor once a fortnight in a grievance session, but all day every day. He feels the union's scrutiny and pressure in everything he does. It is not always easy for him to keep his relations with the union entirely impersonal.

The foreman's task and problems indicate the kind of help and training higher management needs to give him. This phase of supervisory training belongs to the personnel department. Two important subjects make up the curriculum: the labor agreement and what may be loosely called human relations.

The Foreman and the Labor Agreement.   A foreman ought to know the agreement at least as well as the steward who stands opposite him. In addition, he must be drilled in the company's position on any unclear or controversial provisions. If the personnel department does not give the foreman this understanding, he can only learn by the costly way of trial and error. He will meet with reversals of his actions in grievance cases; and that never adds to a foreman's prestige with his men. Other supervisors above the foreman need to know the agreement, too, but none in such intimate and accurate detail, for none of them is as directly on the firing line as the foreman is in front of his workers. The foreman shares with the personnel department the most vital role in collective bargaining after the actual negotiation of the agreement—that is, living with the agreement.

The Foreman and Leadership by Persuasion: Human Relations.
Human relations, the other main subject in the curriculum, aims at teaching the foreman how to get results from his people with the limited
resources left to him either of compulsion or reward. In essence, he has
to learn to lead by *persuasion.*

Leading by persuasion alone, without the equivalent in hand of either
the carrot or the stick, tends to become quite an art. The economist, whose
premises giving money wages as the motivator for better and faster work
once guided industry, and the psychologist, whose tests of aptitude and
measures of mental efficiency were a sensation in their day, have given
way of late to teams of social scientists probing the mysteries of interaction and group behavior.

There is no science that has not contributed in some way to industrial
progress. No doubt the behavioral sciences are due to have their day in
setting the premises of employee relations. Without waiting for detailed
findings, it would seem safe at this point to say that in industry the
success of leadership by persuasion at the foreman's level depends on two
things. One is the pull of the enterprise as a whole on the worker; the
other, the foreman's ability to make the worker see, feel, and appreciate
this pull.

What economic incentives does the enterprise offer? What is the
structure of wages? The level? The method of wage payment? What are
the job advancement opportunities? What are the chances of security and
what are the fringe benefits? What psychological satisfactions come from,
and in, employment with the enterprise? Does the enterprise give outlets
that appeal to the individual? Does it absorb him in group efforts toward
a common goal?

Answers to questions like these determine the total effect employment
with an enterprise has on the employees. Only the central administrative
organs of a company can today provide the answers, for the questions all
involve matters of policy that belong to top management. To the extent
that collective bargaining affects policy, part of the answer comes from
the union, acting at top level jointly with management in policy making.

Leadership by persuasion consists, then, first in creating a situation
today's generation of workers regards as at least satisfactory and then
showing the worker his part in it and how to benefit from it. The whole
enterprise thus becomes one great big carrot. The stick is in the threat of
banishment from the feast, not by anyone's arbitrary decree, but by the
failure to meet the group's standards, to measure up, to "get along with
people," in a word—in self-banishment. The foreman, no longer a driver,
no longer a keeper of the key to reward, walks alongside the worker as a
guide; an older, wiser, successfully integrated fellow employee showing
the way.

Not all the results are in from the investigations conducted in the behavioral sciences, but it is still not premature to report that the results to

date hint strongly at the importance of leadership by persuasion. The first hint comes from a historic piece of research called the Hawthorne Experiments. These were a series of studies carried out at the Hawthorne Works of the Western Electric Company by the management in cooperation with a team of Harvard University social scientists headed by Elton Mayo, an anthropologist. The experiments were started in the late 1920s and brought to an end by the onset of the depression, but the results remained unpublished until 1938, although Mayo had hinted at some of them in an earlier book. The official report, entitled *Management and the Worker*, by Roethlisberger and Dixon, is the acknowledged landmark and point of departure for the human relations school of thought.

One of the important concepts springing from the findings published in this book is that the face-to-face work group, and not the individual, is the real unit with which management has to deal in the industrial situation. The work group has cohesion, continuity, and control over its members. It can set and enforce standards of individual conduct, including production norms. It has its natural informal leaders. It can enhance or it can retard management objectives and cooperate with or oppose the formal leadership given by line management. This is true with or without the presence of a union; there was, in fact, no union organization at the Western Electric Company when the experiments took place.

The book which brought these facts before the public does not make easy reading. It is formidable in size. It might have had little immediate effect on management thinking if it had not followed as closely as it did the sweep of the CIO unions through manufacturing industry. This union storming of the nonunion fortresses had a shock-wave effect and left factory management bewildered, seeking for an explanation and for guidance in coping with the unfamiliar problem. Some of the popular management journals spread the word about the Hawthorne experiments. The experiments did contain clues to an explanation of what had happened, but they did not give specific guidance on how to deal with the new unions. They also put to work a multitude of laborers in the field across which Hawthorne plowed the first furrow: the field of human relations in industry and behavioral science research.

A generation later, the literature of management, the teaching of management, the practice of management, have all been thoroughly imbued with the lessons of Hawthorne. Management by shared objectives, participative management, democratic management, such are the phrases currently in vogue. As such, they are topics of foreman training.

EMPLOYER ASSOCIATIONS

As noted in Figure 3–3, some important personnel management activities may be contracted to consultants or employer associations or special representational organizations. It is not uncommon for small employers to contract out their collective bargaining negotiations to an employer association.

Management associations, like unions, are membership organizations. The members are the enterprises which pay the expenses and support the activities of the association.

Businessmen organize for many reasons besides collective bargaining. Only a minority of their associations do, in fact, directly engage in it. Others, which do none of it themselves, carry out representational activities (lobbying, public relations, and the like) that may affect the collective bargaining process generally, or they may give aid and advice to member firms involved in specific negotiations, strikes, or other relations with unions. The term "employer association" to designate management groups that directly engage in collective bargaining, will differentiate this type of organization from other management associations.

Conditions for Association Bargaining

No employer association enters in directly when collective bargaining takes place between a single local union and a single employer, or between a number of locals and a single employer. Employer association bargaining takes place only in two situations:

The first is when a number of employers each hire workers who are members of the same local, or group of locals organized in a joint board or district of the same international. This occurs, for instance, in the trucking industry; not universally, but in those localities where employers have succeeded in forming an association. It occurs in the garment industry as a normal and regular thing. An untypical but outstanding instance of the same nature shows up in the coal mines. Regional and national employer associations bargain jointly with the United Mine Workers' International.

The unions in this picture are industrial unions, or industrial amalgamations of craft unions, as in the garment trade; and in every case a big union deals with a lot of small companies, all of which are in competition with each other. In all these industries except mining—mining is always an exception—labor costs are a high proportion of total costs. The effect of this industrial union type of multiemployer, or Association, bargaining is to eliminate or reduce competition between companies based on wage differences.

The second situation occurs when a number of employers each hire workers who are members of different locals of as many different internationals. This is the characteristic situation in the construction industry. It is the craft-union type of association bargaining, which is not only multiemployer, but multiunion as well. The association negotiates and signs agreements with each of the locals, and these agreements bind all the members of the association in their dealings with each of the unions.

The reason for this is that the employers need and use different kinds of labor at different stages of their construction projects, and so deal with the local representing that particular craft at the time when its members are on the job; and not before, and not after. Their association gives them the protection of a valid agreement with established rules and terms at the time they have need of that particular trade, or class of employee. It relieves all of the employers from having to negotiate separate agreements with each of the many craft unions.

Not to be confused with true association bargaining is employer *cooperation*. An example of this might be the agreement between New York City newspaper publishers that if any one of their papers is hit by a strike, all the others will suspend publication. This is certainly a strong pledge of support for an enterprise to get from its competitors, but the bargaining, and the agreements signed, are separate.

Problems of Association Bargaining

All bargaining involving more than one employer raises problems of representation. The National Labor Relations Board will, on request, designate by means of an election among workers, the union representation for a given group whether or not all workers in the unit belong to the union. Employers who bargain jointly must, on the other hand, do so by agreement among themselves and on a voluntary basis. A bargain made by the union is binding on all the workers in the bargaining unit, but a bargain struck by the organized employer group is in no way binding on other employers who are not members of the association. In any practically enforceable legal sense, it is not even very binding on Association members.

The employer association has problems that parallel in several curious ways the problems of a union, and are often even more acute. Among the more troublesome are organizing, leadership, and the administration and policing of the labor agreement.

Organization.   Employer associations are strictly voluntary since there is no law that compels an enterprise to abide by decisions of a body to which it does not belong. The first hard job in forming an association is to round up members. The next is to keep them in line.

Unions are also, technically, voluntary associations, but through arrangements worked out in collective bargaining (closed shop, union shop) they have found ways of making workers want to join the union—or at least, want not to *refrain from* joining—and to maintain their membership. In any case, a union that has won an election and gained recognition has the legal right to bind the nonunion minority in accordance with the decisions of the prounion majority.

Certain employers, in contrast, may have powerful motives rooted in competition for staying out of the association, or personal inclinations against risking a reduction of accustomed freedom of individual action. In particular, if it is the larger operators who want to play the lone wolf role, the holdouts can cripple the association's effectiveness. Concessions granted to the union by a nonmember can force the hand of the association.

The businessman, more accustomed to competition than cooperation between enterprises—indeed, often dedicated by conviction to that view—is harder to organize than workers who are conditioned to cooperation on the job and accustomed to joint action and discipline.

Leadership. Under a union constitution all employees are equal, but to paraphrase George Orwell's quip, some employers are "more equal" than others: that is, some enterprises are larger, or are under more vigorous management, or make a greater financial contribution to the employer association. Though they may temporarily sink their differences on matters that have to do with the union, they remain in competition with each other. An elected leadership may consequently be subject to distrust or jealously, and the necessity for consultation over decisions may hamper the speed and decisiveness of action.

As a remedy for these difficulties, many associations turn to the employment of professional labor relations experts to conduct the business of the association. The member firms set general policy and review the results of the neutral hired manager's activities. Assuming an able manager, this seems to be a satisfactory plan.

Administration. It is sometimes easier to negotiate a joint agreement than to make sure of observance of its provisions by those who are party to it. In pursuance of this aim the employer association frequently gets help from the union, which has, perhaps, an even more direct interest than any employer in uniformity of performance and strict adherence to the agreed terms.

Greater difficulty arises when the union, instead of helping, hinders proper enforcement. It may attempt to take advantage of the separation of the enterprises to seek local gains or set precedents that can be used against other signatory employers. This is a variant of the old union game called "whipsawing." It sets the members of the association against each other.

The professional manager proves his worth in this kind of situation. Between negotiations he can devote a great deal of his time to policing the agreement, advising and assisting member firms in the handling of grievance cases, and in many ways assuring uniform application of the agreement terms.

Another device associations also use is the employment, jointly and by agreement with the union, of an impartial umpire, or arbiter. To this man they submit disputes that arise during the life of the agreement, and both sides bind themselves in advance to abide by his decisions. The arbiter's role, which does not differ much whether the agreement is multilateral or bilateral, receives more detailed explanation in Chapter 9.

Essentials of Association Bargaining

Association activity of any sort in the labor relations field always follows the rise of unions and is a reaction against it. It is either a specific response to a need for united employer action to meet an immediate union threat, or a generalized answer to the growth of union influence in the community, state, or nation.

There would seem to be need for united action by employers whenever the union is bigger than the enterprises with which it deals. Now, when is the union "bigger"?

"Big" Unionism. The union is bigger than the employer when the union body with which he deals brings to bear, in the bargaining process, the bargaining power of members who work for all the employers in a given labor or product market. This is true when the union controls the pool from which they all draw their workers, so that labor could be withheld from one employer while his competitors went on unhampered. Obviously, a craft union is in such a position in relation to its employers. An industrial union, ordinarily, is not, for the source of factory labor is open to all, and workers hired in the employment office do not come under union influence until they are part of the factory working force.

The union is also bigger when the union body with which employers make their bargain controls the supply of materials an enterprise needs, or the market to which it sells, or the channels of distribution to the market. A perfect example of this is the Teamsters, an industrial union, which can cut the channels of distribution or supply by refusing deliveries.

Either one of the two situations sketched out above cries out for employer organization. Unless employers facing such situations bargain through an association they are simply inviting exploitation by the union, and may lay the industry open to racketeering. The size of the employer association needs to be exactly proportioned to the size of what was called above the "union body."

This union body may be a local, as in the building trades. It may be a joint board of locals, as in the garment trades. It may be a district, as in the trucking industry. It may be an entire international, or a major part thereof, as in the coal mining industry.

Without the protection of an association, employers face the prospect of having the union "knock down" the individual enterprises of the industry one by one. The first bargain with the union may consist of seeing an organizer walk in with a printed agreement and say, "Sign here." If the employer signs, knowing that the penalty for not doing so would be a shutdown of his business while competitors continued to operate, the next bargain might be: "Sign here. And slip a C-note into the papers when you hand them back: cash, no checks." Before long an entire industry could get into the hands of racketeers who used the employers to keep the workers in line and beat each of the employers over the head with the threat implied in control of all the others. Once such a condition arrives it is harder than ever for the employers to organize. Association bargaining balances the strength of the opposing forces.

Equality in Bargaining. Some see the union as always bigger than any employer because it organizes all the enterprises in an industry or all the practitioners of a single skilled trade whose craftsmen work for many employers.

The union is not bigger just because it has a million members while the enterprise employs only a thousand workers, if the interprise bargains only with a local composed of its own thousand employees. The union's other members in other plants have managements of their own to bargain with; every enterprise in the industry could conceivably be evenly matched with its own segment of the union. That seems, in fact, to be generally the case in mass-production manufacturing. It is undoubtedly one of the reasons why association bargaining is rare in manufacturing outside the garment industries.

Even the "Big Three" auto companies, General Motors, Ford, and Chrysler, only began to approach joint and simultaneous bargaining as a thinkable but potentially dangerous possibility, in their dealings with the challenge of the UAW in 1958, the year the auto agreements expired without renewal and the plants operated without a contract. The Big Three companies would seem, offhand, well suited to engage in association bargaining. Together they produce more than 90 percent of the nation's cars. They face a common adversary in the big and powerful UAW. They maintain headquarters in the same city of Detroit, where the UAW International also has its offices, and the auto company top managers are personally acquainted and in frequent cordial social contact with each other. Time and again in the past the UAW played off one or another of the three companies against its two competitors to win important gains the others had to match; yet the Big Three held off.

They have held off, in part, perhaps, for fear of antitrust action, always a delicate subject in their circles. Another reason certainly must be competition for the new car market, in which the customer takes performance pretty much for granted and spends his money for style and conveniences. Any one of the companies, convinced that its designers have come up with styling that will catch on with the public, meets an immediate union demand without too much regret, confident that whatever it gives the union, the union will make the other two grant in time. Thus it was, for instance, with the "S.U.B." unemployment benefits plan, first put to

General Motors by the union, but first granted by Ford. The UAW is a big union, but the giant corporations of the auto industry are pretty big themselves and are confident and willing to take a chance. Why should they tie their own hands by being timid?

In spite of this, some observers claim to see a trend toward multi-employer bargaining on an industry-wide scale with industrial unions even in the largest enterprises. The logic of events would seem to favor this, but it will probably not come until the big employers are convinced the union really is bigger than they are. Certainly the unions have little to gain by pushing it; they have been doing very well without it. Would the UAW really welcome a united front of the Big Three auto companies against itself?

Despite this auto industry exception, the trend is certainly setting in the direction of association bargaining. Besides the industries already mentioned in this chapter, a number of others have engaged in it for years, while some have come to it comparatively recently. The garment unions have been doing it for a long time. The lumber industry, the shipping industry, the canneries on the West Coast, have been at it for two decades or more. In fact, association bargaining is prevalent as a regional phenomenon on the West Coast to an extent unknown as yet in the East or Middle West.

Most notable example of industry-wide bargaining is probably the steel industry negotiations. Technically, this is still only cooperative bargaining, in which the United Steelworkers discusses terms jointly and simultaneously with the huge steel employers; but one product of the 1962 contract was an *industry-wide* seniority pool from which all the firms would draw workers, these workers having gone into the pool as they were displaced from any of the firms by technological improvements.

The standard European practice from the start has favored association bargaining. It would appear that American practice tends in the same direction; but the process still has far to go. The greater portion of the mass-production and mass-distribution industries has not come to it yet.

OTHER MANAGEMENT ASSOCIATIONS

Unions engage not only in collective bargaining but in "representational" activities such as lobbying and public relations, and service activities such as workers' education and research. These kinds of activity, directly or indirectly, frequently supplement collective bargaining. They encourage helpful, or ward off harmful, legislation affecting the process. They promote a favorable climate of public opinion. They provide training for improved union leadership and functioning, and information useful to locals engaged in negotiations. The bulk of this representational activity goes on at levels above the local union (which is the primary collective bargaining organization) in any given international, and in the mixed bodies such as city centrals, state centrals, and the national union federation.

Similarly, certain management organizations specialize in representational and service activities for employers, and these are likely to be of greater than local scope and mixed in character. Those that unite enterprises of a single industry, unless formed for the express purpose of collective bargaining, are likely to center their attention on technological or marketing problems peculiar to the industry rather than on labor relations.

The National Association of Manufacturers

The employer counterpart of the AFL-CIO, the national union federation, is the National Association of Manufacturers, commonly called the "NAM." Of all employer groups engaged principally in representational activity the NAM takes the greatest interest in labor relations. It carries on the most vigorous and massive "pressure-group" activity—similar, but counter to, union pressure tactics—aimed at influencing the legislative and executive branches of government. It conducts the most extensive public relations work and does the most research in the labor relations field. Its network of affiliates throughout the country includes industry groups that contain employer associations for collective bargaining as well as mixed, nonbargaining associations of manufacturers and other industrialists organized on a geographical basis. This heightens the resemblance of the NAM to the organized labor movement opposite which it stands. The NAM structure is much looser than the unions', but the prestige, power, and financial resources of its employer members gives it great influence.

The Chambers of Commerce

Another important network of management associations is the Chamber of Commerce, or "C of C," units of which exist locally and affiliate on a state-wide and national scale. Throughout its structure the C of C is of mixed composition, and so does no bargaining. Local Chambers are largely service and promotional organizations, which are drawn into the representational type of activity that supplements collective bargaining only occasionally, by virtue of the stake and interest many of the member enterprises have in the field. Membership in the C of C, as in other management associations, is voluntary.

In addition to these two nationwide federations of employees, many local and unaffiliated associations, some of a quite informal nature, others well organized and enduring, bring together groups of employers for collective bargaining or representational and service functions. They may be considered analogous to unaffiliated local unions.

SUMMARY AND CONCLUSIONS

Previous systems for the management of labor have shown only two parties in the relationship: the "employer" (slaveowner, lord of the manor) and the "employee" (slave, serf). The present free-labor system shows in addition a third element, the union. The employer may be an individual or a company of people incorporated as an artificial "person," and acting through agents with delegated authority. The union is always an association of people, acting through representatives. Only the worker is always an individual, full-blooded person. Collectively, he is the flesh-and-blood link between the company and the union.

The "Four Sets of Relations"

Between these three elements there are three sets of relations, and perhaps a fourth that encompasses them all:

1. *The company and the worker.* This is a freewill contract in which the worker exchanges work against wages, under conditions laid down by the employer and accepted by the worker, or agreed upon between them.

2. *The worker and the union.* Here the relationship is a free association between the worker as a member and the union to which he belongs. Technically, at least, it is a voluntary association and the right to enter it comes from the Bill of Rights of the Constitution.

3. *The union and the company.* The relation between the union and the company is usually thought of, and referred to, as a "contract," but it is more nearly analogous to a *treaty* between two sovereign powers. It is an exchange of pledges and promises that have to do with the contract between the company and each of its individual workers.

4. *The "encompassing fourth" relationship.* The company and the union are linked so intimately by the body of the workers, who are at the same time employees of the one and members of the other, that they may be thought of as a three-link chain, or perhaps more appropriately symbolized by overlapping circles.

The "Key" Element

The *key element* that brings the other two into association with it is the company. The *company* organizes the working force around its production processes. The union has to take the workers as it finds them in their relations with each other and with the company, their employer.

But labor-management relations, expressed in bargaining for agreements and in administering the agreements, is a process of interaction. Companies bring unions into existence by creating work groups for the union to organize. Unions act on the company, and the company registers their impact in terms of management organization structure and functioning. Internal change is the result, but there are also external effects. Union pressure on separate, independent enterprises forces them into united action and mutual dependence.

Multiemployer bargaining, which long ago reached maturity in the handicraft sector of the economy, spread into mass production and distribution with the growth of industrial unions. Industry-wide bargaining, not yet much developed, seems to be almost in sight, and, some say, sure to come.

Industry-wide bargaining involving the big and decisive mass-production and distribution units of the economy will surely affect management structure and functioning within the enterprise, and the relation of enterprises to the society they sustain with their products and services. The enterprise will no longer be as free and independent as before. The local union, which is a direct, responsive membership organization, will yield its rights and powers in collective bargaining to the international, which is a delegate organization remote from local control.

While these possibilities unfold, the employer remains the key element. He will hardly remain passive but will act as well as be acted upon. It is to be hoped that in association he will act as effectively as when he stood alone, to help sustain a vigorous economy and provide the material basis for a good society.

QUESTIONS FOR DISCUSSION

1. Foreman training in human relations is a major development of the post-World War II period. Why?

2. What is the influence of the prevailing form of ownership of capital on management organization, objectives, and methods?

3. How do you explain the fact that there frequently is substantial friction between line and staff organizations in the handling of personnel matters in large-scale enterprises?

4. Compare and contrast management objectives and methods in handicraft industry and mass production.

5. In 1947 several proponents of the Taft-Hartley law favored outlawing multiemployer bargaining. Although this proposal continues to crop up occasionally, it is less frequently heard nowadays. What do you think of this proposal and why does it seem to have gone out of style?

CASES: 5, 6, 7, 8.

SELECTED ANNOTATED BIBLIOGRAPHY

ALLEN, A. DALE, JR. "A Systems View of Labor Negotiations," *Personnel Journal* (February 1971), pp. 103–14.

An attempt to develop a systems model for collective bargaining with a view to improving the goal setting, forecasting, and decision making of industrial relations executives. Allen stresses the flexibility of his model to various situations.

ANTHONY, PETER, and CRICHTON, ANNE. *Industrial Relations and the Personnel Specialists.* London: B. T. Batsford Ltd., 1969.

An extensive reevaluation of the industrial relations process in light of recent findings in the field of organizational behavior, particularly socio-technical systems theory. Authors see a need to integrate the industrial relations process into line management.

BAKER, HELEN, AND FRANCE, ROBERT R. *Centralization and Decentralization in Industrial Relations.* Princeton, N.J.: Industrial Relations Section, Princeton University, Research Report Series, No. 87, 1954.

Discusses management and union preferences for centralization and decentralization in industrial relations responsibility and authority in multi-plant firms and the actual practice of centralization or decentralization in these companies.

BELCHER, A. L. "How Top Management Views the Industrial Relations Function," *Personnel,* Vol. XXXIV (March–April 1958), pp. 65–70.

Results of a personnel director's survey of some 200 executives and university professors to determine the factors necessary for success as a personnel man.

BROWN, DOUGLASS V., and MYERS, CHARLES A. "The Changing Industrial Relations Philosophy of American Management," *Proceedings of the Ninth Annual Meeting of the Industrial Relations Research Association,* pp. 84–99. Madison, Wis.: The Association, 1957.

Discusses five forces causing changes in the approach of management to industrial relations in the last decade.

HILL, LEE H., and HOOK, CHARLES L., JR. *Management at the Bargaining Table.* New York: McGraw-Hill Book Co., Inc., 1945.

A comprehensive review of the issues and practices of collective bargaining from a management viewpoint. Provides a penetrating insight into management thinking at the end of World War II.

LYNCH, EDITH. "The Personnel Man and His Job: An AMA Survey," *Personnel,* Vol. XXXII (May 1956), pp. 487–97.

A profile of "the average personnel man" derived from an American Management Association questionnaire survey of 450 participants in a personnel conference.

McCAFFREE, KENNETH M. "A Theory of the Origin and Development of Employer Associations," *Fifteenth Annual Meeting of the Industrial Relations Research Association* (December 1952), pp. 56–68.

McFARLAND, DALTON E. *Cooperation and Conflict in Personnel Administration.* New York: American Foundation for Management Research, 1962.

Discusses attitudes of cooperation and conflict between line and staff organizations performing the personnel function in large-scale enterprises.

———. "The Labor Relations Consultant as Contract Negotiator," *Personnel,* Vol. XXXIV (May–June 1958), pp. 44–51.

Discusses the advantages and disadvantages to a company in the use of outside consultant as contract negotiator. Interesting observations on the impact of this practice on internal management organization.

McGREGOR, DOUGLAS. *The Human Side of Enterprise.* New York: McGraw-Hill Book Co., Inc., 1960.

Argues for greater participation in decision making by subordinates in business enterprise.

McMURRAY, ROBERT N. "The Case for Benevolent Autocracy," *Harvard Business Review,* Vol. XXXVI (January–February 1958), pp. 82–90.

A leading management consultant argues against participative management and in favor of his proposed "benevolent autocracy."

———. "War and Peace in Labor Relations," *Harvard Business Review,* Vol. XXXIII (November–December, 1955), pp. 48–60.

A leading management consultant takes issue with the "philosophies" growing out of "causes-of-industrial-peace" type of thinking and advocates a preventive labor relations policy to maintain a balance of power between company and union.

MYERS, CHARLES A., and TURNBULL, JOHN G. "Line and Staff in Industrial Relations," *Harvard Business Review,* Vol. XXXIV (July–August 1956), pp. 113–24.

Professor Myers of M.I.T. and Professor Turnbull of the University of Minnesota survey the organizational placement of the industrial relations in management and propose methods of clarifying the relations between the industrial relations department and line management.

PATTEN, THOMAS H., JR. "Personnel Research: Status Key," *Management of Personnel Quarterly,* Vol. 4 (Fall 1965), pp. 15–23.

Reviews the personnel research carried out by specific large corporations.

———. "Revitalizing the Role of the Foreman," *Management of Personnel Quarterly,* Vol 5 (Summer 1966), pp. 34–43.

Outlines a program for identifying supervisory potential, recognizing supervisory performance, and retaining in the employ of the enterprise employees who have demonstrated proficiency as line supervisors.

ROETHLISBERGER, F. J. "The Foreman: Master and Victim of Double Talk," *Harvard Business Review,* Vol. 43 (September–October 1965), pp. 22–26.

Reprints the author's 1954 analysis of the foreman's role, with retrospective commentary on the article and its significance.

RYDER, MEYER S., REHMUS, CHARLES M., and COHEN, SANFORD. *Management Preparation for Collective Bargaining.* Homewood, Ill.: Dow Jones-Irwin Inc., 1966.

An analysis of personal interviews with approximately 100 officials from 40 companies about how they forge policy, strategy, and tactics for collective bargaining.

SCOTT, WILLIAM G. *The Management of Conflict: Appeal Systems in Organizations.* Homewood, Ill.: Richard D. Irwin, Inc., and the Dorsey Press, 1965.

Examines appeal systems in business and nonbusiness organizations without unions.

SLICHTER, SUMNER H.; JAMES J. HEALY; and LIVERNASH, E. ROBERT. *The Impact of Collective Bargaining on Management.* Washington, D.C.: Brookings Institution, 1960.

See Chapter 2, "Issues for Management in Industrial Relations" and Chapter 29, "Line and Staff Cooperation and the Position of Foreman."

SOMERS, GERALD G. "Pressures on an Employers' Association in Collective Bargaining," *Industrial and Labor Relations Review,* Vol. VI (July 1953), pp. 557–69.

Compares experience under multiemployer bargaining in the bituminous-coal and flint-glass industries.

WALKER, CHARLES R.; GUEST, ROBERT H.; and TURNER, ARTHUR N. *The Foremen on the Assembly Line.* Cambridge, Mass.: Harvard University Press, 1956.

Examines the roles and points of view of foremen in an automobile plant.

WHYTE, WILLIAM H., JR. *The Organization Man.* New York: Simon and Schuster, Inc., 1956.

Examines the ideology, training, neuroses, testing, and behavior of the organization man in business, government, and professional employment.

WORTMAN, MAX S., JR. "Influences of Employer Bargaining Associations in Manufacturing Firms," *Fifteenth Annual Proceedings of the Industrial Relations Research Association* (December 1962), pp. 69–82.

Chapter 4 | UNION ORGANIZATION FOR COLLECTIVE BARGAINING

Each worker has a separate employment contract with his employer; but work is social. Any enterprise of moderate size organizes and integrates its tasks so closely that every job is interdependent with all others. The individual cannot bargain for changes in his own job or conditions without affecting others in varying degree so that individual bargaining is ineffective. Changes in individual employment contracts usually depend upon a *general* review of the conditions of employment which can be obtained only by collective pressure on the employer. To exert this pressure, workers form unions. In the factory and other large-scale organizations with a high degree of job specialization, they form industrial unions. In other cases, where skilled craftsmen perform substantially the same work for an employer, or employers, and bring to their work the same qualifications, it seems natural to seek the same employment bargain for all workers possessing the same skills. Again the means of doing this is to form a union, and for skilled men in the handicraft trades, a craft union.

Physicians, attorneys, engineers, and other members of the professions often form professional associations. Although these associations typically do not engage in collective bargaining and shun the label of "unionism," some of their activities tend to parallel the behavior of unions.

Craft unions, industrial unions, and professional associations seek somewhat different ends and use somewhat different means for accomplishing these ends. In addition to discussing the ends and means of unions and professional associations, this chapter will describe some of the major characteristics of the structure of American labor organizations.

THE GENERAL OBJECTIVES OF UNIONS

Unions are *service* organizations; they produce no tangible product. The profit motive which plays such an important role in business enterprise is irrelevant to a discussion of labor organizations.

The general objectives of American unions can best be understood by starting with an assumption deeply imbedded in the tradition of American law and unionism, that is, that unions are *voluntary* and *private* institutions. Under this assumption, it is fairly obvious that the objectives of American unions are two:

1. To raise the living standards *of their members*, that is, to raise wages, shorten the hours of work, and improve working conditions, and
2. To protect *their members* from arbitrary employer actions in the course of employment.

The voluntary and private institution assumption is helpful in: (1) providing a rationale for the flow of authority or consent in unions, (2) putting no constraints whatsoever on the nature of union behavior, i.e., leaving unions free to pursue the welfare of their members either by collective bargaining or political activity, and (3) excluding utopian ideological schemes from the realm of union activity. Each of these advantages of the voluntary and private institution assumption merits brief discussion before the assumption itself is modified.

If unions are voluntary and private associations, the members "own" the union and the will of the members must be paramount in all union activities. Thus authority must flow upward in unions from the owner-members to the elected officers. Majority rule and town hall democracy provide the foundation upon which unions must be built. The individual member's inherent right to withdraw from the union provides a constant check on any undemocratic practices of the union leadership. If oligarchy develops, it has been approved through the apathy of the membership. In theory at least, the membership always possesses an absolute veto on any action of the leadership.

The private side of the assumption gives unions great discretion in the means they adopt to achieve their ends. So long as unions do not exceed the freedoms guaranteed to individual citizens, they would be free to engage in all sorts of fraternal and political activities, just as a lodge could endorse a political candidate or contribute to his campaign expenses. Carried to the extreme, as private organizations unions could even become political parties.

Students of the labor movement have argued the relative merits of "bread-and-butter" unionism versus "utopian" unionism for almost a century now. Within the labor movement itself considerable controversy has raged over the obligation of unions to act as the protectors and advocates of the downtrodden in the society. It probably is not an exaggeration to say that the principle which split the labor movement in the formation of the CIO in 1935 was the question of the obligation of the labor movement to bring the benefits of unionism to unorganized workers. If one firmly supports the voluntary and private assumption, the question of organizing the unorganized beyond the immediate jurisdiction of existing unions is largely irrelevant. Certainly the voluntary and private assumption excludes any necessity for action seeking to modify the existing politico-economic structure of society. Today it is fashionable to criticize the failure of American unions to organize the real victims of poverty in the United States, and the authors of this book have frequently joined this lament. However, if the voluntary and private assumption were completely accepted, there would be little justification for this criticism. Under the voluntary and private assumption, union activity in organizing the victims of poverty could be judged a failure only if unorganized poverty-stricken workers posed a threat to the prosperity of the present members of unions.

Although the voluntary and private institution assumption about unions is helpful in explaining union activity and is deeply imbedded in tradition, it must be abandoned today simply because *it is contrary to fact.* Under current law, unions are obligated to represent *all* the workers under an NLRB certification whether they are union members or not. Thus American unions have become instrumentalities of the state at least to some degree. The significance of the quasi-public nature of unionism is discussed in Chapter 5.

Quite apart from the legal obligation to represent some nonmember workers, American unionism has interests which go beyond the simple representation of present members. These interests are dictated by the market context and the broader ideological objectives of *some* unions. Market conditions dictating union activity beyond the representation of present members are fairly noncontroversial. Low-wage, nonunion textile plants pose an obvious threat to the jobs and wages of unionized textile workers; the interests of the members of textile unions can be protected only by organizing the nonunion workers or raising their wages to union levels by law. On the other hand, the obligation of unions to represent the downtrodden in the society is a highly controversial question which ultimately is decided on the ethical standards of the discussants. In the discussion which follows, consideration will be given to the organizational elements best suited for serving these broader representational interests.

Because the voluntary and private institution assumption does not square with present-day facts, this book argues that the *general* objectives of unions are four in number. Individual unions may adopt a mixture of all four of these objectives or they may concentrate all of their energies on only one or two of them. Both the degree of intensity in seeking these objectives and the organizational components established for the purpose of achieving them vary between individual unions. The general objectives of unions are:

1. To influence the wage and effort bargain; to take labor out of self-competition,
2. To establish a system of individual security; to obtain justice at the workplace,
3. To influence the rules for rule making; by the process of political

representation to obtain legislative, executive, and judicial actions which promote the interests of individual unions, unions in general, and the welfare of the constituency of unions, and
4. To obtain power in the state and over the economy; by political means to create an economic and political environment conducive to the welfare of labor.

Public acceptance of union activity depends, in part, on the objective sought. Although some citizens might argue that union wages are too high or that a particular seniority system is contrary to the general welfare, very few citizens would argue that workers should be denied the right to *influence* the wage and effort bargain or to seek to establish *some* system of individual security. On the other hand, it seems likely that a larger number of citizens would criticize union political activities.

One might suppose that unions would encounter little difficulty in setting their operational objectives; that the goals would be dictated by a democratic vote of the membership and that union officers would be relatively impotent to modify these objectives. This idealistic fiction collapses because of the complexity of union organizational structures and the issues in collective bargaining, the ambition and manipulative skill of union leadership, and the apathy of rank-and-file union members. A few words about the problems of achieving union democracy are in order before discussing the elements of union organizational structure.[1]

Complex union organizational structures and complex issues in collective bargaining tend to frustrate latent union democracy of the town hall variety. Power is where the money is. For reasons to be discussed below, there is a growing tendency in the labor movement for money to be concentrated above the local union. A natural outgrowth of this is to reduce the autonomy of local unions and the influence of the members of a union on its policy. One of the factors contributing to the centralization of power in unions at levels above the local union is the complexity of collective bargaining issues. It probably is fair to say that a majority of union members would like to have pensions; but pension bargaining requires the services of a highly trained expert and this bargaining is beyond the competence of rank-and-file union members. Once an expert enters the bargaining the influence of union members on the final settlement diminishes.

This book argues that the basic determinants of union structure are Dunlop's contexts and that the technology context is the most important single determinant of union structure. Nevertheless, it is obvious that union organizational structures are influenced by the personal characteristics of union leaders. Although the general welfare of the people defines

---

[1] In his classic study of radical *Political Parties* and working-class movements, Robert Michels concludes that every system of leadership is incompatible with the most essential postulate of democracy.

the position of President of the United States, the Presidency itself during the tenure of Calvin Coolidge was quite different from what it was under Franklin D. Roosevelt. A Teamsters union under James R. Hoffa would undoubtedly be quite unlike a Teamsters union under Walter Reuther or George Meany.

Probably the greatest deterrent to town hall democracy in unions is the apathy of rank and file. A good many union members have little interest in union affairs so long as the union is effective in negotiating wage increases and processing their personal grievances. These members pay their dues and expect the union to do a job for them, just as they may hire a neighborhood boy to mow the lawn. As long as the grass gets cut they are satisfied, and they couldn't care less about who cuts it or what methods he uses to do the job.

Union democracy is hard to define. Two dimensions of the meaning of union democracy are suggested by a substantial body of scholarly literature. The legalistic dimension of union democracy is the existence of procedures for fair and regular elections, reasonable trial procedures in applying union discipline, and guarantees that members of the union have a right to express reasoned dissent from union policy.[2] Another, more humanistic, dimension of union democracy deals with the extent to which individual members of unions feel that they are capable of influencing union policy, and their satisfaction with the policies established.[3] It seems fair to say that rank-and-file apathy, the ambition of powerful leaders, and centralization of union decision-making power at levels above the local tend to dilute union democracy in both the legalistic and humanistic dimensions.

The wage and effort bargain and systems of individual security always originate at the level of the enterprise and the local union. Political activity more frequently is conducted at higher levels of union organization than the local.

ELEMENTS OF UNION ORGANIZATIONAL STRUCTURE

The basic elements of union organizational structure in the United States are: (1) the local union, (2) the international union, and (3) the AFL-CIO. Auxiliary elements of union structure which are directly engaged in the negotiation and administration of collective bargaining agreements include: (1) districts, (2) joint boards, (3) conference boards, and (4) trade councils. Two auxiliary elements of union structure which are engaged primarily in representational or political activity are: (1) city centrals and (2) state centrals. Each of these elements of union

---

[2] For example, see Philip Taft. *The Structure and Government of Labor Unions* (Cambridge, Mass.: Harvard University Press, 1954).

[3] A classic human relations study is Leonard R. Sayles and George Strauss, *The Local Union* (New York: Harper & Bros., 1953).

structure will be considered separately and then integrated into the overall structure of the American labor movement.

THE TWO KINDS OF LOCAL UNIONS

This book argues that there are two basic kinds of local unions: craft locals and industrial locals. Before emphasizing the differences between these types it is well to consider the common characteristics of most local unions.

The local union is a voluntary association of workers who, as free citizens with economic interests in common, have banded together for mutual advantage. The members of the local work for an employer or for several or many employers, but the union exists as an organization independently of any employer, under the constitutional guarantee of freedom of assembly.

The members "own" the local and control it by majority vote: one vote per member. They elect officers and an executive board to act for them between meetings. They hold their meetings, ordinarily, at intervals of a month or less, and conduct them by the rules of order of democratic deliberative assemblies.

The membership meeting is the highest authority of the local union. All members in good standing have voice and vote there. A member maintains good standing by paying dues and assessments and observing the discipline of the union as laid down in the local constitution and bylaws, and in decisions of the local at membership meetings. New members gain admission to the union by complying with the conditions and qualifications of the constitution, paying the required initiation fee, and, if the constitution requires it, receiving the affirmative vote of the members.

In structure and the routine conduct of its business a local union resembles countless other private and independent organizations to which Americans belong: clubs, lodges, church groups, recreational, educational, and service associations. The difference is in the aims the local union sets itself and the functions it carries out.

The primary aim of the local union is to represent its members in relation to their employer or employers. Like any other membership association it also carries on social and subsidiary activities, but in pursuit of its primary aim, the most important functions it performs with employers are collective bargaining and grievance handling.

As independent entities, the local union and the employer of its members negotiate through authorized agents for an agreement defining the terms of the individual work contracts of the employee-members. Negotiation takes place at the policy-making level of the two organizations involved. In the local union, the membership meeting makes policy and selects agents to negotiate on policy with policy makers in management.

Corollary to the process of negotiating the agreement is grievance handling or administration of the agreement. The local union provides employees with a channel for complaints arising under the agreement and for solving problems not foreseen in the negotiations. An administrative organ of the local union sees to the application and enforcement of agreement terms.

Both craft locals and industrial locals devote their main efforts to influencing the wage and effort bargain and establishing systems of individual security at the workplace. Because their membership base is relatively small, they are capable of exerting only insignificant political influence on either the rules for rule making or power in the state.[4]

The Craft Local. "One craft, one union" is the slogan of the craft union. Craft unions dominate the building construction industry and also play an important role in printing and publishing and in the barbering trade. The "tie that binds" a craft union local is the mastery by its members of an entire recognized trade, such as plumbing, lithography, or barbering.

A worker typically masters a trade by serving an apprenticeship consisting of classroom instruction and on-the-job training of several years' duration. Approximately 800 detailed trades and occupations or crafts are recognized by government, unions, and employers as eligible to participate in the national and state apprenticeship programs. Figure 4–1 lists some apprenticeable trades in various industries and indicates the normal duration of the apprenticeships.

A craft union local typically seeks to enroll in its membership all practitioners of its trade in the immediate geographic vicinity regardless of who the employers of its members are. That is, a typical Carpenters' local would seek to organize all the carpenters in Peoria, Illinois, or in Tompkins County, New York. Journeymen carpenters who had served an apprenticeship or acquired journeyman status by long experience would be joined by apprentices in training and carpenter helpers in a single local union. One of the major functions of this local might be joint administration of an apprenticeship program with employers of carpenters in the area. An exception to this general rule might occur when a single employer had a large regular force of craftsmen, for example, a local of the Electrical Workers' Union composed solely of skilled electrical workers employed by a power and light company.

The key man in a craft union is the business agent. A full-time paid employee of the local union, he plays a critical role in the negotiation of the collective bargaining agreement and in its administration.

Bargaining Activities of Craft Locals. The business agent is influential

---

[4] Although some local unions are truly massive organizations and politicians eagerly seek their endorsements, single locals are typically inundated even in city elections. For example, the 40,000 members of Ford Local number 600 of the UAW are lost in a metropolitan Detroit electorate approaching 1 million.

FIGURE 4–1.   Some Apprenticeable Trades and the Duration of Apprenticeship

Representative Trades in the Building Construction Industry

Bricklayer	3 years	Painter and decorator	2–4 years
Carpenter	4 years	Plasterer	3–4 years
Cement mason	3 years	Plumber-Pipefitter	4–5 years
Electrical worker	4–5 years	Rigger	2 years
Ironworker	2–4 years	Roofer	2–3 years
Lather	2–3 years	Sheet-metal worker	3–4 years
Millwright	4 years	Stonemason	3 years
Operating engineer	3–4 years	Tile setter	3 years

Representative Trades in Printing and Publishing Industry

Electrotyper	5–6 years	Printer	5–6 years
Engraver	4–5 years	Printing pressman	5–6 years
Lithographer	4–5 years	Rotogravure engraver	5–6 years
Mailer	4–5 years	Stereotyper	5–6 years
Photoengraver	5–6 years		

Representative Trades in Service Industries

Arborist	3–4 years	Cosmetician	2 years
Barber	2 years	Photographer	3 years
Cook	3 years	Telephone worker	4 years

Representative Trades in Manufacturing Industry

Aircraft fabricator	3–4 years	Machinist	4 years
Brewer	2–3 years	Metal polisher and buffer	3–4 years
Butcher-Meat Cutter	3 years	Model maker	4 years
Candy maker	3–4 years	Pattern maker (foundry)	5 years
Draftsman-Designer	3–5 years	Pottery worker	3 years
Fabric Cutter	3–4 years	Tool- and Die-Maker	4–5 years
Furrier	3–4 years	Upholsterer	3–4 years

Source: U.S. Department of Labor, Manpower Administration, *The National Apprenticeship Program*, 1965, pp. 9–27.

in both the *policy-making* and *policy-enforcement* phases of collective bargaining. Policy making consists of negotiating a collective bargaining agreement with the employers of the local's members. Policy enforcement consists of checking on employer compliance with the terms of the agreement after it has been negotiated.

The business agent typically is the chief negotiator for the craft union local. He and other officers of the local meet with the representatives of the employer association and hammer out a basic collective bargaining agreement. This agreement is then presented to a general membership meeting of the local where it is ratified or rejected by a vote of the membership. Once ratified, this agreement becomes the policy of the signatory employers and the union.

Labor agreements negotiated by craft unions and internal craft union procedures fulfill the four basic functions of: (1) union security and management rights, (2) the wage and effort bargain, (3) individual security, and (4) administration. Typically, union security is achieved by a clause in the agreement which obligates the business agent to refer members to signatory employers when they seek to hire additional hands.

The wage and effort bargain is settled by establishment of a standard union scale of wages and the tradesman's traditional control over the tempo of his work. Individual security may be defined by the incorporation into the agreement of rules for employee conduct and by union practices in distributing available work among its members. Administration of the agreement is provided for by a system of on-the-job representation and the arbitration of unresolved grievances. The contents of a typical craft-union agreement are discussed in detail in Chapter 9.

The fact that some carpenter employers in the vicinity may not be members of the employer association imposes an additional negotiation responsibility on the business agent. After the basic agreement is printed, he then visits nonassociation member employers and insists that they sign a document identical to the basic agreement.

On-the-Job Representation in Craft Locals. An agreement setting forth wages, hours, and working conditions has been signed between the local and all the contractors employing carpenters in a given city. In response to the request of one of these contractors, the business agent of the local sends union members to work on a construction project. The first man he puts on the job customarily acts as "steward" for the Carpenters' union. The business agent chooses him by sending him out first; or, if the policy of the local is to refer members to jobs on a strict seniority basis, he is the most senior member of the local who happens to be looking for work. The craft union job steward is chosen, then, either by the business agent or by chance.

On the job, the steward's duty is to make sure that the contractor lives up to his agreement with the union in the way he pays and treats his carpenters. If the steward observes a violation of the agreement (a copy of which the business agent has given him), he calls it to the attention of the foreman in charge of the carpenters. If the foreman does not correct the violation, the steward reports the matter to the business agent, who takes it up with the contractor. The business agent is often empowered to call the carpenters off the job if the contractor does not adjust the grievance, and keep them off until the dispute is settled.

This system constitutes a simple and effective machinery for enforcing the agreement. It gives the business agent, an administrative official of the union, a live contact with every one of the many jobs on which members of his local are working. He gets information from them, and can pass out information to the members through them. Several points about this system deserve notice.

Stewards representing different unions on a construction job have no official contact with each other, but only with the business agent of their own local: carpenters with the Carpenters' union, bricklayers with the Bricklayers, and so on. This need not prevent informal consultation between stewards of different unions, but there is little point in such contact since the members of each union work under a separate agreement. There is no one body of union representatives, or channel of communication, for all the workers employed on the construction project in dealings with their common employer. This will appear as one of the significant differences between craft and industrial unions.

All the stewards representing any one union—again the Carpenters, for instance—on all the projects where members are employed make up a potential "council." That is, they could be called together without calling a meeting of the local and provide contact with all the working carpenters in town. Calling them together would have little point, however, because each works for a different employer. The only things they would have in common are matters internal to the union; and for the purpose of considering internal union matters a meeting of the local would serve the same purpose and would have what the steward body would lack—power to take action affecting policy. This will appear as another of the significant differences between craft and industrial unions.

Craft union stewards, furthermore, do not represent the men on the job. They represent the business agent, who is responsible for enforcing the agreement. The steward personnel is constantly changing as the work on one project comes to an end and the men shift to other jobs in new and random groupings.

The practical consequence of all this is that the craft union stewards, as a group, do not constitute a separate, functioning organization within the structure of the local union and are not a continuing body. They are simply an extension of the authority of the business agent; an extension, in fact, of his person—his eyes and ears on the jobs where the members are employed. They do not influence the nature of collective bargaining.

Craft-union locals seldom find it necessary to take unresolved grievances to arbitration. Business agents and employers in handicraft industry share the tradition of the craft and settle their differences among themselves. The business agent, as the sole supplier of the employer's critically needed tradesmen, often holds the ace of trumps in these discussions.

The major activities of both craft and industrial local unions are influencing the wage and effort bargain and establishing a system of individual security. However, their bargains and systems are quite different from each other, as are their organizational structures for achieving these ends.

The Industrial Local. "One shop, one union" is the slogan of the industrial union. Industrial unions dominate manufacturing industry and also play important roles in trade, transporation, finance, and mining. It seems reasonable to expect that industrial unions will play an increasing role in government employment. The "tie that binds" an industrial local union is the workplace and the workers' common employer. In the industrial union all the employees working for a given enterprise at a given workplace belong to the same local union without regard for what they do in the plant.

An industrial local union typically seeks to enroll in its membership all production and maintenance workers at the place of employment, with the legally imposed exceptions of supervisors and guards. Although many industrial local unions would very much like to obtain representation rights for white-collar workers employed at their plants, such efforts have been largely unsuccessful to date.

Industrial local unions, unless very large, typically do not employ full-time business agents. Instead the major activities of the union are handled by elected officers who also are working employees at the plant. When a full-time professional union man helps an industrial local he usually is an international representative, a full-time employee of the international union, not the local.

Bargaining Activities of Industrial Locals. Perhaps with the assistance of an international representative, the officers of the industrial local and a bargaining committee negotiate an agreement with the management of an enterprise. This agreement is then presented to a general membership meeting of the local where it is ratified or rejected by a vote of the membership. Once ratified, this agreement becomes the policy of the employer and the union.

Industrial union collective bargaining agreements are much more comprehensive and complex than craft union agreements, although they fulfill the same four functions as craft bargains, as will be discussed in detail in Chapter 8. Industrial unions achieve union security by a clause in the agreement requiring the employees of the enterprise to pay union dues. The agreement may also contain a lengthy section describing management rights or managerial prerogatives. Industrial unions find it necessary to negotiate an entire structure of wages, perhaps with as many as 50 different wage rates for a wide variety of jobs in contrast to less than half a dozen wage rates found in the typical craft union agreement. While a craft union agreement may make no reference whatsoever to work tempo, an industrial union agreement may contain several pages of principles and rules by which production standards are established and modified. Industrial union agreements invariably contain long sections on seniority and due process designed to provide the industrial worker with the individual security which a craft unionist receives from the internal operating procedures of his local union. The industrial union agreement also contains detailed provisions for on-the-job representation and the arbitration of certain unresolved grievances.

For the purpose of enforcing or administering its collective bargaining agreement the industrial local union makes use of a steward system and a grievance committee. The steward system, sometimes called a shop committee, provides on-the-job representation to the members of the union and sometimes asumes the character of a "union within the union."

On-the-Job Representation in Industrial Locals. Shop stewards in an industrial union are elected by the union members in the departments where they work. The term of office is usually six months or a year, but most unions permit a department to depose its steward by majority vote and elect a new one. (This seldom happens, but the fact that it can is supposed to keep the steward on his toes.) The steward's election may be a very informal affair, done by a show of hands at a department meeting held on the shop floor during noon hour, or it may be by a solemn secret ballot vote at the union headquarters. A steward may be reelected indefinitely.

(1) *The department steward.* The steward is the eyes and ears of the union in the shop, and its voice as well, and its strong right arm. The stewards as a group provide a two-way flow of communication, information, instructions, sentiment, and advice between the union and the members working in the plant, to its remotest reaches. They enforce not only the union agreement, which is company policy, but union discipline. If there is not yet a "union shop" clause in the agreement, requiring all workers to join the union as a condition of employment, the stewards are the union's organizers, all day and every day in the departments, striving to get nonmembers to join the union or to "make 'em wish they had." If there is no checkoff, the stewards collect dues from the union members and turn the money over to the local. For their trouble, they usually receive a small percentage of what they collect: five or ten cents on the dollar.

Each steward has a personal constituency. He knows the people who elected him, and they know him. They see each other every working day. They look to him for leadership. In case of strike, they rally around him as their picket captain. There could hardly be more direct or personal contact, or greater confidence, between leader and followers. Unlike the foreman, who works for management, the steward is one of the gang. His fellow workers see him as "on our side."

(2) *The steward council and the chief steward.* The steward council brings together and coordinates the efforts of these natural, elected leaders of the working force. It provides the local with a "line organization" in the shop that is (or can be) as efficient, and more cohesive, than the company's own management hierarchy. It ties the local organically to the workers in the shop and to shop operations in a dynamic, reciprocal relationship.

Typically—or at any rate, ideally—the union elects a steward wherever members work under the direction of a first-line supervisor. The stewards then elect a chief steward from among their ranks. In a shop where there are several echelons of management, such as, for instance, division superintendents under a works manager and over groups of department (first-line) foremen, the stewards of a division may select a "chief division steward." If there is a night shift, the night shift stewards will have a chief night steward. All of these smaller "chiefs" are subordinate to *the* chief steward. The union's aim is to place a representative opposite every member of line management—to parallel the line organization of the enterprise. The chief steward—and through him, the local union—thus has "line" channels exactly similar and equivalent to management's, which lead into every part of the enterprise where members of the union work under supervision.

The chief steward's election by the department stewards has to be ratified by a majority vote of the members of the local at a union meeting. That is because he is an *ex officio* member of the grievance committee, a highly important committee of the local which deals centrally with the personnel department (or equivalent authority) on matters of administration of the labor agreement. Ratification of the chief steward's election by the membership also asserts the local's discretion and authority over those who are to represent it in official dealings with management, and is a token of the subordination of the stewards to the local union.

All of the stewards, including the chief steward, are and remain full-time working employees of the company. Their election to the job gives them certain special rights and duties, which the union agreement defines. They get their authority, therefore, from the union's agreement with the company, and exercise it within prescribed limits.

(3) *The steward in grievance adjustment.* The man who wears the badge of a department steward is entitled to take time off his company job without loss of pay, under most agreements, in order to investigate, discuss, and adjust grievances. His name goes to the top of the seniority list in his department, regardless of his actual length of service, so that he is the last man in the department to be laid off if work gets slack. This is called "superseniority." Elected officers of the union also get superseniority in most agreements. The aim is to keep the union administrative apparatus in the shop intact, despite fluctuations in the level of operations, just as the company keeps intact its management cadres. Of course, an individual loses his superseniority if he ceases to be a steward or is not reelected to union office.

Grievance adjustment, for which the steward is given paid time off, is the primary function stewards perform in the shop. Most grievances consist of claims that the company has failed to live up to the terms of the agreement in its dealings with an individual or a group of workers. The steward is the union watchdog over contract compliance at the department level. For this purpose—and this purpose only—he is the equal of the company foreman who supervises the group that elected him steward. In all other aspects he is merely one of the foreman's subordinates, like any other worker in the department.

It has been shown, but may be repeated here, that the union's agreement with the company has the effect of setting *company* policy in the areas it touches. Foremen and supervisors do not *make* policy for the company. They exercise delegated management authority in directing operations in accordance with company policy. Because they hold this delegated authority, workers under their supervision are bound to carry out their instructions and accept their decisions, but if—through error, ignorance, or other causes—these run counter to policy as set forth in the agreement, the union steward files a grievance.

Filing a grievance means that the steward formally requests the foreman to reverse some action he has taken, or do something he has failed to do, or alter some action or decision affecting workers under his supervision. The foreman, whose challenged action stands until he, or someone in authority over him, alters it, then has to decide whether the steward's demand is justified, and should be granted; or unjustified, and should be rejected. If the foreman says yes, that settles the grievance. If he says no, the steward has the choice of dropping the demand, and thereby accepting the foreman's determination of the issue, or sending the case up to the grievance committee (see Figure 4–2).

There may be stages or grievance-procedure "steps" at intermediate levels between the department steward and the grievance committee, but these are relatively unimportant. The number of these intermediate (and often superfluous) steps depends on the size of the enterprise and the extent to which management desires to give its various echelons a chance to "get in on the act," and slow down the process. The two really vital steps are the *first*, in the department where the grievance originated, and the one that puts the issue before the executive responsible for *centralized* administration of personnel policy for the enterprise as a whole, usually the personnel director.

If a grievance remains unsettled after it has been appealed to the central personnel department, it goes to the local union, and the stewards drop out of the case. They do not have the power to make policy decisions. The local union, which has the power, must decide whether to accept the company's determination of the issue or carry the case up another step to the policy-making level of management and thereafter—or directly—to arbitration or a strike.

Grievance handling is a duty the steward carries out as much for the benefit of the company as for the employees. Its aim is to ensure compliance with company policy. That is the reason most companies pay the union steward for time spent in grievance activity. The steward has other duties for which the company does not pay; duties the union demands of him as part of his job as steward.

(4) *The steward and the local union.* Under the chairmanship of the chief steward, the department stewards meet together, either on call, or more commonly at regular intervals, to discuss problems that arise in the course of their grievance activity, and other problems bearing upon the union's relation with the company, and the union's internal affairs. There is often a danger that the steward council will encroach upon, or even usurp, the powers of the local union. Attendance at the council meetings is sometimes better than at membership meetings of the local, and the council is by its nature representative of the whole plant. Whether the

:URE 4–2. An Industrial Union Grievance Procedure

This diagram represents a four-step grievance procedure in a manufacturing plant with an industrial union steward system. Grievance procedures may have few or many steps. The only essential requirements are at least one policy-*administration* step and at least one policy-*making* step. Almost without exception the first policy-*administration* step in a grievance procedure is a conference between the supervisor and a steward. The top and final policy-*making* step is either arbitration or a strike.

The department, at the bottom of the diagram, consists of workers managed by a supervisor, who have elected a steward. The supervisor and the steward are responsible for policy *administration*. If a grievance is not settled at the first step, it proceeds upward in the grievance procedure until it is settled. Grievances may enter the process initially at the second step, when they affect more than one department, or as in the case of a peremptory discharge, when the department supervisor has taken action that puts the case out of range of the department steward.

If a grievance remains unsettled until it involves the top management of the company and the local (and, sometimes, international) union officers, it becomes a policy-*making* matter because of its company-wide implications. Every grievance ultimately must be settled. Over 90 percent of all American collective bargaining agreements provide for arbitration as the final means of settlement of grievances. However, many of these agreements specify that certain grievances are not arbitrable and, consequently, the strike remains as an alternative final policy-*making* step in the grievance procedure.

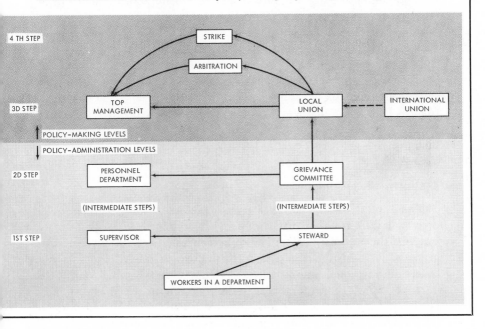

steward council tail will wag the union dog depends on the strength of leadership of the officers of the local, who are entitled to attend steward council meetings. Most of them are graduates of the council, and having reached leadership in the chartered local by way of experience as a steward or chief steward, know how to keep the council in its place.

At council meetings, members report on events and developments in the shop. A steward whose foreman has rejected a grievance may bring his problem to the council for advice. The chief steward reports on the activities of the grievance committee, and may ask the council to endorse a recommendation to the local union on a grievance case unsolved at the last session with the company's personnel department. Officers of the local explain union policies or outline union programs which the stewards are to support in the shop. As the time for renewing the union agreement rolls around, there is discussion of that. The stewards make suggestions for improving the terms or wording over the old one. After the new agreement is signed, the stewards receive an explanation of its provisions and of the union's interpretation of the way it should be understood. They ask questions about it and plan strategy towards issues that it raises.

The union-linked steward system in industrial relations is unique to the American (U.S. and Canadian) labor movements. Other industrial countries have shop committees operating in the enterprises, but the relation of these committees both to the unions and the workers differs from the steward system. Their existence seems to prove only that some kind of shop committee is a necessity of modern manufacturing and the large enterprise.

The foregoing discussion of craft and industrial local unions strongly suggests that unaffiliated and totally independent local unions could influence the wage and effort bargain and negotiate systems of individual security with employers. And, indeed, they can and do. Current membership in such unaffiliated and independent local unions has been estimated to be as high as 500,000 workers.[5] If unaffiliated, independent local unions exist and operate, why do most local unions affiliate with an international union?

The International Union

The typical local union is a part of an international union. A few present-day local unions may originally have joined with other locals in forming the international union of which they are now a part. Most present-day locals, however, were themselves organized and established by the international union with which they are affiliated. Even in those instances where a local took part in the founding of the international, the local, in so doing, gave up its original identity and took on a new identity by receiving a charter from the international, like any other local. This charter recognizes, and in a sense *creates*, the local union.

The international union is a federation of local unions, usually in the same trade (such as carpentry) or industry (such as steel). The international union stands as "parent" to the local union, which it creates by issuing a charter. An individual worker does not hold his membership

---

[5] U.S. Department of Labor, Bureau of Labor Statistics, *Directory of National and International Labor unions in the United States 1967*. Bulletin No. 1596, 1969.

directly in the international union, but in the local union. The local union is a member of the international. It supports the international financially by contributing a fixed proportion of the dues paid, or per capita. The amount of per capita is set by the international constitution.

The international union is much like a local union on a grander scale. Its highest policy-making body is the convention, called together annually, biennially, or periodically at some other interval according to the provisions of the international constitution. Delegates elected from the locals, usually with voting rights proportional to the local membership, take part in the convention and transact its business. They elect officers and an executive board to act for them between conventions in accordance with policies and instructions laid down by majority vote in the convention.

Craft, Industrial, and Mixed International Unions. The fundamental tie between a local and an international *should* be based on services rendered. An international union composed of craft locals renders somewhat different services to its constituent locals than the services rendered by an industrial international to its locals. Today many international unions have both craft and industrial locals, a situation which puts considerable stress on their structure or results in the neglect of the needs of the minority group of locals. In this discussion, international unions composed of significant numbers of both craft and industrial locals will be referred to as

FIGURE 4–3. Selected International Unions: Number of Locals, Claimed Membership, 1967

Organizations	*Locals*	*Membership*
Craft		
In Manufacturing Industry		
Lithographers and Photoengravers (AFL-CIO)	170	53,000
Printing Pressmen (AFL-CIO)	750	114,000
Typographical Union (AFL-CIO)	750	106,646
In Government*		
Fire Fighters (AFL-CIO)	1,014	115,000
Teachers (AFL-CIO)	650	125,000
In Service Industries		
Barbers, Hairdressers, Cosmetologists (AFL-CIO)	850	72,000
Musicians (AFL-CIO)	654	252,487
In Transportation Industries		
Locomotive Engineers (Ind.)	871	39,600
Railroad Trainmen (AFL-CIO)	1,125	185,000
Railway Carmen (AFL-CIO)	831	125,615
In Construction Industry		
Boilermakers, Iron Shipbuilders, Blacksmiths (AFL-CIO)	425	140,000
Bricklayers, Masons, and Plasterers (AFL-CIO)	917	149,000
Carpenters and Joiners (AFL-CIO)	2,643	800,000
Engineers, Operating (AFL-CIO)	335	330,000
Ironworkers, Bridge, Structural and Ornamental (AFL-CIO)	330	162,006
Laborers (AFL-CIO)	900	474,529
Painters, Decorators, and Paperhangers (AFL-CIO)	...	200,569
Plumbing and Pipefitting (AFL-CIO)	750	284,707
Sheet Metal Workers (AFL-CIO)	...	100,000

FIGURE 4–3. *(Continued)*

Organizations	Locals	Membership
Industrial		
In Manufacturing Industry		
Automobile Workers (Ind.)	1,383	1,402,700
Clothing Workers (AFL-CIO)	749	382,000
Electrical, Radio, and Machine Workers (AFL-CIO)	610	320,000
Electrical, Radio, and Machine Workers (Ind.)	164	167,000
Garment Workers, Ladies' (AFL-CIO)	480	455,164
Meat Cutters (AFL-CIO)	390	353,059
Mine Workers, District 50 (Ind.)	1,604	232,000
Oil, Chemical, and Atomic Workers (AFL-CIO)	575	165,329
Pulp, Sulphite, and Paper Mill Workers (AFL-CIO)	723	171,118
Rubber, Cork, Linoleum, and Plastic Workers (AFL-CIO)	499	170,437
Steelworkers (AFL-CIO)	3,483	1,068,000
Textile Workers (AFL-CIO)	678	182,000
In Trade		
Retail Clerks International Association (AFL-CIO)	262	500,314
In Government*		
Government Employees (AFL-CIO)	1,180	199,823
Letter Carriers (AFL-CIO)	6,399	189,628
Postal Clerks (AFL-CIO)	6,776	143,146
In Service Industries		
Building Service Employees (AFL-CIO)	342	348,500
Hotel and Restaurant Employees (AFL-CIO)	505	449,974
In Transportation and Public Utilities		
Communications Workers (AFL-CIO)	808	321,117
Maintenance of Way Employees (AFL-CIO)	1,400	141,000
Railway and Steamship Clerks (AFL-CIO)	1,542	270,000
Teamsters (Ind.)	837	1,651,240
Transit Union (AFL-CIO)	374	103,000
Transport Workers (AFL-CIO)	100	135,000
Mixed		
Electrical Workers, International Brotherhood of (AFL-CIO)	1,716	875,000
Machinists, International Association of (AFL-CIO)	1,950	836,163

Source: U.S. Department of Labor, Bureau of Labor Statistics, *Directory of National and International Labor Unions in the United States,* 1967. Bulletin No. 1596 (1969), pp. 17–39.

* Significant increases in these figures for government employees since date of survey, not available when publishd in 1969. See Chapters 15 and 16.

"mixed" internationals. Internationals composed primarily of craft locals will be referred to as craft internationals, while the term industrial international will be applied to internationals composed primarily of locals organized on the basis of workplace.

There are approximately 180 international unions in the United States, ranging in size from less than 1,000 affiliated workers to giants claiming over 1 million dues-paying members. Figure 4–3 attempts to classify some of the larger international unions according to the primary organizational units of their constituent Locals: craft, industrial, and mixed. The *sole* criterion for the classification of internationals shown in Figure 4–3 is the organizational unit of the majority of their constituent locals. Thus, the United Automobile Workers and the United Steelworkers are classified as *industrial* internationals, despite the fact that both organizations have locals in many industries and a few locals composed of workers who possess an apprenticeable trade. Although the Carpenters' International has a few locals composed of assembly-line workers engaged in the manufacture of furniture, it is classified as a *craft* international because of the predominant role played by its craft affiliates in the building construction industry. The International Brotherhood of Electrical Workers is classified as a "mixed" international because of its extensive apprenticeship orientation in the construction industry paralleled with substantial industrial organization units in the field of public utilities.

Before attempting to differentiate the services provided by craft and industrial internationals, it is well to discuss the general services which either international might provide to its constituent locals. To a substantial degree, the difference in services rendered is a matter of the blend of services required by the constituent locals.

Services Performed by International Unions. The most important service rendered by any international union is organizing the unorganized workers within its jurisdiction. Most local unions formed in the United States since the 1940s have been organized by the initial expenditure of effort and funds of some parent international union. This means that the international has assigned organizers to the community or place of employment of the potential members, sought to enroll workers in the union, and, frequently, conducted the negotiations with the employers and NLRB prior to obtaining the first collective bargaining agreement. As will be discussed in Chapter 6, this can be a long, difficult, and expensive process. The price that a newly formed local pays for this service is affiliation with the international union.

Suppose that a local had been organized by an international in 1942. Why is organizing the unorganized important to that local in 1972? It really is not very important to the local or its members *if* the product market served by the employer of the local's members is fully unionized. On the other hand, any significant number of nonunion competitors poses a vital threat to the conditions of employment that can be established by collective bargaining in unionized enterprises. Even in highly organized industries like automobiles and steel, the international unions spend large sums of money every year for the purpose of maintaining and consolidating a high degree of unionization. If organization is permitted to crumble, locals will be undercut in their negotiations. Probably the best current example of the impotence of locals in a partially organized industry is textile manufacturing, where nonunion southern plants pose a constant threat to the prosperity of unionized textile workers.

Many international unions also provide a variety of expert research, negotiation, and educational services to their constituent locals. Complex issues such as pensions, health and welfare plans, and the legal intricacies of various hiring hall, strike, and picketing situations require professional research of a variety beyond the competence of the membership of a local union. International unions often provide this research and the services of a full-time professional negotiator to their locals as one of the benefits of affiliation.

One of the initial purposes of unionization in the days before the Wagner Act was the provision of insurance benefits for members at a time when insurance benefits were not readily available in the general market. Some international unions continue to provide these services as supplements to the more recently developed employer-financed insurance and pension arrangements or in the form of retirement homes for members or special union-supported medical centers.

The strike benefits provided by many international unions might be considered to be another form of insurance. Because of their huge membership base compared to the membership base of any local union, International unions provide a means of pooling the costs of strikes. A local union with even 5,000 members has at its disposal relatively insignificant funds for the financing of a strike compared to the taxing power of its parent international with perhaps several hundred thousand potential contributors.

International unions also may perform important political and representational services in behalf of their constituent locals and their members. Leonard Woodcock, speaking as the president of a 1-million member UAW, is likely to get more attention from a congressional committee on social security than a letter written by the president of a 500 member local union. Among the many political programs important to local unions and their members are campaigns for minimum wage legislation, social security, workmen's compensation, the income tax, unemployment compensation, and medicare. In many of these fields, the international can provide highly professional representational services at a fraction of the cost of less effective local efforts.

Services provided by the international are financed from the per capita revenues of the international. The more services provided, the higher the per capita tax must be, and the higher the per capita tax, the less autonomous the locals and the less influence rank-and-file members of the locals have on their own fates. Although the members of a local can properly feel reassured by the promise that the international may pay them substantial strike benefits, the price that must be paid for these benefits is international approval of their proposed strike.

Both craft and industrial internationals provide bargaining and representational services to their constituent locals. However, the blend of these services provided, and the degree of autonomy of the two kinds of locals, differs significantly.

Services Performed by Craft Internationals. Craft union locals tend to have greater autonomy and to receive fewer services from their internationals than industrial union locals. This tendency is attributable to the nature of the product market and the history of craft unionism.

As noted above, the business agent, a full-time paid employee of the local union, plays a key role in craft union bargaining. This role is conditioned by the fact that the product market of craft unions is typically local in nature. Craft unionists earn high hourly rates and pay high union dues which are kept by the local for the important purposes of negotiating and enforcing the agreement and organizing the unorganized in the community served by the union.

Craft unions have a longer history than industrial unions in the United States. Typically they organized at the local level first and then affiliated with their international organizations. They have been jealous of their local autonomy and have surrendered very little of it to their internationals.

Craft internationals provide important representational services to their locals by attempting to influence the rules for rule making which have been particularly cumbersome for craft unions since the passage of the Taft-Hartley Act in 1947. Craft internationals also provide a militant voice for their constituent Locals in the defense of jurisdictional claims within the AFL-CIO. Craft internationals also play an important role in the national apprenticeship program.

Services Performed by Industrial Internationals. The typical industrial international provides all the services discussed above for its local unions in substantial degree. Because of a tradition of "top down" organizing of industrial locals they typically possess less autonomy than their craft union counterparts.

International unions are completely autonomous bodies usually affiliated with the federation of international unions, the AFL-CIO. Both craft and industrial international unions are members of the AFL-CIO.

The AFL-CIO

The American Federation of Labor and Congress of Industrial Organizations, or the AFL-CIO, represents the interests of labor and its constituent international unions at the highest national level. The federation itself engages in no collective bargaining. It serves and advises the internationals which make it up. Membership by internationals is voluntary. The federation gets per capita from its member internationals.

The formation of the merged AFL-CIO in 1955 modified the AFL's traditional policy of noninterference in the internal affairs of constituent internationals. Under the AFL-CIO constitution international unions can be tried and expelled from the federation if proven corrupt or communist dominated.

The Department of Organization of the AFL-CIO assists affiliated internationals in the organization of the unorganized. Besides this, various internationals have cooperated in seeking to organize nonunion areas and enterprises.

In addition to membership in the AFL-CIO itself, most affiliated international unions have elected to pay an additional per capita tax required for affiliation with one or more of the nine trade and industrial departments of the AFL-CIO: (1) Building and Construction Trades Department, (2) Industrial Union Department, (3) Maritime Trades Department, (4) Metal Trades Department, (5) Railway Employees' Department, (6) Union Label and Service Trade Department; and (7) Government Employees Council, (8) Scientific, Professional and Cultural Employees Council; and (9) Railway Labor Executives' Association. Internationals pay a department per capita tax according to the number of their members who fall within the particular department's jurisdiction.

Each department is free to manage and finance its own affairs. Between the merger of the CIO with the AFL in 1955 and the year 1969 the Industrial Union Department was probably the best-financed and most active department in the federation. It was, in fact, a federation within the federation, consisting as it did of most of the CIO Internationals that entered into the merger. In 1968 Walter Reuther, then president of the Industrial Union Department as well as of the Automobile Workers Union, resigned from the department, and soon thereafter the Auto Workers withdrew from the AFL-CIO. In 1969 they joined the other large independent union, the Teamsters, to establish the Alliance for Labor Action which has subsequently drawn into its ranks other independents, notably District 50 of the Mine Workers.

The Alliance for Labor Action

The unification of labor which seemed to have been achieved with the merger of the AFL and CIO in 1955 was substantial, but never complete, and signs of possible disintegration and realignment appeared in the late 1960s. Walter Reuther, the man who, as president of the CIO had led it into the federation, took his International out of the federation in 1968 and in 1969 joined with the Teamsters in what they called an Alliance for Labor Action. The Alliance held its first convention in Washington, D.C., in May 1969, electing as co-chairmen Reuther and Frank Fitzsimmons, acting president of the Teamsters. Other sizeable unions which joined the Alliance were District 50 of the Mine Workers with a membership of 232,000; District 65 of the Retail, Wholesale and Department Store International Union with about 50,000 members; and the International Chemical Workers Union with 91,000 members. These, added to the 1.6 million Teamsters and the 1.4 million Auto Workers, gave the new Alliance a respectable membership base at its start. Although Reuther died in a plane crash in 1970, the UAW under his successor, Leonard Woodcock, maintained its support of the Alliance.

The founders of the Alliance claimed that the AFL-CIO, under conservative leadership, had done too little to extend unionization to the unorganized agricultural workers, the "working poor," and white-collar workers. They vowed to extend the benefits of organization to these groups. It is too early to assess the impact and results of the establishment of the Alliance, but it may be surmised as possible that it might become a rallying-point for other industrial union internationals, particularly those which were formerly in the CIO, if they should find themselves uncomfortable or dissatisfied in the still-dominant AFL-CIO federation.

Auxiliary Bargaining Elements of Union Structure

Auxiliary elements of union structure which are directly engaged in the negotiation and administration of collective bargaining agreements include: (1) the district, (2) joint boards, (3) conference boards, and (4) trade councils. Although these units appear in only a few industries, they are of great importance in these specific cases.

The District. The district is an administrative division of the international union, usually defined on geographical lines. It has the same structure, on a smaller scale, as the international. Not all internationals subdivide into districts, but in some unions the district is a very important and powerful body. The Teamsters union is an example. Truck hauls on the highway are for the most part more than local but less than nationwide. Certain areas, such as New England, the West Coast, the Chicago area, and the areas around Detroit, Minneapolis, St. Louis, Nashville, and other cities, have well-defined trucking routes that radiate from rail and water terminals of long-distance freight hauling. Effective union control over trucking can best be exercised from the strategic points these terminals create, and must extend over the entire area they serve. Local unions, whose activities cover only a single city, would be impotent beyond their own city limits when trucks took to the road if they did not have the cooperation of other locals in the area. The district acts as the coordinator, and becomes thereby a center of union authority which is much stronger, of course, than any local; strong enough almost to be independent of the international. District leaders of this union become very powerful figures, as exemplified by Dave Beck, who came to the presidency of the International from the West Coast dstrict, and James R. Hoffa of Detroit, who succeeded him.

Joint Boards. The joint board is an affiliation obligatory only in a certain kind of union, the "amalgamated" union. The best examples are the garment workers' unions. In these amalgamations, former separate craft unions have fused into an industrial union international without completely giving up their craft identity. In a given city where there are enterprises of the industry, the locals elect a joint board to carry on collective bargaining for all locals, since members of each local are employed in all the firms. The need here is for *joint action* on a common problem.

Joint boards are seldom formed, and never on an obligatory basis, by local industrial unions whose members work in separate enterprises with which the separate locals bargain. They have no need for joint action.

Sometimes local unions of the same craft form a joint board, but this is on a voluntary basis. It occurs in cities which, because of their size or for historical reasons (such as the affiliation of a former independent union in a body with the craft international), support not just one craft local in a given trade but several. The joint board in such cases is a substitute or makeshift for the normal situation of having only one local union of a craft in a locality and often is a prelude to the actual merger of the locals that made up the joint board.

Conference Boards. Local industrial unions belonging to the *same* international and bargaining with the *same* employer, as in a multiplant manufacturing company, form conference boards, under the auspices of the international, to centralize their collective bargaining. Two examples of this would be the General Motors Conference Board of the United Auto Workers and the Westinghouse Conference Board of the International Union of Electrical Workers. The locals elect delegates who meet before negotiations, draw up a proposed master agreement to cover all the plants of the enterprise, plan strategy, select spokesmen, and then carry out negotiations. After the master agreement has been ratified and signed, each local negotiates supplements applying the terms of the master agreement to its own separate plant. The conference board is not a permanent body, has no constitution or officers, gets no per capita, but usually establishes a permanent "secretariat" at the international headquarters, which is made the responsibility of a specific international officer or representative.

A variant on the conference board organizational element may be emerging in the electrical products industry. Several international industrial unions have collective bargaining relationships with the General Electric Company. In recent years these unions have found bargaining there to be extremely tough and have suspected that the company has played one union off against the others. In order to strengthen their bargaining position these unions, e.g., the International Union of Electrical Workers, the United Auto Workers, and the Machinists, have entered an informal "alliance" that no one union will settle with the company without the concurrence of the other unions.

Trade Councils. Local unions belonging to *different* internationals in the building construction industry frequently form locality councils. The local Building Trades Council groups together the locals of the construction industry for the purpose of coordinating their activities and controlling jurisdictional claims. Facing it, almost inevitably, is to be found an association of building trades employers with a name such as the General Contractors' Association which groups the construction enterprises of the same locality. These two organizations together initiate and oversee the bargaining for the separate trade agreements signed between the locals and the employer association. Administration of these separate agreements then devolves upon the separate locals, with the Council (and the Association) standing by to help the locals and the enterprises keep the wheels turning smoothly.

Districts, joint boards, conference boards, and trade councils are important auxiliary elements of union structure for collective bargaining activity. There are other auxiliary elements of union structure which emerge primarily in political activity.

Auxiliary Political Elements of Union Structure

The city central and state central are important political spokesmen for organized labor and engage in a wide variety of welfare activities.

The City Central. The city central is a federation of local unions in a given city or county. The AFL City Central traditionally called itself the "Central Trades and Labor Council," and its CIO counterpart, the "Industrial Union Council." Now they are merged as AFL-CIO City Councils.

The city central includes locals of all the internationals which have chartered locals in the area. It does no collective bargaining, but focuses and coordinates the activities of organized labor generally in relation to the community. Elected delegates of the various locals exchange information; engage in programs of mutual aid (such as "Buy Union" campaigns) or they help to organize boycotts of "unfair" firms; give aid to locals on strike; and carry on other cooperative activities. Elected officers of the city central represent labor in civic affairs, bring labor influence to bear on local governmental bodies and officials, and advise local unions on community problems. If a political candidate wants labor's endorsement for his campaign, he tries to get it from the city central. This in itself wins him few votes, but opens the door for him to the affiliated locals, the votes of whose members he is courting.

The city central holds its charter direct from the AFL-CIO and sends a delegate (or delegates) to the AFL-CIO Convention. Through its direct affiliation, it brings news and directives of the federation to the locals in its community.

It is customary for all AFL-CIO local unions to join their appropriate city central. The city central gets its financial means by a per capita tax on the member locals.

The State Central. The state central is a "city central" on a statewide scale. It is composed of delegates from local unions of all internationals, plus delegates from city centrals. Some local unions that maintain affiliation with their city central do not bother to affiliate with the state central, which seems more remote from them.

The main activity of the state central is to bring labor influence to bear on the state legislature and executive. This activity may be very important in connection with such matters as unemployment compensation, workmen's compensation, factory inspection codes, minimum wage legislation, and when the legislature is considering a "right-to-work" law.

THE STRUCTURE OF THE AMERICAN LABOR MOVEMENT

The American labor movement claims about 18 million members in approximately 75,000 local unions. About 85 percent of this total membership is claimed by the affiliates of the AFL-CIO. Probably somewhere between half and three quarters of all union members belong to industrial locals as defined in this chapter, with the remainder organized along craft or occupational lines.

Figure 4–4 is a schematic diagram of the structure of the American labor movement. Organizations shown in the middle and left of this diagram exert most of their efforts in collective bargaining activity, while the organizations shown to the right of the diagram are primarily concerned with representational and political activities.

In Figure 4–4 special attention is called to the membership figures on international and local unions not affiliated with the AFL-CIO.

Since the beginning, American unions and the American labor movement have concentrated their efforts on the problems of obtaining, keeping, and improving collective bargaining agreements which set the conditions of employment for their members. Representational and political activity has been regarded as a secondary and reenforcing means of achieving the basic objective of influencing the wage and effort bargain and establishing systems of justice at the workplace. In sharp contrast to the experience in other countries, the present-day AFL-CIO could hardly be called a "movement" dedicated to sweeping economic and political reconstruction of the whole society. The organizational structure which has evolved seems well suited to the achievement of these "bread-and-butter" objectives.

In what sectors of the economy does the labor movement exert direct influence on the conditions of employment and how powerful is the influence exerted? Unfortunately, this very basic question cannot be answered with much statistical authority because of the paucity of data.

Industrial Distribution of Union Membership

Over 40 percent of all American union members are employed in three major industry groups—metal and machinery, transportation, and construction. Other industry groups with at least 1 million members each are food and tobacco, clothing and leather, transportation equipment, and retail and wholesale trade.

FIGURE 4–4. The Structure of the American Labor Movement

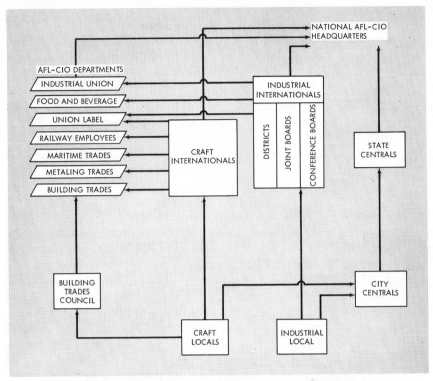

Some Important International Unions Not Affiliated with the American Federation of Labor and Congress of Industrial Organizations

Union	1967 Claimed Membership
Automobile Workers	1,402,700
Bakery and Confectionery Workers	61,000
Electrical, Radio, and Machine Workers	167,000
Life Insurance Agents	1,900
Rural Letter Carriers	40,340
Locomotive Engineers	39,600
Longshoremen's and Warehousemen's Union	60,000
United Mine Workers' Union	N.A.
United Mine Workers Dist. 50	232,000
Railway Conductors and Brakemen	18,780
Teamsters	1,651,240
Telephone Unions: Alliance of Independent	75,000

The U.S. Bureau of Labor Statistics is unable to provide detailed data on the extent of union membership by industry, e.g., that 90 percent of employment in over-the-road trucking is unionized. Instead, it is only able to list industry groupings in rank order of unionization as follows:

1. Transportation
2. Transportation equipment
3. Contract construction
4. Food, beverages, tobacco
5. Telephone and telegraph
6. Mining and quarrying
7. Electric and gas utilities
8. Furniture, lumber, wood products, and paper
9. Stone, clay, and glass
10. Metals, machinery and equipment except transportation equipment
11. Printing and publishing
12. Petroleum, chemicals, and rubber
13. Clothing, textiles, and leather products
14. Federal government
15. Trade
16. Service industries
17. State and local governments
18. Finance and insurance
19. Agriculture and fishing

The Bureau further estimates that about one half of manufacturing employment is unionized, as compared with one fourth of nonmanufacturing and one seventh of government employment.[6] These estimates tend to understate substantially the significance of union influence because: (1) they are estimates of union membership while the coverage of collective bargaining agreements would be larger (unfortunately, it is impossible to say how much larger), (2) the divisor of each estimate includes employees whom unions do not seek to represent, e.g., managerial and salaried employees who frequently represent as much as 50 percent of an enterprise's employment,[7] and (3) some enterprises provide employment conditions parallel to unionized enterprises for the purposes of remaining nonunion.

Geographical Influence of the Labor Movement

The geographical distribution of union membership is important both as a measure of political influence and as an indication of the significance of organized labor in the economies of the several states. Union officials argue that certain areas, e.g., the South, are particularly hard to organize because of local custom.

Union membership is heavily concentrated in a few states having the largest number of workers in nonagricultural establishments. In 1967, six

---

[6] U.S. Department of Labor, Bureau of Labor Statistics, *Directory of National and International Labor Unions in the United States, 1967*, Bulletin No. 1596 (1969), p. 62. (But see Chapters 15 and 16 on government employment, now near one-third unionized.)

[7] Unfortunately, no data are available on the extent of "organizable" employment within industries. A *crude* approximation could be made from the ratio of production employees to total employment. Such data are not available for transportation, telephone, and telegraph, government, services, finance and insurance, and agriculture and fishing. Of the other industries listed here, the percentages range from a low of 63 percent in printing and publishing to a high of 89 percent in clothing, textiles, and leather products.

FIGURE 4–5.   Union Membership as a Proportion of Nonagricultural Employment by States, 1967

Rank	State	Membership as a % of Employees in Nonagricultural Establishments
1	West Virginia	44.1%
2	Michigan	40.5
3	Washington	40.3
4	Pennsylvania	37.7
5	New York	37.3
6	Indiana	36.5
7	Illinois	36.0
8	Missouri	35.6
9	Ohio	35.5
10	Montana	34.0
11	Minnesota	32.8
12	Oregon	32.7
13	Wisconsin	32.1
14	California	32.0
15	New Jersey	31.3
16	Alaska	30.2
17	Nevada*	29.8
18	Kentucky	27.1
19	Rhode Island	26.8
20	Hawaii	26.6
21	Massachusetts	26.2
22	Connecticut	26.1
23	Maryland–District of Columbia	22.8
24	Colorado	22.2
25	Delaware	21.8
26	Iowa*	21.4
27	Wyoming*	20.4
28	Maine	19.9
29	Alabama*	19.2
30	New Hampshire	19.0
31	Tennessee*	18.9
32	Nebraska*	18.8
33	Idaho	18.4
34	Louisiana	18.3
35	Arizona*	17.9
36	Kansas*	17.5
37	Vermont	17.1
38	Arkansas*	17.0
39	Utah*	16.6
40	New Mexico	15.8
41	Virginia*	15.5
42	Oklahoma	15.0
43	North Dakota*	14.2
44	Georgia*	14.2
45	Texas*	13.7
46	Florida*	13.6
47	Mississippi*	12.3
48	South Dakota*	10.4
49	North Carolina*	6.9
50	South Carolina*	6.7

Legend:
States without Right–to–Work laws
States with Right–to–Work laws

Source: U.S. Department of Labor, Bureau of Labor Statistics, *Directory of National International Labor Unions in the United States,* 1967, Bulletin No. 1596 (1969), p. 64.

states, New York, California, Pennsylvania, Illinois, Ohio, and Michigan, accounted for 55 percent of the nation's total union membership.[8]

The top-ranking states in terms of total membership are not necessarily those in which unions have scored their greatest penetration among non-

[8] Ibid., p. 63.

farm employees. As shown in Figure 4–5, New York ranked fifth, California ranked fourteenth, and Pennsylvania ranked fourth in terms of degree of union penetration. The highest proportions of unionized workers were recorded in West Virginia, Michigan, Washington, Pennsylvania, New York, Indiana, Illinois, and Ohio. Figure 4–5 graphically reveals the low percentages of union penetration into the economy of the South and, in general, states having right-to-work laws.

Collective bargaining as traditionally defined takes place between employers and employees organized into unions. In the main, unionists are hourly rated employees engaged in blue-collar occupations. Exclusive concentration on traditional collective bargaining overlooks another very important aspect of the world of work—people engaged in white-collar and professional occupations either as self-employed entrepreneurs or as employees. Professional and white-collar occupations are growing more rapidly than the labor force as a whole. Organizations of persons engaged in professional and white-collar occupations are in a state of ferment and it is reasonable to expect that organizational activity in these areas will expand as these occupations continue to increase their significance in the national economy.

PROFESSIONAL ASSOCIATIONS

The word "professional" is all too loosely used. In one sense it merely connotes a person's occupation: a professional entertainer, fisherman, football player, burglar, soldier. The professional entertainer may be a belly dancer in a carnival or the star of a dozen box-office movie hits; the professional soldier, a private or a general. What makes them professionals in this sense of the word is their attachment to a particular source of livelihood. This attachment is usually lifelong, or for a goodly stretch of time; longer, for instance, than a conscript's term of army service. It is not what these people do that makes them professionals—amateurs and draftees do the same things—but the fact that they do it for a living. In this shade of its meaning, the word "professional" is always an adjective.

It becomes a noun as soon as we think of such typical figures as the lawyer, the doctor, the engineer, the teacher, the accountant. To say that a man is a professional surgeon would be redundant; he could not be a surgeon without being a (noun) professional. An amateur surgeon had better not take the knife to a patient; he would quickly wind up in jail, and the patient, probably, in the cemetery.

This substantive meaning of the word is clear enough, but presents its problems, too. A registered nurse is surely a professional; not on a plane with a medical doctor, but still a professional. How about the licensed practical nurse? And how about mama, nursing her child through an illness with the essential tender, loving care no hired professional could provide? The work done is very much the same, but somewhere between mama and the R.N. runs the line of true professionalism. Where does it put the practical nurse? On mama's side of the line, or the R.N.'s? A union of registered nurses would certainly be a professional association: an association of professionals. If the practical nurses insisted on calling their organization a professional association, who would deny them the courtesy of the term?

Another example: the National Education Association (NEA) with its state branches calls itself a professional association. The bulk of its members are classroom teachers: licensed professionals. So are the members of the American Federation of Teachers (AFT) with its locals, affiliated with the AFL-CIO. The AFT calls itself a union.

The AFT bargains collectively with school administrations; so does the NEA, nowadays, though it didn't use to. For years the NEA held itself aloof from bargaining and categorically renounced the right to strike, concentrating instead on the "purely" professional issues of educational standards. From the very start the AFT asked for higher pay and tenure for teachers, and early-on, picketed and struck for its demands. Today it also professes concern for educational standards. Today the NEA also pickets and goes out on strike. Which is the union, which the professional association? Or are they both both?

Most professionals are white-collar workers, but not all white-collar workers are professionals: insurance agents, for example, or bank tellers, or punch-card operators. Organized white-collar workers undoubtedly see themselves as standing closer to professionals than to manual workers. Traditionally, they shy away from blue-collar union membership, ideology, and method. When they form an organization they are likely to call it a Guild (American Newspaper Guild) or an Equity (Actors Equity) or an Institute (American Institute of Banking) but most commonly, an Association; not a union. The minute they start bargaining collectively, however, they behave like unions.

What's more, they correspond to the models, industrial and craft, described and analyzed in the last chapter. Newspapermen bargain through their Guild (which, incidentally, is an affiliate of the AFL-CIO) not just for reporters, but for the people in the business office and advertising department: for everyone except the print shop and the paper boys. The basis of organization here is the newspaper—the employer. Organization and behavior follow the model of the industrial union. Whether (adjective) professional reporters are (noun) professionals is a nice question. They certainly have expertise in writing the news, which is why people buy newspapers, but they include with them all the other employees who play a part in the operation. A union of registered nurses is indubitably an association of (noun) professionals, but follows the craft model. The basis of organization is the analogue of skill: professional training, certification, and status. People who are not registered nurses do not belong. The association bargains (when it bargains) for nurses as a special group in any hospital or clinic where they may be employed and for no others.

The union or association of teachers is a little different from both of these, but corresponds to the amalgamated union, like the unions in the garment industry. Teachers are trained and credentialled to teach in a particular field or discipline. The separate disciplines appear simultaneously and together in a balanced curriculum and may be thought of as analogous to the coordinated subcrafts in a garment factory. All teachers in a university or city school system work for a common employer. Their professional association behaves in collective bargaining like an industrial union.

Thus the phrase conveys several meanings. A professional association may be an organization devoted entirely to the technology or discipline practiced by its members—for example, the Mississippi Valley Historical Association whose members are mostly university historians. These professionals do not bargain collectively with their employers through the association.

It can be an organization that does bargain collectively with the employers of its members, like the Newspaper Guild, though most—perhaps even all—of the members are nonprofessionals.

It can be an organization of the self-employed, like the American Bar Association whose members are lawyers—professionals—but which does not bargain collectively. It can be an organization of employed professionals, like the NEA or AFT, which bargain; or like the AAUP (American Association of University Professors) which has only begun to bargain directly, having traditionally sought by other means and tactics the ends sought in bargaining: pay levels, tenure, teaching loads, and other aspects of "wages, hours, working conditions, and other conditions of employment."

A reader should be on guard then, at sight of a phrase, to make sure what kind of professional association is in question and in what phase of activities it is involved. The discussion in this chapter from this point on will center on the type of association of employed professionals which engages in collective bargaining with enterprises, public or private, that employ professionals.

Spread of Professional Associations

In 1965 one eighth of all United States workers were engaged in what have been loosely defined as professional, technical, and related occupations. These occupations—employing about 8.9 million people—accounted for more than one quarter of all white-collar employment.[9]

People in administrative and related occupations who run the nation's

---

[9] U.S. Department of Labor, Bureau of Labor Statistics, *Occupational Outlook Handbook: 1966–67 Edition*, Bulletin No. 1450, p. 23. If the definition of a profession were limited to clergy, physicians, lawyers, teachers, engineers, registered nurses, and certified public accountants, this figure would shrink to about 4 million. See Figure 4–6.

businesses and manage a wide variety of other organizations, both private and governmental, numbered more than 7,500,000 in 1965. This classification includes corporate officers, supervisors, industrial foremen, and persons who direct the work of others. All of these people are specifically *excluded* from the discussion of professional people here. This exclusion is based on the indefiniteness of educational requirements for entering this field, the lack of licensing requirements, and a belief that economic progress is dependent upon maintaining freedom of enterprise in the form of open entry to managerial positions.

Characteristics of a Profession

Neither white-collar occupations nor professional occupations are easy to define. There are few, if any, white-collar or professional "industries" because industries must be defined in terms of the product produced or service rendered. Medical care and education would appear to be identifiable professional industries, but the identification is blurred by the fact that large segments of both industries are government operated. Some professionally qualified persons practice their professions as employees of nonprofessional enterprises, many sole proprietorships are found in the practice of medicine, nonprofit private institutions play a major role in both industries, and both industries employ significant numbers of persons in subprofessional occupations.

An attempt to define professions on the basis of the professional qualifications of the persons engaged in particular occupations is almost as frustrating as the attempt to identify professional industries. Almost everybody wants to be called a professional and almost every occupation or career field has staked out a claim to professional status. Thus, any definition of a profession is arbitrary. It seems best to start with a very restrictive definition. From this base additional occupations can be added, but it should be recognized that each addition dilutes the basic definition.

For purposes of this discussion, a profession is an occupation with *all* of the following characteristics: (1) the requirement of a postgraduate college education, (2) governmental licensing of practitioners of the profession, (3) a primary commitment to the service of humanity by the members of the profession, (4) the acceptance of a code of ethics by the members of the profession, and (5) the existence of a professional association dedicated to the enforcement of the code of ethics. Only a handful of occupations approximate the requirements for professional status enumerated here, i.e., physicians, dentists, lawyers, and clergymen. As the requirements for professional status are relaxed, occupations such as engineering, teaching, certified public accountants, pharmacy, registered nursing, and social work would be included in the professions. From this second wave, the professions flow outward through such categories as chartered life underwriter, certified professional secretary; perhaps even to certified shopping center manager.

Professional Occupations and Educational Requirements

Figure 4–6 reveals 1965 employment in the major professional occupations. Employment in the basic professions of religion, medicine, and law totals less than 1 million persons. Elementary, secondary, and college teaching employs over 2 million persons. Engineering and technical employment approaches 2 million. Both accounting (not limited to certified public accountants) and registered nursing are larger occupational callings than any one of the basic professions.

The educational preparation required for entry into the ministry has a wider range than that for most professions. Some religious groups have no formal educational requirements, and others ordain persons who have received varying amounts of training in liberal arts colleges, Bible colleges, or Bible institutes. An increasingly large number of denominations, however, require a three-year course of professional study in theology following college graduation.

FIGURE 4–6. Employment in Selected Professional Occupations and Membership in Related Organizations

Occupation	Employment*	Related Organization(s)†	Membership†
Teachers			
Elementary and secondary...	1,850,000	National Education Association‡	813,000
		American Federation of Teachers§	100,000
College.................	200,000	American Association of University Professors	62,000
Engineers.................	1,000,000	American Institute of Electrical and Electronic Engineers‖	156,500
		American Society of Mechanical Engineers‖	59,500
		American Society of Civil Engineers‖	49,000
		American Institute of Aeronautics and Astronautics‖	36,000
		American Institute of Chemical Engineers‖	22,000
Registered engineers.........	250,000	National Society of Professional Engineers‖	60,000
Registered nurses............	550,000	American Nursing Association	170,000
Clergymen.................	300,000	No relevant organization	
Physicians.................	275,000	American Medical Association	176,000
Lawyers...................	275,000	American Bar Association	115,000
Dentists..................	100,000	American Dental Association	100,000
Certified public accountants....	80,000	American Institute of Certified Public Accountants	48,000

° U.S. Department of Labor, Bureau of Labor Statistics, *Occupational Outlook Handbook,* 1966–67 Edition, Bulletin No. 1450, pp. 23, 72.

† Frederick G. Ruffner, Jr., R. C. Thomas, Ann Underwood, and H. C. Young (eds.), *Encyclopedia of Associations,* Vol. 1 (Detroit: Gale Research Company, 1964).

‡ NEA membership includes elementary and secondary schoolteachers, college and university professors, administrators, principals, counselors, and others interested in education. Bulk of membership composed of elementary and secondary teachers and administrators.

§ U.S. Department of Labor, Bureau of Labor Statistics, *Directory of National and International Labor Unions in the United States, 1965,* Bulletin No. 1493, p. 32.

‖ Membership includes students.

Physicians, attorneys, and dentists face substantial educational requirements. Physicians must complete a four-year course in a medical school after three or four years of premedical college training. In 32 states, physicians must also complete a one-year internship in a hospital before being licensed to practice medicine. Lawyers are admitted to the bar by a written examination which is taken after graduation from an approved four-year law school course which is preceded by three or four years of prelaw college training. Dentists obtain a license by examination after the completion of a four-year approved dental school program. A minimum of two years of predental college work is required for admission to dental school.

Of all the professions, teaching is the largest, and no other profession offers so many employment opportunities for women. Almost 1,500,000 women are teachers, more than twice the number employed in nursing, the second largest field of professional employment for women. Only about one fifth of all college and university teachers are women.[10] The large number of women in elementary and secondary school teaching might have a significant effect on the behavior of teacher organizations. It is frequently said that women are hard to organize into unions because they look on their employment as a short-time experience preparatory to marriage or as a second career after their children are reared. To the extent that women teachers are secondary breadwinners this fact would tend to reduce their militancy. On the other hand, labor force participation rates for women are steadily rising, women now represent a majority of the adult population, and, as a result, steadily increasing numbers of them are undertaking lifetime employment careers.

All states require every teacher in the public elementary and secondary schools to hold a certificate issued by the State Department of Public Instruction. Several states have this same requirement for teachers in parochial and other private elementary and secondary schools. In 1964, 45 states and the District of Columbia issued regular teaching certificates only to persons with at least four years of approved college preparation.[11] Although college teachers are not required to possess teaching certificates, a master's degree is usually required to qualify for beginning positions in college teaching, and a doctor's degree for advancement and tenure.

Engineering and technical occupations provide employment for approximately 2 million persons.[12] Approximately 1 million persons are considered to be "engineers," more than half of them employed in manu-

---

[10] Ibid., p. 210.

[11] Ibid., p. 212.

[12] This figure includes approximately 900,000 engineering and science technicians and excludes 400,000 scientists. Jobs like engineering and science technicians usually require post-high school education but less than a college degree. Technicians frequently do work which otherwise would be assigned to engineers. Work as a scientist almost always requires a minimum of a bachelor's degree. Neither scientists nor engineering and science technicians are registered or certified by state agencies.

facturing industry. A bachelor's degree in engineering is the generally accepted educational requirement for entrance into engineering occupations. Although some persons without a degree are able to become engineers after long experience in a related occupation, more and more engineering specialties are now requiring postgraduate college training. All 50 states and the District of Columbia have laws providing for the licensing (or registration) of those engineers whose work may affect life, health, or property. In 1964, about 250,000 engineers were registered under these laws in the United States. Generally, registration requirements include graduation from an accredited engineering curriculum, plus at least four years of experience and the passing of a state examination. Examining boards may accept a longer period of experience as a substitute for a college degree.[13]

A license is required to practice professional nursing in all states and in the District of Columbia. To obtain a license, a nurse must have graduated from a school approved by a state board of nursing and pass a state board examination. Approved schools of nursing require a minimum of two years' study beyond high school graduation.

All states require that anyone practicing in the state as a certified public accountant hold a certificate issued by the State Board of Accountancy. By 1970 almost half the states had laws that require CPA candidates to be college graduates.[14]

The professional and managerial occupational groups engaged 8 in every 10 workers with a college education in 1964. Both the numbers of college graduates and their concentration in these occupational groups is steadily increasing. Projections prepared by the United States Office of Education in 1964 indicate an increase from 502,104 bachelor's degrees granted in 1964 to 731,000 in 1970 to 815,000 in 1975. According to the same projections, the number of master's degrees conferred per year may exceed 160,000 and the doctorates may approach 25,000 per year in 1975.[15]

Ethics, Licensing, and the Role of the Professional Association

All of the occupations discussed here are based on a primary commitment of their practitioners to the service of humanity. Unethical conduct by a member of one of these professions will result in his disbarment from practice, usually by revocation of his license. In unlicensed professions like the clergy and college teaching, disbarment procedures may be less formalized but they are operational.

Each of the professional associations shown in Figure 4–6 has a committee or commission on ethical standards and a similar group responsible

---

[13] Ibid., p. 72

[14] Ibid., p. 29.

[15] Ibid., pp. 24–25.

for advising schools and licensing agencies on educational standards. Members and officers of the appropriate professional association serve as members of examining and licensing boards for their professions and as judges in disbarment proceedings.

Clearly the primary purpose of licensing requirements and ethical standards is to protect the public from incompetent and unscrupulous practice of professions which vitally affect the physical, mental, and spiritual health of humanity. At the same time, the number of persons licensed to practice a particular profession has a profound effect on the price of professional services and the economic welfare of the seller of those services. Each of the professional associations listed in Figure 4–1 has a committee or commission on the economic status of the profession. Are collective bargaining practices applicable to the maintenance and improvement of the economic status of members of the professions?

The Professions and Collective Bargaining

Professional people would turn to collective bargaining practices only if they felt that their economic status were deteriorating or that, as employees, they needed an individual security system providing job rights and a procedure for due process. Two developments in the economy in the last 20 years suggest that professionals would be well advised to consider what aspects of collective bargaining practices would be useful to them. The first development is the success of unionism in substantially upgrading the status of blue-collar workers. Today union members possess through collective bargaining many of the economic benefits and status symbols which 20 years ago were the sole possession of professionals and white-collar workers, e.g., paid vacations, pensions, severance pay, and hourly wage guarantees which approach the security provided by a salary. Although the conditions of professionals have improved substantially over the last 20 years, the success of unions has narrowed the gap between professionals and union members. In some cases union members have outstripped the incomes of professionals. The second development is the changing structure of markets for the sale of professional services.

The applicability of collective bargaining practices to professionals is dependent upon the market structure for the sale of professional services and the ideology of professionals. Market structures and ideology tend to interact.

The Markets for Professional Services. The markets for professional services are conglomerate. Physicians, lawyers, and certified public accountants typically offer their services on an ad hoc basis to anyone needing them; most physicians, lawyers, and CPA's are entrepreneurs and employers rather than employees. In sharp contrast, most teachers, engineers, and nurses practice their professions as employees of a school, business, or hospital. There are many exceptions to both rules, but the professions do seem to divide between entrepreneurs and employees. Within both classifications the structure of markets is dynamic.

The dynamism of markets for professional services is well illustrated in the practice of medicine. Thirty years ago, practically all medical service was sold on an ad hoc fee for service basis, the fee being paid directly by the recipients of the service. Today most physicians perform a large portion of their work for Blue Shield and private insurance companies, frequently being paid according to a schedule of fees established by the insuring agency. Under the medicare amendments to Social Security, it is reasonable to expect that physicans are receiving an increasing proportion of their income from sources other than the recipients of services. Prices are influenced by the structure of the market. It hardly seems an exaggeration to say that the market for medical care is undergoing dramatic change from almost atomistic competition between buyers a generation ago toward something approaching monopsony in the foreseeable future. The problems of a seller in a monopsonistic market are not too different from the problems of an employee.

To the extent that physicians, lawyers, and CPA's can learn anything from collective bargaining practice, their "text" would be the program of craft unions. Their economic interests could best be served by maintaining very high standards for admission to the profession, the collective withdrawal of service, and tight control over the methods of "production" in their "industry." Through licensing requirements and a code of professional ethics, they possess the means needed to accomplish their economic ends, as well as to fulfill their basic commitments to the service of humanity.

Teachers, engineers, nurses, and other employed professions have a legitimate interest not only in their salaries but also in a system of individual security which provides job rights and due process. The need for a system of individual security seems to intensify as the size of the employing institution increases and the mobility of its employees declines. Thus the need for a system of individual security seems to loom particularly large in nursing and teaching. One would expect organizations like the National Education Association, the American Federation of Teachers, the American Association of University Professors, the engineering societies, and the American Nursing Association to take an "industrial union" view of their "industries."

For the past few years elementary and secondary education have been in a national state of ferment with the American Federation of Teachers, an out-and-out union, and the National Education Association, a professional association whose membership includes principals, administrators, and others interested in education as well as teachers, vying with each other in many communities to prove who can bargain best for teachers. In this ferment, the issues are not limited to salaries but include such items as teaching loads, tenure policies, the assignment of teachers to "subpro-fessional" duties, and the claims to preferential assignment within school districts based on length of service. In a more restrained but nevertheless persistent manner, the American Association of University Professors is pressing for more faculty participation in the government of institutions of higher learning and giving wide publicity to institutional differences in salary levels. The American Nurses' Association's economic security pro-gram authorizes state associations to act as exclusive spokesmen for nurses and encourages them to develop bargaining techniques. In several states, state associations have negotiated formal written agreements with indi-vidual hospitals and hospital associations. With the exceptions of the Amer-ican Association of University Professors and the engineering societies, the basic issues for the employed professionals are almost a carbon copy of the basic industrial union program.

Despite the ferment among professionals, which appears to run deep, there are several strong ideological deterrents to the overnight emergence of a professional (labor) movement. These deterrents are the interpretation of professional ethics by the individual members of the respective pro-fessions, the law, and public opinion. Each of these deterrents merits some discussion.

Ethics as a Deterrent to Unionism.   All of the professions discussed here are based on a service to humanity, but the severity of human needs for these services varies between the professions and within the profes-sions. The most severe need of humanity is for medical care *at the instant* of serious illness or injury. Some medical needs are less essential and can wait for some time before they are treated. It is a disturbing thought, but nevertheless a genuine possibility, that a community could survive for some time if its physicians chose to provide only "essential" medical services. Although society's need for legal and educational services is basic, these needs are deferrable. The ethics of a profession ultimately must come to grips with the question of propriety of a strike or its equivalent—the mass withholding of the services of the profession for the purpose of improving the economic condition of its practitioners.

The strike issue seems to be central to the question of unionization of professionals. During 1965 and 1966 some physicians and a good many teachers concluded that their personal interpretation of the ethics of their profession justified strike activity. Although teachers' "professional days," mass "sick leaves," and strikes engendered a good deal of bitterness in many communities and certainly created some conflicts for teachers who are also parents, it appears that at least some teachers have decided to take direct action.

The Law as a Deterrent to Unionism.   Teachers and nurses employed by government or nonprofit hospitals had until recently no legally pro-tected right to organize under federal law, i.e., their employers had the right to discharge them for union activity. All federal employees and most state employees are specifically denied the right to strike. This means that any legal union activity by these groups had to take the form of lobbying activity or persuasion based on public opinion. While the law has not prevented either unionization or strikes, it remains something of a practical as well as psychological deterrent.

Public Opinion as a Deterrent to Unionism. Present-day methods of communication and the market structure for professional services have a strong impact on public opinion. The government and private foundations have generated a good deal of information on the teacher supply and role played by hospitals in community welfare. The steady stream of public information generated by these sources probably has developed some public sympathy for the plight of teachers and hospital employees. At the same time, fees for medical and hospital services have been undergoing a change from a *personal* fee-for-service experience to an insurance premium (frequently paid by the employer) or governmentally provided services. These concurrent developments probably have a net effect of substantially reducing public resistance to improved compensation and conditions of employment for members of the profession. If present, the reduced resistance tends to relieve professionals from taking the strike route to improved conditions of employment. Public resistance to strikes by professionals who hold the welfare of the community in their hands remains strong.

Some Conclusions

There are deterrents to the emergence of collective bargaining in the union pattern, but the dynamics of the employment relationship seem to push employed professionals into collective bargaining activity. This takes forms analogous either to the craft or industrial union organization and bargaining. The trend, which seems to be international in scope, for more members of the traditionally self-employed professions to become employees, promises to intensify the move towards collective bargaining by professionals. If accelerated, this trend might bring about major changes in the policy of even such old, established professional associations as the American Medical Association and the American Bar Association.

SUMMARY

This chapter has examined the structure of unions and professional associations as instruments for achieving the goals of employees in collective bargaining. Craft union locals and industrial union locals have somewhat different goals in collective bargaining and differ radically in their organizational structures.

At the local level union structure is greatly influenced by the structure of enterprises in particular industries. Industrial union locals need complex organizational structures to match the generally large employers with whom they bargain. Craft union locals on the other hand are organized in such a way as to provide service to workers who have intermittent employment with many relatively small employers.

Above the local level, union structure is conglomerate. In general, industrial international unions provide more service to, and exert more control over, their constituent locals, which operate in national product markets, than craft international unions do over their constituent locals, which operate in local product markets.

The political and representational interests of union members are served by the AFL-CIO, the state federation, and city central organizations. None of these organizations is homogeneous in terms of either the industrial attachment or of the occupational calling of the workers who form their ultimate constituency.

QUESTIONS FOR DISCUSSION

1. The text argues that the enterprise and the local union are the most important elements in American collective bargaining. Some American scholars argue that the international is the most important element of the labor movement while others focus on the local. Discuss the rationale of choosing either the local or international for study.

2. American unions seem to put somewhat less emphasis on representational activities than do their counterparts in other countries. Why? Do automation, chronic unemployment, and recent developments in social security suggest that representational activities by American unions will increase in significance?

3. Assume that an independent local union has been collecting per capita monthly dues of $5 and that this local has been invited to affiliate with an AFL-CIO international. If it affiliates, its dues income will be allocated as follows: (1) for the local union, 60%; (2) for the international, 40%; (3) from its own share, 10 cents, to the state federation and (4) to the city central, 10 cents. Carefully show why affiliation would be a "good buy" or a "bad buy" on the basis of benefits received in exchange for payments made.

4. Both the AFL-CIO and international unions perform lobbying activities at the national level. Sometimes congressmen are confronted with *conflicting* labor representation, e.g., the AFL-CIO generally has supported freer trade and lower tariffs while some of its international unions have argued for higher tariffs in their particular industry. As a congressman, how would you react to this conflicting testimony? Why? What kinds of problems does this situation cause for the AFL-CIO president?

CASES: 4, 5, 6, 8, 30, 31, 32.

SELECTED ANNOTATED BIBLIOGRAPHY

BAMBRICK, JAMES J., JR., and HAAS, GEORGE H. *Handbook on Union Government and Procedures.* New York: National Industrial Conference Board Studies in Personnel Policy No. 150, 1955.

————. *Sourcebook of Union Government Structure and Proceedings.* New York: National Industrial Conference Board, 1956.

A companion volume to the *Handbook,* the *Sourcebook* summarizes the 194 union constitutions and contains verbatim texts of pertinent sections of these constitutions.

BARBASH, JACK. *Labor's Grass Roots: A Study of the Local Union.* New York: Harper & Bros., 1961.

A description of the organization and functions of the local union, its scope and evolution, its formal constitutional foundations, and its relationships to the international union, other unions, and city and state labor federations. Membership characteristics and attitudes, duties and behavior of business agents, stewards, and other leaders; and internal conflict, controversy, and democracy in the local are studied.

————. *The Practice of Unionism.* New York: Harper & Bros., 1956.

Examines the reasons why workers join unions and why unions seek to organize; methods by which unions are governed and administered; the nature of collective bargaining; the role of the professional in union affairs; the problem of Communism and racketeering; and the challenge to union leadership today.

———— (ed.). *Unions and Union Leadership: Their Human Meaning.* New York: Harper & Bros., 1959.

A collection of articles representing the views and comments of a wide range of observers. The material covers both such broad concerns as the status of the labor movement today, where it is headed, its impact on society, and also more specific issues as the bargaining relationship, racketeering, communist penetration, the black worker in unions, and government intervention.

BLOCH, HERMAN D. *The Circle of Discrimination.* New York: New York University Press, 1969.

Thoroughgoing historical study of craft union exclusion of black members, from colonial days to the present.

BLUM, ALBERT A. (ed.). *White Collar Workers.* New York: Random House, 1971.

The book contains intensive case studies of various groups of white-collar workers from sales clerks to professional engineers and nurses and their behavior regarding unionization and collective bargaining.

ESTEY, MARTEN S. "The Strategic Alliance as a Factor in Union Growth," *Industrial and Labor Relations Review,* Vol. IX (October 1955), pp. 41–53.

A study of interunion alliances in the retail trades. Relates growth of retail union membership to the "strategic alliance" between weaker retail unions and unions having control over strategic positions such as truck drivers, warehousemen, and retail butchers.

ESTY, MARTIN. *The Unions, Structure, Development, and Management.* New York: Harcourt, Brace and World, Inc., 1967.

A good outline and overview of the design and operation of American unions. Emphasis is on management of unions as organizations striving to achieve a variety of objectives.

GALENSON, WALTER (ed.). *Trade Union Monograph Series.* New York: John Wiley & Sons, 1962.

Each volume in this series describes the government of a major American trade union. The emphasis is on those aspects of government which may be said to further or retard internal democracy. The volumes in this series are:

HARRINGTON, MICHAEL. *The Retail Clerks.*

HOROWITZ, MORRIS A. *The Structure and Government of the Carpenters' Union.*

KRAMER, LEO. *Labor's Paradox—The American Federation of State, County, and Municipal Employees AFL-CIO.*

PERLMAN, MARK. *Democracy in the International Association of Machinists.*

ROMER, SAM. *The International Brotherhood of Teamsters: Its Government and Structure.*

ROTHBAUM, MELVIN. *The Government of the Oil, Chemical and Atomic Workers Union.*

SEIDMAN, JOEL. *The Brotherhood of Railroad Trainmen: The Internal Political Life of a National Union.*

STIEBER, JACK. *Governing the UAW.*

ULMAN, LLOYD. *The Government of the Steel Workers' Union.*

HARDMAN, J. B. S., and NEUFELD, MAURICE F. (eds.). *The House of Labor.* New York: Prentice-Hall, Inc., 1951.

More than 40 union officials contributed papers on the internal operations of labor unions. Divided into eight parts (American labor movement; unions and political activity; American labor abroad; union publicity and public relations; union research and engineering; welfare, health, and community services; union administration; union education activity; the union staff), this volume is a most comprehensive collection on union organization in the United States.

KENNEDY, VAN DUSEN. *Nonfactory Unionism and Labor Relations.* Berkeley: University of California, West Coast Collective Bargaining Systems Series, 1955.

A study of service-industry unions on the West Coast. Author emphasizes the differences between "factory" and "nonfactory" labor relations. Professor Kennedy's emphasis might be compared with the "industrial union" and "craft union" distinction drawn in this book.

KLEINGARTNER, ARCHIE. *Professionalism and Salaried Worker Organization.* University of Wisconsin, Madison: Industrial Relations Research Institute, 1967.

An excellent review of the occupational characteristics of professionals and how these vocational traits relate to the organization of an effective collective bargaining representative.

MARSHALL, RAY. *The Negro and Organized Labor*. New York: John Wiley and Sons, 1965.

A comprehensive analysis of the discriminatory behavior of many American unions. Marshall says that remedial action is occurring but at a painstakingly slow pace.

MILLIS, HARRY A., and MONTGOMERY, ROYAL E. *Organized Labor*. New York: McGraw-Hill Book Co., Inc., 1945.

Volume III of the authors' brilliant Economics of Labor series, this book covers labor history through the early 1940s, union government, structure, and policies. Reference to this volume should be one of the early steps in any research undertaking on American unionism.

NATIONAL INDUSTRIAL CONFERENCE BOARD. *White Collar Unionization*. Studies in Personnel Policy No. 220, 1970.

A recent survey of 140 white-collar organizing campaigns reveals both union and management strategy and tactics in approaching the ever-increasing numbers of white-collar workers.

ROBERTS, BENJAMIN C. *Unions in America: A British View*. Research Report Series No. 96, Princeton University Industrial Relations Section, 1959.

A discussion by a leading British authority on labor problems of such contemporary labor issues as corruption in unions, the impact of unions on price inflation, internal union democracy, and the political role of unions.

SAYLES, LEONARD, and STRAUSS, GEORGE. *The Local Union*. New York: Harper & Bros., 1953.

Based on extensive field research, this volume presents a penetrating insight of the place of the local union in the industrial plant.

SEIDMAN, JOEL, and CAIN, GLEN G. "Unionized Engineers and Chemists: A Case Study of a Professional Union," *Journal of Business* (University of Chicago), Vol. 37 (July 1964), pp. 238–57.

Presents a case study of unionism among professional engineers and chemists in a large oil refinery to learn their view of unionism and to compare it with the concept held by blue-collar workers.

STRAUSS, GEORGE. *Unions in the Building Trades: A Case Study*. Buffalo, N.Y.: University of Buffalo Series No. 24, 1958.

A field study of building trades unions in a community of 400,000 population. Major emphasis is placed on the functions and attitudes of business agents.

TAFT, PHILIP. *The Structure and Government of Labor Unions*. Cambridge Mass.: Harvard University Press, 1954.

An in-depth study of union elections, dues, discipline, and appeals. Essays on the internal procedures of the unlicensed seafaring unions, the Autoworkers, the Steelworkers, and the Teamsters.

U.S. DEPARTMENT OF LABOR, BUREAU OF LABOR STATISTICS. *Directory of National and International Labor Unions in the United States*. Washington, D.C.: U.S. Government Printing Office.

Issued biennially, this bulletin contains a detailed listing of international unions, officers, location, conventions, publications, and claimed membership of the approximately 200 unions headquartered in the U.S.

WOLMAN, LEO. *Ebb and Flow in Trade Unionism.* New York: National Bureau of Economic Research, 1936.

A study of trends in trade union membership in the United States between 1897 and 1934. Gives considerably more attention to the impact of cyclical factors and government policy on the rise and decline of union membership than does the author's 1924 volume on the same subject.

Chapter 5

THE GOVERNMENT AND THE PUBLIC INTEREST

This chapter deals with the most important third actor in the industrial relations system, the government, and its influence on the other two actors, managers and unions. Although laws have influenced collective bargaining in America ever since colonial times, the first general nationwide labor relations law, the Norris–La Guardia Act, did not come to pass until 1932. The exercise of the judicial and executive powers of government in labor relations has a longer history, but today it appears to follow the guideposts set by the more recent legislation. This chapter examines the current status of legislative, executive, and judicial regulation of the actors and their interaction in collective bargaining.

Government may take many forms, from absolute monarchy to pure democracy. Regardless of its form, a government draws upon the resources of society and organizes the people in it by the exercise of moral authority and the possession of power. In a democracy, the moral authority of government derives from its efforts to represent what is called the public interest. The public interest may be conceived of as a delicate balancing of pluralistic private interests for the common good or as an overpowering, unified popular objective. In either case, a government claiming to promote the public interest cannot be neutral toward the private interests of management and unions or toward the activity in which they engage their separate, and often opposing, interests: collective bargaining.

In a democratic state, defining and interpreting the public interest is the responsibility of those representatives of the public who wield governmental power: legislators, executives, and judges. Every citizen has a right to his own interpretation of the public interest and the right also to advocate that interpretation, but only the appropriate officials of government have the final say, so long as they retain their position of public trust. Thus at any particular time the public interest is what the legislators say it is when they pass a law, and what the executives say it is when they enforce the provisions of a law, and what the judges say it is when they rule on disputes under the law. The public interest, then, is not something eternal and unchanging. This chapter seeks to show that the public interest has, in fact, changed over the years. It will go on to explain how the

146

present-day public interest, as reflected in present-day law and its enforcement, regulates unions and management. It will point out some areas in which controversy over different interpretations of the public interest has not yet settled down into a determination of law.

CONCEPTS OF THE PUBLIC INTEREST

At various times, different groups of people have viewed labor relations legislation as a vehicle for achieving one or more of the following social goals, which were conceived to be in the public interest: (1) preserving property rights; (2) advancing the civil rights of working people; (3) keeping the government out of economic affairs; (4) lessening or eliminating public inconvenience resulting from labor disputes; (5) controlling monopoly power; (6) controlling the business cycle; (7) equalizing bargaining power between conflicting private interests.

Although several of these goals conflict, each has found some expression in present-day labor relations legislation. A brief statement of each of these concepts will explain the thinking behind them and help evaluate their influence on law.

Preserving Property Rights

The right of an individual to hold property is enshrined in the Constitution; it is not the right that is in question here, but rather various interpretations of what constitutes its proper exercise in management. Some see it as an "inalienable" right not only to set prices and to determine what goods or services to produce and the way to produce them, but also to set wages and employee performance standards, to hire and fire at will and without challenge, to set rules and regulations governing the conduct of employees. So sweeping a view of the management prerogatives derived from property rights would naturally call for the elimination of collective bargaining and for laws prohibiting or severely limiting union activity.

Advancing the Civil Rights of Working People

In contrast to the above, an extreme view of the civil rights of working people would require their participation and consent in every act of management. A more moderate statement of this position would give employees the right to bargain collectively only over the conditions of their employment. Once collective bargaining becomes the method of establishing these conditions, a simple extension of the civil rights concept would insist that workers also have a right to full democratic participation in the affairs of their unions. Further, if racial or religious or age or sex discrimination violates civil rights, unions themselves must be clean of any taint and must open their membership rolls and activities without discrimination.

A twist to this civil rights concept is the "right to work"—the right of an individual to hold a job, whether or not he elects to join a union.

Keeping the Government out of Economic Affairs

Classical political economy makes out a very strong case for keeping the government from interfering with labor-management relations in a democratic state with a free enterprise economy. The presumption is that free employers and free unions know what is best for them and have a primary interest, which should not be disturbed, in settling their own affairs.

As a matter of fact, American law on collective bargaining today rather follows this concept and is largely *permissive*, both with regard to the terms and to the methods by which the parties reach agreement. Indeed, if a group of workers and an employer, in total ignorance of the law, were to sit down and bargain out an agreement, it is unlikely that they would agree to anything prohibited by existing laws.

The concept of governmental noninterference must not be confused with neutrality. In terms of the total effect of government policy at any given time, nonintervention in labor-management relations strengthens the hand of either management or the union.

Lessening Public Inconvenience

Most citizens have at one time or another been inconvenienced by a strike. Some strikes go beyond mere inconvenience and may imperil public health or jeopardize the national defense. Public policy, under this concept, looks toward preventing strikes; or if they occur, toward lessening their impact.

It is sometimes forgotten that the Wagner Act (seldom viewed as a strike control measure) virtually eliminated what had been, before its passage, the principal cause of strikes in the United States: the strike for union recognition. The Taft-Hartley law went further and tackled the problem of national emergency strikes. Experience has shown that the attempt was only moderately successful. The legislative quest continues for a solution to the problem of lessening public peril and inconvenience.

Controlling Monopoly Power

This concept has two contradictory aspects. On the one hand there are those who claim that the employer has monopoly—"monopsonistic"— power over job opportunities, so that the individual worker is helpless in bargaining for his labor. Collective bargaining restores the balance. Against this, on the other hand, there are those who see *unions* as the real monopolies and believe they should be broken up under the antitrust laws.

Controlling the Business Cycle

There is little doubt that the idea of increasing purchasing power as a step toward ending the Great Depression won many congressional votes for the passage of the Wagner Act in 1935. It has also been argued that the Taft-Hartley restraints on union power were aimed at controlling inflation in 1947. Both concepts hold that labor relations law is a proper field for countercyclical legislation.

Quite apart from law, government action taking such form as the Presidential "guidelines" of 1965 (withdrawn in 1967), which looked toward wage-price stability, went on the presumption that collective bargaining had a bearing on the health of the economy. The guidelines clearly stated the national objective to be noninflationary full employment and asked employers and unions to conduct their affairs in harmony with this objective. President Nixon's wage-price freeze of 1970 made an even more explicit move toward the same end.

Equalizing Bargaining Power

Probably the most venerated concept of the public interest in labor relations is the idea that government should equalize the "bargaining power" of management and unions. This concept implies that labor's interests conflict with management's; that they are bound to fight; and that the stronger will most likely win, to the detriment of broader interests. If, however, government backs up the weaker and thus makes them equal, they may settle their differences without a fight, and if they fail, at least the fight will be fair. Thus the Wagner Act prohibited unfair labor practices by employers, who at the time were felt to be stronger. The Taft-Hartley Act, some 12 years later, turned the same argument around to prohibit unfair labor practices by unions.

Another application of this argument, never enacted in law, holds that some big unions dealing with many employers should be broken into smaller units, just as business combines sometimes are required to divest themselves of their holdings. An example is the United Automobile Workers, which has members working for Chrysler, Ford, and General Motors. Public policy would oppose a merger of the Big Three; why should not the UAW, it is argued, break down into units that would equalize bargaining power?

These concepts of the public interest have had their partisans, and perhaps all have some validity, though taken together they would be hard to apply to any specific labor-management relationship, or even to any particular piece of legislation. Too frequently an individual's zeal for a particular principle, or his interest in a specific legislative proposal, blinds him to equally valid aspects of the public interest. Somewhere, sometime, the powers that be in government have to make a decision. It is rarely one-sided, but it is never—and it cannot be—completely neutral.

Before discussing the substantive regulation of the parties, it is well to identify the agencies of government currently active in the industrial relations field. In this brief survey of agencies, their major functions and their points of contact with the other actors will be emphasized.

GOVERNMENTAL AGENCIES ACTIVE IN THE INDUSTRIAL RELATIONS FIELD

American government is organized around the legislative, executive, and judicial functions at the federal, state, and local levels. Under the commerce clause of the Constitution, federal authority has emerged as the dominant force in the regulation of collective bargaining.

Legislative Agencies

Since 1932, the U.S. Congress has shown substantial interest in regulating the collective bargaining process. The basic federal law on collective bargaining today is incorporated in three statutes: the Norris–La Guardia Act of 1932; the Taft-Hartley Act of 1947 which amended the Wagner Act of 1935; and the Landrum-Griffin Act of 1959. The Norris–La Guardia Act deals with the use of injunctions in labor disputes. The Taft-Hartley Act provides procedures for establishing union recognition and preventing "unfair labor practices" by management and unions. The Landrum-Griffin Act regulates the internal affairs of unions and managements.

Beyond the direct regulation of the collective bargaining process, Congress has enacted a substantial body of federal legislation in the social security, wage and hour, taxation and tariff fields which is a legitimate concern of managements and unions. This legislation is considered in an Appendix to this book.

Congress is subjected to continuous pressures from management and labor organizations. Most major corporations maintain legislative liaison departments or offices in Washington and these voices are supplemented by such organizations as the U.S. Chamber of Commerce and the National Association of Manufacturers plus a multitude of associations concerned with the affairs of individual industries. The fact that 55 international unions maintain their headquarters in the city of Washington is some evidence of union interest in legislative affairs. Beyond the individual internationals, the AFL-CIO and its departments engage in lobbying activity at the federal level.

Under the police power, state legislatures have played a major role in the field of protective labor legislation—child labor, minimum wage, factory inspection, fair employment practices, protective hours limitations, wage payment and collection, time off for voting, and the regulation of private employment agencies. Although much of protective labor legislation is peripheral to the collective bargaining process, unions and managements have a vital interest in state unemployment compensation and workmen's compensation statutes and, where operative, state labor relations statutes regulating collective bargaining relations which are excluded from the coverage of federal law. Although the federal law is supreme in most collective bargaining areas, the Taft-Hartley law, in ceding jurisdiction to the states for laws restricting union security (so-called right-to-work laws), set the stage for some bitter legislative battles at the state level.

Lobbying at the state level finds local unions and the state federation representing organized labor, while enterprises speak for themselves or use the services of state-wide industry associations.

County commissions and city councils almost never regulate the collective bargaining process or the affairs of managements and unions, but they spend a good deal of money on building construction and they employ many civil servants. Enterprises and unions affected by their activities are engaged in attempting to influence their deliberations.

Executive Agencies

As chief executive, the President of the United States is concerned with all aspects of American life. His public pronouncements on labor relations have a great weight of authority. Perhaps even more important is the influence which his office carries in behind-the-scenes conversations with the captains of industry and with labor leaders. Most Presidents of the 20th century have used the power of their office in at least some labor-management crises.

Presidents Wilson, Roosevelt, Truman, Eisenhower, Kennedy, Johnson, and Nixon have all personally intervened in major labor disputes. Although their interventions have taken different forms and their personal philosophies of the desirability of intervention have differed, their actions have demonstrated the significant role which the President himself plays in labor-management relations. It seems that the times in which we live require at least some Presidential participation in labor-management relations. The form that this intervention will take depends upon the personality of the incumbent of that office.

Presidents Wilson, Truman, Kennedy, and Johnson have used the authority of their office in attempts to reconcile the interests of labor organizations and management for the national welfare. President Wilson's first Industrial Conference in 1919 and President Truman's National Labor Management Conference in 1945 failed. The president's Advisory Council on Labor-Management Policy, established by President Kennedy and reactivated by President Johnson was not much more successful.

Three independent agencies of the executive branch of the federal government concern themselves directly with labor relations. They are: (1) the National Labor Relations Board, (2) the Federal Mediation and Conciliation Service, and (3) the Department of Labor.

The National Labor Relations Board. First established by the passage of the Wagner Act in 1935, the National Labor Relations Board, its regional offices, and its General Counsel's office are responsible for administering the basic federal law of management-union relations. Many enterprises and unions find it desirable to use the facilities of the NLRB for resolving representation questions even before they negotiate their first collective bargaining agreement. The NLRB also possesses broad authority for investigating charges of noncompliance with the law, and enforcement. Every effort possible to secure voluntary compliance precedes formal action, but in case of controversy NLRB investigators gather evidence and Board lawyers prepare cases for a hearing before a trial examiner appointed by the Board or the Board itself.

The Federal Mediation and Conciliation Service. Formally established as an independent agency by the Taft-Hartley Act of 1947, the Federal Mediation and Conciliation Service is the successor organization to the Labor Department's Conciliation Service which was established in 1913. The Federal Mediation and Conciliation Service works entirely through the voluntary cooperation of enterprises and unions. It has no power to prosecute anyone or to issue orders; it is even chary of comment and criticism. The function of the Federal Mediation and Conciliation Service is to assist managements and unions in reaching collective bargaining agreements, by the procedures of conciliation and mediation. For many years efforts at conciliation and mediation started only when labor or management were on the point of having a strike or even after a strike was on. Lately mediators have been called in to help much earlier in the game, even in the process of adjusting grievances. The role of mediators is discussed in Chapter 9.

United States Department of Labor. Although the main activity of the U.S. Department of Labor lies in the protective legislation field and in research activities, it is the President's official liaison with organized labor and with employers in their collective bargaining capacity. The Landrum-Griffin Act of 1959 greatly expanded the functions of the Secretary of Labor in the new field of protecting inner-union democracy.

State Executive Agencies. In the 15 states with labor relations statutes, these laws are administered by either the state labor department or a state labor relations board similar to the NLRB. Most states have an executive agency charged with responsibility for assisting in the mediation of labor disputes. Every state has an executive agency responsible for the administration of its unemployment compensation and workmen's compensation laws and, where applicable, the administration of factory inspection, minimum wage, child labor, and other protective legislation. Particularly serious intrastate strikes, either because of their impact on the state economy or the exceptionally rare violent strikes, often involve the governor of the state.

Local Police. Every strike poses a threat of traffic disruption and possible violence. Although strike violence has largely disappeared from the American scene, the local police force plays a vital role in maintaining order in those exceptional cases where violence does erupt. The role of the police will be discussed in Chapter 9.

The Courts and Collective Bargaining

Judges have at varying times been the villains, and alternately the heroes of the drama of collective bargaining in the eyes of both labor and management. The last word in interpretation of the law comes from the courts.

Before the passage of the Norris–La Guardia Act in 1932, the courts, through the interpretation of the common law, often "legislated" in the collective bargaining field. The subsequent passage of a substantial body of statutory law on collective bargaining has reduced the participation of the courts in labor relations. Today the courts have the very important function of ruling on the constitutionality of labor relations legislation and providing the final say on the interpretation of whatever legislation is enacted by the legislative branch of government and enforced by numerous executive agencies.

Managers and union leaders come in contact with a wide variety of governmental representatives who are responsible for the law of collective bargaining. What is the substance of that law?

FEDERAL LABOR RELATIONS LAW

All American labor relations law that has been written into the federal statutes dates from the 20th century. That part of it which remains currently valid is embodied in five laws: (1) The Railway Labor Act of 1926, as amended; (2) the Norris–La Guardia Act of 1932; (3) the Wagner-Connery Act of 1935; (4) the Taft-Hartley Act of 1947; and (5) the Landrum-Griffin Act of 1959. Some authorities argue that the antitrust laws are labor relations legislation, but their applicability to labor relations has been severely restricted by Supreme Court rulings. Excluding the Railway Labor Act and the antitrust laws, the Appendix contains the full text of current federal labor relations statutes applicable to industry in general.

FIGURE 5–1. The Emerging Substance of American Labor Relations Law

Norris–La Guardia Act (1932)	*Wagner–Connery Act* (1935)	*Taft–Hartley Act* (1947)	*Landrum–Griffin Act* (1959)
1. "Yellow dog" contract made unenforceable at law	Outlaws "yellow-dog" contract (Sec. 8[B][3])	No change	No change
2. Severely restricts use of injunctions in labor disputes	No change	NLRB empowered to obtain injunctions: (a) in national emergency disputes (Sec. 208–210) and (b) to prevent unfair labor practices (Sec. 10[E]–[M]).	No change
	3. Established NLRB (Sec. 3–6)	Separated General Counsel functions from Board functions (Sec. 3–6)	Representation questions delegated to Region Directors (Sec. 3
	4. Empowers NLRB to resolve questions of representation (Sec. 9)*	Special treatment for foremen, guards, and professional employees (Sec. 9[B])* Only one election per year (Sec. 9[C][3])* Decertification elections (Sec. 9[C][1])*	No change
	5. Prohibits management actions aimed at frustrating employee free choice of representatives and organizational efforts (Sec. 8[A]-[1]–[4])	Employer "free speech" amendment (Sec. 8[C])*	No change
	6. Require management to bargain with union (Sec. 8[A][5])	No change	No change
		7. Requires union to bargain (Sec. 8-[B][3])	No change
		8. Prohibits union actions aimed at frustrating employee free choice of representatives (Sec. 8[B][1])	No change
		9. Outlaws closed shop (Sec. 8[B]-[4]‡)	No change
		10. Authorizes State "Right to Work"	No change

FIGURE 5–1 (Continued)

Norris-La Gaurdia Act (1932)	Wagner-Connery Act (1935)	Taft-Hartley Act (1947)	Landrum-Griffin Act (1959)
		Laws 14[B])‡	
		11. Outlaws secondary boycott (Sec. 8[B][4])*	Outlaws "hot cargo" Agreements except in garment and construction industries.
		12. Require 60-day notice of contract termination (Sec. 8[D])	No change
		13. Created Federal Mediation and Conciliation Service (Sec. 202–205)†	No change
		14. National Emergency Disputes procedures (Sec. 206–210)†	No change
		15. Makes union subject to suits in federal courts (Sec. 301)	No change
			16. "Bill of Rights" for union members (Title I)
			17. Responsibilities of union officers (Titles II, III, IV)
			18. Safeguards on union funds (Title V)

° Discussed in greater detail in Chapter 6.
† Discussed in greater detail in Chapter 7.
‡ Discussed in greater detail in Chapter 10.

The discussion of labor relations law in this chapter focuses on several substantive areas of regulation. Figure 5–1 traces the emergence of American legislation on labor relations.

Positive Nonintervention: The Norris–La Guardia Act

The Norris–La Guardia Act was a very modest piece of legislation. It created no new governmental agencies and had the net effect of reducing the work of the courts in labor relations matters. Although addressed only to restricting the use of injunctions in labor disputes and making the "yellow dog" contract unenforceable in the courts, the Norris–La

Guardia Act did state a new policy for the United States on the employment relationship and freedom of contract.

Noting the protection given to property owners in the corporate form of enterprise and other ownership associations, the Norris–La Guardia Act stated:

. . . the individual unorganized worker is commonly helpless to exercise actual liberty of contract and to protect his freedom of labor . . . though he should be free to decline to associate with his fellows, it is necessary that he have full freedom of association, self-organization, and designation of representatives of his own choosing, to negotiate the terms and conditions of his employment and that he shall be free from interference, restraint, or coercion of Employers of labor. . . .

The words "full freedom of association," "representatives of his own choosing," and "free from interference, restraint, and coercion" were to become the cornerstones of American public policy on labor relations.

The Norris–La Guardia Act made the question of representation a private matter between workers, employers, and the unions, not subject to intervention by the courts. It provided no penalties for employer actions seeking to prevent unionization, but it stripped such actions of all legal protection.

The act attacked two abuses that seemed to give management an unfair advantage in fighting unions: the "yellow dog" contract and the unrestricted use of injunctions in labor disputes. Neither of these management abuses had any basis in statutory law, but got their sanction from common law and judicial precedent; they were admittedly not crimes against the unions, only inequities. The act provided positive statute law which deprived these abuses of legal sanction.

The Yellow Dog Contract.   Employers opposed to the unionization of their workers hit upon an ingenious idea, somewhere around the turn of the century, of making workers "take the pledge" against the union. As a condition of employment, each employee had to sign a card in which he affirmed that he was not a union member and would not join a union as long as he went on working for the company. He acknowledged that if he did join or became active on behalf of a union, he would have broken his contract with the company and given cause for terminating his employment. The worker forced to sign the pledged to hold his job, union men said, felt like a dog with his tail between his legs—a yellow dog, at that!

It seemed to many Americans outside the labor movement as well as in it that employers who required the yellow dog contract were forcing men to waive a portion of their inalienable civil rights in order to make a living. This, they argued, deprived a man of freedom. The issue reached the courts and was tested in United States Supreme Court case of *Hitchman Coal and Coke* v. *Mitchell* (1917). The Supreme Court upheld the legality of the yellow dog contract. Since this decision rested on interpretation of the common law, the remedy was a specific statute—the Norris–La Guardia Act of 1932.

Section 3 of the Norris–La Guardia Act declared yellow dog contracts to be contrary to the public policy of the United States. The law simply stated that such contracts "shall not be enforceable in any court of the United States and shall not afford any basis for the granting of legal or equitable relief by any such court."

The Norris–La Guardia Act did *not* outlaw yellow dog contracts, it merely made them unenforceable at law. Under the Norris–La Guardia Act employers were still free to require yellow dog contracts and to fire any worker who joined a union. An official outlawing of the yellow dog contract had to wait until the Wagner Act of 1935 made it an unfair labor practice for an employer to discharge or discriminate against a worker because of his union activity.

Norris–La Guardia Restrictions on the Use of Injunctions. Injunctions are preventive court orders issued at the discretion of a judge *before* a case has been heard.

A judge issues an injunction to forestall some threatened or contemplated act that is not inherently illegal but that might cause "irreparable" harm. This allows time to examine the case in court by the due processes of law to determine whether the damage that is feared will indeed result if the act is carried out.

The judge may then either withdraw the injunction or make it permanent.

For example: A man might learn that his neighbor intends to cut down a shade tree on or near the unmarked dividing line between their properties. In discussion with the neighbor it might develop that each contends that the tree is growing on his side of the line. One wants to cut it down because the roots are ruining his garden plot; the other wants to keep it for its shade and beauty. Supposing that they fail to settle the argument in reasonable fashion, and that the tree lover has reason to believe his neighbor intends, perhaps out of spite, to cut the tree down anyway; he could ask for an injunction to prevent it. This would restrain the neighbor (under pain of contempt of court) from using the ax until a resurvey of the boundary established ownership. If in truth it belonged to the neighbor, he would then be free to cut it down; but if he had done so before the survey, and the survey went against him, he would have done irreparable damage which would be hard to measure in money and which he could not replace; for it might take a century to grow a new tree.

Following similar reasoning, an employer threatened with strike action (before the Norris–La Guardia Act) would ask a judge for an injunction against the union, on the ground that the strike would do irreparable damage to his business. Or, with a strike actually in progress, the employer would allege that damage and disorder were imminent if picketing and other strike activity continued, and ask the judge to enjoin the complained-of activities. If the judge agreed—and judges seemed prone to agree on what often seemed very slight grounds—the strike was delayed, frustrated, or brought to a close as soon as police or sheriff's deputies moved to enforce the injunction.

Thus while strikes were not in themselves unlawful and could not legally be forbidden outright, the terms of an injunction could so hamstring the union's activities as to have the effect of outlawing the strike. It must be remembered that before the passage of the Wagner Act in 1935 a union could not ordinarily win recognition without a strike. In recognition strikes, timing is often a crucial element of failure or success. Even if after a hearing the injunction was withdrawn, the damage to the union's cause might have been done—irreparably—with union members demoralized and intimidated, the union weakened or destroyed.

As with the yellow dog contract, many citizens who were not themselves union members found the abuse of the injunction in labor disputes unfair. It seemed to pervert the law's wise provision for protecting a citizen against threatened harm to his property or person by turning it into a tricky and oppressive device for depriving other citizens, the union members, of rights that were lawfully theirs under the Constitution.

The act did not outlaw the use of the injunction, even in labor disputes when necessary, but made the conditions for getting an injunction so stiff that the effect was almost the same.

Impact of the Norris–La Guardia Act.   Professor Charles O. Gregory sees the Norris–La Guardia as the culmination of the philosophy of laissez-faire in union-management relations.[1] Its meaning in the 70s is very different from what it was in the 30s.

The net impact of the Norris–La Guardia Act on the society and on unions and managements depends upon the legal and economic environment of the time in which it is evaluated. At the time of its passage in 1932, the impact of the Norris–La Guardia Act was little more than sweet talk to the unions. Even without a yellow dog contract, the employer's powers of persuasion (the perfectly lawful threat and exercise of discharge for union activity or membership) were indeed effective. In those very rare cases where unions were strong enough to force employers to recognize them, they were free to exert their full power. The Norris–La Guardia Act gave little direct help to unorganized workers and weak unions. In 1932 union membership was at an all-time low. If the Norris–La Guardia Act were to become the sole industrial relations statute in effect in the 70s the net effect of the law would be quite different. Many of the unions in America today could defend themselves quite adequately in a fair fight with management. Under the Norris–La Guardia Act alone, the unions would have full use of the strike, boycott, and picketing. These

---

[1] Charles O. Gregory, *Labor and the Law* (rev. ed.; New York: W. W. Norton & Co., Inc., 1958), p. 185.

weapons are very potent indeed when they are supported by a union membership in being, and when potential allies are available in the union movement. These weapons were substantially less effective when, as in 1932, the union membership existed only in the hopes of labor leaders.

Positive Protection of the Right to Organize: The Wagner Act of 1935

The Great Depression was three years old, and at its deepest, when Franklin Roosevelt took office in 1933. Almost his first official act was to close all the banks. For reasons fully understandable only to people who lived through those days, this ultimate gesture of economic collapse gave the nation its first breath of confidence. It seemed to wipe the slate clean for a fresh start, or, to use the imagery of those days, it called off all bets and broke out a new deck of cards. In quick succession other measures followed. Preeminent among these was the National Industrial Recovery Act, or NIRA, the predecessor of the Wagner Act of 1935.

The NIRA aimed to build public confidence by halting the decline of prices and encouraging production and jobs. It called upon industry to adopt codes of "fair competition," which were to be drawn up and administered by the participants, promulgated and policed by the government. To this end it authorized the formation of industry associations and suspended the antitrust laws. Minimum prices were part of the plan of fair competition and also minimum wages. As a means toward keeping wage levels up, and hence maintaining purchasing power, the act guaranteed to unions the right of collective bargaining. This was the famous Section 7a.

Worker response to Section 7a was overwhelming. Unions formed spontaneously in plant after plant, the internationals which mounted a vigorous organizing campaign (like the mine workers and the clothing workers) got an enthusiastic response. The newly formed CIO began its campaign to organize the unorganized in mass-production industry and met with unheard-of success.

In 1935, the Supreme Court declared the NIRA unconstitutional. Immediately, Senator Robert Ferdinand Wagner of New York introduced a bill in Congress that reaffirmed, with amplifications, the substance of 7a.

The Wagner Act passed easily in Congress, but for two years its constitutionality remained in doubt, under challenge of litigation headed for the Supreme Court. This proved no check on the union drive. In 1936, the auto industry sit-down strikes broke out in the Detroit area.

As with the bank closings, one must have lived through this experience to understand fully the impression the sit-downs made on the public mind. American labor relations seemed to be rushing to the brink of violence—and who could be sure?—maybe revolution. In the relative calm of a "cease-fire" between the auto industry and the union, negotiated by the governor of Michigan, the same Supreme Court that had thrown out the NIRA upheld the constitutionality of the Wagner Act. Militant unionism abandoned the sit-down and, for its most pressing aim of recognition, turned to the ballot box in Labor Board elections. Since the Supreme Court's validation of the Wagner Act, industrial unions have fought their strikes out at the plant gate instead of on the factory floor.

The Wagner Act solved three hard problems that had been plaguing American labor relations for many years: union recognition, company unionism and discrimination against unionists, and company refusals to bargain. Because of the large sector of economic life covered by the Wagner Act and the need for flexibility in administration, the Wagner Act created the National Labor Relations Board to implement its provisions.

The National Labor Relations Board. The National Labor Relations Board is an independent administrative agency. It is empowered to investigate, to hold hearings, and to issue decisions and orders. The orders and decisions of the Board are subject to court review for their final enforcement, but the courts have shown considerable reluctance in setting aside the orders of the NLRB. The NLRB can impose no penalties for the violation of the laws that it administers. The Board is empowered to prevent unfair labor practices by cease-and-desist orders and to require affirmative action to effectuate the law.

Although the Taft-Hartley law of 1947 and the Landrum-Griffin law of 1959 modified the organization of the Board and its jurisdiction, the present day NLRB is a direct lineal descendent of the organization created by the Wagner Act.

Jurisdiction of the NLRB. Federal regulation of collective bargaining is based on the commerce clause in the Constitution. As the Supreme Court has interpreted the commerce clause, the federal government has very wide jurisdiction in regulating collective bargaining activities in enterprises of all sorts. This broad constitutional authority is limited by the statutory provisions governing the NLRB and minimum standards which the NLRB has established governing the volume of business that an enterprise must do before the NLRB will exercise its power over an enterprise.

Under Taft-Hartley and the Landrum-Griffin law, the following employers and employees are specifically *excluded* from the jurisdiction of the NLRB:

1. Employers:
   a) The U.S. government and the states or any political subdivision of either.
   b) Federal Reserve bank.
   c) Wholly owned government corporations.
   d) Nonprofit hospitals.
   e) Any employer who is subject to the terms of the Railway Labor Act.

2. Employees:
   a) Agricultural laborers.
   b) Domestic servants.
   c) Any person employed by his parent or spouse.
   d) Any individual employed by an employer who is subject to the Railway Labor Act.
   e) Independent contractors.
   f) Supervisors.
   g) Government employees, federal or state, including government corporations and Federal Reserve banks.
   h) Employees of completely nonprofit hospitals.

Although the Board has legal jurisdiction over enterprises that affect commerce, it has, with the approval of Congress and the courts, limited the exercise of its jurisdiction to enterprises whose effect on commerce, in the opinion of the Board, is substantial. The Board's standards for determining those enterprises over which it will exercise jurisdiction are based on the total annual volume of business done by the corporation, or the total annual volume of sales or of purchases, and these standards are different for different kinds of business. In addition, the Board exercises jurisdiction over all enterprises that affect commerce when their operations have a substantial impact on national defense. The Board, in its discretion, may decline to exercise jurisdiction over any class or category of employees where a labor dispute involving such employees is not sufficiently substantial to warrant the exercise of jurisdiction. The Board has refused to exercise jurisdiction over hospitals operated for profit, or over racetracks, and real estate brokers.

Section 701 of the Landrum-Griffin Act gives to state labor relations agencies and courts full jurisdiction over any dispute which the NLRB declines to hear, and directs the NLRB to hear every case that was covered by its jurisdictional standards in effect on August 1, 1959. The NLRB is empowered to broaden its jurisdiction up to the full coverage of the law, but is forbidden from reducing its jurisdiction from the coverage in effect on August 1, 1959.

Organization of the NLRB. The Taft-Hartley Act divided the functions of the NLRB into a trial section and an investigative section headed respectively by a Board of five members and by a General Counsel—all appointed by the President. The Board makes decisions on cases which the General Counsel, who is not responsible to the Board, investigates and prepares for hearing. This separates the executive and judicial functions in the enforcement of national labor relations policy.

The work of the National Labor Relations Board consists of two parts: (1) representation cases and (2) unfair labor practices cases. Representation cases deal with the question of union recognition. The Wagner Act prohibited five unfair labor practices by management. Retaining the

Wagner Act's unfair labor practices by management, the Taft-Hartley Act added six unfair labor practices by unions and the Landrum-Griffin Act added a seventh.

Union Recognition and Representation Issues. The Wagner Act stated that "Representatives designated or selected . . . by the *majority* of the employees in a *unit appropriate* . . . (for collective bargaining), shall be the *exclusive representatives* for the purpose of collective bargaining." (Emphasis added.) Thus in representation cases, the Board has three problems to solve:

1. What is an appropriate unit?
2. What is the will of the majority of the employees in this unit?
3. How can a change in the will of the majority be accommodated?

These questions and the evolution of Board policies are discussed in some detail in Chapter 6.

The important things to note now about union recognition and representation issues are: (1) *employees* are the sole judges of whether or not they should be represented by a union; (2) a *majority* of the employees can commit what may be a very unhappy minority to representation by a particular union; and (3) it is the job of the NLRB to determine what the majority wants.

The Board may certify a union as the exclusive bargaining agent either by an election or by other means of determining the majority's will. In the early days of the Wagner Act, the Board often placed reliance on union dues books or authorization cards as a means of determining the majority's will. Elections, however, have since the very early days of the act been the principal method of determining the will of the majority. This democratic procedure greatly eased the unions' job of organizing the unorganized. Before the Wagner Act, union members usually had to strike to obtain union recognition. Under the Wagner Act and its successor legislation, all the union has to do is to convince a majority of the employees to vote for it in a secret ballot election conducted by the government. Once the union has won the election and been certified by the Board, the employer has no choice but to deal with the union.

"Ballot box organizing," initiated by the NLRB under the Wagner Act and continued to this day, is unique in the United States. This procedure, which Congress has seen fit to continue and strengthen through 35 years of industrial relations legislation, indicates a strong endorsement of the assumption that collective bargaining is in the public interest.

Unfair Labor Practices by Management. The unfair labor practice section of the Wagner Act specifically protected only employees from interference, restraint, and coercion. The unfair labor practices prohibited by the Wagner Act were all *employer* actions. The Wagner Act sought to balance the position of employees and employers by restricting the activities of employers.

Section 8 of the Wagner Act prohibited five unfair labor practices by management. The prohibited practices were:

1. To interfere with or restrain or coerce employees in the exercise of their right to self-organization.
2. To dominate or interfere in the affairs of the union.
3. To discriminate in regard to hire or tenure or any condition of employment for the purpose of encouraging or discouraging union membership.
4. To discriminate against or discharge an employee because he had filed charges or given testimony under the act.
5. To refuse to bargain with chosen representatives of his employees.

The unfair labor practices section of the Wagner Act was one-sided in that it attacked excesses by management only. At the same time, it is very important to note what the Wagner Act did *not* do. First and foremost, it did *not* make the unfair labor practices a crime; that is, it did not impose any penalties or fines for violation of the act. The "teeth" in the Wagner Act became apparent only when the courts began to uphold NLRB orders instructing employers to reinstate *with back pay* employees who had been discharged in violation of the act. Second, the Wagner Act did *not* require an employer to concede to the demands of a union for higher pay or for anything of substance; but only required acceptance of the act of bargaining. Probably the most difficult problem confronting the NLRB even today is giving practical meaning to the obligation to bargain. This important problem is discussed in Part V, Case 1.

Redressing the Balance: The Taft-Hartley Act of 1947

Preserved in the Taft-Hartley law, as stated, are all the fundamental principles of the Wagner Act. To these the new law added some things that dismayed union leaders, pleased many management people, and kept the issue simmering just below the boiling point in politics from the day of passage almost to the present.

During the 12 years following the Wagner Act, unions enormously increased their strength. In advocating his bill to amend the Wagner Act, Senator Taft leaned implicitly on the concept of balancing bargaining power. The employer, he said, had now become the underdog. Union leaders promptly replied that his supposed equalizing measures put the employer on top again. There was probably exaggeration in both views.

The year of reconversion to civilian production following World War II brought on more strikes, and bigger ones, than any previous year in American history. In contrast to the strike wave following World War I when management shook off the slight hold unions had gained in the factories during the war, this time the unions, for the most part, won their strikes. They won them because they were organized industrially and because, on the crucial recognition issue, the law was on their side. That is, recognition was no longer at stake; the unions could hold concrete, attainable economic issues before the strikers' eyes.

But the American public, newly released from the pressures of war, did not take kindly to the strikes. Many people not hitherto opposed to unions became alarmed at the magnitude and duration of strikes which they saw the big industrial unions were capable of bringing about. In this climate of reaction against the spectacle of union power, the Taft-Hartley bill passed in Congress. President Truman vetoed it, but it passed again over his veto and became law.

What follows is a brief statement of the substance of the new law. Its fuller implications for managements and unions will be discussed in later chapters.

Changes in the Right to Union Representation. Section 7 of the Wagner Act was explicitly amended to give a majority of the workers the protected right to *refrain* from union organization and collective bargaining. The Taft-Hartley law also contained new election procedures which were designed to permit workers to refrain from collective bargaining. In the case of foremen, plant guards, and professional employees, the Taft-Hartley law defined specific permissible and nonpermissible forms of union recognition. Last but not least, the Taft-Hartley law gave employers a strong voice in influencing workers in their free choice of union representatives.

The Taft-Hartley law provided that the NLRB could hold only one election in any year for a single group of employees. Thus if a union lost an election or employees wanted to rid themselves of a nonrepresentative union, the *status quo* was frozen for one full year. Strikers who had been replaced were not eligible to vote in NLRB representation elections. The Taft-Hartley law created the decertification election by which employees could use the facilities of the NLRB to remove a union which was no longer representative.

Under the Taft-Hartley law, foremen were denied all protection of the law in seeking union recognition. The NLRB was directed to allow plant guards to be represented only by unions composed exclusively of plant guards. Professional employees could be represented by plant unions only if a majority of the professional employees had voted for such representation.

Obviously, employers might very well have preferences about whether or not their employees were represented by a union and which union would represent them. The Wagner Act and NLRB interpretations of that law took the position that employer attempts to influence the outcome of NLRB elections were "interference, restraint, and coercion" of employees in the exercise of their guaranteed right to free choice of representatives. The Taft-Hartley law, Section 8(c), called the "free speech" amendment, stated:

The expressing of any views, argument, or opinion, or the dissemination thereof, whether in written, printed, graphic, or visual form, shall not constitute or be evidence of an unfair labor practice under any of the provisions of this Act, if such expression contains no threat of reprisal or force or promise of benefit.

This free speech amendment substantially increased the influence which employers could exert on the outcome of NLRB elections. We shall discuss the free speech problem in some detail in Chapter 6.

The net effect of the Taft-Hartley law in the area of union recognition was to encourage employees and employers who wanted to avoid collective bargaining. The right to collective bargaining was retained, but the implicit right to refrain from bargaining was made explicit in the words of our national industrial relations policy.

Unfair Labor Practices by Unions. The Wagner Act defined and prohibited certain unfair labor practices *by management.* That was on the theory that employees and their unions were weaker and needed protection. The Taft-Hartley law extended the concept of unfair labor practices to *unions,* and brought them under the same sanctions and penalties for infractions as were applicable to management. The prohibitions on unfair labor practices by unions were designed to protect employees and employers.

Section 8(b) of the Taft-Hartley law enumerated six unfair labor practices by unions:

1. To restrain or coerce employees in the exercise of their guaranteed rights to engage in, or to refrain from, collective bargaining.
2. To cause an employer to discriminate against an employee who is not a member of a labor union for any reason other than his failure to tender the periodic dues and initiation fees uniformly required as a condition of acquiring or retaining membership.
3. To refuse to bargain with an employer, provided the union is the representative of his employees.
4. To engage in or to induce employees to engage in strikes or concerted refusal to work or boycotts—refusal to use, process, or handle certain goods or materials—when an object of such action is:
    a) forcing or requiring an employer or self-employed person to join any organization or forcing anyone to cease using the products of, or doing business with, any other person,
    b) to force recognition by any other employer of a union unless certified by the NLRB,
    c) to exert pressure against any employer to recognize a particular union when another union has been certified by the NLRB, and
    d) economic pressure in a jurisdictional dispute.
5. To charge an excessive or discriminatory fee as a condition precedent to membership in a union under a union shop clause.

6. To cause or attempt to cause an employer to pay or deliver any money or other thing of value, in the nature of an exaction, for services which are not performed or not to be performed.

The prohibition on unfair labor practices by unions protected employees in several ways. First, employees were protected from union restraint and coercion, just as the Wagner Act had protected them from employer coercion. Employees were also protected from union pressure exerted through their employers—with the sole exception of the obligation to pay union dues under a valid union shop agreement. Section 8(b)(4) protected nonunion workers in nonunion firms from union pressure even if they had obtained business by undercutting the conditions that existed in unionized firms. Under the union shop, employees were also protected from excessive or discriminatory initiation fees and dues.

The protection given to employers by the Taft-Hartley Act was certainly as significant as the protection given to employees. Unions were stripped of their power to induce employers to discharge persons who were antiunion. Section 8(b)(4) gave nonunion employers very substantial new insulation from unions that sought to organize their employees through boycotts. Section 8(b)(3), which required unions to bargain, and Section 8(b)(6) which was aimed at eliminating featherbedding were not to prove as significant. The new obligation for unions to bargain was somewhat frivolous since a union's reason for being is to bargain. The prohibition against featherbedding proved to be too vague to be meaningfully interpreted by the NLRB and the courts.

Obligatory Bargaining Procedures. The Taft-Hartley law changed the definition of the obligation to bargain, which the NLRB and courts had formulated, in only one important way—it provided a cooling-off period in the termination of agreements. Section 8(d) requires the party intending to terminate or modify a collective agreement to serve a written notice of such intention on the other party to the agreement 60 days prior to the proposed date of termination or modification. Thirty days after the serving of a termination notice, the Federal Mediation and Conciliation Service and the state mediation agency must be notified of the existence of the dispute. A strike or a lockout before the expiration of this 60-day period or the termination date of the agreement, whichever occurs later, is an unfair labor practice. An employee who strikes in violation of this provision loses all protection of the law and may be discharged for this kind of union activity. We shall discuss the functions of the Federal Mediation and Conciliation Service later.

Regulating the Internal Affairs of Unions. Many of the legislators who supported the Taft-Hartley law were deeply concerned over Communist infiltration of labor unions, the misappropriation of union funds, the monopoly aspects of the closed shop, and undemocratic procedures in unions. These concerns provided a basis for a new legislative departure in regulating the internal affairs of unions.

The Taft-Hartley attack on Communist influence in unions made the services of the NLRB available only to internationals and locals whose officers swore out "non-Comunist affidavits." This indirectly, for the first time, told unions how to run—or at least how *not* to run—their business. (The Landrum-Griffin law has gone further on this issue by a direct and positive prohibition and added a ban on racketeers.)

Congressional concern over the use of union funds was evidenced by the reporting requirements imposed on labor organizations and the prohibition on political expenditures by unions and corporations. Unions which failed to file annual reports on their finances with the Secretary of Labor were denied all access to the facilities of the NLRB. Violation of the ban on political expenditures was punishable by fines and imprisonment.

The Taft-Hartley ban on the closed shop deprived unions of the time-honored right to *effectively* set their own rules for admission to the union. Although the unions' rights to set their own admission standards were explicitly excepted from the union unfair labor practice of restraint and coercion of employees, the real power to set admission requirements ultimately resides in the ability to force the discharge from employment of the nonmember. In the closed shop ban and the Taft-Hartley's provisions for discharge only for nonpayment of dues, Congress severely restricted the power to set admission requirements. Even the question of "excessive and discriminatory" initiation fees came under the scrutiny of the NLRB. We shall have more to say about the importance of the ban on the closed shop and Section 14(b) which authorized state "right-to-work" laws in Chapter 10.

The Taft-Hartley Act's regulations of the internal affairs of unions were primarily aimed at the disclosure of union rules and procedures to governmental officers and the union membership. The Landrum-Griffin law goes beyond disclosure in prescribing affirmatively how unions shall operate.

National Emergency Strikes. As defined in the Taft-Hartley Act, a national emergency dispute has two essential features: (1) it affects an entire industry or a substantial part thereof *and* (2) it imperils the national health and safety. In such a dispute, the President is empowered to appoint a board of inquiry to ascertain the causes and circumstances of the dispute. Upon receipt of the report of the board of inquiry, the President may direct the Attorney General to petition any district court for an 80-day injunction against the strike or lockout. The district court will issue the injunction if the dispute has *both* of the features required. The board of inquiry is reconvened when the injunction is issued. If the dispute is not settled in the next 60 days, the board of inquiry reports the positions of the parties and the employer's last offer to the President who in turn makes the report public. The NLRB within the next 15 days conducts a secret ballot of the employees involved to determine if they wish to accept the employer's last offer. If no settlement is reached by the eightieth day, the injunction is discharged. The President then reports to the Congress and *may* recommend legislation to deal with the dispute.

It needs to be emphasized here that after the 80-day injunction the union is free to strike and the management is free to lock out. *Neither* the President *nor* the board of inquiry is empowered to recommend terms of settlement. The procedure consists of an 80-day cooling-off period, extensive publicity to the positions of the parties (but no official judgment of the propriety of those positions), and the permission for Presidential petition of Congress for *ad hoc* legislation if all else fails.

It is neither unfair nor premature to say that the Taft-Hartley provisions did not solve the problem of national emergency strikes. The Landrum-Griffin law did not amend the Taft-Hartley Act on national emergency disputes.

Remedies under the Taft-Hartley Act. Besides substantially increasing the scope of governmental regulation of collective bargaining, the Taft-Hartley law imposed new sanctions in addition to the remedies provided by the Wagner Act, on persons and organizations who violated its provisions. The new sanctions were: criminal penalties of fine and imprisonment, injunctions, and private suits for damages. The criminal penalties applied to violations of the ban on political contributions, false non-Communist affidavits, violations of the rules on checkoff and welfare funds, and willful interference with an agent of the Board. The Board was empowered to obtain injunctions to prevent the occurrence of unfair labor practices. In the case of boycotts, this injunction process was mandatory on the Board. Federal courts were empowered to hear private damage suits against labor unions for violations of collective bargaining agreements.

Just as the substance of the Taft-Hartley law was directed mostly against unions, the new remedies related primarily to union activity. It is important to note that the NLRB (*not* private parties) was empowered to get injunctions against unfair labor practices. The Norris–La Guardia Act was not repealed, it was merely amended, in that a specific governmental agency was empowered to use injunctive relief against specific unlawful acts. As has been indicated above, the injunction is a particularly potent weapon in labor relations. Congress very wisely limited the use of this weapon to a governmental agency.

The Taft-Hartley Act in Perspective. The Taft-Hartley law was passed in a climate of postwar reaction against the upsurge of union power. Time and experience have dissipated much of the emotion that enveloped earlier discussions of the Taft-Hartley Act. What is important about the law today is quite different from what appeared to be most important in the late 40s. The law's lasting impression on society and collective bargaining in the enterprise can be briefly summarized.

From the viewpoint of society, the Taft-Hartley Act leaves some unsolved problems as well as some clear failures and some clear progress.

Experience with the Taft-Hartley law clearly illustrates the futility of trying to exactly balance the bargaining power of managements and unions in society as a whole. General remedies cannot provide the much sought balance between such diverse relationships as the small union against the giant corporation or the giant union against the tiny employer. Although the Taft-Hartley's legislative recognition of the national emergency disputes probably served the public interest well, the remedies provided by the Taft-Hartley Act leave much to be desired. For better or for worse, the free speech amendment, the ban on secondary boycotts, and the regulation of union security both in the Act and in right-to-work states retarded the spread of unionism in nonunion areas and industries. The seed for the governmental regulation of the internal affairs of unions found in the Taft-Hartley Act sprouted in the Landrum-Griffin Act. It is still too soon to make firm predictions about exactly where the governmental regulation of internal affairs of unions will lead society. Probably the most significant conclusion that can be drawn from the operation of the Taft-Hartley Act is that unions have been recognized as a permanent institution in society.

From the viewpoint of bargaining in the enterprise, the impact of the Taft-Hartley Act was relatively slight. The total fabric of the Taft-Hartley law made organizing more difficult for unions in their formative stages than in earlier years. The Taft-Hartley prohibition on the closed shop in industries with casual and intermittent employment was so unrealistic that it encouraged widespread violation which had to be (at least partially) patched up in the Landrum-Griffin Act. The statutory bargaining procedures provided by the Taft-Hartley Act probably have been helpful to the parties in establishing a better plan for negotiations.

The Landrum-Griffin Act of 1959

When it was first enacted newspaper headline writers called this act the labor reform law. This reflected the hope of some of its sponsors and a large segment of the public that it would bring about inner-union democracy and honest leadership where these might be lacking or in danger. Other observers, not so confident, admitted at least that it put the means for doing this within the grasp of rank-and-file union members. Still others sardonically called it the lawyers' full employment act because of its precedent-shattering provisions, some of which are most obscurely and ambiguously drafted and seemed headed for years of test and challenge in the courts.

It will be helpful to look into the events that brought about its passage.

Background of the Act. The issue which split the AFL and called the CIO into being—the issue of industrial unionism—soon ceased to be a difference in practice. Unions of both federations organized industrial locals where that form was appropriate. Reunification of the labor movement thus became thinkable soon after the split, and unfriendly overtones in Taft-Hartley gave unions common cause to heal the breach. Before the merger in 1955, some leaders in both camps opposed reunification. Others who wanted it hesitated, because each side imputed to the other a tolerance of certain evils that were barriers to unity. These were: Communist leadership and influence in some CIO unions; and racketeering in some unions of the AFL.

Reunificaton, therefore, seemed to call for action on both these inner-union problems; and effective action proved difficult. Neither the AFL nor the CIO could step in to straighten out the internal affairs of an autonomous International. Expulsion, the strongest disciplinary measure available, merely drove out the per capita paying members as well as their offending officers, without accomplishing reform. Outside authority was needed.

From 1957 to 1959, a committee headed by Senator John L. McClellan of Arkansas conducted hearings that uncovered evidence of crime, corruption, collusion, malpractices, and dubious dealings in a few old-line AFL unions, notably the Longshoremen (East Coast) and the Teamsters. It was at the height of public excitement over these revelations that the Landrum-Griffin Act became law.

What does it aim to do? How does it propose to do it?

Aims of the Law. The Landrum-Griffin law has two aims: (*a*) to set minimum standards of democratic procedure, responsibility, and honesty in the conduct of the internal affairs of unions and (*b*) to clarify congressional intent on basic labor relations policy as stated in the Taft-Hartley Act. The first six titles of the Landrum-Griffin Act, taken together, lay down a comprehensive program dealing with three problem areas of inner-union democracy: (1) the rights of union members; (2) responsibilities of union officers, and (3) safeguards on the use of union funds. Parenthetically it should be stated that Title II also requires employers to file reports on their financial relationships with union leaders and payments made to persons for the purpose of influencing employees in the exercise of their rights under the law. Title VII amends the Taft-Hartley Act by (1) tightening up the Taft-Hartley regulation of secondary boycotts and hot cargo agreements, (2) liberalizing the Taft-Hartley law on union security and the right of economic strikers to vote in NLRB elections, and (3) imposing additional restrictions on the rights of unions to picket for recognition.

Inner-Union Democracy and Responsibility. Before the passage of the Taft-Hartley Act, no agency except the courts was ever responsible for regulating the internal affairs of unions. It probably is not an exaggeration to say that, in general, unions were viewed as private clubs or fraternal organizations. Like college fraternities, they were free to set their own qualifications for membership and to exclude from membership anyone who violated their rules or incurred the indignation of the officers or the membership. In some unions, particularly the old-line craft unions, racial discrimination played a role in admission to membership. Most unions also took a very dim view of a member who crossed its picket lines. However, racial discrimination in employment was perfectly legal in many states and even churches have been known to crack down on members who violate their rules.

Many persons both sympathetic and hostile to the labor movement were gravely concerned about civil liberties in labor unions. By 1947, many unions were powerful enough to negotiate agreements which made membership in the union a condition precedent to employment. Under a closed shop agreement, the union literally could deny a job to a worker. This concentration of power in the hands of the union could be viewed in three ways. First, it could be argued, as most union leaders did argue, that this power held by unions was no greater than the power held by any employer. This argument, if it carried, would result in no governmental regulation of unions' internal affairs. Second, it could be argued—and this argument carried in the Taft-Hartley Act—that no unions should be permitted to possess this power. The Taft-Hartley Act simply outlawed the closed shop. No matter how distasteful a worker might be to the union, his right to work could be upheld by his employer so long as the worker paid his union dues. Third, it could be said that union members had a legitimate interest in who worked alongside them and that any legislation should be directed at the arbitrary, discriminatory, or antisocial exercise of the power that the closed shop created. Although supported by many public-spirited authorities on labor-management relations and civil liberties, the third argument has not been accepted in legislation. The Taft-Hartley law sought to protect workers from undemocratic unions by depriving all unions of effective control over the act of employment.

The Landrum-Griffin law carries the basic civil liberties rationale of the Taft-Hartley law one step further. It seeks to guarantee union members democratic procedures inside their unions. The Taft-Hartley law's protection of the worker who wants to refrain from membership in a union is unchanged.

a) Rights of Union Members. Title I of the Landrum-Griffin Act sets forth a bill of rights for members of labor organizations. These rights are summarized in Figure 5–2. Members are guaranteed the right to vote on union matters and to engage in political activity within the union. Union dues can be increased only by following a prescribed procedure. Members are given the right to sue the union and its officers in federal courts for deprivation of their guaranteed rights. Title VI makes it a criminal offense punishable by fines and/or imprisonment to use violence or the threat of violence to interfere with a member's exercise of his guaranteed rights.

b) Responsibilities of Union Officers. The Landrum-Griffin Act extended the regulation of union officers started by the Taft-Hartley law

FIGURE 5–2. The Landrum-Griffin "Bill of Rights" for Union Members

Under Title I, every member of a labor organization engaged in an industry affecting interstate commerce is to have the following rights and privileges:

1. *Equal rights* to nominate candidates for union elections, attend membership meetings, and vote on union business.
2. *Freedom of speech and assembly* in and out of union meetings, so long as such conduct does not interfere with the union's performance of its legal or contractual obligations.
3. *Dues and initiation fees* can be increased, and assessments can be levied, only as follows:

      a) by locals, by secret vote of the membership.
      b) by internationals,

         (1) by majority vote of the delegates to a convention, or
         (2) by majority vote of the members in good standing voting in a secret ballot referendum, or
         (3) between conventions, if authorized by the union constitution, by the majority of the executive board, but effective only until the next regular convention.

      c) The AFL-CIO and similar federations of unions are specifically excluded from these regulations.
4. *Members' right to sue.* Unions are prohibited from limiting the right of any member to bring a court action or administrative proceeding against the union. However, union members may be required to exhaust reasonable hearing procedures within the union (but not to exceed a four month lapse of time) before instituting a legal or administrative proceeding against the union or any of its officers.
5. *Procedural safeguards.* No member may be disciplined by a union or any of its officers, except for nonpayment of dues, without being served with written specific charges, given a reasonable time to prepare his defense, and afforded a full and fair hearing.
6. *Retention of existing rights.* Nothing in Title I limits the rights of any union member under any state or federal law or before any court or other tribunal, or under any union's constitution or bylaws.
7. *Right to copies of collective bargaining agreements.* Local unions must supply every member who requests it a copy of any agreement made by the local which directly affects his rights as an employee. International unions are required to supply their constituent units with copies of agreements directly affecting the constituent unit's membership.

Any person whose rights under Title I have been infringed may bring action for appropriate relief including an injunction in a United States District Court.

Section 610 of the law states: "It shall be unlawful for any person through the use of force or violence, or threat of the use of force or violence, to restrain, coerce, or intimidate, or attempt to restrain, coerce, or intimidate any member of a labor organization for the purpose of interfering with or preventing the exercise of any right to which he is entitled under the provisions of this Act. Any person who willfully violates this section shall be fined not more than $1,000 or imprisoned for not more than one year, or both."

and changed the method of applying congressional pressure on the unions. Taft-Hartley denied the use of the NLRB to *unions* whose officers refused to swear out non-Communist affidavits. The Landrum-Griffin Act imposed its penalty on the union *officer* who violated its provisions and repealed the Taft-Hartley's penalty on unions which had noncomplying officers. The Landrum-Griffin Act prohibited former Communists and felons from holding union office for five years after they left the Party or were convicted of crime, or were released from jail after conviction. Labor organizations and their officers were charged with the responsibility of excluding such persons from union office. Persons who willfully violate this section of the Landrum-Griffin law are subject to fines of up to $10,000 and/or one year in prison.

Title IV of the Landrum-Griffin Act is devoted to the regulation of union elections and internal political campaigns. International unions are required to hold elections for officers at least every five years and more frequently if required by their constitutions. Such elections must be held by secret ballot among the members in good standing or at a convention of delegates chosen by secret ballot. Local unions must elect their officers not less often than once every three years by secret ballot among the members in good standing. If the Secretary of Labor finds that a union constitution does not contain adequate provisions for the removal of officers guilty of misconduct, any officers guilty of such misconduct may be removed, after notice and hearing, by a secret ballot of the membership. A member of the union is authorized to enlist the assistance of the Secretary of Labor and the courts in invalidating improper elections after the member has exhausted the remedies available to him within the union. Title IV also gives candidates for union office an opportunity to examine lists of eligible voters and prohibits the expenditure of the union's funds to support candidates for union office.

Many international constitutions permit the executive board of the convention to establish a "trusteeship" or provisional government over a local union or other subordinate union body. The power to create a trusteeship has been used in the past for such laudatory purposes as preserving a local's funds from embezzlement or to eliminate Communist or other officers who were undermining the legitimate activities of the local. The trustee device is also a powerful means of suppressing democracy within the local, or destroying opposition to the international officers at the grass roots level, or the milking of a local by the international officers. Title III of the Landrum-Griffin law brings the trustee device under statutory control. Trusteeship may be established only in accordance with the union's constitution for the purposes of: (*a*) correcting corruption or financial malpractice, (*b*) assuring the performance of collective bargaining agreements, (*c*) restoring democratic procedures, or (*d*) "otherwise carrying out the legitimate objects of such labor organization." During a trusteeship the votes of a local union may be counted in a convention or union election only if the delegates have been chosen by secret ballot in which all members of the local could vote. The funds of a local in trusteeship cannot be transferred to the international. The Secretary of Labor must be informed when a trusteeship is imposed and semiannual reports on the operation of the trusteeship must be submitted to him.

c) Safeguards on Union Funds. The officers, agents, shop stewards, and other representatives of a labor organization occupy positions of trust in relation to the union and its members as a group. Title V of the Landrum-Griffin law requires persons holding such positions to hold the union's money and property solely for the benefit of the union and its members. Persons holding offices in unions or employed by unions are prohibited from holding or acquiring any pecuniary or personal interests which conflict with the union's interests. Every union representative who handles union money must be bonded for at least 10 percent of the funds which he normally handles in a fiscal year, but need not be bonded for more than $500,000. Labor organizations may not loan any officer or employee more than $2,000. Unions may not pay the fines of their officers or employees convicted of violating the Landrum-Griffin Act. Theft or embezzlement of union funds is a federal crime subject to a fine of up to $10,000 and/or imprisonment for up to 5 years.

Before leaving the comprehensive code for the regulation of the internal affairs of unions, a word should be said about new powers and duties of the Secretary of Labor. The Secretary of Labor is not only required to receive a large number of reports of internal union affairs, he also is empowered to conduct investigations on a wide range of union affairs and to assist union members in court cases. Under the Landrum-Griffin Act, the Bureau of Labor-Management Reports of the Department of Labor has become a great depository of all kinds of information on the internal operations of labor unions. The files of the Bureau are a gold mine for persons interested in research on unionism. It is to be hoped that researchers will give us a much better understanding of union operations by taking full advantage of the Bureau's policy of encouraging scholarly research.

In addition to regulating the internal affairs of unions, the Landrum-Griffin Act carried forward the legislative intent of the Taft-Hartley law.

Taft-Hartley Amendments. Secondary boycotts, the rights of economic strikers to vote in NLRB elections, and recognition picketing were regulated by the Taft-Hartley Act. Apparently Congress was dissatisfied with the application of the Taft-Hartley provisions because it substantially amended the previous regulations in all three areas.

a) Secondary Boycotts and Hot Cargo Agreements. Section 8(b)(4)(A) of the Taft-Hartley Act was aimed at "secondary boycotts." Secondary boycotts are not easy to define, but in general they are attempts by a union to induce some other party (union members, consumers, or an employer) to cease doing business with someone. As the NLRB and the courts interpreted Section 8(b)(4)(A) several kinds of activities were not in violation of the Taft-Hartley law, e.g., (1) inducements of a *single* employee to strike or to refuse to handle goods; (2) inducements of employers directly, instead of through a strike of their employees; and (3) inducements of employees excluded from the definition of employees in the Taft-Hartley Act, i.e., railroad workers or municipal employees.

The Landrum-Griffin Act amended Section 8(b)(4)(A) of the Taft-Hartley and closed the secondary boycott loopholes tight, by substituting the word "person" for "employees."

A hot cargo clause is an agreement between an employer and a union that the employees covered by the agreement will not be required to handle "unfair" goods, e.g., struck work or nonunion goods. The Landrum-Griffin Act outlawed hot cargo agreements except: (1) in the construction industry agreements relating to "the contracting or subcontracting of work to be done at the site of the construction, alteration, painting or repair of a building, structure or other work," and (2) "persons in the relation of a jobber, manufacturer, contractor or subcontractor working on the goods or premises of the jobber or manufacturer or performing parts of an integrated process of production in the apparel and clothing industry."

The Landrum-Griffin amendments on secondary boycotts and hot cargo restrict a union's power to make its strike effective. Under Landrum-Griffin a struck employer is free to transfer work to other plants and to subcontract the work that otherwise would be performed by the people on strike. The hot cargo ban restricts the power formerly held by the Teamsters' Union to help strikers by cutting off the flow of goods and services to a struck plant. Although unions have some protected activity in advertising to their members and the general public the presence of unfair goods, they no longer are permitted to picket an employer who is selling unfair goods or who is performing operations on struck work.

b) Union Security and Economic Strikers. There was very little in the Landrum-Griffin Act that could be termed prounion. Still, building trades union leaders could be heartened by the new union security provisions, garment union leaders could be encouraged by the exemption of their industry from the hot cargo and secondary boycott bans, and industrial unions could get some comfort from the revised right of economic strikers to vote in NLRB elections.

In 1947, the Taft-Hartley law outlawed the closed shop and thereby threatened to upset long-established ways of doing business in the construction industry. It is not inaccurate to say that the Taft-Hartley law failed to destroy the closed shop practice in many industries. Landrum-Griffin took a step backward toward the realities of life in the construction industry. A new Section 8(f) permits employers and unions primarily engaged in the building and construction industry to enter into agreements before workers are hired and to establish a seven-day union shop. The prehire contract coupled with the seven-day union shop certainly approximates the closed shop *modus operandi* in the construction industry.

Under the Taft-Hartley law strikers not eligible for reinstatement were denied the right to vote in NLRB decertification elections. Under this provision it was possible for an employer to provoke an economic strike, to replace the strikers, and then obtain an NLRB election in which the union members on strike could not vote. Obviously, the assured result of such an election would be the decertification of the striking union. Landrum-Griffin sought to remedy this unfair situation by providing that the NLRB was empowered to permit economic strikers who had been replaced to vote in an NLRB election held within 12 months after the beginning of the strike.

   c) Organizational and Recognition Picketing. The Landrum-Griffin Act adds a new Section 8(b)(7) to the National Labor Relations Act. This section makes it an unfair labor practice for a union to picket, or to threaten to picket, where an object is to gain recognition or promote organization of the employees, under three circumstances: (A) where the employer has recognized another labor organization; (B) for 12 months following a valid representation election lost by a union; and (C) where, apart from the foregoing circumstances, "such picketing has been conducted without a petition under section 9(c) being filed within a reasonable period of time, not to exceed 30 days." The circumstances described in (C) are qualified in two respects: (1) the union need not demonstrate "a showing of substantial interest" or claim recognition, and (2) picketing beyond the 30-day period, or other publicity addressed to the public and consumers, is permitted if the effect of the picketing is not to induce a disruption of services at the employer's place of business.

   Although the primary aim of Section 8(b)(7) was probably to protect employers from harrassment picketing, this provision does enable a union to obtain a quick NLRB election by the method of picketing.

   Section 602 of Landrum-Griffin outlaws extortionate picketing. Any person who carries on picketing for the purpose of personal profit or the enrichment of any other individual (except a bona fide increase in wages or other employee benefits) by taking or obtaining anything of value from an employer against his will is subject to a fine of up to $10,000 and/or imprisonment up to 20 years.

   The Significance of the Landrum-Griffin Act.   When the Landrum-Griffin Act was passed in 1959, the meaning of many provisions of the Taft-Hartley Act of 1947 was still uncertain because of a lack of full judicial review. It is still too soon to state the impact of the Landrum-Griffin Act except in the most general terms.

   The provisions of the Landrum-Griffin Act that strictly belong in the field of labor-management relations are relatively minor. They seek to plug up the loopholes in the Taft-Hatley ban on secondary boycotts; they prohibit hot cargo agreements of the Teamsters and others (but not the garment unions); they restrict organizational and recognition picketing. They potentially extend the jurisdiction of the states in making labor law and improve the speed of case handling by the NLRB. They also meet some long-standing union demands. Economic strikers get the right to vote in NLRB elections. The closed shop, for all practical purposes, is reauthorized in the construction industry.

More important to the future of collective bargaining than these changes in labor relations law is the fact of direct government intervention in the affairs of unions. Unions heretofore were private organizations. Normally they were democratic; sometimes not. In either case, government regulation touched only their relations with other organizations. As long as they kept within the laws of the surrounding democratic society, it was no business of anyone in government whether they were democratic or autocratic, honest or corrupt, run by the members or by self-perpetuating bosses, or, indeed, by thugs. The Taft-Hartley Act provided only minimal regulation of the internal affairs of unions.

The Landrum-Griffin Act changes all that. In the most positive fashion, under the threat of heavy penalties, it *directs*, specifically and in detail over a wide range of issues, that unions shall be democratically administered. Whether it succeeds or fails to reach its aim, there will be repercussions in the years to come not only in the union hall but at the bargaining table.

SUMMARY

The third main actor in the collective bargaining system is the government, personified by many different elected officials and civil servants, each charged with responsibility for protecting the public interest. In some areas, like the obligation to bargain and the right of employees to be represented by representatives of their own choosing, the public interest has been clearly articulated by statutes and administrative rulings. In other areas, like strikes, mediation, and noninflationary wage settlements, the public interest has not been so clearly defined. The public interest changes over time.

Statutory law on labor relations in the United States is largely permissive in nature. The first labor relations law applicable to all interstate commerce, the Norris–La Guardia Act of 1932, restricted the issuance of injunctions in labor disputes and made the yellow dog contract unenforceable by law. The Wagner Act of 1935 created the National Labor Relations Board and gave it broad powers in formulating administrative law. The Wagner Act introduced the ballot box as the basic way of obtaining union recognition and protected employees' right to organize by prohibiting unfair labor practices by management. The Taft-Hartley law of 1947 amended the Wagner Act by protecting the right of workers to refrain from union organization and redressed the balance of power between management and unions by prohibiting unfair labor practices by unions. The Landrum-Griffin Act of 1959 was a major innovation in labor relations legislation in that it provided detailed regulation of the internal affairs of unions.

QUESTIONS FOR DISCUSSION

1. Since American labor relations law is largely permissive, why study it?
2. Show how the Norris–La Guardia Act, the Wagner Act, the Taft-Hartley Act, and Landrum-Griffin Act succeeded or failed in "balancing" the bargaining power of management and unions.
3. Does *protective* labor legislation have any influence on collective bargaining?
4. By reference to specific pertinent provisions of the Wagner Act, Taft-Hartley Act, and Landrum-Griffin Act, trace changes in American public policy on the regulation of the internal affairs of unions. Have American unions become instrumentalities of the state?
5. The Railway Labor Act is noteworthy for the fact that it represented a consensus between management and unions. How might a consensus between managements and unions be developed for future collective bargaining legislation?

CASES: 1, 2, 3.

SELECTED ANNOTATED BIBLIOGRAPHY

AARON, BENJAMIN. "The Labor-Management Reporting and Disclosure Act of 1959," *Harvard Law Review*, Vol. LXXIII (March–April 1960), pp. 851–907 and 1086–1127.

   An authoritative discussion of the Landrum-Griffin Act.

BAKKE, E. WRIGHT; KERR, CLARK; and ANROD, CHARLES W. (eds.). *Unions, Management and the Public*, 3d ed. New York: Harcourt, Brace & World, 1967.

   A classic book of readings on the role of unions, management, and the institution of free collective bargaining in the United States. Readings deal with the full spectrum of issues relating to collective bargaining.

BARNES, STANLEY N.; GOLDBERG, ARTHUR J.; and MILLER, LAMBERT H. "Unions and the Anti-Trust Laws," *Labor Law Journal*, Vol. VII (March 1956), pp. 133–36, 178–86, 186–92.

   Three papers on unions and the antitrust laws. Mr. Barnes, Assistant Attorney General in charge of the Anti-Trust Division of the Department of Justice, sketches the present statutory pattern and raises problems posed by possible extension of antitrust action to the labor relations area. Mr. Goldberg, special Counsel to the AFL-CIO, examines monopoly charges against individual unions and the AFL-CIO, and boycotts, jurisdictional disputes, and featherbedding as grounds for antitrust action. Mr. Miller, general counsel of the National Association of Manufacturers, compares the structure of modern unionism and modern business and argues that there should be no "double standard" in the application of the antitrust laws.

BROWN, LEO C., S.J. "Consensus in Labor Relations," chap. 8, *Arbitration and Public Policy*, SPENCER D. POLLARD (ed.). Proceedings of the Fourteenth Annual Meeting of the National Academy of Arbitrators, Washington, D.C.: Bureau of National Affairs, 1961, pp. 193–202.

Father Brown argues that industrial relations problems are rapidly increasing in their complexity, that the parties are doing a good job of settling them, and that the purpose of legislation should be to force the parties to face up to the responsibility of settling their own problems.

CHERNISH, WILLIAM N. *Coalition Bargaining: A Study of Union Tactics and Public Policy*. Philadelphia: University of Pennsylvania Press, 1969.

An analysis of one of the most controversial developments in collective bargaining. The study looks at union coalition behavior in several companies and industries including General Electric. Also contains a review of relevant NLRB and court decisions regarding coalition bargaining.

COHEN, SANFORD. "An Analytical Framework for Labor Relations Law," *Industrial and Labor Relations Review*, Vol. XIV (April 1961), pp. 350–62.

The author suggests that the timing and character of labor law can be regarded as a variable which is dependent upon the "resultant of the prevailing ideology of property rights and the degree of access to political power enjoyed by private power blocks." This two-variable framework is applied to an analysis of the American legal experience; the concept of "countervailing power" as an alternative explanation is also considered.

COX, ARCHIBALD. "Internal Affairs of Labor Unions under the Labor Reform Act of 1959," *Michigan Law Review*, Vol. LVIII (April 1960), pp. 819–54.

Following a summary of the legislative background of the Labor-Management Reporting and Disclosure Act of 1959, the author discusses and evaluates the provisions of the act that deal with the internal affairs of labor organizations.

———. "The Duty to Bargain in Good Faith," *Harvard Law Review*, Vol. LXXI (June 1958), pp. 1401–42.

Professor Cox analyzes NLRB decisions having the effect of enlarging the scope of substantive issues in collective bargaining.

CUSHMAN, EDWARD L. "Management Objectives in Collective Bargaining," ARNOLD W. WEBER (ed.), *The Structure of Collective Bargaining: Problems and Perspectives*, pp. 59–75. New York: The Free Press of Glencoe, Inc., 1961.

Mr. Cushman, vice-president of American Motors Corporation, argues that sound public policy would be (1) dissolution of very large firms under the antitrust laws and (2) limiting the responsibility for collective bargaining with an employer in a basic industry to a union composed solely of the employees of that company. Discusses the decentralization of collective bargaining within American Motors Corporation.

DUNLOP, JOHN T. "The Arbitration of Jurisdictional Disputes in the Building Industry," *Arbitration Today*, JEAN T. McKELVEY (ed.). Proceedings of the Eighth Annual Meeting of the National Academy of Arbitrators, pp. 161–65. Washington, D.C.: Bureau of National Affairs, 1955.

Discusses the early history of the National Joint Board for the Adjustment of Jurisdictional Disputes in the Building and Construction Industry.

EVANS, HYWELL. *Governmental Regulation of Industrial Relations: A Comparative Study of the United States and British Experience.* Ithaca, N.Y.: New York State School of Industrial Relations, 1961.

A critical analysis of the development of public policy in the field of labor-management relations in the United States by a British observer. Attempts to explain the comparative increase in government intervention and control of collective bargaining in the U.S. since the late 19th century; comments on the success of mediation, arbitration, and emergency-disputes procedures, and appraises the status of unionism since the passage of the Taft-Hartley Act.

GREGORY, CHARLES O. *Labor and the Law.* 2d rev. ed. New York: W. W. Norton & Co., Inc., 1958.

A scholarly and very readable account of American labor relations law with heavy emphasis on the common-law background.

INDEPENDENT STUDY GROUP, COMMITTEE FOR ECONOMIC DEVELOPMENT. *The Public Interest in National Labor Policy.* New York: CED, 1961.

Clark Kerr, Douglas V. Brown, David L. Cole, John T. Dunlop, William Y. Elliot, Albert Rees, Robert H. Solow, Philip Taft, and George W. Taylor compose the membership of the Study Group. George P. Shultz, Abraham Siegel, and David Burke compose the staff. Discussion of, and recommendations on: the public interest and private responsibilities; function and control of strikes and lockouts; collective bargaining, inflation and effective use of manpower; private power and its control; and individual rights in effective institutions.

MILLIS, HARRY A., and BROWN, EMILY CLARK. *From the Wagner Act to Taft-Hartley: A Study of National Labor Policy and Labor Relations.* Chicago: University of Chicago Press, 1950.

A landmark in labor legislation scholarship. Part I, The Wagner Act, by Professor Brown. Parts II and III, the Taft-Hartley Act, planned and partially written by the late Professor Millis, former Chairman of the National Labor Relations Board. Parts of this book provide a statement of Professor Millis's philosophy of industrial relations. The book includes detailed analyses of a number of the NLRB's major policies and their change over time.

SEIDENBERG, JACOB. *The Labor Injunction in New York City: 1935–1950.* Ithaca, N.Y.: New York State School of Industrial and Labor Relations, 1953.

An exhaustive study of the issuance of labor injunctions by the courts of the state of New York after the passage of the Norris–La Guardia Act.

SHISTER, JOSEPH; AARON, BENJAMIN; and SUMMERS, CLYDE W. (eds.). *Public Policy and Collective Bargaining.* New York: Harper & Row, 1962.

A volume published by the Industrial Relations Research Association. Specialists in industrial relations and law analyze the following: "An Historical Evolution of Public Policy in Labor Relations," by DOUGLASS V. BROWN and CHARLES A. MYERS; "Employer Free Speech," by BENJAMIN AARON; "The Obligation to Bargain in Good Faith," by ROBBEN W. FLEMING; "The Union Security Issue," by PAUL E. SULTAN; "Picketing and Boycotts," by DONALD H. WOLLETT; "Collective Bargaining and the Antitrust Laws," by GEORGE H. HILDEBRAND; "Legal Regulation of Internal Union

Affairs," by JOSEPH R. GRODIN; and "A Comparison of U.S. and Canadian Experiences," by HARRY D. WOODS.

SMITH, RUSSELL A. "The Labor-Management Reporting and Disclosure Act of 1959," *Virginia Law Review*, Volume XLVI (March 1960), pp. 195–251.
An authoritative discussion of the Landrum-Griffin Act.

"The Taft-Hartley Law after Ten Years: A Symposium," *Industrial and Labor Relations Review*, Vol. XI (April 1958), pp. 327–412.
Seven experts discuss experience under the Taft-Hartley law. Contents:
AARON, BENJAMIN. "Amending the Taft-Hartley Act on Union Strength tration."
SHISTER, JOSEPH. "The Impact of the Taft-Hartley Act on Union Strength and Collective Bargaining."
TAFT, PHILIP. "Internal Affairs of Unions and the Taft-Hartley Act."
ABELOW, ROBERT. "Management Experience under the Taft-Hartley Act."
KLAUS, IDA. "The Taft-Hartley Experience in Separation of NLRB Functions."
ISSAACSON, WILLIAM J. "Federal Preemption under the Taft-Hartley Act."
SUMMERS, CLYDE W. "A Summary Evaluation of the Taft-Hartley Act."

WELLINGTON, HARRY H. *Labor and the Legal Process.* New Haven: Yale University Press, 1968.
A comprehensive examination of the national policy toward labor-management relations and the role of law and legal institutions in accomplishing of that policy.

PART II

Collective Bargaining Activities

Part II of this book considers the activities of employers, workers, and government representatives in establishing the collective bargaining relationship and arriving at the collective bargaining agreement; the nature of the collective bargaining agreement; and living with the collective bargaining agreement.

| Chapter 6 | ESTABLISHING THE COLLECTIVE BARGAINING RELATIONSHIP |

The collective bargaining relationship always starts with the recognition of a union by the management of an enterprise. Recognition is preceded by a decision of some of the employees of an enterprise that they will seek union representation, or a union decision that a non-union enterprise must be organized, or a manager's decision that a unionized operation is the best way to run his newly established business. No matter whether employees, a union, or management takes the initiative in establishing the collective bargaining relationship, an "outside" agent, the union, appears on the scene and solicits members from the employees or prospective employees of the enterprise. What happens in this period *before* the first collective bargaining agreement is negotiated is of great importance to the managers, employees, and union(s) involved. These activities are regulated by law. Prenegotiation activities sometimes generate hostility which leaves a long-lasting scar on the collective bargaining relationship. This chapter describes how a collective bargaining relationship comes into being.

THE INITIATIVE IN ESTABLISHING THE COLLECTIVE BARGAINING RELATIONSHIP

Typically management is the initiating force in all employment activities and the preservation of the right of managerial initiative is generally considered to be essential to enterprise efficiency. The major exception to the rule of management initiative is the activity of establishing the collective bargaining relationship. With one small exception, in the contemplation of the law, the initiative in establishing a collective bargaining relationship belongs either to employees or to a union.

Employee Initiative

Every job holds some potential of real dissatisfactions for anyone who might hold it: the pay is too low, the boss is unfair, the pace is too fast, the job itself is insecure or potentially short-lived, the hours are too long, the working conditions aren't as good as they should be, or the fellow workers aren't friendly. Each employee has his own "boiling point" and his own evaluation of the qualities of the job, but for some reason a group of employees becomes dissatisfied with the conditions of their employment and conclude that the only way they can get "justice" is to form a union. These employees call a union and an organizing drive begins.

Probably no two union organizing drives are exactly alike, but some general rules do seem to apply. At the early stages of the drive, organization is conducted in secret, the union contacting employees who might join the union through other employees who have shown interest in forming a union. Only after a fair number of employees have shown an active interest will the organization conduct its campaign for members in the open. The secrecy aspect protects the early joiners from management retaliation and gives the union an idea about the prospects of a successful organizing drive before overcommitting itself or its new members. Secrecy also has the advantage of preventing management from killing an incipient union with kindness.

When a group of employees has taken the initiative in calling in a union, the union's organizing job is simplified. The employees who took the initiative can supply the union with information about grievances in the enterprise and the names of employees who most likely would favor a union as well as the names of employees who should be avoided because of their loyalty to the enterprise and the probability that they would inform management that a union organization drive was under way. Employees sympathetic to the union cause also can supply information about the sometimes vital matter of enterprise organizational structure. As a rule, an industrial union seeks membership in all production departments of the enterprise and it is desirable to have union members under the supervision of every foreman in the enterprise. Most important of all, the employees who took the initiative in calling the union serve as union organizers in the shop.

Most union organizing drives are initiated by dissatisfied employees, but some union organizing drives are initiated by unions and managements.

Union Initiative

A union is an institution to some degree independent of both its members and the enterprise which provides jobs for its members. As an independent institution, the union has ambitions for growth and an important defensive strategy of organizing all enterprises which compete with enterprises that it has organized. A pure union initiative in an organizing drive springs from the growth motive or the defensive strategy of organizing the unorganized.

Most international unions keep an eye on developments in their industry. Two examples will suffice: The International Ladies' Garment Workers' Union and the amalgamated Clothing Workers' Union operate in industries where it is very easy to open a small shop. Both unions expend a substantial portion of their resources on finding these new shops and organizing them. A different kind of situation arises when a huge industrial combine like General Motors, General Electric, or United States Steel opens an entirely new facility. The unions which have collective bargaining relationships with the parent organization watch these developments closely and launch organizing drives as soon as they learn of the company's plans.

In all of these cases the motive to unionization is different from when employees take the initiative, but the techniques of organizing are similar. In a union initiated drive, the union looks for, or "manufactures" employee grievances, sells the advantages of union membership, and seeks to start an internal chain reaction among the employees of the enterprise.

Management Initiative

A management initiative in establishing a collective bargaining relationship is extremely rare and poses a serious problem at law. *Only* employers engaged "primarily in the building and construction industry" can take the initiative in establishing a collective bargaining relationship with reasonable immunity from unfair labor practice charge of interference, restraint, coercion, or company domination of the union.

In the construction industry, new enterprises usually come into being when a unionized tradesman bids successfully for a subcontract. The natural thing for this new entrepreneur to do is to contact a union business agent as the source of his potential employees. Under the Landrum-Griffin Act, except in states with general right-to-work laws, employers and unions in the building and construction industry are free to:

1. Make collective bargaining agreements *before* the majority status of the union is established under Section 9 of the law,
2. Require membership in the union as a condition of employment after the *seventh day* following employment or the effective date of the agreement, whichever is later,
3. Require the employer to notify the union of job opportunities or give the union an opportunity to refer qualified applicants for employment, and
4. Specify minimum training or experience qualifications for employment or establish priorities in opportunities for employment.

These provisions of the Landrum-Griffin Act are a substantial step toward reauthorizing long-established methods of doing business in the building trades. The prehire agreement and seven-day union shop are a close approximation of the old-time closed shop. Although the NLRB has ruled that the Landrum-Griffin prehire contract shall not stand as a bar to a petition for an NLRB certification,[1] employers in the building and construction industry have very substantial immunity under the law in taking the initiative in establishing a collective bargaining relationship.

Employers not engaged in the building and construction industry are well advised *not* to take the initiative in establishing a collective bargaining relationship. In the early days of the Wagner Act employers frequently sought out "responsible" and "cooperative" unions and entered into "sweetheart" agreements with them. When there is evidence of union and management collusion in the signing of a collective bargaining agreement, the NLRB voids the agreement and brings unfair labor practice charges against the management. Although employer initiatives in establishing collective bargaining relationships are on the outer fringe of lawful employer activity, it is likely that a few employers do take these actions and are able to do so within the bounds of the law or without getting caught. Because union representation is so vitally significant to enterprise welfare and the wide variety of unions which might organize a single employer, it seems fair to expect that many employers are sorely tempted to take the initiative in establishing the collective bargaining relationship even though such action is of questionable legality.

Regardless of whether employees, a union, or the employer takes the initiative in establishing the collective bargaining relationship and whether the union organization drive is conducted openly or in secret, eventually there must be a union and management confrontation on the question of union recognition. Today there are two methods by which union recognition may be established.

THE TWO METHODS OF ESTABLISHING UNION RECOGNITION

Before the passage of the Wagner Act in 1935, a union could obtain recognition only by persuading an employer to grant such recognition voluntarily. Although statistics are not available, it seems quite fair to say that most unions found it necessary to persuade employers through the use of strikes, picketing, and boycotts.

Today there are two methods by which a union may obtain recognition from an employer: (1) *without* governmental intervention, and (2) through the processes of the National Labor Relations Board. The law severely restricts the use of picketing by unions as a means of persuading employers to grant recognition. At the same time it provides orderly procedures for obtaining recognition. Governmental intervention is the rule of the day, but the law still protects the rights of the parties to settle their own problems without governmental intervention so long as those private settlements do not violate public policy.

---

[1] *Twenty-Sixth Annual Report of the National Labor Relations Board for Year Ended June 30, 1961*, p. 42.

Union Recognition without Governmental Intervention

If a majority of the employees in an enterprise want a certain union to represent them in collective bargaining and that union can satisfy the employer on this point, the employer may voluntarily recognize the union and bargain with it. In such cases, the union usually satisfies the employer by showing authorization cards or petitions signed by a majority of the employees in the unit. This method may be followed in any employee group whether or not the business affects commerce.

In those exceptional cases which are not subject to federal or state labor relations statutes, the union is free to strike, picket, and boycott to obtain recognition. For example, supervisors, agricultural workers, and the employees of completely nonprofit hospitals (none of whom are "employees" under the Landrum-Griffin Act) are free to strike, picket, and boycott for recognition unless prohibited by state law.

Unions of employees who are covered by the Landrum-Griffin law are subject to restrictions on how they may persuade employers to grant recognition. These restrictions on picketing and jurisdictional disputes were designed to curb abuses of the past and to protect employers from conflicting claims for union representation.

Picketing for Recognition. Under the Landrum-Griffin Act, picketing by a union that is not recognized as bargaining agent and has not been certified by the NLRB, for the purpose of securing recognition or of forcing the employees to select it as bargaining agent, is sharply restricted. Organizational picketing is forbidden altogether where a valid NLRB election has been held within the previous 12 months or the employer lawfully recognizes another union. In such cases, an election petition will not be entertained by the NLRB. In other circumstances, e.g., a nonunion shop with no recent NLRB election, the picketing may not continue for more than 30 days without the filing of a petition for an NLRB election.

Union jurisdiction is a direct concern of the labor movement. Employers can assert only an indirect influence in the resolution of jurisdictional disputes. The old AFL attempted to control interunion competition by issuing mutually exclusive charters to international unions and deciding disputes between unions. When the CIO was born, all restraints on the issuance of overlapping charters lapsed. The high cost of jurisdictional warfare was a major inducement to the merger of the AFL and the CIO in 1955. Because of the high cost of jurisdictional warfare to union treasuries, many unions have entered into "no-raiding" agreements under the auspices of the AFL-CIO. Thus a new form of jurisdictional rights based on established collective bargaining relationships seems to be taking shape from the merger of the AFL and CIO.

The Taft-Hartley law imposes several restrictions on the freedom of unions to fight it out over jurisdictional claims. The law differentiates two types of jurisdictional strikes: (1) strikes for recognition and (2) work assignment disputes. The strike for recognition involves the attempt of a union to establish an initial collective bargaining relationship with the employer. The work assignment dispute is an attempt by a union already having a collective bargaining relationship with the employer to assert its control over certain jobs.

Jurisdictional Strikes for Recognition. The Taft-Hartley law prohibits one union from calling a strike against an employer who is dealing with another union under an NLRB certification. It also prohibits a union from strike action against Employer A for the purpose of forcing Employer B to recognize or bargain with any union which has not been certified by the NLRB as the representative of the employees of Employer B.

The NLRB's interpretation of these provisions may be illustrated by three cases:

1. Employer A deals with Union A under an NLRB certification. Union B violates the law if it calls a strike of A's employees. Union B also violates the law if it pickets A's premises because this is an inducement to strike.
2. Employer A deals with union A and purchases materials from Employer B. Employer B is nonunion or deals with Union B which has been certified by the NLRB. Union A violates the law if it strikes Employer A for the purpose of forcing Employer B to deal with any union other than Union B. Union A also violates the law if it proposes to call off the strike on the condition that Employer A refuses to place further orders with Employer B.
3. The Meat Cutters' Union represents meat buyers in a number of markets. The union wants to organize the meat salesmen of Packer A. The union violates the law if it instructs its meat buyer members not to purchase Packer A's products.

Work-Assignment Disputes. Work-assignment disputes need not involve an employer's original refusal to recognize a union. After recognition has been achieved, two rival unions may both insist on the right of their members to perform a particular task. These disputes most frequently occur in industries like building construction, organized by craft unions. A classic example of this type of dispute is the disagreement between the carpenters and the concrete workers as to who should build the necessary wooden forms. The carpenters claimed the work because the forms were wood and constructed with carpenters' tools. The concrete workers insisted that the forms were incidental to concrete work and, therefore, were within their jurisdiction.

The Taft-Hartley law provides for ultimate NLRB determination of work-assignment disputes if the disputants fail to settle them by themselves. Section 8(b)(4) forbids a labor organization from engaging in or inducing strike action for the purpose of forcing any employer to assign particular work tasks "to employees in a particular labor organization or in a particular trade, craft, or class rather than to employees in another labor organization or in another trade, craft, or class, unless such employer is failing to conform to an order or certification of the Board determining the bargaining representative for employees performing such work."

The Board may not intervene in a work-assignment dispute until certain statutory requirements are fulfilled. Section 10(k) requires that the parties to a jurisdictional dispute be given 10 days, after notice of the filing of charges with the Board, to adjust their dispute. If at the end of that time they are unable to "submit to the Board satisfactory evidence that they have adjusted, or agreed upon methods for the voluntary adjustment of the dispute," the Board is empowered to hear and determine the dispute. Section 10(k) also provides that "upon compliance by the parties to the dispute with decision of the Board or upon such voluntary adjustment of the dispute," the charge shall be dismissed. A complaint issues only if there is a failure to comply with the Board's determination. Also, a complaint may be issued in a case of the failure of the method agreed upon to adjust the dispute.

Before the passage of the Taft-Hartley law, the American Federation of Labor had made several attempts to establish machinery for the adjustment of jurisdictional disputes within the "house of labor." At best, this machinery was able to survive only a short time.

The jurisdictional disputes provisions of the Taft-Hartley law were completely unacceptable to building trades unions. They motivated the formation of a National Joint Board of Adjustment in the Building Construction Industry. This Board is composed of equal numbers of labor and contractor representatives. Its major functions are the arbitration of local jurisdictional disputes and the negotiation of national jurisdictional agreements between unions in the construction industry. The chairman of the Board has a vote to break deadlocks, but has been extremely reluctant to use it. Instead he has used his influence as a mediator of disputes. Because of the reasonably successful operation of the Board, the NLRB has received only a very few construction-industry jurisdictional disputes for arbitration. It seems fair to say that the Taft-Hartley provisions have done a good job in forcing the building trades unions to settle their jurisdictional disputes without resort to extensive strike action.

Union Recognition through the NLRB

If an employer covered by the Landrum-Griffin Act refuses voluntary recognition of a union, and there is a question as to whether the union represents a majority of the employees in the unit, or if there is a dispute over the appropriateness of the unit, the matter can be settled by filing a representation petition with the Regional Office of the NLRB.

Filing a Representation Petition. A petition can be filed by an employee or group of employees or any person or union acting on behalf of a substantial number of employees. An employer who is presented by a union with a claim that it represents a majority of his employees, or with competing claims by two or more unions each seeking recognition, can file a petition to determine the question.

If a union is currently acting as bargaining representative, any employee or group of employees, or any person or union acting on their behalf, can file a petition asking that the current union be thrown out. This is called a "decertification" petition.

A representation petition contains: (1) description of the unit of employees in which an election is sought; (2) the approximate number of employees in the unit; and (3) the names of all unions that claim to represent the employees in the unit.

When a representation petition is filed at the Regional Office, a field examiner is assigned to get answers to determine the following questions of fact:

1. Are the employer's operations within NLRB jurisdictional standards?
2. Is the proposed unit appropriate for collective bargaining?
3. Is there a sufficient showing of employee interest?
4. Is the filing of the petition timely?

In answering these questions the field examiner applies the facts of the particular case to standards that have been established by the NLRB. For a discussion of NLRB jurisdictional standards and the coverage of federal industrial relations legislation see Chapter 5.

The Appropriate Unit for Collective Bargaining. The law requires an employer to bargain with the representatives of his employees. In some instances all of the employees in a plant will want the same union to represent them because their interests are essentially the same. In other cases, different employees in a manufacturing plant may have different interests. For example, the clerical employees in an enterprise may have interests in collective bargaining substantially different from those of production employees in the same plant. In those situations each group of employees, called a "unit" for collective bargaining purposes, is entitled to have a different union represent the unit in bargaining with the employer. Acting through its Regional Director, the NLRB determines which employees should be included in the appropriate unit for collective bargaining.

The Importance of the Unit to Workers, Management, and Unions. The bargaining unit is of considerable importance to employees, management, and the unions seeking representation rights. The wage concessions available to particular groups of employees can be influenced by the bargaining unit established. For example, a small group of skilled employees might be able to negotiate substantially larger wage concessions for themselves (at the expense of the larger less skilled group) in separate bargaining. Such a separate bargaining unit in a factory might be able to impose standard rates prevailing in less regular construction employment. This would not necessarily impose excessive costs on the employer, since he might be able to trim his wage concessions to the larger group of semiskilled (and perhaps nonunion) employees.

The employer may favor small bargaining units in the hope that he can play one unit off against the other and thereby minimize his costs. Or he may favor large units because he thereby avoids the hazards of union "whipsawing" and the costs of multiple agreements and negotiations. The employer may have a particular interest in excluding a few key jobs from the bargaining unit because he feels that such workers should be identified with management, e.g., the chef in a restaurant.

From the union viewpoint, the bargaining unit determination of the NLRB may have a decisive influence in deciding who (if anyone) wins representation rights. A craft union would almost certainly be doomed to failure in an election contest with an industrial union if the NLRB decided that the appropriate unit included all production and maintenance workers. The probable fate of an industrial union in a contest with a craft union over the representation of a small group of employees who had served a traditional apprenticeship is equally certain. Of course, union election units are also potentially subject to the gerrymandering game. The inclusion of groups of employees known to be antiunion in an appropriate unit would have an important influence on the outcome of the election, as for instance the lumping of office staff with manual employees.

Given these diverse interests, what criteria does the NLRB apply in carrying out its statutory obligation to determine the appropriate unit for collective bargaining? The Board is governed by limited statutory guidance and its own long experience in dealing with the unit question.

Statutory Limitations on the Appropriate Unit. The law directs the Board to establish the appropriate unit for collective bargaining "in order to assure to *employees* the fullest freedom in exercising the rights guaranteed by this Act." (Emphasis added.) Beyond this injunction that the *employees'* interest shall prevail over the interests of employers and unions, statutory law on the bargaining unit is sparse, dealing only with: (1) professional employees, (2) plant guards, (3) craft severance, and (4) extent of employee organization.

Section 9(b) of the Taft-Hartley law prohibits the NLRB from including professional employees in a bargaining unit with nonprofessional employees unless a majority of the professional employees vote for inclusion in such unit.

Individuals employed as guards to enforce rules against employees and other persons to protect property of the employer or to protect the safety of persons on the employer's premises may be included only in a unit composed exclusively of guards. No labor organization that admits nonguard employees to membership or is associated with a nonguard organization may be designated as a representative for a guard unit.

Section 9(b)(2) of the Taft-Hartley law governs "craft severance" cases. Aimed at restricting the Board's authority to include craft workers in an industrial unit, this section provides that the Board should not "decide that any craft unit is inappropriate . . . on the ground that a different unit has been established by a prior board determination, unless a majority of the employees in the proposed craft unit vote against separate representation."

The Board is also prohibited from giving controlling weight to the extent to which employees have organized in determining the appropriate unit. If during an organizing drive a union has enrolled in its membership production workers, craft workers, salesworkers, and office workers who have diverse interests, the NLRB is prohibited from ruling that a single unit is appropriate solely because workers in these different groups have all joined the same union.

Before leaving statutory limitations on the Board's authority to establish appropriate units, it should be recalled that certain workers are not "employees" under the law and are therefore excluded from appropriate units and the protection of the law. These excluded persons are supervisors, agricultural workers, and independent contractors.

The Board makes bargaining unit determinations in three types of situations: (1) It establishes new bargaining units when a representation issue arises for the first time; (2) It reconsiders the propriety of established units in "craft severance" cases; and (3) It establishes units for expedited elections in recognition and organizational picketing cases coming under Section 8(b)(7)(C) of the Landrum-Griffin Act. An adequate understanding of the complexity of the Board's problem in determining the appropriate unit can be acquired by a brief consideration of some of the criteria used by the Board in original unit cases and craft severance cases.

NLRB Criteria in Initial Unit Determinations. The Board customarily accepts units agreed to by unions and management, but it does not recognize such stipulations as establishing Board policy. Moreover, union-management agreements to exclude certain individuals from the unit have been set aside by the Board where it believed that the persons involved should properly be included in the unit.

In exercising its power to determine appropriate units, the Board strives to give meaning and practical effect to the actual day-to-day relationships among employees. This aim, the Board has stated, "is best served by giving controlling effect to the community of interest existing among employees." This "community of interest" criterion is certainly basic to any Board determination of the appropriate unit.

Besides the community of interest criterion, the Board has, in different cases, considered such criteria as: union organizational structure, management organizational structure, extent of union representation interest, methods of wage payment, and regularity of employment. Comment on the frequently used criteria of bargaining history, craft or departmental units, and multiemployer units may be helpful.

Bargaining history frequently is a major factor in the Board's considerations. The Board is primarily interested in the bargaining history of the employees directly involved in the petition, but the bargaining history of similar employees in the area or industry may be considered on occasion. In several cases the Board has listed as one factor militating against a single-plant unit the fact that such a unit did not conform in scope to the pattern of relationships for that type of business in the particular area.

The Board will establish craft or departmental units only when the petitioner can show that employees in the proposed unit are functionally distinct *and* that they can be represented effectively as a separate group.

The Board will not establish multiemployer units unless the employers have chosen to bargain jointly and have held themselves bound by the results of these joint negotiations. An employer may withdraw from multiemployer bargaining and thereby reestablish his employees in separate appropriate units. A single-employer unit will be deemed appropriate in such circumstances when the employer manifests an intention to withdraw from group bargaining and to pursue an individual course of action in his labor relations. The Board has found separate single-employer units appropriate where, following a breakdown in association-wide negotiations, individual employers: (1) abandoned group bargaining, (2) did not pay dues or assessments to the association—resulting in automatic termination of membership under the association's bylaws, and (3) indicated their desire to pursue an individual course of action by executing contracts on a single-employer basis.

Craft Severance Cases. Craft unions use the facilities of the Board in gaining recognition but often prefer the direct approach to the employer. When craft unions use the facilities of the Board, they usually are involved in craft severance cases. In these cases, the craft unions are asking the Board to upset an existing collective bargaining relationship between an employer and an industrial union. The Board's responsibility is to decide the issue in the best interests of the employees. In craft severance cases, the Board's problem is to decide which employees—all the employees or the craft employees—are benefited or hurt most by severance. The authors of the Taft-Hartley law sought to restrict the Board's authority to include craft workers in the industrial unit. Section 9(b)(2) stated that the Board should not "decide that any craft unit is inappropriate. . . on the ground that a different unit has been established by a prior Board determination, unless a majority of the employees in the proposed unit vote against separate representation." In the National Tube Company case,[2] the Board dismissed the petition of a group of steel industry brick-

---

[2] 76 NLRB 1999.

layers for separate representation. The Board reasoned that the only restriction imposed by the law was that a prior determination by the Board "may not be the sole ground upon which the Board may decide that a craft unit is inappropriate without an election."

In passing on petitions for either the establishment of craft units, or the severance of craft or craftlike groups from existing larger units, the Board applies the American Potash rules.[3] Under these rules: (1) A craft unit must be composed of true craft employees having "a kind and degree of skill which is normally acquired only by undergoing a substantial period of apprenticeship or comparable training; (2) A noncraft group seeking to be severed must be functionally distinct and must consist of employees who, "though lacking the hallmark of craft skill," are "identified with traditional trades or occupations distinct from that of other employees . . . which have by tradition and practice acquired craftlike characteristics"; and (3) A union which seeks to sever a craft or quasi-craft group from a broader existing unit must have traditionally devoted itself to serving the special interests of the type of employees involved.

Craft severance poses a knotty problem for the Board, for employees, employers, and unions. The Taft-Hartley provisions on craft severance reflected a congressional suspicion that the NLRB has displayed a pro-CIO bias in unit determination. There can be little doubt that many skilled workers believed that they could get better terms of employment if they were represented by craft unions instead of being swallowed up in industrial unions. Many employers were seriously concerned about the prospects of craft severance upsetting long-established and effective collective bargaining relationships. Craft severance was a threat to industrial unions, a promise of new hunting ground for craft unions, and a potential trump card for dissident factions within industrial unions.

Experience with craft severance has been significantly less unsettling than expected. American Potash rules restrict the number of severance cases likely to arise. Both industrial unions and employers dealing with them have given more attention to the problems of quasi-craft workers covered by industrial union agreements. Newly formed craft unions drawing their membership from dissident factions in established industrial unions have had tough sledding.[4]

---

[3] 107 NLRB 1418 (1954).

[4] An example of the problems confronting dissident factions was the 1958 experience in the automobile industry. Newly formed, independent craft unions petitioned for severance of certain skilled employees from individual plants of the General Motors Corporation. Over the years before the petition, the NLRB had established single-plant industrial units at GM. The NLRB dismissed the petition of the new unions on the grounds that individual-plant craft severances would disrupt long-established collective bargaining relationships. In making this decision, the Board disregarded the technicality that it had established plant units and based its decision on the reality of a corporate-wide bargaining unit which had been established by the practice of both the company and union. Simultaneously, the UAW changed its structure to give a greater voice to quasi-craft employees. Although a newly formed

Last but not least, where craft severance has occurred, it has not disrupted stable labor relations to the extent feared; and, generally speaking, it has not seriously harmed the welfare of production workers.[5]

After the NLRB field examiner has decided that the petition is within the jurisdiction of the NLRB and has made a tentative finding on the appropriate unit, he seeks to ascertain if a substantial number of employees want the union to represent them and if the petition is timely.

Sufficient Showing of Interest. This showing of interest is usually made by producing cards signed by employees authorizing the union to represent the signer-employee, or authorizing the petitioner to seek decertification. This evidence must be filed with the petition or submitted to the regional office investigator within 48 hours thereafter. Normally the petitioner must establish that at least 30 percent of the employees in the unit have designated the union as their representative.

If it is the employer who files the petition, the NLRB does not require this sort of a showing of interest. The Regional Director usually proceeds with the matter, provided one or more unions have made a demand on the employer for recognition. Such a demand need not be expressed in words but can be implied from union conduct.

Timeliness of the Petition. The law provides that no election can be conducted in any bargaining unit (or any subdivision of one) in which a valid election has been held during the preceding 12-month period. This provision of the act guarantees to both the employer and employees for this period of time stability in their relations and freedom from disruptions that attend an election.

To further insure stability of industrial relations, the NLRB has established what is called the "contract bar" doctrine. The contract bar doctrine states that a valid collective bargaining agreement between an employer and a union representing his employees will ordinarily prevent the holding of an election among the employees covered by the agreement. In general, the contract bar doctrine rules a petition untimely if it is filed during the term of an existing contract with a three-year maximum in the case of contracts that run for more than three years. Under the rules of the Board, a petition may be filed at least 60 days, but no more than 90 days, before the expiration of a contract. This filing period makes it possible to upset a contractual relationship at an appropriate time.

If the petition meets the Board's requirements on jurisdiction, the appropriate unit, a sufficient showing of interest, and timeliness, the Regional Director either issues a notice of formal hearing or approves a consent agreement made by the parties.

---

union probably could effectively organize on a plant-by-plant basis, such a union would have a hard time in a frontal assault on a corporate-wide unit.

[5] For a careful study of the empirical results of craft severance, see Dallas L. Jones, "Self-Determination vs. Stability in Labor Relations," 58 *Michigan Law Review* (January 1960), pp. 313–46.

Consent Election Agreements. A consent election agreement between the parties to a representation question includes: (*a*) a description of the appropriate unit; (*b*) the time and place of holding the election; and (*c*) a basis for determining who is eligible to vote. A consent election agreement, when approved by the Regional Director, eliminates the formal hearing prior to an election.

Formal Hearing on Representation. The representation case hearing is a formal proceeding. It aims to obtain information which the Regional Director needs in order to determine: (1) the appropriateness of the unit; (2) the adequacy of the showing of interest; (3) the timeliness of the petition; (4) the eligibility of employees to vote; and other pertinent matters. All parties who establish their interests are given full opportunity to produce facts to support their positions on the matters to be determined.

Following the hearing, the Regional Director determines the need for an election and the procedures to be followed if an election is directed. In some complex cases the record is furnished to the entire NLRB for consideration before ordering an election.

The Election. Section 9(c)(1) of the Taft-Hartley Act provides that if a question of representation exists, the NLRB must resolve it through an election by secret ballot. The elecion details are left to the Board. Many observers have cited Board-conducted elections as examples of the best operation of the democratic process. Before discussing the important, and frequently neglected, question of what an employer can do to influence the outcome of an election, it will be well to consider the election mechanics and the election environment.

Election Mechanics. The Board's rules on election mechanics are designed to encourage workers' participation in the election and to assure the integrity of the election process. The arrangements and voting procedure in all elections are the same, whether they are consent elections or elections directed by the Regional Director or the Board.

Under the *Excelsior Underwear* rule,[6] within seven days after the Regional Director has approved or ordered an elecion, the employer must supply the Board with a list of the names and addresses of all persons in the unit. The Board then gives this list to the union in order that both the union and the employer have equal access to persons eligible to vote in the election.

A regional office official will arrange for the posting of notices containing a sample ballot and information about the location of voting places, the timing of the voting, and eligibility rules. The actual voting is always conducted and supervised by Board agents. Secrecy in voting is assured. Either the Board agents or the authorized observers of the parties may challenge for reasonable cause any employee who applies for a ballot. To be entitled to vote, an employee must have worked in the voting unit

---

[6] 61 *LRRM* 1217–22.

during the eligibility period and on the date of the election. Challenged employees may mark ballots, but their ballots are not counted until the challenges have been resolved.

Section 702 of the Landrum-Griffin Act states, "Employees engaged in an economic strike who are not entitled to reinstatement shall be eligible to vote under such regulations as the Board shall find are consistent with the purposes and provisions of this Act in any election conducted within twelve months after the commencement of the strike." Generally the Board has ruled that an economic striker forfeits his right to vote under Section 702 when he obtains permanent employment elsewhere before the election.

Ordinarily the Board directs that elections be held within 30 days from the date of direction of the election. However, where an immediate election would occur at a time when there is not a representative number of employees in the voting unit—because of such circumstances as a seasonal fluctuation in employment or a change in operations—a different date will be selected in order to accommodate voting to the peak or normal working force.

Important as the mechanics of an election are, it is obvious that the outcome of an election can be influenced by improper electioneering, threats of violence, or other environmental influences.

The Election Environment.   The area of legitimate employer and union conduct during an election campaign is one of the most difficult problems confronting the NLRB. It seems obvious that an employer's opinion on the probable consequences if a union should win an election would not always be free of bias, but would carry great weight with his employees. This would be particularly true if his "opinion" was that widespread layoffs would result, or that he would be forced to close the plant permanently. The NLRB has the delicate task of protecting the employer's freedom of speech and at the same time protecting his employees from undue interference, restraint, or coercion that his speech might exert on them as they express their choice about union representation. Although Section 8(c) of the Taft-Hartley Act, commonly called the "free speech provision," has broadened management's freedom to try to influence the outcome of an NLRB election, management participation in the election process is still limited by law and NLRB rulings.

For more than 30 years, the NLRB has walked this tightrope. An example of two NLRB rules, both now abandoned, may help to illustrate the Board's problem. At one time the NLRB held that a "captive audience" (employees required to listen to the employer's autiunion statements during working hours) was a cause to set aside an NLRB election. At a later time the Board held that a captive audience was legitimate if the employer paid his employees for "equal time" while the union attempted to refute his speech.

Another recurring question is whether foremen or other supervisors exert undue influence on the outcome of an election when they talk about it to individual employees and groups of employees. The Board has consistently set aside elections where the employer resorted to the technique of calling upon all or a majority of the employees in the unit individually, in the employer's office or at their homes, to urge them to vote against a proposed bargaining representative, regardless of whether the employer's remarks to the employees were coercive in character.

Under present rules of the Board, an election will be set aside if it is accompanied by conduct which, in the Board's view, creates an atmosphere of confusion or fear of reprisals and thus interferes with the employees' free choice of a representative guaranteed by the act. In determining whether specific conduct amounts to such interference, the Board does not attempt to assess its actual effect on the employees but concerns itself with whether it is reasonable to conclude that the conduct tended to prevent a free expression of the employees' choice.

Electioneering is vigorously controlled by NLRB rules and the provisions of the law. Under the *Peerless Plywood* rule, the Board prohibits election speeches on company time to massed assemblies of employees within 24 hours before the scheduled time for conducting an election. Electioneering near the polling places during the election is also prohibited. All participants in an election are prohibited from using any document purporting to be a copy of the Board's official ballot, unless the document is completely unaltered in form and content.

The Board will not police and censure the parties' election propaganda except to prevent fraud or coercion. However, in the *Mosler Safe Co.* case, the Board ruled "when one of the parties deliberately misstates material facts which are within its special knowledge, under such circumstances that the other party or parties cannot learn about them in time to point out the misstatements, the Board will find that the bounds of legitimate campaign propaganda have been exceeded and will set aside an election."[7]

Although the Board tolerates intemperate, abusive, and inaccurate statements made by the union during attempts to organize employees, it does not interpret the act as giving either party license to injure the other intentionally by circulating defamatory or insulting material known to be false. In *Linn* v. *Plant Guards Local 114*, the U.S. Supreme Court ruled on February 21, 1966, that a Federal District Court has jurisdiction of a civil action for alleged libel instituted under state law by an official of an employer subject to the Federal Labor-Management Relations Act for defamatory statements published by a union during an organizing drive if the employer's official pleads and proves that the statements were made with malice and injured him.[8]

---

[7] 129 NLRB 747.
[8] 61 *LRRM* 2345–53.

Many an employer has felt abused in the course of establishing the collective bargaining relationship. Typically the employer finds himself in a surprised, passive, and defensive position when he is first confronted by a union demand for recognition and the processes of the NLRB. Instead of occupying his usual role of planner, decision maker, and allocator of the enterprise's resources, he frequently is swamped by the demands of "ungrateful" employees, the intrusion of "outsiders" who appear to threaten the future of the enterprise, and a governmental proceeding where the "shall nots" outnumber the "shalls" by 1,000 to 1. What can he do?

The Employer in the Rules for Establishing the Collective Bargaining Relationships. Although collective bargaining relationships have worked amazingly well in vast segments of the American economy, the typical employer undoubtedly would prefer to operate his business on a nonunion basis. Any manager who sought out a collective bargaining relationship would be considered a wild-eyed idealist by the most generous of his colleagues. How does an employer go about staying nonunion, defeating the union in an NLRB election, or getting rid of an unwanted union after it has been certified?

Unions lose about 40 percent of the NLRB elections held each year. This fact means that some employers *can* and *do* launch effective programs against unionization. There is no easy sure-fire formula to beat the union in an NLRB election, but several possibilities are open to an intelligent and aggressive management. A successful program could be built around the following steps:

1. Long before there is a union organization threat, do a good job of managing personnel. This would include:
   a) Good wages, hours, and working conditions.
   b) A *genuine* "open door" on grievances and perhaps a formal grievance procedure, the latter being particularly important in a large-scale enterprise.
   c) Economic education of employees, not in the abstract, but realistically, in the problems and prospects of the specific enterprise and its industry.
   d) Effective supervision of the labor force with a heavy emphasis on *fair* treatment of employees in disciplinary cases especially.
   e) Effective *upward* communication in the enterprise, with management really listening for employee grievances and suggestions.
2. When the union enters, vigorous campaigning against the union in the election.
   a) This campaigning has to be based on the *substance* of the enterprise being a good place to work, e.g., wages *are* good, the treatment of employees *is* fair, and, in fact, there is little that the employees can gain from unionization. The big hazard of a "hard

sell" on how good things are is that if the union wins, the items that management has sold them become the starting point of negotiations. In later negotiations, management cannot claim credit for what the employees had in the preunion period.

b) Publication of the fact that unionism may mean lost paydays due to strikes and that union membership costs money in terms of dues, assessments, and initiation fees.

c) Take advantage of any derogatory information about the union which has been revealed in investigations or publicity.

d) Emphasize the idea that the union is an outsider or third party that comes between the employees and the enterprise management.

e) Adopt and enforce a uniform rule against all solicitations during working hours and in work areas. Prohibit the distribution of union literature in work areas.

f) If union organizers can contact employees on public property near the plant, prohibit them from entering the company parking lot or the plant area.

3. Scrupulously *avoid* any actions that are contrary to law and would result in an invalidation of the election. A full list of the "dont's" would be very long indeed. The following items are examples only:

a) Don't threaten to close the plant if the union wins.

b) Don't raise wages or benefits prior to the election.

c) Don't promise to increase wages or benefits on condition of the union losing the election.

d) Don't reduce wages or benefits prior to the election.

Probably the most critical matter in the outcome of NLRB elections is timing. An election ordinarily will be held within about 30 days of the union's first filing with the NLRB. If the union's petition comes as a genuine surprise to the employer, and it frequently does, there really isn't much he can do about putting his house in order. In most cases, the employer has to stand or fall on the policies and practices he has used *before* the union makes a formal appearance.

Turning a union out after it has won an NLRB certification election is usually much harder than beating the union in its initial organizing drive. NLRB union decertification procedures will be discussed below.

Certification of Election Results.   Where a valid election has been held, the Regional Director or the Board will issue to the participants a certification of the results. If a union has been chosen by a majority of the employees in the unit, it will receive a certificate showing that it is the official bargaining representative of the employees in the unit. If a majority of the employees have voted that no union be designated as their bargaining representative, the certificate will so state. This certificate protects both the employer and the winning union from a trial by election for 12 months. If an agreement is negotiated, the agreement provides even larger protection under the NLRB's contract bar rules.

The foregoing is an enterprise view of the rules for establishing a collective bargaining relationship in the United States. It is now appropriate to make a few observations about the process from a national and public policy viewpoint.

THE NATIONAL EBB AND FLOW OF UNION RECOGNITION

As discussed above, union recognition may be won either by voluntary action of management or by an NLRB election. Union recognition is lost either through business mortality or an NLRB decertification election. The 35-year trend in industrial relations legislation is a steady upgrading of the importance of an NLRB election as the major method of obtaining union recognition.

Figure 6–1 summarizes the outcome of NLRB elections from 1936 through 1970. Several observations on the experience with NLRB elections are in order:

1. Consistently, workers have shown great interest in NLRB elections. Note that in every year but one over 80 percent of the workers eligible to vote in NLRB elections have chosen to exercise their right to vote.
2. Since 1955, between 350,000 and 590,000 workers have been eligible to vote in NLRB elections each year. NLRB election activity seems to have declined rather steadily since a high-water mark in the early 1940s.
3. Although union success in elections has been slipping since the mid-1950s, unions continue to poll about 60 percent of the valid votes cast each year. The percentage of votes cast for the unions would be the most accurate measure of the popularity of unions among workers where representation rights were sought. Note the close relationship between the numbers of votes cast for unions and the number of employees in units selecting a union as representative.
4. The number of employees in units selecting a union as agent is the most important figure for measuring the dynamics of union recognition. This figure shows how many additional workers come under the potential coverage of collective bargaining agreements each year. If a union wins an election by only one vote, it still wins the right to represent all workers in the unit. The number of workers in units selecting the union as a representative is the potential membership base won by the union.
5. Figure 6–1 shows that NLRB elections since 1955 have enabled unions to increase their potential coverage of collective bargaining agreements from less than 200,000 workers in the 1957–58 fiscal year to over 300,000 workers in 1965–70. Although unions could be encour-

FIGURE 6–1. Results of NLRB Representation Elections, 1936–65

Fiscal Year Ending	Number of Elections Held	Number of Employees Eligible to Vote	Percent of Eligible Employees Voting	Valid Votes Cast for Union Representation	Percent of Total Vote Cast for Union	Number of Employees in Units Selecting Union as Agent
6/30/36*	31	9,512	79.6	6,162	59.1	N.A.
6/30/37*	265	181,424	90.5	142,428	69.1	N.A.
6/30/38*	1,152	394,558	87.1	282,470	82.8	N.A.
6/30/39*	746	207,597	85.4	138,032	77.9	N.A.
6/30/40*	1,192	595,075	89.5	435,842	81.9	N.A.
6/30/41*	2,568	788,111	92.6	589,921	80.9	N.A.
6/30/42*	4,212	1,296,567	82.3	895,091	83.9	N.A.
6/30/43*	4,153	1,402,040	80.3	923,169	81.9	N.A.
6/30/44*	4,712	1,322,225	81.1	828,583	77.2	N.A.
6/30/45*	4,919	1,087,177	82.8	706,569	79.1	N.A.
6/30/46*	5,589	846,431	82.6	529,847	75.8	N.A.
6/30/47*	6,920	934,553	86.2	621,732	77.2	N.A.
6/30/48	3,222	384,565	86.8	256,935	77.0	N.A.
6/30/49	5,514	588,761	87.7	377,360	73.1	N.A.
6/30/50	5,619	890,374	87.8	649,432	83.1	753,598
6/30/51	6,432	666,556	88.2	442,066	75.2	505,322
6/30/52	6,765	771,346	86.6	503,143	75.3	584,030
6/30/53	6,050	737,998	86.7	497,286	77.7	584,450
6/30/54	4,663	511,430	87.9	314,701	70.0	343,092
6/30/55	4,215	515,995	87.9	335,393	74.0	378,962
6/30/56	4,946	462,712	89.6	268,531	64.8	291,292
6/30/57	4,729	458,904	89.5	261,762	63.7	264,920
6/30/58	4,337	351,217	89.8	190,558	60.4	196,334
6/30/59	5,428	430,023	89.7	247,867	64.2	257,028
6/30/60	6,380	483,964	90.2	280,140	64.1	286,048
6/30/61	6,354	450,930	89.4	239,693	59.4	229,283
6/30/62	7,355	536,047	89.8	299,547	62.1	305,976
6/30/63	6,871	489,365	90.3	264,727	59.9	265,747
6/30/64	7,309	538,019	90.4	281,483	57.9	286,897
6/30/65	7,576	531,971	90.3	300,144	62.5	325,698
6/30/66	8,103	582,212	90.1	305,891	51.0	334,998
6/30/67	7,882	611,006	88.0	332,950	54.5	349,406
6/30/68	7,618	550,610	89.5	205,642	57.8	276,499
6/30/69	7,700	570,990	90.0	273,157	52.0	287,557
6/30/70	7,773	588,214	82.1	296,637	50.1	307,104

* During some of the years before 1948, data were presented as a composite of election and payroll checks or cross checks by NLRB. After the passage of the Taft-Hartley Act in 1947, the NLRB was empowered to certify a union for collective bargaining only on the basis of an election. Source: *Annual Reports* of the NLRB.

aged by NLRB election trends since 1962, the 60s are a hollow shell of the period before 1955. Of course, any *actual* increase in collective bargaining agreement coverage would equal only this *potential* gain minus any losses due to business mortality, declines in employment in unionized firms, and the employment of firms where unions lost decertification elections.

Union recognition is lost either by business mortality or an NLRB decertification election. Indices of business mortality do not include information on whether or not the business was unionized.

The authors of the Taft-Hartley Act wanted to provide a means by which employees could rid themselves of unwanted unions. The method provided was the NLRB decertification election. Figure 6–2 summarizes the outcome of NLRB decertification elections since 1947. It should be noted that decertification elections have released fewer than 10,000 workers per year.

Since 1955, American unions have been substantially less successful in extending union recognition than they were in early periods. At least part of this decline can be attributed to the high level of unionization already achieved in many segments of the economy. At the same time, since 1955, unions have usually won the right to represent about 250,000 new employees through NLRB elections each year, while losing the right to represent fewer than 10,000 each year through decertification elections.

A number of important public policy questions on the rules for establishing the collective bargaining relationship are unresolved.

FIGURE 6–2. Results of NLRB Decertification Elections, 1947–65

Fiscal Year Ending	Number of Elections Held	Number of Employees Eligible to Vote	Percent of Eligible Employees Voting	Valid Votes Cast against Unions	Percent of Valid Votes Cast against Representation	Number of Employees in Units Choosing Decertification
/30/48	97	8,836	88.9	3,914	49.8	N.A.
/30/49	132	18,773	91.0	7,262	42.5	N.A.
/30/50	112	9,474	89.6	4,164	49.1	4,034
/30/51	93	6,111	87.5	2,954	55.2	3,429
/30/52	101	7,378	88.6	3,465	53.0	4,045
/30/53	141	9,945	90.0	4,389	49.1	5,076
/30/54	150	10,244	88.7	4,774	52.5	5,935
/30/55	157	13,002	90.0	5,936	50.2	5,524
/30/56	129	11,289	91.9	4,761	46.3	5,598
/30/57	145	11,018	92.9	5,516	54.3	6,888
/30/58	153	10,124	89.7	4,787	52.7	4,499
/30/59	216	16,231	90.3	6,984	47.7	7,705
/30/60	237	17,421	88.1	6,817	44.4	8,695
/30/61	241	18,364	90.4	6,570	45.6	10,607
/30/62	285	12,323	86.8	7,365	68.8	6,930
/30/63	225	13,256	87.9	5,208	53.3	8,033
/30/64	220	13,732	90.4	5,562	44.8	5,399
/30/65	200	12,565	88.9	4,618	41.3	4,718
/30/66	221	10,510	89.3	4,905	52.5	6,061
/30/67	234	12,705	87.6	4,744	42.6	4,997
/30/68	239	15,554	88.6	4,628	33.6	4,804
/30/69	293	21,771	86.5	8,316	43.8	9,349
/30/70	301	20,344	88.3	8,025	44.6	8,558

Source: *Annual Reports* of the NLRB.

UNRESOLVED PROBLEMS IN PUBLIC POLICY ON UNION RECOGNITION

By now it should be clear that in the United States the government sets the terms of union recognition. It does so by defining the bargaining unit and conducting elections. Although the role of government is firmly established, several unresolved problems remain to plague the Congress, the NLRB, and the courts. The solutions developed to these problems may well have an important long-range effect on the structure of collective bargaining in America. Four major problems deserve attention: (1) employees excluded from NLRB jurisdiction; (2) the peculiar problems of union recognition in industries characterized by casual and intermittent employment; (3) free speech; and (4) the sometimes conflicting objectives of self-determination, stability, and effectiveness in union recognition.

Employees Excluded from the Protection of the Law

In aggregate, a very large number of American workers are excluded from the law's protection of the right to union representation. The largest single group of workers excluded are agricultural employees. Also excluded are the employees of small interstate and all intrastate enterprises, hospital employees and persons in supervisory positions.

It is possible that some of the employees excluded from the protection of the law are the object of deep-seated political pressures which are unlikely to yield. In the case of governmental employment, the systems of union recognition are, of necessity, grafted on established procedures for protecting the employees' interests. In the case of small employers, the administrative costs of extending the protection of the law seem to be greater than the benefits which society would gain.

Government Employees. On January 17, 1962, President Kennedy issued Executive Order 10988, Employee-Management Co-operation in the Federal Service. This order extended to some 2 million employees of the executive branch of the government a unique form of the right to union representation.[9] President Nixon reaffirmed its principles in Executive Order 11491 in 1969. The problems of government unions are considered in Chapters 15 and 16, Part IV of this book.

Organizations seeking to represent governmental employees must: (1) disavow the right to strike against the government, (2) not advocate the overthrow of the government, (3) not discriminate with regard to the terms or conditions of membership because of race, color, creed, or national origin, and (4) be free of corrupt or undemocratic influences which

---

[9] U.S. Department of Labor, Bureau of Labor Statistics, *Directory of National and International Labor Unions in the United States, 1965*, Bulletin No. 1493, p. 55.

are inconsistent with the purposes of the order. When an employee organization has been recognized as the exclusive representative of employees, it shall be entitled to negotiate agreements covering all employees in the unit and shall be responsible for representing the interests of all employees in the unit without discrimination and without regard to employee organization membership.

Union recognition under Executive Order 11491 is required to be consistent with the standards of the Civil Service Commission, the rights of veterans, and the rights available to an individual governmental employee in the absence of union recognition. Heads of agencies are empowered to deny union recognition where they decide that this order cannot be applied in a manner consistent with national security requirements and considerations.

Agriculture, Hospitals, Small Firms. It is probably fair to say that agricultural workers and the employees of hospitals and very small firms usually work under employment conditions less advantageous than those found in most unionized industries. On a humanitarian basis, it might be argued that these employees *need* union representation more than other employees.

It might be argued that hospital employees should be asked to renounce the right to strike, as is required of governmental employees. Obviously, the health and safety of a community depends on the continuous operation of hospitals. On the other hand, hospital employees certainly have interests *as employees* which should be heard.

The exclusion of small employers, hospitals, and agricultural employees from the basic law of union recognition usually is justified on the basis of protecting employers who could not remain in business if they had to meet the demands of unions. The authors of this text, nevertheless, wholeheartedly agree with the recommendations of a distinguished independent study group,[10] working under the auspices of the Committee for Economic Development, that the self-determination principle should be extended to cover hospital, farm, and small firm employees.

One of the problems in drawing up agricultural labor legislation comes from the intermittent and casual nature of employment. This problem also arises in certain other industries.

Casual and Intermittent Employment and Union Recognition. From its very beginning, the NLRB has tried to establish fair rules for getting and keeping union recognition in industries characterized by casual and intermittent employment. The Taft-Hartley ban on union hiring halls and the closed shop aggravated the Board's problems. The Landrum-

---

[10] Clark Kerr, Chairman; Douglas V. Brown, David L. Cole, John T. Dunlop, William T. Elliott, Albert Rees, Robert M. Solow, Philip Taft, George W. Taylor, Members; George P. Shultz, Staff Director, and Abraham Siegel, Associate Staff Director. See *The Public Interest in National Labor Policy* (New York: Committee for Economic Development, 1961), pp. 74–79, 84–85.

Griffin law cleared the air a little by permitting prehire contracts in the building construction industry.

As a minimum, the authors of this book believe that the Landrum-Griffin prehire and seven-day union shop permission should be extended to all industries characterized by intermittent and casual employment. Given the extensive protection of the right to membership in unions which is guaranteed by Landrum-Griffin, it is most likely that the best solution to the problem of all industries characterized by casual and intermittent employment would be any hiring hall, closed shop, or other arrangement which employers and unions in those industries worked out together.

Free Speech.   The problem of guaranteed free speech at the same time that employees are protected from interference, restraint, and coercion has occupied the NLRB, the Congress, and students of labor relations for over 30 years.[11] Any policy on free speech influences the outcome of elections and the prevalence of collective bargaining in society. Individual congressmen and members of the NLRB have deep convictions about both free speech and the desirability of extending collective bargaining. Changes in policy probably reflect changes in the composition of Congress and the Board.

We believe that most of the argument about free speech can be summarized in the commonplace statement: "It's not only *what* you say, but *how* you say it." Such an interpretation requires that actions be considered in their frequently complex context. The context of election statements varies between regions of the country, the histories of particular enterprises, and the education and attitudes of particular groups of employees.

Free speech is an emotion-laden issue in public policy on labor relations. It probably will remain as an unresolved problem in public policy. This is as much a tribute to the institutions of freedom as it is a source of continued frustration to the parties to collective bargaining and to men of goodwill who are charged with the responsibility for maintaining an environment consistent with a fair election process.

Most of the remaining unresolved problems in public policy on union recognition have to do with the relative weight to be given to three sometimes conflicting objectives of labor policy: self-determination, stability, and effectiveness of representation.

The Objective of Self-Determination, Stability, and Effectiveness

Probably the cornerstone of American public policy on union recognition is *self-determination* by employees (and, to a lesser degree, by em-

---

[11] For a definitive statement of the history of this problem and observations on the propriety of various NLRB rulings, see Benjamin Aaron, "Employer Free Speech: The Search for a Policy," chap. 2 of Joseph Shister, Benjamin Aaron, and Clyde W. Summers (eds.), *Public Policy and Collective Bargaining* (New York: Harper & Row, 1962), pp. 28–59.

ployers) of the method of union recognition. Employees are given the right to vote on what union, if any, will represent them. NLRB unit determination policy on multiemployer bargaining protects the right of individual employers to decide whether they wish to go it alone or be represented by an association. Decertification elections protect the right of employees to "run the rascals out" when they wish to reject a union which they had previously embraced. Craft severance and professional employee elections preserve the right of self-determination for particular groups of employees.

The objective of self-determination sometimes runs afoul of the objective of *stability* in labor relations. NLRB contract bar rules, the statutory 12-month limitation on elections, and NLRB criteria for craft severance are outgrowths of a desire for stability in labor relations. It is obvious that subjecting employees and employers to an election every time a dissident group could muster a following would spell chaos for the employment relationship. At the same time a 12-month ban on elections may deprive employees of the right to representation on a permanent basis. Occasionally unions have lost NLRB elections by a very small margin and have been unable to maintain a semblance of organization for 12 months after the election. The contract bar rules of the NLRB occasionally have enabled an unrepresentative union to maintain its position in a collective bargaining relationship.

The fundamental purpose of national labor policy is to minimize obstructions to the flow of commerce. This would imply an objective of *effectiveness* in labor-management relations. Effectiveness in employee and employer representation might very well dictate a substantial reduction in the freedom of self-determination granted to the parties. For example, one powerful corporate-wide union probably would be most effective in dealing with management, regardless of how poorly it treated the interests of skilled workers or professional employees. It is not altogether certain that management would find such an arrangement distasteful. In a similar vein, in highly competitive industries with many small employers, effectiveness in collective bargaining might be achieved by governmental policing of the membership of an employers' association. There have been numerous cases where both an employer association and the union(s) representing workers in the industry would welcome government support in keeping wayward employers in line. As a final example, few objective observers would argue that archaic lines of jurisdiction over work in the railroads, airlines, and building trades foster efficiency in representation.

The basic problem in union recognition is a delicate balancing of the interests of employees and employers in the pursuit of the objectives of self-determination, stability, and effectiveness in labor relations. Unfortunately, neither society nor the parties can have all their cakes and eat them, too.

QUESTIONS FOR DISCUSSION

1. "Ballot box organizing" is unique to the North American continent. Does ballot box organizing fulfill any particular needs of a politically democratic private enterprise society? Does it pose any challenges to free institutions? What might be substituted for ballot box organizing?

2. The Landrum-Griffin Act permitted the NLRB to delegate more authority to its Regional Directors for the handling of representational issues. Do you think it would be a good idea to give the Regional Directors authority to rule on unfair labor practice charges? Justify your position.

3. Since employers have a real interest in the determination of bargaining units, is it fair to make the interests of employees the controlling factor? By the same token, why is the employer's interest considered to be controlling in multiemployer units?

4. "Employers and the general public are always the innocent victims in jurisdictional strikes." Discuss.

5. Attack or defend the proposal that the closed shop be authorized by law.

6. The text recognizes several unresolved problems in public policy on union recognition. What are these problems? How would you resolve them? Why?

SELECTED ANNOTATED BIBLIOGRAPHY

Collective Bargaining Today. Proceedings of the Collective Bargaining Forum, 1969; sponsored by the Institute of Collective Bargaining and Group Relations. Washington, D.C.: The Bureau of National Affairs, Inc., 1970.

The first set of proceedings from a newly founded institute gives a panorama of views by prominent management and labor officials as to their current objectives in collective bargaining. These proceedings are to be published annually and will provide a continuing up-to-date compilation of attitudes toward collective bargaining by those actually practicing it.

HEALY, JAMES J. (ed.). *Creative Collective Bargaining: Meeting Today's Challenge to Labor Management Relations.* Englewood Cliffs, N.J.: Prentice Hall, 1965.

The book contains eleven case studies of collective bargaining situations which are felt to illustrate fresh and creative approaches to bargaining. Each of the studies was completed by a graduate student of the Harvard Business School.

MYERS, M. SCOTT. "Overcoming Union Opposition to Job Enrichment," *Harvard Business Review* (May–June 1971), pp. 37–49.

A leading exponent of the behavioral approach to labor relations looks at cases where the union has been induced to cooperate rather than fight improvements in job design.

NORTHRUP, HERBERT R., and YOUNG, HARVEY A. "The Causes of Industrial Peace Revisited," *Industrial and Labor Relations Review.* Vol. XXII (October 1968), pp. 31–47.

In the wake of post-World War II strike activity the National Planning

Association did a series of case studies of peaceful relations to isolate its causes. Those cases are looked at again in the context of the affluent society of today and the original conclusion is reassessed.

WEBER, ARNOLD (ed.). *The Structure of Collective Bargaining*. New York: The Free Press of Glencoe, 1961.

A collection of essays dealing with the question of the size, scope, shape, and interrelationships of bargaining units. The essays are subdivided into four parts: theory, union and management interests, industry case studies, and finally questions of public policy.

Chapter	THE PROBLEM OF
7	REACHING AGREEMENT

Once the collective bargaining relationship is established, the actors must bargain out a collective bargaining agreement and live with it. This chapter deals with the problems and procedures involved in reaching agreement. Chapter 8 explores the nature of the labor agreement, and Chapter 9 discusses the problems of living with whatever agreement the parties reach. Although the end result of negotiations is largely economic in nature, the activities involved in reaching agreement have many political overtones and may be compared to the practice of international diplomacy on a small scale.

Those who own property or legally control it have one-sided authority to dispose of their property as they see fit and to set the conditions under which others may use it. Without collective bargaining, management unilaterally sets the "wages, hours, working conditions, and other conditions of employment" of those who work in and for the enterprise. They may do this without consulting anyone, including those who work for them, so long as they do not violate any specific laws such as, for instance, the minimum wage law.

When a union wins an NLRB election and certification the situation changes significantly. In theory, a manager still possesses unilateral rights to set the conditions of employment. In practice the certification of a union alters power relationships. The manager still determines policy and administers it at his own discretion *unless the union persuades him to do otherwise.*

The law requires an employer to recognize and bargain "in good faith" with a certified union, but it does not force him to agree with the union. He is free to yield to the union's persuasions, but he does not have to be persuaded; providing, always, that he has given the union an opportunity —in good faith—to persuade him.[1]

The union's task is to persuade the employer to accept policies and

---

[1] Case No. 1 deals with some of the legal and policy implications of the obligation to bargain in good faith.

administrative procedures the union wants. If the union's attempt succeeds and the two parties reach agreement, then the law requires that, at the request of either party, they must reduce their agreement to writing. The universal practice is to put the agreement in writing.

This written document, signed by the employer or his agent and by the union representatives, is commonly referred to as a "contract," but in many ways it more closely resembles a treaty between two sovereign powers, the company and the union. It sets the conditions under which the employer offers each individual worker in his employ (that is, within the bargaining unit) a work contract; and it binds him to abide by these conditions. The labor agreement becomes, in effect, company policy, just as a treaty between nations becomes national policy to which the signatory is bound.

Treaties are usually negotiated peacefully by persuasion and diplomacy. The vast majority of collective bargaining agreements are worked out by peaceful labor-management diplomacy with no resort to force. Occasionally, however, an agreement can be reached only by resort to force. To paraphrase Karl von Clausewitz on war, strikes may be considered a continuation of diplomacy (negotiations) *by other means*. Negotiations may temporarily break off during a strike, but a strike cannot be settled without negotiations. Although the threat of strike invariably surrounds negotiations, it is well to consider negotiations first and then to consider the strike.

Various models from the social sciences have suggested themselves to scholars who have studied labor negotiations as a phenomenon of organizational behavior in an attempt to formulate theory. Economics offers the concept of supply and demand; and there are, indeed, economic issues at stake in labor-management negotiations. Ideas drawn from economic principles would seem to apply most clearly to craft union bargaining. The ideas and analogies that seem to be most applicable to industrial union bargaining come from political science.

Recently attempts have been made to apply game theory, cost-benefit analysis, and highly sophisticated models from the behavioral sciences to labor negotiations.[2] Studies of this sort are bound to enrich understanding of the dynamics of labor-management interaction at the bargaining table, but to go deeply into theory at this point would be a needless digression. The discussion that follows here looks upon collective bargaining as in the broadest sense a political form of activity with, amongst others, economic ends in view.

---

[2] See, for example, Richard E. Walton and Robert B. McKersie, *A Behavioral Theory of Labor Negotiations* (New York: McGraw-Hill Book Co., 1965). The authors put forth four models of bargaining behavior: distributive, integrative, attitudinal structuring and intraorganizational. For a more traditional approach see Carl M. Stevens, *Strategy and Collective Bargaining Negotiations* (New York: McGraw-Hill Book Co., 1963).

NEGOTIATIONS: LABOR-MANAGEMENT "DIPLOMACY"

Today most labor-management negotiations are concerned with the revision of *existing* collective bargaining agreements which regularly expire at intervals usually ranging from one to three years. An *initial* collective bargaining agreement between an employer and a union poses somewhat different substantive problems, but the procedures for either renewing an existing agreement or negotiating the initial agreement are essentially the same.

The People Who Do the Bargaining

Preceding chapters have explored the various combinations of separate, and usually opposing, interests present in negotiations. But negotiating is an activity, carried out by people who meet at a definite point in time and space. These people stand in definite organizational relationships to the interests they represent, and perform definite functions. They come from the ranks of unions, enterprises, and, sometimes, from the government.

The Union Negotiating Committee. There is no set rule about who is to negotiate with the company for the union.

It may be the committee that drew up the demands and saw them through to ratification. It may be a standing committee, such as the union's executive board, or, at the other extreme, a committee elected specially, and at large from the whole membership, expressly for the occasion. It almost always includes, in any case, certain ex officio members such as the president, one or more vice presidents, the secretary, the chief steward. If the local has a business agent, he (or she) will certainly accompany the negotiators.

Also accompanying the negotiators in most cases will be someone who is not a member of the local union: the international representative.

The International Representative. On the union side in negotiations sits an "outsider," the international representative. Of all the participants, often he is the only one who does not make his living by working for the company. He does not work for the local union either, as a paid officer or business agent does, but only in its behalf. He is answerable to the executive board of the international union.

Status of the International Representative. He is there in negotiations by request of the local union, to guide and counsel; usually, in fact, to act as spokesman, strategist, and tactician for the union side. The company cannot keep him out, despite his outsider status, for the law permits workers to be represented by "agents of their own choosing."

He is a professional negotiator, perhaps the only professional in a group whose business, and respective positions, require that they engage in collective bargaining, but only so rarely, and so incidentally to their other concerns, that in comparison they are amateurs. They meet each other to make these solemn agreements no more often than once a year; he engages in like activity, with other groups as well as this, day after day. For everyone else present, the outcome of negotiations will be felt as dollars-and-cents additions to income, or added production costs; he loses not a cent nor, for that matter, stands to gain a penny by what transpires, though if he is successful it will be a feather in his cap.

He may have entered the negotiations only when he stepped in the door of the conference room, but more likely he had been working with the local through all the stages or at least the later stages of preparations. The chances are he shared in shaping the demands and putting them in draft-agreement form, and it was through him that the research department of the international channeled information to aid in the negotiations.

Role of the International Representative. This outsider to the group that meets for negotiations is, in a sense, the only full-time "insider" to the collective bargaining process: it is his life and living. He has no authority except the prestige of his position, but he is the key man in negotiations, the professional who really makes collective bargaining work and keeps it going. As will be seen, he is also the key man in strikes. In single-employer bargaining (which accounts for most of industrial unionism) he has no regular counterpart on the employer side. In most negotiations he is the one who calls the signals and sets the tone.

During the discussions with the company he gives tactical leadership to the union committee. His role varies with the circumstances, his own talents and personality. Sometimes he spearheads the attack on the company, perhaps with the aim—and frequently with the effect—of making the local's committee of company employees look reasonable and moderate to their employer, so that the company will offer them concessions to keep them from following his extremes. Or, with a militant committee, it is he who may seem moderate, receptive to "reasonable" offers of concessions, which he implies he will use his influence to try to "sell" the committee in the recess that he then calls.

He may be a vain and stubborn fellow, or smart or stupid, or sly or sincere—actually; or he may only appear so. Often he has to be an actor, playing a role. Only when he has had a number of encounters with a given management, gotten to know them and be known, can he drop into a consistent natural pattern of behavior with them. He will usually then be found a shrewd and sensible fellow with a good deal of personal integrity, who prides himself—for it is a professional asset—on being a man of his word. Sometimes he becomes almost a mediator between company and union, who soothes ruffled feelings, saves people's faces, and harmlessly grounds dangerous emotional charges that have built up in a labor relations situation. Sometimes he serves the useful function of the scapegoat, who assumes the "sins" of the community—both sides—and carries them away with him, to leave the local people cleansed and reconciled for the next period of the life they have to live together.

There are negotiations in which not one but two or several outside representatives participate, either alternately or together. One may deliberately build up tension, concentrating company hostility on himself so that a colleague, blandly smiling, can walk in and, in the ensuing relief and atmosphere of cordiality, reach the settlement.

The Employer Representatives. Union agreements set or affect company policy. A line executive responsible for policy—president, vice president for industrial relations, or at the very least a works manager—sits in directly on this policy-making process, or designates someone with authority to act for him.

Single-Employer Bargaining. In any single-company negotiations, then, the delegation of authority is a simple matter. The person exercising this authority and speaking for the company is usually a production man and line executive, but he has staff advisers such as the personnel director, and perhaps a public relations expert, and a company lawyer. Of all these, the lawyer has least to contribute, in most cases, to the progress of negotiations.

In contrast to the union representatives, the negotiators for the employer are usually armed with full authority to conclude an agreement, though in some cases the Board of Directors may have to ratify results. There is a simple reason for this: in the company, authority flows downward; in the union, upward. At the policy-making level where negotiations take place, authority is already concentrated on the company side, while in the union there has to be a specific act of delegation, and the delegation is not complete but only provisional and temporary.

Multiemployer Bargaining. Multiemployer bargaining, as has been noted, is more common in the trades, with craft unions, than in manufacturing. There are some notable exceptions—perhaps enough to constitute another rule, and not just exceptions.

In the garment industries, for instance, employer associations bargain as a group both with the Amalgamated Clothing Workers and with the International Ladies' Garment Workers' Union. These two well-known and well-organized industrial unions are the composite modern form of older separate craft unions. Some of these crafts were once truly skilled —cutters, for instance, who are direct descendants of custom tailors— while others formed satellite unions of the unskilled—"floor boys," for example—and of the semiskilled, as new machines created specialties. This is a situation comparable in some ways to the construction unions where skilled men and their unskilled satellites form a complex of closely related unions under the Building Trades Council. The garment workers did not stay separate; they fused; and now they act together just as if they were a single union, though they are still enrolled in locals based on craft and occupation, not on workplace.

Garment-industry employers, faced with the problem of dealing with the huge, fused union, followed the lead of other similar employers throughout history and organized. The producing units of their industry are small and many; together in an association they are somewhat like a counterpart of the union with which they deal. Member firms promise to abide by bargains the association makes with the union.

The small size of the enterprises seems to be a factor in bringing employers together, but an equally compelling one seems to be competition; competition in both the product market and the labor market. Labor costs are so high a percentage of total costs that once the bulk of the industry was unionized the organized firms found themselves sharing the union's own interest in fighting cutthroat nonunion competition based on lower wages. In this, again, they are like the building trades. They are also like highway transportation, for the pattern already clear in the garment industries appears to be spreading to the trucking industry which is also an area of small firms and a big union.

The Employer Association Representative. This kind of multiemployer bargaining—of "employer unionization"—has brought forth a type of man who may fairly be called the equivalent of the international representative. That is the labor relations adviser and negotiator on the employer side. He is not universally present in multiemployer bargaining, for many associations speak through respected senior member-firm executives; but the neutral expert is coming to the fore.

His title is likely to be executive secretary or labor relations director of the association. His duties are analogous to those of an international representative, and so is his function in negotiations. He organizes—gets firms to join the association. He helps draw up employer counterproposals to union demands. He directs or arranges for research to back up the proposals. He negotiates. He also inspects the member firms' administration of the agreement, helps take care of grievances and arbitration, and polices the rules of the association. Wherever he is active, he, like the international representative, is the key man.

(This is a field, incidentally, where the college graduate enamored of the labor relations "game" may find it possible to break in. The unions bring their representatives up from the ranks, while even in a medium-sized corporation it is a long way up from management trainee to industrial relations director. But the employer association often has room for a man from the outside who has had experience or training in labor relations work. Being from the outside is, in fact, an advantage. The future may see more professionals, on both sides of collective bargaining, as this trend continues. Even the unions may have to turn to the colleges for representatives as the employers "wise up" and as the union old-timers die off.)

The Government Representative. As long as labor and management obey the law, the government regards collective bargaining between them as a private matter.

But it is not a matter of indifference to the government, nor to the public which government represents, particularly if a strike seems in prospect. In order, therefore, to assist the bargainers reach constructive results that are satisfactory to both, and compatible with the public interest, the government provides—*on a strictly voluntary basis*—the services of its Mediation and Conciliation Service.

The Mediator in Negotiations. The interchangeable terms "conciliator" and "mediator"—not to be confused with *arbiter* or *arbitrator*—apply to anyone who seeks to bring labor and management to agreement in a dispute; but the field is passing to the professional. In some disputes a mayor or other public official, or even on occasion a presidentially appointed board, may step in with an offer of good offices. More likely, though, it will be an obscure and not overpaid civil servant, a state or federal employee, who makes a career of mediating and conciliating in labor disputes. He comes at the call of either party, or even at his own initiative, but he can do little without the consent of both parties, who must at least agree to talk to him. His job is to help them find a way out of their impasse.

As with negotiation itself, there are no set rules for conciliation and mediation. Much depends on circumstances, and the personalities involved, including the personality of the mediator. Wisest procedure usually seems to be for him to meet with each side separately before attempting to get them both together. In that way he hears the uninhibited viewpoint of both sides, and gets a grasp of the problem.

The Mediator's Methods. The mediator listens. He is neutral, and he can sympathize impartially with each disputant in turn as he hears the story of the iniquity and unreasonableness of the other. This allows him to size up the people, who are part of his problem, as well as the facts, and it undoubtedly has cathartic and therapeutic value for the complainants, who are often pretty well fed up with each other by the time the mediator arrives. He acts as a lightning rod for charges of mutual hostility between them.

He has more to offer than emotional release, however, for like the "rep" he has had varied experience, and is a pro. He can suggest ways out of what appear dead ends to the negotiators, because he has seen these ways work in analogous situations before. He had no emotional "blocks" that blind him, as the participants are sometimes blind to unconsidered possibilities. He talks the language of either side, and both. He can help both "save face" when they have gotten into untenable positions.

Frequently it is he who finds the magic formula that will resolve the dispute. If he is skillful he will bring both sides around, unconsciously, to thinking it was their idea. Successful mediation can avert a strike or settle a strike when one has broken out, for mediation can occur at any stage. If the strike settlement happens to coincide with the formula the mediator suggested to avert a strike, he never says "I told you so." As smoke comes out of the factory smokestacks again and workers troop through the gates to start drawing paychecks once more, he packs his battered briefcase and smilingly bids goodbye. There is a telegram in his pocket, probably, calling him on to another situation in which a company and local union are at loggerheads.

Good mediators, like union "reps" come from all kinds of varied backgrounds. Personal qualities count for more than formal qualifications. Some of the best are former union officials. Mediation is a form of government service open to college-trained men or women with a consuming interest, as well as background, in active labor relations work; but it is not for the person who has his mind made up in advance about labor's rights, or management's prerogatives. It is not for the show-off or know-it-all.

Skillful, patient mediation can do a lot toward preventing strikes, or settling strikes amicably once they have broken out.

PREPARATION FOR NEGOTIATIONS

The men (and women) who carry on labor-management negotiations shoulder a heavy responsibility. Their work sets policy. Its results are bound to affect the welfare, the earnings, the chances for promotion, the security, the job satisfaction of every member of the union, every employee of the company in the bargaining unit (and some outside it) for the next year, or two years, or even three or five. Equally affected are company profits, productivity, and competitive position, as well as prices and production available to the public.

Negotiating the agreement is the very heart of collective bargaining. Proper discharge of the responsibilities it lays upon the bargainers calls for preparation.

The Union Initiative

Unions prepare more or less carefully for negotiations. Big national negotiations, such as those between the United Auto Workers and General Motors, have repercussions throughout the national economy and are carefully prepared for a year or more in advance, with full attention to public relations as well as to keeping the members informed. Many smaller local unions make little or no preparation other than to draw up demands.

Preparation for negotiations involves: (1) drawing up demands or formulating what the members want; (2) assembling information to support the demands; and (3) publicizing and explaining the demands. This last point usually means merely informing the members, and the workers in the plant, but often requires spreading the information to the public in the community at large.

Drawing up Demands. The union ordinarily initiates negotiations. To the union member the most important thing is what he, personally, will get out of the agreement. Sometimes he knows exactly what he wants. At other times he knows only that he wants "more" than he has, but does not recognize it in concrete form until his union leaders formulate and explain it to him.

If he has had "nothing"—that is, if he has not worked under a union agreement before—then he wants what workers in other shops and unions have already secured: such things as seniority, grievance procedure, a raise in wages, vacations with pay, and the like. If he is already working under a union agreement granting concessions of this sort, he wants more of the same.

"New" Demands. Sometimes union demands appear to be new, but almost invariably they turn out, upon examination, to be merely novel forms and extensions of older ideas. The 1955 demand for a "guaranteed annual wage" worked out in practice, in the "S.U.B." plan of Supplementary Unemployment Benefits, as no more than a strengthening of the existing seniority system with increased pay (from private funds, to supplement public funds) for laid-off workers. The aim of the plan was to satisfy the worker's age-old demand for individual job security. Its proponents also hoped that it would promote steadier employment and cushion the impact of automation. The 1958 demand for profit sharing aimed at least in part to increase worker income by a supplement to wages. This is akin to many bonus schemes that preceded it. Ironically enough, the idea of giving workers a share in profits is one that had often been advanced by management as an antidote to unionism!

A new demand once raised and won by a union in one enterprise, or the enterprises of one industry, gets copied by other unions trying to follow the leader—or outdo him. Thus after the auto workers pioneered the S.U.B. plan the steelworkers took it up and secured even greater concessions based on the same idea. In neither case was the actual program a spontaneous creation that welled up, fully formed, out of the minds of the workers in the shops. In both cases, sophisticated professional labor leaders formulated proposals that appealed to the members' formless and inarticulate yearnings: the human desire to be secure in what one has, and to have a little more.

Spread of a Pattern. The leaders exercise their foresight and inventiveness to devise plans and formulate demands that the members will recognize as corresponding to their needs. Political, and even personal, interunion rivalries spread first worker, and then company, acceptance of those demands that do successfully evoke worker response and support. The most recently organized local union therefore tends to adopt for its program of demands the schedule of gains registered, step by step, by others organized before it, just as a newly built factory gets the benefit of the latest technological progress.

There is no doubt that some union programs (S.U.B., for example) exert a far-reaching influence on the economy that may affect society in permanent and important ways, for good or ill. If he thinks about this at all, the worker and rank-and-file union member tends to minimize the question. This is only human, and on the order of the well-known fact that a flood in China drowning a whole province is a disaster that does not hit home quite as hard as a leaky pipe that floods a man's own basement. In asking for a raise, the worker undoubtedly likes to have his mind set at ease that he is not sending the national economy into an inflationary spiral—and his union leaders gladly oblige with the necessary assurance—but the question of whether he will get a raise in his next pay envelope is of more immediate interest to the worker. He tends to ignore the possible economic and social effects of an accumulation of separate union demands shaped to the same plan; he pays attention chiefly to the special effects that flow from his own local's direct action.

Restraints on the Demands. Perhaps, in the back of his mind, he looks to the company to keep the situation from getting out of hand, just as he relies on the company to secure orders, maintain production, and pay wages. He regards the pressing of demands as a test of strength, and a necessary one, for it does not seem likely that he will get what he does not ask for, whereas he feels sure that the company will not give him more than it can truly afford. He is embarked, he feels, with management, on an enterprise making its way upon the vast and sometimes stormy economic sea. He does not want his own ship to sink under him or strike a rock, but he is convinced that the men on the bridge want that no more than he does, and that they will not let it happen. He knows there are profits to be made from the voyage and for his part clamors for what he considers a just return for his work, and a good living. And so he draws up demands, or adapts the demands others like him have drawn up, and presents them; and, if need be, strikes for them.

Some small companies and their unions, and some "sick" industries, have been forced to take a more careful look, and act more cooperatively toward union demands that would raise costs beyond the danger point. Higher wages and other concessions to the union in some situations could depress business and result in unemployment. Wage cuts, instead of wage raises, might even be in order.

Some Problems. This question has many ramifications. Should a union subsidize inefficiency in a small or backward company by permitting low wages and substandard conditions? Or should it force the small-scale, low-pay producer out of business to make way for more progressive enterprises? Can the union help the company increase efficiency by boosting worker productivity? Should the union fight against technological improvements that would throw members out of work?

A consideration of these questions, and others equally pertinent, would lead away from the problem of *drawing up* demands into the *content* of the demands. Such questions might, in a given case, condition the nature of the demands, but the union negotiator is more likely to have to deal with them as they come up during the course of negotiations.

Assembling Information.   A strike threat frequently hangs over negotiations from the start. When this is so, the negotiations are a test of strength, and the end result is likely to register not so much the merits of the case on either side as the relative strength of the parties.

But the parties carry on negotiations by discussion: they talk, they use arguments, they reason and try to convince. In spite of, as well as because of, the strike threat that lurks in the background, in the foreground men sit around a table and try to persuade each other.

They do persuade each other in many things. It is their function to reach an accommodation and reduce it to writing. Even when the general terms of their bargain reflect relative underlying strength rather than abstract objective judgment, these terms must at least be rationalized in wording acceptable to both sides. In order to reach common ground as well as to define their differences, the union and the company negotiators must exchange views and come to a meeting of the minds. Each side must show the logic of its position.

Both sides, therefore, build up information to support their arguments. The union negotiators want, basically, two kinds of information: (*a*) what might be called, by analogy with the military, "intelligence" that will help them gauge the company's strength and intentions, and (*b*) facts to back up arguments in favor of the union's specific demands. Under this heading would also come, of course, facts for rebuttal of possible company arguments.

"Intelligence."   The union negotiators stand at a disadvantage unless they can find out something about matters on which the company already has a good deal of information: the state of the industry and the firm's position in the industry, competition, profits and sales, orders and prospects: in a word, economic and financial data. Some of these factors will indicate the company's ability to pay, others may give an inkling of the company's ability to withstand a strike, or willingness to make concessions. Such data remains confidential with the company, unless the company refuses union demands solely on the grounds of inability to pay. In such cases, the NLRB has ruled the company must open its books and show the union proof of its contention.

The international's research department provides most of the general economic information and financial data on the company. Experts and specialists employed by the international assemble and evaluate the information and make it available to the negotiators as part of the service provided local unions by the international. Local information along the same lines and word of specific innercompany developments may "leak" to the union from friendly office workers or sources in the community. The reports of shop stewards keep the negotiators abreast on actions taken by management in the various departments. These and other scraps of isolated information, fitted together and evaluated, may give clues to the company's intentions.

Ordinarily the company may be expected to know more about economic and financial prospects than union intelligence can unearth and correctly put together, but unions have steadily gotten better at the game. Through its international, a local draws on the services of economists, lawyers, and accountants no less expert in their fields than the company's own specialists.

Facts for Argument. Here again economic and financial data have a bearing, particularly when the costs of specific concessions are at issue, but a great deal of information comes from the shop itself. Experiences gained under the past agreement suggests changes in some of the provisions. The grievance records or other data drawn from practice provide facts for argument. The steward apparatus probably constitutes the main source of information in this category.

On the company side the assembling of information for negotiations shows the same twofold nature: the need to try to gauge the union's strength and determination; and the need for facts and figures to counter union arguments and support the company's position. Sources of information for the company are analogous: employer associations, which correspond to the union international, and the company's own supervisory apparatus and personnel department.

Publicizing and Explaining the Demands. Both sides have a public to which they appeal for understanding and support, and the most important segment of that public is the working force of the enterprise.

The union keeps its members informed by means of meetings, printed or mimeographed bulletins of various kinds distributed at the plant gate or circulated by union stewards, and, on occasion, mass media such as radio or television. The union also—and most importantly—"talks up" its information through its steward system and circulates it by word of mouth. The department stewards are in daily personal contact with the entire body of employees. They are elected representatives who have the confidence of their constituents. The workers turn to them for facts, advice, and direction as the negotiations proceed.

The wider public which consists of the community does not usually hear much about specific demands under negotiation unless there is a strike. Then both sides take to the newspapers with their versions of the issues and wage a propaganda battle to win, or at least neutralize, public sentiment.

The Employer Defense and Counterinitiative

It still seems to be the practice of some employers to wait until the union has presented its demands before getting ready for negotiations. This is a purely defensive strategy. There is some justification for it in that decisions go by default to the employer unless the union requests a part in making them, and that most changes that could be made represent concessions by the employer to the union. Why give the union, as it were, things the union does not first ask for? Why not just sit back, see what they want, and say "No"?

Active Preparation for Negotiations. Nonetheless more and more employers are finding it wise to prepare more carefully and to anticipate union demands or deflect them with proposals of their own. Some of these counterproposals may actually be things the union has not asked for! Employer preparation for negotiations gives management an active, instead of a passive, function.

The farsighted employer or employer association calculates in advance the cost and relative desirability of various alternatives and meets the union with concrete proposals rather than a monotonous "No, no, no" followed, perhaps, by a reluctant "Yes" to an arrangement shaped entirely by union initiative. The General Electric Company has been a leader of this trend. It has come to be known as Boulewareism, after a former G.E. vice president who initiated it.[3]

This does not mean that the employer gives up the defensive position, which is a strong one despite some disadvantages. It means that he plans his defense and supplements it with counteroffensive strategy that does not leave all the issues, or points of attack, entirely to the union.

The Area to Be Defended. The area of company policy where employees usually desire changes are those defining the employees' individual work-contracts with the company. The standard phrase used to designate this area is "wages, hours, working conditions, and other conditions of employment." It does not normally include, for instance, company sales policy; it does include such policies as layoff order, and practices that have to do with conveyor speeds or the way time studies are taken.

The union's aim is to influence the terms of the individual work-contract the company has with each of its employees. In effect, what the union seeks is to get the employer to *promise* that certain agreed-on conditions affecting wages, hours, working conditions, and other conditions of employment, will become part of this work contract. When the union signs its eventual agreement with the company, that does not make the union itself a party to the individual employee's work contract. The individual still holds that with the company, and holds it directly, delivering work in exchange for wages at certain conditions. The amount of the

---

[3] On Oct. 28, 1969, the U.S. Circuit Court of Appeals in New York, acting in a legal process started in 1960, ruled that General Electric's "unbending patriarchal posture" violated the National Labor Relations Act. The company appealed the ruling to the U.S. Supreme Court, but lost.

The Circuit Court's decision came one day after the IUE and 12 other unions struck in General Electric plants all over the country. In 1966 the company had refused to engage in coordinated bargaining with the IUE and seven other unions. This form of bargaining—one large firm with a number of different unions acting jointly, or as a coalition—was held to be proper in an NLRB decision of Oct. 24, 1968, when the Board upheld a trial examiner's decision that GE had acted illegally in refusing to bargain.

wages and the nature of the conditions become those the company has promised the union it will pay and perform.

PRESENTING THE DEMANDS

The union starts by drawing up its draft demands and presenting them to the company.

The nature of this process varies between craft and industrial unions, and the demands themselves differ. What follows will describe the process in the typical industrial union situation of the single-union single-employer pattern.

Procedure in the Local Union

At a meeting of the local industrial union the members charge a committee, or a group of officers, with the task of drafting proposals for negotiation. In due course this group reports back to the membership with the draft demands they have drawn up. These demands are in the form of a proposed agreement that sets forth the terms the union wants the company to offer and incorporate in the individual work-contracts with each of its employees in the bargaining unit and to adopt as policy in its dealings with all of them. Influences that shape the content of these draft demands have been discussed earlier in this chapter.

The members of the local discuss the recommendations. They suggest additions, deletions, alterations, and improvements in the terms and wording. Following parliamentary procedure, they go over the document paragraph by paragraph and vote, first on its separate provisions, then on the document as a whole. When they are finished with this procedure they have ratified the demands. Once ratified, the draft agreement becomes the official union program of proposals for the forthcoming negotiations with the company, and the union's instructions to its negotiating committee.

In the case of a new union and an initial agreement, the draft demands usually take for their pattern a standard form recommended by the international union, or copy the model of some similar agreement known to the local union. The committee fills in specific items, such as wage rates or seniority rules, to make it applicable to local conditions.

In the case of an established union already working under an agreement, the deliberations center on proposed changes and improvements. Perhaps the history of grievance adjustment over the past year points out loopholes that need to be plugged, or too-rigid wording that needs to be relaxed to give the union some leeway. Experience may suggest the addition of new clauses, the deletion of inoperative or undesirable ones. Words may be weighed, punctuation revised. Generally, the agreement grows at least a little every year. Clauses that have stood the test of time remain;

new ones, to cover previously unforeseen contingencies, are added. Eventually, the draft demands are ratified and ready for negotiation. The union sends or presents them to the company as a basis for discussion.

THE ACT OF NEGOTIATION

The union presents its demands and asks for a meeting. The employer, ready or not with counterproposals, designates a spokesman and agrees on a date. The two sides meet and start negotiating. They continue to meet until they have achieved some result.

The Context of Negotiations

The union may be newly organized, seeking its first agreement. Negotiations then are new, exceptional to the experience of both management and labor, surrounded with hopes, fears, and uncertainty. They may be charged with tension; there will certainly be a feeling of strangeness. Or, they may be routine renewal talks in an established and stable collective bargaining relationship; expected, understood, and taken very calmly. In any case the workers in the plant or bargaining unit follow them closely, and even the general public may take an interest.

If a strike is in prospect—and this threat lurks somewhere in the background in any negotiations—then union members, other employees of the company, their families, their creditors, and the community in which they live wait anxiously for the outcome. Stockholders of the company may, and the board of directors certainly will, be on the alert. The negotiators on both sides are bound to feel the pressure and to realize that what they do will have repercussions. Much is at stake for many, at the bargaining table.

Because of this interest from the outside, the negotiations sometimes attract a good deal of publicity. The sessions themselves almost invariably take place behind closed doors, but the union delegates have to report back to their members, and a union meeting—even a closed one—is no place to tell a secret. Reporters may try to question the participants on either side as they leave the bargaining sessions, or later, and this brings the temptation for the parties to carry their case to the newspapers.

So long as no confidence is violated, the propriety or the wisdom of such a course is a matter of judgment, but it has its dangers. There is, for instance, the danger of being misquoted, or the opposite one of being caught off guard and quoted all too accurately in a rash statement. There is the danger of taking a stand publicly from which it may be necessary later to retreat—publicly. But there are also occasions when a word to the press can become an effective tactical weapon in the bargaining. It all depends. The real negotiating still has to be done in the conference room.

THE CONDUCT OF NEGOTIATIONS

Negotiating is so personal an art, and its practice so dependent upon the mixture of personalities present, as well as the circumstances and issues, that little of a general nature can be said that would be valid in all cases. A few remarks may still be hazarded.

Privacy of the Negotiations

The presence of outsiders seems to inhibit fruitful negotiation, and so does the making of a written or taped record. Real human conflict takes place at the bargaining table, with moments of high suspense and drama. This is part of the process. When an audience is present, participants tend to speak for the effect they hope to make on the audience; that is, instead of making progress with each other, they spout propaganda. Sessions degenerate into ham acting, posing, clowning, or name-calling. Something of the same sort happens when there is a stenographer taking down what people say, or it is known that the proceedings are going on a sound track that may be played back someday. Under such circumstances, only a trial lawyer would feel at ease. Speeches "for the record" take the place of honest bargaining. Spontaneity, and the flexibility of give-and-take disappear; the people "freeze" and act unnaturally.

Informality and an atmosphere of freedom, on the other hand, seem to produce the best effect. People are then not afraid to express themselves; and more important, lest they be made to appear later as ridiculous, or wrong, to reverse themselves if necessary. It is much easier to eat one's words when they have been uttered in private, in the presence of opponents who may also have to eat a few ill-chosen words of their own.

Negotiation Strategies

As for negotiating strategy—that is, the narrow strategy of how to present or defend a case—that depends greatly on the counterstrategy it has to meet, but there are two typical approaches.

The Piecemeal Approach.   The first is the piecemeal, or step-by-step approach. This tries to settle the issues one by one in some order such as "easiest" first, or from the beginning to the end of the draft demands. It is the approach that comes naturally to the practical-minded worker, who knows that you do a job by finishing the first task before going on to the second, and so on to completion. Each item arises as a separate issue, is argued out, disposed of, and tucked away, while attention turns to the next.

The Total Approach.   The second is the "total" approach, or just the reverse of the piecemeal. This regards nothing as settled until everything is settled. Bargaining "points" are offered and discussed, then laid aside as others are brought forward; every question remains open until suddenly the whole complex is ready to crystallize into a total agreement. This is frequently the company approach. Legal fiction supports this concept of bargaining, for no part of an agreement is valid until the whole has been signed. Management people generally are accustomed to thinking in terms of a complex of interrelated factors, interdependent variables, no one of which can be fixed until its effects on all the others have been calculated.

Combining Strategies. It can readily be seen that there must usually be something of both approaches in any given strategy. The company is understandably reluctant to tie itself down irrevocably on Point A until it sees how great a concession it has to make on Point X. The employees are prone to view with distrust a juggling of issues, as if they are colored balls flying through the air all at once and never coming to rest.

Here is where the easy-to-hard sequence often provides a middle way. The union gets the company fairly well tied down on minor matters, one by one, until there are only a few big issues "up in the air." This provides opportunity for serious efforts at compromise. Offers combining elements of the unsettled issues in different proportions are tried out, considered, rejected, reshuffled, and reworked until finally the mix is right. When that occurs, negotiations are almost over, and successful.

The final formula may be the result of some pretty tall horse trading at the end. Anticipating this, the union's demands and the company's counterproposals usually contain from the start a certain number of built-in bargaining points that are intended to be thrown away, or swapped for something else, at the last moment. Part of the problem for each side is to feel out the other to find out which "vital" demands have been put in just for trading purposes and which are really vital—so much so that they may take a strike to settle. Often these bargaining points are obvious "phonies," but there is enough difference between the outlook and mentality of both sides to lead to occasional serious miscalculations.

Personality in Negotiations

Negotiations are a contest, and like any contest put a strain on the participants. "The union" and "the company" are abstractions, but their representatives at the bargaining table are human beings. Human beings differ in knowledge, skill, attitudes, systems of values, temperament, endurance. It would be hard to overestimate the influence of individual personalities on negotiations.

Different men get their results in different ways. What are the personal characteristics of a good negotiator?

Patience, intelligence, stamina, a level head, an open mind, and integrity; these would seem to be minimal qualities for a good negotiator; and he must be able to express himself well and convincingly. A sense of humor always helps.

Not all men have these qualities, and even those who have are subject, under strain, to emotional influences. Bargaining sessions coop men up together and pit them against each other. Tempers wear thin. "Bargaining fatigue" resembles the combat hazard of battle fatigue.

Broadly speaking, here is where the international rep (or in multi-employer bargaining, as pointed out, his management counterpart, the employer association secretary) is at an advantage, like a professional athlete among amateurs. The outcome of the contest is never as deadly personal to him as to the others. It is all part of the day's work, and the stage of frustration and exhaustion may be the very moment he has been waiting for. Gone now is the time when to keep things moving he would crack a joke. Now the negotiations are not moving; they have stalled and show no immediate prospect of getting further. Ugly remarks have passed across the table. Nerves are raw.

At such a moment—always depending on the personalities involved— the rep may rub the raw nerves of an overstrained company official to the point of provoking anger. In anger many men lose their heads. Or, again depending on personalities, this may be the time when anger drives both sides to greater stubbornness, or exasperation threatens to undo all that has been accomplished. The rep calls a retreat—a recess or adjournment for a day or two—and takes his men outside to cool off and recuperate.

A CLIMAX IN NEGOTIATIONS

With or without conciliation and mediation, the negotiations have to run a course. Perhaps the parties come to an agreement. They put it down in writing, piecing the text together, perhaps, from parts of the original union draft, the company counterproposals, and notes made during the course of the argument. They initial it, or even sign it.

But sometimes they fail to agree, by contract expiration date or by some other deadline. What then?

Then there may be a strike.

Negotiations now break off, to be resumed under the new conditions and added pressure of strike action. Aside from this added pressure, there is no basic change in the process of negotiation, though the results reflect not just the reason and logic of the parties but the fortunes of the strike. Interest shifts, therefore, to what is going on *outside* the conference room, in the streets, at the plant gate.

THE DECISION TO STRIKE

Although the actual calling of a strike is the union's move, strikes result from decisions made independently by the employer, the union, and the workers involved in the negotiations.[4] Management could always avoid

---

[4] The authors are indebted to Professor Thomas W. Gavett of West Virginia University for suggesting much of the material in this section.

a strike by giving in to the demands of the union and unions could avoid strikes by capitulating to management. In the end, it is the workers who must hit the bricks so their decision is also of great importance. Although some strikes are emotional outbursts, it seems likely that most strikes are the result of at least partially rational decisions made under conditions of uncertainty.

The Management Decision to "Take a Strike"

In negotiations, management seeks "reasonable" labor costs and the flexibility needed to run the enterprise in an efficient manner. If the union's demands represent what management considers to be reasonable labor costs and adequate freedom for unilateral management decisions, management signs up and there is no strike. But union demands are not drawn up for the purpose of being reasonable in management's eyes and they very seldom turn out that way. Methods of determining the costs of a union agreement will be discussed in Chapters 8 through 14.

Typically, then, management is confronted with the difficult choice between accepting "excessive" union demands or incurring the costs of a strike. While the cost of a strike to management depends entirely on the circumstances of the individual enterprise; nevertheless, most strikes at least threaten the loss of anticipated profits during the strike, continuing fixed costs of operation, shutdown and reopening costs, and permanent loss of customers. These costs can—to some degree—be minimized by building inventories in anticipation of a strike, continued operations during the strike, and profit pooling arrangements between employers when only some of them are struck. In turn, each of these methods of minimizing strike costs involves some additional costs of its own. These include interest and storage costs when building inventories, the costs of obtaining and maintaining replacements for strikers if operations are continued during the strike, and the "premium" on strike insurance or profit pooling arrangements.

The costs of taking a strike also depends on the *duration* of the strike. A stoppage of one week's duration might only be an inconvenience, while a 30-day stoppage might be catastrophic for the enterprise. Once started, neither management nor the union nor the workers can say for sure when the strike will end. To complicate matters further, the union may up the price of an agreement if it has been necessary to strike.

The Union's Decision to Strike

The leadership of the union is usually confronted with an unhappy choice similar to that confronting management: They can accept an agreement not wholly satisfactory to the membership (and a vociferous dissatisfied group is almost always present); or they can face the potentially high costs of a strike.

When a union strikes it risks some very heavy costs. The union's greatest risk is that the employer will replace the strikers or go out of business. If the strikers are replaced, the union is dead. Even if the employer makes no attempt to replace the strikers, a strike involves costs for the union in terms of strike benefits, administrative costs, and the possible disaffection of its members if the strike lasts too long or isn't "won big."

The Worker's Decision to Support the Strike

The worker expects the collective bargaining process to provide him with high wages and an opportunity to participate in the decision making of the firm. He is mightily unimpressed by competitive conditions which may depress his wages or any need for flexibility which interferes with his "right" to his job. Although accommodations are imperative, the worker's goal in collective bargaining appears directly contrary to the manager's objectives.

The worker's choice is probably the most difficult decision to be made by any of the decision makers. The decision to strike puts the worker's livelihood on the line, and few things are less willingly undertaken than personal hardship. All the decision makers in negotiations must rely on incomplete information, but the individual worker does not have even the full knowledge of what transpired in negotiations to base his decision on. At very best, his decision must be based on secondhand interpretations of the company's stand and the union's goals and resources. Part of the worker's choice comes when the strike actually begins.

The Strike Vote

At some time during negotiations, and very commonly at the outset, a union is likely to strengthen the hand of its negotiators by taking a strike vote. In many cases this is almost a ritual. Unless it sets a specific date and time, the strike vote taken early in the negotiations is almost always a maneuver: a mere threat, a psychological weapon, a "cold-war tactic." The threat may even be pure bluff.

Any bluff raises the danger of being called, but the strike threat, when it is a bluff, happens to be a fairly safe one just as long as it does not turn into action, because the company has no effective counterbluff. The threat of lockout, potent enough in the craft situation, does not usually fit the factory. All the company can do in the face of a strike threat is to tell the union, in effect, that if the threat turns into action, the company is ready to withstand the strike.

Purpose of the Strike Vote.   Taking a strike vote therefore does not inevitably mean that there will be a strike. It conjures up, in visible and dramatic form, the specter that hovers in the background anyway, and pointedly reminds the company (and incidentally, the union) of what may come if negotiations fail. It puts a sense of urgency into the effort to reach agreement.

It is doubtful whether agreements embodying many concessions would ever be reached if the strike threat did not hang over negotiations.

The strike threat does not need to be explicit. The coal miners, for instance, have a slogan that expresses a tradition of their union: "no contract, no work." Neither the mineowner nor union representative in negotiations ever need doubt that there will be a strike if they do not succeed in coming to agreement before the expiration of the current contract.

Other industrial unions have not developed such a binding tradition. With some exceptions, they bargain not on an industry-wide basis as the miners do, but enterprise by enterprise. The history and experience of a given local union and the labor relations policy and record of the company with which it deals have much to do with the union's militancy, its willingness to strike. The current level of activity in the enterprise, or highly local and temporary conditions, may affect a union's readiness, its ability to strike.

Effect of the Vote on Union Members.   The threat expressed in a strike vote does not bear solely against the company; it has its psychological effect on the minds of the union members, too. It reminds them of the price they may have to pay to get their demands and sometimes helps keep the demands within reason. A leadership doubtful of membership support in rough going may call for a strike vote early, when conflict seems far away and unlikely, in order to condition the members' minds to the idea, in case it later becomes necessary to mobilize them for strike action.

"Insurance" for the Committee.   Again, an early strike vote is a form of insurance for the committee. It puts responsibility back where the authority remains: in the members' hands. Most workers shrink from the perils and inconvenience a strike involves, unless pushed to it, or desperate. Once they have gone on record by a vote, the committee can take the position of urging acceptance of compromises from the original demands, as they develop in negotiations. This is frequently a sounder and more comfortable position than that of having to try to cajole a reluctant membership to strike in support of the committee.

A Form of Referendum.   Besides the initial strike vote, others may be taken at crucial points during the negotiations, according to (but sometimes against) the recommendations of the negotiators. They constitute a sort of referendum of member sentiment, registering the reaction of the workers to the course of negotiations. It can readily be seen that this can have a strong effect upon the negotiations themselves. A committee armed with a fresh and overwhelming vote of confidence returns to the bargaining table for the next session with new strength. There is nothing quite like it on the management side.

Because of the strength that comes from the unique, one-sided value of the strike threat (up to the point where it turns into strike action) union leaders set great store by the strike vote. It would not be to their advantage as negotiators to face the company with poor membership support, so they are careful not to take a strike vote that does not pass. When, on the other hand, they can feel fairly sure of an enthusiastic endorsement by an overwhelming vote, they have nothing to lose and everything to gain by staging a demonstration.

Effect of the Vote on Negotiations.   A strike vote strengthens the union negotiators' hand as long as they are careful not to turn the threat into an ultimatum by setting a date when it will certainly turn into a strike. Much of the psychological value of a threat lies in its uncertainty. Once the term is set, the strike-threat pressure ceases to be directed solely against the company, but bears on the union committee too. Then they are under equal compulsion to come to agreement by the time stated—or else! Setting the term too early may unnecessarily harden the company's position so that it gives up nothing, short of actual "war." The strike threat requires flexibility in use and is ordinarily so phrased as to be an authorization to issue a strike call, not itself a call.

Timing.   Choosing the time to strike (if strike should come) is a question of high strategic value to the union. Unless negotiations are for an initial agreement, the union of course does not have unrestricted freedom in this choice. The expiration date of the existing agreement is a sort of deadline, but even so the union has some flexibility of action. The old agreement can be extended, by mutual consent, for additional stated periods, or on an indefinite basis. In some cases the union can let the contract expire without an agreement to extend it, and thereby restore the conditions of an initial agreement. This, of course, involves risks for a union, which must go on a "war alert" footing, ready to strike; but the tension puts the company under pressure as well.

Retroactivity.   In the past many companies and unions went on bargaining after the expiration date with the understanding that any agreements reached eventually would be retroactive. In more recent years company resistance to this practice has hardened. It relieved the union of all sense of urgency but left the company under pressure—increasing pressure! The trend, therefore, has been toward making the expiration date of the contract the probable date of a strike, *if* there is to be a strike. The strike threat, in negotiations, consists mainly of that "if."

Craft and industrial unions use similar methods in their negotiations with employers, but they seek different kinds of collective bargaining agreements and they strike in different ways to persuade employers to grant these concessions.

UNIONS ON STRIKE

In the conduct of their strikes, craft and industrial unions strike for different aims, follow different strategies, and employ different tactics.

Craft-Union Strikes

The craft union's aim is to get a favorable price for skilled labor and to maintain an acceptable economic supply-demand relation between job openings for workers in the craft and craftsmen seeking jobs. Thus carpenters will strike for a raise in hourly wages or against a cut. They will also strike against the employment of nonunion workers to do carpenters' jobs, usually on the ground that these nonunion workers are not qualified to do the work. This includes the jurisdictional strike in which some other skilled-worker union claims the right to do work which the carpenters consider "belongs" to them. An example might be the job of installing prefabricated windows. The glaziers claim them because they have glass panes; but so do the carpenters, because the frames are made of wood. In this case a decision either way expands the total demand for one kind of skilled labor and diminishes the demand for another kind. While jurisdictional strikes have fortunately become one of the less common kinds of strike, their incidence most clearly demonstrates the economic orientation of craft-union collective bargaining aims.

Strategy and Tactics. Strategy in craft-union strikes springs from this supply-demand relation. It aims simply to withdraw a scarce element of production, skill, from the labor market and withhold it until the price is right. It has been pointed out before that craft unions flourish only where handicraft methods still prevail so that the product is directly turned out—as in the building trades—by a skilled craftsman. This craftsman is a man who has passed through an apprenticeship and taken several years to master a trade. When he walks off the job, the employer cannot replace him with any Tom, Dick, or Harry. In the short run he and his fellow craftsmen are irreplaceable. The more completely and the longer they withhold their skilled labor, the stronger grows the demand for it, until an offer of hourly wages is made that seems acceptable as the price of the labor to be supplied.

Tactics under this strategy can be quite simple. Basically, what the union members do is wait. If the strike is against a single employer, or a few out of many, and the others are complying with union terms, the business agent of the local finds jobs for the striking workers with these other firms. If there are not enough jobs to go around, the union pays individual cash benefits out of its strike fund to the members who are unemployed because of the strike. That is what the fund was built up for—to help the members wait it out.

Employer Answer. Employers are not always willing to let the union pick them off one by one, as just described, but may answer the union's strike against one member firm of an association with a lockout by all the firms. That sharpens the struggle, but does not change the underlying basis of the union's fight. The waiting puts a heavier strain on the strike fund, but also puts a strain on all the member firms. Sooner or later the two sides resume negotiations and find a formula acceptable to both.

Picketing in craft-union strikes is token in nature and may even be done not by union members but by hired sandwich men. It is to advertise the fact that a given employer's union workers are on strike, so that a stranger recruited in another town will not make the mistake of accepting employment on a struck job. Such a mistake could be very costly to a craftsman; it could cost him his union card and any future opportunity to make a livelihood at his trade. And only an out-of-towner would be ignorant of the strike, for the craft-union local organizes all the craftsmen of a given skill in one community.

Instances where violence has flared on craft-union picket lines, are, like jurisdictional strikes today, both rare and illuminating. In most such cases it will be found that the fight is between local people and members of the same craft international from another locality. This underlines the fact that a strike of skilled men can be broken only if other skilled men of the same craft cross the picket line. This, of course, seldom happens. On the contrary, craft-union solidarity is generally so strong that members of one craft will not even cross the picket line of another craft. It takes no violence to restrain them; respect for picket lines is almost a "religion" to the craft unionist. He gives it to others when they are on strike, expects it (and gets it) in return when he is out. It can be said of craft unions: They win their strikes who only stand and wait.

Industrial-Union Strikes

Very different is the situation in the industrial-union strike. To stand and wait would be the surest way of losing a strike. The industrial union goes on strike for economic aims, but gets and holds them by methods that can only be called, for want of a better term, *political*, in the sense of power politics.

The Strike Objective. The immediate strike objective of the industrial union in manufacturing is to control physical access to the workplace. This denies the employer the use of his productive plant until he ransoms it by making a satisfactory settlement. The industrial union in transportation aims to bring the employer's rolling stock to a standstill. Industrial unions in other fields have to select their strike objectives in the light of their particular circumstances, which vary. The underlying stategy in all of them is to prevent the replacement of individual strikers of many varieties and degrees of semiskill, by other individuals who can be taught the strikers' jobs.

Organization for Strike. The exact date and time of the strike may be set by vote of the members, or authorized by vote and set by call of the union officers or committee. Between internationals, and even locals of the same international, practices differ. The range is from a requirement in either the local or international constitution calling for a secret ballot of all the members, with a two-thirds or three-fourths majority in favor of strike necessary to carry, down to a simple majority of members present and voting at a meeting. The practice is likely to lie somewhere between these extremes, probably nearer the latter, or less rigorous, requirement.

In a factory union, mere prudence on the part of union leaders would indicate the desirability of taking a vote before calling a strike. The members are the union's army in the strike, as well as the union's citizenry. In a democracy, it takes a vote of the citizenry as represented in parliament—the local meeting—to mobilize the army. The secret-ballot, every-member method of authorizing a strike goes further yet: it submits the question to a referendum.

Opposing Interests within the Union. At the moment of taking the crucial strike vote, the interests of union leaders and union members may not quite coincide. The leaders are out in front, fighting for concessions the members say they want. The leaders are in direct contact with the company. They have presumably reached the conclusion that it will take more than mere arguments to win concessions, and that there are good chances of success through strike action. Conversely they fear the effect on the morale of the union members if they fail to win concessions by failing to strike. The leaders, therefore, want the strike vote to pass. The members (who may be egging their leaders on) want the concessions they have demanded, but hesitate as individuals to pay the price. That price, they know, means paydays missed, picket line duty, maybe a broken head. Even though reason may tell them they can only win by risking the strike, fear holds them back.

It may well be that at the crucial moment only a minority is actively in favor of strike. The rest—as is all too human—have gotten cold feet. But in a crowd situation a militant minority can get its way against a leaderless and wishy-washy majority. As will be shown shortly, it does not necessarily take a majority to close the factory: a militant minority can do it.

Role of the Shop Stewards. The stewards are a key group at a time like this; and indeed their support and activity are vital throughout that test that negotiations and the strike impose. They see the members in the shop from day to day. If properly informed and inspired, they are a flesh-and-blood, word-of-mouth link between the union leaders and the members. They campaign for the strike, and in the strike act as an officer corps to lead the workers.

Thus the strike vote is a critical test. In the typical, democratically organized factory union it cannot be sidestepped, because the citizen army may be mobilized by its own consent but not conscripted by decree; and yet, unless carefully handled, the conduct of the vote may expose the union to danger.

The Union's Forces. The forces at the union's disposal are the union members, a volunteer army often without experience; they make up the rank and file. Their officers are the shop stewards, who now serve as picket captains, and others who volunteer or are elected by their mates for special strike duties. This group makes up the line organization of the striking union.

The strike committee sets up subcommittees for staff and service functions, mostly service. Among the important activities that have to be carried on during a strike are the following: setting up a soup kitchen to feed the picketers (this draws the strikers' wives into active participation); scrounging supplies and soliciting help from friendly sources in the community; publicity; transportation; a welfare center to provide relief in hardship cases; legal defense if trouble breaks out on the picket line; recreation, if the strike is long drawn out; and others.

Strike Headquarters. The union hall is the headquarters where the members meet, and serves as a base for most of the auxiliary activities mentioned in the last paragraph. In addition, the strikers set up a field headquarters near the plant, handy to the picket line. This may be a vacant store hired for the occasion, or a tent that also houses the soup kitchen, or even a public place like a café or saloon whose proprietor tolerates the strikers' presence (and gets their business), perhaps even making a back room available for their use. Here the picket captains report, and get encouragement, instructions, and advice from the rep and the strike committee. Pickets drop in between spells of sidewalk duty to drink a cup of coffee, warm their toes, and pick up gossip of the strike. To one who has seen service with front-line troops in combat, it is remarkable how much these other "front-line" headquarters reproduce the atmosphere of selflessness, shared perils, and camaraderie.

Allies. The striking local's allies are other locals of the international, and more immediately, other local unions in the town. The strikers' ambassador to the city central informs the other delegates of his union's plight, and the support that comes from the labor movement of the home community is almost always warm and often generous. After all, they are neighbors. Most of them can do no more than contribute to the strike fund, send fraternal delegations to the strike meetings, and pass resolutions of support in their own. Sometimes they can give active direct support, as when the Teamsters refuse to cross a strike picket line. But the Teamsters do not always respect picket lines of other unions, and when they do, or others join in a sympathy strike, the situation takes on a new significance beyond that of the situation being examined here, which is the simple strike of factory workers.

The Striking Worker.   The plant gate channels a human stream, regular as the tide, set into motion daily during the week by the onset of the factory shift. The worker bound for his workplace who finds strike pickets at the familiar gate cannot help feeling an initial sense of shock. Not to walk through the open gate runs against habit and impulse. Man is no creature of blind instinct, and when the shop steward meets his people at the gate and diverts them to picket duty, most of them will respond; but the unspent impulse is strong, and tautens nerves.

Emotionalism.   That check to habit is the first of many emotional experiences of the strike. If the picket line keeps the worker from entering the plant the first day of the strike, and starts him on a new routine—the strike routine—the union has accomplished a great deal toward winning the campaign. It cannot always do this at the first try; if not, the task gets harder with each shift that does not see an empty plant. The union cannot always hold the lines after initial success, but that is another problem. The first task is to close down the plant, "shut 'er up tight."

This is not very difficult to do, nor does it necessarily take a majority to do it. A militant and determined minority is usually enough. Probably no more than a good handful assemble anyway, at dawn of the first day of strike, to get instructions and be posted at the gate or gates. They take their stations at all points where workers normally leave public property and step or drive onto the plant premises—parking lot entrances, street gates, and doors. As the first workers come—for habit is strong, and even those who know a strike is on cannot resist the pull of the current setting plantward at the onset of their shift—the strike leaders pass on the union's instructions. It may be to join the pickets and greet later comers with a bigger force. It may be to go to the union hall for a meeting, in cases where the strike leaders deem it desirable to keep the streets clear of crowds.

Those who act bold and confident carry the others along with them. The active ones are under leadership; the passive, leaderless, drift with the new tide. The mere sight from the head of the street of a crowd around the gate is enough to turn timid souls away. Discreetly they retire and go home (which they will find as strange, during working hours, as the deserted shop). From there, after a while, anxiety and curiosity may draw them to the union hall. At the union hall they are caught in the contagion of mass excitement and brought under organized leadership again. The factory worker, a disciplined person, responds to leadership. In a day or two he is taking his turn on the picket line.

The man who walks the picket line is not quite the same man who walked off the job the day before. After the strike, he will never be quite the same man again.

There is no such type of factory worker as the "hardened striker," but one strike will usually "harden" a union. It gives the members a shared experience that changes their attitude toward management—not individually, but as a group, for striking is a social activity. They are like troops that have seen combat.

Lessons of the Strike Experience. For many, it is an illuminating—even exhilarating—experience to learn that they can collectively defy the authority that normally dominates their individual lives and get away with it. This remains true even when they do not clearly win their strike, so long as they regain their places in the factory after it is over. What they have once dared they may do again. They feel a confidence they could not know before. They have learned caution, too, which tempers ther boasts and threats but makes more meaningful, and to the company, ominous, those they do express. One strike is enough to last most factory workers—and factory managers—a long time. The strike transforms them both.

It changes them because, as has been shown above, a strike is a profoundly emotional experience. That does not mean that it is primarily an emotional outburst (strike causes run deeper than that), but it works strongly on the emotions of everyone involved. Most numerous of those involved, and most directly affected, are the workers.

The Picket Line. The aim of the strike is to deprive the company of production and make management sue for terms to get it rolling again.

The first step is to call the workers off their jobs. This is the formal meaning of the strike vote and is easily accomplished since workers leave the plant anyway at the end of the shift.

Shutting down the Plant. The second step is to shut down the plant, and this may be a little harder. Meeting-hall courage has been known to melt away overnight. A man is not counted absent from work until he fails to show up at the start of the next scheduled shift. The strike is not actually on until the shift fails to report. The union therefore must stop the shift from going on. As has been shown, that is not really difficult to do if there is any appreciable amount of strike sentiment and if adequate organizational measures are taken.

The third step, and the one that may be hardest in the long run, is to keep the workers, and strangers who might replace them, from going in to work. This is the aim that animates every move made by the union in the strike, the object of all its vigilance, the reason for any violence that may occur on either side. The way it is carried out is by means of a picket line.

A picket line consists of union members who walk back and forth in front of the plant gate or gates. They warn their fellows, and any others who might seek to enter the factory to work, not to cross the line. They do this by word of mouth and by carrying signs. If words are not enough, they may resort to deeds.

Blockading of the Gate. The picket line at the factory gate is not a siege of the factory. A besieging force is one trying to get into a defended place to which the gates are barred. The factory gate is open during a strike. People walk in and out of it: guards, executives, and supervisors, perhaps the entire office force; even a skeleton crew of maintenance men —union members—who keep the pipes from freezing or preserve other vital installations.

Picketing the plant is not a siege, it is a blockade. It cuts the plant off from a vital element of production: labor. It defends the approaches to the plant against the entrance of people who might provide the labor. Who are these people who might want to go in the open gate? Anybody and everybody, including union members who weaken.

This is an offensive, not a defensive, strategy. The union picketer does not have to wait until someone does something to him; he has to do something to make the potential replacement refrain from entering the gate, as the replacement has every legal right to do. The weapons available to the picketers for carrying out this offensive strategy are of two kinds: moral suasion and force.

Keeping the Line Solid. Moral suasion appeals to some sentiment or belief such as working man's solidarity, or sympathy, or shame. It may be powerful enough to overcome a man's desire to get a job by which he can make a living—at any rate, in that particular plant. It certainly will do so in most cases in a community where the mores contain a tradition of worker solidarity. It may not do so if the replacement is a "stranger," particularly if he comes from a region (as, for instance, the South) where no such sentiments are common. It runs against the traditional belief that ours is a competitive society in which one man has as much right as another to take or refuse any job that is open and offered to him. Moral suasion can suffice, but it is more effective when it is supported by a powerful emotion, fear—fear of the use of force.

The force may be no more than jostling and getting in the way of a strikebreaker trying to enter the gate. No matter which way he turns, he finds somebody standing in front of him and "accidentally" barring the way. This is sometimes called "belly-bumping" and requires a beefy physique. Force may go further than that, to manhandling and beatings.

Or force may be nonviolent with picketers standing in the way of a car headed into the company parking lot. The driver cannot get through the gate without running down the people and making himself liable for their injuries. Again, force may go further than that, to the point of rocking the car and rolling it over with its occupants inside.

The striker knows that the way to his workplace leads through the gate which he is picketing. If he may not go in, he certainly does not want to see others go in, but his attitude toward these others depends upon whether they too have their "own" workplaces inside, or whether they are strangers, not fellow employees. If the person who goes through the gate is a fellow worker who has given in under the pressure, the picketer treats him with scorn for weakening; but if the strikebreaker is a stranger, he shows fury. Any return to work of former employees and union members raises the prospect of having to settle for less than the desired terms, and possible individual victimization, but the advent of new workers threatens permanent displacement.

Where there is danger that many will try to enter the plant, the union's recourse is to the mass picket line. In fact, the mass picket line is the industrial union's natural and characteristic form of strike activity. It keeps the strikers busy and it keeps them together, so that they can keep an eye on the company and on each other all the time, and it assembles the force necessary to insure closing the gates.

Under the Taft-Hartley law mass picketing has been held to be illegal— an unfair labor practice—but someone has first to forbid it or disperse it: until then, it simply goes on.

Picket-Line Violence. Mass picketing, the industrial union's most effective way of blockading a plant, is probably the kind of picketing least likely to lead to physical violence unless interfered with. That is because the very size of the picket force discourages entry of strikebreakers. Nonviolent "living wall" tactics, in which the pickets lock arms and stand in the way, can keep out cars as well as people, and any overt violence has to come as an attack on the pickets. Of course, once a fight breaks out in a crowd of people already tense and with their livelihood at stake, there is no telling what may happen. The point is, it is not the strikers in such cases who are likely to start trouble.

But mass picketing, besides being effective, is illegal. A company can get a court order against it. With majestic impartiality (as pointed out earlier) the law prescribes for craft and industrial unions alike the uniform conditions of "peaceful picketing": 2 (or 4, or 6) pickets at each gate, spaced 10 (or 20, or 40) yards apart, showing signs to advertise the fact that there is a labor dispute, but not shouting, or calling, or jeering, or threatening any who "in their lawful purposes" may want to enter the plant. With variations, this is the stuff of a court order enjoining mass picketing.

The picketing becomes peaceful by legal definition but, ironically, whatever potential for violence the strike contains may actually build up in proportion to the reduction in the picketers' effectiveness in keeping the plant gate closed. If strikebreakers now feel safe in crossing the picket line, and enough of them do cross it, the union faces the uncomfortable but inescapable dilemma of losing the strike or breaking the law.

How many strikebreakers are "enough"? Only as many as it would take to raise the fear in the minds of the strikers that the company can replace them. If they are strangers that need be only a few, for every striker then feels threatened. If they are employees, perhaps union members, it might be more; but in either case the ones still on strike seek to halt the movement. Breaking the law then becomes one of the risks of battle. It is a risk the union leaders frequently, either out of pure heedless emotion or after due calculation, elect to take.

Financing the Strike. A strike is financed in two ways. Basically, of course, the members support it by their self-denial in giving up their potential earnings for the period of the strike, and by the unpaid services they render on the picket line and in such related auxiliary activities as mentioned in the last section. Workers on strike are ineligible for unemployment compensation.

Strike Funds. The other way is by drawing on strike funds accumulated by the union out of dues and assessments paid in while the members were working. All internationals have such funds, and most locals.

To get support from the international, a local must receive the international's approval before taking strike action. This must not be misunderstood to mean that the local always has to get permission to strike. As long as the strike does not violate an agreement with the company the local is usually free to make its own decision, but if it wants international money during the strike (and the help of an international representative) it has to notify the international beforehand.

Approval by the higher body is usually routine. It would be withheld only in unusual circumstances. Getting this approval is a step the local can use as part of its psychological war of nerves with the company in negotiations. In cases where a strike has been forced unexpectedly on a local, approval may still be gotten *ex post facto.*

The craft-union international, with its relatively fixed membership of skilled workers only a small proportion of whom are ever on strike at the same time or for very long, can afford to pay strike benefits to individuals out of a fund accumulated centrally. The industrial union international is in a different situation. Factory strikes often involve tens of thousands of workers, and sometimes last for months.

Strike funds in the industrial union come from a small percentage, rarely more than 10 percent, of the dues dollar; and dues in turn are a small percentage—perhaps 2 percent—of a worker's pay. To try to support a striker and his family by paying him directly even a fraction of his normal wage sufficient to live on, and to do this for all the workers who may be on strike, would soon deplete the treasury of the international.

Besides, the aim is not to help the worker wait it out in an industrial union strike; such conflicts are not won by waiting. The aim is to keep alive the striker's militancy; and while an empty stomach makes a man abject, a half-filled belly whets the appetite and keeps the man active. Strike benefits, when paid, are therefore nominal—perhaps $10 to $30 a week—just enough to keep a little change jingling in the striker's pocket for coffee, bus fare or a few gallons of gas, newspapers, cigarettes, and the most pressing personal expenses.

Most of the strike funds go to support general activities and to meet needs that are common to the union as a whole. They pay the rent of the field headquarters and purchase supplies for the soup kitchen where the striker can half-fill his belly. They provide hospital care for any strike casualties and buy bail and legal aid for prisoners arrested for activities on the picket line. Such portion of the strike funds as goes to individuals is given frankly as relief for the emergency. Of course the union's committee will eke out its own resources, if possible, by getting relief for needy cases from public or private welfare agencies, but this resource is not always available. In any case, not to take care of members facing real personal disaster through the strike (rather than mere belt-tightening austerity for a time) would hurt morale; and in a strike, which is a form of combat, morale is vital. A striker threatened with eviction from his home may be provided with rent money to stave off the landlord. A family with small children will get milk and groceries.

Besides the established strike funds of the local and international, contributions come in from other unions and from individuals in the form of cash and goods, particularly food. "Scrounging committees" solicit groceries from food stores and farmers. (The advent of the supermarket run by a hired manager is closing off this source of supply, but the trend toward part-time farming by industrial workers, and part-time work in industry by farmers, may have opened up another.) Every little bit helps: a few sacks of potatoes, a carton of eggs, perhaps a side of beef for the stew pot. In an extremity, the strike army "lives off the country" while it carries on its fight.

Employer Strike Strategy and Tactics

Strike action is by nature drastic in the original sense of the word. The company that permits a strike to occur and the union that calls one both expect to receive some hurt, but hope to win concessions by hurting the other side more. The things they are concerned about during a strike show curious parallels. Neither side wants the plant or equipment to suffer any permanent damage, else they will not be fit to turn out production and provide jobs again. Both hope for a short strike and for the return to work of the entire force. Both envisage, as the worst that could happen, complete replacement of the work force by new employees, but by the logic of their conflict both sides are compelled to act as if that worst were bound to come to pass. That is their main defense against its happening.

Strike Costs. A strike denies the company the use of its productive equipment, while overhead costs continue. In a sense that is by no means purely figurative, part of that productive equipment consists of the strikers. The most advanced techniques of personnel selection, placement, and training have gone into getting them together and fitting them into management's grand design that makes the factory as a whole a smooth, efficient apparatus of production. They represent the know-how that the company has developed over the years. The cost in money, time, and organizing efforts of replacing all of them at once would be staggering.

Employer Objectives. Obviously, the cheapest and most satisfactory way of getting the factory back in production calls for the return of all the workers—though there might be a few the management would prefer not to recall. This broadly coincides with the union aim of getting all its members—without any exception—back on the job. The only thing that prevents both sides from doing this at once is the thing that led them to take drastic action in the first place: disagreement over the terms at which workers resume their jobs. Until the strike, which hurts them both, hurts one side badly enough to make it give in to the other on these terms, they cannot do what they both fundamentally desire.

A factory in operation, making profits and providing good jobs, is their mutual aim and reason for existence, and even when they are locked in struggle neither side loses sight of this aim. The striking union gives "safe conduct" across the picket line to maintenance men assigned to protect vital plant installations. Strikers in a spiteful mood may commit malicious damage of the petty kind, such as breaking windows, but they will not blow up or set fire to the factory. Their own jobs would go up in the smoke.

If, then, the union wants to get all its people back to work, and the company wants them back, and only the terms of their return prevent this, why should not the company simply close down the plant, as in a craft employer lockout, and wait for the union to give in on terms?

The Lockout and the Factory Strike. In general, the lockout is not the answer to the factory strike or to the demands of the industrial union.

That is not to say that the employer's cause is lost unless he tries from the very start, in a union-declared strike, to break the picket line around his plant. He will certainly want to keep the gate open at least long enough to make sure the union has been able to keep the work force from entering it; but acceptance of the fact that the plant is shut down, while negotiations continue, would be a sensible course in most cases for a time at least. Such action might have a tempering effect on the negotiations, which broke off, presumably, at white heat. It would give the union a chance to reflect on its course. Reopening the gate later, if initial reasonableness has failed of its purpose, might then have greater tactical effect than belligerence right from the start. A decision here depends on circumstances.

But keeping the gate closed indefinitely plays into the union's hands. Overhead costs continue to mount as long as a strike lasts, whether the gate is locked or left open. Locking the gate against an industrial union does not dispel the picket line, it simply makes the picketing job easier. If the employer has initiated the lockout to counter union demands, the workers may even be entitled to draw unemployment compensation while "on strike," which is not the case when the union calls the strike. Unless the terms are settled in negotiations, the pickets will be right back when the gate reopens. Meanwhile, a portion of the work force—and very likely, the best of it—may have dispersed, found other jobs and moved away. Keeping the gate open not only maintains pressure on the union to come to a settlement but concentrates the hopes as well as the fears of the strikers on the plant gate. The implied threat that a man's job will be given to someone else seems to increase his sense of proprietorship toward it. Instead of wandering off, he is more likely to stay and fight for it.

There may be unusual circumstances in which a lockout would be effective. In a one-factory town, for instance, strikers or potential strikers might be intimidated by the threat. A lockout would still be a dangerous move in any community not sufficiently isolated to be beyond an hour's drive from other employment opportunities. Shutting down the plant would almost certainly transfer to the company a share at least of the public opprobrium that would otherwise have been directed at the strikers. The lockout is a negative and passive answer to the union. Its use restricts more active possibilities open to the company.

Tactics. In most factory strikes the gate remains symbolically open all the time, watched from the inside by company guards, patrolled from the outside by union pickets. One of the first concerns of the company is the number of pickets at the gate or gates, and their conduct. If pickets are few and orderly, chances of getting nonstrikers to cross the line and enter the plant are enhanced. The Taft-Hartley law lists mass picketing as an unfair labor practice, but there is always the problem of determining how many pickets constitute mass picketing, and enforcing the ban against it. The responsibility for assuring legal and orderly picketing rests on the public authorities: city police or, outside city limits, the sheriff and his deputies. It is sometimes necessary to apply for a court order enjoining mass picketing and prescribing the number of peaceful pickets.

Picketer Morale. With the number of pickets cut down to no more than a handful at each gate, it is possible to invite workers to return to their jobs. This is often done by mailing circular letters to all employees, sometimes reinforced by newspaper ads or radio announcements. Successful "infiltration" by a few emboldens others who would like to be at work again. Every person who responds "counts double," in the sense that he simultaneously augments the working force and diminishes the ranks of strikers. There may be little of a useful nature for him to do in the plant, but his presence there, with others who trickle in, undermines the morale of those still outside and tempts them back. They weigh the uncertainties of future settlement against present hardships and the invitation of the open gate, and perhaps the trickle turns to a gradually swelling stream. Eventually the balance may shift so far that the union either has to give in or resort to violence.

Violence at the Gate.   Violence is double-edged; it may hurt the union, but it also hurts the company by checking the back-to-work flow. It takes effective law enforcement to minimize the likelihood of violent outbreaks and cope with them when they occur. Liaison with law-enforcement agencies, as well as skillful public relations work, has to be an important part of the company's activity during a factory strike.

Nowadays only the exceptional strike erupts into heavy and prolonged violence. For a strike to reach that stage, the issues must be practically insoluble, or else there must be an irreconcilable clash of powerful personalities in the leadership of company and union. The 10-year Kohler strike in Wisconsin seems to be an example of the latter. Both sides in the dispute became so deeply involved that neither could retreat and it developed into a "fight to the death." The strike moved on inexorably to the state that is "the worst that can happen": replacement of a decisive segment of the entire working force by new employees. This brought about the defeat of the local union and its disappearance as a viable organization in the plant. Had it not been for the massive and sustained intervention of one of the world's richest and most powerful international unions, the local union and its members would have simply passed from the scene. Although the international union eventually won the largest back-pay settlement in NLRB history ($3 million plus $1,500,000 for restored pension rights), the lesson of the strike seems to be that a company determined not to give in can beat a local union in the field by replacing its members on the job; but the fight may be very long and the cost very high indeed.

The "Back-to-Work" Movement.   The hope of destroying the union may often be present in the minds of management people during a strike —or indeed, at any time when managers feel the restrictions unions put on freedom of managerial action—yet rarely does a company really aim at unconditional surrender by the union. Rather, the company puts the union through its strike paces in the hope of softening the terms of a proposed agreement. A good healthy back-to-work movement will usually soften up the union, though failure of a move in this direction may have the opposite effect. Just how and when to do it are tactical problems that have to be solved in the circumstances of each specific strike. Several techniques have proved successful in certain cases.

During a strike negotiations continue, mediation efforts increase. The atmosphere in which management and union people meet is even more highly charged than before. Emotional reactions often are transferred from the picket line and plant gate to the conference room. Management people have to hold particularly tight rein on their feelings at such times. A lost temper might prolong the strike, or lose it. The union rep they deal with is a cold-blooded professional. It is up to the company representatives to stay cool and keep their wits about them.

Military Analogies. To sum it up: The company's position in a factory strike, by analogy with the military, is defensive, and the defensive position is a strong one. The law is on the company's side in setting the conditions of the battle. The tension and emotionalism that grip the workers during a strike make the morale problem crucial. If the strikers lose their morale, the union loses the strike. Counteroffensive measures open to the company may undermine morale, and the most potent of such measures are those that persuade workers to return to their jobs without waiting for a strike settlement. This forces the union to give in or to resort to violence. Violence as such hurts the company, in most cases, as well as the union, but may be averted, sometimes, by careful coordination of efforts with law enforcement agencies.

If active measures fail to bring the strike to an end, and the company can afford it, waiting it out will eventually result in a settlement. Most industrial workers will have run through their savings and reserves in a few weeks, and each additional week subjects them and their families to greater hardship. Unless bitterness deep enough to offset the personal privations has been allowed to creep in, the strikers will eventually surrender.

Assuming that management has not launched a successful back-to-work movement, as the strike continues pressure on both sides mounts for a settlement. The strikers want to go back to work and to start drawing paychecks again. The management's fears of lost business are beginning to become reality as more and more customers look for more reliable sources of supply. The union's funds are running low and the membership is restive.

Negotiations are resumed, perhaps on the urgings of a mediator. Both sides have new facts to consider now and they weigh them with the intelligence of greater maturity that comes from combat. Eventually the negotiators come to an agreement. They initial it, or even sign it.

CONSUMMATION OF THE AGREEMENT

The negotiators' agreement still remains tentative; it lacks validity until the members of the local, and perhaps also the international union's Executive Board and the company's Board of Directors have ratified it. The local does this in a meeting similar to the one at which the members ratified the draft demands. This time they vote on the agreement as a whole. They cannot ratify parts of it and reject other parts. If any part of the agreement is so objectionable to the members that they will not swallow it, the whole agreement fails and the negotiators have to go back and try again. Their job is not complete until the whole of their work has met with membership approval.

The agreement is finally reached and ratified, the outsiders to the dispute (union professionals, mediators, and company consultants) leave the scene. The workers go back to work, the company resumes operations.

SUMMARY AND CONCLUSIONS

The process of reaching a labor agreement can be compared with the relations between two sovereign national powers. Negotiations are analogous to the conduct of international diplomacy. Strikes, like war, are the continuation of diplomacy (negotiations) *by other means.*

In negotiations, the union seeks benefits for its members which pose a serious challenge to management's need for reasonable costs and flexibility in the operation of the enterprise. Both parties arm themselves with whatever facts they have at their disposal, but the negotiations always involve decision making under conditions of uncertainty, and emotions are likely to prevent a purely rational approach to reaching an agreement.

The writers of this book hold that strikes are part of collective bargaining. They are not inevitable, but neither are they abnormal. Still, strikes bring loss to the participants, their dependents, and those who trade with them. They inconvenience, and may even endanger, nonparticipants. When of great magnitude or in a sensitive sector of industry, strikes can imperil the general health and welfare, and even national security. On the other hand, strikes are only one of many causes of economic waste, and by no means the major offender.

There can be no doubt that strikes can be eliminated by governmental action, but only at the expense of personal freedom and civil liberty, and with the danger of eventual violent revolt. To date, the American people have found the price too high, and are unwilling to assume the risks. The inconvenience, loss, and occasional danger incidental to strikes, and the waste they represent, are recognized as part of the price the public has to pay to maintain those free institutions of our society that go far beyond the strike situation and the industrial situation generally.

Unions go on strike when they cannot get an employer to agree with them on terms they feel are right, and are unwilling to accept his terms. The strike thus becomes an additional argument—a direct and powerful one—to back up the stand the union has taken in negotiations. A strike aims to make it expensive and inconvenient for an employer *not* to agree.

Management may occasionally provoke a strike for basically the same reason to call a union bluff. If the union negotiators fail to get the members to respond to a strike call, or if the vote in favor of a strike is close and unenthusiastic, obviously the argument fails to impress; the strike threat not made good loses its force and softens up, rather than strengthens, the union bargainers.

Craft unions and industrial unions use essentially the same procedures in negotiations, although the agreements they seek are quite different, as will be discussed in Chapter 8. The strike strategy and tactics of craft and industrial unions differ radically.

Craft-union strike strategy consists of withdrawing a scarce skill from the market. Craft unions can win their strikes by merely waiting for supply and demand to come into balance at their desired price.

Industrial union strike strategy depends on closing the plant and keeping it shut *tight*. This is a power strategy, which gets no support from the law and may result in violence at the plant gate. The reason that plant gate violence does not occur more frequently is that most employers do not attempt to operate their plants during an industrial union strike.

Whether invoked by a confident union or provoked by a stubborn management, in either case it is the union that must assume the onus of calling the strike. A strike is the union's move.

Strategically speaking, the union is on the offensive during a strike, the employer on the defensive. The defensive position in a strike (as in classical, pre-H-bomb warfare) is strategically the stronger. An employer defensive, skillfully conducted, may turn into a counteroffensive that puts the union to rout; or the union may prevail, sufficiently (at least) to win an agreement more favorable than had been offered in the preceding negotiations.

The end product of negotiations (diplomacy) and strikes (war) is an agreement (treaty) which management, workers, and the union must try to live with.

QUESTIONS FOR DISCUSSION

1. If you were a plant manager of a firm employing 1,000 persons, would you want a foreman to sit in on negotiations? Why or why not? If you wanted him to sit in, what role should he play?

2. Assume that you are a mediator. How would you go about preparing for your role in a specific set of negotiations?

3. What happens if the local membership rejects the agreement after it has been negotiated?

4. Compare and contrast the strike strategy and tactics of craft and industrial unions.

5. Although craft and industrial unionists need to behave differently to accomplish their strike objectives, the law does not differentiate between them. Is this sound public policy?

6. An attorney for the UAW has proposed that all picketing be outlawed but that employers be prohibited from hiring new employees while a strike is in progress. Evaluate this proposal.

7. Does a strike deadline help or hinder the negotiation process?

8. Discuss the nonstoppage strike. (See Mangum and Marshall in the bibliography.)

SELECTED ANNOTATED BIBLIOGRAPHY

This bibliography consists of two parts: (1) negotiations and (2) strikes.

1. Negotiations

ANON. "How One Company Prepares for Collective Bargaining," *Personnel,* Vol. XXXIII (July 1956), pp. 58–72.

This article provides a step-by-step guide for management preparations for collective bargaining. Includes examples of well-organized notebook pages and exhibit sheets to organize the facts behind management's position. How to organize the management team and select a chief negotiator are discussed.

CARPENTER, JESSE T. *Employers' Associations and Collective Bargaining in New York City.* Ithaca, N.Y.: Cornell University Press, 1950.

A detailed description of how the collective bargaining process works under employer association bargaining. Discusses development and composition of employer associations, union and employer attitudes, power of employer associations, and their internal organization, patterns of group bargaining and their complexity, and negotiation procedures and strategies.

DONNELLY, LAWRENCE. "Toward an Alliance Between Research and Practice in Collective Bargaining," *Personnel Journal* (May 1971), pp. 372–99.

The author develops a frame of reference which he believes will help the practitioner make use of the vast but esoteric research being done on collective bargaining. A good succinct summary of insights that have come from academics.

DOUGLAS, ANN. *Industrial Peacemaking.* New York: Columbia University Press, 1962.

A penetrating psychological analysis of labor-management negotiations under mediation. An intensive study of six sets of negotiations.

FRANCE, ROBERT R. *Union Decisions in Collective Bargaining.* Princeton, N.J.: Industrial Relations Section, Princeton University, Research Report Series No. 90, 1955.

Discusses union preferences for bargaining unit, nature of union decision making under collective bargaining, coordination between international and local unions, and the impact of the level of decision making on the decisions made by 13 international unions and 3 local independent unions.

INDIK, BERNARD P.; GOLDSTEIN, BERNARD; CHERNICK, JACK; and BERKOWITZ, MONROE. *The Mediator: Background, Self-Image and Attitudes.* New Brunswick, N.J.: Research Program, Institute of Management and Labor Relations, Rutgers—The State University, 1966.

Reports on two surveys of the social background, employment conditions, attitudes, and opinions of state and federal mediators.

Labor Law Journal, July 1960. "Proceedings of the 1960 Spring Meeting of the Industrial Relations Research Association."

The following papers all discuss the question of cooperation between employers in an industry in an attempt to meet an industry-wide union: "Mutual Aid in the Airlines," by MARK L. KAHN; "Cooperation among Auto Managements in Collective Bargaining," by WILLIAM H. MCPHERSON; "Company Cooperation in Collective Bargaining in the Basic Steel Industry," by JACK STIEBER; "Cooperation among Managements in Collective Bargaining," by FRANK C. PIERSON.

LEVINSON, HAROLD M. "Pattern Bargaining: A Case Study of the Automobile Workers," *Quarterly Journal of Economics,* Vol. LXXIV (May 1960), pp. 296–317.

The essential points brought out by this analysis are that there has been a considerable degree of flexibility in union's approach; the most important variables affecting the union's wage policy were size of firm, relationship to industry, its financial condition, and the desires of unions to obtain "equitable" settlement; and that neither "economic" nor "political" hypothesis above provides an adequate frame of reference for understanding union's policies.

LIVERNASH, E. ROBERT. "Recent Developments in Bargaining Structure," ARNOLD W. WEBER (ed.), *The Structure of Collective Bargaining: Problems and Perspectives,* pp. 33–55. New York: The Free Press of Glencoe, Inc., 1961.

Discusses the postwar growth of centralization in contract negotiation in the local and national product market structures of bargaining. Emphasizes the great diversity of bargaining structures in the U.S.

MARTING, ELIZABETH (ed.). *Understanding Collective Bargaining: The Executive's Guide.* New York: American Management Association, 1958.

Forty-six authors, most of them industrial relations executives, discuss bargaining and the company's future, getting ready to talk contract, bargaining procedures, the contract and its wording, the issues in collective bargaining, the use of mediation, strikes, and explaining management's position.

McCAFFREE, KENNETH M. "Regional Labor Agreements in the Construction Industry," *Industrial and Labor Relations Review,* Vol. IX (July 1956), pp. 595–609.

Discusses reasons for the changing structure of collective bargaining in the building construction industry.

McKEE, CLINE. Know Your Climate—the Key to Effective Bargaining," *Personnel,* Vol. XXXIV (July–August 1957), pp. 52–62.

The Industrial Relations Officer of the Canadian Broadcasting Corporation describes management's preparation for collective bargaining as consisting of knowledge of the opposition, the agreement, company objectives and organization. He also describes the formulation and uses of the clause comparison chart which incorporates the existing agreement, union proposals, and management counterproposals.

MEYER, ARTHUR S. "Function of the Mediator in Collective Bargaining," *Industrial and Labor Relations Review,* Vol. XIII (January 1960), pp. 159–65.

Question of how mediation actually works has long resisted best efforts to find satisfactory answers. In this brief but penetrating distillation of his own experience, the author reveals the method which he employed as mediator and comes close to defining general principles involved in the conduct of mediation.

National Industrial Conference Board. *Preparing for Collective Bargaining,*

Studies in Personnel Policy: Nos. 172 and 182. The Board, 1959 and 1961.

A survey of hundreds of companies that reveals the similarities and differences in how enterprises plan and carry out contract negotiations. The report gives a comprehensive view of the complex set of interdependencies that make collective bargaining such a challenging event.

NORTHRUP, HERBERT R. "Boulwareism vs. Coalitionism in the 1966 GE Negotiations," *Management of Personnel Quarterly*, Vol. 5 (Summer 1966), pp. 2–11.

Reviews Boulwareism in light of the attempt at coalition bargaining by a group of unions with G.E. in 1966.

PILLSBURY, WILBUR F. *The Use of Corporate Financial Statements and Related Data by Organized Labor*. Bloomington: Indiana University, Bureau of Business Research, Report No. 18, 1954.

Discusses sources of corporate financial data for collective bargaining and the use of these data by union research departments. Suggests a series of financial statements which would prove most helpful in achieving factual collective bargaining.

SLIGHTER, SUMNER H.; HEALY, JAMES J.; and LIVERNASH, E. ROBERT. *The Impact of Collective Bargaining on Management*. Washington, D.C.; Brookings Institution, 1960.

See Chapter 30, "Negotiation of Union-Management Contracts."

STAGNER, ROSS, and ROSEN, HJALMAR. *Psychology of Union-Management Relations*. Belmont, Calif.: Wadsworth, 1965.

An interpretation of bargaining behavior and other aspects of industrial relations in light of modern psychological theories such as those dealing with perception and attitudes.

STEVENS, CARL M. *Strategy and Collective Bargaining Negotiations*. New York: McGraw-Hill Inc., 1963.

Stevens argues that the skill of the negotiator can dramatically enhance or diminish the power each party brings to the table. The book examines how various bargaining strategies affect bargaining power.

TAYLOR, GEORGE W. (ed.). *Industry-Wide Bargaining Series*. Philadelphia: University of Pennsylvania.

This series of monographs by experts in industrial relations provides the most comprehensive discussion of multiemployer bargaining available. The monographs in the series include:

KESSLER, SELMA, compiler. *Industry-Wide Bargaining: An Annotated Bibliography*.

TILOVE, ROBERT. *Collective Bargaining in the Steel Industry*.

FRIEDEN, JESSE. *The Taft-Hartley Law and Multi-Employer Bargaining*.

POLLAK, OTTO. *Social Implications of Industry-Wide Bargaining*.

BAHRS, GEORGE O. *The San Francisco Employers' Council*.

KERR, CLARK, and RANDALL, ROGER. *Collective Bargaining in the Pacific Coast Pulp and Paper Industry*.

PIERSON, FRANK C. *Multi-Employer Bargaining: Nature and Scope*.

FISHER, WALDO. *Collective Bargaining in the Bituminous Coal Industry*.

FEINSINGER, NATHAN. *Collective Bargaining in the Trucking Industry*.

KENNEDY, THOMAS. *The Significance of Wage Uniformity*.

GARRETT, SYLVESTER, and TRIPP, L. REED. *Management Problems Inherent in Multi-Employer Bargaining.*

TAYLOR, GEORGE W. (ed.). *Proceedings: Conference on Industry-Wide Collective Bargaining.*

ABERSOLD, JOHN R. *Problems of Hourly Wage Uniformity.*

LEVY, BERT W. *Multi-Employer Bargaining and the Anti-Trust Laws.*

SEYBOLD, JOHN W. *The Philadelphia Printing Industry: A Case Study.*

THOMSON, ARTHUR A., and WEINSTOCK, IRWIN. "Facing the Crisis in Collective Bargaining," *M.S.U. Business Topics* (Summer 1968), pp. 37–44.
  Discusses the problems that are beginning to arise in bargaining attitudes and goals as managements begin to move more toward accepting McGregor's Theory Y assumptions while most labor unions continue to base their demands on Theory X assumptions about the worker.

WALTON, RICHARD, and MCKERSIE, ROBERT. *A Behavioral Theory of Labor Negotiations.* New York: McGraw-Hill Book Co., Inc., 1965.
  The most ambitious attempt to date to explain bargaining activities by models adapted from social psychology and game theory.

2. Strikes

BAMBRICK, JAMES J., JR. "The Strike Manual," *Management Record,* Vol. XIX (July 1957), pp. 238–39.
  Discusses need for, and content of, management strike manuals with plans for evacuating the plant, maintaining essential services, and minimizing strike-inflicted losses.

———. "Marquis of Queensbury Rules for Strikes," *Management Record,* Vol. XVIII (March 1956), pp. 85–87.
  A Conference Board Study of 92 disputes shows that experienced managers and unionists tend to adhere to certain rules to be sure that the plant can reopen after a strike. Sometimes these rules appear in the contract, but they are more frequently only spoken agreements, sometimes made after the strike is under way.

BAMBRICK, JAMES J., JR., and DORBANDT, MARIE P. "National Union Strike Benefits," *Management Record,* Vol. XX (July–August 1958), pp. 242–45, 267–75.
  This survey of 78 unions indicates that over half provide strike benefits at the national union level. Detailed tables on source of union strike funds and the amount of individual strike benefits.

BERNSTEIN, IRVING; ENARSON, H. L.; and FLEMING, R. W. (eds.). *Emergency Disputes and National Policy.* New York: Harper & Bros., 1955.

BRIGGS, VERNON M., JR. "The Mutual Aid Pact of the Airline Industry," *Industrial and Labor Relations Review,* Vol. 19 (October 1965), pp. 3–20.
  Describes the establishment, principles, and effectiveness of the mutual assistance scheme adopted by a number of carriers to cope with the problem of whipsawing strikes.

CHAMBERLAIN, NEIL W., and SCHILLING, JANE METZGER. *The Impact of Strikes, Their Economic and Social Costs.* New York: Harper & Bros., 1954.
  Discusses the impact of strikes in coal and railroad transportation.

———. *Social Responsibility and Strikes,* New York: Harper & Bros., 1953.

Discusses public opinion on strikes, direct and indirect sanctions in support of public opinion, the reliability of these sanctions, and strikes in a dominant firm and in a public utility.

CULLEN, DONALD E. "The Taft-Hartley Act in National Emergency Disputes," *Industrial and Labor Relations Review*, Vol. VII (October 1953), pp. 15–30.

A review of experience under the Taft-Hartley national emergency provisions and proposed amendments.

FRANCE, ROBERT R. "Seizure in Emergency Labor Disputes in Virginia," *Industrial and Labor Relations Review*, Vol. VII (April 1954), pp. 347–66.

A review of experience under the Virginia emergency disputes law.

HAMMETT, RICHARD S., SEIDMAN, JOEL, and LONDON, JACK. "The Slowdown as a Union Tactic," *Journal of Political Economy*, Vol. LXV (April 1957), pp. 126–34.

Discusses the effectiveness of the slowdown as a union tactic and union members' attitudes toward its use.

HIRSH, JOHN S., JR. "Strike Insurance and Collective Bargaining," *Industrial and Labor Relations Review*, Vol. XXII (April 1969), pp. 399–415.

Article describes impact of strike insurance on bargaining process, noting a probable increase in their use and their tendency to prolong strikes.

KARSH, BERNARD. *Diary of a Strike*. Urbana: University of Illinois Press, 1958.

Story of a strike's effects on individuals directly and indirectly involved, upon the company and entire community. Gives dramatic account or organizing campaign and strike.

KORNHAUSER, ARTHUR; DUBIN, ROBERT; and ROSS, ARTHUR M. (eds.). *Industrial Conflict*. New York: McGraw-Hill Book Co., Inc., 1954.

Experts on sociology, psychology, and economics make an interdisciplinary study of the causes and effects of industrial conflict.

McCALMONT, DAVID B. "The Semi-Strike," *Industrial and Labor Relations Review*, Vol. XV (January 1962), pp. 191–208.

Briefly notes the nature of, and objections to, several proposed nonstoppage strike plans which provide for uninterrupted production of goods and services while the parties to the dispute incur economic penalties, and develops his own semistrike proposal.

McDERMOTT, THOMAS J. "Ten Years of the National Emergency Procedure," *Labor Law Journal*, Vol. IX (March 1958), pp. 227–43.

Effectiveness of procedure adopted in Taft-Hartley Act to handle public interest labor disputes examined in light of its application to specific disputes.

MANGUM, GARTH L. "Taming Wildcat Strikes," *Harvard Business Review*, Vol. XXXVIII (May–April 1960), pp. 88–96.

Argues that "wildcat strikes are management's responsibility—they continue as long as the participants find them profitable; cease when management, through disciplinary action, makes them unrewarding." Experiences with six wildcat strikes are described.

MARSHALL, HOWARD D., and MARSHALL, NATALIE J. "Nonstoppage Strike Proposals—A Critique," *Labor Law Journal*, Vol. VII (May 1956), pp. 299–304.

A comparative analysis of the various plans for the use of the "statutory strike" as a substitute to reduce public inconvenience resulting from work stoppages in essential industries.

PARNES, HERBERT S. *Union Strike Votes: Current Practices and Proposed Controls*. Princeton, N.J.: Industrial Relations Section, Princeton University, Research Report Series No. 92, 1956.

This study evaluates compulsory strike-vote legislation in terms of experience under such laws and describes the processes whereby strikes are authorized by American unions.

ROSS, ARTHUR M., and IRWIN, DONALD. "Strike Experience in Five Countries, 1927–1947; An Interpretation," *Industrial and Labor Relations Review*, Vol. IV (April 1951), pp. 323–42.

Suggests reasons for differences in strike incidence in five countries.

ROSS, ARTHUR M., and HARTMAN, PAUL T. *Changing Patterns of Industrial Conflict*. New York: John Wiley & Sons, Inc., 1960, p. 220.

An analysis of national trends and international differences in strike activity in 15 countries of North America, Europe, Asia, Africa, and Australia. An attempt to explain the "withering away" of the strike in most of the countries of Northern Europe. A discussion of the relation between national patterns of industrial conflict and certain features of the industrial relations system.

SCHULTZ, GEORGE P. "The Massachusetts Choice-of-Procedures Approach to Emergency Disputes," *Industrial and Labor Relations Review*, Vol. X (April 1957), pp. 359–74.

Examines experience under the Slichter choice-of-procedures emergency strike law in Massachusetts.

SLICHTER, SUMNER H.; HEALEY, JAMES J., and LIVERNASH, E. ROBERT. *The Impact of Collective Bargaining on Management*. Washington, D.C.: Brookings Institution, 1960.

See Chapter 22, "Wildcat Strikes and Union Pressure Tactics."

STAGNER, ROSS. *The Psychology of Industrial Conflict*. New York: John Wiley & Sons, Inc., 1956.

A systematic and comprehensive application of psychological principles and concepts to an understanding of the dynamics of industrial relations.

Chapter

8

THE NATURE OF THE
LABOR AGREEMENT

"CONTRACT?" OR AGREEMENT

Any company in the regular course of business enters into many contracts, written, verbal, or implied. The "union contract" would seem, at a casual glance, to be merely one of these contracts, much like all the others.

This is far from the case.

When a company purchases materials it enters into a contract with another company, the vendor, under which the vendor supplies the materials and receives money in return. But under the labor agreement the union supplies nothing tangible, receives no money from the company in return. The union does not "supply" labor; the workers supply that, and draw the wages for it. The union does not contract for the labor of its members. It does not own them. It could no more force them to deliver labor promised to the company than the company itself could exact forced labor from them.

When a company sells its products to a customer it makes a contract to deliver goods of specified quality and quantity for a specified price. But the union buys nothing from the company, pays nothing to it.

When a company engages a contractor (again by contract) to erect a building, or to do some hauling, or to manufacture a component part, it pays the contractor who pays the labor used on the job. The union does not pay its members for the work they do for the company, nor does the company pay its workers through the union as an intermediary.

It is because the union "contract" differs so markedly from ordinary business contracts that this text refers to it by preference as the "labor agreement," or "union agreement." Usage has made the other term so common, however, that it would be pedantic to condemn it and hopeless to try to suppress it. There is no harm in using the term "union contract" interchangeably with "labor agreement," so long as the user, or reader, understands how this special kind of agreement differs from other contracts. To do so it is necessary to get a firm understanding of the nature of the labor agreement.

The Contract with the Employee

The company does not contract for labor with the union, but with the company employees. They are the ones who supply something tangible, hours of labor or pieces of finished work, and who receive money wages in return. The company has a contract with each one of them—as many contracts as there are employees. This contract may or may not take form in writing; it may not even be explicitly expressed verbally, but is inherent in the company's offer of a job and the employee's acceptance of the job. This contract—work for wages—is enforceable at law, and so firmly recognized that a "mechanic's lien," or claim for wages due, takes precedence over the claims of all other creditors of an employer. It must be paid in full even though the other creditors get only partial payment.

The union is not a party to this contract, yet shapes it, under collective bargaining, by establishing its terms. The labor agreement negotiated by the union defines the *company's* offer of wages, hours, and working conditions that are to make up the employee's work contract. Any worker is free to accept or reject these terms. If he accepts them he enters into a contract *directly with the company*. He may terminate this contract at will, just by quitting. The company is also theoretically free to terminate it by dismissing him, but part of the terms is usually a promise by the company not to exercise this right except under certain conditions: seniority, "just cause" for discharge, and other restrictions.

The Agreement with the Union

Without altering, therefore, the direct contractual nature of the employer-employee relationship, the labor agreement collectively sets the terms on which the company offers its individual work contracts to each of the employees in the bargaining unit. The labor agreement thus takes the place of company policy—*becomes* company policy—in all areas that it touches.

A great deal of the literature of collective bargaining consists of attempts to define these areas and their boundaries, and to list and classify them. Most factory agreements (in contrast to craft-union contracts) are bulky, complicated documents. Some of them, printed in handbook form in 8-point type, run to more than 100 pages. Attempts to make sense of the many articles and clauses, sections, subsections, paragraphs, and subparagraphs, are often as confusing as the ponderous and pseudolegal phraseology of the documents themselves.

As a working instrument, every labor agreement has to be studied, by those who live under its provisions, as carefully as a code of laws. Every agreement differs in some respect from every other; there is no standard, no pattern, no universal model; and this is particularly true of industrial union agreements, which tend to be long and complicated. What the student needs is a tool of analysis that will unlock the meaning of any agreement.

A Tool for Analysis

This chapter, with the points it makes, constitutes just such a tool. By its aid the bulkiest or most obscurely worded agreement yields its essential purport to analysis. Despite the dissimilarity in organization or topics and presentation of provisions that is found in different labor agreements, all are reducible to certain common denominators.

These are presented in Figure 8–1, and topics in the remaining part of the chapter are arranged to correspond with the chart.[1] Part III, The Issues in Collective Bargaining, follows the same format.

FIGURE 8–1.   Functions of the Labor Agreement

Function	Category	Scope
I. Union Security and Management Rights	a) The bargaining unit b) Form of recognition c) Duration and renewal d) Management rights	Who speaks for whom With what authority For how long Except in what conditions
II. The Wage and Effort Bargain	a) Pay for time worked b) The effort bargain c) Premium pay d) Pay for time not worked e) Contingent benefits	Day rates and base rates; job evaluation Standards Hours: duration Fixed labor costs Variable labor costs
III. Individual Security	a) Job Rights b) Due process	Relative claim to available work; seniority Absolute claim to fair treatment; grievance procedures
IV. Administration	a) Internal b) External	On-the-job representation; shop stewards Arbitration

---

[1] This presentation is taken from an article by one of the authors of this book, which appeared in the September/October 1962, issue of *Personnel*, journal of the American Management Association, by permission of the copyright owner. Minor changes in terminology have been made in the version given here.

FUNCTIONS OF THE LABOR AGREEMENT

The function of a collective agreement as a whole is to set the terms and conditions of employment for the individual employees it covers.

In common usage, this collective agreement is called a contract, but the real contract is between the company and each of the employees in the bargaining unit, so that there are actually as many contracts as there are individuals. They individually do the work and draw the pay; the union agreement merely lays down rules under which each individual contract takes effect. These rules make up two of the four main sections shown on the chart—the Wage and Effort Bargain, and Individual Security. The other two—Union Security and Management Rights, and Administration—define the union's relationship with management, and provide for administration of the terms agreed to.

The four parts further break down into the 13 functional categories listed in Figure 8–1. Following is a detailed explanation of these various categories and what they cover:

I. Union Security and Management Rights

Every labor agreement constitutes recognition by one party of the other, and defines their relationship—who speaks for whom, with what authority, for how long, and except in what conditions. These four categories are shown in the table as:

a) The Bargaining Unit. The bargaining unit is the people for whom the union speaks and for whom the company recognizes the union as spokesman. At any given moment, these people could be listed as names on a payroll, but because people shift jobs, move on and off the payroll, it is customary to describe the unit in terms of jobs. This may be done positively, by listing jobs or job categories, or negatively, by listing exclusions. Or, as is usually the case, it can be done by both methods.

b) Form of Recognition. The statutory form of recognition is sole and exclusive bargaining rights. Other, stronger forms of recognition are also legal, but go beyond the statutory minimum. Some items that will fall in this category are:

1. Union hiring hall.
2. Checkoff of union dues and contributions.
3. Union participation in apprenticeship control.
4. Provisions giving the union power over employment; that is, the individual's right to join and remain in the bargaining unit.

c) Duration and Renewal. The agreement must run some specific term, and usually contains provisions for renewal. Such, for example, are:

1. Notice of termination or negotiation.
2. "Openers" for wage adjustments during the contract period.

d) *Management Rights.* This balances union security. Many agreements do not contain management rights provisions, on the theory that all rights not specifically bargained away belong to management, but most companies find it more practical to insert reminders that certain specific areas of action and decision remain in management hands. What special rights does management most need to retain? Three stand out:

1. Freedom to select the business objectives of the company.
2. Freedom to determine the uses to which the material assets of the enterprise will be devoted.
3. Power to discipline for cause.

II. The Wage and Effort Bargain

This is the heart of the agreement. It tells the employee how much pay he will get for how much work on a given job. It tells the company how much it will cost—in money—to get desired performance and production. Here we have five categories:

a) *Pay for Time Worked.* This means the hourly, weekly, monthly wage or salary paid for the job, by base rates or day rates. Determining the appropriate rates for the job is part of bargaining, but the technique most commonly used for establishing wage differentials, with or without bargaining, is standard job-evaluation procedure, including such considerations as:

1. Labor grades or classifications and rate ranges.
2. Pay steps within grade.
3. Expected average earnings under piecework systems.

b) *The Effort Bargain.* This part of the basic contract between the company and each of its employees does not always appear explicitly in the agreement, but it is always there, if only by implication. It is as important to management (for it determines costs) as the preceding item is to the employee (since that item determines his income). The effort bargain, in a word, means standards for task performance.

Standards may take very concrete form, as in time studies, or they may be loose and undefined. If management is careless about standards, employees may set them by default. Standards determine the intensity of each hour worked—the miles per hour, rather than distance traveled or hours on the road—the performance expected under the working conditions that surround the task. Incentive plans or piecework may permit variable earnings, but standards are firm. That is, once standards have been properly set, they ought to change only with changes in working conditions, technology, or other alterations in the task itself. The effort bargain makes stipulations such as:

1. Rules for setting standards or making time studies.
2. Crew sizes, manning tables.
3. Quotas.
4. Work rules, including safety rules applying to the task.

   c) Premium Pay. This is what used to be called "penalty pay." Theoretically, it is money that would never be paid if no employee were asked to work outside his regularly scheduled, normal daylight hours. The most common types of premium pay are:

1. Overtime.
2. Call-in pay.
3. Shift differentials.

   d) Pay for Time Not Worked. This item used to be lumped together with the following one, contingent benefits, under the general heading of "fringe benefits." Our outline separates them, putting in category II (*d*) payments that represent fixed labor costs, i.e., costs that are inescapable and predictable—the payments that all employees get such as:

1. Paid holidays and vacations.
2. Christmas or other bonuses.
3. Minor items, such as paid coffee breaks, washup time, and so forth.

   e) Contingent Benefits. These are usually, though not always, variable labor costs. That is, most companies pay for them on a cents-per-man-hour basis, or as a percentage of payroll. (The other way of paying for them is by a flat sum per head per month, which turns them into fixed costs, or semifixed, at all events.) They differ from the preceding category in that not every employee gets all the benefits they offer; also, employees may contribute to the costs. Actuarial calculations will yield quite an accurate prediction as to the number of employees to whom these benefits will be paid, but the individual claims cannot, of course, be foreseen. Management must judge these items by their cost, whereas employees will judge them by their payoff in individual cases. The main types of contingent benefits are:

1. Death benefits.
2. Pensions.
3. Supplementary unemployment benefits.
4. Severance pay.
5. Health and welfare plans.

III. Individual Security

The wage and effort bargain, outlined above, is the fundamental contract offer the employee accepts when he accepts his job. It obligates the company to pay him according to the terms set down. In turn, it obligates the employee to perform as specified in the agreement, or as directed by management in day-to-day operations. But it contains no guarantee of continuance. An employee who finds the bargain satisfactory wants some guarantee of continuity of employment. Broadly speaking, this attitude coincides with management interests, because the company does not want excessive turnover. Nevertheless, the company has to lay people off when work is slack; at times it needs to transfer people from one job to another; and it should have freedom to select good prospects for promotion. Thus, there has to be an accommodation of company and employee interests. The rules whereby the company, on the one hand, maintains a work force of the optimum quality and numbers, and employees, on the other, are assured of their individual security, fall into two categories:

a) *Job Rights.* Probably the most common job rights device is seniority. Other common forms are the closed shop or the union hiring hall. In the latter case, union practices or bylaws take care of individual claims to available work; they are then no concern of management. Seniority within the company, on the other hand, is a vast and complicated field of claims and counterclaims by individuals. Seniority is never absolute; it gives the individual only a relative claim to available work or other benefits flowing from the enterprise. Three types of seniority can be distinguished—protective, opportunity, and privilege—together with a special concept, the seniority unit, that has a bearing on all three.

To take the special concept first, the seniority unit usually consists of a list of employees' names ranked in order of their seniority. What is important here is the size of the list or lists in relation to the total work force in the bargaining unit. Criteria for compiling the list may range from simple job seniority on up through occupational, departmental, divisional, and plant-wide groupings to company-wide seniority. (The 1965 steel settlement even extended the concept to a "seniority pool" for the industry, thus cutting across company lines.)

Of the three main types of seniority, the first—protective seniority—applies in the case of layoffs: The most senior employee (within the specified unit) is the last to be let go and the first to be recalled when work picks up.

The second type, opportunity seniority, gives the most senior employee the first chance to get, or qualify for, a better job—or, in case of a cutback, to stay on the payroll. The "bid and bump" system exemplifies this type. Of course, the broader the seniority unit, the closer opportunity seniority comes to being the same thing as protective seniority, and in the plant or company-wide unit they become synonymous.

The third type, privilege seniority, is the employee's right to contingent benefits, such as pensions. This is probably the only completely noncontroversial kind of seniority, as evidenced by the fact that the unit is almost always company-wide, with pensions calculated according to total years of service.

But union agreements rarely make seniority the sole determinant of job rights. The broader the seniority unit, the more it is likely to be affected by such factors as merit or ability to do the job, particularly in cases of opportunity seniority. Hence, in the job-rights category also fall such items as:

1. Superseniority for shop stewards.
2. Breaks in seniority.
3. Criteria other than seniority, such as merit, for individual advancement.

b) Due Process. This category covers the grievance-handling procedure (though not the machinery)—the rules that have been laid down for handling employee complaints of all types, including allegations of simple injustice as well as contract violations. This covers such items as:

1. Steps in the grievance procedure.
2. Time limits for replies to grievances.
3. Procedure for invoking arbitration.
4. No-strike, no-lockout pledges pending arbitration.
5. Warning notices and reprimands.
6. Disciplinary penalties and appeals.

IV. Administration

This section covers the machinery that is set up to enforce agreement terms and put due process into effect, including the delegation of the requisite authority to specific individuals who have been given certain responsibilities in connection with the agreement. Part of this machinery is internal, in that it involves only employees of the company. Part is external, involving outsiders, such as union representatives, government officials, or private arbitrators. This gives us our two final categories:

a) On-the-Job Representation. Though union members may name their representatives, such as shop stewards, the election of those people does not confer authority upon them. They obtain their authority from the agreement, in which the special activities of shop stewards are recognized. Thus, this category covers such arrangements as:

1. Payment for time spent by stewards in handling grievances.
2. Permission for stewards to leave their workplace to confer with employees and with supervisors.

b) Arbitration. This category encompasses those sections of the agreement covering outsiders on whom it confers a certain authority. It includes such items as:

1. Grants of permission to union officials to visit workplaces during working hours, under certain conditions.
2. Composition of a board of arbitrators, or a disciplinary board, if this draws upon people from outside the company.
3. Duties and powers of the arbitrator and any limitations thereon.

DIVERSITY IN LABOR AGREEMENTS

This chapter purports to be a tool for the analysis of labor agreements. To show how this tool works, two labor agreements will be analyzed. This analysis will require consideration of long-established practices of the parties to an agreement as well as the written words. By noting the substantial diversity in the practices of craft and industrial unions, the basic unity of purpose of all collective bargaining agreements becomes apparent.

A Craft Union-Employer Association Agreement

The first agreement to be analyzed is 30 pages long and contains about 9,000 words. It covers the bricklayers in a major metropolitan area. Three employer associations and four local unions of the Bricklayers, Masons and Plasterers' International Union signed the agreement.

Union Security and Management Rights. To understand the union security provisions of this agreement it is necessary to look beyond the written words of the agreement. Such key words as "Union Security" and "Management Rights" appear nowhere in the agreement.

Bargaining Unit. The agreement contains no explicit reference to the "bargaining unit." However, the bargaining unit is defined in three other sections of the agreement: "Article XI: Scope of Work" (which deals with the nature of covered jobs), "Article XIV: Negotiations: Grievances" (which provides for the settlement of jurisdictional disputes), and "Article I" (which defines the relationships of individual employers to the three Associations who are signatories to the agreement).

Article XI: Scope of Work, reads as follows:

The work covered by this Agreement is described as bricklaying masonry and shall consist of laying bricks, in, under and upon any structure or form of work where bricks are used, whether in the ground or over the surface, or beneath water, in commercial buildings, rolling mills, iron works, blast or smelting furnaces, lime or brick kilns, in mines or fortifications and in all underground work such as sewers, telegraph, electric and telephone conduits; all pointing and cutting of brick walls, fireproofing, block-arching, terra cotta cutting and setting, laying and cutting of all tile, plaster, mineralwool, cork blocks, cement and cinder blocks, glass brick, macotta and metalon, or any substitutes for the above materials where the trowel is used, and setting of all cut stone or artificial stone trimming on brick or stone buildings.

The work defines the jobs covered by the agreement which is the equivalent to the employee side of the bargaining unit question.

Because Article XI might come into conflict with bargaining units defined in other building and construction industry agreements, Article XIV provides for the local settlement of jurisdictional disputes or the ultimate referral of such disputes to the National Joint Board for the Settlement of Jurisdictional Disputes in the Building and Construction Industry.

"Article I" which has no descriptive title provides the answer to the question of what employers are covered by the agreement. The three associations which signed the agreement represent masonry contractors, general contractors who employ other tradesmen as well as bricklayers, and residential construction contractors. Article I states that the associations acted only as agents for their members in the negotiation of the contract and that the associations have an individual, but not joint, obligation to the terms of the contract. Article I also contains a "most favored nation" clause which binds the union not to negotiate more favorable contracts with other employers.

Form of Recognition. The form of recognition or union security provisions of this agreement are contained in "Article VIII: Hiring Employees." The six sections of this article require the employers to notify the union of job vacancies and to give preference in employment to workmen who have previously worked at the trade or to graduates or students in an approved apprenticeship training program. The union agrees to refer qualified workmen to the employer for consideration. Workmen who refuse to join the union within seven days after being hired must be discharged. All this boils down to either a "seven-day union shop" or a "modified closed shop"—neither of which terms can be found anywhere in the words of the agreement.

Duration and Renewal. The provisions for duration and renewal are routine.

Management Rights. The term "Management Rights" is also missing from the written agreement. Article XI, Section 1, states, "There shall be no limits or restrictions as to the amount of work performed by employees," but numerous other paragraphs provide that "No work shall be done which shall destroy the true principles of the trade." All this seems to indicate that management rights are defined by a tradition which places heavy emphasis on judgment of individual tradesmen.

The Wage and Effort Bargain. The wage and effort bargain is the largest single section of the bricklayers' agreement. It covers almost 10 of the 30 pages of the agreement. Nevertheless, it is very brief and very simple compared to the typical industrial union agreement.

Pay for Time Worked. The wage scale contained in this agreement provides base wages for only *four* jobs: journeymen, subforemen, foremen, and apprentices. Foremen are paid 50 cents an hour more than journeymen and subforemen are paid 25 cents an hour more than journeymen. Apprentices receive a graduated percentage of the journeyman rate depending on how long they have served in the apprenticeship, e.g., 50 percent during the first six months of apprenticeship up to 80 percent in the seventh six months.

The Effort Bargain. The bricklayers' contract does not say much about the effort bargain as such. However, it contains quite detailed provisions on the types of scaffolds to be provided, the fact that foremen must be "practical mechanics of the trade," limits on the work activity of foremen, the obligation of workmen to cooperate with one another, and workmanship standards which preserve "the true principles of the trade."

Premium Pay. Work in excess of eight hours per day is prohibited except for a few minutes of work in cases of necessity. Overtime work and work performed on Saturdays, Sundays, and holidays is paid at the rate of double time. Base wages on the second shift and third (or special) shift are 30 cents and 60 cents per hour higher than on the first shift. The "special shift" is any single shift when conditions make it impractical to work a shift wholly between the regular hours of 8 A.M. and 4:30 P.M.

Pay for Time Not Worked. Holiday pay is provided by the Bricklayers' Holiday Trust Fund which is supported by a 4 percent payroll contribution by the employers covered by the agreement. Wash-up time is limited to five minutes before lunch and before quitting time.

Contingent Benefits. The benefits provided by this agreement are described in a separate agreement which has been amended several times since its establishment. The basic agreement, however, provides for employer contributions of 4 percent of the base wages paid to the Bricklayers' Pension Trust Fund. Insurance is provided by the Construction Workers' Insurance Fund which is financed by employer payments of 15 cents per man-hour worked for all hours worked by his employees. It should be noted that the Holiday Trust Fund, the Pension Fund, and the Insurance Fund are all multiemployer arrangements and that the worker is entitled to his benefits by virtue of employment with any unionized employers in the industry rather than by continuous employment with a single enterprise.

Individual Security. Job rights, or the individual's relative claim to available work, is almost entirely absent from the agreement. Since the union refers workers to employment, *union* rules define the individual's job rights. However, if it becomes necessary to reduce the working force temporarily the foreman is directed to divide the work equally among the crew, and no employee is to receive less than two hours' pay on any day on which the work force is reduced temporarily unless the foreman sends the whole crew home for that day. The workers' absolute claim to fair treatment is described in the sections of the agreement dealing with foremen. The agreement provides that foremen shall be selected by the employer and shall represent the employer on the job. Another paragraph of the agreement states: "It shall be the duty of the foreman to abide by terms of this Agreement and he shall not be required as a condition of employment to violate any part of it." Although the agreement provides a method of wage payment for employees who may be discharged, the agreement lists no grounds for discharge and makes no reference whatsoever to disciplinary procedures.

Administration. Article VI of the agreement provides for a job steward on each job. The steward is a member of the union appointed by the business agent to act as steward. The steward and business agent may confer with employees during working hours.

If the steward is unable to settle a grievance with the foreman, he refers the grievance to the business agent. If the business agent is unable to settle the grievance with the employer, the grievance is referred to a Joint Arbitration Board consisting of equal numbers of union and employer representatives. If this Joint Board is unable to render a majority opinion on the grievance, the grievance is then referred to the international union. A representative of the international union and a representative of the associations then designate an umpire (arbitrator) who is empowered to render a final and binding decision.

The foregoing analysis of a craft union collective bargaining agreement shows: (1) the importance of unwritten practices in industries which have a long history of collective bargaining, (2) the omnipresence of the basic functions of the labor agreement, and (3) when compared to the following industrial union agreement, the great diversity in practice in the provisions of the labor agreement in different circumstances.

An Industrial Union–Single-Plant Agreement

The second agreement to be analyzed is 40 pages long and contains about 16,000 words. By industrial union standards, it is a short (many of them run to several hundred pages) and simple (one plant of a multiplant employer) agreement. Nevertheless, it will be obvious from the discussion that follows that this agreement is much more formal and complete than the typical craft union agreement.

Union Security and Management Rights. The industrial union agreement uses most of the terminology in Figure 8–1 in the form presented there.

Bargaining Unit. Article I—Recognition states that "The Company recognizes the Union as the exclusive bargaining agent with respect to wages, hours of employment or other conditions of employment for all production, maintenance and other factory employees, excepting office employees, office building janitors, time keepers, plant police, administrative employees, foremen, and clerks."

Form of Recognition. The form of recognition granted in this agreement is the agency shop, because the plant is located in a "right-to-work" state. The last paragraph of Article II provides that if the state right-to-work law is repealed the union shop clause will be reinstated in the agreement.

Article III of the agreement provides a voluntary and revocable check-off of union dues by the employer.

Duration and Renewal. The provisions for duration and renewal are routine.

Management Rights. Article IV of the agreement is entitled "Management of the Plant." Paragraph 4.0 reads as follows:

The management of the plant and the direction of the working force, including the right to hire; discharge for just cause, suspend, discipline, promote, transfer; to decide the machine and tool equipment, the products, methods, schedules of production, processes of manufacturing and assembling together with all designs and engineering, and the control of raw materials, semi-manufactured and finished parts which may be incorporated into the product, shall be vested exclusively in the Company.

Paragraph 4.1 provides that the rights of the company to discharge for just cause, suspend, discipline, to promote and transfer to jobs within the bargaining unit are subject to the provisions of the agreement and the grievance procedure.

The Wage and Effort Bargain. The wage and effort bargain provisions of this agreement cover approximately 15 of its 40 pages.

Pay for Time Worked. Appendix "A" lists the rates of pay for 124 different job descriptions falling into 13 labor grades. The lowest rate of pay is $2.43 per hour and the top rate is $3.22 per hour. New employees start at ten cents per hour below regular rate and receive a five-cent raise after 30 days on the job and another five-cent raise after 90 days on the job.

The Effort Bargain. The agreement being analyzed here makes no reference to production standards as such, but its grievance procedure is sufficiently broad in coverage to make production standards subject to arbitration.

Premium Pay. Time and one half is provided for work in excess of eight hours in a day, or forty in a week, or for work on Saturdays. Double-time pay is provided for all work on Sundays and holidays. Fifteen cents per hour of premium pay is provided for workers of the second and third shifts. Four hours of call-in pay are provided.

Pay for Time Not Worked. Holiday pay is provided for eight holidays. Vacation pay of from one to three weeks is provided for workers having more than one year's seniority. A 10-minute clean-up period is provided for painters before the end of their work shift.

Contingent Benefits. The company provides Blue Cross and Blue Shield insurance coverage for all members of the bargaining unit. A separate pension agreement provides for company contributions to a pension fund which will permit the payment of a schedule of benefits for workers when they reach the normal retirement age of 65. The pension fund covers only the employees of the company at this one plant.

Individual Security. Article VIII—Seniority describes the workers' relative claim to available work. The eight pages of Article VIII define the seniority unit, the applications of seniority, superseniority for stewards, and reasons for the revocation of seniority.

The workers' absolute claim to fair treatment is described in Article VIII—Discipline and Discharge. This article provides that all discipline shall be for "just cause." Article XIV provides that violation of company rules will provide a just cause for discipline. Appendix "B" lists 22 "Shop Rules and Regulations" and 10 "Safety Rules." Other provisions of the agreement outline the grievance handling procedure which terminates in arbitration.

Administration. Article V provides for on-the-job representation by stewards to be elected by whatever method the union deems appropriate so long as stewards have at least one year's seniority with the company and the number of stewards is agreed to by the company and union. Stewards are paid by the company when engaged in handling grievances but they must be excused from work by their foremen and the company reserves the right to limit the discussion of a grievance to 15 minutes.

The powers of the arbitrator are very broad under this agreement because he is authorized to "rule on all disputes pertaining to the interpretation or application of this Agreement, provided, however, that he shall have no power to add to, nor subtract from, nor modify any terms of this Agreement." The arbitrator is to be selected by the parties from lists provided by the American Arbitration Association.

SUMMARY

Every employment relationship focuses on a wage and effort bargain. When the employment relationship becomes formalized through collective bargaining, the agreement expands to cover four basic functions: (1) Union Security and Management Rights, (2) The Wage and Effort Bargain, (3) Individual Security, and (4) Administration. These four functions are present in every collective bargaining agreement: sometimes the written agreement is quite explicit in defining these functions and sometimes it is necessary to look carefully at the practice of the parties to identify the functions.

This text has emphasized the diversity of the practice between industrial and craft unions. This diversity remains in the contents of their agreements, but the very diversity in these agreements is proof of the unifying significance of the four basic functions of every collective bargaining agreement.

QUESTIONS FOR DISCUSSION

1. Compare and contrast the union agreement with the "employment relation" entered into between a physician and his patient or a lawyer and his client. Compare both of these relationships with the employment relation in a nonunion enterprise.

2. Would the "functions" discussed in this chapter be helpful in preparing for negotiations? Outline the desirable steps in detail.

Chapter 9   AGREEMENT ADMINISTRATION

The collective bargaining agreement states the rights and duties of the parties. It is more than a contract; it is a generalized code to govern a myriad of cases which the draftsmen cannot wholly anticipate. . . . It calls into being a new common law—the common law of a particular industry or a particular plant.

The grievance procedure is . . . a part of the continuous collective bargaining process. It, rather than a strike, is the terminal point of a disagreement.

. . . The labor arbitrator is usually chosen because of the parties' confidence in his knowledge of the common law of the shop and their trust in his personal judgment to bring to bear considerations which are not expressed in the contract as criteria for judgment. The parties expect that his judgment of a particular grievance will reflect not only what the contract says but, insofar as the collective bargaining agreement permits, such factors as the effect upon productivity of a particular result, its consequence to the morale of the shop, his judgment whether tensions will be heightened or diminished. For the parties' objective in using the arbitration process is primarily to further their common goal of uninterrupted production under the agreement to make the agreement serve their specialized needs.

> —Mr. Justice Douglas
> *United Steelworkers of America* v. *Warrior and Gulf Navigation Company*
> June 20, 1960

The quotation at the head of this chapter comes from the majority opinion in a trio of cases decided by the Supreme Court in 1960. As might be expected in a pronouncement from the bench, it reflects the judicial point of view. It regards a collective bargaining agreement as "a generalized code" that spells out rights and duties and sees this code as emerging from amidst a continuing set of customary relations, mutual expectations, and accepted modes of behavior that constitute "a new common law."

There is indeed, as Mr. Justice Douglas points out, an aspect of industrial jurisprudence in the administration of a collective bargaining agreement, but managers and union members know that this is only

271

half—perhaps less than half—the story. The arbitrator and the judge come in on appeal when things go wrong; it is up to the manager and the union official to make things go right, as things are expected to do. An agreement made in good faith is intended to be observed, not violated. Along with the Supreme Court opinion which sanctions the agreement as a "code," it would be well to recall the Dunlop theoretical framework, explained in the first chapter of this book, which calls the terms of the agreement "substantive rules."

In the Dunlop terminology, the two principal actors, management and labor, make the rules and live under them, regulating their relations with each other in accordance with the terms agreed upon. Presumably, they reach an acceptable accommodation that reconciles their separate interests and brings them into a joint relationship conferring mutual advantage. Among the rules they make are rules for implementing and enforcing—in a word, administering—the activities the rules govern. These implementing rules authorize and create a system of on-the-job representation for employees that corresponds to the organization's structure of management and supervision. They also provide for calling in, on occasion, a third actor normally not part of the organization: the arbitrator, one of Dunlop's "regulators." This third actor comes in when the two primary actors find that the machinery for internal administration cannot effectively resolve some problem of application or interpretation of the substantive rules.

AIMS OF AGREEMENT ADMINISTRATION

Ideally, the aim common to both management and the union in administering the agreement is to make the rules work in such ways as to result in mutual benefit. Successful attainment of this joint aim becomes difficult if the rules themselves are one-sided or if either management or the union seeks to take one-sided advantage of them. It may be presumed that when each side acts in its own best interest, both jointly further the common aim given good rules to begin with and good faith in their administration.

This chapter takes for granted a good agreement—one whose rules are well-conceived and well-formulated—as the norm. Even so, as will be seen, the implementing roles, prescriptions, and procedures make demands on both parties to the agreement and require implementing machinery that is both internal and external to the organization. (Please note, by the way, in the discussion that follows, the use of two words spelled almost alike but with very different meanings: *rules*, and *roles*.)

THE SUBSTANTIVE RULES

By definition, the management of an organization consists of a structure, or (to use a more dynamic metaphor) the working machinery, for administering operations that look toward the attainment of organizational objectives. A manager at any level reaches his objectives only when employeees, including subordinate managers, behave toward their tasks and toward each other in ways that he prescribes or expects. In a nonunion enterprise, management makes the rules of employee behavior (as well as the rules of manager behavior), but these rules cannot deviate very greatly from social norms and accepted standards. Even a nonunion firm could not expect an unchanged employee response if wages were cut in half and the work doubled. Implicit then, even in management-formulated rules, is the need for reciprocal benefits.

In a unionized firm, management and the union jointly make the rules. Both have an interest in fair and uniform observance of the reciprocal rights and obligations. A simple slogan expresses this, albeit in a primitive, traditional way: A fair day's pay for a fair day's work. Unionized enterprises make explicit provision in the agreement for a system of employee on-the-job representatives, usually called shop stewards, or committeemen. The steward system that the rules create becomes a *counterpart* or *control* to the management structure in the administrative machinery of the enterprise.

The steward system, brought into being, differs between craft and industrial unions and between organizations and unions in both categories, but serves essentially the same function in all. The internal administrative machinery of *management* remains primarily responsible for implementing the substantive rules, just as the management organization remains responsible for planning, directing, coordinating, and controlling operations. The shop steward's role does not permit him to substitute his judgment for the supervisor's, or exercise supervisory authority. It does give him the right to make sure that the supervisor does, in fact, implement the substantive rules that management and the union have agreed to.

If the union's understanding of a rule, or of its application, differs from the supervisor's action in observing or enforcing the rule, the steward still cannot substitute his interpretation for the supervisor's, or countermand the order. What he can do is set in motion a process to challenge and test the supervisor's action.

Thus, for example, the substantive rule might be that an employee is to perform work "as directed" by his supervisor, in return for the wages and other material benefits he gets from the organization; but there is more to the rule than that. The employee must, indeed, work as directed; he may not pick and choose his tasks; but he does so at a specified wage and at a tempo that has also been specified, or that, unspecified, is the standard or "common law" of the shop. If, now, the supervisor gives him tasks that under other substantive rules call for higher pay or requires him to work faster than the normal pace, the supervisor has broken the rule. The worker can go to his shop steward and lodge a complaint. While waiting for redress of his grievance, the worker must still go on working as directed by the supervisor; but the shop steward, as part of his recognized role, can officially challenge the supervisor's action and set in motion grievance procedures capable of eventually bringing the supervisor's behavior into conformity with the rules.

The administrative provisions of an agreement thus create new roles for policing and enforcing compliance with agreement terms and promoting proper observance, alongside the implementing role that already belongs to managers and supervisors. Chapter 4 has touched on some of these new roles in its account of the activities of shop stewards and grievance committee members. The same set of provisions also gives roles in the administrative procedures to some persons external to the enterprise and independent of it: to arbitrators on occasion, sometimes to mediators; and on a routine or special-occasion basis to certain union officials who are not employees of the organization nor of the local union such as, most commonly, district or international representatives.

If there were no appeal to an external, impartial arbitrator, labor and management would probably find that the machinery for internal administration did not work very well; but neither party would want to have the rules administered entirely by an outsider. "Don't call us, we'll call you" probably expresses (without the snide or contemptuous implication) the attitude of both primary actors to this third actor. They don't need arbitration every day; but when they do, they "need it bad."

Arbitration procedures thus wait at the end of the line in agreement administration. The arbitrator stands outside the enterprise, apart from operations. Most of the labor-management interaction that makes up the ongoing and dynamic content of agreement administration takes place between supervisors and employee representatives directly, at the work place, and goes on from day to day, from hour to hour.

This chapter examines that activity and discusses the roles of the representatives on both sides who carry it out. It then goes on to expain what happens when agreement administration hits a snag or breaks down, bringing the arbitrator on the scene.

CRAFT UNION AGREEMENT ADMINISTRATION

In industries like construction where craft unionism prevails, the norms and standards of behavior on the job are of long standing and are well known to the participants. As a consequence, the substantive rules are either understood or simply stated and simply administered. The implementing structure for agreement administration puts a job steward opposite the foreman or subcontractor supervising a crew of skilled workers, and the local union business agent opposite the employer or general contractor. Any dispute that this latter pair cannot settle between them is likely to result in a strike or lockout.

One kind of dispute that in the past frequently led to strikes arose out of conflicting jurisdictional claims between unions. Most jurisdictional strikes resulted from changes in technology. Who, for instance, should install a new type of prefabricated metal window, already glassed when brought to the building site? Should it be the carpenters, who always have installed the frames, which have always before been made of wood? Or the glaziers, who traditionally glassed the panes? Or the metal workers, who have never worked with wood or glass, but do work with metal? Today, the building trades unions and the associated contractors jointly participate at the national level in a board for the settlement of jurisdictional disputes. On the board an impartial umpire—an arbitrator—casts a deciding vote; the industry and the unions have bound themselves to abide by the board's decisions. Thus a third actor, one of Dunlop's "regulators," finds a place in the administration of the rules under craft unionism.[1] The jurisdictional strike, once the bane of the construction industry, has all but disappeared. Other disputed issues may, under some present-day agreements, go to an interunion body on the one side and an employer association on the other, and from there to arbitration rather than inevitably to a strike or lockout. Craft unions, nonetheless, resort to arbitration over disputes with the employer much less frequently than industrial unions.

Craft union practice at the level of the local gives the business agent discretion to appoint job stewards. Often the job steward is the first man sent out on a job in response to an employer's requisition for skilled workers. The job steward acts as a control over employer observance of the agreement for the union. He checks to see that all men hired are union members in good standing or have a valid work permit from the union. He watches to make sure that bosses, apprentices, laborers, and members of other unions do not perform work that belongs to journeymen of his craft. If he should come across a breach of the agreement—any failure either by management or the men to abide by the rules—he notifies the business agent.

A craft union job steward rarely argues a grievance with the gang boss; he rarely has to. Craft union members are skilled workers. They know their jobs. They control the rate at which they carry out their tasks. They receive uniform pay—the union scale—and carry their seniority or other job rights not with the employer of the moment or the season, but with the union. They have few interests that depend on the discretion of their boss or foreman. For that matter, the boss himself is likely to be a union member—or former member, carrying a withdrawal card entitling him to renew his membership if he should cease to be a boss—so that he knows very well the limits to his authority. He plans and lays out the work, tells the men simply what to do, and when; they do it. If the job steward were not there, the rules might not be quite so

---

[1] Incidentally, the umpire for building trades disputes happens (at this writing, 1972) to be that same John T. Dunlop, in his role as a practitioner.

well enforced, but the important rules are union rules, anyway, and the job steward plays primarily an intra-union role.

The business agent to whom the job steward reports is not an employee of any of the enterprises that employ the union members, but draws his pay from and works for the union. He may still be considered part of the internal administrative apparatus because he represents one of the primary actors, the union, which is a party to the agreement.

INDUSTRIAL UNION AGREEMENT ADMINISTRATION

In any sizeable enterprise where the industrial form of unionism finds appropriate application, agreement administration is not simple, but complex. The wage and salary system, for example, does not consist of a single "union scale" for a single category of skilled workers, but a structure of differentiated rates within a wide and often-changing range. Tasks making up job content also change; tempo of work depends not on the worker alone but may be machine-paced, or may derive from time and motion studies, work sampling, or other techniques not under worker control. A carpenter usually remains a carpenter throughout his working career, but factory workers change jobs; move up, down, and sideways in the differentiated job structure of the enterprise; master no single skill but perform many varied tasks. For these and many other reasons administration of the rules requires a rather comprehensive structure or machinery, creates special roles peculiar to industrial union agreements, and relies heavily on arbitration.

The important roles in industrial union agreement administration are those of the *shop steward, grievance committee member* (individually and as a collective body), and *arbitrator.*

The Shop Steward

The shop steward in the industrial type of union plays a more active and strategic role than his craft union counterpart. While he may carry out some intra-union duties, his primary function is to handle grievances. Arguing grievances with the supervisor is, in fact, his characteristic activity.

There are other differences. Shop stewards are not appointed, but elected. They are chosen by, and serve, a particular constituency consisting, usually, of a department or recognized subdivision of the enterprise headed by a work-group supervisor. The union members in the work group who elect the steward also have the right to recall and replace him; and in any case, he comes up for election again at the end of his term of a year or two.

Management has no say in the selection of shop stewards, but binds itself by agreement to deal, through the work-group supervisor, with the steward the employees elect. The agreement thus creates the role. The steward gets his authority to act in that role and capacity from the terms of the agreement—hence, ultimately, from management. The rules permit him to question and, indeed, to challenge, acts and decisions of the work-group supervisor, as a means of insuring respect for the rules. If complaints or grievances arise that the steward has to handle during working hours, the rules permit him, under most agreements, to leave his work station in order to carry on investigations, interview employees, and negotiate with the supervisor. Usually the company pays a steward at his regular rate for time spent away from work on steward's duties. Often the agreement gives him the special protection of "superseniority," which puts him at the top of the list in his unit, regardless of his actual length of service, as long as he holds office as a steward. This is to guarantee that he will be available to perform his role of on-the-job representation.

The rules providing on-the-job representation thus create a new, nonmanagement role assigned to play a part in the control of management performance. It is a completely internal role: Shop stewards are always enterprise employees.

They are also union members and, in fact, union officials. They are like noncoms in the local union's "army," serving alongside the enlisted members. They give the union a communications net in the enterprise during the working day; a union grapevine; the union's eyes and ears in the shop—and its voice, too, capable of reaching the remotest corner of the working organization.

Unless a union-shop agreement makes membership mandatory and automatic, shop stewards solicit new employees to join the union. When the agreement has no checkoff provision, they collect dues. Meeting together as a steward council, regularly or on call, they become a powerful, compact, functioning auxiliary of the local union. In larger organizations they collectively make up a hierarchy of employee representatives parallel to the management hierarchy: the mirror image of the management structure of the enterprise. Thus opposite a work-group supervisor stands the shop steward, and opposite the supervisor's boss, a chief steward of one sort or another, depending on the structure of the organization. This departmental or divisional chief steward may in turn take part in the election of a chief steward at the next-higher echelon, and so on up the ranks. While the agreement may not explicitly recognize all the intermediate roles, it makes provision invariably for the shop stewards at the bottom of the hierarchy and a chief steward at the top; the others still play a functioning part in administration. The steward *system* may be thought of as a counterstructure to the management organization.

The Grievance Committee

The steward system permeates an organization to provide on-the-job representation for employees throughout the bargaining unit. A *grievance committee.*[2] deals with the central personnel department. Jointly and centrally the union and management representatives deal with matter of administration that a shop steward could not settle with the work-group supervisor, or that affect more than one work group, or that concern all employees in the bargaining unit.

The grievance committee represents the local union and is headed by its president or other designated union officer. If the union employs a business agent, he is a member and often the chief spokesman. As might also be expected, the chief steward is an ex officio member because he heads the steward network.[3]

Additional union officials or elected members may also serve on the grievance committee, depending on the size of the enterprise or as specified in the agreement. Frequently one or more shop stewards may sit in, ad hoc, on sessions of the grievance committee when issues that are to be discussed affect their work groups, and in the same way management may call in the work-group supervisor temporarily.

Neither the grievance committee on the union side nor the personnel department on management's has any policy-making power. They cannot alter the agreement. Their job is to interpret it and apply its terms. Even if they should come to agree that a rule needs changing, they can do no more than recommend the change to the bodies that they represent: higher management or the local union. These higher bodies, having made the agreement in the first place, may agree to change it; but if either one declines, the existing agreement stands. Arbitration, incidentally, cannot change the rules either, but comes in when the two actors disagree about application or interpretation.

The grievance committee meets with management regularly or on call, usually at fixed minimum intervals such as a month or a fortnight. Between these meetings, the business agent may transact purely routine union business with the personnel manager, but any item of an exceptional nature or disagreement over routine affairs goes to the committee and a joint session. The joint sessions deal with accumulated grievances

---

[2] Nomenclature varies: The union may call its committee a "bargaining" or "negotiating" committee, just as management may call its department an industrial or employee relations department. The agreement may refer to it only as a joint committee with both management and union members; and indeed it transacts business in joint sessions; but the two elements are separable and this chapter's discussion deals with the union element. Whatever its local name, this standing committee must not be confused with the special committee or representation that also meets jointly with management to bargain on terms and negotiate the agreement establishing substantive rules. Calling the standing committee a grievance committee, as this chapter does, emphasizes its administrative function. Neither the grievance committee nor the personnel department make the rules; both play a part, during the life of the agreement, in enforcing the rules.

[3] Because the chief steward's duties and position in the steward system make him an essential member of this union committee, most local unions require that his election as chief steward by the stewards be ratified by vote of the members of the local.

unsettled at lower levels in the enterprise and matters affecting the work force as a whole or sizable portions of it or affecting more than one work group. It would be safe to say that the two central administrative organs of management and the union, meeting together and discussing the various issues that arise from day to day manage, with goodwill, to clear up most of the misunderstandings that might affect operations, and deal with most of the instances of misapplication of the rules. As in all human affairs, however, questions do arise from time to time that have no easy administrative answers, and disagreement results. What happens now?

The management decision prevails.

Management is, after all, directly responsible for administration. When management says "No" to the union, and still says "No" after hearing all the arguments, that settles the question—at least for the time being. The grievance committee then has two choices: Take "No" for an answer and drop the issue or take the problem to the local union.

The local union decides whether to take an issue to arbitration or, if there is no arbitration clause in the agreement, to a strike; otherwise, again, the management decision stands. If it should choose either of these alternatives, the issue becomes a matter of *external* administration (arbitration) or renewed bargaining, backed by the strike.

The *arbitrator's* role, which the agreement creates, will be discussed below as part of the external administration of the rules.

EXTERNAL ADMINISTRATION

Before any grievance can be handled, the management and union must agree to a procedure for processing grievances. Regardless of differences in procedures for handling grievances, the methods of investigating grievances and the methods of settlement available to the parties are the same in handicraft and mass-production industry. In this chapter, we will be discussing general methods of grievance settlement. Our hypothetical grievance is drawn from mass-production industry and is handled through a factory grievance procedure. We shall return to some of the differences in procedural arrangements in Chapter 14.

Given the presence of legitimate and unforseeable problems, what avenues for settlement are available to unions and management during the life of the contract? The possible methods of settlement here are just the same as the possible methods for settlement in negotiating a new contract. The critical difference between day-to-day problem settlement and contract renegotiation settlement is the different emphasis which the parties place on the alternative methods under the two sets of circumstances. Either type of dispute can be settled by: (1) arbitration—submitting the issues to an outside party who has been given authority to issue a binding decision, (2) mediation—asking a "friend of the family" to cool tempers and suggest methods of settlement which the parties may accept or reject, or (3) a strike, a lockout, or other resort to force.[4] Of course, none of these possibilities should be considered before both parties have done their best to settle their disagreement within the privacy of their own home.

It is very important to note that all three of these possibilities may be envisaged in the wording of a collective bargaining agreement. Something in the vicinity of 90 percent of all collective bargaining agreements provide for arbitration as a final method of settling *some* disputes over the interpretation of their terms. At the same time, some of these *same* contracts clearly provide that certain disputes will *not* be settled by arbitration. For the items *not* subject to arbitration and *not* finally settled by the terms of the contract, the employer reserves the right to institute changes not agreeable to the union and the union reserves the power to veto his changes by the strike. Even in the case of disputes not subject to arbitration because of *planned* loopholes in the arbitration section of the agreement, strikes are infrequent for several reasons. The infrequency of these strikes, the reasons for which will be discussed below, has caused some students to assume incorrectly that *any* strike during the life of an agreement is an unlawful strike or a strike in breach of the agreement. Many strikes during the life of an agreement are breaches of that agreement, but many are *not* breaches of the agreement because the agreement itself is an agreement to *strike* as the final method of settlement of a very few, but extremely important, kinds of disputes.

Dispute Settlement between the Parties by the Parties Themselves

A grievance is almost always an individual or group human problem. The agreement may define grievances in abstract terms as far as arbitrability goes, but in the day-to-day process of living together the grievances are a human problem. Union stewards' manuals on grievance processing usually contain statements such as the following:

You can usually decide whether a complaint is a genuine grievance by asking yourself two questions:
1. Did the company violate the contract?
   If the answer is "yes," you've got a grievance for sure.
2. Has the worker been treated unfairly by the company?
   If the answer is "yes" to this question, you've probably got a grievance even though you're not sure that the contract has been violated. Sometimes this kind of grievance is hard to win, though, because of a loophole in the

---

[4] The use of arbitration as a means of settling contract negotiation disputes is so exceptional that it must be noted lest it be overlooked. Strikes and mediation, instead of arbitration, are so infrequently used in agreement interpretation disputes that they must be noted lest they be overlooked as possibilities.

contract. When this happens, make a note that this clause in the contract should be improved at the next contract negotiations.[5]

The human aspect of grievances is further borne out by company foremen's manuals. The variety of statements is too wide to present a representative quotation, but almost every manual emphasizes the foreman's job of resolving grievances at early stages and *preventing* situations from arising which cause grievances. The company's preventive program is closely akin to the union's fairness program.

A worker *feels* the company has violated the contract or treated him unfairly. This is the beginning of a grievance. Maybe the company hasn't violated the contract or treated the worker unfairly; if he *feels* he has been treated unfairly we have an embryo grievance which can be run through the dispute-settlement process. Sometimes a union representative will "cook up" grievances for the purpose of embarrassing the company. Sometimes a company will work at creating unfair situations in the hope of provoking the union into a strike that the union can ill afford. But wherever the grievance really came from, its first obvious appearance is usually in a worker protest against some actual or alleged management action or inaction.

Assume, for simplicity of discussion, that a worker feels that his foreman is violating the contract when he instructs him to stack his finished pieces in a new and time-consuming way on the cart used to take the pieces to the packing department. The worker claims that this is work "outside of my classification" and is a management speed-up. Since this is a grievance against the individual foreman, the worker will probably take it to his union steward as the first step. The worker tells his story to the steward.

The grievance is now in the lap of the steward. What does he do with it? The first thing the steward should do is get all the facts. Pertinent facts in this case would include such questions as:

1. When did the foreman first give you orders to stack the pieces in a certain way?
2. Did he give similar *new* orders to the other workers in your department?
3. How long has it been your practice to pile the pieces on the cart without stacking them in a certain way? Has the foreman ever told you to stack them this new way before? When? Do the other men stack them this new way?
4. What did you do in the past when you ran off more pieces than you had cart space for? Who picked up and piled this surplus on the next cart that came along?
5. What does the job description for this job say about preparing

[5] Department of Education and Research, CIO. *The Shop Steward: Key to a Strong Union* (Washington D.C.: CIO Publication No. 271, 1955), p. 21.

finished work for transfer? How do other departments with similar jobs handle the stacking problem?

6. Does the production standard or incentive wage rate for this job provide time allowances or money allowances for stacking?

7. What does the contract say about job reevaluations and changes in production standards?

8. By *actual observation*, what additional fatigue or effort does this new order impose on the worker?

9. What effect would the processing of this grievance have on the overall position of workers in the company? If the grievance were aired and we "lost" would the result be a general speed-up throughout the plant?

In processing the grievance, the steward may consider one other important fact: his own political position within the department and the union. If he is up for reelection, he may show little restraint in processing questionable grievances from his potential political supporters. In a plant without a union-shop agreement, he may show a natural reluctance to energetically process grievances originating with "free riders." When the union is trying to soften up management for impending negotiations, he may even manufacture grievances. Most stewards seldom refuse to process grievances because the individual worker has the right to process his own grievance through exclusively management channels. The steward can ill afford to refuse to process a grievance and have management later grant the individual worker's request for an adjustment. Having noted these possibilities, let us assume that our steward had no political problems and judges this grievance to be fully justified by the facts and the collective bargaining agreement.

The steward's next move is the conference with the foreman. As a general rule, the grievance is not reduced to writing before this conference is held. A steward in preparing for this conference might very well improve his discussion with the foreman by outlining the grievance as it may ultimately be reduced to writing. This process clarifies the grievance in the steward's mind and may suggest further fruitful avenues for discussion. However, both the foreman and the steward frequently prefer to talk it out before the formality of writing out the grievance. This talk before writing gives both sides flexibility in their thinking. If the grievance is clear and justified, both the union and the management profit from better feelings by settling it informally and with dispatch. In the conference with the foreman, the steward requests redress for the alleged injustice.

The foreman listens to the steward's request and asks whatever questions he deems necessary to fully understand the nature of the grievance. Both the foreman and the steward are well advised to control their tempers. The foreman usually postpones his answer to the steward until he has had time to review the agreement and gather his own facts about the situation. One of the critical facts which the foreman usually considers is the opinion of higher management or the personnel department on what disposition should be made of this grievance. It is very important that the foreman do this because any settlement he makes may be used later as a precedent in other departments.[6] After considering these facts, the foreman delivers a decision to the steward. We shall assume that for a good reason he believes this grievance to be invalid and denies the steward's request for an adjustment.

As discussed in Chapter 4, the grievance then moves up through higher echelons of the company and union organizations. We shall assume that our grievance goes through to the top echelon of the company and union organizations without a mutually satisfactory adjustment. What happens next?

Although increased interest has recently been shown in grievance mediation, this method of settling agreement interpretation disputes is still infrequently used. Grievance mediation occurs when the disputants ask an impartial outsider to suggest possible avenues for agreement. The mediator cools tempers, brings a fresh outlook to the dispute, and may propose perfectly acceptable means of agreement which the disputants overlooked. Grievance mediation seems to be uniquely appropriate when the same mediator has played an influential role in the negotiation of the agreement now in dispute. Although either or both of the disputants might for strategic or tactical reasons oppose resort to this method, when it is acceptable to the parties it is probably the *ideal* means of dispute settlement. In questions of agreement interpretation almost anything that the parties will agree to is preferable to a decision made by an outsider or resort to force. Failure in grievance mediation almost always results in a resort to arbitration or the use of force in achieving a settlement.

The final step, beyond company and union organizations, may be established by the terms of the collective bargaining agreement or improvised at the time of the deadlock. When face-to-face agreement proves

---

[6] In the period 1935–45 many managements, confronted with unionism for the first time, centralized all authority for labor relations matters at a high level. This was a natural, and probably necessary, reaction to militant unionism. Dealing with unions was a radical new departure and a few "experts" monopolized this activity in the management hierarchy. The union itself was a new challenge to the foreman's authority and he was disillusioned when management met this outside challenge by stripping him of his authority in labor relations. Once collective bargaining was established and management became competent in its practice, many managements began training foremen in contract administration and restoring their authority in labor relations. At the present time, the main current of progressive management practice seems to be flowing in the direction of giving foremen increased discretion in labor relations matters. Nevertheless, it is quite likely that consultation with higher management on many grievance settlements will remain a necessity because of their potential precedent-making character.

impossible, what *others means* for grievance settlement are available to the parties?

Grievance Settlement by Means Other than Negotiation

Depending upon whether management or the union is the grievant, the nature of the grievance itself, and the provisions of the applicable collective bargaining agreement, the dispute may be settled by arbitration or the use of force. We shall discuss the use of force before the much more commonly used method of arbitration. It must be repeated for emphasis that the vast majority of agreement interpretation disputes are settled by resort to peaceful voluntary arbitration.

Use of Force in Agreement Interpretation Disputes. Both unions and managements occasionally use force as a means of settling their disputes over agreement interpretation or matters not specifically covered by the agreement. Sometimes, as in the case of strikes over nonarbitrable issues, they have agreed in advance to fight it out when disagreements arise. Other resorts to force, such as injunctions, law suits, and disciplinary actions against workers violating the terms of an agreement, result from inadequate advanced planning for handling certain particularly tough disagreements. It is an encouraging sign that resort to force seems to be a steadily declining practice because of increased responsibility in agreement observance by both unions and managements.

Five different forms of resort to force may be delineated: (1) strikes over nonarbitrable issues, (2) law suits by either managements, workers or unions to recover damages suffered as a result of alleged agreement violations, (3) injunctions sought by either managements, workers, or unions to prevent an anticipated breach of the agreement, (4) voiding a contract which has been breached, and (5) disciplinary action against workers who have engaged in strikes, slowdowns, sabotage, or other violations of a collective bargaining agreement. These instruments of force vary in the frequency with which they are used and their utility to each of the disputants.

When an agreement reserves the right to strike for the union over certain nonarbitrable issues during the life of the agreement, management may institute or continue the practice, e.g., higher production standards or a low wage rate on a new job, which the union considers objectionable. The union either "agrees" with the practice by continuing to work under these objectionable conditions or it disagrees by calling a strike. Although the strike power in this situation is a powerful instrument of persuasion, the union is usually extremely reluctant to enforce its claim for "justice." Typically nonarbitrable issues involve only a few workers at a single time. The union leader is frequently confronted with the prospect that hundreds of workers just won't respond to a strike call aimed at obtaining concessions for only a handful of workers. The risks of striking frequently are too great when compared to the possible gains obtainable from winning a strike over contract interpretation.

When workers engage in contract violations such as slowdowns or strikes, management may seek redress through the lockout. Like the strike, this method is seldom used because of the dangers inherent in its use. Although many collective bargaining agreements provide for the right of management to process grievances against the union, such grievances seldom arise except in the case of slowdowns or strikes in breach of the agreement. The infrequency of grievances against the union is due to the fact that management retains the power of initiative in most of the situations unforeseen or not agreed to at the time of negotiations.

Suits for damages and injunctions usually are considered to be the substitute of law for the exercise of force. We have classified them as resorts to force because the initiating party is seeking to enlist the coercive power of government to help it impose its will on the offending party. Enlisting the support of government is perfectly legitimate, but it tends to leave a scar on the collective bargaining relationship just like other resorts to force.

Both unions and managements have the legal right to sue the offending party for breach of contract. From the union viewpoint, there have been a few suits for damages in the case of "runaway" plants, violations of clauses limiting management's right to subcontract or "farm out" work normally performed within the bargaining unit, or for restitution in wage payment cases. From the company viewpoint, suits for damages are possible remedies for such things as boycotts, strikes in violation of the agreement, and slowdowns. Suits for damages are seldom used in present-day collective bargaining because both parties tend to view them as "divorce" actions.[7] Arbitration, strikes, or disciplinary actions against workers are often preferred over suits for damages and injunctions because they leave less severe long-term scars on the company-worker-union relationship.

Injunctions are available, under severely restricted conditions, to either unions or managements as a means of settling disputes over agreement interpretation. The injunction, which stops the threatened misapplication or breach of the agreement, is an *ideal* union remedy against runaway

---

[7] It might be noted that many managements insist that the international union be made a signatory party to the collective bargaining agreement. One advantage of this procedure is that the larger financial resources of the international would be available for the satisfaction of any court-awarded financial damages. It seems likely that international unions' urgings of wildcat strikers to return to work are sometimes motivated by a fear of this consequence.

plants. From the management viewpoint, the injunction (if it is obeyed) is the *ideal* remedy for the wildcat strike in violation of a collective bargaining agreement.

When a union or a management misinterprets an agreement to the extent of violating its provisions, the offended party has the legal right to void the entire agreement. There are few recorded cases where this remedy has been used because its application usually results in an immediate strike, suit, or injunction. A hypothetical example may clarify the possible application of this remedy. Assume that a union engages in a strike in violation of the agreement. Management could then reduce wages, discontinue employee benefits, or deny union security on the basis that the whole agreement had been voided by the union's failure to abide by some of its terms.

In wildcat strikes, slowdowns, or sabotage in violation of a collective bargaining agreement, management may discharge or otherwise discipline the workers involved. The value of this remedy depends entirely upon the individual circumstances. When all the workers are on strike, management's *practical* power to discipline even the strike instigators is severely limited if it wants to resume production promptly. In such cases, the union frequently protects the strike leaders by refusing to return to work until an agreement is worked out on disciplinary action. If the strike has solid support and the management strongly wants to resume production, the disciplinary measures against strike leaders may be bargained down to nothing. Mass disciplinary action against very large numbers of strikers or slowdown participants frequently is a practical impossibility since such managerial action would cause even further interruptions to production.

Before leaving these seldom-used methods, it might be well to note again that all of them involve the infliction of injury on one party by the other, sometimes assisted by government. These methods tend, therefore, to leave more or less enduring scars on the collective bargaining relationship. Arbitration is a process which settles the dispute without the unpleasantness of direct combat. Except where the issues are of vital importance to one or both of the parties, they usually prefer to settle their differences over contract interpretation without direct combat. This peaceful adjudication of disputes is our next topic.

Case No. 3 in Part V of this book deals with the remedies available to the parties in event of breach of the agreement.

Voluntary Arbitration: Peaceful Adjudication of Grievance Disputes

Our worker's grievance over stacking finished parts on the cart might very well be a strikeable issue under some collective bargaining agreements. However, we shall assume that like the vast majority of grievances it is not. Under the circumstances, the normal last step is voluntary arbitration. Usually the collective bargaining agreement itself establishes the broad outline of the procedure to be followed for arbitrating disputes over its interpretation.

In arbitration, the disputants ask an impartial person for a determination of the dispute on the basis of evidence and argument presented by them. The disputants agree in advance to accept the decision of the arbitrator as final and binding. Before discussing the preparation for, and conduct of, an arbitration hearing, we shall briefly note the procedural decisions which precede the hearing.

Procedural Arrangements for Arbitration.   The company and the union must create an arbitration tribunal and submit their dispute to that tribunal before the case can be heard and a decision rendered. In writing their collective bargaining agreement or later submitting their dispute to arbitration, they have several choices to make about procedural matters. There are several public and private organizations which will help them in handling these problems.

Creating an Arbitration Tribunal.   Should a different tribunal be established for each dispute (ad hoc arbitration) or should a single tribunal be established to decide all disputes between the parties (umpire or permanent chairman system)? Ad hoc arbitration is most commonly used in small companies because of the infrequency of arbitration hearings. It has the important advantage of low procedural costs. Even where companies have only a few arbitrations per year, occasionally they establish an umpire system to give continuity to arbitration procedures and decisions. An umpire, like an ad hoc arbitrator, serves only so long as he is acceptable to both parties. The powers of the ad hoc arbitrator or umpire are detailed and limited by the terms of the collective bargaining agreement or the submission agreement.

Should the arbitration tribunal consist of a single impartial member or should representatives of the disputants also be members of the tribunal? An impartial one-member tribunal offers the advantage of a unanimous decision without compromising the position of either of the disputants or the impartial member. The disputants sometimes favor a tripartite tribunal as an opportunity to educate the impartial member in the full complexities of the dispute and to be certain that he considers all relevant facts and arguments. It may give both disputants a fuller understanding of the award than exists under a one-member tribunal. The tripartite tribunal has the disadvantage of frequently handing down only "majority" decisions. Even here, the impartial member may have to compromise his judgment of the issue in dispute to get a decision from the deadlocked tribunal. A tripartite tribunal may tend to shade off from arbitration into the field of mediation.

How is an impartial person selected as sole arbitrator or as a member of a tripartite tribunal? The disputants are free to select any person as their arbitrator so long as they both agree to his selection. Because labor arbitration is a process requiring complete impartiality, high intelligence, and a knowledge of the issues, unions and managements frequently solicit the assistance of public or private organizations in arranging for an arbitrator's services. The American Arbitration Association, a private non-profit organization, the Federal Mediation and Conciliation Service, and several state mediation boards maintain rosters of professional arbitrators for selection by the disputants. These organizations supply information about the arbitrator's qualifications to the parties seeking an arbitrator's services.

The collective bargaining agreement itself frequently details the procedures to be followed in selecting an arbitration tribunal. A commonly used method is the standard arbitration clause of the American Arbitration Association:

Any dispute, claim or grievance arising out of or relating to the interpretation or the application of this agreement shall be submitted to arbitration under the Voluntary Labor Arbitration of the American Arbitration Association. The parties further agree to accept the arbitrator's award as final and binding upon them.

This clause is supplemented by a statement providing for an impartial or tripartite tribunal.

When the American Arbitration Association clause is included in an agreement, either party may initiate arbitration proceedings by filing a Demand for Arbitration with the regional AAA office.

When a dispute arises between parties who are not subject to an arbitration clause, they may bring the matter to arbitration by means of a jointly signed statement setting forth the nature of the dispute and affirming their willingness to abide by the arbitrator's award. This statement is called a submission agreement. Submission agreements may also be used when a collective bargaining agreement terminates and the company and the union are unable to agree to new terms.

Selecting an Arbitrator. Selecting an arbitrator is somewhat like selecting a physician. Just as an ill person needs a physician *now*, the parties with an unresolved grievance need an arbitrator *now*. The minimum qualifications of a physician are reasonably easy to establish, but the selection of the *most* able physician is a tough problem for a medical society let alone an ill person. In selecting an arbitrator, the parties may get some help from government and private agencies as well as their trusted neighbors in management or the labor movement.

The use of the procedures of the Federal Mediation and Conciliation Service, the American Arbitration Association, or a State Mediation Board in selecting an arbitrator assures a timely arbitration hearing. Under these procedures, the management and union usually select their own arbitrator from lists submitted by the agency. If none of the arbitrators listed (on a "panel") is acceptable to one of the parties, the agency may designate an arbitrator to hear the case. Although agency designation of arbitrators is unusual, there must be some final power to appoint an arbitrator in order that neither party may void their arbitration agreement by unreasonable delays.

An arbitrator acts in a quasi-judicial capacity. He should possess the judicial qualifications of fairness to both parties so that he may render a faithful, honest, and disinterested opinion. He must lay aside all bias and approach the case with a mind open to conviction and without regard to his previously formed opinions as to the merits of the parties or the case. His conduct must be free from even the inference that either party is the special recipient of his favor. An arbitrator is expected to disqualify himself from any arbitration if he has any financial or personal interest in the result of the arbitration.

Any arbitrator on the panels of the American Arbitration Association, Federal Mediation and Conciliation Service, or State Mediation Board meets certain minimum standards of impartiality, acceptability, and professional competence. These agencies review the arbitrator's education, experience, and general reputation with management and unions. These minimum standards cannot be stated with exact precision. Although most arbitrators possess either law or other postgraduate degrees, some prominent arbitrators did not graduate from college. Arbitration experience cannot be an absolute requirement for membership on an arbitration panel since most arbitrators get their *first* cases by selection from panels. Industrial relations experience as a member of management might make an arbitrator unacceptable to unions, just as industrial relations experience as a union representative might make an arbitrator unacceptable to management. A *perfect* neutral, for example, a college professor or lawyer with no business, union, or arbitration experience, would be of little value as an arbitrator because he would lack the vital knowledge of union-management practice.

Very frequently both the management and the union enter arbitration with the clear-cut goal of *winning* the case. If you want to win fairly, you are much more interested in how a specific arbitrator is likely to view your case than you are interested in his general reputation for impartiality. This very natural desire to win results in sometimes extensive investigations of arbitrators' backgrounds and awards. Employers' associations and unions frequently keep extensive records of arbitrators' awards which may be used by members in selecting the arbitrators most likely to lean either to the management or the union side.

The records on arbitrators kept by employers' associations and unions have both desirable and undesirable effects on the arbitration process. It is obviously desirable that both parties have access to detailed information on the qualifications of any arbitrator they might select. The best way to evaluate an arbitrator is by a careful review of his awards. An undesirable effect of using records developed by either an employer's association or a union is that these records may be incomplete or inaccurate. Because not all arbitration awards are published, anyone building a record on an arbitrator is working with incomplete data. An obvious inaccuracy in interpretation would be a record based on a "box score": Arbitrator X is good (or bad) because out of 20 cases he decided 18 for managament. Arbitrators can be judged fairly only on an evaluation of the full circumstances of each case.

It seems likely that the desire to *win* will remain as an important criterion for the selection of arbitrators in many collective bargaining relationships. Fortunately for the arbitration process, this attitude is not totally destructive because both parties must accept the arbitrator. Arbitrators who try to play a promanagement or a prounion game find themselves out of the arbitration business.

Preparing a Case for Arbitration. The American Arbitration Association suggests that companies and unions follow 10 steps in preparing a case for arbitration. These steps are:

1. Study the original statement of the grievance and review its history through every step of the grievance machinery.
2. Examine carefully the initiating papers (Submission or Demand) to determine the authority of the arbitrator. It might be found, for instance, that while the original grievance contains many elements, the arbitrator, under the contract, is restricted to resolving only certain aspects.
3. Review the collective bargaining agreement from beginning to end. Often, clauses which at first glance seem to be unrelated to the grievance will be found to have some bearing on it.
4. Assemble all documents and papers you will need at the hearing. Where feasible, make photostatic copies for the arbitrator and the other party. If some of the documents you need are in the possession of the other party, ask that they be brought to the arbitration. Under some arbitration laws, the arbitrator has authority to subpoena documents and witnesses if they cannot be made available in any other way.
5. If you think it will be necessary for the arbitrator to visit the plant for on-the-spot investigation, make plans in advance. The arbitrator will have to be accompanied by representatives of both parties; it is also preferable that the Tribunal Clerk be present.
6. Interview all witnesses. Make certain they understand the whole case and particularly the importance of their own testimony within it.
7. Make a written summary of what each witness will prove. This will be useful as a checklist at the hearing, to make certain nothing is overlooked.
8. Study the case from the other side's point of view. Be prepared to answer the opposing evidence and arguments.
9. Discuss your outline of the case with others in your organization. A fresh viewpoint will often disclose weak spots or previously overlooked details.
10. Read as many articles and published awards as you can on the general subject matter in dispute. While awards by other arbitrators for other cases

have no precedent value, they may help clarify the thinking of parties and arbitrators alike.[8]

If both parties have carefully followed these steps in preparing the case, the arbitration hearing is very likely to run smoothly and provide all the information the arbitrator needs to make a fair decision.

The Hearing. The arbitrator has substantial latitude in establishing the time, place, and conduct of the hearing. His job is to give both sides full opportunity to introduce relevant evidence and argument and to decide the case upon due consideration of that evidence and argument. He may ask whatever questions he deems necessary to the proper consideration of the dispute. All witnesses are subject to cross-examination. Both parties must try to convince the arbitrator of the justice of their positions.

The statements of the American Arbitration Association also provide adequate and concise guidance for the effective presentation of an arbitration case:

Every party approaching arbitration should be prepared with—
1. An opening statement which clearly but briefly describes the controversy and indicates what he will set out to prove. The opening statement lays the groundwork for witnesses and helps the arbitrator understand the relevance of testimony. For this reason it is frequently advisable that the opening statement be in writing, with a copy given to the arbitrator. This opening statement should also discuss the remedy sought.
2. Names of all witnesses in the order in which they will be called, together with a list of the points they are to cover. Questions should be brief and to the point, and witnesses should be instructed to direct their answers to the arbitrators.
3. A list of exhibits in the order in which they are to be introduced and a notation of what each is to establish. It speeds up proceedings considerably and never fails to make a good impression on the arbitrator when copies are available for distribution to all parties.
4. A closing statement. This should be a summation of evidence and arguments, and a refutation of what the other side has brought out.[9]

The American Arbitration Association also lists 10 common errors in presenting an arbitration case as follows:

1. Overemphasis and exaggeration of the grievance.
2. Reliance on a minimum of facts and a maximum of arguments.
3. Using arguments where witnesses or exhibits would better establish the facts.
4. Concealing essential facts; distorting the truth.
5. Holding back books, records, and other supporting documents.
6. Tying up proceedings with legal technicalities.

[8] American Arbitration Association, *Labor Arbitration: Procedures and Techniques* (New York: The Association, 1947), pp. 17–18.

[9] Ibid., pp. 18–19.

7. Introducing witnesses who have not been properly instructed on demeanor and on the place of their testimony in the entire case.
8. Withholding full cooperation from the arbitrator.
9. Disregarding the ordinary rules of courtesy and decorum.
10. Becoming involved in arguments with the other side. The time to try to convince the other party was before arbitration, during grievance processing. At the arbitration hearing, all efforts should be concentrated on convincing the arbitrator.[10]

Before closing the hearing, the arbitrator determines the wishes of the parties concerning posthearing briefs and arranges for their submission to him through a neutral party. The parties do not communicate directly with him except when both sides are present. The hearing is closed and the arbitrator considers the evidence and issues an award.

The Award. In the case of tripartite tribunals there may be some difficulty in preparing an award. If a deadlock seems likely, the union and management members of the Board of Arbitration may authorize the impartial member to write an award without their concurrence. Failing to achieve this sort of an arrangement, the impartial member may have to compromise his judgment of the dispute in order to achieve a majority opinion. We shall assume that our case is heard by a single impartial arbitrator, thereby avoiding this difficulty.

In writing his award, the arbitrator considers the content of the agreement, the practice of the parties, and the evidence and arguments presented at the hearing in exhibits and briefs. The arbitrator usually defers to the wishes of the parties in the form of the award. A simple statement of his findings and the action required by the decision is an adequate award. In our hypothetical case, an award might read: "Machine operators are required to stack finished work on carts for movement to the packing department in the way presently directed by supervision. The grievance claiming that such work is 'out of classification' is without merit and is denied." However, at the request of the parties, arbitrators usually will summarize the pertinent evidence and arguments, their findings, and the reasoning used to reach a decision. As a rule, the parties want the arbitrator to give them a reasonably detailed award. Such an award, often running to as many as 20 typewritten pages, may be more useful to the parties in their future relationships.

Once the award is delivered the matter is settled. It is no longer a bone of contention between the parties and they can get back to the business of living together. If the award is unsatisfactory, they usually can negotiate a more satisfactory arrangement in their next agreement. The arbitrator has enabled both sides to talk the matter out and he alone is responsible for the results of his award. Either the management or the union or both may be angry about the award, but they should not be angry with each other about it.

---

[10] Ibid., pp. 18–19.

Voluntary arbitration deserves much more detailed discussion than it has been given here because it makes a major contribution to harmonious union-management relations.[11] In a few cases, unions and managements have been so satisfied with grievance arbitration that they have adopted voluntary arbitration as a means of settling disputes in contract negotiations. On the other hand, some unions and managements have used arbitration as a means of harassing each other. The act of arbitration may be evidence of good or bad faith. In general, experience with grievance arbitration is a most encouraging sign of increasing trust and mutual respect on the part of American unions and managements. To the authors of this book, an even more encouraging sign is the effort of both parties to avoid arbitration by working hard at settling their disagreements within the grievance procedure. Both of these trends are optimistic signs for the future of collective bargaining.

The Legal Environment of Arbitration. Although labor arbitration is a quasi-judicial process, it is not governed by a comprehensive code of law. There is no United States Labor Arbitration Act, although such legislation has been advocated by the influential National Academy of Arbitrators. Several states have labor arbitration statutes, but these laws provide only minimal guidance to the conduct of arbitration. In decisions in 1957 and 1960, the U.S. Supreme Court has taken the first steps in fashioning a federal law of labor arbitration from the public policy statements contained in the Labor-Management Relations Act of 1947.

The arbitrator derives his power from the agreement of the parties to submit a dispute (or disputes generally) to him for decision. He operates within the specific or general rules established by the parties in their agreement to utilize his services. In several states, he is given the added legal authority to subpoena witnesses if needed to decide the issues before him. In all cases, the courts will set aside his award if there is evidence that it was influenced by corruption, fraud, or other undue means. In some cases, the courts will set aside his award if it is clear that it exceeds the authority vested in him by the parties.

The law of arbitration becomes a vital issue when one of the parties refuses to submit an issue to arbitration on the grounds that the issue is not arbitrable under the terms of the agreement to arbitrate. Although such refusals to arbitrate are indeed rare, either party could emasculate an arbitration agreement if it were allowed to be the sole judge of the meaning of the agreement.

The federal law of arbitration which the Supreme Court is fashioning

---

[11] Students are urged to read from the bibliography at the end of this chapter. Three books, Copelof's *Management-Union Arbitration*, Elkouri's *How Arbitration Works*, and Stone's *Labor-Management Contracts at Work*, are especially recommended. Frequent references to the proceedings of the annual meetings of the National Academy of Arbitrators are made throughout this book. These proceedings offer an insight on current issues in labor arbitration and recent research findings.

from the public policy statements of the Labor-Management Relations Act deals with the question of arbitrability. Four Supreme Court decisions must be mentioned in a discussion of labor arbitration. In 1957 in the case of *Textile Workers Union of America* v. *Lincoln Mills*, the Supreme Court ruled that federal courts were empowered by Section 301(a) of the Labor-Management Relations Act of 1947 to order specific performance of an agreement to arbitrate grievance disputes. In the cases of *United Steelworkers of America* v. *American Manufacturing Company*, *United Steelworkers of America* v. *Warrior and Gulf Navigation Company*, and *United Steelworkers of America* v. *Enterprise Wheel and Car Corporation*,[12] decided in 1960, the Supreme Court dealt in some detail with questions of arbitrability of grievances in different situations.

In the *Lincoln Mills*[13] case, the employer refused to submit to arbitration grievances involving work assignments and work loads under a collective bargaining agreement which provided for arbitration as the terminal step in the grievance procedure. The Supreme Court ruled that the Norris–La Guardia Act does not withdraw the jurisdiction of federal courts to require specific performance of an agreement to arbitrate grievance disputes. Before the Court ruled in this case, the employer had ceased to do business so the questions of job assignments and work loads were held to be moot. However, the Court ruled that monetary damages to the employees who grieved were not moot.

In *American Manufacturing*, the union sought to force the arbitration of the claim of one Sparks that he was eligible for recall to his job after an absence due to a work injury. Sparks had accepted a settlement for the work injury based on a permanent partial disability. The District Court held that Sparks, having accepted this settlement on the basis of a disability, was estopped to claim any seniority or employment rights. The Circuit Court of Appeals upheld the District Court on the grounds that Sparks' grievance was "a frivolous, patently baseless one, not subject to arbitration under the collective bargaining agreement." The pertinent provisions of the agreement were: (1) provision for arbitration of all disputes between the parties "as to the meaning, interpretation and application of the provisions of this agreement," (2) managerial authority to suspend or discharge "for cause," and (3) the requirement that the employer employ and promote employees on the principle of seniority "where ability and efficiency are equal." The Supreme Court reversed the lower courts and ordered arbitration of Sparks' grievance. The Supreme Court commented that, "when the judiciary undertakes to determine the merits of a grievance under the guise of interpreting the grievance procedure of collective bargaining agreements, it usurps a function which . . . is entrusted to the arbitration tribunal."

---

[12] Abstracts of the majority and dissenting opinions in these cases are used as cases in Part V of this book.

[13] 353 U.S. 448.

In *Warrior and Gulf Navigation*, the union sought to force the arbitration of a grievance arising from the subcontracting of work. The agreement contained a general arbitration clause and a provision that "matters which are strictly a function of management shall not be subject to arbitration." The employer refused arbitration of the grievance, and the union sued in District Court to require arbitration. The District Court dismissed the union's complaint after hearing evidence that the agreement did not "confide in an arbitrator the right to review the defendant's business judgment in contracting out work." The Circuit Court affirmed, finding that contracting out fell within the exception of "matters which are strictly a function of management." The Supreme Court reversed the lower courts and ordered that the dispute be submitted to arbitration. The Supreme Court found: "whether contracting out in the present case violated the agreement is the question. It is a question for the arbitrator, not for the courts."

In *Enterprise Wheel and Car Corporation*, the union sought judicial enforcement of an arbitrator's award of reinstatement and back pay to employees who had engaged in a wildcat strike. The District Court ordered the employer to comply with the arbitrator's award. On appeal, the Court of Appeals held that the award was unenforceable because it included back pay subsequent to the termination of the agreement and that the expiration of the agreement made the order of reinstatement unenforceable. The Supreme Court agreed with the Court of Appeals that the arbitrator's award of back pay was ambiguous. However, the Supreme Court ruled that an ambiguity in the award did not render the award unenforceable. The Supreme Court remanded the case to the District Court for proceedings "so that the amount due to employees may be definitely determined by arbitration."

The brevity of the foregoing summaries of leading Supreme Court decisions is intentional. The meaning of these cases will be argued in law journals and court proceedings for some years to come. Our single conclusion from these cases is that the Supreme Court has given arbitrators very substantial discretion in deciding the question of arbitrability *within the provisions of the agreement to arbitrate*. If the parties wish to reduce this discretion, it is within their power to agree to arbitration procedures which accomplish their mutual objective.

SUMMARY

In this chapter we have discussed the problems of administering the collective bargaining agreement. Agreement administration is of vital importance to the parties because actions speak louder than words and the word of the agreement frequently must be somewhat imprecise.

The key roles in agreement administration are played by foremen and stewards in their day-to-day activities. When the parties are unable to agree as to the meaning of their agreement or the proper application of their agreement to a particular set of facts and circumstances, they may use either force or voluntary arbitration to resolve their differences. In some disputes, the parties specifically reserve to themselves the right to resort to economic force. Much more commonly today the parties are placing greater reliance on voluntary arbitration to settle agreement interpretation disputes. Recent court decisions have the effect of encouraging the parties to make use of arbitration.

QUESTIONS FOR DISCUSSION

1. What are the functions of an arbitrator?
2. How can the parties to collective bargaining minimize the use of arbitration?
3. What is the legal status of an arbitrator's award?
4. How would you go about selecting an arbitrator from a panel of five provided by the American Arbitration Association?
5. Discuss the importance of preparation for arbitration on the part of both unions and management.

CASES 3, 30, 31, 32, 33

SELECTED ANNOTATED BIBLIOGRAPHY

AARON, BENJAMIN. "The Uses of the Past in Arbitration," chap. 1, *Arbitration Today*, JEAN T. McKELVEY (ed.). Proceedings of the Eighth Annual Meeting of the National Academy of Arbitrators. Washington D.C.: Bureau of National Affairs, 1955, pp. 1–12. Discussion by Peerce Davis and Lloyd H. Bailor, pp. 12–23.

Discusses the weight that should be given to an employer's past practice in establishing an arbitration award. AHNER, C. W. "Arbitration: A Management Viewpoint," chap. 2, *The Arbitrator and the Parties*, JEAN T. McKELVEY (ed.). Proceedings of the Eleventh Annual Meeting of the National Academy of Arbitrators. Washington, D.C.: The Bureau of National Affairs, 1958, pp. 76–87. Discussion by Maurice S. Trotta, pp. 87–92.

Ahner urges the more widespread use of tripartite mediation as a substitute for arbitration, the simplification of awards, and arbitrators making themselves available to the parties to explain their awards and to educate foremen and stewards on the agreement and its operation. Trotta disagrees with the proposition that arbitrators should shift from arbitration to mediation as the situation dictates and that "education" on lost awards is almost hopeless.

ALEXANDER, GABRIEL N. "Impartial Umpireships: The General Motors-UAW Experience," chap. 6, *Arbitration and the Law*, JEAN T. McKELVEY (ed.). Proceedings of the Twelfth Annual Meeting of the National Academy of Arbitrators. Washington, D.C.: The Bureau of National Affairs, 1959, pp.

108–51. Discussion by Joseph E. Shister and Sylvester Garrett, pp. 151–60.

Alexander, who served as GM-UAW Umpire from 1948 to 1954, discusses the history of the umpireship, the operation of the system, and appraises its successes and failures. Based on personal experience, previously unavailable information supplied by the parties, and extensive interviews with the umpires, this paper is the first of a series of monographs on umpire systems prepared for the National Academy of Arbitrators. Shister emphasizes the uniqueness of the GM-UAW experience as contrasted with ad hoc arrangements. Garrett emphasizes the importance of ideas and personalities in developing a constructive system of arbitration.

————. "Evaluation of Arbitrators: An Arbitrator's Point of View," chap. 4, *The Arbitrator and the Parties*, JEAN T. McKELVEY (ed.). Proceedings of the Eleventh Annual Meeting of the National Academy of Arbitrators. Washington, D.C.: The Bureau of National Affairs, 1958, pp. 93–100. Discussion by James C. Hill, pp. 100–110.

Alexander comments on the failure of labor and management to formulate objective and realistic criteria for the evaluation of arbitrators. Hill discusses the pros and cons of publishing arbitration awards.

BAMBRICK, JAMES J., JR., and SPEED, JOHN J. *Grievance Procedures in Nonunionized Companies.* New York: National Industrial Conference Board Studies in Personnel Policy No. 109, 1950.

Discusses the problem of grievance handling in nonunion companies.

BEAL, EDWIN F. "Origins of Codetermination," *Industrial and Labor Relations Review*, Vol. VIII (July 1955), pp. 483–98.

Based on several year's field study in Germany, this article traces the relationship between German unions and worker representation in the shop from 1918–55.

BERGER, HARRIET F. "The Grievance Process in the Philadelphia Public Service," *Industrial and Labor Relations Review*, Vol. XIII (July 1960), pp. 568–80.

A description of the collective bargaining relationship and agreement between the City of Philadelphia and its civil service employees, who are represented by District Council No. 33, AFSCME, AFL-CIO. Principal focus is upon the grievance process within the operation of the collective agreement.

BROOKS, GEORGE W., and GAMM, SARA. "A Union Steward-Training Program," *Industrial and Labor Relations Review*, Vol. IV (January 1951), pp. 249–56.

A discussion of the subject matter and methods of instruction used in steward training by the International Brotherhood of Pulp, Sulphite, and Paper Mill Workers.

COPELOF, MAXWELL. *Management-Union Arbitration.* New York: Harper & Bros., 1948.

Discusses appropriate questions for arbitration, the selection of an arbitrator, and a wide variety of arbitration cases.

COX, ARCHIBALD. "Rights under a Labor Agreement," *Harvard Law Review*, Vol. LXIX (February 1956), pp. 601–57.

Suggests that union and employer should be permitted to specify in their agreement whether the union or individual employees should have the authority to settle claims or sue the employer. When no specific intent is specified in the agreement, Professor Cox would have the courts apply presumptions, based on the nature of the agreement, as to whether the union or individuals have the right to sue.

DAUGHERTY, CARROLL R. "Arbitration by the National Railroad Adjustment Board," chap. 5, *Arbitration Today*, JEAN T. MCKELVY (ed.). Proceedings of the Eighth Annual Meeting of the National Academy of Arbitrators. Washington, D.C.: The Bureau of National Affairs, 1955, pp. 93–120. Discussion by Dudley E. Whiting and Paul N. Guthrie, pp. 120–26.

Discusses the statutory basis for grievance arbitration in the railroad industry, procedures for railroad grievance arbitration, and the nature of a national industry-wide arbitration system. Suggests methods of improving the statutory basis for grievance settlement and reducing the heavy backlog of unarbitrated cases.

DE VYVER, FRANK T. "Labor Arbitration after Twenty-Five Years," *Southern Economic Journal*, Vol. XXVIII (January 1962), pp. 235–45.

The author's presidential address to the 1961 conference of the Southern Economic Association considers the position of management under the present system of grievance arbitration; how management decision making is affected by arbitration; and suggests alternatives to arbitration.

ELKOURI, FRANK. *How Arbitration Works*. Washington, D.C.: Bureau of National Affairs, 1952.

Discusses scope of labor arbitration, the arbitration tribunal, grievances, standards for determination of contract interpretation and negotiation disputes, evidence and burden of proof, the precedent value of awards, and arbitration and management's rights.

FEINSINGER, NATHAN P.; ROSS, ARTHUR M.; SIMKIN, WILLIAM E.; and SMITH, RUSSELL A. "The Role of the Law in Arbitration: A Panel Discussion," chap. 3, *Arbitration and the Law*, JEAN T. MCKELVEY (ed.). Proceedings of the Twelfth Annual Meeting of the National Academy of Arbitrators. Washington, D.C.: The Bureau of National Affairs, 1959, pp. 68–89.

Ross views arbitration as a potentially creative instrument in the development of better industrial relations under a system of economic freedom. He proposes steps that the parties and the arbitrators should take to revitalize the process. Simkin outlines 14 points which form an outline for a "Practical Philosophy of Arbitration." Smith discusses the advisability of formulating a "model" arbitration statute and the problems inherent in its formulation.

FLEMING, R. W. "Some Problems of Evidence before the Labor Arbitrator," *Michigan Law Review*, Vol. LX (December, 1961), pp. 133–68.

Considers the procedures and processes that have evolved for the protection of the parties in arbitration. Based on arbitrators' replies to hypothetical case situations.

FLEMING, ROBBEN W. *Labor Arbitration Process*. Urbana: University of Illinois Press, 1965.

Reviews the growth and development of grievance arbitration and makes recommendations for some of its current problems: costs, time lag, and formality; predictability; individual rights; and problems of evidence and procedural regularity.

GIVENS, RICHARD A. "Responsibility of Individual Employees for Breaches of No-Strike Clauses," *Industrial and Labor Relations Review*, Vol. XIV (July, 1961), pp. 595–600.

Considers the following questions: Is it wise for employers to bring damage actions against individual employee conduct in a wildcat strike? Do such suits for damages conflict with national labor policies? And is legislation to bar individual damage suits desirable when employees peacefully participate in a strike?

JENSEN, VERNON H. "Dispute Settlement in the New York Longshore Industry," *Industrial and Labor Relations Review*, Vol. X (July 1957), pp. 588–608.

Discusses reasons for recent reduction in wildcat strikes on the New York waterfront and the emerging system for grievance settlement.

KAGEL, SAM. *Anatomy of a Labor Arbitration*. Washington, D.C.: Bureau of National Affairs, 1961.

A "how to do it" volume on preparing for and participating in arbitration proceedings. Principles are illustrated through analysis of an actual arbitration.

KUHN, JAMES. *Bargaining in Grievance Settlement*. New York: Columbia University Press, 1961.

Kuhn's thesis is that the grievance procedure is more than a judicial procedure; it is a way of extending collective bargaining to the lowest organizational levels. The contract becomes the rule for rule-making in the grievance arena of bargaining. Conclusions based on study of grievance process in rubber industry.

McPHERSON, WILLIAM H. "Grievance Mediation under Collective Bargaining," *Industrial and Labor Relations Review*, Vol. IX (January 1956), pp. 200–212.

Discusses increasing use of grievance mediation in U.S.

MITTENTHALL, RICHARD. "Past Practice and the Administration of Collective Bargaining Agreements," chap. 2, *Arbitration and Public Policy*, SPENCER D. POLLARD (ed.). Proceedings of the Fourteenth Annual Meeting of the National Academy of Arbitrators. Washington, D.C.: The Bureau of National Affairs, 1961, pp. 30–58. Discussion by Alex Elson and John A. Hogan, pp. 58–68.

Discusses characteristics which typify most practices, i.e., clarity and consistency, longevity and repetition, acceptability, and the underlying circumstances. Functions of past practice in clarifying ambiguous language, implementing general contract language, modifying or amending apparently unambiguous language, and as a separate, enforceable condition of employment are discussed. Mittenthal concludes that in the problem areas of past practice there are so many fine distinctions that the final decision in a case will rest on any abstract theorizing but rather on the arbitrator's view of the peculiar circumstances of that case. Elson cites examples where past practice may deprive employees of due process. Hogan emphasizes the importance for the parties to try to eliminate inconsistencies between the contract and past practice.

NORTHRUP, HERBERT R., and KAHN, MARK L. "Railroad Grievance Machinery: A Critical Analysis, I and II," *Industrial and Labor Relations Review,* Vol. V (April, July 1955), pp. 365–82; pp. 540–49.

Discusses and evaluates the unique system of grievance adjustment on U.S. railroads.

PRASOW, PAUL, and PETERS, EDWARD. *Arbitration and Collective Bargaining: Conflict Resolution in Labor Relations.* New York: McGraw Hill, Inc., 1970.

The most comprehensive current analysis of the operation of the grievance-arbitration process in print. Relates the process to contract negotiations, labor, and most importantly the decision-making framework used by American arbitrators.

SEGAL, ROBERT M. "Arbitration: A Union Viewpoint," chap. 2, *The Arbitrator and the Parties,* JEAN T. MCKELVEY (ed.). Proceedings of the Eleventh Annual Meeting of the National Academy of Arbitrators. Washington, D.C.: The Bureau of National Affairs, 1958, pp. 47–70. Discussion by Lewis M. Gill, pp. 70–75.

Segal discusses a number of criteria used by unions in evaluating arbitrations and the relationship of arbitration of the courts. Gill comments on Segal's list of reasons for "blacklisting" of arbitrators by unions, i.e., mediating when the parties don't want mediation, excessively long and involved ͬpinions, excessive citation of outside decisions, and slowness in the issuance of decisions.

SLICHTER, SUMNER H.; HEALY, JAMES J.; and LIVERNASH, E. ROBERT. The *Impact of Collective Bargaining on Management.* Washington, D.C.: Brookings Institution, 1960.

Special attention is invited to the following chapters: 23, "The Problem of Grievances"; 24, "Adjustment of Grievance"; 25, "The Grievance Arbitration Process"; and 26, "Arbitration and the Bargaining Relationship."

SMITH, RUSSELL A. "The Question of 'Arbitrability'—The Roles of the Arbitrator, the Court, and the Parties," *Southwestern Law Journal,* Vol. XVI (April 1962), pp. 1–42.

A penetrating analysis of the 1960 Supreme Court decisions and their impact on the courts, arbitrators, and the parties to arbitration.

SOMERS, GERALD G. *Grievance Settlement in Coal Mining.* Morgantown, W. Va.: West Virginia University, Business and Economic Studies, Vol. IV, No. 4, 1956.

A statistical review of the procedures, subject matter, level of settlement, and disposition of 970 grievance cases heard between 1933 and 1954 in bituminous coal mining.

STONE, MORRIS. *Labor-Management Contracts at Work.* New York: Harper & Bros., 1961.

An analysis of American Arbitration Association awards on reduction in force, seniority and ability, stewards, foremen, call-in pay, holidays, vacations, overtime, and discipline.

U.S. CHAMBER OF COMMERCE. *Model Arbitration Clauses to Protect Management Rights.* Washington, D.C.: The Chamber, 1961.

As a response to Supreme Court decisions on arbitrability, this monograph contains sample clauses on management rights, arbitrator jurisdiction, and no-strike and lockout.

WOLFF, DAVID A.; CRANE, LOUIS A.; and COLE, HOWARD A. "The Chrysler-UAW Umpire System," chap. 5, *The Arbitrator and the Parties*. JEAN T. McKELVEY (ed.). Proceedings of the Eleventh Annual Meeting of the National Academy of Arbitrators. Washington, D.C.: Bureau of National Affairs, 1958, pp. 111–41. Discussion by Harry H. Platt and Nathan P. Feinsinger, pp. 141–48.

Wolff has served as the Chrysler-UAW Umpire from the inception of the system in 1943. The UAW-Chrysler system is notable in the few cases that reach the arbitration stage and the formality of Appeal Board Hearings. Platt, Ford-UAW Umpire, contrasts the Chrysler-UAW system with the Ford-UAW system. Feinsinger, GM-UAW Umpire, comments primarily on the exclusion of grievants from Chrysler arbitration hearings. This paper is one of a series on umpire systems prepared for the National Academy of Arbitrators.

WOODCOCK, LEONARD. "Problem Areas in Arbitration," chap. 4, *Arbitration and the Law*. JEAN T. McKELVEY (ed.). Proceedings of the Twelfth Annual Meeting of the National Academy of Arbitrators. Washington, D.C.: Bureau of National Affairs, 1959, pp. 90–97.

A then UAW vice president discusses the need for a more detailed study of arbitrators and arbitrators' awards, more adequate training of the parties in case preparation and presentation, and the rising costs of arbitration.

PART III

The Issues in Collective Bargaining

Part III of this book analyzes the issues in collective bargaining; the areas of disagreement between employers, workers, and unions. The discussion follows the basic format proposed earlier for the analysis of collective bargaining agreements: union security and management rights; the wage and effort bargain; individual security; and administration. Management and union goals in matters of principle and cost are considered in the two "model" types of collective bargaining relationships.

Chapter 10

UNION SECURITY AND MANAGEMENT RIGHTS

The Management of an organization can assemble a work force, and that work force may remain nonunion, but a union—to be a union and not some other kind of association—cannot enroll members who are not actual or potential employees of an organization. To put this in specific terms: The X Manufacturing Co. can hire a thousand workers and bargain with each of them, legally, as single individuals; and go on dealing with them that way as long as the majority of them remain ununionized. Let the thousand—or even a small fraction of them, with the support of the majority—form a union, and under existing labor law the company must bargain with the union on the terms and conditions of employment of the thousand. Theoretically, these terms had hitherto been bargained with each individual, but management practically offered the terms on a take-it-or-leave-it basis. The union concentrates the bargaining power of all its members against the bargaining power of the company. Union security, or an assurance that the union will continue to exist and perform its bargaining function, thus becomes vital both to the union as an institution and to the members whose terms and conditions of employment it protects.

If the company had not put together a work force, there could have been no union. Now that the work force exists and is unionized, the union takes on an existence independent of the company. Labor relations law requires the company to recognize and bargain with it. The union often wants security that goes beyond (without contradicting) the law. Every collective bargaining agreement therefore confirms the recognition of the union, by the employer of the work force the union represents, and defines the relationship of the parties.

Many collective bargaining agreements (though not all) contain sections clearly labeled "union security" and "management rights." Whether labeled and set apart or not, they specify who speaks for whom, with what authority, for how long, except in what conditions. They become a kind of enabling act that gives authority and binding effect to everything else in the agreement.

UNION SECURITY

The union is not secure in its relationship with the employer if there is any doubt about (1) which employees the union does—and does not—represent, (2) the form of recognition, or (3) the duration of the agreement and procedures for renewal or renegotiation.

The sections on union security aim to resolve these doubts.

The Bargaining Unit: Who Speaks for Whom

Rarely, if ever, does a union represent or even claim *all* the employees of a given employer. Often only a part, and not the whole of an employing enterprise or employer association, deals with a union. Who speaks for whom in any collective bargaining relationship appears in the definition of the bargaining unit.

The bargaining unit under existing labor law is a legally defined body or constituency empowered under certain circumstances to make, on behalf of both management and the employees contained in the unit, the crucial decision on recognition.[1]

The law does not leave this issue entirely up to bargaining between the parties but reserves to the government, acting through the NLRB, the right to define the bargaining unit. Public policy trusts neither management nor the union, separately or together, to make this determination in the public interest. When management had the power to make it, employers used their power to deny recognition and deprive employees of freedom of choice. When unions sought the power, they tried to assert jurisdictional claims that were often irrelevant to employer operations and contrary to employee wishes. Still, the bargaining unit is important both to the union and the company—more directly important to them than to anyone else—so, when in a given situation they agree on a specific delimitation as appropriate, the NLRB will usually confirm their jointly-defined unit. If they cannot agree, the NLRB decides. The NLRB has shown itself reluctant to define the unit in ways that would interfere with operations. It will, indeed, "carve out" a craft or professional, from an otherwise industrial, unit, but only if the employees in the carved-out unit vote for separation.

A bargaining unit is supposed to group together those employees who have common interests, and exclude those who do not share these interests. As a rule these groupings correspond to natural divisions brought about by work-place technology. Some commonly accepted units are: hourly paid production and maintenance workers; clerical employees; technicians or professionals; members of a recognized craft or trade. Guards may have a bargaining unit, but may not be represented by the same union as other employees.

---

[1] See Ch. 6, "Establishing the Collective Bargaining Relationship."

The Form of Recognition

Before the passage of the Wagner Act in 1935 the forms of recognition and corresponding degrees of union security that unions won from management ranged all the way from "open shop"—no recognition, no security—to the maximum—closed shop (craft union)—and, in a few rare instances, union shop (industrial union). The range included intermediate forms such as recognition for members only or for specified purposes only—as for the presentation of complaints and grievances. This gamut carried through to the present day in public employment; for the federal service, Executive Order 11,491 on collective negotiations lists some graduated degrees of recognition. In private industry, labor relations law since 1935 has diminished the range.

Until the enactment of a law, actual union security could only be as great—regardless of the form of recognition—as union strength or company weakness made it. A company could refuse to recognize a union even though employees wanted it, or it could choose between rival unions without regard for employee preference, or start a company union and deal with it even though all but a few employees shunned it. To gain recognition from a reluctant company management, therefore, a union had first to lead the employees out on strike. The recognition strike was as much a regular feature of an industrial union's activity as the jurisdictional strike was of the craft union's.

One of the aims behind labor legislation was to eliminate strikes over recognition. The law accordingly gave *employees* the right to choose their own union representatives without interference either from management or from unions with rival jurisdictional claims. Employees do this by majority vote of all those eligible to vote in an appropriate bargaining unit in an NLRB election. Recognition follows automatically for the union that wins a majority. Legal recognition won in this fashion takes a *minimum* form that is already a strong guarantee of union security: exclusive bargaining rights. Stronger forms are permitted, though some of the strongest are limited or technically prohibited by federal or state law. Here, briefly, are some of the common forms.

Exclusive Bargaining Rights. This is the legal mimimum. For a given bargaining unit, the employer recognizes one union, and that one only. Agreements reached with this union apply to all employees in the bargaining unit, whether or not they are union members. Nonmembers are not required to join the union, but the employer can make no deal with any of them that departs from the terms of the agreement.

A union with exclusive bargaining rights is ordinarily secure from rival unions and from withdrawal of recognition for at least the duration of the agreement: a year or more.

Union Shop. The phrase "union shop" is often loosely used to mean any unionized enterprise, even when the form of recognition is no stronger than exclusive bargaining rights. In this loose sense it merely means anything except a completely nonunion enterprise. Here, however —and throughout this book—union shop has a precise and technical meaning, the meaning recognized in labor law and collective bargaining practice. The union shop is the *maximum* form of security for an industrial union.

The union shop contains all the elements of exclusive bargaining rights and goes further. A union shop agreement requires the employer to make union membership a condition of employment for all employees in the bargaining unit. A new employee does not have to be a union member when hired, but within a specified time after hiring must join the union and remain a member in good standing or be discharged.

Because this requirement of the union shop works a hardship on people with religious scruples or strong personal convictions against union membership, the Taft-Hartley law of 1947 modified the forced-membership feature of the union shop: Employees need not actually join and be active in the union, provided they pay the equivalent of the union's initiation fee and regular dues just as if they were members. The minimum probation period before payments begin, under the same law, cannot be less than 30 days, but may be longer.

Agency Shop. The union shop is unlawful in right-to-work states. What takes its place is a resourceful expedient devised to stay within the letter of state law, yet get the substance of union shop conditions. Under the agency shop form of recognition, employees are not required to join the union. Instead, the agreements make it a condition of employment that they pay the union the equivalent of initiation fees and dues as a kind of tax, or service charge, in return for the union's acting as their bargaining agent. This makes a rule out of the exception written into the Taft-Hartley law.

Closed Shop. This is another maximum form, characteristic of craft unions, but also applicable wherever the conditions of the labor market favor operation of a union hiring hall. Such conditions tend to arise in industries that have traditionally depended on nonskilled, casual labor; notably, the maritime industry. Decasualization, or stabilization of employment for a restricted number of workers, is the union's aim in setting up a hiring hall as the central labor exchange. The employers on their side get a dependable labor pool to draw from at need. With the organization of pickers in the vineyards and row-crop farms of the Southwest, decasualization seems to be on the way in agriculture. The closed shop and the hiring hall thus fit the conditions and meet the needs of operations in industries drawing from the two extremes of the labor market: skilled craftsmen; and the unskilled.

The Taft-Hartley Act of 1947 outlawed the closed shop; but merely passing a law did not suppress it as an institution. It persisted without sanction of law in the industries mentioned, for more than a decade before the NLRB started proceedings to enforce the ban.

In 1959 the Landrum-Griffin Act rescued the closed shop and revived it—practically, or de facto, if not legally, or de jure—by exempting the construction industry from the Taft-Hartley 30-day probation period and substituting a 7-day minimum. Not many employers want to try to circumvent the union by hiring nonunion workers they will have to fire and replace in a week; it's easier to take union men or women out of the hiring hall right at the start. Thus unions and employing organizations in construction continue to sign agreements that may seem to have the form of the union shop but provide the substance of the closed shop, and closed-shop conditions.

The wording of an agreement that, while staying within the letter of the law provides closed-shop conditions, calls for the employer to apply first to the union when he needs workers and to look elsewhere only when the union cannot meet his demands. In effect, this means that he may hire only workers who already belong to the union or who have a work permit from the union. When jobs are scarce, the union can reserve the openings for its members. When jobs are plentiful, the union still controls referrals to the job. It issues work permits to nonmembers— a sort of temporary membership without privileges—revocable at the union's pleasure. The union does not have to accept these temporary workers into permanent membership, but after the probationary period —7 days or 30 as the case may be—can require them to pay the equivalent of union dues. They will already have paid the equivalent of an initiation fee for the work permit.

Outsiders, such as college students working at unskilled jobs during vacations, often complain about the apparent injustice of this system. It was perhaps indignation at the supposed injustice that impelled Senator Robert Taft to put the ban on the closed shop into his bill. But justice does not look the same to all. The worker dependent for his living on an industry offering sporadic and temporary job opportunities sees no injustice in a device that gives him something like regular work and protects him from losing income to competitors who have no permanent attachment to the occupation.

Maintenance of Membership. This form of recognition seems to be dying out, but may be met occasionally. It occurs in industrial union agreements and falls somewhere between exclusive bargaining rights and the union shop; a compromise between the two.

Historically, maintenance of membership agreements first appeared in World War II. Unions had given a no-strike pledge. In return for renouncing the strike weapon, they accepted government mediation and, in those instances when they could not reach agreement with an employer, tripartite arbitration. This took place before the emergency National

War Labor Board composed of representatives of labor, management, and "the public." Unions pushed, in their negotiations with employers, for union shop agreements. Some employers gave way, others resisted. The unions took this issue to the NWLB.

On the Board and its subsidiary panels, labor representatives naturally tended to side with the unions; employer representatives, with management. That gave the public representative the deciding vote. This third party, the public member, shrank equally from forcing the union shop on a reluctant employer and denying the union (which was honor-bound not to strike at a time when strikes would have been most effective) more than the minimal protection offered by exclusive bargaining rights.

The upshot (as might be expected) was a compromise. Under a maintenance of membership clause, all employees who are members of the union at a specified time after the signing of the agreement or who later join the union must continue to pay dues to the union for the duration of the agreement.

After the war, when unions were free again to strike for their demands, many of these agreements were renewed in the more clear-cut union shop form. Others reverted to the legal minimum of exclusive bargaining rights. Maintenance of membership today tends to be a transitional form, marking progress or retreat between the current extremes.

Maintenance of membership, like the closed shop, is illegal in right-to-work states.

Checkoff.   The checkoff is really an administrative arrangement, not a form of recognition, since it may be associated with any of the forms. It most commonly accompanies the closed or union shop. It merely provides that the employer withhold union dues from union members' paychecks and transmit the money directly, in a lump sum, to the union. Under the Taft-Hartley Act, the checkoff is lawful only when each individual employee signs a checkoff declaration, which may continue indefinitely if not revoked, but may not be irrevocable for more than one year.

MANAGEMENT RIGHTS

Widespread interest in the proper formulation of management rights clauses in collective bargaining agreements developed after World War II, but the history of the controversy over rights is older. Two presidents of the United States convened well-publicized national conferences without getting management and labor to agree on principles of union security and management rights.

President Woodrow Wilson called the first industrial conference in the fall of 1919. His main purpose was to facilitate the orderly reconversion of the economy to a peacetime footing. Labor, management, and public representatives met but were unable to agree on principles to guide postwar labor-management relations. After 17 days of debate the conference collapsed. The stumbling block was union security. Labor representatives argued that employees should be entitled to representation by unions of their own choosing. Public represenatives favored collective bargaining but thought that no employee should be denied the right to refrain from joining a union. Management representatives steadfastly insisted on the following statement of principles:

There should be no denial of the right of an employer and his workers voluntarily to agree that their relation shall be that of the "closed union shop" or of the "closed nonunion shop." But the right of an employer and his men to continue their relations on the principle of the "open shop" should not be denied or questioned. No employer should be required to deal with men or groups of men who are not his employees or chosen from among them.[2]

As a practical matter, the principle advocated by management meant that unions could function only with the *consent* of management. This provided *no* union security. The failure of the conference resulted in a continuation of the status quo in collective bargaining and labor relations law. This status quo was the "closed nonunion shop" in mass-production industry in 1919. With no legislative protection of the right to organize, unions lost the footholds they had temporarily gained in the factories during the war. Employers successfully extended the "closed nonunion shop" to most of American industry by 1930. Not until the passage of the Wagner Act in 1935 did the unions gain the means of achieving any real measure of union security.

President Harry S Truman called the second national industrial conference in 1945. Again the nation faced problems of harmonious reconversion to peacetime production. This time, with union security already written into law, management rights became the major issue. Again labor and management representatives found themselves unable to agree on principles. Management representatives stated their case this way:

Labor members of the Committee on Management's Right to Manage have been unwilling to agree to any listing of specific management functions. Management members of the Committee conclude, therefore, that the labor members are convinced that the field of collective bargaining will, in all probability, continue to expand into the field of management.

The only possible end of such a philosophy would be joint management of the enterprise. To this the management members naturally cannot agree. Management has functions that must not and cannot be compromised to the public interest. If labor disputes are to be minimized by "the genuine acceptance by organized labor of the functions and responsibilities of management to direct the operation of the enterprise," labor must agree that certain spe-

---

[2] Department of Labor, *Proceedings of the First Industrial Conference (Called by the President) October 6 to 23, 1919* (Washington, D.C., U.S. Government Printing Office, 1920) p. 82.

cific functions and responsibilities of management are not subject to collective bargaining.[3]

Labor's response was to reject the view that in the conduct of enterprise operations any given set of rights belonged inherently to management. According to union spokesmen, management rights were fluid and should be handled on a case-by-case basis by management and the union in each enterprise. They insisted:

> Because of the complexities of these [diverse union-management] relationships the labor members of the Committee think it unwise to specify and classify the functions and responsibilities of management. Because of the insistence by management for such specification the Committee was unable to agree upon a joint report. To do so might well restrict the flexibility so necessary to efficient operation.
>
> It would be extremely unwise to build a fence around the rights and responsibilities of management on the one hand and the unions on the other. The experience of many years shows that with the growth of mutual understanding the responsibilities of one of the parties today may well become the joint responsibility of both parties tomorrow.[4]

Two basic and opposed positions on management rights seem to emerge from these contrasting statements. The one put forward by management looks on the rights as inherent, but alienable; that is, that management may give some of them away. This formulation moves the management position a step back from holding that management rights and prerogatives are inalienable. Thus, though they may be alienable, managers still decline to give them away or to share their exercise with unions.

Labor's position in effect denies that management has any inherent rights and holds instead that management rights arise out of a definition of the relationship between management and labor in each particular enterprise.

To this day, both views have their adherents. One is an ideological approach and has been called the doctrine of the residual rights of management. The other is pragmatic. Before accepting either view, or rejecting both, it might be well to look at the logic of the respective positions.

The Residual Rights Doctrine

The residual rights approach starts from the premise that initially and inherently management possesses total freedom and discretion in ordering the affairs of an enterprise, and that union demands are an encroachment on this freedom or set of rights and prerogatives. It follows that every time a manager makes a concession to union demands he gives away, and

---

[3] *President's National Labor Management Conference,* Vol. III, Doc. 125 II/13 (November 29, 1945), p. 47.

[4] Ibid., Vol. III, Doc 120II/11 (November 28, 1945), p. 45.

therefore loses, a part of the rights that inherently belong to management. What remains to him then are the *residual* rights he did not specifically renounce.

The personal experiences of many managers in their first encounters with unions seem to confirm, and originally may even have given rise to this line of thinking. In the early days of industrial union bargaining, employers often complained that unions were attempting to invade what they held to be the forbidden field of long-accepted management prerogatives. Before unionization, for example, managers had decided who might be allowed to stay and who would be laid off when business was slack. Now, instead, at union insistence they had to follow the seniority principle in layoffs and rehiring. Every time the company gave in to a demand of this sort, the argument ran, management surrendered some of its rights. By this interpretation, agreements signed with unions became, in every section, phrase, and clause, a record of lost management rights. One of the best-known early books on collective bargaining expresses in its very title this point of view: *The Union Challenge to Management Control.*[5]

It is not hard to understand and perhaps even sympathize with the outlook of a manager who has seen power of this sort slip from his grasp. He feels he has lost something; something important to him and to the conduct of his business. Suddenly he finds he cannot make decisions that were his to make before: a countervailing and—it seems to him—inimical power opposes his will. It is natural enough for him to believe that what he has lost the union has gained. Carried to its logical extreme, this line of reasoning might well rouse the fear that unions are on their way to taking over *all* the rights and power of management; getting ready (as the phrase goes) to tell an employer "how to run his business."

That nothing quite so dire has yet materialized does not dispose of the argument. Given the premises, the conclusion logically follows. What stops the unions, if they have indeed been stopped? What is to prevent union erosion of management rights from continuing until, of the residual rights, there is no further residue?

The error may lie not in the logic, but in the premises. What are these lost prerogatives, these threatened rights? At least one highly respected teacher and practitioner, Charles W. Killingsworth, says they are a myth; there are no management rights, and never have been. He gave his views in his inaugural address as president of the National Academy of Arbitrators in 1971.

The Pragmatic Approach

Killingsworth's attack on the residual rights doctrine draws its theme from his practice as an arbitrator and from certain important Supreme

---

[5] Neil W. Chamberlain, *The Union Challenge to Management Control* (New York: Harper, 1948).

Court decisions affecting arbitration. Foremost amongst these is a 1960 set of three decisions on the arbitrability of issues not dealt with in specific terms in collective bargaining agreements. The companies in these three cases had stood on their residual rights in refusing to arbitrate certain issues, claiming unhampered freedom to take unilateral action. The Court rejected the companies' argument.[6]

The outcome of this litigation, as decided by the Supreme Court, would seem to establish that there are no inherent management rights, even residual ones. That puts the matter much too baldly. Killingsworth does not argue from the legal decision alone, but draws on economic theory and practical experience to show that many constraints impinge on management's freedom to act—so many as to nullify any effective force or value to a set of management prerogatives. In general, he seems to agree with the views expressed in the above-quoted statement of labor representatives at President Truman's 1945 industrial conference: There are no management rights, only labor-management relationships; and the relationships are to be read in the aggregation of terms written into any given, specific collective bargaining agreement.

Yet labor agreements—many, though not all—continue to show specific provisions headed "Management Rights" and are likely to go on doing so.

A Synthesis of Opposing Views

The authors of this book take a position that differs from both extremes treated above, but that is not simply a compromise between them. We agree with those who hold that there are certain rights that belong to management, but we believe that union power had not diminished these management rights. Since they remain undiminished in our view, we can agree with the reasoning of those who hold that there has been no change, though not with the premise that they never existed. What has changed is the set of contexts—the climate or environment—in which management exercises its undiminished rights.

To call them rights rather than prerogatives already begins to strip away some of the mystique. Prerogatives—for instance, royal prerogatives—rise out of an ideology, but rest on political power. Thus, by the doctrine of divine right, kings had prerogatives that went with succession to the crown. Those who were subject to the king's power respected the prerogatives. Should the monarchy give way to a republic, the king would retain his prerogatives only in the minds of die-hard royalists. For republicans, he loses his prerogatives with his power.

Managers have never ruled by divine right nor, as managers, wielded political power; but owners of property under any regime have rights,

---

[6] These opinions appear as Case 2 in Part V of this book and were briefly reviewed in Chapter 9.

property rights, defined and guaranteed by the prevailing political power. These property rights are no myth; they are real and enforceable. Owners of property can delegate their rights to managers. Since slavery was abolished, managers have never had any rights over people, only over property.

Property rights never have been absolute. An owner and his agents exercise the rights only under constraints and limitations which vary over the course of time and in different places and conditions. Managers of an enterprise exercise delegated ownership rights within the three contexts into which Dunlop's scheme analyzes the environment in which they operate.[7] When, as an enterprise, they have something to sell, they cannot compel but must persuade customers to buy. When they want to buy, they cannot force anyone to sell but must get the seller's consent and agreement on a price. This holds just as well for the labor market, in which the enterprise is a buyer, as for the product or services market which it enters as a seller.

As long as power relations in the enveloping society prevent or discourage people from organizing into unions, managers bidding for employees in the labor market can deal with them individually. Each work contract concluded and continued with an employee remains separate from the others, even though work is social and operations intricately coordinated. In slack times (to go back to the example already cited), a manager may decide to lay off or retain a particular employee according to any criterion he wishes to apply: efficiency, or family obligations, or pure spite and favoritism, or, indeed, seniority. The choice is open. Nothing in the terms and conditions of the company's work contract with any one person ties the decision on what happens to him with what happens to anyone else. A separate contractual connection, terminable at will, ties each employed person with the employing company and can be served without reference to any of the others. The ability of the company to cut this connection at will is not a unique management right but the right of a contracting party to terminate a contract. Its counterpart is the right of the other contracting party, the employee, to quit his job. What makes it look like management's rights *over* the employee is that in slack times an employee does not usually want to quit his job and thereby lose his source of income.

When power relations in the enveloping social system permit and encourage collective bargaining, and employees unionize, workplace power relations reflect the change. Collectively, now, employees demand terms and conditions in *each* work contract that ties it to the others in some order; usually (for purposes of layoff and recall), an order of seniority. A single thread still connects the company to each employee, but the company agrees that in slack times the threads will be released in

---

[7] See Chapter 1, the discussion of John T. Dunlop's theoretical framework.

a certain sequence, and not at will or at caprice or in some other sequence or order.

Thus far in history power relations in the enveloping social system have not changed so radically that an employer is obliged by law to give in to a union's demands. The employer still retains the right to dispose of his own property and to lay out his material resources, including money for wages, in his own interests. Those interests may be better served in a given instance by accepting the union's demands or by fighting them; the choice is the employer's. Even when he accepts union demands (again, for example, in the matter of layoff and recall), workplace power relations do not deprive him of the right to lay off people when he does not need their services. He simply may not pick by name, but must lay off by category or by an individual's position on a previously-established seniority list. The same number of people go, the same number stay, but the names may differ. It is conceivable, though not inevitable, that the work force that is left will not be as efficient as would one that management might have picked; but it is equally conceivable that most of the time the senior employees are the efficient ones.

Over the years prices of goods and services have risen, and so have the costs incident to changes in the conditions of employment. Would any businessman protest that a supplier's rise in prices was an attack on his management rights? Why argue, then, that a rise in labor costs infringes on management prerogatives?

Perhaps what happens is that the old lord-of-the-manor, slaveholder mystique hangs on. The manager, pragmatic and clearheaded when dealing with physical limitations and with impersonal legal or economic constraints, responds emotionally to personal and human opposition to his will. He seeks to rationalize his feelings in an ideology. The pragmatic approach to management rights usually yields more practical results than ideology.

In Summary

The foregoing exposition of two views of management rights shows that the authors of this book take issue with the residual rights doctrine and favor the pragmatic approach. They agree with Killingsworth that management does not have—and never had—any rights inherent in the manager's role, but hold that in their role managers exercise the delegated property rights of ownership.

The residual school of thought maintains that management starts out with something like total freedom, total discretion; that managers have the ability as well as the right to order the affairs of an organization entirely at will; and that employees have the duty, and are bound, to conform to management's arrangements. By this view, an employer gives away part of the management rights he started out with each time he makes a concession to union demands. Whatever he does not concede and specifically renounce in the agreement remains as management's *residual* rights.

Given the premise, the conclusion logically follows. This book rejects the premise. Managers, like kings, have no prerogatives except as they have power. Power is a relationship, with dependency as its reciprocal. Property rights confer power insofar as people are dependent on the material resources, including money wages, at the disposal of the property-owner. When the dependency ceases or declines—either absolutely or relative to the ability of wage earners to withhold their labor—so does the power decrease. Employees organized in unions are individually less dependent on the employer. The new *collective* bargains by which managers exchange material benefits—property—for human effort expended under specific terms and conditions, register the effect of present-day power relations as reflected in the enterprise. The bargaining is harder, the price is higher, but the exchange remains the same.

MANAGEMENT RIGHTS AS FUNCTIONS OF THE MANAGER'S ROLE

Management, then, has rights: delegated property rights; the right to dispose of, allocate, commit the material resources of the organization (including money) in order to carry on operations toward attaining the objectives of the enterprise. Rights alone do not make a manager; the actual owner (or owners, as in joint-stock companies) may, as a matter of fact, play no part in management. What makes a manager is managerial *use* of the delegated rights and the power and authority derived from them. In the total system of an organization, the rights *reinforce* the manager's role. A management rights clause in a union agreement makes practical sense when it takes the form of a definition of management's role instead of merely expressing an ideology.

An organization must have people who carry out operations. It must also have people who *plan* the operations, *organize* the work flows and work stations or jobs, who *direct* and *coordinate* activities, and *control* results. These are the accepted functions of the manager; their performance constitutes the manager's *role*. In performing his role, a manager at any level—and at all levels—acts for the organization, with and for and through the unit, however limited or however broad, for which he has accepted responsibility. Most likely, he is an employee too. He draws his pay from the same source as the subordinates in the unit he manages, but, organizationally speaking, acts for all. What must he be allowed to do as manager that other people playing the reciprocal nonmanager roles cannot do as part of their roles? What must they allow him in order that he may carry out his role?

As things stand in most enterprises today, in order to survive and meet the needs of members and owners, an organization must allow its managers some flexibility in three areas of activity: (1) discretion to organize, integrate, and coordinate operations; (2) discretion to deploy the work force and maintain discipline; and (3) discretion to deal with the outside world or environment, including (within an organization) other units of the organization.

Flexibility in Operations

Perhaps the most inflexible kind of operation would be an automated, serialized production line. The most flexible, most variable kind, perhaps, might be something like a band of strolling players at a tourist resort. Without going to this informal extreme, however, short-run job-lot production calls for flexibility in operations and might be kept in mind as a contrasting example. Management discretion in the design and layout of the automated line would have to precede operations, and would probably have to be pretty well unrestricted. In job-lot production, discretion has to enter in to daily operations.

At both these hypothetical extremes, the persons occupying management roles have to make decisions—organizational decisions—for others to carry out if the entire unit is to meet its objectives. At various points within the range there is bound to be an appropriate division of discretionary activity between managers and nonmanagers.

Operations integrate tasks. Operations concern people only as people are needed to carry out the tasks. Scientific management unflinchingly shouldered responsibility for ordering tasks and operations as management's role—and claimed it as a management prerogative. Present-day proponents of participative management see the same operations as an activity to be *shared* with nonmanagers.

Pragmatically speaking, collective bargaining makes operations neither a shared function nor a management right, but an activity in which managers and nonmanagers play separate but reciprocal roles. To the extent that both can contribute to a common aim, they parcel out areas of discretion. What has to be determined jointly in collective bargaining is the degree of discretion managers truly need, in a particular enterprise, in order to keep operations going for the good of all.

Flexibility in Deployment and Discipline

Decisions on deployment and discipline affect people rather than tasks; though tasks are carried out, of course, by people. Deployment involves assigning people to tasks and moving people around as operations demand. Discipline implies standards of performance, including task performance, and standards of behavior, including behavior toward other people.

A part of any manager's role is to deploy people to best advantage, but not as if they were inanimate objects. People have individual characteristics, career aims, perceptions of themselves and of others, desires, emotions, personal problems. They also acquire, through collective bargaining, job rights. Getting the best out of people, using their talents where they will do the most good, integrating the contribution of each with the joint efforts of all, would seem to be the very essence of the art of management.

No manager needs absolute power over the livelihood and career of any individual, but within limits needs discretion to fit employees into operations. No employee can fairly demand that the enterprise give him exactly what he wants, regardless of its needs or of the wants of others. A definition of job rights—always relative to the rights of others—gives the employee a measure of security against arbitrary acts of management. Beyond these stated job rights, management discretion rules. It takes effect not as a management right, but as a function of the manager's role in the organization.

When, for instance, it makes no difference to operations who stays on the job and who goes in a layoff, manager discretion need not extend to deciding, by name, who shall stay. When, as in promotion to or within management ranks, it does make a difference who gets the job, management can justify picking the person by name.

Discipline, too, bears upon people. Here the procedures of due process define employee rights. No manager needs the authority to discharge an employee, on the spot and without notice, even for cause, so long as he has authority to suspend, and after investigation make a decision. Every organization needs to be able to protect itself from those who thwart or hinder progress toward objectives and must be able to discharge for cause. Due process protects the individual from arbitrary and unfair treatment, but need not—and in fact does not—prevent a management which observes procedures from following practices conducive to good discipline and countering harmful acts of individuals. Again the rights are individual, the role is management's.

Flexibility in Dealing with the Environment

Groups and collectives act as a unit towards other collectives by means of spokesmen, agents, and representatives. Through its managers an enterprise deals with buyers and suppliers, borrowers and lenders, government and the public, and indeed with unions. Within an enterprise, managers deal with other managers, with staff units, with technicians.

This area of management discretion is so clearly part of management's role that little attempt has yet been made by unions to enter it; in fact, they have shown little interest, at the level of the enterprise, except as management mistakes affect the equilibrium of the enterprise. Unions have sensibly perceived activities in this area as something managers are uniquely qualified to do and charged with doing. This does not make it an inherent management right. Unions are concerned, for instance, with the state of the market, but exert influence upon it, usually, at levels higher than the enterprise and through union organizations greater than the local union.

Management's Freedom to Perform Its Role

A study of the degree of management freedom and flexibility in the performance of its role in the enterprise helps show how things stand in some typical collective bargaining agreements. Although the researchers implicitly adopt the residual rights ideology, it is not necessary to adopt the ideology to grasp the significance of their findings. It makes sense as a record of actual arrangements that managers and unions have come to in defining the constraints and flexibility allowed the manager's role in a number of agreements.

In a study of union participation in decision making in 37 plants, Milton Derber, W. E. Chalmers, and Milton T. Edelman differentiated the *scope* and *depth* of union penetration of management rights.[8] *Scope* of union participation was measured by determining the number of important enterprise activities (e.g., contracting work out, product pricing, job evaluation, etc.) in which the union had a voice either through agreement negotiations or grievance settlement. The *depth* of union penetration was measured in terms of the agreement provision itself or the stage of a decision at which the union became involved. The measurement of *depth* of union penetration may be clarified by comparing two specific measures used by Derber, Chalmers, and Edelman: (1) Union security was judged solely on the terms of the agreement provision, i.e., sole bargaining rights, maintenance of membership, union shop, preferential hiring, or closed shop; (2) making major technological change was judged on the stage of a decision at which the union became involved, i.e., decision made without advance notice, advance notice given by management, management consults union, or changes require prior union agreement. Derber, Chalmers, and Edelman used this system of measurement for interfirm comparisons over time. Although individual enterprises might find it desirable to modify the specific measures used by Derber, Chalmers, and Edelman, the measures of *scope* and *depth* certainly are pertinent to the question of management rights. The framework for an analysis of the collective bargaining agreement outlined in Chapter 8 should be helpful in determining the *scope* and *depth* of union penetration of management rights in an enterprise.

How are management rights protected in the collective bargaining process? It seems to the authors of this book that management rights are

---

, [8] Milton Derber, W. E. Chalmers, and Milton T. Edelman, "Union Participation in Plant Decision-Making," *Industrial and Labor Relations Review,* Vol. XV (October 1961), pp. 83–101.

most effectively preserved by effective and decisive management action in the overall operation of the business, in the negotiation of the whole collective bargaining agreement, and by the religious observance of the terms of the agreement negotiated. If a particular management runs a taut ship in all of its business relations, it will have little difficulty in determining what management rights it needs. With a clear objective in mind, the company's negotiators should be able to sell their position to the union. A good contract *adequately backed up with day-to-day supervisory practices* is within the grasp of any management worthy of its responsibilities.

FIGURE 10–1. Illustrative Management Rights Clauses

Some employers prefer a long-form management rights clause like the Company Responsibility clause below. Other employers prefer a short-form clause like the Management Clause below. Employers favoring the short form feel that the enumeration of rights is dangerous, lest some rights be omitted.

Regardless of the form or content of the management rights clause, management functions may be given away, violated, or undermined by *other* clauses in the agreement or in company practices.

Company Responsibility

The Company retains the sole right to manage its business, including the rights to decide the number and location of plants, the machine and tool equipment, the products to be manufactured, the method of manufacturing, the schedules of production, the processes of manufacturing or assembling, together with all designing, engineering, and the control of raw materials, semimanufactured and finished parts which may be incorporated into the products manufactured; to maintain order and efficiency in its plants and operations; to hire, lay off, assign, transfer, and promote employees, and to determine the starting and quitting time and the number of hours to be worked; subject only to such regulations and restrictions governing the exercise of these rights as are expressly provided in this agreement.

Management Clause

The management of the business in all its phases and details shall remain vested in the Employer. The rights of the Employer and the employees shall be respected and the provisions of this contract for the orderly settlement of all questions regarding such rights shall be observed.

Many management negotiators and the spokesmen for management organizations advocate the inclusion of management rights clauses in the collective bargaining agreement. These clauses may have an educational effect on the employees and the union over the years. When management action is in harmony with the management rights clause, the clause may also be helpful in arbitration hearings. Figure 10–1 contains illustrative management rights clauses.

SUMMARY

In order to serve its members, a union has to have *recognition* as their agent from the employer. The people for whom the union speaks make up a *bargaining unit;* and recognition takes the specific form of the union shop, exclusive bargaining rights, agency shop, or practically speaking (but not formally), the closed shop. Further, the union seeks continuity in its relationship. Management wants to define its areas of discretion in relations with employees.

The sections of a labor agreement on Union Security and Management Rights are a kind of enabling act that give authenticity and authority to the terms and conditions of employment the agreement defines. This answers the questions: Who speaks for whom? With what authority? For how long? With what exceptions?

The exceptions carry the label "Management Rights." Traditionally, managers have looked on their right to manage the affairs of an enterprise as inherent in their status as managers and have regarded concessions made to a union as a dilution of management rights. By this line of thinking, any such rights not given away remained "residual" in management's hands. A more pragmatic approach that seems to be gaining ground concerns itself not so much with abstract rights as with the kinds of discretion management must exercise if the enterprise is to remain viable and employ the union members. These discretionary elements rise out of management's role. They have to do with ordering operations, deploying and disciplining the work force, and interacting with the environment. The terms of the agreement as a whole define the areas of management discretion and flexibility in action.

QUESTIONS FOR DISCUSSION

1. Maintenance of membership was a compromise form of union security suggested by the National War Labor Board during World War II. How do you account for this development at that time and its demise after the end of the war?

2. What are management rights? Why are they important? In a specific situation, how would you go about protecting them from union infringement?

3. Compared to unions in other countries, American unions are preoccupied with union security. Why? Does the law of collective bargaining have anything to do with this?

4. What is the "residual" theory of management rights? What changes in social, economic, and political conditions challenge the residual rights doctrine?

5. What rights (authority) seem most necessary for the exercise of the management role, and why? Do unions challenge these rights? Under what circumstances might they do so?

CASES: 5, 6, 7.

SELECTED ANNOTATED BIBLIOGRAPHY

CHAMBERLAIN, NEIL W. *The Union Challenge to Management Control.* New York: Harper & Bros., 1948.

A landmark study of the impact of the union on the authority of management in the large corporation.

DEMPSEY, JOSEPH R., S. J., *The Operation of Right-to-Work Laws.* Milwaukee: Marquette University Press, 1961.

Based on unreported court cases and interviews with jurists, employers, unions, and attorneys, this book compares the statements of state legislators on the meaning of right-to-work laws and the meaning of these laws as developed by the courts.

GOLDBERG, ARTHUR. "Management's Reserved Rights: A Labor View," *Management Rights and the Arbitration Process,* JEAN T. McKELVEY (ed.). Proceedings of the Ninth Annual Meeting of the National Academy of Arbitrators. Washington, D.C.: Bureau of National Affairs, 1957, pp. 118–29.

The then General Counsel of the United Steelworkers of America proposes some standards for the arbitration of management rights controversies.

JUSTIN, JULES J. "How to Preserve Management's Right Under the Labor Contract," *Labor Law Journal,* Vol. XI (March 1960), pp. 189–215.

Examines the substantive areas where management's rights have been invaded by unions, and presents guideposts to follow in negotiating and administering the labor contract, emphasizing that management must know what its rights are, must understand the political structure of its union, and train its supervision in how to manage within the framework of the contract.

KELLER, LEONARD A. *The Management Function: A Positive Approach to Labor Relations.* Washington, D.C.: Bureau of National Affairs, 1963.

Defines a good labor policy, explores contracts in general, "management rights" clauses in particular, and gives model arbitration clauses which protect management rights. Suggests how to deal with labor attempts to restrict changes in methods, classifications, departments, and work schedules.

MEYERS, FREDERIC. *"Right-to-Work" in Practice.* New York: Fund for the Republic, 1959.

A study of the effects of "right-to-work" legislation on labor and management in Texas over the past several years.

MYERS, A. HOWARD. "Concepts of Industrial Discipline," chap. 5, *Management Rights and the Arbitration Process,* JEAN T. McKELVEY (ed.). Proceedings of the Ninth Annual Meeting of the National Academy of Arbitrators. Washington, D.C.: Bureau of National Affairs, 1956, pp. 59–83.

The author, a professor at Northeastern University and an arbitrator, discusses the meaning of reasonable discipline, the challenge to supervision, the union's responsibility for discipline, and employee conduct off the job. Paper is discussed by Gabriel N. Alexander, Detroit arbitrator and attorney.

PHELPS, JAMES C. "Management's Reserved Rights: An Industry View," *Management Rights and the Arbitration Process,* JEAN T. McKELVEY (ed.). Proceedings of the Ninth Annual Meeting of the National Academy of Arbitrators. Washington, D.C.: Bureau of National Affairs, 1957, pp. 102–17.

An executive of Bethlehem Steel Company proposes some standards for the arbitration of management rights controversies.

SHISTER, JOSEPH; AARON, BENJAMIN; and SUMMERS, CLYDE W. (eds.). *Public Policy and Collective Bargaining.* New York: Harper & Row, 1962.
See "The Union Security Issue" by Paul E. Sultan.

STONE, MORRIS. *Managerial Freedom and Job Security.* New York: Harper & Row, 1964.

A companion volume to the author's earlier *Labor-Management Contracts At Work,* this book addresses itself principally to job security issues, including the subcontracting of work; transfers of work outside the bargaining unit; attempts by the employer to change the content of a job; and out-of-classification assignments to solve special production problems.

Chapter 11

THE WAGE AND EFFORT BARGAIN: JOB STRUCTURE

With or without a union, with or without collective bargaining, there is always a wage and effort bargain; it is the economic and legal substance of the employment relationship in our society. Every employee has a work contract with his employer; every employer has a work contract with each of his employees—as many work contracts as he has employees. The contract is: Work for pay. The employee applies physical and mental effort to the performance of tasks, in exchange for which the employer pays money wages or salary.

The wage and effort bargain costs the employer money, gives the employee income. The effort side costs the employee physical and mental exertion over set periods of time, gives the employer production. Thus the wage and effort bargain is a wealth-producing economic exchange that puts products and services on the market and provides people with a living. Its legal form distinguishes working relationships in our society from preceding bond systems. It rises out of the political reality of a population of free citizens legally competent to contract for their own labor: free to accept or reject an offer of employment or demand for work; free to quit or terminate the contract of employment.

The presence of a union and the practice of collective bargaining does not change either the economic or the legal basis of the relationship, but does affect the terms. Even though an agreement reached between a union and an employer is commonly called a "contract," the agreement does not bring a new contracting party into the old relationship. It merely sets new *terms* to the contract the employer offers and the employee accepts. The employee still exerts the effort and performs the work; the employer still pays the wage or salary.

What kind of changes in the terms of the work contract does collective bargaining bring?

Collective bargaining usually sets new levels of pay for jobs, and hence new levels of income for people performing the jobs, and fixes these levels for stated periods of time. This is bound to affect the employer's costs. Collective bargaining may also regulate the amount of effort employees

325

expend in earning their pay. It does this when it sets standards for task performance. One way or another, collective bargaining affects productivity. Over the course of time it has altered the form of the "pay package" that wraps up the cost and income components of the wage and effort bargain.

This chapter examines the wage and effort bargain as it takes shape at the level of the enterprise. Craft unions and industrial unions approach the bargaining in different ways and with different results. To understand the wage and effort bargain in both settings, it would be helpful first to break down the pay package into its five components.

THE PAY PACKAGE

Chapter 8 gives a breakdown of the wage and effort bargain, showing that it contains the two basic and reciprocal elements of work for pay in the form of five separately distinguishable components: (1) pay for time worked and (2) the effort bargain—the basic elements—*plus* (3) premium pay; (4) pay for time not worked, and (5) contingent benefits, or worker insurance and income-continuity programs. The fifth of these subdivisions, contingent benefits, differs so markedly in form from the others, and has become so complex and so large a proportion of the total package, that it merits separate treatment. It will be discussed in detail in Chapters 13 and 14.

Pay for Time Worked

The enterprise pays its employees to get something done—to perform work. In return for work performed, the worker receives wages or salary. The amount of pay depends upon the amount and kind of work done, and the wage or salary considered appropriate in the given place at the given time. That raises three issues which have come to be described in the following words: (*a*) the job *structure*, (*b*) the wage or salary *level*, (*c*) the *method* of wage or salary payment.

Job Structure. As just stated, the enterprise pays an employee to perform work. The employee earns his pay on the *job;* the enterprise gets its work by employee performance of *tasks.* The employee who carries out tasks which make up his job must possess qualifications appropriate to the tasks. The tasks, furthermore, may vary in difficulty, in the skill or expertise required, or in the conditions under which they are performed. Two tasks of equal difficulty performed under approximately equal conditions and requiring similar or comparable qualifications on the part of the workers involved ought naturally to entitle the workers who perform them to equal pay. If, on the other hand, the tasks involved are of unequal quality, then it would appear to be just as fair to compensate performance unequally, in proportion to the relative value of the tasks. A job consists of a collection of tasks. Just as one task may be compared with another, a job including many tasks may be compared with other jobs. A job requiring higher qualifications or making greater demands in performance should, under the principle just stated, receive higher compensation. The determination of relative differences between jobs in a given enterprise is called establishing the job structure. The most common way of setting up the job structure is job evaluation.

Job evaluation is a well tested and widely accepted technique of analyzing differences in job worth. It is a means of analyzing jobs and *measuring* the differences between them. It results in ranging them in an order of relative job worth from the least difficult up to the most difficult, or the least valuable to the enterprise up to the most valuable.

The Pay Level. The job structure, or relative position of jobs within the enterprise, is independent of the dollar amount paid for any of the jobs in question. The pay level concept applies money values to the job structure in proportion to the worth of the jobs. Whereas the job structure applies only within the enterprise, the pay level implies comparison with jobs, and the pay for these jobs, in other enterprises, usually in the enterprises which compete in a given labor market. For the kinds of jobs usually covered by collective bargaining agreements this is normally a single urban or metropolitan community.

Unlike the job structure, which always compares jobs in terms of relative worth within the enterprise, wage levels are not necessarily set in terms of comparisons. An enterprise may establish its wage level quite without regard for community rates, but this would be unusual.

If, now, the job structure were to be represented by points on a horizontal line, reading from left to right, so that the low rated jobs were on the left and the higher rated jobs on the right, the relative position of the points representing each job, and their distance from each other, would be the job structure of the enterprise. If, again, pay rates expressed in dollars and cents were ranged on a vertical axis intersecting the horizontal line of the job structure at the point of the lowest rated job, then it would be possible to represent the job level by a line or curve correlating structure with money rates. An illustration of this will be given later. The point here is that structure and level are independent of each other. As long as job content remains unchanged, the structure remains the same. The level, on the other hand, may vary. It may rise with a general increase in wages; it may take a different slope; it may even become distorted by temporary abnormalities of the labor market.

Method of Payment. There are two basic ways of paying wages or salary: (1) time wages, or pay by the hour, day, month, or year, without specifying the amount of work to be done; (2) production wages, or pay related to the amount of work the individual or group performs, more or less disregarding the time involved in its performance. In fact, however, the time element cannot be effectively separated from production nor production from time. No employer would want to pay his people for an hour of work without having some idea of the amount of work he could expect to get in return. No employee would care to receive production pay, or pay based entirely on output, unless he had some expectation that he would be able to earn an average wage appropriate to the type of work, that is, to the kind of tasks that made up his job. Production wages are often referred to as piecework. The rates paid for piecework depend upon standards which are often set by time study. In setting these rates, however, there must be some presumption about average expected earnings. It can be seen, then, that time and output are really inseparable, but that for purposes of calculating payment two opposite approaches may be made to this problem.

It now becomes possible to define pay for time worked in the sense intended by the category under the wage and effort bargain. Pay for time worked is the *level*, expressed in concrete dollars and cents terms, of the wage or salary paid for a given job within the job structure of an enterprise; or it is the *expected average earnings* for the same job, even though the method of payment may not consist of straight time wage but of piece rates or production wages.

The Effort Bargain

Pay for time worked, or pay for the job, always appears in concrete dollars and cents form. The effort bargain, on the other hand, is not always so easily identified. It consists of the amount of work expected or required during a given period of time. Another way of saying this is: The effort bargain is the standard or norm expected on a given task. Thus, the effort bargain is always measured in terms of the task. If the entire job consists of a single task endlessly repeated, measuring the time required for that one task in a sense sets the effort bargain on that job. If the job consists of a variety of tasks, then the effort bargain is the sum or composite of the work expected on each and all of the tasks making up the job.

The most obvious and observable way of setting the effort bargain is through time study. At this point only a few important matters need to be noted. The first of these is that the effort bargain implies the working conditions of the phrase: "wages, hours, and *working conditions.*" That is, under one set of conditions the output expected may differ from that under an entirely different set of conditions, even though the productive task, and the finished work turned out, may be the same.

Premium Pay

Premium pay consists of rates, or formulas for determining rates, which are to be paid for extra work performed outside the normally scheduled daylight working hours, or at other personal inconvenience to the employee. Under this heading fall such matters as overtime pay (usually calculated at time and one half) after 40 hours in any 1 week or 8 hours in any 1 day; night-shift differentials; and call-in pay.

Theoretically, this is money the enterprise would never have to pay if it did not work its employees outside the scheduled daylight hours. It used to be called "penalty pay," because it was intended to punish the employer who made extra demands on his employees and encourage him to schedule his operations more carefully. A foreman ought to know at the end of one shift whether he is going to have work for a man at the beginning of the next shift on the following day. If he does, and fails to tell the man; or if, through poor planning on his part or at levels above him, he does not know, the man may come in to work as usual, find no work waiting for him, and have to be sent home. Without a provision for call-in pay, he would have lost not only the day's pay but the free time which he might have used for himself—even if only to go fishing. A union agreement requiring that the company either notify him the day before, or give him at least four hours' work or four hours' pay, serves as a powerful reminder to the foreman not to neglect giving appropriate advance notice when he is *not* going to need one of his regular hourly paid workers.

In practice, overtime pay has come to be regarded as "gravy" which many workers are eager to get. Some companies have even used overtime pay, systematically scheduled, as a means of raising take-home pay for their employees without disturbing the pay rates. Premium pay provisions still remain, basically, a means of regulating not the income to the worker or the cost to the company but the hours worked. This is true whether the maximum (before overtime) is set by law or by union agreement.

Pay for Time Not Worked: Miscellaneous Labor Costs of Doing Business

Pay for time not worked and the miscellaneous labor costs of doing business frequently total between 8 and 10 percent of payroll costs. Pay for time not worked usually runs to a total of about 8 percent of payroll costs.

Pay for Time Not Worked. At least four different types of pay for time not worked can be easily identified: (1) vacation pay, (2) holiday pay, (3) paid rest periods, lunch periods, wash-up time, and (4) special bonuses such as Christmas bonuses. The cost of these different items varies tremendously as does the complexity of the collective bargaining agreement which brings them into being or guarantees their continuity.

Vacations. The high potential cost of paid vacations can be seen from a simple example. Assume that all persons on the payroll worked 50 weeks per year and drew 2 weeks' vacation pay. In this case, vacation pay would equal 4 percent of payroll or 10 cents per hour (assuming an average wage rate of $2.50 per hour).

An adequate agreement on vacation pay must deal with the following problems:

1. Scheduling vacations: Will the plant shut down for a stated period to allow all workers to take their vacation at the same time or will vacations be staggered over the year? If the plant shuts down for vacations and some workers will be needed during the shutdown, which workers will be required to work and what will be their rate of compensation? If some workers are required to work during the vacation period, will they be given an opportunity for a vacation at another time during the year? If management wishes to operate the plant, due to a backlog of orders, during the vacation period, what compensation will be given in lieu of vacations? If vacations are to be staggered through the year, what method is used in determining when an individual takes his vacation? If vacations are staggered, may a worker use his vacation pay during an illness?

2. Eligibility for vacations: How much seniority must an employee have before he is eligible for a paid vacation? Is a worker on temporary layoff eligible for vacation pay? Are part-time workers eligible for vacation pay? Are paid holidays falling within a vacation period a basis for extra compensation? Does an unauthorized absence immediately before or after the vacation period disqualify a worker for vacation pay?

3. Duration of vacation pay: The length of paid vacation time to which an employee is entitled is frequently related to his length of service, e.g., 1 week for 6 months' seniority; 2 weeks for a year's seniority; 3 weeks for 10 years' seniority; and so on. In computing the amount of vacation pay entitlement, what consideration is given to breaks in seniority? Are there any requirements that long vacations must be taken at the convenience of the company or that they must be split so as to minimize interference with production?

4. Computation of vacation pay: Does the vacation pay computation include overtime premium, shift premium, incentive earnings, and personal rates above the base rate for the employee's job? Sometimes vacation pay is computed as a percentage of the previous year's earnings, e.g., 2 percent of the previous year's earnings would equal one week's vacation pay. This percentage method includes overtime premiums paid, incentive earnings, holiday pay, etc., but tends to reduce the vacation entitlement of workers who have had substantial layoffs or absences in the previous year.

5. Vacation pay for workers temporarily or permanently separated: Is a worker on temporary layoff at the vacation period entitled to vacation pay? If a worker quits or dies does he or his family have a vested

right to his "earned" vacation time? Is a worker discharged for cause entitled to his "earned" vacation time at the time of discharge?

The foregoing list of vacation bargaining issues emphasizes the cost element of vacations. This is not an altogether fair emphasis, because some of this cost may be offset by improved employee morale or a saving of unemployment compensation costs. At the same time, it seems logical that the individual employer's gain in employee morale from granting generous vacations has been significantly diluted by almost universal adoption of the practice.

Holidays. Paid holidays vie with vacations as being the most expensive form of pay for time not worked.

Five paid holidays per year would cost about 2 percent of the annual payroll. One day of holiday pay usually costs the employer more than one day of vacation because holiday pay frequently applies to everyone on the payroll regardless of seniority. Like vacations, paid holidays have become so common that the individual employer only succeeds in avoiding poor morale by granting them.

An adequate agreement on holiday pay must deal with the following problems:

1. Eligibility for holiday pay: How long must an employee be on the payroll before he becomes eligible for holiday pay? Is an employee eligible for holiday pay if he is absent on his scheduled shift immediately before or following the holiday?
2. Work on holidays: Are workers obligated to report to work on holidays if advanced notice is given? What rates of pay will prevail for workers required to work on holidays?
3. Holidays falling on nonwork days: If a paid holiday falls on a nonwork day, is the holiday celebrated on the next or preceding work shift or is holiday pay disregarded in this case?
4. What compensation will be given for holiday pay? Is shift premium, incentive pay, and normal overtime included in the pay given for holiday?
5. What days will be observed as holidays? The rather striking increase in the number of paid holidays in recent years has pretty well exhausted the list of national holidays available, e.g., Independence Day, New Year's Day, Labor Day, Memorial Day, etc. As a result an increasing number of religious holidays are being added to the list. This poses a problem where members of the labor force are adherents of different religious faiths.

Miscellaneous Labor Costs of Doing Business. Depending upon the purpose for which the data are collected, miscellaneous labor costs of doing business are totally insignificant, or substantial. Obvious items, such as employer subsidies to cafeterias, supply of special work clothing, and transportation allowances, usually amount to only a very few cents per hour. However, employers frequently wish to impress the total cost of hiring labor on the employees and include such items as unemployment compensation, workmen's compensation, and the employer's share of social security payments and other legally required payments. Although these items are genuine labor costs, it is a matter for discussion whether they should be included in the calculation of the total employment benefits package.

CRAFT-UNION WAGE BARGAINING

When a craft union bargains with an employer, the wage agreement is the essence of simplicity. Worker characteristics and the work to be done are clearly established prior to bargaining by the training of the skilled craftsmen. For example, carpenters perform a variety of operations on wood. The typical agreement with a carpenters' union assigns all wood work to the carpenters' union. Through union rules (written and unwritten) every carpenter knows the content of a "fair day's work" and performs only that amount of work because he controls the tempo of work with his own hands. The only collective bargaining wage problem confronting the skilled craftsman and his employer is what the rate shall be for a known quantity and quality of workmanship. After this problem is handled the auxiliary problems of rates for apprentices and helpers remain. Most employers of craftsmen are specialists employing only one or a few crafts. An employer of several crafts obtains a wage structure which relates the rates of various jobs only after he has carried on several separate negotiations with different unions representing the different crafts. Thus craft-union wage negotiations deal almost exclusively with problems of general wage adjustments.

Collective bargaining in the building trades is an important example of craft-union bargaining. We shall discuss the structure of building-trades bargaining, factors creating a solid community of interest between craft unions and building-trades employers, and the points of disagreement between unions and managements in building-trades wage negotiations.

Structure of Building-Trades Bargaining

Building-trades unions and employers bargain on a local level. Because the product market is local, there is little need for, or benefit to be derived from, bargaining on an area or national basis.[1] Customarily, the

---

[1] An important exception to this general rule must be noted in the relations between the Associated General Contractors of Northern California and California Building Trades Unions. Here a master contract covering a broad geographic area has been negotiated. This arrangement seems to be a natural outgrowth of the tech-

collective bargaining agreement covers many employers and the members of a single local union composed of workers of the same craft, e.g., carpenters, electricians, or plumbers. General contractors have contracts with many unions, while an occasional specialty contractor will have only one contract with one union.

Frequently employers in the same line of business bargain as a group through an employer's association. This employer's association usually includes the largest and most influential firms in the local industry. Very often smaller employers and even a few large employers are not members of the association and, as a result, do not have a direct voice in determining the terms of the master agreement. After negotiations are completed with the employer's association, the nonmember employers usually voluntarily accept the terms of the master agreement or the union forces acceptance of the agreement through strike action. Occasionally, the union permits deviations from the master agreement in the case of nonsignatory employers as an organizational device.

Each craft local union customarily bargains for itself, but it expects, and usually gets, substantial strike support from the local unions in other crafts. Craft international unions usually allow their locals to go their own way on general wage adjustments but may exert powerful influence on working rules and the protection of the union's jurisdictional claims. In those unusual cases where craft international unions have tried to influence wage negotiations, they have met with only very limited success.

Community of Interest between Local Unions and the Construction Industry

In many ways the industry is like one big family. The nature of their work throws construction men into close interaction with each other. Not only are there close social ties among members of a given trade, but the industry as a whole stands apart from the rest of the community.

The class line between employer and employee, supervisor and worker is quite thin. Most contractors and superintendents are former workers. Many still hold union cards. Only a small proportion of the supervisors have had college educations. The social gap which separates management and labor in mass-production industry seems to be lacking. In general they see problems from the same point of view.

As a consequence, relationships are highly personal (in the words of Max

nology of the California construction industry, where general contractors bid on jobs over a wide area, move heavy equipment from job to job over this area, and recruit labor from the area where the particular job is performed. See Gordon W. Bertram and Sherman J. Maisel, *Industrial Relations in the Construction Industry* (Berkeley: University of California, Institute of Industrial Relations, West Coast Collective Bargaining Systems, 1955); and its sequel, Gordon W. Bertram's *Consolidated Bargaining in California Construction: An Appraisal of Twenty-Five Years' Experience* (Los Angeles: Institute of Industrial Relations, University of California, 1966).

Weber, they are particularistic rather than universalistic). Friendships and feuds flourish. To the outsider disputes seem irrational and over-emotional.[2]

The community of interest between building-trades unions and contractors is rooted in both social and economic institutions. The local nature of the product market dictates local day-to-day bargaining. The worker's control of work tempo and the high percentage of labor cost to total cost forces the employers, workers, and union to be cost conscious (at least in those segments of the product market where demand is price elastic). Since a significant part of sales in most markets is to governmental agencies or performed under conditions prescribed by the government, the employer and unions are frequently political allies. Because entry to the industry sometimes involves only a small capital outlay, the unions and present employers share an interest in policing the activities of new firms, be they outsiders trying to invade the local market or individual tradesmen who may undersell the union rate.

Even in the knotty problem of union jurisdiction, there may be a community of interest between employers and the union. Like the tradesmen, many employers are specialists in the use of certain materials and thus share an interest in maintaining a demand for their particular type of construction and materials.

Although tradesmen, unions, and employers in the building trades have much in common, they tend to separate on the central issue in craft union bargaining—the "standard rate." Even here, their disagreement is usually over the interpretation of the same facts. Occasionally the union leadership and management are in agreement, with the workers dissenting.

The Wage Dispute

Wages are the central, and frequently the *only*, issue in building-trades bargaining. Union security, production standards, seniority, and other major issues have been settled for so long in most communities that they aren't even discussed in negotiations. Usually these nonwage matters have merely been entrusted to the union's care and negotiations start with the closed shop, union working rules, and jurisdictional claims as settled issues. This normal situation may be upset by new governmental rules or some new union rule or new materials or methods, but such occurrences are exceptional. We turn now to the goals of unions and managements in craft-industry wage bargaining.

Craft-Union Wage Goals. Typically, craft unions seek to increase only the standard rate. Recently many craft unions have shown increased interest in the multitude of wage supplements, such as pensions, health and welfare benefits, and insurance which the industrial unions have pio-

---

[2] George Strauss, *Unions in the Building Trades: A Case Study* (Buffalo, N.Y.: The University of Buffalo Series, Vol. 24, No. 2, June 1958), p. 69.

neered, but primary emphasis continues to be placed on the basic wage rate. Because of the irregularity of employment in the building trades, these programs are administered on a market-wide basis with eligibility for benefits based on continuous employment in the industry which usually means continuity of union membership. As a result, when a union seeks a package it really means so many cents for wage increases and so many cents for welfare benefits. Because of the worker's control over tempo, the employer can almost convert this package into a unit labor cost increase. The entire bargain can be stated as income to the worker versus costs to the employer.

How much of an increase will a building-trades local union demand and strike for in a given year? What factors influence the determination of the union's demands.[3]

Like managers, college professors, and farmers, rank-and-file members of building-trades unions seem to have an insatiable desire for more money. They exert a rather constant pressure on the union leadership to get more. They become particularly insistent when business is good, the cost of living is rising, or other unions have negotiated substantial wage increases. The craft unionist feels that he is entitled to as large a wage increase as other unionists get and frequently he expects his union to get an even larger increase because of his painstakingly acquired skill. On the other hand, the building-trades unionist probably knows more about the general state of business in his industry. This greater industry consciousness can be traced to the building-trades unionist's visits to the union hall for work and his employment on different jobs during the course of the year. Because of this industry consciousness, craft unionists as a group may exhibit some concern over the employment effects of their wage demands.

When a building-trades business agent enters negotiations with employers, he is representing the interests of a more or less fixed number of union members. His job is to get the best possible bargain for those members. Most of his members have a substantial investment in an apprenticeship and can earn a return on that investment only through employment in the building trades. When all of his members are working, the business agent usually presses for a very substantial wage increase. When many of his members are out of work, he tends to be much more conservative in his wage demands. Several students[4] of building-trades wage bargaining have suggested that business agents tend to differentiate "big work" and "small work" in their thinking on wages. For big work such as large buildings and roads, business agents tend to believe that cost

---

[3] Our discussion of some of these factors will be abbreviated in this section. Fuller discussion of some of these factors, especially the cost of living, will be found in the discussion of industrial-union bargaining.

[4] William G. Hosking, "Wage Decisions of Building Trades Unions in Central New York," *ILR Research*, Vol. II (December 1955), pp. 2–5, and Strauss, *op. cit.*

has little influence on the decision to build or not to build. In this case, the business agent would show little regard for the employment effect of his wage demands. In the case of small work, such as residential construction and renovation, business agents may believe that cost is a major determinant of the decision to build. Thus, business agents might show greater restraint in increasing the wage paid on small work than on big work especially in periods when many unionists were unemployed. If this distinction does enter the thinking of building-trades business agents, it is clear that they tend to view the best bargain as consisting of both a wage and an employment component. It should be noted that Strauss indicates that although the business agents he studied seemed to be worried about the employment effect he could not discover a single case where they had reduced wage demands because of fear of loss of employment.[5]

Undoubtedly the major consideration in building-trades demand formulation is the business agent's perception of the willingness and ability of the employers to meet his demands. If the contract comes up for negotiation at the height of a very busy season with lots of work started and more on the drawing boards, the business agent is very likely to make substantial demands. Under these circumstances, even a short strike will hurt the contractors and they will be in a conciliatory frame of mind. If business is slow and no great pickup is expected in the near future, the business agent will probably go slow on his wage demands. In this case, a strike threat loses much of its persuasive power. We turn now to the interests of the building contractors in wage bargaining.

Contractors' Bargaining Goals.   From the foregoing discussion it becomes clear that craft-union wage bargaining concentrates on wage *levels*, or pay for time worked. The effort side of the bargain may not even receive mention. The reason for this apparent oversight is that effort is under the control of the worker, who thus sets tempo; and the employer can do little about it.

The man who has served a trade apprenticeship learns, among other things, how fast he should work to maintain traditional standards of quality and quantity. He will not slacken his pace, but is not easily driven to quicken it. A bricklayer, for instance, will on the average lay so many bricks per hour and per day, and not many more or many less. From this known rate (which has varied over the years and may vary from one locality to another), a contractor can estimate quite accurately how much it will cost him to put up a wall containing a given number of bricks: the unit labor cost per brick. If he wants to reduce this unit labor cost he must either persuade his bricklayers to take a pay cut while continuing to work at the same tempo, or, without cutting pay, to speed up the work. Neither wage cuts nor speedups are popular with unionized crafts-

---

[5] Strauss, *op. cit.*, 76.

men. Although muscle-saving machinery has made its way into the technology of the construction industry and lowered total costs, skill-saving devices and machinery have met adamant opposition from the craft unions. Unit labor costs for tasks requiring the work of skilled hands remain tied to the pace or work tempo of the craftman who applies the effort.

Other elements of the five-point package follow almost automatically from the outcome of the bargaining on pay for time worked. Premium pay simply applies time and a half or double time to the agreed hourly rates. Pay for time not worked, the fourth item, was not traditionally a part of the craft union bargain. A holiday was a layoff day; now it may be paid, or worked at premium rates. Contingent benefits, if any, came not from the employer but from the union or, after the passage of the social security laws, from the government. Craft workers typically are temporary employees. In successive seasons, or even a single season, they work for many employers. Now that industrial unions have won contingent benefits, craft unions negotiate agreements that call for employer contributions—so much per hour worked—to an industry fund administered by the union or jointly by the union and representatives of the employer association.

Setting the wage level, therefore, sets unit labor costs uniformly for the industry in a given locality, and gives no one employer a competitive wage advantage over another. Each contractor tries instead to cut total costs by finding more efficient methods of carrying out unskilled operations, such as materials handling. He looks outward to the structure and economic health of the industry, and supports measures that encourage the expansion of business generally. Large contractors usually have an influential voice in the decisions of the employer's association. Sometimes smaller employers don't bother to belong to the association because they fear being outvoted by their larger associates or believe that their interests will be represented even if they don't pay their dues.

Typically the union and the employer's association work closely together to police the industry for compliance with the master agreement. This is a service to the employers in that it protects each employer who abides by the agreement from being underbid by some employer who uses nonunion labor or who shades the prevailing wage scale by other methods. Although each employer probably would like to bid on projects with a personal wage cost advantage, the best interest of all employers is served by eliminating such advantages. The activity of the employer's association and the union, if effective, guarantees an equality of competition in the industry as far as labor costs go.

When building activity is slow, employers naturally start a serious search for methods of generating new business. One means of generating new business is to increase governmental building. Here the employers and unions are complete allies. Another way of stimulating new business that is likely to occur to the contractors is a "bargain sale." Since all building construction is on a made-to-measure basis, the employers seek ways of reducing their costs, by greater use of precut materials and gentle urging of the craftsman to pay less attention to unimportant details.

When building is booming the contractor is likely to be quite generous in wage bargaining. After all, customers are waiting at his door and they only frown when he quotes a price. He and the customer both bemoan the high prices but the customer buys and the contractor adds on the customary profit (which is sometimes figured as a percentage of cost). Like the business agent, the employer may worry about the sales effect of high prices, but in periods of good business he is unlikely to do anything about them.

Although the building-trades unions represent the elite of American unionists and compose a substantial portion of the labor movement, the typical building-trades contract is negotiated with little public notice or concern because of the local nature of bargaining. Once the contractors and the unions in a locality have made their peace, the contract goes into open operation and exerts practically no influence whatever on bargaining in other segments of the economy.

INDUSTRIAL UNION WAGE BARGAINING

Wage bargaining is not as simple for industrial unions as for the crafts. Each craft union, in effect, bargains for a single, standard job: the job of carpenter, or electrician, or printing pressman. A job structure for the industry (and hence for the enterprises in the industry) emerges as an incidental result and takes the form of a range of different union rates. This range encompasses the levels set for each of the separate crafts, some of which are more highly paid than others.

In mass-production and analogous enterprises, workplace technology imposes quite different demands. Instead of bargaining job by job on the pay level and only incidentally arriving at a job structure, unions and management have to establish, at a single stroke, an *enterprise* structure for a range of differentiated, mainly nonskilled, nonstandard jobs.

Instead of setting a single union rate or simple union scale, they must resolve complicated issues to arrive at a wage curve (which may be a straight-line "curve") that will relate the pay levels with job worth as evaluated in the structure.

Instead of starting from an effort bargain that is known and can be taken for granted, they have to establish *procedures* for setting standards on a multitude of frequently-changing tasks. Instead of bargaining for workers who follow a lifelong trade from one employer to another they must provide for a permanent work force and seek contingent benefits for workers whose career attachment is to a specific enterprise.

Industrial union wage bargaining thus faces four issues: (1) establishing an *enterprise* job structure (pay for time worked); (2) setting *task* standards (the effort bargain); (3)paying *differential* wages (pay levels); and (4) devising contingent *benefits* appropriate to a given work force and a specific enterprise.

This chapter now proposes to discuss the first two issues, leaving the question of pay levels to the following chapter, Chapter 12, and contingent benefits to Chapter 13.

The Enterprise Job Structure

The rather misleading term "semiskilled" has come into use to distinguish factory jobs from those that require a trade apprenticeship. It is misleading because the prefix "semi" implies a *half* of something and would seem to imply further that all semiskilled jobs are equal. Common observation, not to mention industrial experience, belies this logic. Jobs in factories—and jobs in offices, hospitals, banks, mines, lumber camps; wherever people work—vary through a wide and finely graduated range of what can only be called *job worth*. A better way to put it is to say that jobs call for a broad range of *expertise*. Chapter 3 in this book makes the distinction between skill and expertise.

Jobs differ, too, in the degree of responsibility they carry, in the risks they entail, in the amount of physical and mental energy they demand for satisfactory performance. These sometimes intangible variables all contribute to job worth and different degrees of job worth tend to demand corresponding differences in pay. The method most commonly used for measuring job worth is *job evaluation.* Job evaluation arranges jobs into a structure showing their relation to each other by quantitative measurement of the intangible, job worth.

Job Evaluation

What is job evaluation? What are its aims? Its principles?

The principle behind job evaluation, which is acceptable to management and employee alike, could not be better phrased than in the simple slogan: Equal pay for equal work.

But work is not equal; different jobs have different worth. When jobs are unequal, they should not get equal pay. Hence the corollary: Unequal pay for unequal work *in proportion to the inequality.* The problem is to measure the inequality.

The employee gets his income from the *job,* but the enterprise gets its work—its production, or its services—from employee performance of *tasks.* A job may consist of a single task, endlessly repeated, or it may include a variety of different tasks.

The enterprise pays an employee for *doing:* for carrying out a task or a prescribed round or variety of tasks. It is irrelevant in theory whether the tasks call for physical or mental activity, even up to brainwork of the highest intellectual or creative order. The enterprise pays to *get something done*, at some point in time and space, by some person to whom the manager expects to have to pay real money. This person, then, must perform; but he must be capable of performing the kinds of tasks that make up his job—all the tasks, from the simplest to the most difficult.

That means that he must possess certain necessary *qualifications*. He is paid for what he *is* as well as what he *does*—not what he is as a person, but what he is, or has to be, in what he does as a performer on that job. Now, how does job evaluation theory define qualifications? Qualifications for satisfactory performance of a job consist of either (1) *ability* or (2) *aptitude.*

Ability—present ability—consists of qualifications that a person already possesses when he starts on a job. They are things he was born with, or acquired by education, training, or experience. A bizarre example of innate qualification for an element of a job came in the airframe industry during World War II. The job of bucking rivets from inside the wing of the plane required workers of small stature. Midgets came to the job with this qualification; persons of normal height and girth could not even acquire it. Examples in abundance of acquired qualifications come from those skilled crafts that can only be learned through a trade apprenticeship. Thus, if the job calls for wiring a circuit from blueprints, only a certified electrician can give acceptable performance. Only a surgeon would be allowed to remove someone's appendix; only a trained accountant assigned to audit a company's books. Present ability for jobs whose tasks require them is a finite and often scarce resource in the labor market.

Aptitude—the other kind of qualification—is the innate capacity to acquire ability, after instruction or experience. Ability is always specific, but aptitude is general. Ability may be inborn, but is generally acquired; aptitude is inborn. It remains undeveloped and plastic until given form and specific direction. Many people have it in a wide range of potentialities. These are almost infinitely present in the population, not rare or scarce in the labor market.

The scarcity factor is negligible, then, for initial hiring on jobs whose tasks require only aptitude plus on-the-job training. Ever since industry broke away from handicraft methods, the trend has been toward designing production jobs to this description. The undeveloped aptitude the worker brings to the job turns, under training and experience, into present ability *for that job*. Developing this ability has cost the enterprise time and money for training, and slow or substandard work during the learning process. It would cost no less to train and develop another worker.

The labor market for potential candidates for that job now consists of a sea of undifferentiated aptitude, plus only that person or those people who have acquired present ability. Present ability on a semiskilled job may be slight as compared with that of the skilled craftsman, the graduate engineer, or the research physicist, but *for that job* it is greater than anyone else's. It sets the possessor off from his competition; gives him comparative scarcity value. His services are worth more than theirs; but not too much more, for the enterprise could always train a replacement— at a cost.

The wage bargain thus consists of three elements: (1) the worker characteristics (e.g., skill, knowledge, strength, etc.) required to perform the assigned task, (2) the amount of work done by the worker, and (3) the amount of compensation exchanged for the type of work and the amount of work performed.

Union Attitudes toward Job Evaluation. Union attitudes on job evaluation vary considerably. Some unions have decided on a job evaluation program jointly with management; they have analyzed jobs and written job descriptions, evaluated jobs, determined labor grades and rate ranges, all on a joint basis. These unions believe that the best way to protect the interests of their members is to know the system "inside-out" and to actively participate in the formulation and administration of the system. An outstanding example of this attitude is the United Steelworkers of America, who cooperated with management in developing a nationwide system of job evaluation for the basic steel industry. Some managements actively seek union participation in the hope of relieving employee distrust of the program. Because union participation in job evaluation may put the union in the embarassing position of arguing against a specific rate increase, some unions have allowed management to install job evaluation unilaterally, but have reserved the right to challenge the results of each step through the grievance procedure. Other unions simply reserve the right to bargain on the results of any management wage determination, regardless of how the determination is made.

The general importance placed on individual job rates by industrial unions is illustrated by the rather common contract provision making the rates on new jobs subject to the grievance procedure but *not* subject to arbitration. This means that the union retains its right to strike over rates on new jobs, even during the life of a collective bargaining agreement.

The overall union attitude toward job evaluation might be termed healthy skepticism. For example, consider the following advice which the *AFL-CIO Collective Bargaining Report* gives its union readers:

> Development of a wage structure and determination of wage rates for each job is a fundamental area in which unions must protect members' interests through collective bargaining. This responsibility is not eased or changed where formal job evaluation is used.
>
> As long as unions morally and legally have the right to collectively bargain on wages they must subject every aspect of job evaluation to close

scrutiny and question. If they are working with job evaluation, voluntarily or otherwise, they must recognize that no part of the evaluation process, either in its development or application, can be removed from the bargaining table.[6]

Unions thus assert an interest not only in the outcome of job evaluation—that is, in the pay levels eventually assigned to evaluated jobs—but in the procedures themselves, or the methods used for measuring job worth. They rest this claim on Section 8 (a) (5) of the Taft-Hartley Act.

Section 8 (a) (5) makes it an unfair labor practice for an employer to refuse to bargain in good faith about "wages, hours, and working conditions." The NLRB and the courts have generally upheld union demands for such things as: copies of a company's job evaluation program; job descriptions and specifications; individual employee merit raises; and occasionally, wage survey data. The rationale seems to be that since unions have a right to bargain on the outcome of job evaluation, they cannot be prevented from having a say about procedures.

Many unions regularly participate in the procedures, from start to finish. Jointly with management, they check the validity of job descriptions and specifications, which state the facts about the jobs to be evaluated. They help select the evaluation plan and adapt it to the enterprise. They rate the jobs according to the plan; that is, they measure relative job worth by holding each job up against the plan's "yardstick." They group the rated jobs into appropriate clusters, classifications, or labor grades, to simplify administration and make the structure manageable: all this, perhaps, without a word about money. Instead, the members of the joint evaluation team talk about the intangible: job worth. Figuratively and for the moment they assign these units a money value of algebraic *x*.

Union and management representatives thus jointly work out *principles of equity* for paying different jobs different rates. Once agreed on principle, they fix the actual rate—the pay level—by giving dollar values to the algebraic *x*, or unit of job worth. If 100 points, or units, is worth $2.40 an hour, a job evaluated at 150 points is worth $3.60, and so on.

At this stage of setting pay levels, labor and management representatives may do some hard bargaining from different points of view. They are now no longer discussing abstract principles, but cold cash: costs to the company, income to the workers. They may find an agreement hard to reach, but once they do agree on price, the structure they set up before the bargaining distributes pay to all jobs in proportion to evaluated worth. Employees more readily accept the differential rates as fair, because their union helped set up the *system*. Management and the union can now settle disagreements over individual cases without disturbing

---

[6] "Need for Bargaining on Job Evaluation Plans," *AFL-CIO Collective Bargaining Report* Vol. II (June 1957), p. 36.

the structure. Many managers welcome and invite union participation.

Others, of course, do not; and many unions decline to take part even when invited. They prefer to leave full responsibility in management's hands while they remain free to challenge any rate for any job, by way of the grievance procedure. A unionized company without a job evaluation plan has to justify the rate on every wage grievance the union presents. By going after one job, then another, union committees sometimes whipsaw rates to higher levels than were bargained for, or get the structure so badly out of line that the company cannot justify any of its rates. Management averts this danger when it installs a plan, even without union participation. Wage and salary policy becomes more defensible. Changes in pay levels, when they have to be made, follow more systematic and predictable directions.

Whether a union helps shape its company's program, then, or just sits back and snipes at it, managers in enterprises dealing with industrial unions find that job evaluation brings system and rationality to the complex issues of wage and salary administration. There are four standard job evaluation plans: (1) ranking, (2) classification, (3) point, and (4) factor comparison.

Ranking. Ranking is the simplest method of job evaluation. The persons evaluating jobs merely arrange them from most important and difficult to least important and difficult. The ranking system guarantees that wages are higher for more difficult and important jobs. To this extent, it is superior to highly informal systems of paying each job whatever it appears to be worth with no comparison to other jobs. However, ranking does not tell us *how much* more important a tool-and-die maker is than a janitor. The simplicity of the ranking system commends it to situations involving few jobs that are well known to the evaluators.

Job Classification. Job classification consists of grouping jobs of comparable content and difficulty into "classifications." Classifications are then compared and ranked. Rates are assigned to each classification on the basis of the importance and difficulty of the jobs in the classification. The classification system is a refinement of the ranking system. It further rationalizes the rate structure, but is less complex and, therefore, *possibly* less accurate than the point and factor comparison systems.

Point System. The point system is the most widely used formal system of job evaluation in private industry. In the point system, a number of "compensable factors" are clearly defined. For example, in the National Metal Trades Association point system there are 11 compensable factors: education; experience; initiative and ingenuity; physical demand; mental or visual demand; responsibility for equipment or process; responsibility for safety of others; responsibility for material or product; responsibility for work of others; working conditions; and unavoidable hazards. After the factors are selected and defined they are broken down into smaller units called degrees. For example, in the NMTA system, responsibility for the work of others is broken down into five degrees. The low, medium, and highest degrees are defined as follows: First degree—responsible only for own work; Third degree—responsible for instructing, directing, or setting up for a small group of employees usually in the same occupation, up to 10 persons; Fifth degree—responsible for instructing, directing, and maintaining the flow of work in a group of over 25 persons. After degreeing the factors, it is necessary to weight the factors and the degrees. This is a process of assigning a number of points to each factor and degree which represents its relative value to the company. In NMTA, for example, "experience" is weighted as a maximum of 110 points, while "education" gets a maximum of 70, and "unavoidable hazards" gets a maximum of 25.

FIGURE 11–1. Digest of a "Tailor-Made" Job Evaluation System

Factor	Minimum Points for First Degree	Maximum Points for Sixth Degree
Work of others	0	90
Complexity	6	90
Physical skill	1	30
Experience	0	30
Education	0	20
Physical effort	1	20
Errors	0	25
Hazards	1	30
Working conditions	0	15
Outside contacts	0	40
Inside contacts	0	15
Safety of others	1	35
Funds or property	0	10
Supervision received	0	20

The variety of factors, degrees, and weights that can be used in a point system is almost infinite. For this reason, many managements and unions prefer to establish a job evaluation program that is "tailor-made" to the needs of their particular business. For an idea of the variety of point systems, a tailor-made plan which has worked to the satisfaction of one management and union is shown in Figure 11–1. In the basic steel industry, management and the United Steelworkers have cooperated in establishing a form of job evaluation which is used nationally.

Union interest in the factors used in job evaluation programs has been intensified by automation. As new processes dilute "experience" and "physical demand," union leaders have argued that greater weight should be given to such factors as "responsibility for equipment," "responsibility for material and product," and "visual effort."

The final step in establishing a point system is evaluating jobs. Jobs are evaluated by comparing job descriptions and specifications to the "yardsticks" which have been incorporated in the job evaluation manual. Each job is evaluated at the total of the points it is assigned for each factor.

Relative job worth now appears as points on a scale. This is the *job structure*, graphically represented, after formal evaluation. Once it has been determined with maximum possibly accuracy, it is customary to simplify it, for convenience in administration, by grouping the jobs

FIGURE 11–2.   Job Structure, Labor Grades, Rate Ranges

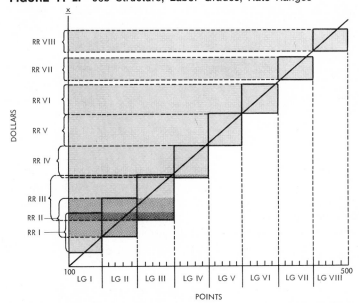

In this diagram, the points on the horizontal axis represent evaluated job worth. The jobs have been classified into Labor Grades (LG). The rate ranges (RR) for each classification appear on the vertical axis. Note that RR I, II, and III overlap. That means that the highest paid (perhaps most senior) individual on a job in LG I, for instance, might receive more pay than a beginner on a LG II job. RR IV, V, and VI are contiguous. RR VII and VIII are discrete. Rarely would an enterprise show a pattern quite like this; it is intended to show all possible variations. Labor Grades never overlap; a job falls in one LG or another—never in between.

into *labor grades* or classifications. It is now possible to assign a money rate, or *rate range* corresponding to each labor grade. This chapter treats the money rate as an unknown, *x;* but whatever the actual value of *x,* a line or curve expressing the relationship between points in the job structure and rates of pay keeps them always in accord with the principle: unequal pay for unequal work in proportion to the inequality. Figure 11–2 shows this in graphic form.

Factor Comparison.   Under the factor comparison system, the first step is the selection of a number of "key" jobs. Key jobs are selected from the complete range of jobs. Each key job must be a job which it is believed is receiving the *right* wage rate now. Each key job is broken down into a number of factors (similar to the factors in a point system) and the money paid for the job is allocated among the various factors. All other jobs are compared to the key jobs on the basis of the factors and rates are imputed to these jobs from the factor comparison with the key jobs.

The Effort Bargain: Task Standards

Thus far in our discussion we have assumed that the method of wage payment was time. Pay by the hour, day, week, month, or year is far more common in the United States than production pay (by the piece, value of sales, or time or material saved). Time wages and production wages are each uniquely suited to certain kinds of business operations. However, two managements in the same line of business may have radically different views as to the desirability of production wages. Also unions are split on their attitude toward incentive wages.

Time wages are particularly suited to situations where:

1. The tempo of production is not under the control of the operator.
2. Quality considerations far outweigh quantity considerations in production.
3. Management is unable to schedule production so that the operators receive a steady flow of available work.
4. Operators perform a wide variety of short-cycle operations instead of repetitive uniform tasks.

Aside from these organizational considerations, time wages offer certain advantages. Time wages are easy and inexpensive to compute. The insistence of some unions on time wages can be attributed to a feeling that they are fair because they are equal. In other cases, management has abandoned production wages when the particular incentive system failed to provide the expected reductions in unit labor costs. In the case of white-collar workers, salaries (which are nothing more than long-term time wages) represent important status symbols. The rationale might go something like this: "Because I can be trusted to make my own work, management doesn't need to pay me on the basis of the number of units of work that I finish." Another white-collar argument goes like this: "My work is so varied and complex that it is impossible to accurately measure the true value of my contribution to the company."

Production Standards. It should be noted that time wages are always accompanied by some form of quantity of labor consideration.

Production standards for skilled craftsmen working under a craft union collective bargaining agreement are established during the apprenticeship period and through written and unwritten union rules. These standards plus a uniform hourly rate give employers of union craftsmen roughly equal unit labor costs.

In assembly line production, the speed of the line establishes the rate of production. Workers who don't finish their assigned tasks as the line moves along are subject to disciplinary action. A typical collective bargaining agreement on production standards is a clause like the following:

The right of the Company to establish and enforce production standards is recognized. Such production standards shall be fair and equitable and shall be set on the basis of normal working conditions, the quality of workmanship, and the normal working capacities of normal experienced operators, with due consideration to fatigue and the need for 'personal' time.

Such a clause is usually accompanied by a provision making production standards subject to the grievance procedure. Because of the importance of production standards, some unions insist that they are not subject to arbitration. Failing to reach a satisfactory settlement with management, the union reserves its right to strike over this critical issue during the life of a contract. Management's vital interest in production standards is illustrated by the great reluctance of management to bargain over them in the past.

There have been a number of instances when unions have made exceptionally good bargains with management on production standards under the threat of a strike at a crucial time such as model changeover time in the automobile industry.

Time Study. Time study is a method of determining the time which should be allowed for a worker to perform a defined task according to a specific method and under prescribed conditions. Time studies are usually made by timing workers with a stop watch while they are doing the task. This time is then adjusted for such factors as delays, fatigue, personal needs, and incentive factors. The task or time standard thus derived may be expressed in terms of units per hour, standard hours per 100 units, or time per unit. If an incentive wage plan is used, the standard may also be expressed in monetary terms, such as one cent per piece produced.

Since most time studies are taken of an individual worker or a small group of workers, disagreements over time studies are usually expressed as grievances on specific task standards at the local union level.

While international unions can provide expert assistance to their locals, the investigation and processing of time-study disputes remain primarily a local problem. *AFL-CIO Collective Bargaining Report* outlined various local union approaches to time study as follows:

1. Some locals prevent the use of time study altogether.
2. Some locals allow management to use any method of setting job standards it desires, but the locals reserve the right to bargain on the results.

3. Some locals participate directly with management in making time studies and in setting standards.
4. A majority of locals allow management to make time studies but insist on bargaining oñ both the methods and their applications.[7]

Since its introduction in the 1880s, most unions have opposed the use of stop-watch time study. Union opposition probably stems from early abuse of time study in the form of speed-ups. Today union opposition and distrust of time study can be rationalized on the basis of research findings on the scientific limits of the accuracy of time study. Industrial unions have been conspicuously unsuccessful in preventing the introduction of time study because time study is almost essential to the successful operation of a factory. Time study was deeply entrenched as a management technique in factory production long before effective industrial unions had been organized.

In recent years somewhere between one fifth and one quarter of all grievances taken to arbitration by unions have been on time study. When we also consider the number of nonarbitrable grievances on production standards, it is obvious that time study is a major issue in labor-management relations.

The reader can obtain an excellent insight of present-day union thinking on time study by reading Figure 11–3. This figure is a verbatim copy of AFL-CIO advice on the handling of time-study grievances. The entire tone of this advice is to show errors in management's study rather than to try to prove a new union time study is a proper one.

Incentive Wages

Time-study data may be used to establish incentive wage rates. However, incentive wage rates may be determined without recourse to time study. Incentive wage rates are based on the assumption that workers *can* increase their output substantially and that they *will* increase their output in exchange for higher earnings. The purpose of incentive wage rates is to reduce unit labor costs by allowing workers to earn substantially higher wages in exchange for more production than would be forthcoming under time wages.

The major types of incentive wage plans are:

1. Piecework. Employees are paid a fixed amount for each unit of production completed. (Piecework is frequently accompanied by a minimum guarantee regardless of the number of units produced.)
2. Differential piecework. These plans follow the famous Taylor Differential Piecework System. They pay a lower piece rate for the first units of production and a higher rate for all units produced beyond a

---

[7] "Time Study," *AFL-CIO Collective Bargaining Report,* Vol. II (September 1957), p. 50.

FIGURE 11–3. Union Handling of Time Study Grievances

Time study grievances should be handled the same as any other grievances. The most important factor is that of getting the facts.

While some knowledge of time study is helpful, it is not necessary for the shop steward or other union representative to be a time study man in order to process a time study grievance.

The union representative should:

(1)   Secure a copy of the company's record of the operation in dispute.

(2)   Make certain that the record of job conditions and the job descriptions is complete. If either is incomplete, it will be impossible to reproduce the job as it was when the time study was made and therefore the company's time study cannot be checked. *This alone is grounds for rejecting the study.*

(3)   If the time study sheet does contain sufficient information as to how and under what conditions the job was being performed when the time study was made, then it is necessary to determine whether the job is still being performed in exactly the same way now.

Check to see if there has been any change in machines, materials, tools, equipment, tolerances, job layout, etc. Any change should be checked to see if it affects the ability of the operator to produce at the same rate as that achieved during the time study.

(4)   Usually the total operation or job cycle is broken down for timing purposes into parts which are called elements.

Check the elemental breakdown of the job on the time study sheet. See that the beginning and ending point of each element is clearly defined. *If it is not, any attempt to measure elements and give them a time value was pure guesswork.*

(5)   Check the descriptions of each element to see if they describe what the operator is presently required to do. *Any change invalidates the original study.*

(6)   Make sure that everything the operator is required to do as part of the job has been recorded and timed on the time study sheet. Watch for tasks which are not part of every cycle.

Such things as getting stock, adjusting machines, changing tools, reading blueprints, and waiting for materials are examples of items most frequently missed.

(7)   Check for "strike-outs." A time study finding is based on a number of different timings on the same job. The time study man may discard some of his timings as "abnormal."

If the time study man has discarded any of his recorded times he must record his reasons for doing so. This enables the union to intelligently determine if the "strike-out" is valid. The fact that a particular time is larger or smaller than other times for the same element is not sufficient reason for discarding it.

(8)   Determine if the time study was long enough to accurately reflect all of the variations and conditions which the operator can be expected to face during the job. Was it a proper sample of the whole job? *If not, the time study should be rejected as its results are meaningless.*

(9)   See that only a simple average, and not the median, mode or other arithmetic device was used in calculating the elemental times. The average is the only proper method for time study purposes.

(10)   Check the rating factor on the time study sheet. Try to find out if the time study man recorded his rating factor before leaving the job or after he computed the observed times. Ask the operator who was time studied if he feels the rating factor is a proper one.

Watch the worker who was timed work at the pace he considers proper and then at the pace required to produce the company's workload. *The judgment of the worker and the steward are as valid as that of the time study man.*

(11)   Make sure that allowances for personal time, fatigue and delays have been provided in proper amounts.

(12)   And finally check all the arithmetic for errors.

A final note:

Most union representatives have found it unwise to take additional time studies themselves as a check, except as a last resort. It is more effective to show the errors in management's study than to try to prove a new union time study is a proper one.

A time study taken even by a union is still only the result of judgment. Even when proper methods are used, they tend merely to reduce the inconsistencies of time study, not eliminate them.

Source: "Union Handling of Time Study Grievances," *AFL-CIO Collective Bargaining Report,* Vol. 2 (September 1957), pp. 53–54. (Italics added) certain standard. Taylor designed this plan to attract top producers and quickly eliminate workers who do not produce at a high rate. The Taylor Differential Piecework System is very rare in present-day practice.

3. Sharing plans. Under these plans, workers and management share in the gains and losses resulting from varying output. "Normal" production is established for a given wage. When production exceeds or falls short of the "norm," employees and management share the gains or losses on some predetermined basis. *Diminishing* piece rate systems of this type are more common in American industry than the Taylor *increasing* piece rate system.

Time wages are more commonly paid in the United States than are incentive wages. This is primarily due to the organizational, psychological, and engineering difficulties in the effective operation of an incentive system of wage payment. These factors are reinforced by a rather general union opposition to incentive wage plans.

Incentive wage plans are suitable to operations where:

1. Output is controlled by the operator (or group of operators).
2. Output is measurable.
3. Quality considerations are secondary to quantity considerations *or* quality is subject to the direct control of the operator.
4. Production scheduling makes a steady flow of work available to incentive workers.
5. Changes in operations to be performed are relatively infrequent.

In addition to these organizational considerations, it is important that the incentive rates be established in such a way as to win the support of employees. It seems that the major factor in the almost universal practice of restriction of output is a deep-seated fear that rates will be cut when production exceeds a certain level.

For a successful incentive plan to exist under collective bargaining, it must satisfy the needs of the three parties to the agreement: the employer, the employees, and the union.

From the employer's viewpoint the sole requirement for a successful incentive plan is unit labor costs lower than those existing in his competitors' plants or those existing in his plant before the plan was installed.

The employee has more varied requirements for a satisfactory incentive plan. Just earning more money isn't enough. In addition, the plan must be simple enough for the employees to understand it. There must be genuine confidence in management's customary pledge that rates will not be cut because earnings exceed a certain level. The firm's sales picture must be good enough that increased production does not result in substantial layoffs. Most difficult to define, but probably most important, the employees must feel that the plan is "their" plan and that they actively participate in its establishment and operation.

Some unions oppose incentive wages as a matter of international union policy. This position could be traced to several origins. Incentive plans might frustrate a union desire to establish some kind of competitive equality between employers in the industry. Any reduction in actual employment or employment opportunities resulting from higher man-hour production reduces the union's membership base. Incentive plans which cause workers to compete among themselves may weaken union solidarity. The complexity of various incentive plans makes it difficult for local union negotiating committees to conform to a single "industry practice."

On the other hand, incentive wage rates are used by some unions as a major stabilizing factor in the industry. The International Ladies' Garment Workers' Union, the Amalgamated Clothing Workers of America, and the Textile Workers Union of America each take an active part in the establishment of incentive wage systems in their industries.

Most collective bargaining agreements provide safeguard clauses against management abuse of incentive wage systems. The more common of these clauses include: minimum earnings guarantees; guarantees against rate-cutting; negotiation and arbitration or the right to strike on the rates for new jobs; and, occasionally, work-sharing arrangements.

The wage and effort bargain thus consists of three parts: the quality of the labor sold, the quantity of labor sold, and the price of labor sold. Job evaluation is used to compare the quality of labor sold by various operators on diverse jobs. Production standards or incentive wage rates (frequently determined through the technique of time study) determine the quantity of labor delivered by each operator. The price at which labor is sold is a wage rate *plus* a series of wage supplements (e.g., vacations with pay, overtime premiums, pensions, unemployment benefits, etc.). These wage supplements constitute an important part of the wage bargain and impose a heavy cost burden on management. However, we shall consider these elements of the wage bargain (which frequently are not directly related to the quality or quantity of labor sold) in our discussion of worker insurance and income-continuity programs in Chapter 13.

SPECIAL COLLECTIVE BARGAINING PROBLEMS ON WAGES

Job evaluation, production standards, and, to a lesser degree, incentive wages are integral parts of the operation of a factory. The most militant union cannot realistically expect to turn back the clock by eliminating these basic tools of industrial management. Because of the vitality of these techniques and their impact on employee welfare, issues related to them are a permanent part of the collective bargaining process. Future bargaining on these issues may take any number of possible directions. We shall briefly discuss four illustrations of possible future trends: (1) guaranteeing personal rates against job restudy, (2) wage structures as a cause of internal industrial union stresses, (3) automation and wage structures, and (4) job enlargement, sometimes called job enrichment.

Job Restudy

The problem of job restudy can be a major problem to a union. The chief union negotiator for a firm confronted with an adverse industry outlook sees the problem like this: "We are opposed to the job evaluation system in principle, but we are living with it. . . . In good times there's no pressure for job reevaluation because the labor market in our industry is too tight. . . . In a slack period like this, if the company brings its job evaluation system to bear in a plant where technological changes have gone ahead faster than reevaluation of jobs, wage rates could be cut drastically." The union answer to this problem was to concentrate on the company's job evaluation program instead of pressing wage increase demands in negotiations. The union's demand was that all workers on specific jobs for six months prior to negotiations be "red-circled" and their rates be unchanged even if the job were downgraded after evaluation. The union also sought to protect certain job rates by urging greater emphasis on certain factors in the job evaluation system.[8]

Industrial Union Internal Stresses

The wage structure problem is almost exclusively the problem of the factory-type employer and the industrial union. One of the major problems of job evaluation is fitting the comparatively small number of skilled jobs into a wage structure which is dominated by the many semiskills of the factory. Skilled workers in a factory are usually represented by an industrial union in which they are only a small political minority. Because of the need for the militant support of the vast majority of the membership, industrial unions tend to negotiate across-the-board wage increases which reduce the skilled-unskilled wage differential. Many of the wage supplements initiated by industrial union bargaining also tend to reduce or conceal the skilled-unskilled wage differential.

The skilled worker in the factory may have a different type of employment relationship than his counterpart represented by a craft union. Factory employment is not subject to some of the severe seasonal fluctuations in such craft-union industries as building construction. The factory employer tends to retain his skilled craftsmen as long as economically feasible in adverse business conditions because of the difficulty of replacing them in periods of business upturn. Many skilled factory workers have acquired their skills at their employer's expense in specialized training programs.

---

[8] "UAW Pratt & Whitney Local Seeks Wage Stability Instead of Boosts," *Wall Street Journal* (Chicago Ed.), Thursday, October 10, 1957, p. 24.

Nevertheless, the wage scales negotiated by craft unions look quite attractive to the skilled factory worker. Also, in periods of booming business activity, most factory skilled workers could find other jobs at higher rates of pay, in job shops or elsewhere. Thus market pressures exert powerful influences on the factory wage structure. Skilled factory workers become restless and begin to believe that they are the "forgotten men" of the industrial unions. They talk about secession from their union and pose a very serious problem for the union leadership.

Wildcat strikes of skilled tradesmen belonging to the UAW plagued the automobile industry for several weeks in 1955 and delayed the ratification of the UAW agreements with General Motors, Ford, and Chrysler. This dissension plus the formation of a dual union, the Society of Skilled Trades, resulted in the UAW giving skilled workers a greater degree of representation in bargaining than they had possessed previously. It is quite certain that the problem of compensation for skilled workers will plague both employers and industrial unions for some years to come.

Automation and Job Evaluation

The exact impact of automation on job assignments in different plants is impossible to predict. However, in almost all cases, automation results in very large increases in man-hour productivity, a greater emphasis on rapid machine maintenance, and a reduction of the physical exertion and an improvement in physical working conditions. Such radical changes undoubtedly will change much of our conventional thinking about job evaluation.

Two trends are already discernible. First, unions are advocating greater emphasis on certain "compensable factors" or the introduction of entirely new factors. In an attempt to justify substantially higher rates for automated jobs such factors as "monotony," "visual effort," and a myriad of others are cropping up in negotiation sessions. It seems likely that these or other factors will be recognized by management as a moderate cost for union acceptance of radical new production methods. Second, several cases of negotiation on automated jobs have resulted in a radical reduction in the number of different jobs and job rates. In one case, several hundred different jobs were eliminated for two new jobs: "automation tender" and "automation equipment maintenance technician." This bargain meant very substantial wage increases for all of the workers in the automated plant. From management's viewpoint, such a bargain provided for maximum flexibility in the assignment of workers in the plant.

Job Enlargement

Industrial managers for many years have believed that maximum output could be achieved at minimum cost by breaking jobs down into the smallest possible tasks. Recent experience, especially during and since

World War II, has radically changed this traditional thinking. "Job enlargement," i.e., the combination of several tasks for a single worker, is receiving increasing attention. This new trend is supported by two factors: (1) extreme job simplification actually reduces total output because of monotony and (2) the need for varied skills in certain maintenance jobs. In the case of maintenance work, "down time" on machinery can be extremely costly and waiting for a skilled worker in a particular classification can prevent other maintenance workers from finishing their part of the repair work. Whichever motivating factor is present, job enlargement changes job content (almost always in the direction of increased complexity) and necessitates reevaluation of the job. When two jobs are combined, should the rate for the new job be equal to the rate of the more complex element? Or an average of the two elements? Or even higher than the sum of the two elements?

SUMMARY

Employer and employee come together in our society under no compulsion, but in a voluntary, mutually beneficial relationship that finds expression in a wage and effort bargain.

The employer pays wages and salaries, which to him are *costs of operation*, and gets work—*production*—in return. The employee performs *tasks* on which he expends physical and mental effort, and gets income—*a livelihood*—in return. The essence of the bargain at any given moment is the *amount* of pay agreed on as acceptable for the *amount and kind* of effort that goes into the performance of the *tasks* that make up the employee's *job*.

Craft unions concentrate on bargaining for a standard rate of pay; that is, on the *pay level*. That is because skilled workers control their own work tempo—the effort side of the bargain—and members of the same craft do substantially the same job.

Industrial unions and the employers with whom they deal face more complicated problems. Management tends to control work tempo by such devices as the man-machine mix, conveyor-line speed, schedules, layout, and production controls. Semiskilled employees work at jobs that are nonstandard and unequal. Thus labor and management have to establish a *job structure* relating different jobs in terms of their comparative *job worth*, and set up procedures for measuring and comparing different *kinds* and *degrees* of physical and mental effort required. Agreement on pay levels cannot precede, but must accompany or follow resolution of these other issues.

Managers have turned to various methods of *job evaluation* as a means of establishing a job structure, often (but not always) with union participation. Managers and unions alike have found that job evaluation systematizes the job structure and simplifies bargaining on pay levels.

Managers also attempt to prescribe and control the effort bargain by various means, of which the most evident and best known is probably time study. Unions thus have to bargain on effort day by day and task by task, resorting to the grievance procedure or, on occasion, to the traditional strike, to set the effort bargain. At enterprise level, therefore, an industrial union is likely to be more directly concerned with the effort bargain than with the absolute pay level. This does not mean that pay level means nothing to industrial unions and their members, or that the problem of determining the level is not difficult and complex.

The next chapter deals with pay levels, general and individual, as unions and managers encounter them in industrial union bargaining.

QUESTIONS FOR DISCUSSION

1. What elements of the "pay package" have unions added to the fundamental wage and effort bargain? To what extent, if any, does the trend in this direction seem irreversible?

2. Why are craft unions primarily interested in the pay level? Is the same thing true and to the same extent of industrial unions? Why?

3. As a principle of equitable compensation, in what way can the slogan, "Equal pay for equal work," justify wage differentials?

4. How do job evaluation techniques lend themselves to assuring equity through different rates of pay for different jobs?

5. As a manager, would you want the union to take part in a job evaluation study and help administer the program? Why? As a union leader, would you want to participate? Why?

6. Does time study primarily affect pay levels, or the effort bargain?

Chapter   THE WAGE AND EFFORT

12   BARGAIN: PAY LEVELS

Pay levels, like prices, vary. For a business enterprise or other organization employing people, the pay level is the current price of hiring labor. This current price per unit of job worth (the algebraic x of Chapter 11) will be unequally distributed over the different jobs in the job structure; but even when structures remain substantially unchanged over a period of time, pay levels vary.

They vary from place to place, industry to industry, enterprise to enterprise as well as year to year. Company executives have always made more money than clerks, engineers than draftsmen, foremen than laborers, and probably always will. Such differences arise from evaluated job worth: the *structure*. All of these jobs in the 1970s pay more than they did in the 1950s or the 1920s, pay more in some companies, industries, and regions than in others. These are differences in *pay levels*. Not all the increase over the years comes from inflation; real wages have risen, too.

The process of setting pay levels turns that algebraic x into a specific sum of money: concrete dollars-and-cents figures on the wage or salary check an employee cashes to meet weekly expenses or pay monthly bills. The amount on the face of the check is highly visible to the recipient, and strongly felt; it both confers and limits command over the range of goods and services money can buy. It directly measures a person's economic, and indirectly, social status in relation to the world outside the shop and after working hours. This is a *comparative* measure, and the comparison involves standards that are *external* to the enterprise.

Pay levels fluctuate—mostly upward—with changes in the labor and product markets and shifts in power relations. These outside forces generate pressures that make themselves felt within the enterprise, whether it be unionized or not. In a nonunion firm management has to estimate the pressures and act accordingly. In unionized firms, unions and their managements jointly negotiate the pay levels. From opposite sides of the table the bargainers apply—each according to their own outlook and interests—standards of *consistency*.

Consistency does not necessarily mean equality, or paying the average, or area, or industry rate. A given firm might, as a matter of policy, decide to pay consistently more; another, consistently less than the going rate. Most firms probably try to match what others pay in order not to be at a disadvantage in competing for labor. Unions try for consistency with the better, or above-average levels of pay.

EXTERNAL CONSISTENCY

Depending on the particular situation, managers and unions may favor either consistency in the labor market or consistency in the product market. While they appeal to the same abstract standard, they may actually be talking about two different things. A firm that sells its product nationally but manufactures in a low-wage region might argue for consistency with community rates; that is, consistency with rates in the local labor market from which most of the employees are recruited. The union, concerned about the jobs of members working for competing firms in high-wage areas, would be likely to argue just as agressively for consistency with the product market. The union's aim is not simply to get raises for members in the lower-paid community, but to equalize labor costs between firms and take wages out of competition. In negotiations between firms and their unions in higher-paid areas, the bargainers often reverse themselves: The union argues for consistence with the local labor market, the firm for the industry or product-market rate. This sounds, and is, opportunistic. Both sides indulge in it. What they eventually agree on tends to affect pay levels both in the labor and product markets—the local community, and the industry—and in the long run tends toward equalizing labor costs.

A building trades union normally shows less concern about industry rates because its product and labor markets roughly coincide. When a craft union negotiates a master agreement with a contractors' association, the result equalizes labor costs for all contractors in the area and takes wages out of competition. The typical industrial union confronts a more complex problem because of the many variations in job content between employing enterprises and their geographic dispersal in areas of differing pay levels.

No matter from which angle it may be interpreted, does external consistency mean that all jobs are to receive rates consistent with the pay levels used as a standard of comparison? No. Only rarely are the jobs perfectly comparable or conditions identical; it still makes sense to arrive at a job structure by internal comparisons. Some jobs may prove to be hard to fill locally. Other factors of the particular situation may enter in. Complete consistency is unattainable. What is attainable is a rather rough approximation: consistency for most jobs most of the time; consistency with standards not entirely unacceptable either to management or the union.

Sources of Wage Data

The informal, sporadic, and occasional exchange of wage information between employers has a long history. Impetus toward systematizing wage comparisons came from the policies of the National War Labor Board in the 1940s. In order to make sure that firms doing priority work for the wartime government could compete effectively for essential workers in the labor market without aggravating inflation, the NWLB required firms and unions requesting wage adjustments first to show that they had installed a formal job evaluation program and made careful wage surveys. Since World War II the quality of data gathered to compare interfirm wage rates has improved; the quantity available is still not overwhelming.

The major sources of wage rate information on individual jobs may be classified as follows:

1. Governmental wage surveys.
2. Employer association wage surveys.
3. Union wage surveys.
4. Individual company wage surveys.

We shall discuss each of these sources before discussing the problems of interpreting what limited data are available.

Governmental Wage Surveys. The Bureau of Labor Statistics gathers wage rates in two important series: Occupational Wage Surveys and the annual Union Wages and Hours surveys. In discussing wage structure problems, we are interested only in wage *rates*. Valuable as detailed *earnings* statistics may be for other purposes, they are irrelevant to questions of wage structure.

Occupational wage surveys are conducted regularly in a number of important industrial centers. In each area, data are obtained by personal visits of BLS field agents to representative firms within six broad industry divisions: manufacturing; transportation (excluding railroads); communication and other utilities; wholesale trade; retail trade; finance, insurance, and real estate; and services. Only firms employing 51 or more workers are surveyed. These surveys are conducted on a sample basis. A greater proportion of large than small establishments is studied. However, all establishments are given their appropriate weight in combining the data.

The occupations selected for study are common to a variety of manufacturing and nonmanufacturing industries. Occupational classification is based on a uniform set of job descriptions designed to take account of interestablishment variation in duties within the same job. A BLS Occupational Wage Survey job description for a tool-and-die maker is presented in Figure 12–1. Factory jobs surveyed are frequently limited to those in maintenance and power plant and custodial and material movement occupations.

Rate data exclude premium pay for overtime and for work on week ends, holidays, and late shifts. Nonproduction bonuses are excluded also, but cost-of-living bonuses and incentive earnings are included. Information is presented also on selected establishment practices and supplementary benefits as they relate to office and plant workers.

Several characteristics of Occupational Wage Surveys limit their usefulness for achieving external wage consistency:

1. They are conducted only in major industrial centers.
2. Surveys are conducted in specific areas only infrequently, e.g., every five years.
3. Frequently the group of jobs studied is small compared to the number of jobs in any particular firm.

FIGURE 12-1. Job Description From BLS Occupational Wage Survey

---

Tool-and-Die Maker

(Diemaker; Jig Maker; Toolmaker; Fixture Maker; Gauge Maker)
Constructs and repairs machine-shop tools, gauges, jigs, fixtures or dies for forgings, punching, and other metal-forming work. Work involves *most of the following:* planning and laying out of work from models, blueprints, drawings, or other oral and written specifications; using a variety of tool-and-die maker's handtools and precision measuring instruments; understanding of the working properties of common metals and alloys; setting up and operating of machine tools and related equipment; making necessary shop computations relating to dimensions of work, speeds, feeds, and tooling of machines; heat-treating of metal parts during fabrication as well as of finished tools and dies to achieve required qualities; working to close tolerances; fitting and assembling of parts to prescribed tolerances and allowances; selecting appropriate materials, tools, and processes. In general, the tool-and-die maker's work requires a rounded training in machine-shop and toolroom practice usually acquired through a formal apprenticeship or equivalent training and experience.

For cross-industry wage study purposes, tool-and-die makers in tool-and-die jobbing shops are excluded from this classification.

We shall discuss the problem of job comparability as it applies to Occupational Wage Surveys later.

BLS conducts annual surveys of wage rates and scheduled hours of work for specified crafts or jobs as provided in labor-management agreements in four industries: building construction, printing, local transit, and local trucking. The studies present the wage rates in effect as of July 1 of each year as reported to the Bureau by the appropriate labor organizations in each of the cities.

Union scales are defined as the minimum wage scales or maximum schedules of hours. Rates in excess of the negotiated mimimum are not included.

These surveys have the important advantage of frequency. For negotiations in noncovered industries, the rates on particular jobs might give a rough indication of the "going" rate in industries competing for the same skills. These surveys also provide bases for comparison between surveyed cities. The careful selection of a surveyed city might provide a rough guide for wage determination in nonsurveyed communities.

Employers' Associations. Employers' association collect and distribute to their members vast quantities of wage-rate data. In 1952, Professors N. Arnold Tolles and Robert L. Raimon published the first general guide to nongovernmental wage surveys.[1] Tolles and Raimon present digests of surveys conducted by 120 associations, with 60,000 employer members, employing 10 million workers, surveying the wages of 4 million

FIGURE 12–2. Numbers of Associations Known to Conduct Wage Surveys, by Industry or by Area Orientation

Association	*Number*
Industry-oriented associations	105
Food and kindred products	7
Textile mill products	6
Lumber, wood, furniture, fixtures	13
Paper and allied products	5
Chemicals and allied products	6
Products of petroleum and coal	2
Leather and leather products	3
Stone, clay, and glass products	7
Primary metal industries	7
Fabricated metal products	8
Machinery, electrical products	13
Miscellaneous manufacturing	2
Transportation	4
Trade: wholesale and retail	7
Finance, insurance, and real estate	3
Medical and health services	4
Miscellaneous nonmanufacturing	3
Area-oriented associations	61
Area employer associations	36
Chambers of commerce	25

Source: N. Arnold Tolles and Robert L. Raimon, *Sources of Wage Information: Employer Associations* (Ithaca, N.Y.: Cornell University, 1952), p. 233.

employees. Figure 12–2 shows the wage surveying associations that they uncovered in their research. It seems to be a safe guess that the coverage of wage surveys has increased rather than decreased since they made their study.

An area-oriented survey cuts across industry lines within a local labor market. Employers seeking wage consistency in the locality need the data supplied by an area-oriented survey. Employers can conduct their

---

[1] N. Arnold Tolles and Robert L. Raimon, *Sources of Wage Information: Employer Associations*, Cornell Studies in Industrial and Labor Relations, Vol. III (Ithaca, N.Y.: Cornell University, 1952), xvi.

own individual surveys, as some large companies do, or they may utilize the services of an employers' association. A well-managed association survey provides detailed information at minimum cost. However, well-managed association surveys cost money and are most commmonly available only in metropolitan centers.

Figure 12–3 is a digest of one well-managed metropolitan wage survey. This survey covers approximately 50 percent of the employment in the area surveyed. Wage data are collected by job description instead of job title. Rates are reported by four averages and a frequency table. This particular survey does not report on fringe benefits. We shall return to this survey in discussing the use of wage survey data.

As shown in Figure 12–2, the industry-oriented survey is more common than the area-oriented survey. Perhaps the greater number of in-

FIGURE 12–3. Digest of a Metropolitan Wage Survey

Coverage: 129 firms; 50 percent of local labor force; 30 industries (a cross section of area industry).

Jobs Surveyed: 81 jobs: Some jobs broken into as many as four difficulty levels.

Pay Period Covered: March 15, 1956.

Specimen Job Data:

Tool-and-Die Maker 1 (most difficult of four levels)

Plan and construct highly intricate tools, dies, fixtures, gauges, to extremely close tolerances. Considerable development work.

Highly skilled fitting, timing, and adjusting. Construct tools where no design is available. Select allowances, devise mechanism details, e.g., multistation progressive and deep forming dies, complex indexing fixtures, subpress dies for parts of delicate outline, optical gauges.

Straight Time		*Incentive*	
Number firms.........	23	Number firms.........	1
Number workers......	1,010	Number workers.......	2
Average rate.........	2.89	Average rate..........	3.00
Weighted average.....	2.74	Weighted average......	3.00

Firms reporting ranges, 17; Average minimum rate, 2.63; Average maximum rate, 2.87; Firms reporting males only, 24; Firms reporting females only, 0; Firms reporting both, 0.

Frequency Table: Straight Time

Rate	*Number Workers*	*Rate*	*Number Workers*	*Rate*	*Number Workers*
2.56.......	30	2.76.......	576	3.00.......	17
2.57.......	18	2.77.......	29	3.03.......	3
2.61.......	42	2.79.......	18	3.06.......	4
2.66.......	67	2.84.......	6	3.11.......	1
2.68.......	1	2.85.......	1	3.15.......	2
2.69.......	2	2.86.......	13	3.18.......	1
2.71.......	142	2.88.......	6	3.21.......	2
2.73.......	7	2.90.......	5	3.47.......	1
2.74.......	4	2.92.......	3	3.80.......	1
2.75.......	8				

dustry-oriented surveys is a response to the needs of employers dealing with the same union. Although no wage survey can compute comparative unit labor costs, an industry-oriented survey offers a more fruitful opportunity for speculation in this direction than does the area-oriented survey.

Union Wage Surveys. Formal wage surveys conducted by unions are not available to employers. However, unions do have access to wage rates paid in companies having contractual relations with them. These data are sometimes introduced into negotiations in a union attempt to win a particular point. Unions probably would have the most detailed wage information on competitors that would be available from any other source. However, these data (like all data for collective bargaining) can be selectively edited. Thus both unions and managements are best advised to regard such data with some caution.

Individual Company Wage Surveys. Many large companies conduct their own wage surveys. Such surveys serve a particularly important function in small communities without other wage data collection agencies. Some companies prefer to conduct their own surveys because they can independently validate the data so collected. Finally a general wage survey is of limited value to a firm requring highly specialized skills, e.g., certain oil refinery jobs, or in the case of women employed by public utilities companies.

Interpreting Wage Survey Data

Wage rate data are *not* generally available. Although we have emphasized the widespread wage survey work done by employers and unions, it is important to remember that these data are always considered at least partially *confidential* and available only to co-operating firms. Only under very exceptional circumstances would an association reveal wage data for a particular firm. The governmental data are available generally, but only with adequate safeguards to the identity of the individual firm.

Job Comparability. Figures 12–1, 12–2, and 12–3 should now be considered as a unit in attempting to resolve the problem of job comparibility. Figures 12–2 and 12–3 are job descriptions for a tool maker's and a die maker's job in our hypothetical plant. Figure 12–1 is a tool-and-die maker's job description used in a BLS Occupational Wage Survey. Figure 12–3 includes the tool-and-die maker's job description used in a metropolitan wage survey. An employer confronted with this array of current wage rate information would be in an *extremely* fortunate position. He would possess much more "comparative wage data" than is usual. However, he is confronted with a serious problem because of the obvious variations in job content between these four descriptions. If this difficulty seems minor, we need only remember that each of the job descriptions surveyed has been interpreted independently by each of the respondents to the survey. Only in that extremely rare situation when employers actually assign similar duties to workers in a single job is anything approaching real job comparability achieved.

Which Rate? Cheerfully assuming that we have resolved or ignored the problem of job comparability, we proceed now to the selection of a "going rate." Referring to Figure 12–3, which "average rate" do we want to use? The "weighted average" is the rate most nearly approximating the rate received by the "average employee" on the job. However, this rate would be inflated if a majority of the employees surveyed were at the top of the respective ranges for the job. This average is also heavily weighted by the largest employers in the area surveyed. Or we might select the "average rate." In this case a firm employing 1 tool-and-die maker is considered just as important as a firm employing 500 tool-and-die makers. The "average minimum rate" would be the impression of opportunities that a worker seeking employment would acquire from a careful job hunt. The "modal" rate can be determined by examining the frequency table. Here again, we are giving weight to the position of workers in the rate range.

Despite all the difficulties, management must decide that one of these rates *is* the "going rate." Wage decisions are then based on this choice. To the extent that both unions and management realize the shortcomings of the data available, the ultimate decision is probably improved.

Achieving and Maintaining External Consistency

External consistency and internal consistency may be opposing concepts in some situations. For example, the engineer shortage of the early 50s can be contrasted to the fear of an engineer glut in the immediate postwar period. Has the value of an engineer doing a particular job in a particular company *changed* because of these market pressures? More practically, just what can management do to assure itself of a reasonably contented and adequate supply of workers in a shortage calling? Should internal consistency be completely abandoned?

In his study of "Wage and Salary Administration in a Changing Labor Market," Professor Preston P. LeBreton found that management was gravely concerned with the problem of maintaining both internal and external consistency. Wage and salary administrators referred to the problem as "frustrating" and "plagueing." At least eight alternative approaches are available to management in solving the problem. As shown in Figure 12–4, management has at least flirted with each of these approaches. In passing it should be noted that several of these approaches vitally effect nonwage clauses in the collective bargaining agreement. For example, subcontracting and use of agency help would undoubtedly arouse substantial union opposition.

FIGURE 12–4. Management Approaches to Maintaining an Internally Consistent Wage Structure When Faced with Heavy Labor-Market Pressure

Approach	*Number of Companies Using This Approach**
Ignore market conditions and concentrate on maintaining internal consistency. Emphasize fringe benefits and other advantages rather than money rates	18
Bring new workers in at market price regardless of its relationship to company rates	17
Bring new workers in at market price unless it falls out of the established range for the job class	73
Deliberately evaluate the job higher than its objective worth	12
Eliminate the job by contracting out or distributing the work internally	6
Use outside agency help at the required rate (agency workers perform their duties on company premises)	11
Add work to job content thereby increasing its worth to the company	19
Raise the level of all wages in the company	18
Other approaches	23

* The total of the right-hand column does not correspond to the total number of participants because some of the correspondents selected several choices.

Source: Preston P. LeBreton, assisted by Thomas R. O'Donovan, *Wage and Salary Administration in a Changing Labor Market* (Detroit, Mich.: University of Detroit, March 1957), p. 2.

BARGAINING ON WAGE LEVELS

Newspaper accounts of labor-management negotiations almost always emphasize wage demands and wage settlements. Reports of the outcome of almost any strike give prominence to the agreed-on pay package. Occasionally a strike continues even after agreement on the pay package, over what the papers refer to vaguely as "work rules." It is not always possible to tell from the newspaper accounts whether the work rules at issue are task standards; that is, the effort bargain; or other things such as seniority and kindred elements of individual security. In the popular view, at any rate, the pay package or pay level *is* the issue at stake in labor-management negotiations.

It is not as simple as all that. Pay level is always important, but does not by itself tell the whole story. It is directly and primarily important in craft union negotiations because effort is under the control of the skilled worker and individual security under the control of the union; productivity per hour is practically fixed, and can be taken for granted. Industrial unions have to be concerned with work rules as well as with the pay level. If these work rules were taken for granted or left to management, changes in work rules and procedures could practically nullify pay level gains.

As already noted, then, industrial union wage bargaining remains complex. It is not a simple contest over the amount in the pay package. Pay levels tie in with other issues just as important both to union members and to management.

Previous editions of this book have dealt at some length with these complexities in the chapter corresponding to this one. Explicitly and by implication the treatment included the "bargaining" that goes on *within* the union and management sides as they set out to formulate their respective demands and later when they approve the settlements reached. A provocative new book by Walton and McKersie draws special attention to this intra-agency bargaining and attempts to analyze negotiations by constructing models.[2] Walton and McKersie offer four models of collective bargaining negotiations: *distributive, integrative, attitudinal structuring,* and *intra-agency*. The third and fourth models are the ones with which they illustrate the dickering and calculating and maneuvering that go on within the union and within the management away from the bargaining table—before, during, and after the joint negotiations.

In their analysis, these authors make no distinction between craft and industrial unions. They do not recognize, or seem to be aware, of any difference; yet the difference works its way to the surface in the course of their exposition. Their distributive model turns out to apply quite well to craft, but not so well to industrial union bargaining. Their integrative model, on the other hand, applies more to industrial than craft union behavior.

The *distributive* model presents wage level bargaining as a zero-sum game in which gains for one side are losses for the other: Higher wages mean lower profits, and vice versa, unless the market permits a rise in prices to offset the rise in unit labor costs. Actually, this zero-sum affect can only occur when productivity depends *directly* on employee effort. The effort bargain is under worker control in craft, but not industrial, unions. In the industrial union enterprise productivity depends less on actual worker effort than on such variables as layout, materials handling, work scheduling, man-machine mix, and degree of automation. The zero-sum model does not apply.[3]

The *integrative* model deals with negotiations over issues on which the accomodations reached benefit both sides. A seniority plan, for example, gives employees a measure of security and assures the employer a stable work force.[4] A grievance system protects employees from unfair treat-

---

[2] Richard E. Walton and Robert B. McKersie, *A Behavioral Theory of Labor Negotiations* (New York: McGraw-Hill Book Co., 1965), 437 pp.

[3] Under mass-production or automation technology it is even possible (though not easy) to *simultaneously* raise wages, lower production costs, lower prices, and increase profits. Henry Ford did exactly that when he started making the Model T on a serialized assembly line.

[4] It is worth noting here, once more, that seniority rights appear in industrial, not craft union agreements; the employer of craft unionists, in most cases, does not

ment and the organization from flare-ups and friction caused by unheard, unadjusted complaints. Clearly the integrative model fits industrial better than craft union bargaining. The issues dealt with are more nearly behavioral, in the social-psychological sense, than economic.

It may be said, then, that the Beal-Wickersham-Kienast models, starting from *structure* (craft and industrial), illustrate, in action, differences in behavior. The Walton-McKersie models (distributive and integrative) start from *behavior* but end up by confirming differences rooted in structure.

Their third and fourth models are something else again. They try to illustrate and explain what goes on before, behind, and beyond the bargaining table negotiations. They deal with interests, influences, and pressures that bear on the behavior of the bargainers: a different range of phenomena.

For reasons which need not be detailed here, the authors of this book do not entirely accept the Walton-McKersie system as a whole, but it has stimulated them to revise and systematize what had been a rather discursive treatment of the same range of phenomena and make more explicit the attitudinal structuring and intra-agency aspects of bargaining in the treatment to follow.

Union Goals in Pay Level Bargaining

How does a union decide in a particular year that it will seek a 40-cent package raise in wages, and not a 20-cent or 60-cent package? And having decided that, how does it break the package down into general demands, wage inequity demands, demands for wage supplements such as medical care and pension improvements, or paid holidays, or longer paid vacations?

Or does the union build up a package by adding its minimum demands in each of these areas to arrive at a total? Does the union carefully apply economic formulas and estimates, or pull the figures out of thin air? Do the leaders have full and free discretion? Or do rank-and-filers, indirectly or directly, play a part in the decisions? What happens *inside* the union?

What happens inside the company? How does the management decide to counteroffer a 30-cent package, or meet the union's 40-cent demand, or even (in exchange, perhaps, for other concessions) exceed the union's wage demands?

Customarily, the union initiates collective bargaining by announcing and justifying its comprehensive demands. Management appears to play the purely defensive part of resisting; and, in some instances, this is probably the actual management policy. Increasingly, however, management

---

want a stable work force. He wants, instead, to be able to assemble a work force of qualified craftsmen when he gets a contract, to change its composition as the work progresses, and to disperse it when the project is completed.

tries to anticipate the union's moves and comes prepared with its own formulation of an offer that is not simply a counteroffer and reaction to the union initiative. Whether the company program be independently arrived at or only a defensive rejoinder to the union, what information, estimates, and hazards shape the management decision?

Both sides have to face certain economic facts of life, whatever their aims or desires. Some of these constraints and possible contingencies are known or can be forecast with reasonable assurance. Others are hidden, or dubious, or unpredictable; and in any case, they shift and change. Decision making under conditions of uncertaintly is an old story to management; unions have had to learn to face the uncertain future, too. One of the elements of uncertainty for each is what the other will do. Whenever there is interaction between human beings, psychological and political and social motivations that are quite distinct from economic processes are bound to enter in. Union demands and management response thus take place in the contexts of both economics and power relations.

The Economic Context

Economic facts pertinent to the union and management positions have to do with the situation of the workers, the union itself, the company, the industry, and possibly the general state of the economy. Knowledge about these facts is never complete on either side, but in some matters the union may be better informed; in some, the company.

The Workers. A worker tends to take primary interest in his take-home pay and its purchasing power. Over the course of a year, take-home pay depends on whether the worker is laid off part of the time, and when working, how many hours he works. The cost of living thus has a bearing on the wage demand he deems appropriate—or indeed, essential.

Historically, money wages have tended to rise in periods of rising prices. For a number of years many unions followed the lead given by General Motors and the UAW in 1948 when they signed a long-term agreement containing an "escalator" clause. Escalator clauses provide for changes in wage rates to parallel changes in the Consumer Price Index. The Index, as everyone knows, has risen steadily, year by year. Although escalator clauses cover less than 25 percent of unionized workers, the national publicity given to such arrangements made many workers (and workers' wives) acutely conscious of the cost-of-living issue. Where escalators have not been negotiated, unions instead have asked for general wage adjustment aimed at catching up with—or, as management would say, anticipating—increases in the cost of living.

Nonetheless, tenure and continuity of employment outweigh the importance to a worker of the hourly real wage. If he suffers periods of layoff, or has only a part-time job of short work weeks, he will need high hourly wages when he is working in order to average out; yet widespread layoffs or short work weeks discourage hopes for higher hourly pay. Confronted with the *personal* and *certain* choice of low hourly wages, or no work, most workers could be expected to choose the low wage. In terms of income, workers do not live literally from day to day, but many live from week to week with little or nothing in reserve, often in debt, and with installment obligations. Few see the choice as certain, but the possible consequences of a fight for higher wages, if it should involve a strike, are always personal. The worker's perception of pay level issues includes an acute consciousness of his precarious financial situation.

The Union. A union's ultimate weapon is the strike. A union's ability to strike successsfully does not depend directly on the amount of money in the strike fund, but financial resources enter into the reckoning when a union formulates its *real* demands. In illustration of this point, we give the frank comments of a delegate to a Special Convention of the UAW.

I work at a GM plant and am ready to hit the bricks for our demands, and I am sure the members of Local 645 are determined to get a much better contract than they have now.

When we do hit the bricks, we want to have the money in the strike fund. The $16 million that will be raised by this dues increase will not be sufficient to carry on a successful strike this year.

The book prepared by the financial secretary on strike assistance lists 350,000 GM workers and 200,000 auto parts workers who would be involved in a GM strike, thus taking 550,000 off the dues-paying list. This means a balance of only 650,000 dues-paying members not on strike.

The dues from 650,000 workers will not carry the GM workers who are on strike. This book on strike assistance says it will cost $80 million plus to carry on an eleven week strike at GM, and $11,400,000 a week beginning with the twelfth week. If the strike lasts as long as 16 weeks, like the last one did, the cost would be more than $136 million.

I think we should be realistic and have a strike fund that will take care of any trouble that comes up. A $25 million strike fund is too small, and any monies placed in the fund by this dues increase should stay there.

Dues should be found to increase the amount to at least $50 million. I would like to see a fund of $80 million. Then we would have the power to back up our just demands.[5]

The arithmetic would be different for other unions or for the UAW at another time or under different circumstances. For example, if the union found it necessary to strike Chrysler, Ford, and GM at the same time, the delegate's $136 million would only be a drop in the bucket. Nevertheless, this kind of economic arithmetic problem must be worked out by any union as a part of the formulation of its final demands.

---

[5] *Proceedings: Special Constitutional Convention, United Automobile, Aircraft and Agricultural Implement Workers of America, January 22–24, 1958,* p. 134.

A striking union may receive economic support from other unions in the form of gifts or loans. These are probably less important in most cases than assurances or expectations of direct action by other unions to reinforce the strike. Refusal to transport goods across a picket line is worth more to a striking union than any amount of money—and more visible to the strikers. Less visible, but equally welcome to the union would be another union's refusal to do work "farmed out" by the struck firm, or an effective boycott.

The Company. Probably the most important economic facts about the firm for collective bargaining purposes are: (*a*) sales forecasts, (*b*) inventories and orders on hand at a probable strike date, (*c*) alternative methods of meeting customer demands during a strike, and (*d*) break-even points under different wage cost assumptions.

Sales Forecasts. Sales forecasts are critical to sound managerial decision making. The economic concepts of elasticity of demand, expectation of profit yields, and competition in the product market are all reflected in the managerial sales forecast. Most sales forecasts also reflect management's general thinking about the short-run economic future. When management is producing a brand-name product with substantial customer loyalty for what appears to be an expanding market, management may conclude that it can pass any wage increase along to the customer in the form of a price increase. This interpretation of the facts is particularly final in cases where labor costs are a relatively small proportion of total costs of production. When a company has just experienced a record-making sales and profits year, the management often assumes that prosperity is here to stay.

Inventories and Orders on Hand. Large inventories and few orders on hand tend to make management less receptive to union demands. Many unfilled orders and an empty warehouse have the opposite effect.

Sometimes the composition of inventories is as important as the size of inventories. Most manufacturing concerns produce a number of products. An inventory shortage of a product insignificant from the viewpoint of the company's total production may become the central issue in company thinking on the union's demands. For example, a very small order for an experimental product from a major customer accompanied by the prospect of large "add-on" orders may prove to be the union's strongest bargaining point without the union's even knowing it. Similar situations exist when the company is the sole source of supply to a major customer of some apparently insignificant bit of hardware. These situations take on even more gravity when they are enmeshed with a defense industry contracting and subcontracting structure.[6]

---

[6] Persons familiar with military procurement procedures are fully aware of the importance of inventory composition as a factor in collective bargaining strategy. In 1953, the U.S. Supreme Court ruled that a strike of some steelworkers at the Dunkirk, New York, plant of the American Locomotive Company was a "national-

Alternative Methods of Meeting Customer Demands. In a variety of situations, a strike imposes only minor inconvenience on the customers of the firm or industry struck. In these cases, management can put up stronger resistance to union demands because it runs a smaller chance of losing its regular customers as a result of failure to deliver during a strike.

In the petroleum industry, the interchange of products between competitors in various markets is a long-established practice aimed at reducing transshipment costs. This same system could be used to satisfy customer demand in the event of a strike against a single firm or refinery. Many firms produce their own brand-name products and have licensing arrangements with other firms. By careful management advanced planning, these licensing arrangements could enable the licensor to continue to supply his brand-name customers almost indefinitely even though his own production facilities were closed down by a strike. Similar potential advantages are available to multiplant, single-product manufacturers who have different unions or contract expiration dates at different plants each one of which is fully integrated. In this case, the employer merely shifts orders from the strike-bound plant to his plants which are operating during the strike.

In each of these situations management can be tough because the employer has insured himself against the *long-range* cost of actually losing his customers to competitors.

Break-even Points under Different Wage Cost Assumptions. Break-even analysis under different wage cost assumptions is primarily important for the economic long run. In the short run, a management may minimize its losses by continuing to produce even though the revenue per unit sold is less than the average total cost of producing that unit. In the short run, management is "stuck" with its fixed costs, e.g., plant and equipment depreciation, property taxes, inventories of materials on hand, etc. As a result, it is good business to incur variable costs, e.g., wages, sales promotion expenses, etc., so long as the product can be sold at a price which exceeds these variable costs. In such a situation, the management may incur substantial losses, but these losses are *less* than the losses that would be incurred if the management chose not to produce. In the economic long run, however, a management will not continue to operate unless it anticipates that sales income from its product will exceed the total (variable plus fixed) costs of production. This is true because in the long run, management has the opportunity of eliminating fixed costs through sale of plant and equipment or simply not replacing plant and equipment as it wears out.

---

emergency" strike within the meaning of the Taft-Hartley law. This strike was only a part of a national steel strike which was *not* considered to be a national-emergency strike. The court ruled that the strikers in Dunkirk were closing a substantial part of an entire industry (the atomic reactor manufacturing industry) and that their strike imperiled or threatened to imperil the national health and safety. Not even all of the employees of the Dunkirk plant were engaged in work on the A.E.C. order.

Break-even analysis brings together all business judgment about sales expectations and cost expectations. If it is believed that prices can be raised without adverse effects on the volume of sales, the break-even point is lowered and the promise of profits is enhanced. If it is believed that prices can be raised without adverse effect on the volume of sales, wages can also be increased with a minimum reduction of profits. On the other hand, if prices can't be raised because of the elasticity of demand or competition in the product market or a general business slump, wages can be increased only at the expense of profits. At the same time, there is always the possibility that such wage increases will cause management to discontinue certain lines of production or actually liquidate the business in its entirety. Or management might find it advisable to change the man-machine mix in such a way as to provide substantially less employment. To be sure, as wages rise, the vital *relative* cost of laborsaving machines certainly declines.

This situation is further complicated by the fact that many costs of production are really matters of accounting *judgment*. Two examples, depreciation expense and cost of materials used, will suffice as illustrations. When management purchases a machine for the price of $100,000 it is merely converting cash into another form of asset. The $100,000 becomes a cost only as it is charged against production in the future. If the machine is *judged* to have no scrap value and a life of 10 years or for a total production of 100,000 units, it may be charged off as an expense at the rate of $10,000 per year or $1 per unit produced. In the first year, only 1,000 units are produced because of a general business slump. If the accountant charges the machine off on a straight-line annual depreciation basis, each unit contains $10 of machine cost (as compared to $1 per unit if he uses a unit-produced accounting method). These two possibilities represent only a very small portion of the many variations which give radically different results and are all within the limits of conventional accounting practice. Similar problems arise in *estimating* the cost of materials used in production. No one *really* knows what the cost of materials or machine time is until such time as the business is totally liquidated. Important as it is to know what costs really are, they are impossible to determine with finality as long as the business continues to operate. Obviously, the curiosity of management and the union stop short of wanting to liquidate the business in order to get the full truth. Accounting methods do become a point of dispute, however, when management pleads inability to pay higher wages.

The Power Relations Context

While corporations are by no means immune from internal political power struggles that affect external relations, economic considerations would appear to take precedence, in most companies, over political aims.

Industrial unions, on the other hand, are basically political organizations. They seek economic ends by political means. Union leaders approach negotiations under political pressures of at least four kinds: (*a*) rival union gains, (*b*) opposition within the union, (*c*) demand for uniformity within the international union's jurisdiction, and (*d*) the strike temper of the rank and file.

Rival Union Gains. Union members look to their leaders to make gains for them and evaluate their leaders on the basis of how the gains won compare with those of other unions. What makes an acceptable bargain in the eyes of the union members?

The answer to that question depends partly on how the new rates compare with former earnings, and partly on what members of other unions have gained. If I. W. Abel of the United Steelworkers of America gets a sizable increase from the steel companies in wage negotiations, auto workers will expect their Leonard Woodcock to do at least as well for them when he bargains with the Big Three. Steelworker gains pose no threat of secession of UAW Locals to join the USA, but do put pressure on the UAW leaders. In another year, the pressure may bear in the opposite direction, with Mr. Abel expected by his members to match Mr. Woodcock's performance. A union leader cannot fall short of expectations too many times, and continue to hold his job.

Rival union gains also strongly influence the contents of the package. In times of business recession, some unions tend to place greater stress on wage supplements than straight wages. In part, this may be attributed to the necessity of matching rival union gains even when wage increases are very hard to come by. For example, a very modest wage increase *plus* "sweeping improvements in pensions, S.U.B., seniority, etc. costing seventy cents per hour according to union estimates" might give the impression of a great victory to the rank and file without involving any substantial and immediate increase in labor costs for the company if spread out over several years. At some particular times, worker insurance and income-continuity benefits can be substantially liberalized with little or no cost to management. This situation sometimes enables a union leader to accept a moderate increase and to save face with rank and file by selling the great importance of the improved wage supplements. Cents-per-hour can be *easily* compared between unions by members of the rank and file; some forms of wage supplements are not so easily compared.

Opposition within the Union. The less secure the political future of the union negotiator, the more likely he is to insist on excessive wage demands. This situation is illustrated by the preference, frequently expressed by managers, for dealing with international officers rather than local officers. The typical international officer is quite secure in office through control of appointive jobs and in the frequent practice of electing international officers by convention roll call votes. As a result, he can afford the political luxury of responsibility in dealing with employers. A local officer who becomes too "responsible" also tends to become an ex-officer. Even international officers do face occasional opposition at the polls and when they are confronted with this prospect they usually become somewhat less responsible in the eyes of the managements with which they deal.

Need for Uniformity within the Jurisdiction of the Union. A union leader who negotiates substantially different wages for members doing similar work for different employers within the same industry is asking for political trouble. "Equal pay for equal work" has an almost universal political appeal. The application of this principle may force a union leader to bargain for less than the full amount that could be obtained from the richest employer within the union's jurisdiction. If this absolute maximum victory were attained and the union leader could not follow through with other employers, he might be in a very unfavorable political position.

Strike Temper of the Rank and File. The union leader's ultimate weapon is the strike. The strike is also a crucial political test. In the strike, the worker plays for the stake of his most valued economic asset—his job. Workers pay union dues with little protest and *vote* to strike almost automatically, but when they strike on a union call they show the absolute maximum of faith in the union leadership. If they return to work before a settlement is negotiated, they are casting the most telling "no-confidence" vote that any union leader can ever receive. True wildcat strikes are also no-confidence votes. If the leader is to survive as a political leader, he must be closely attuned to the willingness (and in some cases, eagerness) of the rank and file to strike. This willingness on the part of the rank and file is undoubtedly the most significant political influence on the union side in the formulation of demands. At the same time that the union leader is the victim of the rank and file willingness to strike, he is also a force in determining that willingness. He does not want to lead a reluctant army. It is his job to make sure that the desires of the union rank and file for higher wages or other improvements in their agreement with the company equals their willingness to hit the bricks.

Formulating Strategy for Wage Level Bargaining

The foregoing discussion has touched on some of the economic and political elements of the situation management and the union face as they begin to draw up their demands, counterproposals, and bargaining positions. Each has imperfect knowledge of the facts. Management is likely to know the economic facts about the situation of the workers and the union almost as well as the union leaders, and economic facts about the company's position much better; but may find the political considerations harder to gauge. Union leaders are in a position to take meaningful, frequent soundings of the political situation, but may not be able to estimate with much accuracy the management's economic resources or its weaknesses.

Major employers maintain large industrial relations research staffs to make continuous studies on trends in union demands, the cost of living, employee attitudes, and other questions that might have weight in bargaining strategy decisions. International unions also maintain research staffs to do what amounts to the same thing from an opposite point of view. The final company position before entering negotiations appears usually to be the decision of the top management (president, chairman of the board) after consultation with senior officers of the enterprise, e.g., vice presidents of industrial relations, finance, production, and sales. Shifts or changes in position during negotiations—in particular, the decision on whether or not to accept the challenge of a strike—probably require the same procedures. By this time company negotiators may come to feel that they have a solid knowledge of what the union will really accept in the way of a wage settlement.

Management people tend to be reticent about how they come to their strategic and tactical decisions, although public and private utterances often contain some clues. One student of management bargaining behavior makes the following inferences:

> The factors which move the more influential segments of industrial management to a wage decision are: (*a*) the compulsion to maintain production, (*b*) the need to maintain a feasible price, and (*c*) the sine qua non profit.
> My theme is simple: *production, price, profit, and the greatest of these is production.*[7]

Obviously, production is important to management. If there are to be sales, there has to be production. There are times, however, when production gets out of balance with sales. This occurs from time to time in the auto industry, as in the years of bulging dealer inventories, when cars are slow to move off the sales floors. At such times the industry is under no urgent pressure to produce more cars. New model tooling during the summer months must, of course, go on uninterrupted, but production of cars is of slight significance. Dealers would, in fact, welcome a stoppage of production. Other years, when cars are selling like hot cakes, both tooling and production are imperative.

Unions are probably equally concerned with production as the key to strategy. They prefer to press their wage demands when management's need for production is high, because the potency of a strike is its ability to stop production. They tend to soft-pedal when the need for production eases. The union position on entering negotiations is undoubtedly

---

[7] Leland Hazard, "What Economists Don't Know about Wages," *Harvard Business Review*, Vol. 35 (January–February 1957), p. 49. See also Hazard, "Wage Theory: A Management View," chap. 2 of George W. Taylor and Frank C. Pierson (eds.), *New Concepts in Wage Determination* (New York: McGraw-Hill Book Co., Inc., 1957), pp. 32–50.

less of a top-level decision then management's; rank-and-filers, and their strike temper, have to be much more of a consideration. During negotiations, in fact, rank and file response to the reports of union negotiators bears directly on the efforts of the negotiating team. In the last analysis, *any* increase in general wage levels is a gain for the union members, but the amount of the raise is not as important for either the members or the leaders as its consistency with expectations and comparisons with what others unions get.

Negotiations

No matter how economically sound the union's demands, they must be sold to the members and to employers before an agreement can be made. Management, in turn, must sell its position to the employees and the union before an agreement can be made. Most collective bargaining negotiations are private affairs between the union and the management. In pattern-making bargaining, the union and/or management sometimes seek public support for its position. We shall discuss this public bargaining after we have dealt with the semiprivate negotiation process.

Special Problems of the Union. As goods-producing or services-rendering organizations, most private enterprises are primarily units of the economic system, but they are subject to political constraints. One of these—and probably the most immediate—is the union, possessing as it does the power to shut down operations with a strike. The union is primarily a political organization (in the power-political sense) subject to economic constraints of which undoubtedly the most immediate is the company's market and financial position. A company facing a particular set of negotiations, not surprisingly, determines its strategy largely on the basis of calculations from economic estimates and data, on which (as has been brought out) it usually has better information than the union. What it seeks in negotiations is a political settlement consistent with its economic prospects.

In pay level bargaining the union leaders seek an economic settlement consistent with political relationships in the union. By formulating and presenting demands they have aroused expectations in the members' minds. The expectations are not always rational; but rational or not, they must be reckoned with. Union leaders usually have a better "feel" than the company for what the members want and how far they are willing to go to get it.

High expectations flow, for one source, from the union movement's own propaganda—usually called "educational activity." Year in, year out, union journals and union-leader oratory call attention to firms which make excess profits, to the rising cost of living, to the social need for strong, sustained, consumer purchasing power. Rival union gains may also raise the members' expectations. The common strategy of asking for more than you expect to get may fix the members' hopes on high demands and trap the leaders when the time comes to climb down.

At such times—and at other times when a company's sales or competitive or financial position puts limits on possible economic gains—high expectations meet with disappointment. Members lose faith in their leaders; for faith, by definition, is not rational. Union leaders very often have to face the hard political problem and dilemma of rousing and holding firm support for high demands that it may take a strike to win, or getting members to accept a settlement that shatters their high hopes. Or both, in succession.

At the same time, clever leaders can often pick up political support for an otherwise moderate settlement in the negotiation of the wage supplements. Pensions are clearly something extra for the older, high-seniority workers. Unemployment benefits appeal to those low on the seniority lists, subject to frequent layoffs. Special pay concessions for strategic groups such as skilled workers who, if dissatisfied, might disrupt a settlement, can sometimes sweeten an otherwise disappointing flat cents-per-hour raise such as is typical of industrial union bargaining. Flat raises are the rule because at union meetings the least-skilled member's vote carries as much weight as that of the most highly skilled; and there are more nonskilled members.

Presenting Demands.   In presenting union demands to an employer, union negotiators use both positive and negative arguments. On the positive side, there is the moral argument: The union's demands are *right*.

Most employers, especially pattern-setting employers, want to do what's right by their employees. They may differ with the union over what *is* right, but there is little ground for cynicism about their motives. (After all, who willfully wants to do *wrong?*) But profits from missionary work are at best illusory. The same union leader who has argued fervently for some pioneering concession, and convinced a not-unwilling employer, may prove to be quite capable of going back to the members with a story of how hard he had to wrestle with the devil to convert the heathen boss. Pioneering employers have discovered that initial gains quickly evaporate; before long the novel concessions, copied in other agreements, become commonplace. Memories are short. Unions and union leaders change with the passage of time, and the "good guy" employer's past performance will not protect him from the "bad guy" image some time in the future.

Union Arguments.   There are also some positive economic arguments. One often advanced is that the union will impose the same conditions on competitors. To the degree that an employer finds this assurance credible, it carries weight. In general, managers feel confident of their ability to compete successfully if they are not handicapped by excessive costs.

The stumbling block is credibility. Big industrial unions like those in steel, autos, and the needle trades can virtually guarantee approximate pay-level equality in domestic industry, but they cannot control foreign competition. Nor can they exert much influence over the total market. A rise in the price of cars might make some people, who in the past have traded for a new car every other year, decide to drive the old car for a year or two longer and spend the money saved on other things instead. Buyers can also substitute one product for another. Steel competes with wood, aluminum, and plastics for certain uses: an increase in the cost of making steel could mean a worsening in some degree of the *industry's* competitive position, even if labor costs were equal throughout.

Other positive arguments appeal to management's concern with the effort part of the bargain: higher morale as a result of higher pay; readier cooperation; increased productivity. Management has to treat all such persuasions with a certain amount of skepticism. Undoubtedly, the union's most telling arguments are of the negative sort.

On the negative side the union can hint at—or point out in so many words—the undesirable consequences of the company's *not* agreeing to the union's demands: a strike, the cost of idle plant and equipment, loss of sales and customers, employee dissatisfaction, ill will, and hostility. Workers in the plant sometimes reinforce the bargaining table arguments with well-orchestrated slowdowns, errors, lapses from quality standards, all of which are costly, and hint at costlier things to come.

If management has done its homework in preparation for the negotiations, it has estimated strike costs and is aware of possible consequences. It does not take much imagination for the company negotiators to clothe the union's veiled or open threats with a clear notion of what might happen. The union cannot guarantee a more productive work force in return for higher wages, but it is within the union's power to lighten a manager's fear of organized obstruction.

Employer Arguments. Employers, too, can offer both positive and negative arguments. The most telling negative argument is a clear showing—or success in giving the impression—of readiness to endure a strike, even a prolonged strike. This threatens workers with loss of income, and the union with a heavy drain on its strike fund, perhaps with the depletion of its financial resources. If coupled with a reasonable company counteroffer, it puts before union leaders the prospect of perhaps having to send their members back, after prolonged hardship and sacrifice, on terms they could have settled for without a strike. Management's threat gains credibility and force if union leaders know, or can be brought to believe, that the company could hold its customers by farming out work, or transferring operations, or resuming production with nonunion labor.

The company's best positive argument is often the proposal (or counterproposal) itself: wage rates that are in step with raises won by other unions, and the prospect of uninterrupted and continued employment for the union members.

Pattern Setting. Union and company negotiators often start their bargaining with a tacitly accepted pattern to guide them. (Of course, in key negotiations like basic steel or the auto industry, there is no previous pattern: They are themselves the pattern setters.) Information on terms reached in key agreements nationally is available to both sides from governmental sources, private reporting agencies (such as the Bureau of National Affairs, Commerce Clearing House, Prentice-Hall), and many trade associations. Employers frequently supplement such data with information which they get directly from competitors, while unions draw on other locals or other unions, including those dealing with competing firms.

The bargainers may, however, disagree over which pattern to apply. Food processors in coal-mining towns, for example, may encounter demands paralleling the national coal settlement from noncoal unions. Even when there is no dispute over the appropriate pattern, both sides will ordinarily seek modifications to fit local conditions. Management is more likely to break from the pattern; a less-than-pattern settlement would favor the company's interests. The union finds it harder to deviate from pattern terms: It cannot gracefully demand the pattern which it is holding up to the company as a model to follow, and at the same time deny it by trying to better its terms.

Management finds many arguments for deviating from the pattern. They are not all consistent with each other, but can be selected to fit the particular situation. Here are a few: Community labor market rates are lower than pattern rates; company wages compare with or exceed wages paid for comparable work in competing firms; company nonwage benefits (pay for time not worked, and contingent benefits) are better than the pattern, or than those offered by competitors, or than those prevalent in the community; competitors have lower nonwage costs, such as transportation; the company has had financial losses and profits are down; or even, the company is operating in the red.

Companies using these or kindred arguments have to bear two things in mind: First, they must be sure of their facts and able to document them, or the argument backfires; Second, each point, if accepted, tends to become a long-term commitment. Thus if the company pleads financial straits in a year when profits are down and gains concessions from the union for that reason, it must expect above-pattern demands in a year when profits are up. Similar long-term commitments grow out of wage-rate, fringe benefit, and productivity comparisons.

Just as the union may reinforce verbal efforts at the bargaining table with carefully coordinated action on the shop floor, management supplements negotiations by direct and indirect appeals to the employees. Most large companies carry on regular, often extensive, information and education programs. Company periodicals are not backward about reminding employees of the benefits they receive, and presenting the company's point of view, however baldly or however subtly, on issues that arise in labor-management relations. Special letters may go out on special occasions—and negotiating the agreement is a special occasion. Communications aimed at employees sometimes take the form of a direct appeal to accept the company's offer in collective bargaining. The company presents its proposals as generous, "final," and in the best interests of employees. If union leaders reject the offer (the message may suggest), employees will suffer layoffs or permanent loss of jobs, or loss of earnings through a futile strike that nobody wants.

Boulewareism. Just how far a management will go in making an offer directly to employees seems to depend on management philosophy and the state of business. The management philosophy expressing an extreme use of this approach, Boulewareism—for many years the General Electric policy—has been declared an unfair labor practice: refusal to bargain "collectively and in good faith." The NLRB and court decisions that struck down Boulewareism seem to draw a distinction between management's legitimate right to speak freely to employees, and a policy that would base bargaining strategy entirely on a direct appeal to each employee, and bypass collective bargaining with the union. Such an approach, the agencies finally concluded, was an attempt to circumvent public policy and the law.

Companies that make direct presentations to employees on a year-around basis seem to believe that little can be accomplished at the bargaining table without also getting the company's message across to employees over the heads of the union leaders. Special appeals seem to multiply in periods of poor business, probably on the presumption that from fear of unemployment, employees at such times will be more "reasonable" than their representatives. In all these special appeals, management tries to bring to bear on the leaders the kind of membership pressures that will favor the company position.

Appeals for support from the public, beyond the bargaining table and beyond the union, almost always accompany pattern-setting bargaining. Both sides make an effort to get public approval for their respective positions.

Enlisting Public Support. To the extent that people who make up the entity vaguely called "the public" take an interest in labor-management negotiations, they start by thinking of themselves as consumers. That puts the public, at the outset, squarely on management's side. To say this is not to imply that the public is antiunion. Unionists and their families make up, in fact, a sizeable part of the public; but every consumer wants lower prices, and no one welcomes the inconveniences that sometimes accompany a strike. Naturally, management plays this advantage for all it's worth.

The union has a trickier public relations problem. It has to convince the public that higher wages will not boost prices, or that, even if prices rise, the needs of the workers involved justify the cost or the inconvenience to the public. Failing either of these, the union tries to divert resentment and put the blame on management. Post office workers, for example, took action that in 1971 raised the price of sending a letter—something everybody does, and often—from 6 to 8 cents, or a 33⅓ percent raise, yet escaped the public wrath and even the stigma of blame. At a time of rising living costs they pictured the men and women who move the mail as having been underpaid for years, and the public responded with sympathy. Other unionists making the same appeal might not be able to succeed as well, perhaps, because the public would not regard them as underpaid. The public half suspects—with or without adequate grounds for the belief—that union-negotiated wage increases are not caused by, but cause, increases in the cost of living.

Another union appeal for public support is to point to the rise in labor productivity. Credit for higher productivity over the course of the years properly belongs to technological innovation; the individual worker has not, in the main, increased his effort. A case can still be made for cutting the worker in on a share of the higher productivity. This shades into the purchasing-power argument: the more money workers earn, the more they will buy, and the better business will be for everyone.

Still another union appeal tries to direct public attention away from wages to high profits. The figures cited need not be those that appear on a company's financial statements, though drawn from them. Profits may be recalculated by using accounting procedures that make them look as big as possible: percentage return on investment, perhaps, instead of sales; or more "realistic" calculations of depreciation. If these interpretations show gains that much exceed 10 percent, the union will argue that the industry is exploiting the consumer and could easily meet union demands out of the excess profits.

Management counters with its own public relations claims. It tries to create and maintain the image of acting as representative of the public and guardian of the public interest. By fighting against excessive wage demands, the industry people say or imply, they are trying to keep costs, and hence prices, reasonable; they are also fighting inflation, which hits everybody's pocketbook. The public relations man who coined the phrase, "wage inflation," and fixed it in the public mind, gave management a potent slogan of persuasion.

In this rivalry for favorable public opinion, what are the stakes for management and the union? After all, the public has no seat at the bargaining table, no voice in negotiations, no veto over the outcome.

It is not so much the general public, but government as the executor of public policy, that the parties have their eyes on. Government is always more or less responsive to public opinion. If government should intervene "in the public interest" as it does sometimes when a strike threatens or breaks out, each wants, if possible, to prevent its coming in on the other's side. It also seems probable that a good part of management's appeal, while ostensibly directed at the public, is really meant to reach employees; and the union's appeal is meant to hearten and rally the members.

SUMMARY

Union-management negotiations reach their greatest intensity when wage adjustments are discussed. Although the nature of the wage question differs in the handicraft and manufacturing segments of the economy, it is a major issue in strikes in both segments.

Successful collective bargaining is based on facts. In this chapter we have reviewed the major sources of economic data for collective bargaining. Management possesses most of the vital economic facts that are needed for bargaining. What economic data employers refuse to supply, unions try to obtain by other methods. Economic data for collective bargaining are not cut and dried figures; they are sometimes vague and almost always subject to diverse interpretations.

Unions and managements, as organizations, must cope with certain internal and external pressures on their wage decisions. These economic, political, and social pressures vary from firm to firm, industry to industry, and union to union. The final agreement on general wage adjustments reflects these pressures.

In times of emergency, such as war, the decision-making power in wage controversies may be taken over by the government. Under these conditions, the interest of the consumer receives greater *conscious* consideration than when wages are set through the market pressures of collective bargaining. However, there is little evidence to prove that governmental wage decisions are actually better for the community at large than decisions which emerge from rough-and-tumble collective bargaining.

QUESTIONS FOR DISCUSSION

1. Recently there has been some talk about negotiating a "sabbatical leave" for unionized employees. How would this development fit into the wage and effort bargain?
2. Discuss the role of government in influencing the wage and effort bargain.
3. Develop a set of task standards for a teacher.
4. In compensating teachers, what relative weights would you give to "merit" and "length of service"? Would you encounter any problems in applying these standards?
5. Why do employers frequently follow a policy of external wage consistency? What problems are encountered in following this policy?

SELECTED ANNOTATED BIBLIOGRAPHY

AULEPP, WILLIAM W. "Work Standards and Labor Costs," *Management Record*, Vol. XVIII (July 1956), pp. 240–42, 254.

Ford Motor Company manager of industrial engineering discusses practical principles for establishing work standards developed at Ford.

BACKMAN, JULES. "The Size of Crews," *Labor Law Journal*, Vol. XII (September 1961), pp. 805–15.

Reviews the nature and impact of state laws which specify the size of train crews; surveys the evolution and character of contractual arrangements which affect the size of crews on the railroads; examines the experiences of other industries with respect to size of crew and reduction of work force; and estimates the cost of full crew requirements on the railroads.

BACKMAN, JULES. *Wage Determination: An Analysis of Wage Criteria.* Princeton, London, Toronto: D. Van Nostrand Co., Inc., 1959.

Discusses current practices in wage negotiation, including such factors as the structure of wages, cost-of-living changes, worker budget data, ability to pay, and nonwage benefits.

BAMBRICK, JAMES J., JR., and BLUM, ALBERT A. "Productivity and Wage Negotiations," *Management Record*, Vol. XIX (October 1957), pp. 352–59.

Discusses questions such as: who causes productivity and who should get the benefits? The results of a Conference Board survey of major unions and 239 U.S. and Canadian firms.

———. "Comparative Wage Data in Collective Bargaining," *Management Record*, Vol. XIX (February 1957), pp. 38–41, 69–76.

Discusses gathering and use of area and industry wage rates and wage supplements for employee information and collective bargaining negotiations.

BEHREND, HILDE. "The Effort Bargain," *Industrial and Labor Relations Review*, Vol. X (July 1957), pp. 503–15.

Through interviews with (British) management and union representatives, the author examines the underlying assumptions of wage incentive systems in the context of labor-management relations.

DANKERT, CLYDE E.; MANN, FLOYD C.; and NORTHRUP, HERBERT R. (eds.). *Hours of Work.* Industrial Relations Research Association, Vol. 14. New York: Harper & Row, 1965.

Contents include:

NORTHRUP, HERBERT R. "The Reduction in Hours."

MARSHALL, RAY. "The Influence of Legislation on Hours."

DYMOND, W. R., and SAUNDERS, GEORGE. "Hours of Work in Canada."

MOTT, PAUL E. "Hours of Work and Moonlighting."

MEYERS, FREDERICK. "The Economics of Overtime."

MANN, FLOYD C. "Shift Work and the Shorter Work Week."

BERRY, DEAN F. "Automation, Rationalization and Urbanization: Hours of Work in the Office."

BROWN, DAVID G. "Hours and Output."

DANKERT, CLYDE E. "Automation, Unemployment and Shorter Hours."

DAVID, LILY MARY, and SHEIFER, VICTOR J. "Estimating the Cost of Collective

Bargaining Settlements," Vol. XCII, *Monthly Labor Review*. (May 1969), pp. 16–26.

The article describes the BLS method of estimating the cost of the economic package. Includes a sample worksheet for calculation plus examples.

DOOHER, M. JOSEPH, and MARQUIS, VIVIENE (eds.). *The AMA Handbook of Wage and Salary Administration*. New York: American Management Association, 1950.

Provides step-by-step advice on establishing and operating wage and salary administration programs and keeping them current.

DUNLOP, JOHN T. *Wage Determination Under Trade Unionism*. Oxford: Basil Blackwell, 1950 ed.

Establishes a model for union behavior which encompasses union wage policies, bargaining power and intermarket relations, and the impact of the business cycle on wages. A landmark in wage theory.

FOLEY, JAMES J. "How Not to Handle Productivity Disputes," *Harvard Business Review*, Vol. XXXVII (September–October 1959), pp. 68–80.

Four cases where grievances over output standards were submitted to arbitration are used to illustrate the author's belief that all that technical arbitrators can and should do is establish proper output potentials. Suggests that management's responsibility is to motivate workers to realize their potentials.

HABER, WILLIAM, and LEVINSON, HAROLD M. *Labor Relations and Productivity in the Building Trades*. Ann Arbor: Bureau of Industrial Relations, University of Michigan, 1956.

Report of a field survey in 16 cities in 10 states and the District of Columbia. Discusses economic characteristics of the building trades, nature of collective bargaining, the problem of unstable employment, union security, apprentices, new techniques, working rules, wages and hours, and jurisdictional disputes. This volume may be considered as a partial updating of Professor Haber's *Industrial Relations in the Building Industry*, published in the 1930's.

HOROWITZ, MORRIS A. *Manpower Utilization in the Railroad Industry: An Analysis of Working Rules and Practices*. Boston: Northeastern University, Bureau of Business and Economic Research, 1960.

An analysis of the complex web of working rules that have developed in American railroads over the past four decades. The author presents an objective definition of "featherbedding" and "make-work," and examines working rules to see which have and do not have make-work or featherbed effects. He has selected for close examination the rules and practices that are considered to have the effect of restricting the economic utilization of manpower.

"Inflation: Wages, Productivity, Bargaining Issues," Special Issue, *Management Record*, Vol. XIX (August 1957).

Papers include:

GARBARINO, J. W. "Wages, Prices, and Inflation."

HAGEDORN, GEORGE E., National Association of Manufacturers. "Are Wages Inflationary? I."

MULLENDORE, W. C., Southern California Edison Company. "Are Wages Inflationary? II."

DUNLOP, JOHN T., Harvard University. "Are Wages Inflationary? III."

Ross, ARTHUR M., University of California, Berkeley. "New Concept of Compensation?"

PIERSON, FRANK C., Swarthmore College. "Postwar Structural Wage Strains."

TAYLOR, GEORGE W., University of Pennsylvania. "Wage Incentives and Productivity."

HEINEMAN, ROBERT K., Aluminum Company of America. "What Happens in Pattern Bargaining."

ZORN, BURTON A. "Pattern Bargaining: Why It Developed and What to Do."

LELAND HAZARD. "Management Action on Wage Inflation."

JOHN POST, Continental Oil. "The Squeeze on Production, Prices, and Profits."

FREDERICK HARRISON, Princeton University. "Summary."

KAHN, MARK L. "Wage Determination for Airline Pilots," *Industrial and Labor Relations Review*, Vol. VI, pp. 317–36.

Discusses the combination of economic and political factors which contributed to the Airline Pilots Association's success in wage bargaining.

KENNEDY, VAN DUSEN. *Union Policy and Incentives Wage Methods.* New York: Columbia University Press, 1945.

A comprehensive survey of union attitudes and policies toward wage incentive methods through the World War II period.

KILBRIDGE, M. C. "The Effort Bargain in Industrial Society," *Journal of Business* (January 1960), pp. 10–20.

Discussion of factors that influence determination of industrial effort. Shows that bargaining enters at both general pace level and level of specific output requirements. Automation and process-paced work are turning discussions of work loads more toward manning assignments, less on output requirements.

LESIEUR, FREDERICK G. (ed.). *The Scanlon Plan: A Frontier in Labor-Management Cooperation.* A publication of the Industrial Relations Section, Massachusetts Institute of Technology. New York: John Wiley & Sons, Inc., 1958.

Presents and evaluates a plan for labor-management cooperation in increasing productivity worked out by a man who had been a steel union official and a member of the Industrial Relations Section at M.I.T. The plan includes a formula for dividing the benefits of increased productivity.

NUNN, HENRY L. *Partners in Production: A New Role for Management and Labor.* Englewood Cliffs, N.J.: Prentice-Hall, Inc., 1961.

Outlines the Nunn-Bush Shoe Company's program for labor-management amity and cooperation. Describes the share-of-production plan, how it works, how it compares with the generally accepted plans of compensation, and how it differs from the Rucker and Scanlon plans.

Ross, ARTHUR M. *Trade Union Wage Policy.* Berkeley, Calif.: University of California Press, 1953 ed.

Major topics include: the trade union as a wage-fixing institution, the dynamics of wage determination under collective bargaining, responsible union wage policy, union-management relations and wage bargaining, and the influence of unions on earnings. A landmark in wage theory.

SALKEVER, LOUIS R. "Toward A Theory of Wage Structure," *Industrial and Labor Relations Review*, Vol. VI (April 1953), pp. 299–316.

Establishes theoretical concepts which contribute to the understanding of the emergence and change in size of occupational wage rates in America.

SCHULTZ, GEORGE PRATT. *Pressures on Wage Decisions: A Case Study in the Shoe Industry*. New York: Wiley and the Technology Press of M.I.T., 1951.

An attempt to demonstrate how "market forces" and "human decisions" are synthesized in the process of wage determination under collective bargaining.

SLICHTER, SUMNER H.; HEALY, JAMES J.; and LIVERNASH, E. ROBERT. *The Impact of Collective Bargaining on Management*. Washington, D.C.: Brookings Institution, 1960.

Special attention is invited to the following chapters: 17, "Wage Incentives"; 18, "Measured Day Work"; 19, "Evaluated Rate Structures"; and 20, "Wage Structure Considerations."

TAYLOR, GEORGE W., and PIERSON, FRANK C. (eds.). *New Concepts in Wage Determination*. New York: McGraw-Hill Book Co., Inc., 1957.

Twelve authorities (GEORGE W. TAYLOR, FRANK C. PIERSON, LELAND HAZARD, NATHANIEL GOLDFINGER, EVERETT M. KASSALOW, JOHN T. DUNLOP, E. ROBERT LIVERNASH, ARTHUR M. ROSS, RICHARD A. LESTER, LLOYD G. REYNOLDS, CLARK KERR, and MELVIN ROTHBAUM) discuss recent developments in wage theory and the influences of collective bargaining on wage determination.

WAITE, WILLIAM W. "Problems in the Arbitration of Wage Incentives," chap. 2, *Arbitration Today*, JEAN T. MCKELVEY (ed.). Proceedings of the Eighth Annual Meeting of the National Academy of Arbitrators. Washington, D.C.: Bureau of National Affairs, 1955, pp. 25–34. Discussion by John W. Seybold and S. Herbert Unterberger, pp. 35–44.

Discusses problems of determining the agreement requirements for arbitrating incentive wage rates and the technical problems in establishing a sound incentive rate.

WHYTE, WILLIAM FOOTE. *Money and Motivation*. New York: Harper & Bros., 1955.

A comprehensive analysis of the impact of financial incentives in the factory. The author has drawn on the works of MELVILLE DALTON, DONALD ROY, LEONARD SAYLES, ORVIS COLLINS, FRANK MILLER, GEORGE STRAUSS, FRIEDRICH FUERSTENBERG, and ALEX BAVELAS.

WOLF, WILLIAM B. *Wage Incentives as a Managerial Tool*. New York: Columbia University Press, 1957.

Discusses the nature of wage incentives, impact of wage incentives on manufacturing costs, the theory and logic of wage incentives, and understanding the use of wage incentives.

Chapter 13

THE WAGE AND EFFORT BARGAIN: CONTINGENT BENEFITS

Contingent benefits are payments made to an employee who suffers some particular misfortune: layoff or permanent separation from a job; illness or accident; early or untimely death; superannuation. Each of these is an income-threatening hazard or contingency to be feared by anyone whose lifeline is the wage or salary earned by working at a job. Contingent benefits provide safeguards against them. Previous editions of this book referred to them by the accurate but unwieldy term, "worker insurance and income-continuity programs." Perhaps "contingent benefits" is no better, but it is shorter.

Like wages, contingent benefits are costs to the employer, but unlike wages, they are not in the usual sense income to the employee. Only those who run afoul of the specified contingency—who suffer the misfortune—draw the benefits; others do not. Thus, for example, if an unlucky worker runs his hand into a buzz saw and loses a thumb, he cannot get his thumb back but is entitled to medical care and financial compensation for his permanent disability. Fellow workers who were luckier or more cautious get no compensation, but still have their thumbs. Similarly, a worker who lives beyond retirement age gets social security and perhaps a private pension, which he would never have drawn if he had died young. If he dies young, his widow may claim death benefits. If he leaves no widow or dependent children, only the undertaker benefits. Everyone knows that death is inevitable, but old age is not; and no one knows when death may come. A worker wants protection against the consequences of either contingency and against other hazards of a working life.

Actuaries can predict for a given population the number of claims that will be made for benefits, hence, calculate the probable costs, but cannot tell in advance who will make claims. Neither can the eventual claimants. Starting from estimated costs, a company providing contingent benefits spreads the risk over the whole work force that is exposed to the hazards and specifies conditions under which an individual will be entitled to receive benefits. The work force covered by a plan may, in fact, share the costs—another difference between contingent benefits

386

and wages—though almost always the employer, when he does not carry the full load, pays the larger share.

Life is full of hazards and those that threaten to cut the income lifeline do not by any means exhaust the list. At various times in the past, right up to the present day, people have coped with the uncertainties and dangers of the future—and more specifically, the economic future—in one or more of three basic ways: (*a*) reliance on personal resources, family assistance, or charity; (*b*) governmental action; and, more recently (*c*) collective bargaining.

Personal Resources, Family Assistance, and Charity. All men are mortal (Socrates said) and some die when they are young and vigorous; some linger into senility and decrepitude. Some people live out their years in health; some fall prey to accident, illness, or disease. These things happen to rich and poor alike as fate decrees, but there is one hazard that does not threaten the person of means: unemployment. Other dangers are as old as human life; unemployment is modern, a plague of industrial society. It threatens all who are dependent on a wage or salary; and, most acutely, it threatens the manual worker.

Against the contingency of becoming unemployed (as against other hazards), the moralist of a century ago counseled workers to "save for a rainy day." The theory was that out of savings put aside from earnings the worker would accumulate reserves to tide him over a period of unemployment. This was, in fact, pretty much what the skilled worker did, or tried to do: worked at high wages during the season, tightened his belt a bit, and waited out the lean days until the following season.

Factory workers of early times found it hard to keep body and soul together even when working and quickly dropped to the starvation level if they lost their jobs. Today, when factory wages are high, the new moralists—merchant and advertiser—urge workers to buy to the limit of their credit and make it easy for him to do so by selling on the installment plan. They tell him not to save, but to go into debt.

Results of the two opposed moralities are about the same. A spell of unemployment soon depletes a worker's personal resources and exhausts his credit; the goods he went into debt for, and used but never owned, are repossessed. Where then can he turn?

And how about other misfortunes: accidents, illness, old age? The traditional recourse was—and still is—the family. Children went back to stay with the old folks; old folks might go to live with their grown-up children. Beyond the family (in disasters exceeding family means), the recourse was help from friends and neighbors, or help from a church or fraternal order—beyond that, public charity.

This system worked quite well in the early American agricultural and handicraft economy. It has not died out even today, though the forms have changed. Putting a few extra pennies in the sock has developed into bank savings, private insurance policies, shares in mutual funds (perhaps bought, like a car or refrigerator, on the installment plan), and kindred schemes. There are echoes of the old-time neighborhood mutual help in the present-day Community Chests. Overtones of the old morality still animate debates over welfare and public assistance. It seems to be a rather generally held belief that a person *should* assume primary responsibility for his own and his family's security.

Governmental Action. As the economic system grew more complex and interdependent and as individuals found their livelihood more closely tied to the prosperity of particular business enterprises—particularly factories—they began to turn to the government to provide security. This trend, which began in the 19th century led to the enactment, early in the 20th, of factory inspection and workmen's compensation laws in a number of the states. It culminated in the New Deal social security programs, enacted at federal level in the 1930s. Subsequent legislation has updated and improved the programs, but has not added much that is really new.

The principle that justifies governmental action to provide safeguards against the hazards of a working life seems to be that for individuals overtaken by misfortune a complex industrial society should do what they cannot any longer do for themselves. There are some indications that the public has accepted a broadening of this principle to embrace those things government can do better or less expensively than the individual. Government programs offer two advantages: (1) They increase the number of people covered; that is, the statistical population, thus making risks more predictable and lessening the costs of insuring against the hazards; and (2) They tend to levy the taxes that support the programs (which are analogous to insurance premiums) on a progressive basis, so that low-income wage earners pay less for what they get than more prosperous individuals or business enterprises.

The federal social security programs, integrated with and supplementing the various state systems, now offer workers a measure of protection against unemployment (Unemployment Compensation); against old age and untimely death (Retirement, Survivors, and Disability Insurance); against job-connected accidents or industrial diseases (Workmen's Compensation); and now, more recently, ill health in general after age 65 (Medicare). Many nonunion enterprises, and even more unionized ones, augment these governmental programs with supplementary private plans.

Collective Bargaining. As described in Chapter 2, early-day craft unions actually grew out of the "friendly benefit" societies, that men who worked together in the same trade formed for mutual insurance. Widows and orphans and disabled fellow-craftsmen received help from these funds. After the evolution of the societies into craft unions, the tradition continued. These early union programs were by no means comprehensive. A man's main source of personal security continued to be his skill, and union efforts went toward keeping the skill scarce and in demand.

Strategy suitable to craftsmen did not fit the situation of the semiskilled worker in the rapidly expanding factory system. Factory workers did not become unionized in any large numbers until the 1930s. New Deal legislation in that decade gave them not only social security but a collective bargaining law, the Wagner act, which protected their right to organize in unions. The industrial unions did not immediately demand contingent benefits. Instead, they concentrated on wage raises and work rules, and pay for time not worked. Paid holidays and vacations had hitherto been practially unheard-of for blue-collar workers.

Collective bargaining for contingent benefits really began only after the United States entered World War II, in the decade of the 1940s. War times are boom times. Factories work full-blast and still cannot keep pace with orders. Qualified workers are scarce, and employers eager to bid for their services. But a wartime economy, unless controlled, leads to inflation.

Aware of the threat of inflation, the wartime government enacted wage and price controls. Labor and management gave reciprocal no-strike, no-lockout pledges. Unions which would gladly have negotiated raises, and employers who would gladly have met or exceeded union wage demands found themselves restricted in what the government would allow them to do. Contingent benefits, hitherto unknown to collective bargaining agreements, were not wages, and did not fall under the strictures of the wage freeze. In most cases, besides, actual payment of benefits could be deferred. Pensions agreed on today, for example, become payable some time in a perhaps far-off tomorrow. Not surprisingly, therefore, unions and managements which found themselves unable to bargain on current wage rates turned to bargaining on promises redeemable in the future.

The bargains reached, in general, *supplemented* governmental programs. Pensions augmented or complemented social security; health and welfare programs extended protection to family members as well as to the already-protected wage earner. Unemployment was no problem at this time; but later, after the war, it became an important issue. Unions succeeded in getting privately financed supplementary unemployment benefits, severance pay, and other forms of protection.

Some employers made efforts after the war to remove contingent benefits from the range of issues subject to collective bargaining; but they were unsuccessful. The NLRB and the courts ruled that benefits are bargainable issues. They remain part of the pay package—an ever growing part—and are a prime topic of collective bargaining negotiations.

THE HAZARDS OF A WORKING CAREER

In the course of a lifetime, any person dependent on wages or a salary faces four main threats to a livelihood: (1) unemployment; (2) accident, pregnancy, or ill health; (3) permanent total disability, or untimely death; or (4) old age. Measures to deal with these four kinds of hazard have to take account of the differences in the nature of the threat and the consequences of the misfortune, but also must recognize some characteristics the four hold in common.

All of them *cost* money; so there are problems of funding and finance. All of them *pay out* money—not to every person covered, but to those who fall victim to the contingency—so there are problems of benefits, eligibility, and claims. All of them are costs to the employer and some, also, to the individuals covered. Thus those who pay for the programs and those who get the protection have a common stake in them, but often opposing interests. So there are problems of policy—management policy, union policy—and problems of administration. Finally, there are problems of social concern that go beyond the particular unions and enterprises. The magnitude and widespread incidence of the plans, their impact on the economy, their relationship to governmental programs and to matters of public policy, need to be assessed.

These last-mentioned social implications of collectively bargained contingent benefits had best be considered last, after the programs have been examined. Issues that grow out of the problems common to all four categories of hazard ought to precede discussion of the hazards themselves. The plan of presentation, therefore, is as follows:

1. Principles and policy.
2. Administration.
3. Benefits, eligibility, and claims.
4. Funding and finance.
5. The four hazards.
6. Social implications.

Principles and Policy

An organization ordinarily formulates policy in terms of its interests and objectives, in the light of principles perceived—rightly or wrongly—to govern the outcome of action towards objectives. By analogy, an individual might work toward the personal objective of financial security in any one or more of many possible ways. He might purchase stocks and securities, start a savings account, buy land, or, indeed, bury his valuables in a hole in the ground. Any of these policies—even the last-mentioned, during a war or revolution—might succeed. Any of them could lead to disaster—even the first-mentioned—as investors found out at the time of the stock market crash. The future is always uncertain and full of change, yet one principle holds true. Benjamin Franklin expressed it most succinctly in *Poor Richard's Almanac:* "Save and Have." It is a more reliable guide to policy aimed at security objectives than its opposite: Let tomorrow take care of itself. One thing is sure: Set nothing aside, and there will be nothing left.

Policy in bargaining for contingent benefits similarly grows from interests and objectives of the bargainers and rests on principles which they perceive as applicable. It would be surprising if unions and management did not have different, often opposing interests and objectives, though it does not follow that these must needs be irreconcilable. It might even happen that unions and management would take different and perhaps opposing views about relevant principles. Certainly principles derived from clashing ideologies could put them in conflict. Just as likely, however, unions and management may find that they accept the same principles and differ only on objectives. Sometimes they will agree both on principles and objectives.

Whether they like it or not, both have to accept one general principle that public policy has laid down as binding upon them; that is, that workers are entitled to protection from the consequences of misfortunes not their own fault or under their control, which destroy or diminish their ability to make a living. Governmental programs provide a start in this direction in the private sector of the economy, and tax private enterprises and individuals to support them.

Not yet a part of public policy is an extension to this principle—that an employer *must* assume the added financial burden of supplementing the governmental programs; but that he *may* do so and thereby wins esteem, has become clear. It is part of the accepted perception of the employer's role in our society. It may become a practical necessity if he is to continue to attract and hold a work force. While not required to do it, then, or condemned if he does not, he can no longer refuse *on principle* (as some employers did, on ideological grounds) to bargain with a recognized union on contingent benefits.

Bargaining then proceeds on other principles: those that apply to the general nature and specific demands of worker insurance and income-continuity programs, regardless of the particular form they take. The most important principles affecting policy in contingent benefits bargaining seem to center around the following issues; (a) noninterference with operations; (b) adequate benefits; (c) actuarial soundness; and (d) appropriate allocation of the financial burden.

Noninterference with Operations. A business enterprise does not exist for the purpose of providing benefits, though it may have to provide them to carry out its operations and achieve its purposes. Operations are a first priority.

Sickness, for instance—real sickness—interferes with operations. It causes absenteeism, disrupts schedules, often means working short-handed. Granting paid leave to a sick employee does not solve the immediate operating problem the absence creates, but alleviates the personal misfortune and by providing timely care may bring a sick employee back to productive work the sooner. A sick leave plan so overgenerous as to encourage a person with a slight headache or hangover to stay home rather than report for work would be of dubious benefit to the individual and interfere needlessly with operations. So would a benefits program so ill-considered or so costly as to tie up a major portion of a company's working capital.

A company is not, and cannot afford to be, a philanthropic institution. To stay in competition, it has to remain solvent and operate efficiently. Few people would expect contingent benefits to *directly* increase efficiency of operations, but at least they must not seriously interfere. The same could be said, of course, of any provision of a union agreement, but is especially true of benefits bargaining, where the negotiators often tend to lose sight of operational effects. Benefit programs seem to the bargainers to be remote from operations and in a separate compartment. Managers might be expected to be more alert to this danger, but they sometimes disregard it. They tend to reckon the impact only in dollar costs, not in effects on operations. Money saved by refusing paid sick leave, for instance, could be lost many times over, not in cash, but in lowered productivity.

Adequate Benefits. If that careless worker of a few pages back had lost his thumb in an industrial accident in the state of Connecticut he would have received in compensation for it (in the late 1960s) not less than $3000; in the state of Oregon, $600. Who is to say which of the two amounts is adequate—or inadequate—or overadequate? How much is a human thumb worth? To the worker who loses it, moreover, it is not *a* thumb, but *my* thumb.

Measures of adequacy emerge somewhat more definitely in establishing pensions. A company pension of $10 a month to supplement social security would add more to the bitterness than to the means of a retired couple, in the face of rising costs of living. Under inflation and despite past increases, social security is already—and remains chronically—inadequate. Barring future inflation, a pension equal to full pay at retirement date would be *more* than adequate. But with inflation, how long will even so overgenerous a provision for retirement (far in excess of current practice) remain adequate? Unions naturally judge adequacy from the point of view of the recipient of benefits. Management tends to judge by the level adequate to gain acceptance for the agreement as a whole.

The same issue of adequacy arises in all four areas of contingent benefits. Various standards of adequacy have been tried in each of them, and will be discussed under the specific categories of hazard. Whatever the category, benefits bargaining starts from the principle of adequacy; though notions of what is adequate may differ.

Actuarial Soundness. A program of inadequate benefits could be actuarily sound, and so could a program offering more-than-adequate benefits. No program can be actuarily sound, whatever the level of benefits, if it does not generate enough funds and maintain sufficient reserves to pay off on its promises. Actuarial soundness is a *calculation*. It matches anticipated payoffs, which are an estimate and forecast of the future, against necessary contributions to be set aside in the present. The future is always uncertain. Predictions of the future are never exact, but have to be expressed in probabilities. Within the range of probability, over the long run, costs must support the expected benefits, payoff must not exceed reserves.

Devising plans that are actuarily sound demands the professional services of actuaries, who are experts. Bargainers absorbed with immediate problems often feel tempted to ignore long-run possibilities, and just take a chance. (Even on an actuary's predictions they take a chance, but it is a calculated chance.) A program that is actuarily sound is more likely to meet employee expectations of benefits and employer expectations of cost. This holds true in any category of hazard.

There are many ways to implement the principle of actuarial soundness. Issues of policy that most frequently come up under this heading are whether a program is *funded* or *nonfunded,* and if nonfunded, whether it is insured or pay-as-you go.

Appropriate Allocation of the Financial Burden. The main issue here is whether the plan should be *contributory* or *noncontributory;* that is, whether employees who are to benefit from the protection shall share part of the cost (contributory) or whether the enterprise shall carry it all (noncontributory).

Governmental programs presently in effect are of both kinds. Social security (RSDI) is contributory; workmen's compensation (in most states), noncontributory. Private supplements do not have to copy the governmental pattern. Many private pension plans are noncontributory, entirely paid for by the employer, though the social security pensions they supplement are contributory. Family health and hospitalization plans such as, for instance, Blue Cross, are usually contributory. The employer's contribution consists of so much per enrolled employee, with the employee making up the rest of a variable total based on the size of his family. In some programs, such as certain forms of group life insurance, employees pay the full premium, but get the insurance more cheaply by virtue of their attachment to the employing organization.

Unions and management often hold different views of principle over the contributory/noncontributory issue. Arguing from the principle of individual responsibility, managers contend that employees should share the burden of providing for their own personal security. This seems to be part of the conventional morality of our culture. Practical considerations reinforce the principle: For the same level of benefits, a contributory plan will cost the employer less. Besides, many employers believe that their employees will appreciate the benefits more if they have to pay for them, and that an awareness of their own contribution will make them more aware of (and perhaps, more grateful for) the employer's.

While union negotiators may explicitly accept the principle of individual responsibility, they tend to take a more pragmatic approach. Their members expect *both* raises and contingent benefits. A contributory program reduces the apparent amount of the raise; noncontributory benefits increase it. Implict and unrecognized, perhaps, behind the union approach there also stands a counter-principle: Provide for contingencies at the *source* of security, the enterprise. Enterprise operations, in which all engage, produce the wealth that is the source of security for all.

A subsidiary issue in allocating the financial burden is the relation of the privately financed benefits to governmental programs; that is, whether the governmental programs (obligatory, and supported by a form of payroll tax) are to carry a greater or lesser share of the total burden for various items of the benefits package. This is the *costs* side of the issue already encountered in its *payoff* form under the heading of adequate benefits.

Administration

A retirement fund can build up over the years to a temptingly large sum of money. Even a fairly small company can accumulate reserves for this and other purposes that run into the millions of dollars, and larger companies into the tens—indeed, the hundreds—of millions. It does *not*, unfortunately, go without saying that those who administer the funds will always be honest, and able, and will take a trusteeship view of their responsibilities. The law (specifically, the Landrum-Griffin act of 1959) had to spell out rules of conduct and standards of administration to safeguard the interests of those for whom such funds are built up: the workers. Certain union leaders, and others, are serving time in prison today for mishandling funds that had been entrusted to them. Even more serious losses to supposed beneficiaries of funded programs may come not from dishonesty so much as inexperience and ineptitude of those who administer them.

Safeguarding the integrity of administration thus becomes part of the responsibility of the bargainers. One issue they have to face is: *Who* will administer the program? Four answers to this question have been found: (1) the employer; (2) the union; (3) the employer and the union jointly; and (4) neutral outsiders such as a bank, an insurance company, or a foundation.

Employers. They are accustomed to administering financial affairs and have an interest in both the honesty and efficiency of administration. At the same time, as employers they have a partisan interest in many questions that could arise and that might possibly run counter to the interests of the beneficiaries. An objection to employer administration, then, is possible conflict of interest.

Union Administration. Subject to the same objection as employer administration, unions have gotten a bad name as sole administrators, chiefly because of a few well-publicized cases of embezzlement and shady dealing. Yet, in some circumstances, unions are the logical administrators. When one large union deals with many small employers, as in construction or the coal mines or the needle trades, the union would seem to be the natural agent of administration. Not as strong a case can be made when a single local union deals with a single employer.

Joint Administration. This is a common arrangement. Issues of principle and practical arrangements having been taken care of in collective bargaining, both sides presumably have a common interest in effective administration.

Outsider Administration. Finally, a solution that minimizes influence from either side and takes administrative decisions out of the hands of both parties is administration by an outsider. It makes use of the experience and expertise of a financial institution such as a bank or insurance company, but also subjects administration to the conservatism and sometimes excessive caution of these organizations. A compromise between this way and direct joint administration sometimes takes the form of establishing a foundation. Management and the union name representatives to the board, which also draws from banks or other outside institutions.

Issues arising from administration of a program (whatever the form chosen) have to do with such matters as: investments; standards of eligibility for benefits and level of benefits paid (when this is discretionary, or depends on the amount of reserves); mergers, acquisitions, dissolutions of employing companies; and many other matters. On investment policy, for example, management usually thinks first about the safety of the investment and the expected earnings. Union policy may favor investment in socially desirable projects such as low-cost housing, which may not be as profitable as other possibilities but provide, as the union sees it, a double benefit.

Generally speaking, issues arising in the course of administration are less important both to the union and the company than provisions for responsible trusteeship and efficient operation.

Benefits, Eligibility, and Claims

A worker who gets a union-negotiated wage raise can spend the extra money at once; but to be able to comprehend the gains from an improvement in contingent benefits he has to make an effort of imagination. A young man, for instance, rarely looks far enough ahead to appreciate the value of a pension plan. If the plan is contributory, he may resent having to pay into a fund just for the benefit (as he sees it) of a few broken-down old-timers. The old-timers look on it differently. Yet neither they nor the youngsters ever give a thought to what it would cost out of pocket or paycheck as individuals, if they had to buy the protection that this or any other benefits plan provides from a private insurance company.

The worker's eye is not on costs but on benefits: the dollar amount of the pension, the number of days of free hospitalization in case of accident or illness, the sum of money to be paid survivors if "anything should happen" to the breadwinner. Consequently, union negotiators also approach benefits bargaining with an eye on benefits, the best possible benefits, or at least such as the members will perceive as adequate. It is the manager who worries about costs. The union may, indeed, publicize the costs as part of a package raise, but convinces members to accept the benefits instead of a higher cash raise, in terms of the potential payoff. Adequacy of benefits is one thing that unions and management bargain over. Eligibility is another.

Eligibility. This has to be established by or for an individual in advance of his drawing the benefits and requires careful definition. No one can expect to collect damages for an automobile accident by insuring the car after it has crashed. Defining eligibility for various kinds of benefits opens up many complicated questions.

How many years of service, for example, entitle an employee to a pension? Are periods of layoff to count against this, or be ignored? Is retirement at, say, age 65 to be compulsory or discretionary; and, if the latter, at whose discretion? The worker's or the company's?

Or: How close must the relationship be to entitle a person to medical care under a family health plan? A spouse, of course; but children to what age? And how about dependent parents or other kin? Must they be living under the family roof? May they be in a nursing home?

Each of the four hazard categories poses problems in defining eligibility. It is not hard to see how important the definitions are both to the company and the union. In multiemployer bargaining, eligibility for benefits may be independent of any continuing relationship with a single company. Employers naturally want assurance that they are not going to have to support people who, directly or indirectly, have no proper claim on them.

This raises the related, important eligibility issue of whether benefits are *vested.*

Vesting. Vesting means giving the individual a right to the benefit independently of a continuing relationship with the employer. All governmental programs are vested. A worker who leaves one employer and goes to another takes his social security rights with him. Each successive employer adds to the account credited to the worker's number and makes payroll deductions of the worker's own contributions. When the worker becomes eligible for benefits in accordance with legally established standards, he draws against the accumulated total.

Some privately financed benefits programs, like the governmental, are vested; most of them are not. Because workers often change jobs and employers in some industries, multiemployer plans to fit them practically have to be vested; single-employer plans do not. A trend towards vesting of private plans seems to be setting in, but has by no means swept all before it. Many companies still find it to their advantage to offer plans, as a matter of policy, that are nonvested.

A company with a nonvested pension plan (for example) pays pensions only to eligible employees who at retirement age are still in its employ. Anyone who quits, is fired, or otherwise becomes separated from the company loses whatever pension rights he may have accumulated. If the plan is contributory, the departing employee may draw the amount of his own contributions, often with nominal interest, but loses the company's matching contribution for which he would otherwise have become eligible.

A nonvested plan of this sort acts as a brake on worker mobility, and for that reason may fit in with an employer's objective of reducing turnover. It gives long-service employees an increasingly strong incentive to stay with the company. It builds a stable though perhaps aging work force, if that is what the company wants. If not, a vested plan might be the better policy.

Claims. Benefit claims depend on eligibility standards, but present some problems of their own. Of those not purely administrative, fraud and malingering are amongst the touchiest. The number of cases is relatively slight, but investigation is embarrassing and control difficult and costly. Partly to avoid the bother of dealing with fraudulent claims, the auto companies tied the administration of their privately financed S.U.B. plans (to be discussed) to the public unemployment compensation agencies. A laid-off worker otherwise might all too easily have gone on drawing his check from the company while working at another job.

Malingering (or feigning injury or illness in order to claim compensation) may arise in connection with industrial accidents where public agencies play a part and help evaluate and control; or disabilities not job connected that are wholly covered by a private plan. As between paying for medical care or granting paid sick leave, most employers would probably prefer to spend their money for medical care. They reason that medical care would be more likely to promote health and fitness in the work force, less likely to reward and hence encourage idleness. In addition, they undoubtedly presume it would be harder for a malingering worker to fool a doctor with fictitious symptoms than to "call in sick" and fool the supervisor. Paid sick leave is more commonly granted to salaried workers.

Funding and Finance

Essentially, benefits bargaining is bargaining over promises. The money to redeem the promises must be available when the specific contingency arises, or the promise might just as well not have been given. If an insurance company, for example, could not or would not pay a policyholder's claim when his car got wrecked, he might just as well not have taken out collision insurance. The insurance company meets claims by collecting and investing the premiums paid by its many policyholders in order to compensate the statistically predictable few who are victims of accident. For given levels of compensation, actuarial calculations determine the premiums; but having the money ready to pay out is a matter of funding and financial management.

Taking for granted actuarial soundness (or setting it aside for the moment as irrelevant), there are two basic approaches to financing benefits: (1) *funded* or *trusteed* plans and (2) *nonfunded*, that is, *insured* or *pay-as-you-go* plans.

Funding. Governmental programs are funded; so are many—but by no means all private plans.

Funding means setting aside money in a fund that may not be touched except to pay the promised benefits and administer the program. A prime example is the social security system, which has accumulated vast reserves in the treasury of the United States out of taxes and contributions. This money may be spent only for meeting the obligations of the law to eligible beneficiaries and for administering the system. No other agency of government may draw on these funds, nor may they be diverted to any other purpose. Money needed for carrying out other intentions of government has to be raised from other sources, such as taxation and borrowing, not from the social security fund.

The government could quite conceivably provide social security benefits on a nonfunded basis, in the form of promises to meet claims out of future income. The Nixon administration, in fact, proposed exactly that in 1971. Acting on the recommendations of the 1971 Advisory Council on Social Security, the Secretary of Health, Education, and Welfare asked Congress to replace the current conservative, funded method of financing with a pay-as-you-go plan. Whether the change will be made, and if so, when, cannot at present be foreseen, but the funding method will not be without defenders. To them, the danger is that an administration unsympathetic to social security, or short of funds, might fail to carry out the promises made over the years to contributors and claimants. The personal stake in the existing fund that all now have who hold social security numbers tends toward conservatism. The existence of the fund makes people feel secure; it takes much of the terror and anxiety out of the hazards of an uncertain future.

A privately financed program can also be funded and provide the same kind of assurance, yet many are not and still offer protection. The difference is somewhat analogous to that between making purchases only with money already saved and in the bank, and buying the same thing on the installment plan; or again, between building for one's heirs a personal estate consisting of a portfolio of stocks and securities, and buying life insurance, for the same beneficiaries, out of earnings. The analogy is not complete, but indicative of the different ways of financing benefits. For some purposes, in some situations, management will prefer one approach, the union another; or they may agree on different methods of finance for different programs.

Nonfunded Plans. From the point of view of an enterprise engaged in benefits bargaining, nonfunded plans tend to fall into two categories: insured and pay-as-you-go.

Insured Plans. As the name implies, these plans finance the promised benefits by purchasing insurance from an insurance company.

Pay-as-You-Go Plans. They are like self-insurance. The company promises to make benefit payments out of its earnings and general resources as occasion arises.

Risks are easier to calculate for some categories of hazard than for others, and the financial arrangements for meeting them differ accordingly. Thus, pensions are usually easier to foresee and plan for than unemployment, which may result from economic forces quite beyond the control of the enterprise. Risks differ, too, in the seriousness of possible consequences. Plans for financing any program of contingent benefits have to consider the hazards.

THE FOUR MAIN HAZARDS OF A WORKING LIFE

Anyone who works for a living, no matter in what capacity or degree, spends on the job between a fourth and a third of all the time fate allots him. The income that makes the rest of the time livable, and more or less agreeable, comes from the job; so do most of the hazards that can cut it short or threaten it, or make it disagreeable and precarious. These hazards can be classified, as already noted, in four categories, for each of which there is a governmental program and each of which provides scope for collectively bargained contingent benefits.

The exposition that follows takes the four categories in this order: (1) unemployment; (2) illness and accident; (3) death and disability; and (4) old age.

The treatment of each hazard starts with: (*a*) the governmental program. It goes on to present, (*b*) collective bargained supplemental or complementary programs. It then discusses (*c*) special issues, trends, and tendencies.

Following the presentation of the four hazards is a brief discussion of their economic, political, and social impact on present-day society, and some implications for the future.

Unemployment

The unpleasant contingency that wage and salary earners fear the most and can personally do the least about is probably unemployment. No matter how much a worker may dislike the job he is on, he prefers it to not having any job at all. He is most likely to lose it when others are losing theirs and when, consequently, jobs are hardest to find and competition the keenest. The older he gets, the slighter his chances of opening up new opportunities and the more catastrophic the consequences of being without a job. If such fears lurk in the background of a worker's mind today, consider what they must have been before the federal government, in 1938, enacted its program of Unemployment Compensation.

Unemployment Compensation. Unemployment Compensation is a federal-state program providing a degree of income security to unemployed workers. Within a federal framework, each state is free to work out its own eligibility standards, benefit structure, and financing methods. At present about 80 percent of American wage and salary workers are covered by Unemployment Compensation. Several of its characteristics should be noted:

1. Unemployment Compensation is *noncontributory*. This means that U.C. taxes are assessed against the employer. (There is substantial question about who ultimately pays for U.C. benefits. Some authorities argue that the employer passes U.C. costs along to the consumer in the form of price increases. Others argue that the employer must absorb this cost. Still others maintain that employees pay the cost because only so much is available for total labor costs. It seems likely that in competitive industries employers can pass on only the average cost of U.C. in price increases. Employers with very irregular employment probably are forced to absorb their extra U.C. costs under experience rating discussed below.)
2. Unemployment compensation is *funded*. Because future needs for unemployment compensation benefits cannot be predicted with a high degree of accuracy, funding of U.C. is not actuarially sound.
3. Most states use *"experience rating"* in assessing U.C. taxes against the individual enterprise. This means that an employer pays a higher tax rate when he has irregular employment than when he has stable employment.
4. The cost of U.C. fluctuates rather sharply between a minimum tax rate as low as zero in a few states to relatively high maximum rates.
5. Benefits vary widely between the states.

Collective Bargaining on Unemployment. No single enterprise can expect to find measures effective against cyclical unemployment; only the government has resources sufficient to cope with that. Even the existing governmental plan would be no more than a buffer if there should again be a large-scale, widespread, long-lasting depression of national or international scope. More amenable to control at company levels are periods of temporary unemployment such as result from seasonal fluctuations, model changeover and retooling, or variations in market demand; and to some extent, adjustment to technological change. The hazard remains unpredictable. There is not yet a *unified* national program of unemployment compensation, retraining, and relocation. Although unemployment occurs at the enterprise, absolute control is beyond the enterprise's power. A few managements and unions have nevertheless developed schemes for cushioning the impact of unemployment, and most labor agreements establish seniority rights that give individuals *relative* protection against layoff in terms of their length of service.

Some of the devices that have found their way into labor-management agreements as measures against unemployment are the following: (1) work sharing; (2) seniority; (3) severance pay; (4) retraining, relocation, early retirement, and other combinations; (5) guaranteed annual wage plans; and (6) supplemental unemployment benefits.

Work Sharing. "Sharing the misery" is what some cynics have called the plans that call for shorter work weeks when there is not enough work to keep everyone employed. It was a common device during the depression of the 1930s, and occasionally finds application in high-wage occupations, as when painters or carpenters adopt a "30-hour" rule. This spreads the work and pay over a larger number of union members during temporary slack periods. When unemployment compensation became available, and particularly after the spread of supplemental unemployment benefits, work sharing lost much of its already dubious attraction. No worker could see the point of spreading the work until wages dropped to, or near, the level of unemployment compensation.

Seniority. Like work sharing, seniority can hardly be classed as an unemployment benefit, but is rather a device for giving individuals a measure of security against layoff in terms of their relative position on a seniority list. A person low on the list expects to be laid off in slack times while those ahead of him stay on the job and also to be recalled when business picks up. Over the years he climbs the rungs of the seniority ladder and may reach a point where he is safe against all but the most catastrophic reduction in force.

Severance Pay. This is a true contingent benefit for those who are to be permanently separated from employment with a company. Technology, in making jobs obsolete, makes the workers on those jobs redundant if they cannot qualify for new jobs or if the reduction in force made possible by technological advance cuts too deep. A lump-sum payment to the technologically displaced worker is his compensation for the permanent loss of his job.

Most severance pay agreements require that an employee have a specified minimum length of service to be eligible. Benefits are graduated upward on the basis of length of service in the company. A fairly common arrangement is one week's pay for each year of service.

Unions prominent in negotiating severance pay plans include the Steelworkers, Autoworkers, Communications Workers, Ladies' Garment Workers, Electrical Workers (IBEW), and lately, the Railway Workers. A number of companies have extended severance pay plans to their non-union white-collar employees, equally threatened by technological change.

Severance pay plans are seldom funded. This puts an unpredictable and theoretically unlimited liability on the employer, and hence may be presumed to encourage companies to be conservative in planning for technological change that will displace many of their employees. Some severance pay plans have been grafted onto supplemental unemployment benefit plans, which are funded.

Retraining, Relocation, Early Retirement. The railway strikes of 1971 and the years immediately preceeding made most people aware of the work rules that modern technology have rendered obsolete. A day's run for a train crew is no longer, realistically, 100 miles, but nearer 300. The rule that a train must change crews every 8 hours or 100 miles no longer accords with the industry's technology, but the problem remains of what to do about the redundant crews. In another instance, cargo for ships at sea no longer consists of miscellaneous boxes, barrels, and sacks, but arrives on the dock in containers, which are quicker and easier to load, with modern equipment that has taken the place of the old donkey engines, nets, and slings.

In an agreement with the powerful longshoremen's union providing a benefit fund (initially $29 million, built up over five and a half years), the longshore employers of the West Coast obtained freedom to introduce the labor-saving devices. The benefit fund finances guaranteed annual wages and early retirement benefits for a limited number of *registered* longshoremen, excluding a group of workers whose attachment to the industry was still more or less casual.[1]

The railways met the same problem of reducing the numbers employed while providing for those who were to be permanently separated from railway employment by a combination of measures: attrition (or not replacing those who quit, withdraw, die, or retire); displacement al-

---

[1] For a discussion of this agreement, the factors leading up to its negotiation, and its probable long-term effects, see Charles C. Killingsworth, "The Modernization of West Coast Longshore Work Rules," *Industrial and Labor Relations Review*, Volume XV (April 1962), pp. 295–306.

lowances (or early retirement) and severance pay; retraining; and preferential hiring.[2]

Guaranteed Annual Wage Plans. A true guaranteed annual wage would provide income for 12 months of the year regardless of how many or how few of the 2080 potential hours an employee might actually work. Salaried white-collar workers have traditionally enjoyed the security and convenience of regular pay throughout the year while manual workers, paid by the hour and only for hours worked, endured unpredictable fluctuations of income. Union demands for a guaranteed annual wage (G.A.W.) are therefore understandable and not surprising. One big industrial union, the United Auto Workers, made a historic breakthrough in October 1967 by getting a guaranteed wage as part of its agreement with the Ford Motor Company. The steel workers have had comparable successes.

Employers should not have found the union demand surprising, but when it was first raised they did consider it unreasonable. They had been treating their white-collar salaried and blue-collar hourly workers differently not just because of custom or on ideological grounds, but because of real constraints rooted in economics and work-place technology. The work done by white-collar workers affects and is affected only indirectly by production work. It can and often must go on whether or not the machines are running. It is a kind of overhead, a fixed charge against total costs, in contrast to production-worker wages, a variable cost.

Consider this extreme case: A cannery, operating only three months a year during the harvest season, needs few more clerical employees—if any—during the rush period than during the slack time. Operations in the busy season, on the other hand, call for a large temporary work force which the company could not afford to support during nine months of idleness. At most, it keeps together a small maintenance gang and warehouse crew when the factory is not working.

Other industries have a more stable pattern. At the opposite extreme, a public utility or perhaps an oil refinery might well be able to guarantee its relatively small force of manual workers the kind of regular income over the year that the much larger salaried group enjoys. In fact, that is

---

[2] Developments in the railways over the past decade have followed fairly closely the recommendations of the Presidential Railroad Commission, agreed to by the carriers and labor organization in the fall of 1960. Anyone interested in the general problems of unemployment, and technological unemployment in particular, will find the Commission's report rewarding. See *The Report of the Presidential Railroad Commission* (Washington, D.C., U.S. Government Printing Office, February 1962), 327 pp. This volume is supplemented by four Appendix Volumes: I, Index-Digest to the Record of the Commission's Hearings; II, Pay Structure Study, Railroad Operating Employees; III, Studies Relating to Railroad Operating Employees; and IV, Studies Related to Collective Bargaining Agreements and Practices Outside the Railroad Industry.

what often happens even without a written guarantee. The collective bargaining problems connected with demands for the guaranteed annual wage come up between the two extremes.

Employers are finding that production-worker wages can no longer be considered a simple variable cost. In their growth and spread, contingent benefits and pay for time not worked (taken together, the "fringe") have made wages much more an item of fixed cost, or overhead, than in the past. At least for an essential core of the blue-collar work force of many enterprises (as perhaps for that maintenance gang and warehouse crew in the cannery) and for high-seniority employees, guaranteed annual wages are within reach. The union's "G.A.W." demand is no longer as unreasonable as it once seemed.

On their side, unions may have to give up work-rules arrangements they once cherished in order to give management the flexibility it needs in assigning the permanent force to whatever work may be available. Penalties for overtime work may have to be reduced. Younger and newer employees may have to wait for the protection until they have acquired seniority and developed versatility to qualify for the guarantees. There may even have to be, eventually, some changes in the laws with employees presently nonexempt from the maximum hours provisions of the wage and hour law moving into the exempt category. Spread of the programs may be slow, but seems to be on the way. Such programs may require the establishment of funds or reserves, though the more stable industries may operate them on a pay-as-you-go basis.

True G.A.W. plans—those which provide the full 52-week, 40-hour guarantee of work or pay—are still rare. The most famous of the early plans, i.e., Nunn-Bush, Procter and Gamble, and Hormel, contain limitations on eligibility and allow overtime offsets. The Hormel plan, for example, takes advantage of a provision of the wage and hour law permitting enterprises in a seasonal industry, by agreement with a bona fide union, to waive the overtime requirements of the law so long as employees do not work more than 1,040 hours in any six months or (according to the agreement reached) 2,080 hours in a year. Meat packing is a year-round industry with seasonal peaks. Its raw material, farm animals, reaches the market somewhat sporadically, when the farmers decide to sell, and consequently the company's stockyards are sometimes empty and sometimes overcrowded. Live animals lose weight unless watered and fed, and feeding before slaughter raises the cost. The company therefore worked out with its union a plan to pay employees a regular wage whether they were idle or working overtime (up to the legal limit). In return, they got a flexible work force, standing by when the yards were empty, able to man the production lines when the pens were full.

Though not a "true" plan, the Hormel program showed what unions and management can do to adapt the G.A.W. principle to a particular industry or enterprise. The Teamsters Union, fairly early in the game, negotiated some true G.A.W. plans. What may perhaps be expected is that industries which adopted plans for supplementary unemployment benefits (S.U.B.) will tend as time goes on to transform their S.U.B. programs into G.AW plans. The auto industry and union have, in fact, taken the lead in this as they did in S.U.B. A brief summary of the UAW-General Motors plan follows.

The General Motors Plan. The 1970 General Motors agreement with the United Auto Workers does not guarantee hourly paid workers the equivalent of a regular salary (as would a true guaranteed annual wage plan) but is a step in that direction, and greatly increases a worker's protection against fluctuations in employment and income. It amends the S.U.B. plan already in effect.

The S.U.B. plan eased the hardships of unemployment for laid-off workers; the amendment supplements the income of workers not laid off, but working short time.

Hourly paid employees under the new plan accumulate Guaranteed Annual Income credits (just as they build up S.U.B. credits) to be applied against short work weeks. Thus an eligible worker not laid off, but called in for less than 40 hours of work in any one week, automatically gets a supplement of 80 percent of his base pay for the hours *not* worked, just as if he had worked them. He can, of course, exhaust his credits if there are too many short work weeks; thus it is not a true guaranteed annual wage; but management has a strong cost-saving incentive to smooth out production schedules so that not many short work weeks occur. As a result, the hourly paid worker can look forward to a more stable level of income. Practically speaking, the skilled workers and high-seniority semiskilled workers get a guaranteed annual wage.

The plan is funded, and nonvested.

Supplemental Unemployment Benefits. In 1955–56 the automobile and steel industries negotiated Supplemental Unemployment Benefits, or S.U.B. plans. By 1970 the coverage of various forms of S.U.B. extended to approximately two million workers represented primarily by the United Automobile Workers, the United Steelworkers, the National Maritime Union, the United Rubber Workers, and the International Ladies' Garment Workers' Union. Although these plans proved to be efficient in operation and not prohibitively costly, their coverage seems to have stabilized with little additional growth to be expected. Extension to workers in other firms and industries of the kind of protection offered seems likely to take the more outright G.A.W. form discussed above. It is still desirable to take a look at the S.U.B. arrangement.

S.U.B. plans start from a presumption that unemployment compensation (U.C.) is inadequate to the needs of workers displaced from jobs in high-wage industries. These plans do not aim to make up the difference between "rockin' chair money" and full pay, but up to as much as but generally not more than 75 percent of gross pay for 40 hours of work per week of unemployment. Beneficiaries may in some cases continue to draw S.U.B. pay for as long as 52 weeks even when, under state laws, their U.C. expires after 26 weeks.

An employee eligible for U.C. becomes eligible, in addition, for S.U.B. This tieup of S.U.B. with the governmental program probably explains why no troublesome problems have arisen in administering the plans. The Ford Motor Company, for example, had to add only five extra people to establish its original plan covering 140,000 employees.[3]

The typical S.U.B. plan is funded by employer contributions up to a Maximum Trust Fund Position, established at the start by agreement with the union on the basis of the company's unemployment experience record. Once Maximum position is reached, the employer replenishes the fund as claims are made on it. This follows the experience rating principle of U.C. and is intended to encourage an employer to stabilize employment.

Experience generally with S.U.B. revealed little interference with operations, but some influence on the wage and benefits differential between skilled and nonskilled workers. The worker most likely to become unemployed, and hence to draw from the fund, is the nonskilled, low-seniority worker. The skilled employee rarely becomes eligible for a benefits check. Besides tending to stabilize current employment, S.U.B. tends to slow down technological advances by making the new installations more costly; that is, the cost of benefits for those displaced must be considered in the calculations. As a rule, however, rapid technological advance occurs in periods of high employment as a response to high demand for a firm's products. Thus in times of high business expectations S.U.B. is not much of a deterrent, and appears to work in harmony with the major determinants of technological progress.

On the union side, S.U.B. brought about a change of attitude towards work sharing, which many industrial unions practiced during the depression when they got their start. Unions with S.U.B. agreements prefer a reduction in the work force to a reduction in the scheduled work week.

Accidents and Illness, Health and Welfare

The earliest governmental measures aimed at protecting industrial workers came in the form of Workmen's Compensation, a state-by-state system without federal counterpart. Starting at the turn of the century in Massachusetts, New Jersey, and other northeastern industrial states, the system spread until by mid-century laws were in effect in every state of the union. Even today they are not uniform, but follow a general pattern. They make the employer responsible for accidents occuring at the work place and illness or disease traceable to working conditions, and thus financially liable for the consequences. This substitutes statute law

---

[3] W. C. Hampton, "Administering an S.U.B. Plan: The Ford Experience," *Personnel*, Vol. XXXIV (July–August 1957), pp. 76–83.

for older common law doctrines under which employers often escaped liability for employee injuries. It gives employers a financial stake in safety on the job.

Most of the state programs are noncontributory, with the employer paying all the costs. Some are funded under state administration, some insured, some pay-as-you-go with the employer self-insured; indeed, some states give a company its choice of financing methods. Eligibility arises out of the accident or disease and claims are heard by a board, on medical evidence, or taken to court. Benefits vary greatly between states (remember that severed thumb, "worth more" in Connecticut than in Oregon) and within a state, particularly if appealed to the courts.

Workmen's Compensation is wholly governmental and does not figure in collective bargaining. Any effort unions or employers make to alter its policies or affect its operations consists of lobbying at the state legislature or representations to boards and commissions.

Workmen's Compensation stops far short of providing comprehensive protection against the hazards that threaten a worker's health and physical fitness, and hence his earning ability. It does not compensate for accidents that take place off the job, or illness not directly job-connected, yet either of these could be disabling. It does not extend to members of a worker's family. The only other governmental program dealing with health, Medicare, does not become available to a worker until after age 65. Unions have consequently raised the demand for benefits that give protection during a worker's active earning career, that include his family, and that arise from sources not directly job-connected.

Collective Bargaining on Health and Welfare. Health and welfare bargaining deals with contingencies against which almost anyone who earns a regular income could protect himself by buying insurance from a private company; but doing it as a group is cheaper and in many ways better. Because the risks are spread, a group can get protection against a greater range of hazards, at lower cost, with higher benefits. Persons who might be denied insurance, or have to pay dearly for it if they applied as individuals, can get it on equal terms as members of a group. These are the main considerations reinforcing the union drive for health and welfare programs.

Historically, the early American craft unions got their start as providers of health and welfare benefits. Later, some progressive companies instituted health and welfare plans in the as yet nonunion factories of the prosperous 1920s, though the depression of the 1930s wiped out most of these plans. A few industrial unions—notably the Ladies' Garment Workers—set up comprehensive health and welfare programs for members and their families. More recently, however, unions have pretty much gotten out of the business of *directly* providing health and welfare benefits from union funds because contingent benefits have become available from other sources. Collective bargaining on health and welfare benefits began to open up these sources after World War II, and the movement has yearly gathered impetus. The bureau of Labor Statistics estimated that the number of workers covered by collective bargained health and welfare programs skyrocketed from 0.5 million in 1945 to 7 million in 1950 to 14.5 million—about 78 percent of all workers under collective bargaining agreements—in 1960. The figures are even higher today.[4]

Issues in Health and Welfare Bargaining. The issues that unions and management have to resolve in health and welfare bargaining are much the same as for other contingent benefits; but three issues of principle stand out and a complex of substantive issues making up the problem of what may be called *design.* To be discussed are the following four topics: (1) actuarial soundness; (2) the contributory versus noncontributory principle; (3) level of costs versus level of benefits; and (4) design of the program.

Actuarial Soundness. It would not be unfair to say that only the most restricted and conservative health and welfare programs can be actuarily sound. There are so many possible contingencies, of such unpredictable consequence and duration to so wide a potential population, that no program drawn up in advance can be considered settled, adequate, and reliable. Just how to assure payoff on promises—whether by funding, insurance, or self-insurance on the pay-as-you-go principle—becomes controversial.

The needs for health care are so many and diverse that there is always room for pioneering; and the management even of a company which in its business affairs is innovative and progressive tends to be reluctant to pioneer in the benefits field. Getting health care and protection are an end to the union, but to management they are means to other ends. By their benefits they may advance, but by their costs they burden, progress toward those other management ends. Any initial advantage one company gets by pioneering is soon lost as others find themselves compelled to follow suit, while gratitude for the effort from its beneficiaries soon gives way to the attitude best expressed in the query: What have you done for us—lately?

Health and welfare bargaining will probably continue to push out into the areas beyond the safe bounds of actuarial soundness. Programs adopted will not be necessarily come to grief, but it would be well to remember what the depression of the 1930s did to many well-intentioned plans.

The Contributory Principle. On the ground that individuals should be self-reliant, and responsible in whole or in part for their own welfare, management tends to insist that the programs be contributory. Unions

---

[4] U.S. Department of Labor, *Analysis of Health and Insurance Plans under Collective Bargaining, Late 1955* (BLS Bulletin No. 1221, 1957), p. iii; and *Health and Insurance, and Pension Plan Coverage in Union Contracts, Late 1960* (BLS Report No. 228), p. 1.

argue against this. A noncontributory plan makes the total wage package look bigger; in addition, it has tax advantages. The tax collector allows an employer's contribution to go tax-free as a business expense, but considers an employee's contribution part of personal income which is taxed. A noncontributary plan also gives better protection and in itself costs less because it assures full coverage of employees and does not require individual solicitation.

Fixed Costs versus Guaranteed Benefits. Unions generally prefer a cents-per-hour method of paying for a benefits program. This fixed contribution makes savings from experience with the plan available to employees. It widens their choice of possible benefits.

The kinds of benefits available from various sources provide a wide and tempting range of choice; the beneficiaries would like a free hand in shopping for the benefits they want, and, if they find a bargain, to be able to spend the money saved on something else. Management tends to want to guarantee benefits and have a free hand in seeking to get them at the least possible cost. This enables a company to recover the savings from favorable experience. A company policy of restricting its guarantee to benefits also permits it to limit the program to the types of benefits generally available from insurance companies and nonprofit service organizations such as Blue Cross and Blue Shield.

In multiemployer bargaining, management usually has to give in to the union's cents-per-hour or percentage-of-payroll demand in order to provide for employees who move from job to job. The larger the group covered, the lower the cost of providing any medical, hospital, or cash indemnity benefit other than life insurance. As the employer enters a larger group, his personal influence diminishes over the amount of benefits to be granted.

Design of the Benefits Program. No two companies, even if they stand side by side on the same street, or operate in the same industry, or deal with the same union, are likely to have identical benefits programs. The variety of benefits available from many sources at different prices matches the variety of situations for which managements and their unions design the programs. The ultimate shape of a given company's program usually has to take account of several or all of the following: (*a*) comprehensiveness, (*b*) form of the benefits, (*c*) coverage, (*d*) freedom of choice, (*e*) integration with community services, and (*f*) special problems.

Comprehensiveness. The scope of protection offered or risks and hazards provided against by the plan is its comprehensiveness. This can range from emergency surgery or long-term hospitalization to routine ambulatory care; the group as a whole is not properly protected except by a comprehensive program. Even so, there may have to be limits, with an expectation of pressure to expand the limits. Can a plan include, for instance, extended psychoanalysis?

Form of the Benefits. This is analogous to payment "in cash or kind." Both management and union probably prefer the form of benefit payment to be in kind: actual, direct medical services, rather than cash. Money paid to beneficiaries is all too easily diverted to uses other than those intended by the plan, leaving the needs the plan was devised for unfulfilled.

Coverage. This has to be defined in terms of numbers and of time: who is to be entitled to the benefits, what family members, what other dependents; and for how long in their lives. For the employee, a plan might cover his active working life; for an employee's widow, perhaps a good deal younger than her mate, benefits might have to extend for years beyond the date when he would have retired; for children, to age 18, or later; and so on.

Freedom of Choice. Giving the beneficiary more or less wide discretion in selecting a doctor, a hospital, or treatment defines freedom of choice. This issue, in a more generalized form, created the greatest controversy over the government's Medicare program. Unions and management have to face it, too, when they design their programs.

Integration with Community Services. Generally this saves costly duplication, avoids waste and lessens friction, and strengthens the community services as well. It may require the negotiation of contracts for services with community agencies. There may be situations, however, in which integration is not possible or may not be desirable.

Special Problems. All sorts of special problems can, of course, arise, but among the most common are provisions against catastrophe, and the inherently "inflationary" nature of health and welfare plans. One benefit gained tends to call for others to be added; all this with the costs of health care steeply on the rise. As with the argument over what is called the "wage-price spiral," there is no agreement over which is cause and which effect: rising medical costs or rising health and welfare benefits.

The most common form of catastrophe insurance is "major medical." Major medical insurance was designed to help meet medical expenses that in some cases might run as high or higher than an employee's annual earnings. Major medical extends basic coverage such as that provided by Blue Cross or Blue Shield to guarantee, with certain reservations, all medical expenses, whether incurred in outpatient care or in a hospital. The reservations are: (1) deductibility, (2) co-insurance, (3) total maximum benefits, and (4) requiring that medical charges must be "reasonable and necessary."

The *deductible* feature (like deductible auto insurance) means that for any year in which benefits are claimed, the insured must pay the first $50 or $100. The *co-insurance* feature means that even beyond the deductible amount, the insurance company pays only 75 or 80 percent of the bill, the insured paying the rest. The *total maximum benefits* feature sets an absolute limit—which can, however, be very high: $10,000 or $25,000 or even more—on the insurance company's liability. Finally, *reasonable and necessary* medical expenses could be matter for argument, but are usually interpreted broadly as those prescribed by competent physicians in the area where the service is rendered.

Reducing the cost of benefits has become a special problem rather than a purely administrative one because it is a chronic problem in the face of rising medical costs. Management and unions share a common concern in this, and have almost identical interests. One public-minded corporation and the union with which it dealt established and jointly administer a foundation dedicated to research and planning in the field. The corporation is U.S. Industries, Inc., which designs and manufactures automation equipment and systems. The union is the International Association of Machinists. They agreed that savings in labor costs from the corporation's own automation measures should be turned over to a Foundation on Employee Health, Medical Care and Welfare, Inc. This foundation has published the result of studies in benefits and costs, which are available to unions and management engaged in health and welfare bargaining and administration of the collectively bargained plans.

To go into the details of the many arrangements that have been tried, altered, improved, found wanting, reorganized, expanded, stabilized, or cut down again—but almost never abandoned—would open up, as the saying goes, a long subject. Those who have a particular interest in the field, or who face bargaining on specific issues, would be best advised to consult the books and authorities that devote full attention to it. References to sources of detailed information may be found in the bibliography.

Death and Disability

This category of hazard follows in close relationship with the preceding one, but the emphasis here falls on *loss of earnings* because of disability or untimely death rather than medical treatment, either as prevention or cure.

In the cosmic scheme of things, death may never be "untimely," but when it comes during a person's active working career it is untimely to dependents and survivors. The federal government's social security program dealing with death and disability also provides old age pensions. A person who lives long enough to draw a pension has escaped the hazards of incapacitating disability and untimely death. This discussion leaves the pensions to be examined later and confines its attention to the provisions for the contingency of having one's life or active working career cut short of normal expectations.

Social Security. The governmental program for survivors and disability insurance is part of the contributory, funded, federal system called by the catch-all title, social security. As part of a total program it provides regular monthly income to eligible workers who become disabled, to widows and dependent children, and may also provide a lump-sum cash payment after a worker's death.

The Social Security Administration, under the Department of Health, Education, and Welfare gives out public information so complete and up-to-date that it would be presumptuous to try to present any of the details here. Standards of eligibility, claims, benefits, policies and procedures are all set by statute or administrative law. In addition to the official documents, the Social Security Administration issues brief, clearly written pamphlets explaining the law and its workings. By reference to one of these, for instance, it is possible for anyone who has a social security number to calculate the benefits he or she is or will be entitled to.

Collective Bargaining on Death and Disability Benefits. Unions and management frequently negotiate supplements to social security death and disability benefits. Such benefits are often linked—as social security is linked—with pensions, since there is an *either-or* character about the twin hazards of untimely death or disability and old age.

A common answer to the either-or dilemma is to combine life insurance (including provisions on dismemberment and disability) with a retirement annuity. The life insurance component starts out at a high figure early in a person's working career, decreasing as the years go by. The annuity component to provide a retirement income starts out low, but increases as the life-and-disability part of the protection diminishes. This corresponds with the needs of the breadwinner and his family. When a couple is young with growing children, loss of earned income is the catastrophe to be feared. As children leave home and become independent, what the parents have to fear is loss of income in old age.

Some plans provide for a cash payment to a widow or dependents in case of a worker's death. The arrangements worked out in this area can take many forms. There seem to be no special problems worthy of note in bargaining collectively for death and disability contingent benefits.

Pensions

A folk song of the labor movement in the depression years expresses the predicament of the industrial worker before the days of social security:

> Too old to work, too old to work,
> Too old to work, and too young to die.
> Who will take care of me, how'll I get by?
> When I'm too old to work and too young to die.

The songwriter seems actually to have had in mind the situation of the Detroit auto worker who, according to a cliché of the times was "on the scrap heap at 40." Only a young man in his vigorous prime could keep up with the implacable, constantly increasing pace of the mechanized conveyor lines. The moment his physical efforts began to flag, he was out of a job and not rehired.

Unionization of the automobile industry gave workers some control over the speed of the conveyor, and seniority rights kept them on the job into and through middle age, but only postponed the day of separation. By general agreement a person aged 60 or 65 is getting to be too old to work, yet with increasing life expectancy, too young to die. To such a person, the question is still pertinent: How'll I get by?

Traditionally, business enterprises granted pensions to executives and to long-service white-collar workers. Some firms—a very few—voluntarily included hourly paid manual workers in their pension plans. Civil service systems, whether federal or state or local, gave pension rights to public employees. Only the hourly paid blue-collar workers in industry, for the most part, lacked comparable protection.

They did not get it until 1938, when the social security system of the federal government came into being. Social security initially provided retirement income after age 65, though later amendments reduced this to age 62 in certain cases. Collective bargaining on pensions followed the lead given by social security. Today, collectively bargained pensions may be said to have in many ways outstripped the model.

Retirement, Survivors, and Disability Insurance. This is a federal program providing cash benefits to retired persons (as well as to totally and permanently disabled persons) who have worked in "covered" employment for certain periods of time. Ever since 1955, RSDI has covered more than 90 percent of all American citizens who were gainfully employed.

Past earnings and marital status determine RSDI benefits. To be eligible, no one needs to work more than 10 years (or 40 quarters) in covered employment, although some who are presently close to retirement age may qualify as "fully insured" in a shorter length of time. Examples of monthly cash benefits now in effect appear in Table 13–1.

In the light of figures shown in Table 13–1 both for average annual earnings and for monthly benefits, it may be interesting to look back and remember that in the early years of the program unions commonly negotiated pensions for long-service employees that would *make up the difference* between social security and a *total retirement income* of as little as $100 a month. Figures are higher today. The use of the government pension as a *complementary* element of a private pension plan has virtually ceased, but it remains the base for pension bargaining to *supplement* social security.

With this in mind, certain characteristics of RSDI as compared with privately financed pension plans need to be noted:

1. RSDI benefits are *vested*. Private plans need not be.
2. RSDI benefit levels reflect a person's *average earnings* rather than

TABLE 13-1.   Examples of Monthly Cash Payments

Average Yearly Earnings after1950*	$923 or Less	$1,800	$3,000	$4,200	$5,400	$6,600	$7,800
Retired worker—65 or older ⎫ Disabled worker—under 65 ⎭	70.40	111.90	145.60	177.70	208.80	240.30	275.80
Wife 65 or older...........	35.20	56.00	72.80	88.90	104.40	120.20	137.90
Retired worker at 62........	56.40	89.60	116.50	142.20	167.10	192.30	220.70
Wife at 62, no child........	26.40	42.00	54.60	66.70	78.30	90.20	103.50
Widow at 60...............	61.10	80.10	104.20	127.20	149.40	171.90	197.30
Widow or widower at 62....	70.40	92.40	120.20	146.70	172.30	198.30	227.60
Disabled widow at 50.......	42.80	56.10	72.90	89.00	104.50	120.30	138.00
Wife under 65 and one child	35.20	56.00	77.10	131.20	181.10	194.90	206.90
Widowed mother and one child...................	105.60	167.90	218.40	266.60	313.20	360.60	413.80
Widowed mother and two children...............	105.60	167.90	222.70	308.90	389.90	435.20	482.70
One child of retired or disabled worker..........	35.20	56.00	72.80	88.90	104.40	120.20	137.90
One surviving child........	70.40	84.00	109.20	133.30	156.60	180.30	206.90
Maximum family payment...	105.60	167.90	222.70	308.90	389.90	435.20	482.70

° Generally, average earnings are figured over the period from 1951 until the worker reaches retirement age, becomes disabled, or dies. Up to 5 years of low earnings or no earnings can be excluded. The maximum earnings creditable for social security are $3,600 for 1951–1954; $4,200 for 1955–1958; $4,800 for 1959–1965; and $6,600 for 1966–1967. The maximum creditable for 1968–1971 is $7,800, and beginning in 1972, $9,000; but average earnings usually cannot reach these amounts until later. Because of this, the benefits shown in the last column on the right generally will not be payable until later. When a person is entitled to more than one benefit, the amount actually payable is limited to the larger of the benefits.

SOURCE: U.S. Department of Health, Education, and Welfare. *Your Social Security.* Social Security Administration, March 1971, p. 12.

duration of continuous employment or seniority. Private plans often make the number of years of continuous service, as well as average earnings during all or some portion of that period, a factor in the formula that determines level of benefits.

3. *Marital status* affects RSDI benefits; private plans usually ignore this.
4. RSDI is *contributory.* So are some private plans, but many are not.
5. RSDI is *funded.* So are many private plans, but some are not.

Collective Bargaining on Pensions. As brought out earlier in this chapter, pension plans are promises made today against the future. Pensions became a prominent element in the pay package in collective bargaining during World War II. Not long after the war's end, when the promises began to come due, both management and the unions, started to take a good look at the subject of pensions. In 1950 the executive council of the American Federation of Labor (not yet merged in the AFL-CIO) set up a special committee to study pension trends, while management organizations and consultant firms analyzed existing plans and made recommendations for the future.

The AFL committee took a rather cautious approach, saying:

Whether or not a pension plan is actually a good idea, and the type of plan that ought to be set up, are questions with no single answer that would apply to all groups alike.[5]

The committee went on to caution against haste, but it would appear that unions—particularly industrial unions, including industrial locals of AFL unions—must have ignored the cautionary advice; for in the same year a management consultant organization had this to say: "To put it rather extremely, very little credit is now given for instituting a pension plan, but vigorous criticism may result from not having such a plan."[6]

Today there can be no question that pensions are more than a trend: They are a firmly fixed part of collective bargaining.

Issues in Pension Bargaining. Management and the unions face the same issues of principle and policy as on other contingent benefits when they bargain collectively on pensions, but standards for determining the substantive arrangements are more readily available. Thus in deciding on the adequacy of a pension, the bargainers do not have to appeal to abstract principle or seek new absolutes, they have concrete reference points: the pensioner's before-retirement earnings as a ceiling, and social security as a floor. The benefit level will fall somewhere between these points. Experience with pension plans exceeds that with any other type of benefit, and in addition, the contingency itself is more predictable.

It would be well, however, to glance briefly at certain issues of pension bargaining as they present themselves under the following headings: (*a*) adequacy, or level of benefits; (*b*) eligibility (vesting; and compulsory versus discretionary retirement); (*c*) finances and funding.

Adequate Benefits. A pension always represents a lower income than the recipient earned on the job: To be "on half pay" is almost the accepted figure of speech for retirement. A worker accustomed to living at or near the limit of his full income has to adjust to a lower standard of living when he retires, even though he will also find some reductions in the cost of living and reduced personal and family obligations. How much less than full pay will suffice? How little would not be enough, even in retirement, to maintain a "modest and decent" living?

One standard that unions use as a base for bargaining is the elderly couple budget of the Bureau of Labor Statistics. Beyond this, they ask allowances for such things as improved housing, locally higher variations in the Consumer Price Index, and items not included in the BLS budget such as car maintenance, essential to an "American" standard of living. Management tends to take a more cost-conscious view. "About all that can be said," remark Couper and Vaughan, quoted above, "is that bene-

---

[5] Lane Kirkland, *Pension Plans under Collective Bargaining: A Guide for the Trade Unions* (rev. ed.; Washington, D.C.: American Federation of Labor, December 1954), p. v.

[6] Walter James Couper and Roger Vaughan, *Pension Planning: Experience and Trends* (New York: Industrial Relations Counselors, Inc., 1954), p. 172.

fits must be large enough to enable a company to retire its superannuated employees without any adverse reaction from other employees or the community."[7]

Pensions are notoriously fixed income, which inflation hits hardest. Keeping retirement income in step with rising costs of living is a chronic problem.

Eligibility. Unions assert that pensions are deferred compensation and not (as management spokesmen sometimes imply) a favor from the employer given out of the kindness of his heart. If the union premise is accepted, the union conclusion logically follows: Pension rights "belong" to the individual and hence should be vested. The contrary premise does not logically preclude vesting, but allows nonvested pensions.

A nonvested pension tends to tie a worker to a company by depriving him of benefits if for any reason he leaves its employ before reaching retirement age. An employee with vested rights in a pension may or may not want to change employers, but if he does he suffers no penalty. Vesting, however, makes pension plans more expensive, often much more expensive. An employer who declines to agree to a vested plan is not necessarily hardhearted, only cost-conscious; and he may have other quite legitimate ends in view. Nonvested pensions tend to cut down turnover of employees and build a stable work force. A trend, nonetheless, seems to be setting in toward vesting of privately financed pensions.

Nonvested plans do tend, indeed, to stabilize a company's work force, but (as they spread through the economy) tend also to decrease labor mobility and reduce job opportunities for younger workers and minority-group workers entering, or seeking to enter, the labor market. In a time of rapid technological change, too close an attachment of workers to their enterprises tends to slow down progress and could result in painful dislocations. The rigidity of nonvested plans thus begins to run counter to the public interest. As a consequence, the weight of public policy may come down eventually on the union side in favor of vesting.

In certain industries, moreover, private plans cannot help but be vested. The worker employed in building construction, clothing manufacture, or the maritime occupations rarely works long for any one employer. If such workers are to get retirement income through collective bargaining, the employers must either offer separate vested plans at prohibitively high cost or join together in multiemployer plans.

Multiemployer Plans. These are either fully integrated programs providing equal benefits and equal employer costs, or special arrangements providing some financial pooling but allowing variations between employers in costs or benefits.

Fully integrated plans flow naturally from the logic of multiemployer bargaining. They commit employers to identical pension costs (as they

---

[7] Ibid., p. 53.

are already committed to identical wage rates). This takes pension bargaining out of competition. Fully integrated plans pool the risks of employing older with younger workers, and so reduce age discrimination; and they pool investment resources and opportunities.

Special arrangements sometimes meet the needs of a number of small companies engaged in single-employer bargaining. As a function of their small size, such companies face higher costs in providing benefits. They find it to their advantage to pool certain risks and to pool funds for investment, without necessarily making either costs or benefits uniform. Here, where employees do not move from job to job, there is no need for vesting, though nothing inherently prevents it.

Multiemployer plans do not attract large firms that bargain with industrial unions, for here they increase rather than reduce the risks. Age and sex distribution of the separate work forces almost inevitably results in the probability that some firms will subsidize the benefits of others. A multiemployer plan of this type would also lessen each firm's control over investment policy and eligibility standards, and weaken the presumed, though nebulous element of employee loyalty to the firm which provides his pension.

Compulsory Retirement. Another issue of eligibility is: Should a person still able and willing to do productive work have to give up his place? On the other hand, should someone younger, with lesser resources, greater obligations, and smaller benefits entitlement have to stand and wait while another who could draw retirement income continues to hold a job at full pay? There is much to be said on both sides, and the age of the person saying it seems to determine which side he argues.

Two demographic facts of the 70s bring opposite pressures to bear on this issue: (1) life expectancy continues to increase and the number of old people in the population continues to rise; and (2) young people, including minority-group youths hitherto all but excluded from employment opportunity, are pressing for jobs in growing numbers, and with growing militancy. The older worker tends to dread the day when he will be "on the shelf," and even when eligible for a pension prefers to go on working. Every older worker eligible to retire who keeps his job by seniority deprives a younger worker of the opportunity to displace him. As a pensioner, on the other hand, this same older worker becomes a drain on the resources available to active participants in the labor force. There seems to be neither a clear-cut and consistent union or management position on this issue. The age of the work force currently active in the enterprise probably gives the bargainers their cue.

Finances and Funding. The actual out-of-pocket costs of operating a pension plan will in the long run be determined by:

1. The amount of money paid to each retiring worker per month or other benefit period.

2. The number of workers qualifying for benefits.
3. How long retirees live to receive benefits.
4. The rate of return on investment of money held in the pension fund (whether held by a trustee or an insurance company).
5. The expenses incurred in administering the pension system.

The employer with an older work force will incur higher costs than if the work force were younger; the company with a higher percentage of women than of men, because women live longer; and so on. Vested pensions cost more than unvested pensions. A benefits formula based on fixed maximum earnings or years of service costs less than a formula allowing unlimited accrual of rights. These few examples illustrate the problem of computing the reserve needed to provide pensions for any specific work force. Making the computation is work for an actuary. The actuary works from data on the number of employees, their age and sex distribution, their seniority, average earnings, rate of turnover, level of benefits to be provided, and a decision on what vesting, if any, is to be provided. Discounting probable employee separations before acquiring eligibility, he estimates the total fund required to pay projected benefits to present employees when they become eligible.

The entire fund need not be established at the time the initial agreement is made; it may take 20 years to accumulate. As money accumulates in the fund, it is invested and begins to earn interest, which is also part of the calculation. The actuary tells the parties what he estimates they will have to pay in costs and contributions for different levels of benefits for the work force being considered.

Methods of Financing. The two most common methods of financing pensions are: (1) insured plans, which arrange to purchase benefits from an insurance company, and (2) trusteed plans which employ a bank or trust company to invest the funds and administer them for the union and management under the collective bargaining agreement. Both types of plan subdivide into limitless variations. Each has its peculiar advantages and disadvantages.

As an illustration of how they work, a brief discussion follows on two insured plans (group annuity and deposit administration) and a self-administered trusteed plan.

The *group annuity contract* is the oldest form of insured pension plan. Every year the employer buys an increment of annuity, or retirement income, for each employee covered by the plan; which the insurance company guarantees. A contract can be written for a firm of any size, with no minimum premium requirement; thus the plan eminently suits the employer of fewer than 50 persons, and is easily vested. The insurance company guarantees the benefits, but not the premium rate, which may be adjusted upward or downward after five years of experience under the plan.

The *deposit administration contract* offers flexible funding. The employer contributes yearly, but nothing is set aside for an individual employee until he actually retires. The pension purchased at that time is guaranteed as in a group annuity contract. The advantages are: (1) more flexible funding than in trusteed plans; (2) guaranteed benefits for retired employees; (3) competent handling of investments by the insurance company's experts; (4) guaranteed integrity of the principal, plus fixed earnings; and (5) small companies can write their own benefit plans. The disadvantages are: (1) low earnings on investment reflect conservative practices of insurance companies; (2) insurance company retentions are usually higher than a trustee's management fees; and (3) higher original costs and lower original benefits than in most trusteed plans.

The *self-administered trusteed plan* deposits money with an outside agency other than an insurance company, usually a bank or trust company, which becomes the trustee. The trustee does *not* guarantee the benefits prescribed in the collective bargaining agreement, but assumes legal liability against fraud or gross negligence. The advantages of this plan are: (1) possible higher income from investment because the law does not limit a trustee, as it does insurance companies, on the extent that they can invest in corporation stocks; (2) some flexibility in funding; slower for past service credits which have been earned by older employees brought into the plan, heavier funding in good profit years, with resultant tax savings; (3) lower *initial* costs; (4) greater responsiveness to changes in benefits and eligibility bargaining; and (5) possible avoidance of certain administrative costs included in an insurance company's premiums. The disadvantages are: (1) possible loss from bad investments; (2) unsuitability for small groups of employees because of higher actuarial risk; and (3) possible inadequate funding because of overoptimistic assumptions about mortality, earnings, expenses, and employee turnover.

To sum up on finances and funding: The great diversity in plans and variety in financing methods calls for the services of a full-time expert to advise the negotiators. Probably the best way for the company and union to make financing decisions is to hire a pension consultant and to get competitive bids from several insurance and trust companies. With the consultant's advice, the principals then consider the bids and decide on the basis of long-term cost, quality of services rendered, and the flexibility offered by the various alternatives.

SOCIAL IMPLICATIONS OF CONTINGENT BENEFITS

The impact of today's pension bargaining will be felt 20 to 40 years from now. In a period as long as 20 or more years, both technological change and business mortality can bring about upheavals and dislocations of employment relationships. Only full vesting, a costly policy, truly protects earned pension rights. Small employers in stable or expanding industries can provide partial protection from the risk of business failures by multiemployer plans. No matter what precautions today's bargainers take, however, only control of inflation would give people on fixed incomes real protection. Collective bargaining cannot control inflation; indeed, some hold it to be a factor in inflation. Some workers covered by pension plans today will not retire before the year 2000. If present trends continue, companies and unions will liberalize their pension plans from time to time—but usually for those who are to retire in the future, not those already in retirement. Management usually resists union attempts to negotiate for retired workers, and lengthening life expectancy rates will probably increase this resistance. Yet the absolute and relative number of pensioners continues to grow. The funds to pay the pensions keep accumulating.

With assets running into billions of dollars, pension funds exert weight in the capital market. Unions increasingly insist on participating in the investment decisions. Future government regulation of pension funds may well extend beyond ethical trusteeship to investment policy and question the propriety of certain types of investment.

Medicare has already influenced collectively bargained health and welfare plans, and since many unresolved issues still surround Medicare, will have further impact. The influence can also work the other way: toward a more comprehensive governmental program of medical care, perhaps on a group-practice basis.

The guaranteed annual wage and supplemental unemployment benefits have also made their mark on economic and social life. They involve people who remain attached to the labor force; thus, unlike pensions and disability benefits, they affect manpower utilization and the labor force. Unemployment remains the greatest hazard. It seems to strike when least expected, and affects the largest number of people who work for a living. Because of its scale, complexity, and unpredictability, employers and workers find it hard to cope with. Only the government has power to mimimize its severity, but there is still no general agreement on what government should do about it.

Collective bargaining for contingent benefits points out the problems and finds partial solutions. For the employed worker it is better—much better—than what he had before, but for society it does no more, at present, than provide experience in dealing with the problems, and perhaps some guidelines for the future.

SUMMARY

Daily and hourly the American economic system creates an abundance of goods and services in which not all Americans share, but which puts within the reach of workers employed in industry, beyond the wage or salary, a means of gaining through collective bargaining a measure of personal security hitherto unknown. The employed worker no longer has to rely solely on personal and family resources for protection against contingencies arising out of the four main hazards of a working life: unemployment, accident and illness, disability and untimely death, or old age.

Governmental programs put a floor under benefits gained through collective bargaining in each of the categories of hazard: Unemployment Compensation, Workmen's Compensation, and Retirement, Survivors, and Disability Insurance.

Management and the unions hold sometimes conflicting, sometimes identical views on the principles behind contingent benefits, and come to accommodation jointly on costs and the level and scope of worker insurance and income-continuity benefits. Public policy accepts this as a legitimate, and indeed, commendable subject for collective bargaining.

The programs adopted so far have had varying impact on economic and social life and on the life styles of those who participate in them. They do not solve all social ills, but may point the way to more fundamental solutions.

QUESTIONS FOR DISCUSSION

1. The text argues that unions and managements have developed certain principles in bargaining over worker insurance and income-continuity programs. Would you agree that principles exist in this field?

2. Are collectively bargained worker insurance and income-continuity programs compatible with a system of social security?

3. Is it socially desirable to permit the development of worker insurance and income-continuity programs which tie the worker to his employer, or vice versa? Are the ties different in different worker insurance and income-continuity programs?

4. How do you plan to provide for your needs in old age? What will those needs be? What contribution (if any) do you expect your employer to make toward fulfilling those needs?

5. What are the unique advantages and disadvantages of multiemployer pension plans? Multiemployer health insurance plans?

6. Some authorities have advocated governmental reinsurance of private pensions, i.e., freedom to purchase any amount of benefits desired from the social security system. How do you feel about this idea?

SELECTED ANNOTATED BIBLIOGRAPHY

This bibliography consists of four parts: (1) General, (2) Pensions, (3) Health and Welfare, and (4) Unemployment Benefits.

General

Burns, Eveline M. *Social Security and Public Policy*. New York: McGraw-Hill Book Co., Inc., 1956.

A penetrating analysis of the major policy questions involved in providing economic security through the instrumentality of government.

BUTLER, ARTHUR. "The Relationship Between Public and Private Economic Security Plans," *Proceedings of the Tenth Annual Meeting of the Industrial Relations Research Association*, pp. 139–45. Madison, Wis.: The Association, 1958.

Discusses possible incompatibility of privately established economic security plans with governmental programs and economic welfare of the society.

LINER, JOHN. "Self-Insurance of Group Welfare Plans," *Harvard Business Review*, Vol. XXXIV (January–February 1956), pp. 95–100.

Discusses the pros and cons of self-insured welfare plans, privately handled, as opposed to plans administered by insurance companies. The author presents his proposed self-insurance program and outlines its administrative features, economies, and possible limitations.

MACINTYRE, DUNCAN M. "Regulation of Employee Benefit Programs," *Industrial and Labor Relations Review*, Vol. X (July 1957), pp. 554–78.

A Cornell professor of industrial and labor relations and occasional staff member of governmental investigating committees on health and welfare programs summarizes the findings of these investigations and proposes some dozen points as guideposts for remedial legislation.

MILLER, GLENN W. "Appraisal of Collectively Bargained and Governmental Programs for Employee Security," in Harold W. Davey, Howard S. Kaltenborn, and Stanley H. Ruttenberg, *New Dimensions in Collective Bargaining*. New York: Harper & Bros., 1959, pp. 117–33.

Analyzes the relationship between public and private employee security programs. Concludes that from the viewpoint of the society as a whole, public programs are preferable to private programs.

MYERS, ROBERT J. "Experience of the UMWA Welfare and Retirement Fund," and "Further Experience of the UMWA Welfare and Retirement Fund," *Industrial and Labor Relations Review*, Vol. X (October 1956), pp. 93–100, Vol. XIV (July 1961), pp. 556–62.

Analyzes the experience of Mine Workers program over time. Plan worthy of special consideration because of financing methods, multiemployer form, and pioneering work in medical treatment of most severe occupational injuries.

SLICHTER, SUMNER H.; HEALY, JAMES J.; and LIVERNASH, E. ROBERT. *The Impact of Collective Bargaining on Management*. Washington, D.C.: Brookings Institution, 1960.

Special attention is invited to the following chapters: 13, "Pension Plans"; 14, "Health and Welfare Plans"; 15, "Employee Benefits"; and 16, "Income Security and Severance Pay Plans."

TURNBULL, JOHN G.; WILLIAMS, C. ARTHUR, JR.; and CHEIT, EARL F. *Economic and Social Security: Public and Private Measures Against Economic Insecurity*. 2d ed.; New York: The Ronald Press Co., 1962.

A comprehensive discussion of the hazards of ill health, old age, and unemployment and the governmental and private programs for alleviating the distress of these hazards.

WILLCOX, ALLANSON W. "The Contributory Principle and the Integrity of Old Age and Survivors' Insurance: A Functional Evaluation," *Industrial and Labor Relations Review*, Vol. VIII (April 1955), pp. 331–46.

Discusses the extent to which the method of financing and other elements of OASI are interrelated.

Pensions

ACKERMAN, LAURENCE J. "Financing Pension Benefits," *Harvard Business Review*, Vol. XXXIV (September–October 1956), pp. 63–74.

Outlines the main cost factors involved in pensions and compares the various possibilities under both insured and trusteed funds.

BARTLETT, H. ROBERT, JR. "Patterns of Pensions Fund Investment," *Eighteenth Annual Proceedings of the Industrial Relations Research Association*, pp. 302–11.

Compares fund investment practice of corporate and multiemployer pension funds.

CORSON, JOHN J., and McCONNELL, JOHN W. *Economic Needs of Older People*. New York: Twentieth Century Fund, 1956.

This book deals with the need of older persons for continuing income. Earnings from employment, social insurance and public assistance, private pension plans, and other sources of income are carefully considered. The adequacy of the various income sources to the economic needs of older people and their impact on the national economy are appraised and assessed.

DEARING, CHARLES LEE. *Industrial Pensions*. Washington, D.C.: Brookings Institution, 1954.

A study of the economics of pension programs, occasioned by the Supreme Court ruling (1950) which made pensions an aspect of "wages" subject to collective bargaining under the Taft-Hartley Act. A good summary of the problem and plans for meeting the various difficulties.

HARBRECHT, PAUL P. *Pension Funds and Economic Power*. New York: Twentieth Century Fund, 1959.

Pensions are charged with being vast aggregations of wealth upon which many have claims but of which none can call himself owner. To remove ambiguity of ownership and to restore line of responsibility, it is proposed that pension funds be treated as deferred wages. This would establish certain rights for the worker and would return to him some of the economic independence the pension system has taken away.

KIRKLAND, LANE. *Pension Plans Under Collective Bargaining: A Reference Guide for Trade Unions*. Rev. ed.; Washington, D.C.: American Federation of Labor, December, 1954.

The basic union source book on collective bargaining on pensions.

LESSER, LEONARD. "Tax Aspects of Collectively Bargained Pension Plans," *New York University Seventh Annual Conference on Labor*, EMMANUEL STEIN (ed.), pp. 617–26. Albany, N.Y.: Matthew Bender & Co., Inc., 1954.

A legal consultant of the UAW Social Security Department discusses tax aspects of different pension contribution bases, termination of pension plans, and pooled pension plans.

McGILL, DAN M.   *Fundamentals of Private Pensions.* Homewood, Ill.: Richard D. Irwin, Inc., 1955.

The general approach of this book is to analyze plan provisions, funding media, and funding methods. Emphasis is placed on rationale, concepts, and guiding principles. The book is not intended as a survey of existing plans.

MURRAY, ROGER F.   "Management Interests in the Investment of Pension Funds," *Eighteenth Annual Proceedings of the Industrial Relations Research Association,* pp. 312–16.

Defines the primary objective of management in the investment of pension funds as that selection of investment opportunities which will maximize future returns and minimize the costs of retirement benefits within the range of acceptable risks.

OTIS, HENRY W.   "Comparing Pension Costs," *Harvard Business Review,* Vol. XXXV (July–August 1957), pp. 58–66.

Comparison of insured and trusteed type pension plans as to security, flexibility, the makeup of costs, and the different factors which can cause different results in the plans.

TILOVE, ROBERT.   "Multi-Employer Pension Plans," *New York University Seventh Annual Conference on Labor,* EMMANUEL STEIN (ed.), pp. 639–58. Albany, N.Y.: Matthew Bender & Co., Inc., 1954.

The Director of the Pension Department of Martin E. Segal & Company outlines the forces which make the establishment of a multiemployer pension plan particularly attractive to small employers and unions whose members have only intermittent employment with a single employer.

————.   *Pension Funds and Economic Freedom.* A Report to the Fund for the Republic, New York: Fund, 1959.

Discusses the implications of American private pension plans for the mobility of labor, and for the concentration of economic power through the acquisition of common stock by pension funds.

STEIN, EMANUEL (ed.).   *New York University Tenth Annual Conference on Labor.* Albany, N.Y.: Matthew Bender & Co., Inc., 1957.

Most of the volume devoted to pension plans. Partial contents.

HOLLAND, DANIEL M.   "The Pension Climate."

COLLINS, ROBERT D.   "Economics of Pension Planning."

TILOVE, ROBERT.   "The Organization of a Pension Plan."

MEUCHE, A. J.   "Past Service Benefits."

MELNIKOFF, MEYER.   "Actuarial Bases: The Interest Rate."

WHITE, WILLIAM K.   "Actuarial Bases: Mortality Tables."

WILLIS, E. S.   "Administration of Single Employer Pension Plans."

VLADECK, STEPHEN C.   "Public Regulations of Pension Plans."

SHELDON, HORACE E.   "Regulation of Pension Plans."

SERGENT, DWIGHT S.   "Planning for Retirement."

HINES, JOHN M.   "Split-Funding and Insurance Company Plans."

KEARSHES, ANTHONY J.   "Method of Funding in Pension Planning: The Trustee Plan."

GOLDSTEIN, MEYER M.   "Inflation and Deflation in Pension Planning."

OLMSTEAD, R. G.   "The Variable Annuity."

BERNSTEIN, PETER L. "The Financial Aspects of Pension Funds; Problems of Investments."

HOWELL, PAUL L. "Investment Management of Union Pension Funds; Problems of Administration and Sources of Assistance."

O'BRIAN, JAMES J. "Investment Management of Pension Plans: Selection of Investment."

FARNUM, C. WADSWORTH. "Pension Fund Investment Media: Bond Investments."

BUEK, CHARLES W. "The Investment Media: Equity Investments."

JOHNSON, RALPH B. "The Continuing Supervision of Investments."

Health and Welfare Plans

FOUNDATION ON EMPLOYEE HEALTH, MEDICAL CARE AND WELFARE, INC. *Studies* (of Health and Welfare Problems). 477 Madison Avenue, New York 22, New York.

Jointly sponsored by the International Association of Machinists and U.S. Industries, Inc., the Foundation has conducted a number of studies of problems in providing the best medical care benefits at minimum cost. Studies cover financing methods for various plans, types of coverage, e.g., medical, dental, hospitalization, and efficiency of various kinds of carriers. Specific reference to two studies are made in chapter on Health and Welfare. Future studies by the Foundation are in progress.

GARBARINO, JOSEPH W. *Health Plans and Collective Bargaining*. Berkeley, Calif.: University of California Press, 1960.

Study of the provisions of hospital and medical care through collectively bargained health plans, with emphasis upon the attempt by these plans to meet important social problems largely through voluntary, privately administered action.

"Hospital Insurance, Supplemental Medical Insurance, and Old-Age Survivors and Disability Insurance; Financing Basis under the 1965 Amendments," *Social Security Bulletin*, Vol. 28 (October 1965), pp. 17–28.

Discusses the three systems, financed separately, made possible by the 1965 amendments to the Social Security Act.

MYERS, ROBERT J. "The Mine Workers Welfare and Retirement Fund: Fifteen Years Experience," *Industrial and Labor Relations Review*, Vol. 20 (Jan. 1967), pp. 265–74.

The article calls attention to difficulties in designing elaborate welfare and retirement programs, especially the pitfalls present in financing such plans on a nonactuarial basis.

SOMERS, HERMAN MILES, and SOMERS, ANNE RAMSAY. *Doctors, Patients and Health Insurance*. Washington, D.C.: Brookings Institution, 1961.

A study of the organization, distribution, and financing of personal medical care. Considers efficiencies of various methods of health insurance and various methods of organizing the distribution of medical care.

Unemployment Benefits

BACKMAN, JULES. "High Cost of Liberalizing SUB Plans," *Harvard Business Review*, Vol. XXXIV (November–December 1956), pp. 69–75.

Outlines a statistical method for estimating the ultimate cost of reducing eligibility standards for S.U.B., lengthening the duration of eligibility, increasing the weekly benefit amounts and other proposed liberalizations of the pioneer S.U.B. plans.

BECKER, JOSEPH M. "Twenty-Five Years of Unemployment Insurance: An Experiment in Competitive Collectivism," *Political Science Quarterly*, Vol. LXXV (December 1960), pp. 481–99.

A survey and discussion of the U.S. unemployment insurance program as an amalgam of capitalistic and socialistic elements. Discussion concentrates on "two most distinctively competitive aspects of the American program— the existence of separate state systems and the use of that tax technique called experience rating."

————. *Guaranteed Income for the Unemployed: The Story of SUB* Baltimore: Johns Hopkins Press, 1968.

An intensive analysis of experience with SUB since the Ford agreement of 1955.

FOX, HARLAND, and WORTHY, N. BEATRICE. *Severance Pay Patterns in Manufacturing*. New York: National Industrial Conference Board Studies in Personnel Policy No. 174, 1959.

Study gives broad general picture of severance pay practices in manufacturing. It also outlines patterns in several important industries.

LATIMER, MURRAY W., Research Director, U.S. Office of Temporary Controls. *Guaranteed Wages, Report to the President, by the Advisory Board, Office of War Mobilization and Reconversion*. Washington, D.C.: Government Printing Office, 1947.

An exhaustive study of guaranteed wage proposals, contains estimates of the cost of such plans and nine case histories of guaranteed wage arrangements.

LESTER, RICHARD A. *The Economics of Unemployment Compensation*. Princeton, N.J.: Princeton University Industrial Relations Section, Research Report No. 101, 1962.

An analysis of state and federal experience during the period 1948–61. Recommendations for improving the system.

McCONNELL, JOHN W. "Supplementary Unemployment Benefits," *Proceedings of the Eighth Annual Meeting of the Industrial Relations Research Association*, L. REED TRIPP (ed.), pp. 167–81. Madison, Wis.: The Association, 1956.

Discusses the impact of S.U.B. on employees, management, and the unemployment compensation system.

STIEGLITZ, HAROLD. "Financing the Ford Plan," *Management Record*, Vol. XVII (September 1955), pp. 350–53, 372–74.

Certainly the most comprehensive, and probably the most authentic, explanation of the thinking of Ford Motor Company executives on the problems of financing a supplemental unemployment benefit plan. Emphasis is placed on statistical tools adapted by Ford for testing the funding of the company's proposal and safety factors built into the plan.

UNTERBERGER, HERBERT S. *Guaranteed Wage & Supplementary Unemployment Pay Plans*. Chicago: Commerce Clearing House, Inc., 1956.

An excellent handbook for the study of G.A.W. and S.U.B. plans.

Outlines labor's demand for the G.A.W., management opposition to the G.A.W., and the emergence of S.U.B. Deals with major problems in the operation of a S.U.B. plan: estimating the cost, minimizing the cost, financial problems in operating under a G.A.W. or S.U.B. plan. Appendix includes full text of Ford, American, and Continental Can S.U.B. agreements.

WICKERSHAM, EDWARD D. "Controlling Unemployment at the Company Level," *Industrial and Labor Relations Review*, Vol. XIV (October 1960), pp. 68–82.

Discusses changes in methods of controlling unemployment at the company level since the Great Depression.

Chapter	INDIVIDUAL SECURITY: JOB
14	RIGHTS AND DUE PROCESS

Besides good pay and working conditions, most workers want some kind of a guarantee of continuity of employment and a fair appraisal of their job performance. As we emphasized in Chapter 10, management needs the freedom to lay off workers when business is slack, to transfer workers between jobs, to select good prospects for promotion, and to discipline for just cause. The worker's desire for job rights and fair play roughly coincides with the manager's desire to avoid excessive turnover and to maintain discipline. Workers and unions recognize management's need for flexibility and efficiency. At the same time managers understand the worker's need for security and fair play. These needs of workers and managers are accommodated through the negotiation of rules for job rights and due process under collective bargaining.

Collectively bargained rules protect the types of work usually assigned to union members and establish the individual worker's *relative* claim to available work. Craft unions and industrial unions follow somewhat different methods of establishing job rights.

Collectively bargained rules for due process establish the individual worker's *absolute* claim to fair treatment in the employment relationship. The worker's claim for fair treatment is the *quid pro quo* for his acceptance of the obligation to perform his job as specified in the agreement or as directed by management in day-to-day operations. Rules for due process are similar in the domains of craft and industrial unions.

JOB RIGHTS

It is important to note that union jurisdictional claims and union security arrangements may play an important part in establishing the individual worker's job rights. Union security is a major concern of the union *as an institution*, sometimes totally divorced from its members. At the same time, the effectiveness of the union's claim to all available work sets the outside limits of what job rights are available to its members.

Craft unionists obtain job rights through custom and practice, while industrial unionists obtain job rights through the provisions of their collective bargaining agreements. The cornerstones of the craft union's program of job control are exclusive union jurisdiction, the closed shop, and the hiring hall. The industrial union obtains job rights through agreement clauses restricting the assignment of work to nonrepresented employees and a system of seniority. Both systems aim at protecting work for assignment to union employees and establishing the individual worker's *relative* claim to available work.

Job Rights in Craft Unions

The craft union's claim of jurisdiction becomes a device of job control as soon as an employer signs a collective bargaining agreement. Under the terms of a typical agreement with the Carpenters union, the employer assigns all of his work "within the jurisdiction of the Carpenters union" to members of the union. An employer who tries to subcontract carpentry work or to assign it to other craftsmen finds that no carpenters are available to perform duties requiring the skills of a carpenter. Frequently the employer also finds that no plumbers, masons, electricians, or structural steelworkers are available either until he reassigns carpentry work to the carpenters union.

Craft workers establish their *relative* claim to available work through the union. When the closed shop or the "seven-day union shop" is operative, members of the union have exclusive rights to all available work on unionized jobs. Most craft-union collective bargaining agreements make little or no reference to seniority. This is to be expected because the typical craft unionist has only an intermittent relationship with a single employer. The craft unionist may seek his own job opportunities or use the union hall as his employment office. If he uses the union hall as his base of operations, and craft unionists frequently do, he may find that the business agent gives job opportunities first to the unemployed members with the most dues stamps in their union books. If the business agent uses this system of allocating job opportunities, the craft unionist carries his seniority in the union. This is a noncontractual seniority system, but it is a seniority system and it works well for workers in industries with intermittent employment relationships. If the business agent distributes job opportunities on the basis of how well he knows the members at the union hall, he is following a less formalized seniority system but it probably reflects the relative seniority of unemployed members. Finally, of course it is possible that the business agent does not believe in seniority and distributes jobs to his friends regardless of their seniority or to the highest bidder. The only check on this discriminatory action by an unscrupulous business agent is the fact that someday he comes up for reelection and an infuriated rank and file can deprive him of his abusive power. When jobs are hard to find, the rank and file probably scrutinize the business agent's allocation of jobs with some care.

Job Rights in Industrial Unions

While the craft union's methods of job control are informal, the industrial union obtains job security through a highly formalized contractual arrangement. Industrial unions protect their total claim to available work by collective bargaining clauses which restrict the freedom of management to assign work to nonmembers of the bargaining unit. These clauses take the form of limitations on the amount and type of work that may be performed by foremen and salaried employees, full crew clauses, and restrictions on the freedom of management to subcontract work normally performed in the bargaining unit.[1] In the absence of detailed contractual provisions, industrial unions are sometimes successful in forcing the continuance of management's past practices in the assignment of work through the arbitration process. Almost universally seniority clauses are the method of establishing the individual industrial unionist's *relative* claim to available work.

Seniority Defined. Seniority is a vast and complicated field of claims and counterclaims by individuals. It confers on its possessor only a *relative* claim to available work or other benefits flowing from the enterprise. The collective bargaining agreement tends to be a fine balancing mechanism between the interests of various groups of workers. Seniority grants certain preferential treatment to long-service employees almost at the expense of short-service employees. In times of business distress, the seniority rights of long-service employees may be diluted by work sharing. For example, instead of 80 percent of the employees with high seniority working 40 hours per week, all of the employees might be scheduled for 32 hours per week. Another example of the dilution of seniority rights is the rather common procedure of compulsory retirement under a pension plan. In this case, the high seniority employee is forced to convert his seniority rights to pension benefits at the prevailing rate of exchange. Retirement of the high seniority employee, in turn, creates a job opportunity for a lower seniority employee or a new hire.

In the most general terms, seniority is defined as length of service. A worker usually does not acquire seniority until he has served a probationary period. Probationary periods usually range from the first week to the first six months of employment. After the probationary period, the

---

[1] A full crew clause specifies the number of persons who must be assigned to a work group. For example, an airliner must have so many crewmen in the cockpit before the plane is permitted to operate. Subcontracting clauses have been very important in the garment industries and building trades for many years. In a 1959 BLS study of subcontracting clauses in agreements covering over 1,000 workers each, less than one in four agreements contained a subcontracting clause. See *Subcontracting Clauses in Major Collective Bargaining Agreements* (BLS Bulletin No. 1304, 1961), 33 pp. Some arbitrators have ruled that subcontracting was restricted by other provisions of the agreement even in the absence of a subcontracting clause. Prohibitions on work of nonrepresented employees, full crew rules, and subcontracting clauses are most important to unions in periods of general unemployment.

worker is credited with seniority equal to the probationary period. Seniority usually is broken or eliminated by such events as discharge for cause, layoffs of very long duration (say, over one year), retirement, or unauthorized leaves of absence. The definition of seniority is completed by reference to the "area" of seniority or seniority "unit." The area of seniority may be as broad as the trade in the case of the craft union, where seniority may be defined as years and months of union membership. Or the area of seniority may be as narrow as the time that an employee has spent on a particular job in a particular plant of the General Electric Company. Between these two extreme areas of seniority is a whole spectrum of "occupational group," "departmental," "plant," "company," "company-community," and other variations. A single worker may possess different "seniorities" (in terms of time of service) in different areas concurrently. Figure 14–1 illustrates various areas of seniority taken from different collective bargaining agreements.

Divergent definitions of the area of seniority take on meaning only when we attempt to apply seniority against the benefits which it bestows on its possessor. We turn now to the problems in the application of seniority.

The Application of Seniority. In Chapter 8 we referred to seniority of protection, opportunity, and privilege. Protective seniority establishes the relative job rights of employees in layoff and recall. Seniority of opportunity involves job promotions and transfers. Seniority of privilege establishes workers' relative claims to wage supplements and worker insurance and income continuity benefits, such as pensions.

Layoff and Recall. Seniority is most frequently used as a criterion in worker layoff and recall. The usual arrangement is that workers with the greatest length of service will be the last to be laid off when business is poor and the first to be recalled when business picks up again. This simple rule poses extremely serious problems for management. The major modifications in the application of the general rule are the area of seniority and "bumping" rights. If length of service were not qualified by a statement of area of application, management might find itself in a position where the high seniority employees still on the job were incapable of performing essential tasks. Because of this potential problem, the areas of seniority described in Figure 14–1 become a critical issue in seniority as applied to layoffs. While areas of seniority determine who is available for layoff, bumping rights are the final determinant of which workers are actually laid off.

Areas of seniority are defined by a union-management compromise within the rather rigid limits established by the work flow of a particular group of employees. From the union point of view, the *ideal* area of seniority would provide the maximum possible security for the senior worker. This would be achieved if the area of seniority were defined as any employment within the jurisdiction of the union regardless of employer, job assignment, or geographic area attachment. For the industrial union employer, this broad seniority area would pose frequently insurmountable problems. From the employer's viewpoint, the *ideal* area of seniority would be defined so as to minimize interference with efficient operations. The best method of achieving this goal would be to limit the

FIGURE 14–1. Illustrative "Areas" of Seniority

Occupational Seniority

Noninterchangeable occupational groups will be established on a plant-wide basis. In case of layoff, the Company agrees to give preference to the employee with the greatest seniority in his established noninterchangeable occupational group. Laid-off employees shall be recalled to work within their respective occupational groups in order of their seniority before any new employees are hired by the Company within the same group.

Departmental Seniority

Straight seniority by department for all employees shall be the rule, except as necessarily modified in connection with classification of tasks. If an employee is transferred from one department to another, his seniority shall be determined in the following manner: He shall be considered a new employee in the new department and should a layoff be necessary in the new department before he has worked in the new department a period of time exceeding the amount of time in the previous department, he shall return to the previous department with accumulated time from both departments. However, should an employee have worked in the new department an amount of time exceeding that of the old department, the entire seniority shall be transferred to the new department and he shall have no more seniority in the old department.

Plant-Wide Seniority

Strict plant seniority shall prevail from the original date of hiring on any job the employee is capable of handling. Employees may be retained or recalled on a temporary basis for special jobs out of line with seniority after consultation with the Shop Committee.

Special Variants of above Types

Plant seniority shall be observed and determined by the last hiring date of each employee. Seniority shall operate as follows: First as to occupation within the department; second on a departmental basis; third on a plant-wide basis.

Seniority lists shall be set up by divisions within the plant. Each intraplant division may include one or more departments. Each employee in the intraplant division shall exercise his seniority in the various occupations within such divisions for which he has been classified by the foreman of the department included in the divisions. The divisions are listed as follows:

(*There follows a detailed listing of company divisions.*)

area of seniority to workers doing identical jobs within a single plant. Under such a system, the worker would have little security in a plant employing only a few workers on each of many different jobs. Most seniority agreements are commonsense compromises of the union's desire for worker security and management's desire for efficiency in production. Industrial unions are able to broaden the area of seniority from the single plant and the single job only in cases where many jobs tend to be interchangeable. In general, industrial unions lack the employment-office type of facilities needed to broaden the geographic area of seniority beyond all the plants of a single corporation. Further, the broadening of the area of seniority to cover more than one employer has generally been vigorously opposed by managements dealing with industrial unions. The area of seniority indicates the order in which employees become available for layoff. The question of whether a particular employee is separated from the payroll remains to be settled.

Workers who are available for layoff within their seniority area are not necessarily actually laid off. Whether they are or not depends upon their bumping rights. "Bumping rights" are the contractual privileges of employees available for layoff within their own area of seniority to displace employees with less seniority on jobs in other areas of seniority. For example, if tool-and-die makers and machine-tool operators were separate areas of seniority and a tool-and-die maker with five years' seniority were available for layoff, he might possess the bumping right to displace a machine-tool operator with three years' seniority. The machine-tool operator, in turn, might possess the bumping right to displace a sweeper with two years' seniority. It can readily be seen that unlimited bumping rights might cause a chaotic chain reaction of job reassignments. We are reminded of the case of a two-plant company which granted sweeping seniority rights as an inducement to union cooperation in the first contract after an NLRB election. One plant was located in Brooklyn and the other was located in Garden City, Long Island. At the time of negotiating the first contract, the company had very large government contracts and was expanding employment and production. Three years later the unforeseen cancellation of several government contracts necessitated a 20 percent reduction in force. Under the seniority arrangements which had been agreed to, it was necessary to reassign some 800 of the 1,000 employees who survived the first layoff. Many workers were reassigned from Garden City to Brooklyn and vice versa. Needless to say, it required several weeks before these reassigned workers could be integrated into an efficient work team. Eventually the seniority provisions of this union contract were renegotiated so as to provide both a degree of security to the workers and needed flexibility to management. However, the management of this company had paid a very dear price for the fair-weather thinking which had dominated in the negotiation of its first union contract. The confusion caused by these transfers may have been partially responsible for further contract cancellations which the company experienced.

If the workers in the Garden City and Brooklyn plants had all been doing *identical* jobs, the bumping experience would have caused no more inconvenience than a longer subway ride or drive for some of the 800 workers who were transferred. But our two-plant company employed its workers on a great variety of different jobs. Most of the jobs were simple, but it required some time for workers to be fitted into a production team.

Because of the differences in jobs and the large number of small jobs in most factory situations, bumping rights are usually limited or qualified in the collective bargaining agreement. The exact nature of the restrictions of bumping rights depends upon the individual employment relationship. Usually one or more of the following restrictions on bumping rights are contained in collective bargaining agreements:

1. The area of seniority itself may be narrowly defined. If so, this means that the original impact of reductions-in-force is minimized.
2. Bumping rights may be declared inoperative for short-term (say, less than two-week) layoffs.
3. Before an employee can bump another he may be required to establish proof that he is capable of performing the job into which he wishes to bump.
4. Employees may be permitted to bump only into jobs which they have previously performed satisfactorily.
5. Bumping rights may be conferred only on workers who satisfy a minimum service requirement greater than the probationary period from the date of original hire.
6. Employees may be permitted to bump only into seniority areas in which they have previous experience.
7. Employees wishing to bump may be required to have a specified amount of longer service than the employee they wish to replace.
8. Displaced employees may be placed in a labor pool where they have seniority claims on new jobs which they are capable of performing as created by turnover.

The foregoing list of possible limitations on bumping rights offers several potential problems in administration. For example, should employees claiming ability to perform jobs claimed by bumping rights be given a trial period on the new job? What is a *reasonable* trial period? If an employee fails in the trial period, is he discharged, or laid off, or given another trial period on another job?

Recall rights of seniority workers pose other serious problems in administration. Do recall rights apply only to the specific job from which the worker was separated? or his seniority area? or any new jobs of which he might be capable? How much and what kind of recall notice must be given to a laid-off worker? What reasons for failure to return when a recall notice is received are sufficient to preserve the seniority rights of the worker who fails to report back for work?

Before leaving seniority and its application to layoffs and recall, it is important to note that most industrial unions insist upon "superseniority" for local union officers and shop stewards or committeemen. A reasonably typical contract clause reads as follows:

The President, 1st and 2nd Vice Presidents and Financial Secretary shall be given top seniority in their occupational group during their term of office if they have three (3) years' service with the Company and it is agreed that they shall not perform duties of their office during working hours.

The members of the Executive Shop Committee, Chief Stewards, and Stewards will have top seniority in the Department or occupational groups which they represent. Such representatives, in order to receive seniority as specified, must have one (1) year's service with the Company. If there is no work in their classification in the departments or occupational groups which they represent, they must, in order to remain employed, be able to qualify for some other job classification within their jurisdiction. Upon such transfer, they will be paid the average hourly rate being paid at the time in the job classification to which they have been transferred.

Such a contract clause preserves union representational rights in the shop even in periods of very high unemployment.

Managements often succeed in trading superseniority for stewards for similar privileges for a group of "key" employees or jobs. Such key employees might include management trainees, setup men, or maintenance experts. A key-employee clause which was obtained in trade for the above superseniority concession for union representatives reads as follows:

Exceptional employees may be retained irrespective of seniority. Exceptional employees are employees whose work in the judgment of the Management and Executive Shop Committee is of exceptional value to the department. The Company agrees to limit the number of such employees to two (2) percent of the total on the payroll. A list of such exceptional employees is to be furnished to the Executive Shop Committee.

The major application of seniority is in the area of layoffs and recall. Seniority provides *substantial* individual security against the uncertainties caused by business fluctuations. The disciplinary factor has pretty much been removed from layoffs caused by poor business conditions. Whatever jobs are available go to the senior workers capable of performing them. Although seniority is also applicable in promotions and transfers, it is generally of less importance here than in layoffs and recall.

Promotions and Transfers. Seniority also provides a degree of individual opportunity when business is good. It not only protects its possessor in bad times, it gives him some degree of preference when business is improving. Thus seniority may establish certain preferences in the area of job promotions and transfers.

Promotions and transfers are differentiated in many collective bargaining agreements. Generally a "promotion" means a job carrying a higher rate of pay. "Transfer" may be applied to any change in job assignment. In an effort to minimize the interferences to production caused by many shifts in job assignments, management frequently seeks to limit seniority preferences in job assignment to the area of promotions. For the same reasons, management may seek to restrict the application of seniority in such matters as shift preference, leaves of absence for vacations, and overtime allocation.

Seniority is almost universally qualified in its application to promotions. Three examples of promotional arrangements illustrate the variety of possible applications:

1. "When new jobs are created, management shall fill these jobs with the most able and meritorious persons available. Present employees shall be considered before an attempt is made to recruit new employees from outside the plant." (Such an arrangement places a minimum of emphasis on seniority in filling new jobs.)

2. "When new jobs are created, management shall attempt to fill these jobs with the most able and meritorious persons presently in the employ of the company. Notices of new jobs shall be posted and any employee on a lower-graded job may apply for consideration. Such applications shall be carefully considered by management. When two or more employees applying for the new job possess equal merit and ability, management shall award the job to the employee with the greatest seniority. In the event that no person applying for the job possesses the required abilities, the company may seek to fill the job by outside recruitment." (Such an arrangement continues to place primary emphasis on merit and ability, but formalizes the rights to consideration and preference conferred by the possession of seniority.)

3. "When new jobs are created, management shall attempt to fill these jobs with persons presently in the employ of the company. Notices of new jobs shall be posted and any employee on a lower-graded job may apply for consideration. New jobs shall be awarded to the applying employee with the greatest seniority capable of performing the job. Outside recruitment may be used to fill jobs when no capable employee applies." (Such an arrangement places near-maximum emphasis on seniority in filling new jobs. In *very* exceptional cases, even greater emphasis may be placed on seniority by granting the senior applicant preference for whatever training may be necessary for him to learn the new job. Such arrangements are found almost exclusively in situations where outside recruitment of needed skills is impossible.)

The foregoing arrangements introduce two new terms, "merit" and "ability," which must be defined either by custom and usage or in the contract itself. The meaning of these terms determine the actual value of seniority preference in promotions.

"Ability" may mean many things: Able to learn? Able to produce at full efficiency on the day of assignment to the new job? Able to produce at full efficiency after a break-in period?

Perhaps even more important than the meaning of the term "ability" is the question of whose judgment shall be controlling in the case of the individual applicant. If tests of ability are used, is management the sole judge of the reliability and validity of the tests? If tests are not used, may management insist that the only valid proof of ability is previous successful experience on the exact vacancy to be filled?

Many managements feel that a merit consideration alleviates some of the difficulties inherent in the ability criterion and improves the chances of filling jobs with satisfactory persons. "Ability" normally implies a *prediction* of future performance. "Merit" is the evaluation of past performance. By adding a merit consideration, promotions become a reward *earned* by efficient performance in the past. It seems reasonable to expect that an employee who has a record of good performance will work out better on a new job than an employee with a poor record and possessing the same ability to perform the new job.

The more refined the criteria for promotion, the greater the difficulties in finally determining the person eligible for promotion. Merit, like ability, is an evasive concept. In many factory situations, formal merit rating has been abandoned because of difficulties in administration. Without effective merit rating, an attempt to apply merit to promotional situations boils down to disqualifying persons with many disciplinary actions in their personnel records for promotion. Obviously, under these circumstances merit is being measured only in a negative manner.

Many detailed studies have been made of the difficulties inherent in merit-rating systems.[2] We may briefly summarize these difficulties as follows:

1. Determining and defining the factors to be rated. The major consideration here is that the factors rated should be precisely defined and valid as a measure of efficiency. For example, a vaguely defined "attitude" factor might, in application mean that the employee being rated did or did not have the same political affiliation as the rater. Unless political affiliation were a major determinant of productive efficiency, such interpretation of the factor would grievously thwart the purpose of merit rating.
2. Assuring objectivity in rating. Untrained raters begin the rating process with widely different interpretations of the meaning of the factors and personal standards of excellency. Further, most of us are rather poor observers of human behavior. We tend to put undue emphasis on the *last* thing we have observed or have failed to observe. Finally, we usually fail to analyze people's behavior. We may erroneously attribute observed low production to "poor attitude," or "low intelligence."

To a degree, these difficulties in merit rating may be overcome by improving the definitions of the factor rated and training the raters. The

[2] For a discussion of these problems, see M. Joseph Dooher (ed.), *Rating Employee and Supervisory Performance: A Manual of Merit-Rating Techniques* (New York: American Management Association, 1951), pp. 192; Michael J. Jucius, *Personnel Management* (rev. ed.; Homewood, Ill.: Richard D. Irwin, Inc., 1957), chap. 17, pp. 295–329; Dale Yoder, *Personnel Management and Industrial Relations* (4th ed.; Englewood Cliffs, N.J.: Prentice-Hall, Inc., 1956), chap. 16, pp. 561–97.

"critical-incident" method of merit rating developed by the General Motors Corporation is an example of an attempt to improve merit ratings. Dr. John C. Flanagan of the University of Pittsburgh spent a year with the Corporation in the final development of this new approach to merit rating.

The critical-incident approach to merit rating seeks to make the process more objective and to avoid the problem of lapses of memory between rating periods. Briefly stated, it merely provides for the prompt recording of all incidents which reflect favorably or unfavorably on an employee's performance. Each incident is discussed with the employee at the time of occurrence and becomes a basis for periodic performance review. If a supervisor has misinterpreted an unfavorable incident, the employee is allowed to set the record straight.

Spokesmen for General Motors Corporation state that this system has substantially reduced grievance cases in disciplinary decisions in the Delco-Remy Division. At the same time, they believe that as a result of the system, seniority has been applied as a major criterion in fewer promotional cases than would otherwise be necessary.[3]

The balancing of merit and ability considerations and seniority considerations in promotional decisions poses a delicate problem for managements, unions, and arbitrators called in to decide grievance cases. The delicacy of this problem is clearly illustrated by the summary of a workshop held by the National Academy of Arbitrators:

> There was no attempt to formulate conclusions or to arrive at a consensus of views, and it would belie the nature and purpose of this all-too-brief discussion to summarize it in such terms. The most that might be done is to note certain comments and viewpoints which, to this reporter, seemed to stand out by virtue of their frequency, firmness, or artistic flair with which they were expressed. They are: (1) it all depends on how the contract is written; (2) the arbitrator is concerned, not only with the correctness of the conclusions of the employer or the union, but whether the answers given by either were addressed to the proper questions; (3) the determination of relative skill and ability should be based on evidence and standards which are reasonable, demonstrable, and objective—but with a suggestion here and there, "let's not carry this objectivity too far"; and (4) in determining questions of skill and ability, the judgments of management should not be set aside where they have not been shown by the evidence to be arbitrary, capricious, whimsical, or discriminatory—or different from our own.[4]

---

[3] Algie A. Hendrix and Byron Stewart, "Appraisal of Employee Performance," *Addresses on Industrial Relations, 1957 Series* (Ann Arbor: Bureau of Industrial Relations, University of Michigan, Bulletin No. 25, 1957) Sec. 6, 15 pp.

[4] James C. Hill, "Summary of Workshop on Seniority and Ability," in Jean T. McKelvey (ed.), *Management Rights and the Arbitration Process* (*Proceedings of the Ninth Annual Meeting of the National Academy of Arbitrators, January 26–28, 1956*) (Washington, D.C.: BNA Incorporated, 1956), p. 49.

Seniority is difficult to apply in the problem of promotional opportunities. At the same time, seniority is the essence of simplicity when applied to the question of eligibility for numerous wage supplements.

Eligibility for Wage Supplements. We have discussed the importance of seniority in determining eligibility for, and the amount of, such wage supplements as pensions, health and welfare benefits, and supplemental unemployment benefits. In addition, vacation benefits are usually related to seniority. In some cases, overtime is distributed on the basis of seniority as are shift assignments. Severance pay is also graduated to reflect the individual's seniority.

Modified though it may be, seniority is almost universally applied as at least a consideration in layoffs, promotions, and fringe benefits. We turn now to several complex and important seniority problems which are of less general application.

Problems in Seniority. In this section we will deal with special problems relating to the individual and his seniority status, seniority and automation, and seniority in corporate mergers.

Individual Problems in Seniority. The accumulation or retention of seniority rights is of great importance to a worker who goes on leave of absence, is called into military service, or who accepts employment outside the bargaining unit with the company.

1. Leaves of Absence. Most collective bargaining agreements prescribe conditions requiring the company to grant leaves of absence, upon proper application, to persons for official union business. Other leaves of absence and the accumulation of seniority for their duration are frequently left to management's sole discretion.

A common clause on seniority and leaves of absence is: "Seniority shall accumulate during the period of an approved leave of absence." Sometimes such a clause is qualified by limiting the amount of seniority that may accrue during leaves of absence for various causes, e.g., illness, union business, personal business, etc.

2. Military Service. Since the seniority and reemployment rights of persons in military service are prescribed by law, most collective bargaining agreements contain a clause similar to the following: "Employees now serving in the Armed Forces of the United States or employees who shall hereafter serve in the Armed Forces of the United States shall be entitled to reinstatement upon the completion of such service to the extent and under the circumstances that reinstatement may be required by the applicable laws of the United States." Sometimes such a clause is enlarged with a statement that, "provided that any employee whose discharge from service is other than dishonorable, shall be accorded the same reinstatement rights as such laws provide in the case of persons honorably discharged."

3. Employment outside the Bargaining Unit. Probably the most trou-

blesome question relating to an individual's seniority rights arises when a worker is promoted to supervision or transferred to a job outside the bargaining unit. The worker is frequently reluctant to risk a new job as supervisor or on other work outside the bargaining unit unless he can retain his security by knowing that he has rights to his old job in the event of failure on the new one. Some managements seek to preserve the seniority rights of workers promoted to supervision as an inducement to accepting the new job. On the other hand, some managements believe that the new supervisor's break with the union-guaranteed right of seniority should be complete, thereby avoiding any possible conflicts in interest or loyalty on the part of supervision. Many unions oppose long accumulations of seniority by former union members promoted to supervision or outside the bargaining unit because they fear that management might seek to weaken the union by transferring seniority-holding supervisors back into the bargaining unit. Other unions feel that allowing former unionists promoted to supervision to accumulate seniority is conducive to better foreman-worker relationships.

The following provisions from an automobile industry collective bargaining agreement illustrate one method of handling the problem:

A seniority employee in a classification subject to the jurisdiction of the Union, who has been in the past or will be in the future promoted to Assistant Foreman, Foreman, or any other supervisory position, and is thereafter transferred or demoted to a classification subject to the jurisdiction of the Union shall accumulate seniority while working in a supervisory position and when so transferred or demoted shall commence work in a job similar to the one he held at the time of his promotion with the seniority ranking he had at the time of his promotion plus the seniority accumulated while he was working in the supervisory position in conformity with the seniority rules of plants covered by this Agreement.

No temporary demotions in supervisory positions will be made during temporary layoffs.

Seniority and Automation.   Unions argue that automation necessitates a substantial revision of seniority practices. For example, an AFL-CIO publication states:

It may be necessary, for example, substantially to revise seniority provisions in collective bargaining contracts. Unions are giving much thought to the need for the broadening of seniority areas—company-wide or plant-wide seniority, for example—to assure equitable seniority protection for their members and the right to interdepartment and interplant transfer, based on seniority. Preferential hiring provisions are being considered, which will require all plants under contract with the union to give preference to laid-off workers in the same industry and area.

Also seniority systems should assure senior employees a full opportunity to qualify for new higher-skill jobs. Such employees should not be passed over in favor of new or junior employees simply because of age or an employer unwillingness to provide the training to enable qualification for the job.[5]

The exact form of the new seniority clauses which may develop as a result of automation is hard to predict. However, it seems likely that if automation creates any substantial dislocation of the labor force, unions will intensify their efforts for greater security for seniority workers. A major difficulty in negotiating new types of seniority clauses may be caused by the changes in automated job content. For example, Professor James Bright of the Harvard Business School states that automation creates an entirely new breed of maintenance technicians. Professors Baldwin and Schultz have suggested that "ability to learn" may replace "ability to perform" as the criterion for selecting workers for promotion to automated jobs.

Seniority in Corporate Mergers.[6] The relative employment rights conferred by seniority usually vanish when a business fails. Corporation mergers may cause the transferring of work between plants, changes in the products manufactured, or plant closures. Such developments may reduce the number of available jobs or change the nature of jobs available. Mergers always present new problems in allocating whatever jobs may be available. These problems are particularly acute when the number of jobs is substantially reduced, two or more unions are involved, the jobs involve nontransferable skills, the places of employment are geographically remote, and reemployment opportunities elsewhere are scarce. The solution to these problems is never easy and in some instances may do violence to workers' job rights.

Three basic alternative methods of integrating seniority lists have been defined by Professor Mark L. Kahn. They are: by length of service, by ratio, or by rank. Figure 14–2 is an illustration of these three methods. Length of service integration treats service with either company as equivalent to service with the new corporate entity. Ratio integration preserves the proportionate position held by employees on the premerger seniority lists. Rank integration, which is seldom used, places extreme emphasis on the actual distance that each employee stood from the top of the premerger seniority lists. Of course, integration may be rejected by placing all of the employees of one of the groups in a subordinate position.

In merging seniority lists, management's primary concern is assuring the position of employees with hard-to-replace skills. In addition, management seeks to minimize the dislocation caused by bumping. After these

---

[5] AFL-CIO, *Labor Looks at Automation* (Washington, D.C.: AFL-CIO Publication No. 21, May 1956), p. 23.

[6] For an excellent discussion of this problem, see Mark L. Kahn, "Seniority Problems in Business Mergers," *Industrial and Labor Relations Review*, Vol. VIII (April 1955), pp. 361–78.

FIGURE 14–2.   Rank, Ratio, and Length of Service Methods
of Integrating Seniority Lists

Given: Company A, 10 employees, length of service from 10 down to 1
year, respectively.
Company B, 5 employees, length of service from 5 down to 1 year,
respectively.

```
                              A—10
         ⎧  B—5 ....................
         ⎪                    A—9
         ⎪  B—4 ....................B—5
         ⎪                    A—8
  Rank  ⎨  B—3 ....................
         ⎪                    A—7
         ⎪  B—2 ....................B—4
         ⎪                    A—6
         ⎪  B—1 ....................
         ⎩                    A—5              Ratio
         ⎧  B—5 ....................B—3
         ⎪                    A—4
         ⎪  B—4 ....................
Length of ⎨                  A—3
 Service  ⎪  B—3 ....................B—2
         ⎪                    A—2
         ⎪  B—2 ....................
         ⎩                    A—1
            B—1 ....................B—1
                              B—5
                              B—4
                              B—3    Bottom of List
                              B—2    (seniority from date of merger)
                              B—1
```

Note: In this example, employees of "A" have been given the advantage of any tie in seniority. In a real situation, this problem is not
significant since length of service goes back to a particular date, not a
particular year.
Source: Mark L. Kahn, "Seniority in Business Mergers," *Industrial
and Labor Relations Review,* Vol. VIII (April 1955), p. 374.

two goals are achieved, management may just pass the problem along to
the union(s) involved. With the union(s) distributing the seniority rights,
the interests of a minority group may be roughly overridden.

DUE PROCESS

A worker's *absolute* claim to fair treatment is analogous to the citizen's
constitutional right to due process of law. Under Anglo-Saxon law, the
accused is considered innocent until he is proven guilty. The accused is
entitled to representation by counsel. His guilt or innocence is determined
by a reference to the law by a judge or jury which is free from any personal bias for or against the accused. *Ex post facto* laws and laws aimed at
depriving an individual or group of liberty or property are invalid.
    The collective bargaining agreement establishes both the law of em-

ployee conduct and the judicial system by which the accused is tried. Unions and managements may negotiate a complex system of rules and penalties. More commonly, the collective bargaining agreement merely states that management has the right to discipline workers for "just cause" or to establish "reasonable" rules of employee conduct. The grievance procedure and arbitration provisions of the agreement create the judicial system of the employment relationship.

The Judicial System under Collective Bargaining

Management is vested with the responsibility for maintaining law and order in the employment relationship under collective bargaining. The initial determination of whether an employee has failed to abide by the rules or his obligation to perform his duties as directed is made by management. If the worker feels that management has treated him unfairly, he calls in the union to act as his defense counsel. In almost all collective bargaining agreements, the worker and the union have final recourse to arbitration in the pursuit of the worker's *absolute* claim to fair treatment.

The Law of Fair Treatment

When the worker's claim finally gets to arbitration, how does the "judge" decide if the worker has been deprived of fair treatment? Like a judge, the arbitrator relies on statutory law (the collective bargaining agreement) or the common law of the employment relationship. If the collective bargaining agreement (statutory law) covers the situation, the arbitrator must weigh the facts and administer justice as defined in the agreement. If the collective bargaining agreement does not cover the situation, the arbitrator must formulate "reasonable and just" laws from the practice of the parties and the mores of the present-day employment relationship. These arbitrator-made rules take on many of the characteristics of a new "common law" of the employment relationship.

The common law of the employment relationship is as difficult to define as the common law of liberty. At the same time, this common law exists and provides very substantial guidance to arbitrators, managers, and unions in providing meaning to the worker's *absolute* claim to fair treatment.

Discharge is frequently called the "capital punishment" of the employment relationship. By examining the common law of just cause for discharge, we obtain an insight on the meaning of due process. Professor J. Fred Holly has analyzed 1,055 discharge arbitration cases. On the basis of his analysis, Professor Holly has formulated eight principles for handling discharge cases which have wide applicability in the arbitration process:

1. Policies must be both known and reasonable.
2. Violation of policies must be proven, and the burden of proof rests on the employer.
3. The application of rules and policies must be consistent:
   a) Employees cannot be singled out for discipline.
   b) Past practice may be a controlling consideration.
4. Where employees are held to a standard, that standard must be reasonable.
5. The training provided employees must be adequate.
6. The job rights of employees must be protected from arbitrary, capricious, or discriminatory action.
7. Actions must be impersonal and based on fact.
8. Where the contract speaks, it speaks with authority.[7]

As Holly states, the application of these principles to the individual case is difficult because of extenuating circumstances which are almost always present. However, the principles do provide a useful guide for unions and management. The principles clearly indicate the need for careful training of supervisors in meting out disciplinary penalties.

SOCIAL IMPLICATIONS OF JOB RIGHTS AND DUE PROCESS

The seniority principle in layoffs probably has worked in the direction of lengthening the average "work life" of employees. Before unionism, discharge for old age was rather common. Seniority means that a worker on the rolls is reasonably free from discrimination because of his age up to retirement age. Of course seniority has no influence at all in preventing discrimination against older workers seeking employment.

The substantial rights granted employees under industrial jurisprudence have emphasized the need for the careful selection and training of new employees. After the short probationary period, the burden of proof in discharges tends to shift to management. To a lesser degree, the employee with the greatest seniority also possesses a claim on whatever higher paying jobs may become available. Although seniority isn't the sole criterion in these areas, and frequently isn't the major criterion, the general significance of seniority is widely recognized and has motivated management to carefully select, appraise, and, when necessary, dismiss new employees before the expiration of the probationary period.

Seniority has probably worked in the direction of reducing voluntary worker mobility. The area of seniority rarely extends beyond the plants of a single corporation. Since seniority provides a degree of job security, many workers are reluctant to leave an employer and forfeit their accrued job rights. Unions have indicated some interest in extending the area of

---

[7] J. Fred Holly, "The Arbitration of Discharge Cases: A Case Study," in Jean T. McKelvey (ed.), *Critical Issues in Labor Arbitration—Proceedings of the Tenth Annual Meeting National Academy of Arbitrators* (Washington, D.C.: BNA Incorporated, 1957), p. 16.

seniority to the entire jurisdiction of the union, but little has been done in this respect in any industry with nonintermittent employment relationships. Substantial employer resistance to this union proposal seems likely to continue as long as each employer insists upon establishing his own qualifications for prospective employees. In the society as a whole, we continue to have substantial worker mobility between employers, especially among the new entrants to the labor market.

Seniority tends to favor present employees over new applicants for employment. It may result in a certain degree of "inbreeding" in a business enterprise.

Of course, the major question about the social implications of seniority is its probable effect on business efficiency. This question is probably impossible to answer. Secure workers are perhaps more efficient than workers constantly worried about their status in the employment relationship. On the other hand, the seniority principle blunts the motivation provided by competitiveness among workers.

.Job rights and due process have implications which reach out into the employment relations of nonunion firms. Although workers in nonunion firms do not possess the right to a day in court before an arbitrator, there is little question that many managements have accepted the broad principles of discipline outlined by Professor Holly above. To a lesser degree, many managements also give substantial consideration to an employee's length of service before laying him off or in determining whether he should have a chance at an opportunity for promotion.

SUMMARY

In this chapter we have discussed individual security measures. Individual security measures aim at giving the worker some promise of continuity of employment and fair appraisal of his job performance. Individual security measures are accommodated to the need of management for efficient operations.

The system of establishing a worker's *relative* claim to available work in craft unions may be highly informal. In industrial unions a highly formalized system of seniority establishes the worker's *relative* claim to available work. Both craft and industrial unionists and their unions as institutions are vitally concerned in establishing firm claims to the largest possible number of man-hours of work. In industrial unions, the seniority system establishes the relative claims to available work. In craft unions, the union hiring hall may allocate available work among unionists.

The worker's *absolute* claim to fair play is protected by collectively bargained rules of employment, the grievance procedure, and arbitration. When the collective bargaining agreement provides only general guidelines to fair play, the arbitrator must rely on the common law of the employment relationship.

QUESTIONS FOR DISCUSSION

1. Is it proper to distinguish between an *absolute* right to fair treatment and a *relative* claim to available work?
2. How are job rights distributed in craft unions?
3. Explain the process by which a "common law" of fair treatment has emerged under collective bargaining. Why do few collective bargaining agreements reduce this common law to detailed written "statutory law?"
4. Does a worker have a "property right" to his job? What is the significance of your answer?

CASES: 17, 18, 19, 20, 21, 22, 23, 24, 25, 26, 27, 28, 29, 37, 38, 39, 40, 41.

SELECTED ANNOTATED BIBLIOGRAPHY

BAUMBACK, CLIFFORD M. *Merit and Seniority as Factors in Promotion and In-Grade Progression.* Iowa City: State University of Iowa, Bureau of Labor and Management, Research Series No. 11, 1956.

   Discusses bargaining rights and grievance arbitration as related to seniority versus merit in in-grade wage progression and promotion.

BROOKS, GEORGE W., and GAMM, SARA. "The Practice of Seniority in Southern Pulp Mills," *Monthly Labor Review,* Vol. LXXVIII (July 1955), pp. 757–65.

   Two members of the Research and Education Department of the International Brotherhood of Pulp, Sulphite and Paper Mill Workers examine in detail the seniority system as it works in the southern craft or sulphite pulp mill.

BROWN, RICHARD P. "A New Technique in Seniority Administration," *Industrial and Labor Relations Review,* Vol. IX (October 1955), pp. 32–40.

   The director of industrial relations, Mesta Machine Company, Pittsburgh, describes how his company set up a system to provide accurate and current information necessary to administer their seniority policies for layoff, recall, and promotion.

CRAWFORD, DONALD A. "The Arbitration of Disputes over Subcontracting," chap. 4, *Challenges to Arbitration.* JEAN T. McKELVEY (ed.) Proceedings of the Thirteenth Annual Meeting of the National Academy of Arbitrators. Washington, D.C.: Bureau of National Affairs, 1960, pp. 51–72. Discussion by MARK L. KAHN, pp. 73–77.

   Based on an analysis of published arbitration awards, Crawford concludes that: "The doctrine seems to be that the company cannot undermine the status of the collective bargaining agent by contracting out work primarily to beat union prices, nor can the company contract out permanent work without compelling reasons other than a seeming desire to reduce the status of the exclusive agent." Kahn discusses the arbitrability of contracting out disputes and emphasizes the bearing of past practice on the contracting out decision.

FLANAGAN, JOHN C., and BURNS, ROBERT K. "Employee Performance Record:

A New Appraisal and Development Tool," *Harvard Business Review,* Vol. XXXIII (September–October 1955), pp. 95–102.

The men who developed the "critical-incident" method of performance review discussed in this chapter tell about its development and operation.

FLEMING, R. W. "Due Process and Fair Procedure in Labor Arbitration," chap. 3, *Arbitration and Public Policy.* SPENCER D. POLLARD (ed.). Proceedings of the Fourteenth Annual Meeting of the National Academy of Arbitrators. Washington, D.C.: Bureau of National Affairs, 1961, pp. 69–91. Discussion by DAVID ZISKIND and IRVIN SOBEL, pp. 91–101.

Discusses the reactions of a broad sampling of members of the National Academy of Arbitrators on how they would handle model situations dealing with (1) notice and appearance, (2) surprise, (3) confrontation, and (4) the agreed case. Ziskind urges that further thought be given to laying down guidelines for weighing the fairness of a hearing. Sobel emphasizes that the worst denials of "due process" take place at other points in the collective bargaining process than arbitration.

HEALY, JAMES J. "The Factor of Ability in Labor Relations," chap. 3, *Arbitration Today,* JEAN T. McKELVEY (ed.). Proceedings of the Eighth Annual Meeting of the National Academy of Arbitrators. Washington, D.C.: Bureau of National Affairs, 1955, pp. 45–61.

A professor at the Harvard Business School and arbitrator discusses the findings of a research study on seniority and merit as factors in promotion. Details the problems in measuring merit and the approach of arbitrators to disputes over merit and seniority in promotions. Paper is discussed by Professor J. T. McKELVEY of Cornell and GABRIEL N. ALEXANDER, arbitrator and attorney of Detroit.

HILL, JAMES C. "Summary of the Workshop on Seniority and Ability," *Management Rights and the Arbitration Process.* JEAN T. McKELVEY (ed.). Proceedings of the Ninth Annual Meeting of the National Academy of Arbitrators. Washington, D.C.: Bureau of National Affairs, 1956, pp. 44–49.

Outlines major contentions of a number of arbitrators on the consideration of merit and ability in disputed cases in labor relations.

JENSEN, VERNON H. "Decasualization of Employment on the New York Waterfront," *Industrial and Labor Relations Review,* Vol. XI (July 1958), pp. 534–50.

Discusses the steps taken by the New York Waterfront Commission to decasualize employment by licensing.

JONES, DALLAS L. *Arbitration and Industrial Discipline.* Ann Arbor: University of Michigan, Bureau of Industrial Relations, 1961.

Based on the intensive study of 19 discharge-reinstatement cases, the monograph investigates each phase of the disciplinary process and considers the impact of arbitration upon future policies and worker performance.

KAHN, MARK L. "Seniority Problems in Business Mergers," *Industrial and Labor Relations Review,* Vol. VIII (April 1955), pp. 361–78.

Discusses the problems of some recent experience in integrating seniority units and evaluates alternative methods of seniority unit integration under the circumstances of a business merger.

LARROWE, CHARLES P. *Shape-Up and Hiring Hall.* Berkeley, Calif.: University of California Press, 1955.

A study of the International Longshoremen's Association and the International Longshoremen's and Warehousemen's Union in New York and Seattle and their contrasting methods of hiring workers in a casual employment industry.

MEYERS, FREDERICK. "The Analytic Meaning of Seniority," *Eighteenth Annual Proceedings of the Industrial Relations Research Association,* pp. 194–202.

Compares and contrasts seniority and the closed shop as individual security measures.

PHELPS, ORME W. *Discipline and Discharge in the Unionized Firm.* Berkeley and Los Angeles: Institute of Industrial Relations, University of California, 1959.

A discussion of the rulings of arbitrators which have produced a definite pattern, consisting of proper grounds for disciplinary action, required procedures, and acceptable penalties and how these factors are qualified by such tests as the burden of proof, firm and industry practices, quality of the evidence, condonation, consistency, extenuating circumstances, and so on.

ROSS, ARTHUR M. "The Arbitration of Discharge Cases: What Happens after Reinstatement," *Critical Issues in Labor Arbitration.* JEAN T. McKELVEY (ed.). Proceedings of the Tenth Annual Meeting of the National Academy of Arbitrators. Washington, D.C.: Bureau of National Affairs, 1957, pp. 21–60.

Professor Ross, Director of the Institute of Industrial Relations, University of California, Berkeley, reports findings of research study on the success of discharged workers who were reinstated on the job as a result of an arbitrator's award. Comment on the paper by SIDNEY A. WOLFF, New York arbitrator.

SLICHTER, SUMNER H.; HEALY, JAMES J.; and LIVERNASH, E. ROBERT. *The Impact of Collective Bargaining on Management.* Washington, D.C.: Brookings Institution, 1960.

Special attention is invited to the following chapters: 3, "The Control of Hiring"; 4, "Union Policies on Training and Apprenticeship"; 5, "Basic Concepts of Seniority"; 6, "Work Sharing and Layoff Systems"; 7, "Promotion Policies and Procedures"; 8, "Work Scheduling"; 9, "Work Assignment and Jurisdiction"; 10, "Subcontracting"; 11, "Make-Work Rules and Practices"; and 21, "Disciplinary Policies and Procedure."

TAYLOR, GEORGE W. "Seniority Concepts," chap. 6, *Arbitration Today.* JEAN T. McKELVEY (ed.). Proceedings of the Eighth Annual Meeting of the National Academy of Arbitrators. Washington, D.C.: Bureau of National Affairs, 1955, pp. 127–47.

Professor Taylor discusses the variations in the use of seniority as a security measure and as an allocator of opportunities between unions and industries. Professor Taylor's long and distinguished experience as an arbitrator and advisor to government results in the formulation of the fundamentals involved in the problem of seniority. The paper is discussed by Professors JOHN A. HOGAN of the University of New Hampshire and CHARLES C. KILLINGSWORTH of Michigan State University.

WIRTZ, W. WILLARD. "Due Process of Arbitration," chap. 1, *The Arbitrator and the Parties.* JEAN T. McKELVEY (ed.). Proceedings of the Eleventh Annual Meeting of the National Academy of Arbitrators. Washington, D.C.: Bureau of National Affairs, 1958, pp. 1–36. Discussion by ABRAM H. STOCKMAN, pp. 37–46.

Drawing on cases and the experiences of several arbitrators, Wirtz discusses problems of maintaining procedural due process in arbitration and the relative weights that should be given to individual interests versus group interests in the grievance process. Stockman generally agrees with Wirtz that arbitration procedures are in the main working well, have no basic flaws, and probably tend to overprotect rather than underprotect individual interests.

PART IV

Collective Bargaining in the Public Sector

The first 14 chapters of this book deal mainly with collective bargaining in the private sector of the national economy. Here management and unions have amassed a great deal of experience and established stable, and in the main, satisfactory institutional arrangements. The two chapters that make up Part IV reach into the public sector. Here management consists of various government agencies and jurisdictions, tax-supported schools and hospitals, states and cities, nonprofit public enterprises, and the like. Employees who in the past held back from unionization are now organizing rapidly, and showing unprecedented militancy. They draw from the experience gained in the private sector, but also face problems and issues unique to public employment. This is the fastest-growing field of collective bargaining activity, and one in which, and about which, much has still to be learned.

THE PUBLIC SECTOR

No employee of government is a more familiar figure than the postman shouldering his mail pouch or pushing his cart along the sidewalks of city, town, and village with a faithfulness and regularity that have become legendary. No department of government touches the daily life of more citizens more intimately. Headed by a member of the President's Cabinet, the U.S. Postal Service is as old as the federal government. Excluding the armed forces, it is the biggest government agency, with employees and a branch post office in every community. Business and industry, education, the public services, private welfare and happiness, all depend on the regular delivery of mail. When the postmen and women went out on strike in early 1970 for the first time since—almost —the founding of the Republic, the whole country recognized it as an event of historic importance.

Postal workers (like other federal employees) were forbidden by law to strike; but they did strike. The same law forbade the Postmaster General to bargain with the strikers; but he did bargain—and so, practically speaking, did the President of the United States. According to law, any postal worker who went on strike became liable to summary discharge from the federal service; but none were fired. The President called out troops. Not many soldiers are trained to handle mail, but many are trained to disperse crowds, including picket lines. These soldiers walked through the lines and did not disperse the pickets. Under the direction of postal supervisors they kept some of the most important mail moving; but the mail bags piled up. The strike did not come to an end until after negotiations with the strikers; and the fact that such negotiations, strictly speaking were illegal, was overlooked as quite irrelevant. The strikers, reinstated without prejudice, got a raise in pay. Congress at last agreed to reorganize the postal service. These were immediate results. Longer-lasting effects may appear as time goes on.

The decade of the 1970s promises to open up an era of militant public sector bargaining and of the spread of unions and professional associations of government employees. Signs of this trend appeared in the late 1960s. Teachers went on strike in a number of cities, the largest such strike being that of 50,000 teachers in the New York City system in November 1969. Sanitation workers (garbage collectors) struck in New York and Baltimore. Policemen and fire fighters struck in several major cities. Air Traffic Controllers, barred by law from striking, "called in sick" in such numbers as to cause delays, cancellation of airline flights, and disruption of schedules.

The public sector, long considered to be outside the bounds of conventional collective bargaining, today seems to be taking the center of the stage. The numbers of people involved would be enough to make this new activity significant, but in addition, the nature of the essential services public employees render and their relation to the sources of political power magnify and multiply the impact of everything that happens in public sector bargaining.

Two characteristics distinguish the practice of collective bargaining in the public sector from its private sector counterpart: (1) measured proportionally in relation to the number of workers affected, collective bargaining is expanding in the public sector while slightly contracting in the private sector; and (2) differences in the market and power relations contexts have produced differences in practice and institutional arrangements.

This chapter examines the practice in the public sector in order to make clear and to account for the differences between public and private sector bargaining. The following chapter deals with specific variations between federal, state, and local levels within the public sector. Before looking at either of these topics, it would be well to get some measure of the spread and extent of collective bargaining in this currently most active sector.

THE SPREAD OF COLLECTIVE BARGAINING IN THE PUBLIC SECTOR

While each year a declining proportion of the nonagricultural civilian labor force in the private sector organizes into unions for purposes of collective bargaining, the opposite is the case in public employment. In small part this reflects the fact that public employees are the fastest-growing segment of the labor force: between 1940 and 1968 public payrolls doubled, from roughly seven to fifteen percent of the labor force. In larger part it reflects greatly increasing interest of public employees in organizing to deal with their employing agencies of government through collective bargaining.

In 1956 fewer than one million government workers were members of labor organizations. By 1964 this figure had increased to roughly one and one-half million. By 1970 labor organizations of public employees had around four and one-half million members. State and local government employees made up more than three million of this total, federal employees the remainder. This 4.5 million figure represents over one third of all full-time public employees at the federal, state, and local levels. In comparison, only a little more than one fourth of all private sector employees are currently members of labor organizations; a decrease of about five percent in the last decade.

The proportional difference is probably even greater than these figures reveal. In the private sector, where union shop and agency shop arrangements prevail, very few workers covered by collective bargaining agreements remain outside the unions. Union security provisions other than exclusive bargaining are the exception rather than the rule in the public sector; hence many employees remain outside the relevant labor organization, but are affected by its activities. In the federal service, for example, labor organizations have enrolled approximately one third of all employees, but gained exclusive recognition in bargaining units employing about one half. If the law had permitted these organizations to bargain for union shop agreements, they might well have been able to enroll one half of all employees eligible for membership, or double the proportion in the private sector. Comprehensive figures for state and local government are not available, but would undoubtedly reveal a similar situation. We normally associate collective bargaining with labor-management relations in private industry. The foregoing figures and proportions show that it is just as much a part of the public sector; perhaps more so. This does not imply that collective bargaining arrangements and procedures have penetrated as deeply into the prerogatives of public as of private management. The institutional framework in the public sector puts obstacles in the way of bilateral decision making on a comparable scale.

How are we to account for the dramatic spread of collective bargaining in the public service in recent years? Can we expect it to continue? Will organizations of public employees strengthen their grip and influence over the issues and decisions in governmental labor-management relations?

Undoubtedly, public sector bargaining gets much of its impetus from the example and the impact of unionization and collective bargaining in private industry. The example provided direct guidance, after the impact had transformed the economic, social, and political environment. Not until New Deal days had industrial unions in the private sector come at all strongly on the scene. They spread explosively thereafter throughout the country's basic industries. The wage bargains they drove, the working conditions they imposed, brought change not just to the workplace, but to the whole society. Accumulation of these changes over a generation prepared the ground for a comparable sudden upsurge in the public sector.

The Union Example

Before widespread unionization, public employees enjoyed many advantages over their private industry counterparts. At a time when an office clerk or factory hand could be laid off or discharged at will, the men and women who worked for the city or the state or federal government had the security of job tenure under civil service regulations, and a system of due process for presenting complaints. While they might earn only a modest income, they received fringe benefits in the form of pay for time not worked—vacations and paid holidays—and contingent benefits such as paid sick leave, and a pension after retirement. Some white-collar workers in private industry got the same privileges as a matter of company benevolence, but without a protective guarantee; and factory workers got none at all. The government set itself up as a model employer. A man or woman with a government job often became the envy of the neighbors.

Earlier chapters of this book tell how the industrial unions, year by year, succeeded at the bargaining table and on the picket line in winning for factory workers one after another of these benefits plus higher and higher wages. The comparative advantages of public employment began to disappear. Even in the area of job rights, where civil service had provided appeals procedures (better than no procedures at all, but still employer-dominated), the unions established grievance-handling systems that culminated in binding arbitration by a neutral third party.

Union-negotiated wages and benefits, furthermore, improved at an increasingly faster rate than pay in the public sector, where adjustments came slowly and through cumbersome procedures. Inflation, especially in recent years, put the public employee, who had already dropped below the income levels of private industry, even behind the steady increase in the cost of living, to which the union raises had contributed. In both absolute and relative terms, the government worker saw himself slipping. He still had job security through tenure, but several decades of nearly full employment made tenure almost irrelevant; and the industrial worker had achieved its counterpart, first in the form of seniority, then Supplemental Unemployment Benefits, and finally, a guaranteed annual wage. As for the various forms of "psychic" pay that go with some jobs—such as prestige—the government employee in America has never been much of an idol to the public.

It is hardly surprising that the deteriorating economic position of public service employees became an inducement to action. The once favored, now underpaid, once docile, now militant government worker set out on a drive to catch up with the times and with his private industry counterpart; and by the same means: collective bargaining.

Civil Rights and Social Unrest

Another environmental factor that fostered public employee militancy (and may hold the key to its timing) was the changing social mood of the last third of the century. Americans in significant numbers began to question, openly, the legitimacy of the social system. The civil rights movement, the antiwar movement, both brought increasing numbers of the young and the old—but most decidedly, the young—to challenge the tenets of the conventional wisdom. The civil rights movement in particular gave dramatic witness to the way organized militant protest could influence governmental decision making. The example was not lost on public employees; indeed, they were sometimes participants. One of the most dramatic events of the decade directly linked public-sector collective bargaining with the civil rights upsurge: the assassination of the Rev. Dr. Martin Luther King, civil rights leader and Nobel Prize winner. King went to Memphis, Tennessee, to support the 9-week strike of sanitation workers against the city administration. After his murder the city signed a labor agreement with Local 1733 of the American Federation of State, County, and Municipal Employees, a union of public employees.

In this atmosphere of questioned legitimacy and authority, public employees found the nerve to challenge the prerogatives of their supposedly sovereign employers. The concept of sovereignty had bolstered the traditional objections of those who argued against the propriety of government's bargaining collectively with employees. The argument was simple: Sovereign power, by definition, cannot be shared. In a time of social change and challenge, public employees found themselves in no mood any longer to accept such simplistic logic.

Political Developments

Political developments in the 1960s reinforced the kind of mass activity and direct action that led public employees to seek bargaining rights. Supreme Court decisions upholding individual and civil rights drew attention to the disparity between the rights of workers in private industry, and the lack of them in public employment. Perhaps even more fundamentally, the court's "one man, one vote" reapportionment decisions in 1962 and 1964 strengthened the position of the public employee. Reapportionment resulted in the election of state legislatures more sympathetic to labor. Laws authorizing collective bargaining for state and local government employees began to come out of these legislatures with increasing frequency after 1965.

Even before these developments in the states, the ball had started rolling in the federal government. John Fitzgerald Kennedy won the presidency with heavy labor backing, and within a year of his inauguration issued a presidential decree, Executive Order 10988, which made collective bargaining on a limited scale the policy of the federal government in its relations with its own employees. As limited as were its provisions, the Kennedy order signaled that times were changing in public sector labor relations.

None of these developments could have made much difference if employees themselves had not taken the initiative. A few vanguard public employee groups such as teachers and registered nurses had already provided successful models for others to follow. Both groups broke long-established taboos by going out, when forced to that extreme, on strike. Instead of universal outrage, they received a good deal of sympathy; and both returned to render their professional services as soon as the strikes were settled, without having brought about the catastrophes their employers predicted. The status of teachers and nurses as professionals undoubtedly helped make collective bargaining respectable in the eyes of other public employees. Besides, it escaped no one's notice that typically no legal retribution followed the successful use of the strike weapon, even by employees forbidden by law to strike.

The 1970s opened with every indication of a rising tide of public sector collective bargaining.

CONTEXTS OF PUBLIC EMPLOYEE BARGAINING

Collective bargaining in the public sector differs from its counterpart activity in private industry because of variations in the underlying market and power relations contexts. It resembles the private sector only in the range of technology on which it draws. Thus, for example, a branch office of the Social Security Administration uses the same kind of procedures and equipment as the branch office of a big insurance company, but serves a different market and must conform to different laws and regulations. Or, for another example, a naval machine shop uses the same technology as a privately owned machine shop, and employs workers with the same skills; but market and power relations differ.

It is these market and power relations differences that set off the public from the private sector. Although it is often hard to draw a sharp line between economic and political power, political influence and sanctions tend to dominate the public sector; economic forces, the private. Public-sector participants in the volatile activities of labor-management relations feel the contraints of political forces more directly than their private-sector counterparts, who operate in a simpler and more stable institutional settling.

The Market Context

According to Dunlop's theoretical framework (see Chapter 1), the budget is the market in the public sector, but the market as normally understood in the private sector is absent. For many reasons, government provides services which private industry is unable or unwilling to offer: a military force, for instance; police and fire protection; education and welfare services; street lights and sewers; highways; and mail deliveries. Government takes on the burden of providing these essential services; and, as a consequence, they become a government monopoly. Monopoly removes the restraints of product competition and substitution that put downward pressure on wages and prices and thereby temper the bargaining strategies of both unions and management in private industry. Competitive pressures in the public sector come, instead, from rival organized publics exerting not buying power but political influence. From different directions these groups place demands on a relatively fixed budget administered by vote-conscious politicians.

Some of these organized publics, like taxpayer's leagues, simply try to reduce the size of the budget. Others, including public employee labor organizations, seek a bigger share of the budget for their constituents. In a sense, therefore, the market in public employment is not so much a market as a political tug-of-war between various organized publics and pressure groups. Each tries to get what it wants for itself from what is available for all from the politicians who control the appropriations. The relative political strength of the rival groups, and not competing enterprises, tempers the behavior of the participants in collective bargaining.

In this free-for-all, strategies and tactics commonly resorted to in private-sector bargaining find no place or work with different effect. An example is the traditional strike and its counterweapon—the lockout. Given the character of public service—that is, the expectations people have of their government and their dependence on it—lockouts are impossible. By contrast strikes, while they are illegal in almost every political jurisdiction, are often particularly effective. They succeed almost in direct proportion to the essentiality of the service strikes deny the public, for they quickly generate pressure for settlement of the strike from affected citizens on their public officials.

This is particularly true in the larger political jurisdictions. The average citizen does not see a direct connection between a high-wage settlement and eventual tax increases. Thus in the post office strike of 1970 public outcry for a quick settlement helped bring pressure to get the mails moving again, with little concern for a rise in postage rates. When the price of a 6-cent stamp went up to 8 cents—a one-third increase—there was only minor grumbling.

Many people see the strike as giving organized public employees an unfair advantage over other groups of citizens. Some regard it as a distortion of democratic political processes.[1] The labor organization's special leverage becomes most noticeable when collective bargaining deals with nonmonetary issues, such as school decentralization, welfare policies, police review boards. In 1970 the New York City teachers' union, for example, went on strike and defeated a citizens' plan for decentralized control of schools in the black ghetto area of Brownsville. The issue was not money but job rights—tenure and transfer privileges of teachers—as opposed to the rights that Brownsville parents and citizens were to be granted by a

---

[1] Harry H. Wellington and Ralph K. Winter, Jr., "The Limits of Collective Bargaining in Public Employment," *The Yale Law Journal*, Vol. 78, No. 7, June 1969.

Board of Education plan to bring policy control of education closer to the needs of the community. Further experimentation along these lines had to be abandoned in view of the effective union opposition.

Lobbying. Because the market in public employment depends more on political than on economic factors, labor organizations have historically resorted to lobbying rather than bargaining to attain their goals. Lobbying is preeminently a form of political activity. A group derives lobbying power from the influence it can ultimately bring to bear on getting a politician elected or reelected. Some organizations of public employees have fared very well by lobbying.

In many jurisdictions, for example, skilled workers have won agreements granting pay scales equal to, or very near, the prevailing wage in their trades in private industry such as construction. Although skilled tradesmen constitute only a small proportion of all public employees, they draw on the political influence of their craft unions in the state and city AFL-CIO councils. No politician up for election wants to be known as antilabor.

Other, unaffiliated employee groups have not done as well. One reason the powerful building trades lobbies have not pushed hard for formalized collective bargaining in the public sector is perhaps a shrewd calculation that they might thereby lose their lobbying advantage. A public employer required by law to bargain in good faith with employees other than skilled workers might not be willing, or find it possible, to continue this favored treatment of the skilled.

Behavioral patterns like lobbying and political action are slow to change, and organizations cling to them. This retards meaningful negotiations at administrative levels, as the same groups gain formal collective bargaining rights in an increasing number of political jurisdictions. Employee spokesmen who are accustomed to getting their answers from the city council or state legislature decline to take as final the decision of an agency administrator or the city manager. They know the ultimate decision-making power remains in the hands of elected officials and legislators, even though not directly involved in bargaining procedures. The fear that employee representatives will appeal administrative decisions and take the final resolution out of their hands acts as a damper on the administrator's willingness to bargain in good faith. Many public employee labor organizations have done nothing to allay those fears. Formal bargaining thus comes close to having bad faith built into it when it becomes just a preliminary to a lobbying appeal or escalation of demands by political activity.

The Power Relations Context

Interwoven therefore with the market context is the context of power relations in the industrial relations system of the public sector. The most conspicuous feature of the power relations context is that the government exercises *sovereignty*. Sovereign power is ultimate power, beyond which there is no human appeal.

In any society, government makes the rules regulating the relationships between its citizens, and arbitrates private arrangements they work out between themselves. Government also arbitrates its own rules; it rules others and also rules itself. Previous chapters of this book have shown how government exercises rule-making power to regulate labor-management relations in the private sector, over which it has sovereignty. As an employer, it also exercises sovereignty over its own labor-management relations.

Sovereignty.   The fact of sovereignty has given rise to an ideology deep-rooted in tradition. It is the ideology, quite as much as the fact, that animated government policy, and so shaped power relations in the public sector. Those who believed in the ideology long regarded sovereignty as an insurmountable obstacle to collective bargaining in the government service. Those who opposed collective bargaining appealed to the ideology. And those who favor collective bargaining in the public sector found the ideological argument hard to overcome.

Here is how it goes. Under the American democratic system, government exercises its sovereign power in trust for all the people. To share this power with a segment of the people violates the trust. Therefore, to bargain collectively with organized public employees—a segment of the people, and a small segment at that—not only violates the trust but is a surrender of sovereignty and abdication of responsibility.

This thinking lay behind early legal and administrative prohibitions on *bargaining* in public employment and the laws still on the books forbidding strikes. Proponents of the sovereignty argument declared that organized public employees, at best, could petition the government in the same way as any other group of citizens. It was, they held, a matter of solemn principle.

Principles often set hard and get harder with the years, but practical affairs can sometimes undermine the ideological foundations. As the complexities of operating the vast network of public enterprise multiplied, government turned increasingly to contracting with private persons and corporations for goods and services needed to carry out the governmental mission. Contracts involve at least a modicum of joint decision making. At a pragmatic level, the government found it harder to justify the difference between the negotiation of contracts and collective bargaining agreements. Besides, some labor advocates pointed out: If government really has sovereign power and can do anything it wants, it can bargain with its employees.

Behind the arguments and counterarguments, it seems clear that managers in public enterprises were just as reluctant, as managers, to divest themselves of what they regarded as their prerogatives as any of their counterparts in private industry. The sovereignty argument merely gave them a convenient shield for fending off demands for union recognition and collective bargaining. It let them picture themselves as champions of the public interest, responsible to all the people.

Even that argument began to lose its force with the accumulation of economic, social, and political change dealt with earlier in this chapter. The ever increasing militancy of public employees and their organizations forced the issue. Administrators had to face the question: Is it more logical to permit chaos in the provision of public services by refusing to bargain, or to lay the sovereignty argument quietly to rest? A growing body of public policy clearly favors the second as the more responsible alternative.

Government as Rule Maker.   Disposing of sovereignty as an ideology and rationale for the refusal to bargain does not annul sovereignty as a fact. Above the government or beyond it, no human power holds sway that can step in, as government does in the relations between its citizens, either to make the rules, or interpret and arbitrate. Government is still the rule maker in bargaining with its employees, and at the same time a party to proceedings under those rules. This is particularly true at federal and state levels; less so at the local level, where rules for rule making come down as a mandate from state legislatures. The state does not identify its interests completely with the interests of local government officials; in fact, it has sovereignty over them.

It would appear then that the number of actors in Dunlop's theoretical framework shrink from the three he identifies in the private sector to only two in the public sector industrial relations system. Public employees and their labor organizations tend to regard this as a disadvantage. It gives them no ultimate appeal from management decisions. The current limited scope of collective bargaining in the federal service reveals how government can so set up the rules of the game as to preclude effective bargaining on many substantive issues.

At the local level, in contrast, a rule maker (the state) stands above local public management. As a consequence, meaningful collective bargaining relations have developed much faster.

Managers in public enterprises may not feel as keenly as the employee representative with whom they bargain about the lack of a third actor; but managers are not unaware of the problem nor have they proved entirely unsympathetic. Impasse procedures (to be discussed in the next chapter) aim at creating something analogous to industrial arbitration. In Dunlop's scheme the arbitrator is a third actor, a "regulator," called into being by action and agreement of the two main actors.

The Right to Strike.   Organized public employees would perhaps not feel so keenly the lack of a genuine third actor if the law allowed them the right to strike. When government denies this right to its employees, as it does in most jurisdictions, it tips the balance strongly in its own favor. Unions in private industry have the right to strike. Their freedom to use the strike weapon as an ultimate argument gives weight to the verbal arguments they offer at the bargaining table. No comparable weight of countervailing power backs up the bargaining-table arguments of public employee representatives.

Public employee labor organizations sometimes have the *power* to strike, as has been shown already, but for the most part they still lack the legal *right*. It makes a difference. It limits the bargaining effectiveness of the organization by increasing the risk an employee faces if he goes on strike, and so inhibits willingness to back up bargaining-table demands. A strike is never without risk for strikers, but workers in private industry do not break the law merely by taking the strike decision. Losing a strike usually means no more to them than getting a smaller raise than they had hoped for. To the public employee a lost strike could mean a lost job and permanent ineligibility for further government employment.

While strikes may have special significance to public employees, the challenge they present to public policy makers is a serious one. To date public employees have violated no-strike laws with relative impunity. Faced with growing disregard for its laws, government must either move to uniformly and vigorously enforce strike prohibitions, remove such prohibitions, or provide an acceptable alternative for resolving bargaining impasses.

To date experience suggests vigorous enforcement is not feasible. First, amnesty for strikers is often a condition for settlement of the strike. Second, the sheer numbers or critical skills of employees often make their replacement quite difficult. Third, the punishment of strikers, especially strike leaders, only serves to stimulate union solidarity and militancy, compounding rather than solving the problem. Also public employers, like private employers, shy away from aggravating the long-term bargaining relationship by invoking negative sanctions in response to illegal strike activity. On occasion too, such punitive action only arouses public sympathy for strikers, especially if sanctions are applied against weaker unions while stronger ones go unpunished. For these reasons, public policy makers are currently looking closely at the other alternatives of relaxing strike prohibitions and providing impasse procedures to reduce the number of strikes.

A recent study of strikes in public employment suggests that a more selective strike ban, to apply only where immediate danger exists to public health and safety, is both more pragmatic and equitable than a blanket prohibition against all strikes.[2] Of course the major problem of such a proposal is establishing criteria used to decide when such danger actually exists. The problem is similar to that experienced in determining when a "national emergency" exists in the private sector. But despite these dif-

---

[2] John F. Burton, Jr. and Charles Krider, "The Role and Consequences of Strikes by Public Employees," *The Yale Law Journal*, Vol. 79, No. 3, January 1970.

ficulties a few states are currently beginning to experiment with relaxing strike prohibitions.

Although there is still controversy as to whether public employees should be given the right to strike, there is agreement that the development of sophisticated impasse procedures are a necessity in either case. The discussion on the design of such procedures centers on finding ways to resolve impasses without creating too heavy a reliance on third parties to resolve substantive bargaining issues—issues which the logic of collective bargaining say are better resolved by labor and management through direct negotiation. In the following chapter, the variety of impasse procedures currently being utilized at various levels of government will be examined.

Separation and Diffusion of Powers.   Other uncertainties becloud labor-management relations and hold back meaningful collective bargaining because of the diffusion of decision-making power within the institutions of a democratic government designed with a system of checks and balances.

Ideally, the legislative branch forges public policy and appropriates money from taxes to carry it out. The executive branch implements policy and carries it into action. The judicial branch stands aside, using its powers only to ensure that the executive does not overstep its policy mandates and that acts of both the executive and legislative branches are consistent with the constitution.

The legislative branch customarily determines general pay levels and other economic benefits for government employees. Administrators in the executive branch exercise varying degrees of discretion on other matters affecting personnel policies and practices. A civil service system in most jurisdictions further limits the discretionary authority of government administrators by prescribing standards and regulations. Collective bargaining thus takes place within three sets of limitations, any or all of which, through lack of coordination, could confuse or frustrate the negotiations.

Civil Service.   The civil service system first entered into government late in the last century. Under the spoils system then prevalent, elected officials made party or personal loyalty rather than ability in the duties of the job, their criterion for appointing backers and followers to positions on the public payroll. When a new administration won election on a pledge to "turn the rascals out," they would carry out that campaign promise, by appointing their own rascals instead.

Reformers offered the novel idea that government employees ought to serve, primarily, the public interest. Instead of favoritism as the standard for getting and holding a government job, they proposed the idea of merit. Congress eventually accepted the reform principles and established the U.S. Civil Service Commission to put them into practice. A few states had already instituted the reforms; others followed, along with cities and other units of local government. Most of them did this by legislative action, but some by constitutional provisions or amendments.

Civil service administration unifies and coordinates personnel policies and practices between various branches of the political jurisdiction it serves. Regulations emphasize job tenure, merit promotion, equity in compensation, and due process procedures for hearing employee complaints. The civil service administration may be likened to a benevolent personnel department of the government. The standards and procedures introduced made government, indeed, for many years the model employer.

Given these protections, many public employees saw no necessity for unions or collective bargaining. In fact, some independent associations of public employees, have opposed legislation that would authorize collective bargaining, on the ground that it would be incompatible with the privileges that civil service has accorded personnel in government service. It is noteworthy, however, that once the bills they opposed turned into law, most of these same associations quickly reversed their position and sought bargaining recognition for the members they represented.

With all the acknowledged improvements that it brought, civil service performance fell short of promises in many instances. Politicians with power of appointment sometimes found ways of frustrating the intent of the merit system. Even when civil service operated almost ideally, as planned, employees began to look on it as a form of bureaucratic paternalism; for in the last analysis, it gave them little to say in setting the rules and regulations. Its standards dealt with the important issues in their relation to the government as their employer, but could do little to shield them, in the work group, from the autocracy of a supervisor who might happen to be a petty bureaucrat. Work-group relations, after all, give tone and set the values in a person's daily life. The more general conditions, over which civil service did hold sway, lost their attraction as compared to private industry when, as noted earlier, conditions in the private sector improved. Large numbers of government employees became disillusioned.

As they turned now to collective bargaining for improvements in their lot, they often found themselves bumping head-on against the civil service regulations. These regulations, they were told, were not negotiable, because they carried out a legislative mandate. Administrators too found civil service regulations hamstringing their honest efforts to bargain with employees. When both sides turned to the boards and administrators of the civil service system, they encountered frustration. The guardians of the system all too frequently interpreted requests for change as attacks on the merit principle. In upholding principle, some of them perhaps— humanly enough—were actually springing to the defense of their own personal prerogative.

Who Speaks for the Public Employer? Private industry experience clearly indicates that bargaining is most effective when labor and management speak, from their respective sides of the bargaining table, with a single voice. Achieving comparable unity on the employee side in the public sector appears to be no problem; but as the preceding section showed, the same cannot be said for the management side. This raises a critical question for collective bargaining: Who speaks for the public employer? And, on what issues?

The answer to this double-barrelled question varies from one jurisdiction to another. But at present, and probably for some time to come, the response to the question, who speaks for the public employee, would have to be in the plural; and to the question, on what issues, complex and confusing. It becomes more confusing when employee organizations deliberately—or even reluctantly, as a result of the plurality of employer spokesmen—play one decision-making level of government against another.

A fire fighter union, for example, may first try to bargain with city executives for a reduction in the work week from 56 hours to 48. Failing to get this concession, they carry their case to the city council, where they may exercise sufficient political influence over enough of the council members to win their point. Failing here, however, they carry the issue to the state legislature through their state-wide organization and its labor union allies. They try to lobby through a bill that would make mandatory on the cities the 48-hour week for fire fighters. Often, they succeed.

Little wonder that executives in local government hesitate to make concessions. They can be almost certain the employee organization will make the concessions they grant a floor from which to escalate demands, and then go on to better them at higher levels. It seems more responsible —though less popular—to say no to the union at the very start. This naysaying attitude, carried over a range of issues, can frustrate even reasonable demands. It is hard to convince public employee labor organizations to refrain from such tactics, and probably just as hard to keep the higher-level bodies from going along with them.

Imagine a similar arrangement in private industry. Suppose the private employer should delegate some bargaining authority to production-oriented line managers, some to a professionally oriented personnel director, while reserving ultimate authority to a fiscal-minded board of directors far removed from the workplace. Imagine further the union's having substantial influence with the board by the possession of proxy voting power. Then let any one of the three attempt to write out with the union a collective bargaining agreement satisfactory to the needs and interests of all.

What the public sector situation amounts to is a breakdown—or at least a common defect—in the delegation of management authority. This weakness may be inherent in democratic government. Until government speaks with a single voice in collective bargaining, it is likely to continue.

Winston Churchill (or some other statesman to whom it is customary to attribute wise sayings) is supposed to have remarked: "Democracy is not a very good system of government; it just happens to be the best man has been able to devise." Perhaps the diffusion of decision-making power, which applies to many aspects of government and not just to collective bargaining, is as much a strength as a weakness of the system, but it makes bargaining more difficult and confusing to the participants.

The Public. A final element in the power relations context is the people. In a democracy it is the people—however indirectly, however feebly—who exercise the ultimate decision-making power. The people enter the processes of collective bargaining infrequently, but when they do, they become the court of last appeal. A striking example of public intervention over a noneconomic bargaining issue came in New York City in 1968.

The Patrolmen's Benevolent Association (PBA) demanded an end to the use of a public review board in the police department's disciplinary system. Having failed to get city executives to remove it by administrative action or the board of aldermen to dissolve it by legislative action, the PBA took the issue to the people of the city by initiative referendum. They won an easy victory.

The tactic of going to the people has also worked on bread-and-butter issues such as pay. In 1968 the San Francisco fire fighters' union, unable to convince city officials that firemen should get parity pay with policemen, took the issue to the people. They won their point.

While public intervention of so direct a nature is infrequent, public opinion remains a constant and pervasive element of the power relations context. Labor and management in the private sector do not have to reckon with it to the same extent. More often than not, when they work out arrangements they find satisfactory, they can ignore public opinion, but not so either public management or public employee labor organizations.

Both sides often appeal directly to the public. Since wages and benefits have fallen behind in recent years, employees feel they have a convincing case, which they do not hesitate to lay before the public. As the gap narrows and discrepancies begin to disappear, they will probably be less inclined to do this. A day may come when public opinion could conceivably shift in favor of management. Wry tribute to the power of public opinion came in the action of New York City fire fighters to improve their public image. The leaders of the union launched a quiet campaign to discourage members from such practices as sitting out in front of fire stations in captain's chairs apparently doing nothing while they drew their pay. This undercut the professional fire fighter image the leaders were trying to impress on the public mind.

SUMMARY

The public sector of the economy has become as active an arena of collective bargaining in recent years as the private sector; proportionally, more so. Differences in the market and power relations contexts alter the content and conduct of collective bargaining in the public sector. Market forces, as commonly understood, are absent; instead, there is competition over claims to shares in a relatively fixed budget between rival segments of the public, including organized public employees. Power relations consequently provide the context of greatest significance for the practice of collective bargaining.

Unique to public sector power relations is the nature of the government's sovereign power. Because there is no neutral third actor standing above government (except, perhaps, indirectly and remotely the people), there appear to be only two actors in the public sector industrial relations system, one with sovereignty over the other. Public employees cannot legally resort to a form of sanction, the strike, that is an institutionalized part of the private sector. Though they cannot strike legally, when they do strike they utilize a weapon unavailable to the competing organized rival publics. No satisfactory substitute for the strike in public service has yet appeared.

The separation and diffusion of powers in a democratic system of government inject confusion into collective bargaining procedures and differentiate the practice from its counterpart activity in the private sector.

QUESTIONS FOR DISCUSSION

1. In what sense can it be said that there is no "market" in the public sector? What implications does this have for the practice of collective bargaining?

2. Why have public employees been almost 25 years behind private sector employees in making widespread use of collective bargaining?

3. Why is the question "Who speaks for the public employer?" particularly perplexing? What implications does the answer have for the character of the bargaining relationship?

4. What role has the concept of sovereignty played in the evolution of the public sector industrial relations system?

Chapter	FEDERAL, STATE, AND
16	LOCAL BARGAINING

The preceding chapter drew attention to the diffusion of decision-making power in American government. This traces back to the Constitution which, besides creating a system of checks and balances, divided power between the 13 previously independent states and the federal government they established. Each of the 50 states now making up the federal union differs internally in some respects from every other, but all contain many political jurisdictions with local constituencies and special powers: cities, counties, school districts, port authorities, and so on.

This democratic structure brings governmental actions and decisions close to the people they affect, but does create diversity and sometimes confusion. In France, for instance, a central ministry of education directs, finances, and controls the entire public school system down to the smallest primary school in the remotest village—and, incidentally, bargains collectively with a national union of teachers. By contrast, in the United States the states set general educational standards and license the teachers, but leave the school districts largely autonomous. If teachers unionize, they bargain with the district school board and superintendent.

This chapter discusses labor-management relations at the three levels of government: federal, state, and local.

THE FEDERAL SERVICE

The federal government is the largest single employer—if one may call it a single employer. Different agencies operate almost autonomously, some because of differences in mission and statutory requirements, others because of sheer size. The post office, largest of all, recently gained special status and has its own rules. The Tennessee Valley Authority, for another example, follows policies quite different from most of the others. In all of these agencies, from old-line departments to the newest special agencies, employees today are evincing a growing interest in collective bargaining.

469

Background of Labor Relations in the Federal Service

Large bureaucracies, almost by definition, are rigid and conservative. With few exceptions, federal administrators have run their agencies autocratically, with perhaps a touch of paternalism. Employee attempts to get some say in their working conditions by union organization and activity called forth from the administrations of Presidents Theodore Roosevelt and William Howard Taft what were called at the time "gag orders." In 1912 Congress nullified the gag orders by passing the Lloyd–La Follette Act that gave federal employees the right to join labor organizations and to petition Congress without fear of reprisal. This focused the activities of labor organizations on the legislative branch of government. It encouraged lobbying tactics rather than collective bargaining. The Wagner Act of 1935, while it encouraged bargaining in the private sector, specifically excluded government employees from its benefits.

In the years that followed, government apologists found it increasingly difficult to justify one policy for governmental and another for private employers. The civil rights movement of the 1960s intensified concern for equal treatment. In January 1962 President Kennedy issued an Executive Order, EO 10988, which for the first time granted restricted bargaining rights to federal employees. After several years of experience with Kennedy's order, President Nixon reaffirmed its basic principles and amplified its provisions in EO 11491.

Presidential action thus shifted the initiative for labor relations policy formulation in the federal service from the legislative to the executive branch. Lobbying in the halls of Congress still goes on—but so does collective bargaining in the operating agencies.

Executive Order 10988

Executive Order 10988 and two later implementing directives affirmed the right of federal employees to join or refrain from joining labor organizations. It set up procedures for bargaining unit determination, and for recognition. It required agency heads to bargain in good faith with labor organizations that succeeded in gaining exclusive recognition through these procedures; this was probably the most important provision of the order. It specified unfair labor practices forbidden both to unions and management, and contained a code of conduct to be adhered to by labor organizations. Many of these provisions were similar in content to those enacted for the private sector in the Labor-Management Relations Act (LMRA) or Taft-Hartley law.

Differences from Private Sector Labor Relations Law. With all these similarities, EO 10988 deviated in several important ways from principles and policies laid down in the LMRA. It continued an absolute ban on strikes by federal employees. It prohibited the union shop, in effect, but provided for exclusive recognition and added two lesser forms: formal and informal recognition, which gave unions consulting (but not bargaining) rights in units without an exclusive bargaining agent.

It left implementation to the agency heads, with staff help from the Secretary of Labor and the U.S. Civil Service Commission. It did not establish a separate agency comparable to the NLRB to conduct representation elections and safeguard employee rights. It limited the scope of bargaining by requiring that agreements must conform to existing laws and civil service regulations; and finally, it dictated a strong management rights clause to be included as part of every agreement as follows:

Management officials of the agency retain the right, in accordance with applicable laws and regulations, (*a*) to direct employees of the agency, (*b*) to hire, promote, transfer, assign, and retain employees in positions within the agency, and to suspend, demote, discharge, or take other disciplinary action against employees, (*c*) to relieve employees from duties because of lack of work or for other legitimate reasons, (*d*) to maintain the efficiency of the Government operations entrusted to them, (*e*) to determine the methods, means, and personnel by which such operations are to be conducted; and (*f*) to take whatever actions may be necessary to carry out the mission of the agency in situations of emergency.

Even with these exceptions and limitations, EO 10988 brought governmental labor relations policy more in line with previously affirmed public policy in the private sector.

Response to EO 10988. Federal employees responded dramatically to the promulgation of EO 10988. Before its issuance in 1962, unions represented only 19,000 employees in 26 units of exclusive recognition. By 1968 they had negotiated written agreements for 1,175,542 employees and represented a total of 1,416,073 in 2,305 units; and consultation rights under formal or informal recognition in more than 2,000 additional units.[1] These figures had added significance in view of the lack of experience of agency heads with the mechanics of collective bargaining and their quite frequent lack of sympathy with the idea of bargaining.

Difficulties were anticipated, since the order had been intended as a transitional policy instrument. In 1967 President Johnson appointed a panel to review experience under EO 10988, and to recommend improvements.

The Review Panel. After extensive investigation and public hearings, the review panel issued a preliminary report in 1968. The major recommendations of the panel dealt with four substantive areas: (1) the establishment of a workable third-party procedure for resolving negotiation impasses, because of the ban on strikes; (2) the establishment of a central authority to coordinate administration of the order and issue definitive interpretations of its provisions; (3) simplification of the kinds of recogni-

---

[1] Report of the President's Review Committee on Employee-Management Relations in the Federal Service, *Government Employee Relations Report,* Bureau of National Affairs, January 20, 1969.

tion accorded unions; and (4) widening the scope of negotiations at all levels, primarily through greater decentralization of bargaining authority.

No action was taken on the panel's findings until the new Nixon administration took office the following year and issued Executive Order 11491.

Executive Order 11491

On October 29, 1969, the Nixon administration superseded EO 10988 with EO 11491. The stated purpose was to bring federal labor relations closer to the private sector model and to standardize procedures among the federal agencies. The text of this order appears in the Appendix to this volume.

Nixon's order gives the Assistant Secretary of Labor authority to determine appropriate bargaining units, supervise recognition procedures, rule on unfair labor practices, and promulgate and enforce standards of conduct for labor organizations. There is no mistaking here the analogy to the powers and functions of the NLRB and General Counsel. Under the old order, agency heads had exercised all but the last of the above listed functions. EO 11491 also creates the central agency that had been lacking before: a Federal Labor Relations Council (FLRC).

The Council is composed of the Chairman of the Civil Service Commission, who serves as its chairman, the Secretary of Labor, and any other member of the executive branch appointed by the president. The Council has the final word on: (1) appeals from decisions of the Assistant Secretary of Labor; (2) negotiability of issues; (3) exceptions to arbitration awards; and (4) other matters pertaining to implementation.

While resembling the NLRB, the Council lacks independent agency status, but supervises a wider range of responsibilities. The most notable of these is impasse resolution in the establishment of a Federal Service Impasse Panel.

Federal Service Impasse Panel. The impasse panel consists of three members appointed by the President. They have authority to take any action necessary to settle a dispute.

The panel has wide discretion. It may recommend procedures to the parties, or issue orders. Without the panel's permission, the parties to a dispute may not resort either to fact-finding with recommendations or binding arbitration which would sidestep the panel. This latitude in the choice of methods open to the panel encourages both sides in negotiation to work out their problems jointly, since neither knows for sure how the panel will act.

Recognition and the Bargaining Unit. EO 11491 also drops "formal" and "informal" recognition as defined in the old order. Experience showed that these forms had promoted factionalism and inhibited meaningful relations. With a single exception, exclusive recognition became the only form attainable under the new order. To get exclusive bargaining rights a union had only to win a simple majority of voting employees rather than 60 percent as before. The one exception gives consultation rights, similar to the old formal recognition, but only at the national level. This permits unions with a substantial following at regional or lower levels, but not enough to win agency-wide exclusive recognition, the right to be heard (but not to bargain) at the agency's national headquarters on matters that would affect their members.

The new order added specific criteria for bargaining unit determination and recognition. These criteria follow the NLRB lead in trying to reconcile the needs and interests of the employees in a unit with the agency's need for efficiency in operations. The new order also made an important break with EO 10988 by excluding units of supervisors from achieving exclusive recognition except where historical precedence had been established. Supervisors are similarly denied these prerogatives under the NLRA.

Finally, EO 11491 slightly relaxes restrictions on the scope of collective bargaining in the federal service. It authorizes the negotiation of contract provisions that would protect employees affected by technological change or agency reorganization. It allows grievance procedures that culminate in arbitration and encourages this way of handling grievances—specifying that when negotiated grievance procedures do not conflict with law and civil service regulations, these procedures shall be the only ones the employees in the unit may use. EO 11491 reasserts the requirement that the broad management rights clause quoted above must be part of every agreement, but makes the FLRC the final authority on negotiability of issues. A liberal Council could thereby further extend the scope of negotiations.

Other Provisions. Not all the recommendations of the Johnson panel appear in the provisions of the new order. That panel, for instance, recommended the deletion of the management rights clause; but it remains. While EO 11491 brings federal service labor relations into closer congruity with the practice and structure of the private sector, the council it creates, and the impasse panel, remain arms of the executive branch of government which is also the employer. Management still holds the ultimate power. Whether federal employees without the right to strike will get what they consider equity from these arrangements depends largely on how far the FLRC goes toward creating conditions for real bilateral decision making over a wide range of issues.

The stage for further developments under EO 11491 had been set by experience under EO 10988. As noted, that order set in motion a massive and rapid unionization of federal employees. Out of about one and one-half million organized federal employees, roughly 9 out of 10 belong to labor organizations functioning only in the public sector. Eight out of 10, approximately, are members of unions affiliated with the AFL-CIO.

TABLE 16–1. Twelve Largest Labor Organizations in Federal Government, 1970

Union	Rank	Employees in Exclusive Units
American Federation of Government Employees	1	530,550
United Federation of Postal Clerks (b)	2	301,155
National Association of Letter Carriers	3	203,928
National Federation of Federal Employees (a)	4	77,099
National Association of Government Employees (a)	5	66,615
Metal Trades Council	6	66,089
National Association of Post Office Mail Handlers	7	44,494
National Association of Internal Revenue Employees	8	38,502
International Association of Machinists	9	32,350
Rural Letter Carriers Association	10	31,134
National Association of Post Office and General Maintenance Employees (b)	11	27,219
National Federation of Post Office Motor Vehicle Employees (b)	12	12,781

(a) Independent unions, all others AFL-CIO affiliates.
(b) These three unions merged in July 1971 with two other postal unions into the American Postal Workers Union, AFL-CIO.
Source: U.S. Civil Service Commission, *Union Recognition in Federal Service*, 1970.

The 12 largest unions currently represent over 90 percent of those federal employees who are in units of exclusive recognition. The largest of these in 1970 was the American Federation of Government Employees, AFL-CIO, with more than 350,000 members and exclusive recognition in units with more than half a million employees. Table 16–1 lists the 12 largest labor organizations in federal employment and shows the number of employees they represent in units of exclusive recognition.

Categories of Federal Employees

The federal government distinguishes between three kinds of federal employees: (1) wage board (hourly); (2) classified, or general schedule (salaried); and (3) postal (hourly and salaried, in a special program).

Wage Board Employees. Wage board employees are blue-collar workers in the trades, crafts, and manual occupations. In 1970, 81 percent of wage board employees were covered by exclusive recognition. They earn hourly wages comparable to private sector rates prevalent in the area where they work. Because the various agencies used different methods of wage comparison, inequities developed. So, in 1968 the U.S. Civil Service Commission set up a coordinated federal wage system. The aim was to make sure that no two employees working in the same job class for different agencies would be paid unequally—a chronic complaint of labor organizations representing wage board employees.

Some agencies had negotiated their wage comparisons with unions. The new program permits this practice to continue, but prohibits its spread. Instead, it provides representation for labor organizations on wage board committees at local and national levels. Of the 11-member National Wage Policy Committee, 5 are labor representatives, and 4 of these are appointed by the president of the AFL-CIO. For the first time this gives labor an official voice in wage board deliberations.

It is noteworthy that the Civil Service Commission did not move to establish this program until it seemed likely that union lobbying pressure in Congress would produce legislation threatening the commission's prerogatives.[2]

Classified Employees. More than half of all federal employees—about one and one-third million—are classified or general schedule employees: white-collar workers in clerical, technical, and professional occupations. They are classified in 18 grades for which, until recently, Congress directly set the pay levels. In 1970 the Federal Pay Comparability Act gave the President authority to adjust salaries of classified employees to make them comparable to private sector rates for similar jobs. The act also established a Federal Employee Pay Council to advise the President on the adjustments. This corresponds to the system for wage board employees, except that the salary schedules are uniform nationally and pay level comparisons national in scope. The President appoints five members of the council from labor organizations representing substantial numbers of federal employees.

Classified employees are the least-organized segment of the federal service, with less than 35 percent in units of exclusive recognition in 1970. Associations unaffiliated with the AFL-CIO are strongest in the classified service. The largest of these are: National Association of Government Employees (NAGE); National Federation of Federal Employees (NFFE); and National Association of Internal Revenue Employees (NAIRE) which has about 37,000 members out of approximately 47,000 who work for the IRS. Substantial numbers of classified employees also belong to AFL-CIO unions such as AFGE.

The Postal Service. As a result of the recent reorganization, the postal service is the most distinctive of the three groups. The post office employs over 700,000 workers. Unionism has always been strongest among postal workers and they have spearheaded the drive for collective bargaining rights in federal employment. They showed their strength in the week-long strike in March 1970 when more than 200,000 walked off the job. The postal reform bill that followed this impressive demonstration grants their union rights almost identical to those of unions in the private sector.

Congress acted speedily in the wake of the strike. On August 12, 1970, the Postal Reorganization Act became law. Article 12 of the act deals with labor-management relations. In essence, Article 12 brings postal workers under the provisions of the LMRA and within the jurisdiction of

---

[2] Robert F. Repas, *Collective Bargaining in Federal Employment,* Industrial Relations Center, University of Hawaii, 1970.

the NLRB. It authorizes collective bargaining on wages and other conditions of employment.

The act still bans strikes, but sets up impasse procedures that culminate in binding arbitration over terms of an agreement that are in dispute. It also bans the union shop, but appears to permit the agency shop.

Postal employees are more thoroughly unionized than either wage board or classified employees, with 87 percent in units of exclusive recognition. Almost all of these are in AFL-CIO unions. The traditional form of organization has been by what the postal workers called "crafts" —clerks, carriers, mail handlers, motor vehicle employees, and maintenance employees—but these separate units have taken steps to amalgamate into a single union. In May 1971 four of the former crafts and one rival industrial union, the National Postal Union, merged to form the American Postal Workers Union.

This new amalgamation will represent the vast majority of postal employees. If the National Association of Letter Carriers should also join, the resulting organization will represent virtually all postal employees.

Extent of Bargaining

The extent of bargaining varies greatly in different federal agencies. It is extensive in the TVA, the postal service, and the Departments of Defense, Labor, and Treasury, also in the General Services and the Veterans Administration. At the other end of the scale, it is minimal in the Civil Service and Atomic Energy Commissions and practically nonexistent in the State Department.

Table 16–2 lists the 10 federal agencies in which more than 20,000 workers were in units of exclusive recognition in 1970.

Except in a few agencies (most notably the postal service) collective

TABLE 16–2. Exclusive Recognition by Agency, 1970

Agency	Number of Employees	Percent of Total Employees in Agency
Postal Service	625,730	87
Navy Department	195,555	58
Department of the Army	173,951	47
Department of the Air Force	157,385	58
Veterans Administration	104,313	61
Treasury Department	55,435	62
Department of Health, Education and Welfare	46,351	42
Defense Supply Agency	25,709	49
National Guard Bureau	22,525	54
Tennessee Valley Authority	21,914	91

Source: U.S. Civil Service Commission. *Union Recognition in the Federal Services,* 1970.

bargaining is decentralized. Most agreements cover only a local installation or activity, and deal mainly with working conditions because of the narrow scope EO 11491 permits as subjects of negotiation. Items include hours of work, rest periods, parking, work clothing, safety, discipline, grievance procedures, union prerogatives—that is, the rights of union representatives in agreement administration—and provisions for impasse resolution. The Department of the Army estimates that there are more than 100 substantive items open for negotiation, yet most agreements contain only from 3 to 36. A survey of agreements in the General Services Administration disclosed a similar paucity of items. This does not mean that there were not plenty of substantive issues to bargain about.[3]

Local level bargaining has to steer clear of agency-wide policy and regulations; hence it cannot alter agency personnel practices. Wages and nonwage economic benefits furthermore (except in the postal service) are outside the bounds of collective bargaining. In addition, civil service rules that regulate the most important conditions of employment also lie outside the scope of bargaining.

Somewhat in recompense, wage board and classified employees have gained representation on the councils that set pay levels; and the executive branch has gained greater freedom to establish the basic scales as well as to adjust inequities.

Some notion of the structure of collective bargaining in the federal service arises out of a BLS study of 685 nonpostal agreements covering more than a million employees in 1968.[4]

Structure of Bargaining. Unions of the AFL-CIO negotiated agreements for 97 percent of the employees covered in the BLS survey, with the AFGE accounting for almost half of these. By size of bargaining unit, 63 percent had over 1,000 employees; 18 percent, from 501–1,000. The remainder had fewer than 500 employees per unit. A majority of all these units contained both wage board and classified employees. A similar survey in 1964 had showed mixed units in only 34 percent. A trend toward bargaining based on the industrial union model seems clear.

Grievance Procedures. A great deal of federal service bargaining has focused on trying to get satisfactory grievance procedures. More than half the agreements in the BLS survey provide grievance systems separate from civil service procedures, but give grievants the right to choose either channel. They specify the grounds for grievances and the steps for adjusting them and, almost without exception, provide advisory arbitration as the final step. Civil service data indicate that 62 grievances reached the advisory arbitration stage in 1967–68. They concerned mainly

---

[3] Michael H. Moskow, J. Joseph Loewenberg, and Edward C. Koziara, *Collective Bargaining in Public Employment* New York: (Random House, 1970), p. 57.

[4] *Negotiation Impasse, Grievance and Arbitration in Federal Agreements,* Bulletin 1661, Bureau of Labor Statistics, 1970.

discipline, promotion procedures, and demands for overtime pay. With few exceptions, agency heads accepted the advisory decisions.

Strikes. Strikes have been rare in the federal service. The BLS study records only 8 work stoppages, involving 5,870 federal employees, in the 10 years, 1958–68.

The postal strike of 1970 was the first major walkout. The same year, air traffic controllers carried out a job action that was only technically not a strike. They "called in sick" in large numbers. Their union, the Professional Air Traffic Controllers Association (PATCO), demanded higher wages and the hiring of more personnel. They carried their case to the public and to Congress by publishing a report alleging that insufficient manpower in traffic control towers at the airports had made flying unsafe. This PATCO appeal illustrates the indirect political pressure tactics that unions in the public sector sometimes adopt. The Hatch Act of 1939 prohibits public employees from direct involvement in political party activities and political campaigns.

Impasse Procedures. Because federal employees are forbidden to strike, their unions have tried hard to get satisfactory impasse procedures for deadlocked contract talks. Both of the presidential orders permit the negotiation of such procedures, as long as they stop short of arbitration. Most agreements consequently contain impasse provisions which refer disputed issues to higher authority for binding decision. Another popular arrangement is fact-finding without public disclosure or recommendations. A few specify only mediation.

Regardless of the procedure adopted in a particular agreement, none provide for appeal to a neutral third party. Widespread and growing dissatisfaction with this situation under EO 10988 led to the creation in EO 11491 of the Federal Service Impasse Panel (FSIP). The FSIP does provide an appeals body, but not a neutral or independent one: The President appoints its three members.

The new postal legislation, on the other hand, gives both sides access to final and binding arbitration, if they wish it, within 180 days of a declared deadlock. Mediation and fact-finding must precede. Arbitration is tripartite, with the Federal Mediation and Conciliation Service supplying a roster of arbitrators from which each party selects one member. These two then select a third. If they cannot agree, the conciliation service makes the selection. At first sight, this seems to be as near the private sector practice as the government could possibly offer.

Arbitration versus the Right to Strike. Arbitration in the private sector deals primarily with grievances and agreement interpretation. Unions rarely resort to it in disputes over substantive issues; they have the right to strike. The postal service arrangement substitutes arbitration for the right to strike.

It will be instructive as time goes on to see whether federal employees come to prefer arbitration on the postal service model or the impasse procedures of EO 11491; also, whether either arrangement prevents strikes. Will postal management hang back in bargaining for fear an arbitration board will only add to what they might agree to grant? Will the procedures of EO 11491 really prove to be impartial?

Experience under these two procedures may provide clues to whether any third-party system of conflict resolution can take the place of the strike weapon. This would have implications for the private sector, particularly as it might apply to national emergency strikes.

In Summary

The practice of collective bargaining is spreading rapidly, though unevenly, in the federal service. It approaches the private sector model most closely in the postal service. Wage board employees are strongly organized, but bargain mainly at the local level where agency policies and the provisions of EO 11491 limit the scope of their agreements. Classified employees lag behind the other two categories, but nonetheless show greater interest in collective bargaining than their white-collar counterparts in the private sector. They face the same limitations on the scope of bargaining allowed them as the wage board employees.

It appears almost certain that various pressures will soon force the federal government to liberalize its labor relations policies for wage board and classified employees, more along the lines of the postal service model. Until this occurs there will not be true bilateral decision making over the important substantive issues of working conditions and pay. As it does occur, pressure will also build up over the rule-for-rule-making issue of the federal employee's right to strike.

STATE AND LOCAL PUBLIC SERVICE

State and local governments collectively employ almost eight million full-time employees. These people work for states, counties, cities, townships, school districts, special districts, "authorities," and similar entities. State, school district, and municipal payrolls each accounts for one fourth of the full-time employees; the remaining one-fourth spread out among other local government jurisdictions.

Public labor-management relations policy for state and local government employees comes mainly from legislation rather than executive order as in the federal service. In the degree to which it authorizes collective bargaining, and in terms of the groups covered, it varies greatly among the 50 states and their over 90,000 political subdivisions. While a few states have laws covering virtually all state and local governments, others cover only local government employees, and sometimes only select groups of these, such as teachers and fire fighters. By 1969 more than half the states had some kind of collective bargaining legislation, most of it enacted since 1965.

State Legislation

Some 15 states require public employers, by law, to bargain in good faith. Several of these, notably New York, Wisconsin, Michigan, and Massachusetts have established comprehensive procedures and administrative agencies analogous to those set up by the LMRA to regulate collective bargaining in the private sector. Four states, including California and Minnesota, make it mandatory only for public employers to "meet and confer" with employee organizations rather than bargain. In this they resemble the consultation rights provisions in the federal service. Several other states have moved to permit, but not require, bargaining. Thus far about 20 have made no clear policy declaration at all.[5] In some of these states, however, such as Ohio and Illinois, many local authorities have voluntarily established collective bargaining relations with their employees. All states prohibit strikes in public employment, except Hawaii, Vermont, and Pennsylvania, which grant a limited right to strike to some employees.

Public Employee Unions

In the favorable legal climate of the late 1960s, increasing numbers of state and local employees organized to bargain collectively with their employers. By 1970 more than one third of them were members of labor organizations. These organizations fall into two categories of roughly equal size: AFL-CIO unions; and other unions and independent employee associations. The unions concentrate primarily on collective bargaining; the associations sometimes have other interests as well.

Teachers and nurses in particular, and other professional employees, bargain for wages and working conditions, but also show concern for licensing, training, certification, and other professional matters. Unions try mainly to get written agreements and represent their members at the workplace; the associations often prefer lobbying and seek to use existing civil service procedures. Unions typically charge higher dues and hire more staff to service their members. They are also more militant, willing to strike if need be to enforce their demands.

In recent years, however, differences between unions and associations have diminished. More employee associations are acting like unions, particularly when they actively compete for members and representation rights, as in education. Many associations which used to oppose collective

---

[5] *Labor Management Policies for State and Local Governments,* Advisory Commission on Intergovernmental Relations, Washington, D.C., September 1969.

bargaining now support it. Some have even merged with the unions against which they formerly competed. Table 16–3 gives a broad view of the major organizations currently representing state and local government employees.

The AFSCME. The American Federation of State, County and Municipal Employees (AFSCME) is by far the largest union in state and local government. It is currently growing faster than any other union in

TABLE 16–3. Membership in Unions and Associations in State and Local Government, 1969–70

Unions		Members
American Federation of State, County and Municipal Employees, (AFSCME)		441,000
American Federation of Teachers (AFT)		165,000
International Association of Fire Fighters (IAFF)		132,000
Service Employees International Union (SEIU)		116,000
Teamsters		57,000
Laborers International Union (LIU)		24,000
Other Unions		125,000
	Union Total	1,060,000
Single Occupation Associations		
National Education Association		1,062,000
International Conference of Policy Associations		142,000
Fraternal Order of Police		81,000
American Nurses Association		37,000
Multiple Occupation Associations		
New York Civil Service Employees Association		175,000
California State Employees Association		114,000
Other State Employee Associations		409,000
Other Local Employee Associations		300,000
	Association Total	2,240,000
	Grand Total	3,300,000

Source: Bureau of Labor Statistics, *Directory of National and International Unions in the United States 1969, 1970;* and *Newsletter of the National League of Cities,* July 1971, Vol. 2, Number 7, article by Jack Stieber, pp. 1, 2.

the United States, having more than doubled its membership in the past six years. It represents workers in a wide range of occupations from garbage collectors to psychiatrists. Its industrial union organizing policy often brings it into conflict with other AFL-CIO unions, usually those of craftsmen which have recently tried to organize public employees.

The organizational vigor of AFSCME stems in large part from the leadership of Jerry Wurf, elected president in 1964. The previous administration had operated more in the traditional way by lobbying and trying to reform civil service procedures.

Under Wurf's presidency, AFSCME shifted its policy to demand bargaining rights equal to those that unions enjoy in the private sector including the right to strike. The 1970 union conventions removed a constitutional ban on strikes by police members. Locals of AFSCME have, in fact, conducted many strikes in recent years.

The almost half-million AFSCME members are distributed in some 1,900 local and 72 district councils. Current policy calls for two councils in each state, one for local and another for state employees. District councils exercise certain authority over the constituent locals. In some instances, as in Milwaukee, locals bargain jointly through the district council, often over the protest of some locals which would prefer to bargain separately.

The AFSCME takes a progressive stand on civil rights. Blacks and other minorities make up more than a third of the membership. The union practices what it preaches: Jerry Wurf marched arm in arm with civil rights leader Martin Luther King in support of the striking garbage workers, black members of an AFSCME local in Memphis, on the occasion already noted. This strong civil rights tie has often made it harder for the union to organize some of the more conservative public employees, like policemen.

The American Federation of Teachers.   The American Federation of Teachers is another vanguard union in the public sector. In existence since 1919, it currently represents around 165,000 classroom teachers in 853 local unions. Big city locals in New York, Chicago, Detroit, Philadelphia, and Cleveland make up the bulk of the membership, with smaller locals scattered widely throughout the country. Teachers in Portland, Oregon, for instance, chose the AFT as their bargaining agent in a city-wide election in October 1971.

From its beginnings, the AFT has championed the classroom teacher, and excluded school administrators. It claims—and practices—the right to strike.

Fire Fighters and Others.   The International Association of Fire Fighters (IAFF) currently represents over 80 percent of the full-time paid fire fighters in the United States. Like AFSCME, the IAFF has become more militant in claiming collective bargaining rights. At its 1968 convention, the IAFF removed a 50-year-old voluntary ban on strikes; and in recent years a number of IAFF affiliates have actually gone out on strike. Uniquely, the IAFF enrolls supervisory personnel in the union, often including the chief of the fire department. This arises from the strong occupational camaraderie of the fire service.

Public employees make up roughly one fourth of the membership of the Service Employees International Union (SEIU)—the bulk of them are low-skilled workers in the health and education fields. This large, industrially organized union is most active in public employment in California. Next most active is the Laborers International Union (LIU), also affiliated with the AFL-CIO. It has about one fourth as many public employee members as the SEIU, mostly unskilled blue-collar workers in public works departments. Both SEIU and LIU occasionally compete with AFCSME for members.

The Teamsters union is the largest and most successful independent union which also organizes public employees. They represent some 57,000. The core of the union's public employee membership consists of truck drivers and helpers in highway, streets, and sanitation departments, but the Teamsters cross occupational lines and may be found bargaining for such diverse groups as nurses and policemen.

The Public Employee Associations

While unions have been quite successful in organizing state and local government employees, independent employee associations currently represent a clear majority. They are of two kinds: single occupation associations, such as those representing teachers and nurses; and general associations on the industrial-union model, the best examples of which are the state employee associations.

The National Education Association. The largest professional association of public employees is the National Education Association (NEA), with over a million members. Of these, 85 percent are classroom teachers; the rest, school administrators. Until quite recently, the NEA shunned the activities associated with unionism and held to an image of professionalism, concerning itself with purely educational issues. It welcomed the membership and accepted the leadership of school administrators.

About 10 years ago it began to change its policy. In 1961 the NEA affiliate in the New York city schools lost a representation election to a local of the AFT. The following year, the AFT local, after a successful strike, negotiated an agreement with the school board for some 50,000 classroom teachers. Soon thereafter, the NEA openly endorsed what it called "professional negotiations." Some NEA affiliates in subsequent years followed the AFT example by going out on strike; and while the NEA does not endorse strike action, neither did it repudiate the strikers. Thus in the rhetoric they use there are still differences between the NEA and AFT, but in their behavior as bargaining agents they have become similar.

Nurses. The American Nurses Association (ANA) is the main organization of registered nurses in the United States. Out of a membership of about 200,000, some 37,000 are nurses employed by local and state governments. Like the NEA, the ANA sees itself primarily as a professional organization with broad interests in the field of health care. It admits nursing administrators as well as general duty nurses.

Unlike the NEA, however, the ANA has long promoted collective bargaining by its affiliates. Under the Economic Security Program of 1946, the ANA sought representation for nurses through collective bargaining; and, while the program developed slowly, ANA affiliates today speak for substantial numbers of nurses. The ANA bargaining policy took a more militant tone in 1968 by removing a constitutional ban on strikes. This reflected the reality that several ANA affiliates had struck in the preceding years.

Policemen. Policemen and women are a group apart—even if not strictly professionals like teachers and nurses. Two national independent police associations represent the great majority: the Fraternal Order of Police (FOP) and the International Conference of Police Associations (ICPA). Both are loose confederations of local associations, and both formally oppose affiliation with the AFL-CIO on the ground that it would compromise the professional image of police, and perhaps lead to conflict of interests. Both organizations, however, engage in collective bargaining and many of their affiliates have negotiated agreements. Both organizations repudiate the strike tactic, but have taken no action against striking locals.

State Employee Associations. Independent employee associations dominate state employment. Currently 36 such associations represent about 500,000 employees. Some also organize local public employees, and represent about 120,000 at this level. The two largest, in New York and California, make up approximately one-half the bulk of total organized state and local employees. The Assembly of Government Employees, a loose national federation with which most of the state associations are affiliated, serves as a forum of information exchange between them.

The associations differ widely in activities, and attitudes towards collective bargaining. Where they face union competition, they engage in it; elsewhere, they tend to rely on their traditional practice of lobbying at the state capitol. They give unions tough competition for bargaining rights. In 1969 the New York Civil Service Association beat the AFSCME in four out of five statewide bargaining unit elections. In Hawaii, rivalry between AFSCME and the Hawaiian Government Employees Association ended in 1970 with a merger of the two organizations.

Local independent associations represent about 300,000 additional employees of local governments. Like the state associations, they take varying positions towards collective bargaining, and often reverse former policy to engage in it when faced with union competition. In 1968, for instance, the Los Angeles County Employees Association opposed the passage of a comprehensive collective bargaining law by the county board. Upon passage of the law, the association fired its old director and hired a new one to lead a fight to gain bargaining rights. The presence of a rival local of the SEIU, which also had a substantial number of county employee members, undoubtedly hastened the transformation.

Bargaining at State and Local Levels

Great diversity prevails in bargaining practice and procedures at state and local levels because of the diversity of the specific contexts. These are quite different, for instance, in a city like Chicago, dominated by the Democratic party machine of Mayor Richard J. Daley, and in an affluent, Republican, north-shore suburb. They differ between a school board with wide discretion in personnel matters and a state agency whose head may have little such discretionary authority.

State and local governments also show the same diffusion of authority noted in the federal service, reduced in scale, perhaps, and mitigated by closer proximity. A mayor or city manager normally has greater latitude in personnel matters than the head of a federal agency. One or the other of these administrators may also have influence over the local legislative body. Civil service systems, where they exist, usually exercise more restricted authority than the federal system. School and other special district boards usually exercise broad authority in matters affecting personnel.

Two-Step Bargaining. Collective bargaining in state and local governments typically takes place in two steps. First, the employee organization hammers out an agreement with an administrator. Second, they take their agreement to the appropriate legislative body for validation of its economic portions. Occasionally, they lobby jointly for validation. More often, the employee organization "renegotiates" for better terms at the legislative level by partisan lobbying.

The ideal arrangement would centralize management bargaining authority in a single person or administrative body, but legislatures seem to hate giving up power, particularly over the purse-strings; hence the governmental structure tends to encourage the two-step procedure. This discourages meaningful bargaining at the first step.

Agreements and Negotiations. Written agreements are becoming more prevalent every day, but their number is no measure of the extent of real negotiations. Many public employee labor organizations—particularly associations—content themselves with getting the results of their negotiations codified in a city ordinance, administrative order, or change in civil service regulations. Written agreements, however, usually indicate a greater degree of bilateral decision making than a code or ordinance.

The Schools. Formal collective bargaining and written agreements are most prevalent in the schools. Two things account for this. First, the overwhelming majority of teachers belong either to the NEA or the AFT. Second, school boards usually possess legal authority to conclude agreements. In 1967 a total of 1,531 school districts had signed written agreements covering some 47 percent—roughly three quarters of a million—of the classroom teachers in the United States. Most of these agreements are patterned after private sector models, and are often more than 50 pages long.[6]

The Cities. Next most prevalent after teachers is collective bargaining by municipal employees. Three out of every five municipal workers are represented by labor organizations, as disclosed by a 1968 survey of 1,530 cities of over 10,000 population. More than a thousand of these cities, or two thirds, set wages and other conditions of employment for at least some of their employees by collective bargaining. Most of this

---
[6] Moskow, op. cit., p. 151.

organized representation was in cities with population over 50,000. Fire fighters with about 80 percent, and police with about 70 percent representation, were the most highly organized. Roughly 65 percent of welfare workers and 50 percent of other city employees had gained representation through labor organizations.[7]

Since the majority of these organized municipal employees are represented by unions like AFSCME and the IAFF the number of written contracts is quickly rising. As early as 1967 over 40 percent of cities with council-manager forms of government reported having written collective bargaining agreements covering some of their employees.[8]

State Service. By comparison, collective bargaining is making slowest headway in state service, where the lobbying tradition lingers. Associations of state employees encounter some difficulties in defining bargaining units because of agency size and diffusion of decision-making power. Lobbying activity still pays off, and seems simpler and more reliable than the complexities of contracts and negotiations.

Wage Issues in Collective Bargaining. The core activity in both private and public sectors is wage and effort bargaining. One reason true collective bargaining is more prevalent in the public sector than at state and federal levels is that labor organizations bargain more directly with those who have authority to set the wages. Bargaining at local level tends to focus on two key issues: pay comparability and the ability to pay.

Pay Comparability. Fire fighters want parity pay with policemen; both want comparability with the skilled trades. Skilled workers want parity with the construction union scale and are not impressed with the retort that they get better pension benefits and no slack-season layoffs. Teachers in central cities want parity with the suburbs. Similar arguments in other job classifications stress the reasonableness of the comparisons made.

The Budget. Even when public employers accept the comparative argument, they often plead inability to pay. Fiscal restraints are tightening in more and more local jurisdictions. The employer's line, "We'd like to, but . . ." meets the response, "You could if you'd slow down urban renewal, or don't build a domed stadium, or. . . ." This illustrates the point made earlier that budget constraints, priorities, and taxing limits, rather than market forces, tend to set the wage bargain in public employment.

The problems are real enough. Public employees often go to bat for their employers to try to boost revenues. The Houston fire fighters, for example, helped get additional taxing authority for the city from the Texas

---

[7] Jack Stieber, "Extent of Municipal Employee Representation," *The Municipal Yearbook* (Chicago: International City Managers Association, 1969).

[8] Winston W. Crouch, "Employee Organizations in Council-Manager Cities," *The Municipal Yearbook* (Chicago: International City Managers Association, 1967).

legislature. They got a handsome pay raise in reward. In education, the tie-in between pay and taxing level has made teacher organizations tireless campaigners for millage levies to support the schools.

Grievance Handling. State and local civil service usually provides appeals procedures. Employees typically look on civil service as an arm of management; they would prefer grievance procedures ending in neutral third-party binding arbitration. Unions of public employees are more insistent than associations in pressing for grievance procedures separate from civil service. They oppose having a board that formulates the rules and then adjudicates them.

Union Security. Union security is an important issue at the state and local levels. Most states do not insist on the federal ban against the union shop, but most public employers have resisted it as a threat to the merit principle: They say they do not want to have to fire a good employee because he does not want to join the union. The AFSCME estimates it could double its membership by getting union or agency shop agreements in political jurisdictions where they are not yet authorized. Associations, on the other hand, generally do not make as big an issue of union security.

Strike Militancy

The last decade witnessed a dramatic increase in strikes of public employees. In 1958 there were only 15, with 14 in local governments. In 1968 there were 253; and of these, 235 were local. Teacher strikes were commonest, strikes of sanitation workers next, but strikes occurred in every local government function, including hospitals and the police and fire services. The table below discloses the increase in strike activity in various government services.

Wages and fringe benefits were the issue in more than half the strikes; union security and recognition in another one fourth. The largest number occurred in the Midwest; next largest, the Northeast. Strikes were most frequent in Michigan, Ohio, Illinois, New York, California, and New

TABLE 16–4. Strikes in Government by Service Involved, 1968 and (1958)

Service	Number of Strikes		Number of Employees Involved	Number of Man-Days Idle
Public Schools and Libraries	112	(0)	148,000	2,198,800
Sanitation	63	(7)	27,500	200,000
Police, Fire and Administrative Services	28	(3)	10,600	44,000
Hospital and Other Health Services	21	(0)	11,000	83,500
Other Services	29	(5)	1,930	23,430
Totals	253	(15)	199,030	2,549,730

Source: Bureau of Labor Statistics, *Work Stoppages in Government, 1958–1968,* 1970

Jersey.[9] The AFT and NEA led more strikes than any other organizations; AFSCME was next. Far fewer employee associations than unions were involved. Many strikes took the form of mass resignations or sick calls.

The use of other pressure tactics such as slowdowns, "working to rule," and mass picketing by public employees has also increased rapidly in recent years but remains largely unrecorded. Such pressure tactics are particularly effective for some groups like policemen who often prefer to take action short of striking, such as refusing to write traffic tickets. Similarly, street department workers may refuse to work overtime during a snowstorm. The techniques are many and varied.

Impasse Procedures. The strike is such a controversial measure in public employment that state and local government and labor organizations search for impasse procedures, as in the federal service. Mediation and fact-finding are common in the state laws on bargaining. Agreements sometimes contain provisions for settling substantive issues by means of binding arbitration, but labor and public management tend to resist making it compulsory, by law, except for police and fire fighters.

The reasons are various. A strong union prefers to use the strike weapon, even when strikes may be forbidden. All public employee labor organizations tend to fear that arbitrators will be timid about breaking new ground, and so make progress, such as might come in collective bargaining, difficult. Finally, many labor leaders hold the right to strike to be essential to true collective bargaining; arbitration as a substitute undercuts its foundations. Public employers fear impairment of their ability to manage by giving authority to a third party unfamiliar with their operations. A solution, as in the federal service, has yet to be found.

Political Action. State and local employees also exert pressure in the political arena. They lobby, and take political action under the traditional slogan, "Elect our friends and defeat our enemies." Laws patterned on the Hatch Act, designed to dampen such activities, have proved easy to evade and generally ineffective.

Unions and associations appear equally adroit at politics. The AFL-CIO tie gives unions a great deal of leverage, of which the fire fighters, conspicuously, have taken notable advantage. Police unions, too, often wield strong political influence. By pulling the political levers, both groups have made gains over workers in jobs that require no more education or training. Political action remains an element of strategy in collective bargaining not just for them, but all employees at state and local government levels.

This is probably unavoidable. Bargaining power on one side seeks out the sources of power on the other and will not be put off with underlings. And politicians will probably never shut their ears when an organized body of constituents asks: "What have you done for us . . . lately?"

---

[9] *Work Stoppages in Government, 1958–68*, Bureau of Labor Statistics, 1970.

SUMMARY

Public employee organization is now proportionately greater than in the private sector. Strike militancy has increased dramatically, and if the trend continues, strikes may become as common in the public as in the private sector. Despite legal restrictions and the peculiarities of government personnel systems, meaningful bargaining is also increasing at all levels of government. The scope of bargaining steadily expands at state and local levels, though more slowly in the federal services, with the exception of the postal system.

The right of public employees to strike has become an imminent key question in public policy. A few states have already granted a limited right to strike; their experience will help shape policy in the public sector. Other states have experimented with binding arbitration; their experience with impasse procedures as a substitute for strikes may have an impact on policy in the private sector.

Yet even if public policy for both sectors become indistinguishable, the practice of collective bargaining will not. Differences in the market and power relations contexts will continue to set them apart. The political activity of organized public employees is bound to continue as long as democratic forms of government prevail in America.

QUESTIONS FOR DISCUSSION

1. How has the fact that government exercises sovereign power affected the establishment of collective bargaining relations in the federal service?
2. Discuss the differences in the pattern of bargaining found in the postal service and the classified service.
3. What difficulties are encountered in attempts to substitute impasse procedures for the right to strike by public employees?
4. What features distinguish the practice of collective bargaining in the federal service from that in local political jurisdictions?
5. How comparable will collective bargaining in the public and private sectors be in 10 years?

SELECTED ANNOTATED BIBLIOGRAPHY

BROOKINGS INSTITUTION. *Study of Unionism and Collective Bargaining in the Public Sector.* A five volume series to be published in 1972.

These five volumes will focus respectively on: (1) the varieties of public employee organizations, (2) the economic impact of public employee unionism, (3) the legal process and public sector bargaining, (4) the impact of collective bargaining on civil service, and (5) the scope and process of public sector bargaining.

ELAM, M.; LIEBERMAN, M.; and MOSKOW, MICHAEL H. (eds.). *Readings on Collective Negotiations in Public Education.* Chicago: Rand McNally, 1967.

As the title suggests, this is a book of readings on one of the earliest and most rapidly expanding segments in public sector bargaining.

ADVISORY COMMISSION ON INTERGOVERNMENTAL RELATIONS. *Labor-Management Policies for State and Local Governments.* Washington, D.C.: U.S. Government Printing Office (September 1969).

A comprehensive analysis of the developing public policy toward bargaining in state and local government. The volume also includes analysis of membership data for public employee unions, strikes and recommendations of the commission, and position papers by management and labor representatives.

LIEBERMAN, MYRON and MOSKOW, MICHAEL H. *Collective Negotiations for Teachers.* Chicago: Rand McNally, 1966.

An excellent book to provide an analytic framework for integrating material from the book of readings by Elam, et al., cited above.

LOEWENBERG, J. JOSEPH and MOSKOW, MICHAEL H. *Collective Bargaining in Government.* Englewood Cliffs, N.J., Prentice-Hall, 1972.

This book offers an excellent selection of articles on the developing patterns of bargaining in federal, state, and local government agencies. Of particular interest are articles comparing and contrasting private and public bargaining:

WELLINGTON, HARRY H. and WINTER, RALPH K. "The Limits of Collective Bargaining in Public Employment" and "More on Strikes by Public Employees."

BURTON, JOHN E. and KRIDER, CHARLES. "The Role and Consequences of Strikes by Public Employees."

MOSKOW, MICHAEL H.; LOEWENBERG, J. JOSEPH; and KOZIARA, EDWARD CLIFFORD. *Collective Bargaining in Public Employment.* New York: Random House, 1970.

This volume integrates conceptual models with data analysis of developments in the federal service, state, and local governments. It is an excellent companion volume for the book of readings just cited.

REPAS, ROBERT F. *Collective Bargaining in Federal Employment.* University of Hawaii: Industrial Relations Center, 1970.

A "how to do it" manual for leaders of employee organization in the federal service. Gives an excellent practitioners perspective on the intricacies of federal bargaining policy and practices.

SEIDMAN, JOEL. "State Legislation on Collective Bargaining by Public Employees," *Labor Law Journal* (January 1971).

The article gives an updating of developments since the extensive study by the Advisory Commission on Intergovernmental Relations in 1969.

SPERO, STERLING D. *Government as Employer.* New York: Remsen Press, 1948.

This book is a good starting point for gaining a historical perspective on collective bargaining in the public sector.

STIEBER, JACK. "Extent of Municipal Employee Representation," *Municipal Yearbook.* Chicago: International City Managers Association, 1969.

A thorough analysis of the varieties of employee organizations in municipal governments. Based on a survey of over 1000 cities.

TAYLOR, GEORGE W. "Public Employment: Strikes or Procedures?" *Industrial and Labor Relations Review*, Vol. 20 (July 1967).

An analysis of the unique impasse procedures needed in the public service to meet the challenge of increased employee militancy. Taylor was one of the draftsmen of New York State's public employee relations law.

WARNER, KENNETH O. (ed.). *Collective Bargaining in the Public Service: Theory and Practice*. Chicago: Public Personnel Association, 1967.

A book of readings primarily aimed at assisting public managers in dealing with unions and negotiating contracts.

WOODWORTH, ROBERT T., and PETERSON, RICHARD B. *Collective Negotiations for Public and Professional Employees, Text and Readings*. Glenview, Ill.: Scott, Foresman and Company, 1969.

A fine selection of readings and comments on the problems of professionals, especially those employed in public agencies, utilizing collective bargaining to deal with their work problems.

ZIZKIND, DAVID. *One Thousand Strikes of Government Employees*. New York: Columbia University Press, 1940.

Another good volume to assist in getting a historical perspective on the development of public sector bargaining.

PART V

Cases in Collective Bargaining

CASES

Part V of this book contains 41 cases, all of them true, but with the names of individuals, companies, and unions disguised in a few instances. Questions about the issues the cases raise or illustrate accompany the presentation of the facts. Many of the cases come from arbitration records and appear here by courtesy of the Bureau of National Affairs, which first published them and has kindly permitted their reproduction for student use. Other cases are drawn from the opinions of the courts on important matters.

Now, why study cases?

Arbitration and legal proceedings account for no more than a small part of the sum total of collective bargaining activities, yet for several reasons the study of arbitration and law cases is unusually rewarding.

To begin with, the arbitration and legal processes leave a written record. This is not true of all aspects of collective bargaining. Where such a record is not kept, cases have to be written up in narrative form (like a few of those in this section) and lack the authority of official record. The decision of an arbitrator or court usually concentrates on a single, seemingly narrow point, but the record of the hearing often preserves for scrutiny a range of facts and testimony that illuminates a much broader field of view. Furthermore, an issue that has gone all the way to arbitration or to court usually embodies some aspect of the relationship between the contending parties that is unique, with important implications that touch on fundamental principles.

The cases in this book present concrete issues that have arisen between bargaining partners in spite of their best efforts to settle differences in advance by written agreement. Practical problems rising out of the living process of collective bargaining appear here in all the confusion and fragmentation of the forms in which they confront actual participants.

It will be the student's task to analyze the problems as they come before him in raw form, applying the principles he may have learned from the text, from collateral reading opened up by the text, and from classroom instruction and discussion. The cases, therefore, help the student develop his powers of reasoning, his ability to move from the general to the particular, and, perhaps, back from the particular to strengthen his grasp of the general. They demand logical organization of ideas and clarity of oral and written expression. (This they demand all the more because in their raw state they are themselves not models of clairty or logic.)

Finally, cases permit the student to express and test value judgments based on his own moral and ethical code. So far as possible, value judgments have been kept out of the text, because the aim there was to present only the facts. Where any value judgments have been made, the authors have taken care to label them as only their personal opinion and have not tried to pass them off as gospel. Here, in handling cases, the student can—and should—give thought to what he thinks is right and wrong, what should and should not be. He will undoubtedly find some who disagree with him; he may sway them, or be swayed. Collective bargaining surely cannot stand exempt from ethics and morality, any more than from economic law or any other influence at work in society, and it is only by free exchange of views and values that understanding (if not full agreement) can be reached.

Like almost everything in this book, the cases here presented do not pretend to be exhaustive, but suggestive. There is no limit to the number of true-life cases students could collect and subject to the process of analysis these cases demonstrate. Having started with these cases, let students bring in their own experiences and observations, either in oral or written form, for presentation to the class and for class discussion.

HOW TO USE THE CASES

Chapter 9 contains the valuable advice of the American Arbitration Association on how to prepare for arbitration. This is worth reviewing before tackling a case problem. After that, two ways of using the cases stand open to the instructor and the class.

One way is to take the case as the starting point for a written exercise. The student writes what he considers should be the arbitrator's award, or in the cases not drawn from arbitration records, directly answers the questions. In either event, he should justify his solution.

Another way, and probably better, is the role-playing method. A team of two or three students can take the union side, a similar team the management side, with a student (or the instructor) to sit as arbitrator and act as chairman. The two sides then act out their roles before the class.

Oral presentation in this manner should not neglect the value—perhaps it might be said, the necessity—of written support in the form of a brief of the argument, and perhaps also "exhibits" in lieu of testimony where "evidence" consists of facts drawn from the printed case. After the class has heard the arguments, each member may then write an "award" as if he were the arbitrator. Other variations will undoubtedly suggest themselves.

A word about briefs and a hint on their preparation.

Most college students will have last encountered brief-writing in their freshman English course, or perhaps in high school. Here is a chance to review an important subject and develop a useful skill.

The hint is this: study the *questions* that follow the cases for clues that will lead to the most logically developed argument, along lines indicated by the interest to be defended, or the value judgment to be upheld. Merely to summarize the arguments already put forward in the "union position," or "management position" of the printed case will fail to develop the full strength of either side's position.

This cases section of the book calls for active student participation, and brings the practice of collective bargaining into play in a form as realistic as it is possible to get in the classroom. A mock arbitration hearing or role-playing session should not be allowed to degenerate into clowning or farce, but need not exclude humor and good spirits. This part of the course can be, and ought to be, good fun as well as good instruction.

CASE 1
The Obligation to Bargain under Federal Law

This case consists of three parts: (1) a brief discussion of the obligation to bargain under federal law; (2) opinions of the United States Supreme Court in three leading cases; and (3) two scholarly comments on sound public policy in this area.

PART I. THE LEGAL OBLIGATION TO BARGAIN

One of the most difficult problems confronting the NLRB and the courts in interpreting the Taft-Hartley Act is defining the obligation to bargain in good faith. Sections 8(a)(5) and 8(b)(3) impose the obligation to bargain on employers and unions respectively. Section 8(d) states that collective bargaining

. . . is the performance of the mutual obligation of the employer and the representative of his employees to meet at reasonable times and confer in good faith with respect to wages, hours, and other conditions of employment, or the negotiation of an agreement, or any question arising thereunder, and the execution of a written contract incorporating any agreement reached if requested by either party, but such obligation does not compel either party to agree to a proposal or require the making of a concession: . . .

The words of the statute provide only sketchy guidelines to the definition of the obligation to bargain. The NLRB and the courts have interpreted the statute as applying to both the conduct of the parties in the act of bargaining and the substantive issues in bargaining. Thus the NLRB requires that both parties meet and discuss their proposals, and it determines whether a party may refuse to discuss certain specific proposals.

Substantive issues in collective bargaining are divided into three legal categories: (1) unlawful issues; (2) mandatory issues; and (3) nonmandatory issues. The parties are forbidden to agree on unlawful issues, e.g., the closed shop. Either party is within the law when it demands a mandatory issue and refuses to sign an agreement unless its demand is satisfied. Both parties are required to bargain about any mandatory subject proposed by the other party. Neither party is obligated to agree to any specific mandatory subject. Unions and managements may agree to bargain about nonmandatory subjects, and any agreement they voluntarily reach on nonmandatory subjects is lawful. However, neither party is obligated to bargain on nonmandatory subjects, nor is either party permitted to insist upon a demand for a nonmandatory subject. A few illustrations of mandatory and nonmandatory subjects may help to clarify the significance of these categories.

The following are examples of mandatory subjects for collective bargaining:

1. Employee stock purchase plans.
2. Profit-sharing retirement plans.
3. Group insurance.
4. Pensions.
5. Christmas bonuses.
6. No-strike clauses.

Suppose that the union and management had agreed on wages, hours, seniority provisions, grievance procedures, and all other matters usually in an agreement. The union would not be guilty of refusal to bargain if it demanded, and struck for, an extra bonus to be distributed at Christmas. Nor would the employer be guilty of refusal to bargain if he refused to sign an agreement incorporating these understandings unless the union agreed to include a no-strike clause in the agreement.

The following are examples of nonmandatory subjects for collective bargaining:

1. Demands that a union post a performance bond.
2. Demands that an employer post a performance bond.
3. Demands that a union withdraw an unfair labor practice charge.
4. Demands that a union forego certain appropriate bargaining subjects for all time.
5. Demand that a supervisor be discharged.

An employer may agree with the union that a supervisor will be discharged as a means of improving the labor relations climate, or a union may withdraw its pending unfair labor practice charge against the employer for the same reason. However, the union is guilty of refusal to bargain if it strikes for the purpose of causing a supervisor's discharge; and the employer is innocent of refusal to bargain if he steadfastly refuses to listen to the union's protestations about the supervisor. The employer is guilty of refusal to bargain if he insists that he will not sign an agreement until the union withdraws its unfair labor practice charges.

The real significance of the division between mandatory and nonmandatory subjects is difficult to assess. Nevertheless, it seems reasonable to conclude that an NLRB and Supreme Court labeling of, say, pensions as a mandatory subject for collective bargaining is a tacit governmental approval of a union drive to negotiate such plans. Also, an NLRB and Supreme Court ruling that a union may not strike to force an employer to post a performance bond as a condition precedent to a collective bargaining agreement tends to reduce the prevalence of such provisions in collective bargaining agreements.

In general, statutory law specifically prohibits relatively few collective bargaining clauses, e.g., closed shops and, under the 1959 law, "hot cargo" clauses.

The complexity of the problems confronting the NLRB and the courts in determining mandatory and nonmandatory subjects is illustrated by the following three abstracted Supreme Court rulings.

PART II. THREE SUPREME COURT DECISIONS

The Truitt Manufacturing Company case, decided in 1956, deals with the obligation of an employer to substantiate his claim of inability to pay a wage increase demanded by the union. This case deals with the process of negotiations rather than a new substantive issue like profit sharing or displacement allowances for workers who lose their jobs in a plant closure.

The Borg-Warner case, decided in 1958, deals with the demand of an employer for a "ballot clause" in a collective bargaining agreement. This case requires a decision on whether a new substantive issue is a mandatory subject for collective bargaining.

The Insurance Agents case, decided in 1960, deals with a union slowdown and other harassment of an employer during the progress of negotiations. Do pressures exerted outside the bargaining sessions provide evidence of a refusal to bargain in good faith?

The reports of the cases presented below have been abstracted. Readers are encouraged to read the full opinions available in U.S. Reports. Dissenting opinions have been included in the abstracts because of the richness of their insight.

Supreme Court of the United States
National Labor Relations Board v. *Truitt Manufacturing Company*
May 7, 1956, 351 U.S. 149

Mr. Justice Black delivered the opinion of the Court.

The National Labor Relations Act makes it an unfair labor practice for an employer to refuse to bargain in good faith with the representative of his employees. The question presented by this case is whether the National Labor Relations Board may find that an employer has not bargained in good faith where the employer claims it cannot afford to pay higher wages but refuses requests to produce information substantiating its claim.

The dispute here arose when a union representing certain of respondent's employees asked for a wage increase of 10 cents per hour. The company answered that it could not afford to pay such an increase, it was undercapitalized, had never paid dividends, and that an increase of more than 2 ½ cents per hour would put it out of business. The union asked the company to produce some evidence substantiating these statements, requesting permission to have a certified public accountant examine the company's books, financial data, etc. This request being denied, the union asked that the company submit "full and complete information with respect to its financial standing and profits," insisting that such information was pertinent and essential for the employees to determine whether or not they should continue to press their demand for a wage increase. A union official testified before the trial examiner: "(W)e were wanting anything relating to the Company's position, any record or what have you, books, accounting sheets, cost expenditures, what not, anything to back the Company's position that they were unable to give any more money." The company refused all the requests, relying solely on the statement that "the information . . . is not pertinent to this discussion and the company declines to give you such information; you have no legal right to such."

On the basis of these facts the National Labor Relations Board found that the company had "failed to bargain in good faith with respect to wages in violation of Section 8(a)(5) of the Act." The Board ordered the company to supply the union with such information as would "substantiate the Respondent's position of its economic inability to pay the requested wage increase." The Court of Appeals refused to enforce the Board's order, agreeing with respondent that it could not be held guilty of an unfair labor practice because of its refusal to furnish the information requested by the union. In *Labor Board* v. *Jacobs Mfg. Co.*, the Second Circuit upheld a Board finding of bad-faith bargaining based on an employer's refusal to supply financial information under circumstances similar to those here. Because of the conflict and the importance of the question we granted certiorari.

The company raised no objection to the Board's order on the ground that the scope of information required was too broad or that disclosure would put an undue burden on the company. Its major argument throughout has been that the information requested was irrelevant to the bargaining process and related to matters exclusively within the province of management. Thus we lay to one side the suggestion by the company here that the Board's order might be unduly burdensome or injurious to its business. In any event, the Board has heretofore taken the position in cases such as this that "It is sufficient if the information is made available in a manner not so burdensome or time-consuming as to impede the process of bargaining." And in this case the Board has held substantiation of the company's position requires no more than "reasonable proof."

We think that in determining whether the obligation of good-faith bargaining has been met the Board has a right to consider an employer's refusal to give information about its financial status. While Congress did not compel agreement between employers and bargaining representatives, it did require collective bargaining in the hope that the agreements would result. Section 204(a)(1) of the Act admonishes both employers and employees to "exert every reasonable effort to make and maintain agreements concerning rates of pay, hours, and working conditions. . . ." In their effort to reach an agreement here both the union and the company treated the company's ability to pay increased wages as highly relevant. The ability of an employer to increase wages without injury to his business is a commonly considered factor in wage negotiations. Claims for increased wages have sometimes been abandoned because of an employer's unsatisfactory business condition; employees have even voted to accept wage decreases because of such conditions.

Good-faith bargaining necessarily requires that claims made by either bargainer should be honest claims. This is true about an asserted inability to pay an increase in wages. If such an argument is important enough to present in the give and take of bargaining, it is important enough to require some sort of proof of its accuracy. And it would certainly not be farfetched for a trier of fact to reach the conclusion that bargaining lacks good faith when an employer mechanically repeats a claim of inability to pay without making the slightest effort to substantiate the claim. Such has been the holding of the Labor Board since shortly after the passage of the Wagner Act. . . . We agree with the Board that a refusal to attempt to substantiate a claim of inability to pay increased wages may support a finding of a failure to bargain in good faith.

The Board concluded that under the facts and circumstances of this case the respondent was guilty of an unfair labor practice in failing to bargain in good faith. We see no reason to disturb the findings of the Board. We do not hold, however, that in every case in which economic inability is raised as an argument against increased wages it automatically follows that the employees are entitled to substantiating evidence. Each case must turn upon its particular facts. The inquiry must always be whether or not under the circumstances of the particular case the statutory obligation to bargain in good faith has been met. Since we conclude that there is support in the record for the conclusion of the Board here that respondents did not bargain in good faith, it was error for the Court of Appeals to set aside the Board's order and deny enforcement.

Reversed.

Truitt Manufacturing Company
Concurring and Dissenting Opinion

Mr. Justice Frankfurter, whom Mr. Justice Clark and Mr. Justice Harlan join, concurring in part and dissenting in part.

This case involves the nature of the duty to bargain which the National Labor Relations Act imposes upon employers and unions. Section 8(a)(5) of the Act makes it "an unfair labor practice for an employer . . . to refuse to bargain collectively with the representatives of his employees," and Section 8(b)(3) places a like duty upon the union *vis-à-vis* the employer. Section 8(d) provides that "to bargain collectively is the performance of the mutual obligation of the employer and the representative of the employees to meet at reasonable times and confer in good faith with respect to wages, hours, and other terms and conditions of employment, or the negotiation of an agreement, or any question arising thereunder, and the execution of a written contract incorporating any agreement reached if requested by either party, but such obligation does not compel either party to agree to a proposal or require the making of a concession. . . ."

These sections obligate the parties to make an honest effort to come to terms; they are required to try to reach an agreement in good faith. "Good faith" means more than merely going through the motions of negotiating; it is inconsistent with a predetermined resolve not to budge from an initial position. But it is not necessarily incompatible with stubbornness or even with what to an outsider may seem unreasonableness. A determination of good faith or of want of good faith normally can rest only on an inference based upon more or less persuasive manifestations of another's state of mind. The previous relations of the parties, antecedent events explaining behavior at the bargaining table, and the course of negotiations constitute the raw facts for reaching such a determination. The appropriate inferences to be drawn from what is often confused and tangled testimony about all this makes a finding of absence of good faith one for the judgment of the Labor Board, unless the record as a whole leaves such judgment without reasonable foundation.

An examination of the Board's opinion and the position taken by its counsel here disclose that the Board did not so conceive the issue of good-faith bargaining in this case. The totality of the conduct of the negotiation was apparently deemed irrelevant to the question; one fact alone disposed of the case. "(I)t is settled law (the Board concluded), that when an employer seeks to justify the refusal of a wage increase upon an economic basis, as did the Respondent herein, good-faith bargaining under the Act requires that upon request the employer attempt to substantiate its economic position by reasonable proof."

This is to make a rule of law out of one item—even if a weighty item —of the evidence. There is no warrant for this. The Board found authority in *Labor Board* v. *Jacobs Mfg. Co.* That case presented a very different situation. The Jacobs Company had engaged in a course of conduct which the Board held to be a violation of Section 8(a)(5). The Court of Appeals agreed that in light of the whole record the Board was entitled to find that the employer had not bargained in good faith. Its refusal to open its "books and sales records" for union perusal was only part of the recalcitrant conduct and only one consideration in establishing want of good faith. The unfair labor practice was not founded on this refusal, and the Court's principal concern about the disclosure of financial information was whether the Board's order should be enforced in this respect. The court sustained the Board's requirement for disclosure which "will be met if the respondent produces whatever relevant information it has to indicate whether it can or cannot afford to comply with the union's demands." This a very far cry indeed from a ruling of law that failure to open a company's books establishes lack of good faith. Once good faith is found wanting, the scope of relief to be given by the Board is largely a question of administrative discretion. Neither Jacobs nor any other Court of Appeals' decision which has been called to our attention supports the rule of law which the Board has fashioned out of one thread drawn from the whole fabric of the evidence in this case.

The Labor Board itself has not always approached "good faith" and the disclosure question in such a mechanical fashion. In Southern Saddlery Co., the Board also found that Section 8(a)(5) had been violated. But how differently the Board there considered its function.

Bargaining in good faith is a duty on both sides to enter into discussions with an open and fair mind and a sincere purpose to find a basis for agreement touching wages and hours and conditions of labor. In applying this definition of good faith bargaining to any situation, the Board examines the Respondent's conduct as a whole for a clear indication as to whether the latter has refused to bargain in good faith, and the Board usually does not rely upon any one factor as conclusive evidence that the Respondent did not genuinely try to reach an agreement.

The Board found other factors in the Southern Saddlery case. The employer had made no counterproposals or efforts to "compromise the controversy." Compare, McLean-Arkansas Lumber Co., Inc. Such specific evidence is not indispensable, for a study of all the evidence in a record may disclose a mood indicative of a determination not to bargain. That is for the Board to decide. It is a process of inference-drawing, however, very different from the *ultra vires* law-making of the Board in this case.

Since the Board applied the wrong standard here, by ruling that Truitt's failure to supply financial information to the union constituted *per se* a refusal to bargain in good faith, the case should be returned to the Board. There is substantial evidence in the record which indicates that Truitt tried to reach an agreement. It offered a 2½-cent wage increase, it expressed willingness to discuss with the union "at any time how our wages compare with those of our competition," and it continued throughout to meet and discuss the controversy with the union.

Because the record is not conclusive as a matter of law, one way or the other, I cannot join in the Court's disposition of the case. To reverse the Court of Appeals without remanding the case to the Board for further proceedings implies that the Board would have reached the same conclusion in applying the right rule of law that it did in applying a wrong one. I cannot make such a forecast. I would return the case to the Board so that it may apply the relevant standard for determining "good faith."

Supreme Court of the United States
National Labor Relations Board v. *Wooster Division of Borg-Warner Corporation*
May 5, 1958, 356 U.S. 342

[This case involved the management's insistence on the inclusion in a collective bargaining agreement of a "ballot" clause and a "recognition" clause. The abstract presented here deals only with the "ballot" clause.]

Mr. Justice Burton delivered the opinion of the Court.

. . . The issue turns on whether . . . the "ballot clause" comes within the scope of mandatory collective bargaining as defined in Section 8(d) of the Act. For the reasons hereafter stated, we agree with the Board . . . [this clause does not come] within that definition. Therefore, we sustain the Board's order directing the employer to cease insisting upon . . . [this clause] as a condition precedent to accepting any collective bargaining contract.

The "ballot" clause . . . provides that, as to all nonarbitrable issues (which eventually included modification, amendment or termination of the contract), there would be a 30-day negotiation period after which, before the union could strike, there would have to be a secret ballot taken among all employees in the unit (union and nonunion) on the company's last offer. In the event a majority of the employees rejected the company's last offer, the company would have an opportunity, within 72 hours, of making a new proposal and having a vote on it prior to any strike. The unions' negotiators announced they would not accept this clause "under any conditions."

. . .

The company's good faith has met the requirements of the statute as to the subjects of mandatory bargaining. But that good faith does not license the employer to refuse to enter into agreements on the ground that they do not include some proposal which is not a mandatory subject of bargaining. We agree with the Board that such conduct is, in substance, a refusal to bargain about the subjects that are within the scope of mandatory bargaining. . . .

Since it is lawful to insist upon matters within the scope of mandatory bargaining and unlawful to insist upon matters without, the issue here is whether the "ballot" . . . clause is a subject within the phrase "wages, hours, and other terms or conditions of employment" which defines mandatory bargaining. The "ballot" clause is not within that definition. It relates to the procedure to be followed by the employees among themselves before their representative may call a strike or refuse a final offer. It settles no term or condition of employment—it merely calls for an advisory vote of the employees. It is not a partial "no-strike" clause. A "no-strike" clause prohibits the employees from striking during the life of the contract. It regulates the relations between the employer and the employees. . . . The "ballot" clause, on the other hand, deals only with relations between the employees and their unions. It substantially modifies the collective bargaining system provided for in the statute by weakening the independence of the "representative" chosen by the employees. It enables the employer, in effect, to deal with its employees rather than their statutory representative. . . .

. . .

Accordingly, the judgment of the Court of Appeals in No. 53 is reversed and the cause remanded for disposition consistent with this opinion.

Wooster Division of Borg-Warner Corp.
Dissenting Opinion

Mr. Justice Harlan, whom Mr. Justice Clark, Mr. Justice Whittaker, and Mr. Justice Frankfurter join, dissenting.

. . .

The legislative history behind the Wagner and Taft-Hartley Acts persuasively indicates that the Board was never intended to have power to prevent good-faith bargaining as to any subject not violative of the provisions or policies of those Acts. . . .

It must not be forgotten that the Act requires bargaining, *not* agreement, for the obligation to bargain ". . . does not compel either party to agree to a proposal or require the making of a concession" 8(d). Here the employer concededly bargained but simply refused to *agree* until the union would accept what the Court holds would have been a lawful contract provision. It may be that an employer or union, by adamant insistence in good faith upon a provision which is not a statutory subject under Section 8(d), does in fact require the other party to bargain over it. But this effect is traceable to the economic power of the employer or union in the circumstances of a given situation and should not affect our construction of the Act. If one thing is clear, it is that the Board was not viewed by Congress as an agency which should exercise its powers to aid a party to collective bargaining which was in an economically disadvantageous position.

The most cursory view of decisions of the Board and the circuit courts under the National Labor Relations Act reveals the unsettled and evolving character of collective bargaining agreements. Provisions which two decades ago might have been thought to be the exclusive concern of labor or management are today commonplace in such agreements. The bargaining process should be left fluid, free from intervention of the Board leading to premature crystallization of labor agreements into any one pattern of contract provisions, so that these agreements can be adapted through collective bargaining to the changing needs of our society and to the changing concepts of the responsibilities of labor and management. What the Court does today may impede this evolutionary process. . . .

As unqualifiedly stated [by this Court in American National Life Insurance, 343 US 409] it is through the "good-faith" requirement of Section 8(d) that the Board is to enforce the bargaining provisions of Section 8. A determination that a party bargained as to statutory or nonstatutory subjects in good or bad faith must depend upon an evaluation of the total circumstances surrounding any given situation. I do not deny that there may be instances where unyielding insistence on a particular item may be a relevant consideration in the overall picture in determining "good faith," for the demands of a party might in the context of a particular industry be so extreme as to constitute some evidence of unwillingness to bargain. But no such situation is presented in this instance by the "ballot" clause. . . .

. . . Here the Court recognizes, as it must, that the clause is lawful under the Act, and I think it clear that the Company's insistence upon it violated no statutory duty to which it was subject. . . .

Supreme Court of the United States
NLRB v. Insurance Agents; International Union, AFL-CIO
February 23, 1960, 361 U.S. 477

Mr. Justice Brennan delivered the opinion of the Court.
. . . The precise question is whether the Board may find that a union, which confers with an employer with the desire of reaching agreement on contract terms, has nevertheless refused to bargain collectively, thus violating this provision solely and simply because during the negotiations it seeks to put economic pressure on the employer to yield to its bargain-

ing demands by sponsoring on-the-job conduct designed to interfere with the carrying on of the employer's business.

. . .

In January 1956, Prudential and the union began the negotiation of a new contract to replace an agreement expiring in the following March. Bargaining was carried on continuously for six months before the terms of the new contract were agreed upon on July 17, 1956. It is not questioned that, if it stood alone, the record of negotiations would establish that the union conferred in good faith for the purpose and with the desire of reaching agreement with Prudential on a contract.

However, in April 1956, Prudential filed an 8(b)(3) charge of refusal to bargain collectively against the union. The charge was based upon actions of the union and its members outside the conference room, occurring after the old contract expired in March. . . .

A complaint of violation of 8(b)(3) issued on the charge and hearings began before the bargaining was concluded. It was developed in the evidence that the union's harassing tactics involved activities by the member agents such as these: refusal for a time to solicit new business, and refusal (after the writing of new business was resumed) to comply with the company's reporting procedures; refusal to participate in the company's "May Policyholders' Month Campaign"; reporting late at district offices the days the agents were scheduled to attend them, and refusing to perform customary duties at the offices, instead engaging there in "sit-in-mornings," "doing what comes naturally" and leaving at noon as a group; absenting themselves from special business conferences arranged by the company; picketing and distributing leaflets outside the various offices of the company on specified days and hours as directed by the unions; distributing leaflets each day to policyholders and others and soliciting policyholders' signatures on petitions directed to the company; and presenting the signed policyholders' petitions to the company at its home office while simultaneously engaging in mass demonstrations there.

. . . .

. . . The Board . . . entered a cease and desist order. . . . The Court of Appeals for the District of Columbia Circuit . . . set aside the Board's order. . . .

. . . Obviously there is a tension between the principle that the parties need not contract on any specific terms and a practical enforcement of the principle that they are bound to deal with each other in a serious attempt to resolve differences and reach a common ground. And in fact criticism of the Board's application of the "good-faith" test arose from the belief that it was forcing employers to yield to union demands if they were to avoid a successful charge of unfair labor practice. Thus, in 1947, in Congress the fear was expressed that the Board had "gone very far, in the guise of determining whether or not employers had bargained in good faith, in setting itself up as the judge of what concessions an employer must make and of the proposals and counterproposals that he may or may not make." . . . Since the Board was not viewed by Congress as an agency which should exercise its powers to arbitrate the parties' substantive solutions of the issues in their bargaining, a check on this apprehended trend was provided by writing the good-faith test of bargaining into 8(d) of the Taft-Hartley Act. . . .

. . . It is apparent from the legislative history of the whole Act that the policy of Congress is to impose a mutual duty upon the parties to confer in good faith with a desire to reach agreement, in the belief that such an approach from both sides of the table promotes the over-all design of achieving industrial peace.

. . . It must be realized that collective bargaining, under a system where the government does not attempt to control the results of negotiations, cannot be equated with an academic collective search for truth—or even with what might be thought to be the ideal of one. The parties— even granting the modification of views that may come from a realization of economic interdependence—still proceed from contrary, and to an extent antagonistic, viewpoints and concepts of self-interest. The system has not reached the ideal of the philosophic notion that perfect understanding among people would lead to perfect agreement among them on values. The presence of economic weapons in reserve, and their actual exercise on occasion by the parties, is part and parcel of the system that the Wagner and Taft-Hartley Acts have recognized. . . .

. . . We think the Board's approach involves an intrusion into the substantive aspects of the bargaining process—again, unless there is some specific warrant for its condemnation of the precise tactics involved here. The scope of 8(b)(3) and the limitation on Board power which were the design of 8(d) are exceeded, we hold, by inferring a lack of good faith not from any deficiencies of the union's performance at the bargaining table by reason of its attempted use of economic pressure, but solely and simply because tactics designed to exert economic pressure were employed during the course of the good-faith negotiations. Thus the Board in the guise of determining good or bad faith in negotiations could regulate what economic weapons a party might summon to its aid. And if the Board could regulate the choice of economic weapons that may be used as part of collective bargaining, it would be in a position to exercise considerable influence upon the substantive terms on which the parties contract. As the parties' own devices became more limited, the government might have to enter even more directly into the negotiation of collective agreements. Our labor policy is not presently erected on a foundation of government control of the results of negotiations. . . .

. . . The Board contends that because an orthodox "total" strike is "traditional," its use must be taken as being consistent with 9(b)(3); but since the tactics here are not "traditional" or "normal," they need not be so viewed. Further, the Board cites what it conceives to be the public's moral condemnation of the sort of employee tactics involved here. But again we cannot see how these distinctions can be made under a statute which simply enjoins a duty to bargain in good faith. Again these relevant arguments when the question is the scope of the concerted activities given affirmative protections by the Act. But as we have developed, the use of economic pressure by the parties to a labor dispute is not a grudging exception to some policy of completely academic discussion enjoined by the Act; it is part and parcel of the process of collective bargaining. On this basis, we fail to see the relevance of whether the practice in question is time-honored or whether its exercise is generally supported by public opinion. It may be that the tactics used here deserve condemnation, but this would not justify attempting to pour that condemnation into a vessel not designed to hold it. . . .

. . .

. . . These distinctions essayed by the Board here, and the lack of relationship to the statutory standard inherent in them, confirm us in our conclusion that the judgment of the Court of Appeals, setting aside the order of the Board, must be affirmed. For they make clear to us that when the Board moves in this area, with only 8(b)(3) for support, it is functioning as an arbiter of the sort of economic weapons the parties can use in seeking to gain acceptance of their bargaining demands. It has sought to introduce some standard of properly "balanced" bargaining power, or some new distinction of justifiable and unjustifiable, proper and "abusive" economic weapons into the collective bargaining duty imposed by the Act. The Board's assertion of power under 8(b)(3) allows it to sit in judgment upon every economic weapon the parties to a labor contract negotiation employ, judging it on the very general standard of that section, not drafted with reference to specific forms of economic pressure. We have expressed our belief that this amounts to the Board's entrance into the substantive aspects of the bargaining process to an extent Congress has not countenanced.

It is one thing to say that the Board has been afforded flexibility to determine, for example, whether an employer's disciplinary action taken against specific workers is permissable or not, or whether a party's conduct at the bargaining table evidences a real desire to come into agreement. The statute in such areas clearly poses the problem to the Board for its solution. . . . It is quite another matter, however, to say that the Board has been afforded flexibility in picking and choosing which economic devices of labor and management shall be branded as unlawful. Congress has been rather specific when it has come to outlaw particular economic weapons on the part of unions. . . . But the activities here involved have never been specifically outlawed by Congress. To be sure, the express prohibitions of the Act are not exclusive—if there were any questions of a strategem or device to evade the policies of the Act, the Board hardly would be powerless. . . . But it is clear to us that the Board needs a more specific charter than 8(b)(3) before it can add to the Act's prohibitions here.

. . .

It is suggested here that the time has come for a reevaluation of the basic content of collective bargaining as contemplated by the federal legislation. But that is for Congress. Congress has demonstrated its capacity to adjust the nation's labor legislation to what, in its legislative judgment, constitutes the statutory pattern appropriate to the developing state of labor relations in the country. Major revisions of the basic statute were enacted in 1947 and 1959. To be sure, then, Congress might be of opinion that greater stress should be put on the role of "pure" negotiation in settling labor disputes, to the extent of eliminating more and more economic weapons from the parties' grasp, and perhaps it might start with the ones involved here; or in consideration of the alternatives, it might shrink from such an undertaking. But Congress' policy has not yet moved to this point, and with only 8(b)(3) to lean on, we do not see how the Board can do so on its own.

Affirmed.

Insurance Agents Separate Opinion

Separate opinion of Mr. Justice Frankfurter, which Mr. Justice Harlan and Mr. Justice Whittaker join.

. . .

I agree that the position taken by the Board here is not tenable. In enforcing the duty to bargain the Board must find the ultimate fact whether, in the case before it and in the context of all its circumstances, the respondent has engaged in bargaining without the sincere desire to reach agreement which the Act commands. I further agree that the Board's action in this case is not sustainable as resting upon a determination that respondent's apparent bargaining was in fact a sham, because the evidence is insufficient to justify that conclusion even giving the Board, as we must, every benefit of its right to draw on its experience in interpreting the industrial significance of the facts of a record. . . . What the Board has in fact done is lay down a rule of law that such conduct as was involved in carrying out the "Work Without a Contract" program necessarily betokens bad faith in the negotiations.

The Court's opinion rests its conclusion on the generalization that "The ordinary economic strike is not evidence of a failure to bargain in good faith . . . (because) there is simply no inconsistency between the application of economic pressure and good faith collective bargaining."

This large statement is justified solely by reference to 8(b)(3) and to the proposition that inherent in bargaining is room for the play of forces which reveal the strength of one party, or the weakness of the other, in the economic context in which they seek agreement. But in determining the state of mind of a party to collective bargaining negotiations the Board does not deal in terms of abstract "economic pressure." It must proceed in terms of specific conduct which it weighs as a more or less reliable manifestation of the state of mind with which bargaining is conducted. No conduct in the complex context of bargaining for a labor agreement can profitably be reduced to such an abstraction as "economic pressure." An exertion of "economic pressure" may at the same time be part of a concerted effort to evade or disrupt a normal course of negotiations. Vital differences in conduct, varying in character and effect from mild persuasion to destructive, albeit "economic," violence are obscured under cover of a single abstract phrase.

While 8(b)(3) of course contemplates some play of "economic pressure," it does not follow that the purpose in engaging in tactics designed to exert it is to reach agreement through the bargaining process in the manner which the statute commands, so that the Board is precluded from considering such conduct, in the totality of circumstances as evidence of the actual state of mind of the actor. Surely to deny this scope for allowable judgment to the Board is to deny to it the special function with which it has been entrusted. . . .

. . . One need not romanticize the community of interest between employers and employees, or be unmindful of the conflict between them, to recognize that utilization of what in one set of circumstances may only signify resort to the traditional weapons of labor may in another and relevant context offend the attitude toward bargaining commanded by the statute. . . .

. . . The broadly phrased terms of the Taft-Hartley Law should be applied to carry out the broadly conceived policies of the Act. At the core of the promotion of collection bargaining which was the chief means by which the great social purposes of the National Labor Relations Act were sought to be furthered, is a purpose to discourage, more and more, industrial combatants from pressing their demands by all available means to the limits of the justification of self-interest. This calls for appropriate judicial construction of existing legislation. The statute lays its emphasis upon reason and a willingness to employ it as the dominant force in bargaining. That emphasis is respected by declining to take as a postulate of the duty to bargain that the legally impermissible exertions of so-called economic pressure must be restricted to the crudities of brute force. . . .

The Board urges that this Court has approved its enforcement of 8(b)(3) by the outlawing of conduct *per se*, and without regard to ascertainment of a state of mind. It relies upon four cases: . . . These cases do not sustain its position. . . . To the extent that in any of these cases language referred to a *per se* proscription of conduct, it was in relation to facts strongly indicating a lack of a sincere desire to reach agreement.

. . .

. . . Viewed as a determination upon all the evidence that the respondent was bargaining without the sincere desire to compose differences and reach agreement which the statute commands, the Board's conclusion must fall for want of support in the evidence as a whole. . . . From the conduct of its counsel before the Trial Examiner, and from its opinion, it is apparent that the Board proceeded upon the belief that respondent's tactics were, without more, sufficient evidence of a lack of a sincere desire to reach agreement to make other consideration of its conduct unnecessary. For that reason the case should be remanded to the Board for further opportunity to introduce pertinent evidence, if any there be, of respondent's lack of good faith.

Viewed as a determination by the Board that it could, quite apart from respondent's state of mind, proscribe its tactics because they were not "traditional," or were thought to be subject to public disapproval, or because employees who engaged in them may have been subject to discharge, the Board's conclusion proceeds from the application of an erroneous rule of law.

The decision of the Court of Appeals should be vacated, and the case remanded to the Board for further proceedings consistent with these views.

PART III. COMMENTS ON PUBLIC POLICY

The first following comment was prepared by a distinguished Independent Study Group of nine members under the chairmanship of Clark Kerr, then president of the University of California.

The second following comment is by Stanley M. Jacks, then associate professor of Industrial Management, Massachusetts Institute of Technology.

"The Duty to Bargain in Good Faith"[1]

The present national policy also calls on both employers and unions to bargain in good faith over wages, hours, and working conditions. The original intent of this provision was to ensure a minimal degree of recognition so that efforts to decide the question of representation by an orderly process would not be frustrated. Senator David I. Walsh, then chairman

---

[1] Excerpts from *The Public Interests in National Labor Policy* by an Independent Study Group, Committee for Economic Development, 1960, pp. 81–82.

of the Senate Committee on Education and Labor, in arguing for this provision in 1935, said:

When the employees have chosen their organization, when they have selected their representatives, all the bill proposes to do is to escort them to the door of the employer and say, "Here they are, the legal representatives of your employees." What happens behind those doors is not inquired into, and the bill does not seek to inquire into it.

Senator Walsh's objective was a sensible one, and an appealingly simple one, too. Unfortunately, as time has passed, the simplicity has been lost. It has been succeeded by a flood of litigation and an increasingly complex set of regulations stemming from amendments of the original provisions and from interpretations by the NLRB and the courts. The efficacy of the process is achieving a more ambitious objective—to compel the parties to bargain in good faith—is at best doubtful.

Parties have been told that they must bargain in good faith, and elaborate tests have been devised in an attempt to determine "objectively" whether the proper subjective attitude prevails. The limitations and artificiality of such tests are apparent, and the possibilities of evasion are almost limitless. In the light of the realities of the bargaining situation, distinctions between matters that are subject to "mandatory bargaining" and those that are not have a hollow ring. Basically, it is unrealistic to expect that, by legislation, "good faith" can be brought to the bargaining table. Indeed, the provisions designed to bring "good faith" have become a tactical weapon used in many situations as a means of harassment.

Delays in processing duty-to-bargain cases and in getting final court orders have undoubtedly contributed to the ineffectiveness of the efforts in this area and to the use of economic force *in lieu* of resort to the legal machinery. But, too much cannot be expected in the way of reducing delay, since the area is one in which delays can easily be provoked if one party so desires.

The subjects to be covered by bargaining, the procedures to be followed, the nuances of strategy involving the timing of a "best offer," the question of whether to reopen a contract during its term—such matters as these are best left to the parties themselves. Indeed, the work load of the National Labor Relations Board and of the parties could be substantially reduced by returning these issues to the door of the employer or union, where Senator Walsh wisely left them.

"National Labor Policy and the Duty to Bargain Collectively"[2]

Converting the obligation to bargain collectively toward more limited goals, however, poses problems which the CED Report does not consider

[2] Excerpts from an article by Stanley M. Jacks appearing in *Industrial Management Review*, Vol. III (Spring 1962), pp. 46–59.

and, in fact, tends to obscure. The duty to bargain collectively in good faith serves more than one purpose. It compels acceptance of the principle of collective bargaining as well as good faith at the bargaining table. The principle of collective bargaining excludes unilateral action by the employer or the negotiation of terms and conditions with individual employees. It requires that the employer treat union demands as something more than suggestions to which he can respond or not at his pleasure. If the recommendation in the CED Report that "the effort to legislate bargaining in good faith should be abandoned" is to be implemented, a question arises whether the requirement of good faith acceptance of the principle of collective bargaining is to be retained. Assuming that it is desired to retain this requirement, a point on which the CED Report is not clear, it follows that the good-faith concept cannot be entirely extirpated from the law. The problem becomes one of delimiting the concept so as to leave the parties free to negotiate after their own fashion.

. . .

It is not clear, however, whether the authors of the CED Report seek to contain the law of bargaining or whether they would abolish it. If the Report is read to recommend a policy aimed only at orderly selection of employee representatives (a policy which the Report erroneously attributes to the framers of the Wagner Act) the foundation of the current law of bargaining would be removed. Such a proposal would raise profound questions for the future of labor relations in the unorganized sector of the economy and for parts of the organized sector as well. If the law were now to withdraw the obligation of the employer to deal in any meaningful sense with the representative selected by the employees and impose no constraints upon employer conduct other than the requirement that he not deal with a minority union, the mode of establishing collective bargaining relationships would be drastically altered. While strategically situated employees, particularly those backed by powerful unions, would not feel the full impact of the change, other employees, such as the Southern textile workers, those engaged in agriculture, workers in service trades, etc., would feel keenly the absence of the legal leverage in effectuating collective bargaining which labor has enjoyed for the past quarter century. Even in organized companies the employer would find himself related very differently to the union. While the impact would vary depending on the power of the union and the quality of the relationship between the parties, aggressive managements might be encouraged to force a test of strength.

. . .

. . . The following statutory definition of bargaining, however, would appear to achieve the principal objectives of the CED proposals. The phrase "to bargain collectively" would then be defined as:

The performance of the mutual obligation of the employer and the representative of the employees to meet at reasonable times and confer with respect to wages, hours, and other terms and conditions of employment, or the negotiation of an agreement, or any question arising thereunder, and the execution of a written contract incorporating any agreement reached if requested by either party, but such obligation does not compel either party to agree to a proposal or make a counterproposal or require the making of a concession. Nor shall such obligation limit the right of either party to insist upon the inclusion of any lawful provision as a condition of agreement.

QUESTIONS

1. What is the obligation in good faith?
2. Following the line of thought presented in the dissents and separate opinions in Truitt, Wooster Division of Borg-Warner, and Insurance Agents, how would the Board put proper emphasis on particular subjects for bargaining when considered in a context of bargaining tactics?
3. In creating "nonmandatory" subjects has the Board usurped the power of Congress to create "unlawful" subjects? What alternative was available to the Board?
4. Although Professor Jacks has drafted a clause to implement the Independent Study Group's recommendation, he has serious misgivings about enacting the clause into law. Are his misgivings well founded?

CASE 2
Labor Arbitration and the Courts

Voluntary labor arbitration is widely used in the United States. It has been estimated that over 90 percent of all American labor agreements provide for voluntary arbitration as the terminal point in the handling of some grievances. In some parts of the world, governmentally established labor courts perform the functions assigned to private arbitrators in the United States.

The Supreme Court decisions which make up most of this case deal with the question of the legal enforceability of an agreement to arbitrate and judicial review of arbitrators' awards. In addition to dealing with an important legal question, the opinions in these cases contain interesting comments on the arbitration process and its function in the broader process of collective bargaining.

Supreme Court of the United States
United Steelworkers of America v. American Manufacturing Company
June 20, 1960, 363 U.S. 564

Mr. Justice Douglas delivered the opinion of the Court.

The suit was brought by petitioner union in the District Court to compel arbitration of a "grievance" that petitioner, acting for one Sparks, a union member, had filed with the respondent, Sparks's employer. The employer defended on the ground (1) that Sparks is estopped from making his claim because he had a few days previously settled a workmen's compensation claim against the company on the basis that he was permanently partially disabled; (2) that Sparks is not physically able to do the work; and (3) that this type of dispute is not arbitrable under the collective bargaining agreement in question.

The agreement provided that during its term there would be "no strike" unless the employer refused to abide by a decision of the arbitrator. The agreement sets out a detailed grievance procedure with a provision for arbitration (regarded as the standard form) of all disputes between the parties "as to the meaning, interpretation and application of the provisions of this agreement."

The agreement also reserves to the management power to suspend or discharge any employee "for cause."

It also contains a provision that the employer will employ and promote employees on the principle of seniority "where ability and efficiency are equal." Sparks left his work due to an injury and while off work brought an action for compensation benefits. The case was settled, Sparks's physician expressing the opinion that the injury had made him 25 percent permanently partially disabled. That was on September 9. Two weeks later the union filed a grievance which charged that Sparks was entitled to return to his job by virtue of the seniority provision of the collective bargaining agreement. Respondent refused to arbitrate and this acton was brought. The District Court held that Sparks, having accepted the settlement on the basis of permanent partial disability was estopped to claim any seniority or employment rights and granted the motion for summary judgment. The Court of Appeals affirmed for different reasons. After reviewing the evidence it held that the grievance is "a frivolous, patently baseless one, not subject to arbitration under the collective bargaining agreement." The case is here on a writ of certiorari.

Section 203(d) of the Labor Management Relations Act, 1947, states: "Final adjustment by a method agreed upon by the parties is hereby declared to be the desirable method for settlement of grievance disputes arising over the application or interpretation of an existing collective bargaining agreement. . . ." That policy can be effectuated only if the means chosen by the parties for settlement of their differences under a collective bargaining agreement is given full play.

. . . The collective agreement required arbitration of claims that courts might be unwilling to entertain. Yet in the context of the plant or industry, the grievance may assume proportions of which judges are ignorant. Moreover, the agreement is to submit all grievances to arbitration, not merely those that a court may deem to be meritorious. There is no exception in the "no-strike" clause and none therefore should be read into the grievance clause since one is the *quid pro quo* for the other. The question is not whether in the mind of a court there is equity in the claim.

Arbitration is a stabilizing influence only as it serves as a vehicle for handling every and all disputes that arise under the agreement.

The collective agreement calls for the submission of grievances in the categories which it describes irrespective of whether a court may deem them to be meritorious. . . . The function of the court is very limited when the parties have agreed to submit all questions of contract interpretation to the arbitrator. It is then confined to ascertaining whether the party seeking arbitration is making a claim which on its face is governed by the contract. Whether the moving party is right or wrong is a question of contract interpretation for the arbitrator. In these circumstances the moving party should not be deprived of the arbitrator's judgment, when it was his judgment and all that it connotes that was bargained for.

The courts therefore have no business weighing the merits of the grievance, considering whether there is equity in a particular claim, or determining whether there is particular language in the written instrument which will support the claim. The agreement is to submit all grievances to arbitration, not merely those the court will deem meritorious. The processing of even frivolous claims may have therapeutic values which those who are not a part of the plant environment may be quite unaware.

The union claimed in this case that the company had violated a specific provision of the contract. The company took the position that it had not violated that clause. There was, therefore, a dispute between the parties as to "the meaning, interpretation and application" of the collective bargaining agreement. Arbitration should have been ordered. When the judiciary undertakes to determine the merits of a grievance under the guise of interpreting the grievance procedure of collective bargaining agreements, it usurps a function which under that regime is entrusted to the arbitration tribunal.

Reversed.

Mr. Justice Frankfurter concurs in the result.

Mr. Justice Whittaker, believing that the District Court lacked jurisdiction to determine the merits of the claim which the parties had validly agreed to submit to the exclusive jurisdiction of a Board of Arbitrators, concurs in the result of this opinion.

Mr. Justice Black took no part in the consideration or decision of this case.

Supreme Court of the United States
United Steelworkers of America v. Warrior and Gulf
Navigation Company
June 20, 1960, 363 U.S. 574

Mr. Justice Douglas delivered the opinion of the Court.

Respondent transports steel and steel products by barge and maintains a terminal at Chicasaw, Alabama, where it performs maintenance and repair work on its barges. The employees at that terminal constitute a bargaining unit covered by a collective bargaining agreement negotiated by petitioner union. Respondent between 1956 and 1958 laid off some employees, reducing the bargaining unit from 42 to 23 men. This reduction was due in part to respondent contracting maintenance work, previously done by its employees, to other companies. The latter used respondent's supervisors to lay out the work and hired some of the laid-off employees of respondent (at reduced wages). Some were in fact assigned to work on respondent's barges. A number of employees signed a grievance which petitioner presented to respondent, the grievance reading:

We are hereby protesting the Company's actions, of arbitrarily and unreasonably contracting out work to other concerns, that could and previously has been performed by Company employees.

This practice became unreasonable, unjust and discriminatory in view of the fact that at present there are a number of employees that have been laid off for about 1 and ½ years or more for allegedly lack of work.

Confronted with these facts we charge that the Company is in violation of the contract by inducing a partial lockout, of a number of the employees who would otherwise be working were it not for this unfair practice.

The collective agreement had both a "no-strike" and a "no-lockout" provision. It also had a grievance procedure which provided in relevant part as follows:

Issues which conflict with any Federal statute in its application as established by Court procedure or matters which are strictly a function of management shall not be subject to arbitration under this section.

Should differences arise between the Company and the Union or its members employed by the Company as to the meaning and application of the provisions of this Agreement, or should any local trouble of any kind arise, there shall be no suspension of work on account of such differences but an earnest effort shall be made to settle such differences immediately in the following manner:

A. For Maintenance Employees:

First, between the aggrieved employees, and the Foreman involved; Second, between a member or members of the Grievance Committee designated by the Union, and the Foreman and Master Mechanics. . . .

Fifth, if agreement has not been reached, the matter shall be referred to as impartial umpire for decision. The parties shall meet to decide on an umpire acceptable to both. If no agreement on selection of an umpire is reached, the parties shall jointly petition the United States Conciliation Service for suggestion of a list of umpires from which selection will be made. The decision of the umpire shall be final.

Settlement of this grievance was not had and respondent refused arbitration. This suit was then commenced by the union to compel it. . . . The District Court granted respondent's motion to dismiss the complaint. It held after hearing evidence, much of which went to the merits of the grievances, that the agreement did not "confide in the arbitrator the right to review the defendant's business judgment in contracting out work." It further held that "the contracting out of repair and maintenance work, as well as construction work, is strictly a function of management not limited in any respect by the labor agreement involved here." The Court of Appeals affirmed by a divided vote, the majority holding that the collective agreement had withdrawn from the grievance procedure "matters which are strictly a function of management" and that contracting-out fell in that exception. The case is here on a writ of certiorari.

We held in *Textile Workers* v. *Lincoln Mills* that a grievance arbitration provision in a collective agreement could be enforced by reason of paragraph 301(a) of the Labor Management Relations Act and that the policy to be applied in enforcing this type of arbitration was that reflected in our national labor laws. The present federal policy is to promote industrial stabilization through the collective bargaining agreement. A major factor in achieving industrial peace is the inclusion of a provision for arbitration of grievances in the collective bargaining agreement.[1]

Thus the run of arbitration cases become irrelevant to our problem. There the choice is between the adjudication of cases or controversies in courts with established procedures or even special statutory safeguards on the one hand and the settlement of them in the more informal arbitration tribunal on the other. In the commercial case, arbitration is the substitute for litigation. Here arbitration is the substitute for industrial strife. Since arbitration of labor disputes has quite different functions from arbitration under an ordinary commercial agreement, the hostility evinced by courts toward arbitration of commercial agreements has no place here. For arbitration of labor disputes under collective bargaining agreements is part and parcel of the collective bargaining process itself.

The collective bargaining agreement states the rights and duties of the parties. It is more than a contract; it is a generalized code to govern a myriad of cases which the draftsmen cannot wholly anticipate. . . . It calls into being a new common law—the common law of a particular industry or of a particular plant.

. . .

A collective bargaining agreement is an effort to erect a system of industrial self-government. When most parties enter into contractual relationship, they do so voluntarily. In the sense that there is no real compulsion to deal with one another, as opposed to dealing with other parties. This is not true of the labor agreement. The choice is generally not between entering or refusing to enter into a relationship, for that in all probability preexists the negotiations. Rather it is between having that

---

[1] Complete effectuation of the federal policy is achieved when the agreement contains both an arbitration provision for all unresolved grievances and an absolute prohibition of strikes, the arbitration agreement being the *quid pro quo* for the agreement to strike.

relationship governed by an agreed upon rule of law or leaving each and every matter subject to a temporary resolution dependent solely upon the relative strength, at any given moment, of the contending forces. The mature labor agreement may attempt to regulate all aspects of the complicated relationship, from the most crucial to the most minute over an extended period of time. Because of the compulsion to reach agreement and breadth of the matters covered, as well as the need for a fairly concise and readable instrument, the product of negotiations (the written document) is, in the words of the late Dean Shulman, "a compilation of diverse provisions; some provide objective criteria almost automatically applicable; some provide more or less specific standards which require reason and judgment in their application; and some do little more than leave problems to future consideration with an expression of hope and good faith." Gaps may be left to be filled in by reference to the practices of the particular industry and of the various shops covered by the agreement. Many of the specific practices which underlie the agreement may be unknown except in hazy form, even to the negotiators. Courts and arbitration in the context of most commercial contracts are resorted to because there has been a breakdown in the working relationship of the parties; such resort is the unwanted exception. But the grievance machinery under a collective bargaining agreement is at the very heart of the system of industrial self-government. Arbitration is the means of solving the unforeseeable by molding a system of private law for all the problems which may arise and to provide for their solution in a way which will generally accord with the variant needs and desires of the parties. The processing of disputes through the grievance machinery is actually a vehicle by which meaning and content is given to the collective bargaining agreement.

Apart from matters that the parties specifically exclude, all of the questions on which the parties disagree must therefore come within the scope of the grievance and arbitration provisions of the collective agreement. The grievance procedure is, in other words, a part of the continuous collective bargaining process. It, rather than a strike, is the terminal point of a disagreement.

. . .

The labor arbitrator performs functions which are not normal to the courts; the considerations which help him fashion judgments may indeed be foreign to the competence of courts. The labor arbitrator's source of law is not confined to the express provisions of the contract, as the industrial common law—the practices of the industry and the shop—is equally a part of the collective bargaining agreement although not expressed in it. The labor arbitrator is usually chosen because of the parties' confidence in his knowledge of the common law of the shop and their trust in his personal judgment to bring to bear considerations which are not expressed in the contract as criteria for judgment. The parties expect that his judgment of a particular grievance will reflect not only what the contract says but, insofar as the collective bargaining agreement permits, such factors as the effect upon productivity of a particular result, its consequence to the morale of the shop, his judgment whether tensions will be heightened or diminished. For the parties' objective in using the arbitration process is primarily to further their common goal of uninterrupted production under the agreement to make the agreement serve their specialized needs. The ablest judge cannot be expected to bring the same experience and competence to bear upon the determination of a grievance, because he cannot be similarly informed.

The Congress, however, has by para. 301 of the Labor Management Relations Act, assigned the courts the duty of determining whether the reluctant party has breached his promise to arbitrate. For arbitration is a matter of contract and a party cannot be required to submit to arbitration any dispute which he has not agreed so to submit. Yet, to be consistent with congressional policy in favor of settlement of disputes by the parties through the machinery of arbitration, the judicial inquiry under para. 301 must be strictly confined to question whether the reluctant party did agree to arbitrate the grievance or agreed to give the arbitrator power to make the award he made. An order to arbitrate the particular grievance should not be denied unless it may be said with positive assurance that the arbitration clause is not susceptible to an interpretation that covers the asserted dispute. Doubts should be resolved in favor of coverage.[2]

We do not agree with the lower courts that contracting-out grievances were necessarily excepted from the grievance procedure of this agreement. To be sure the agreement provides that "matters which are strictly a function of management shall not be subject to arbitration." But it goes on to say that if "differences" arise or if "any local trouble of any kind" arises, the grievance procedure shall be applicable.

Collective bargaining agreements regulate or restrict the exercise of management functions; they do not oust management from the performance of them. Management hires and fires, pays and promotes, supervises and plans. All these are part of its function, and absent a collective bargaining agreement, it may be exercised freely except as limited by public law and by the willingness of employees to work under the particular, unilaterally imposed conditions. A collective bargaining agreement may treat only with certain specific practices, leaving the rest to management but subject to the possibility of work stoppages. When, however, an absolute no-strike clause is included in the agreement, then in a very real sense everything that management does is subject to the agreement, for

---

[2] It is clear that under both the agreement in this case and that involved in American Manufacturing Co., the question of arbitrability is for the courts to decide. Where the assertion by the claimant is that the parties excluded from court determination not merely the decision of the merits of the grievance but also the question of its arbitrability, vesting power to make both decisions in the arbitrator, the claimant must bear the burden of a clear demonstration of that purpose.

either management is prohibited or limited in the action it takes, or if not, it is protected from interference by strikes. This comprehensive reach of the collective bargaining agreement does not mean, however, that the language, "strictly a function of management" has no meaning.

"Strictly a function of management" might be thought to refer to any practice of management in which, under particular circumstances prescribed by the agreement, it is permitted to indulge. But if courts . . . determine what is permitted and what is not, the arbitration clause would be swallowed up by the exception. Every grievance in a sense involves a claim that management has violated some provision of the agreement.

Accordingly, "strictly a function of management" must be interpreted as referring only to that over which the contract gives management complete control and unfettered discretion. Respondent claims that the contracting out of work falls within this category. Contracting out work is the basis of many grievances; and that type of claim is grist in the mills of the arbitrators. A specific collective bargaining agreement may exclude contracting-out from the grievance procedure. Or a written collateral agreement may make clear that contracting out was not a matter for arbitration. In such a case a grievance based solely on contracting out would not be arbitrable. Here, however, there is no such provision. Nor is there any showing that the parties designed the phrase "strictly a function of management" to encompass any and all forms of contracting out. In the absence of any express provision excluding a particular grievance from arbitration, we think only the most forceful evidence of a purpose to exclude the claim from arbitration can prevail, particularly where, as here, the exclusion clause is vague and the arbitration clause quite broad. Since any attempt by a court to infer such a purpose necessarily comprehends the merits, the court should view with suspicion an attempt to persuade it to become entangled in the construction of the substantive provisions of a labor agreement, even through the back door of interpreting the arbitration clause, when the alternative is to utilize the services of an arbitrator.

The grievance alleged that the contracting out was a violation of the collective bargaining agreement. There was, therefore, a dispute "as to the meaning and application of the provisions of this Agreement" which the parties had agreed would be determined by arbitration.

The judiciary sits in these cases to bring into operation an arbitral process which substitutes a regime of peaceful settlement for the older regime of industrial conflict. Whether contracting out in the present case violated the agreement is the question. It is a question for the arbiter, not for the courts.

Reversed.

Mr. Justice Frankfurter concurs in the result.

Mr. Justice Black took no part in the consideration or decision of this case.

Warrior and Gulf Dissenting Opinion

Mr. Justice Whittaker, dissenting.

Until today, I have understood it to be the unquestioned law, as this Court has consistently held, that arbitrators are private judges chosen by the parties to decide particular matters specifically submitted; that the contract under which matters are submitted to arbitrators is at once the source and limit of their authority and powers; and that their power to decide issues with finality, thus ousting the normal functions of the courts, must rest upon a clear, definitive agreement of the parties, as such power can never be implied. . . . I believe that the Court today departs the established principles announced in these decisions.

Here, the employer operates a shop for the normal maintenance of its barges, but it is not equipped to make major repairs, and accordingly the employer has, from the beginning of its operations more than 19 years ago, contracted out its major work. During most, if not all, of this time the union has represented the employees in that unit. The District Court found that "(t)hroughout the successive labor agreements between these parties, including the present one, . . . (the Union) has unsuccessfully sought to negotiate changes in the labor contract, and particularly during the negotiation of the present labor agreement, . . . which would have limited the right of the (employer) to continue the practice of contracting out such work."

The labor agreement involved here provides for arbitration of disputes respecting the interpretation and application of the agreement and, arguably, also some other things. But the first says: "(M)atters which are strictly a function of management shall not be subject to arbitration under this section." Although acquiescing for 19 years in the employer's interpretation that contracting out work was "strictly a function of management," and having repeatedly tried—particularly in the negotiation of the agreement involved here—but unsuccessfully, to induce the employer to agree to a covenant that would prohibit it from contracting out work, the union, after having agreed to and signed the contract involved, presented a "grievance" on the ground that the employer's contracting out work at a time when some employees in the unit were laid off for lack of work, constituted a partial "lockout" of employees in violation of the antilockout provision of the agreement.

Being unable to persuade the employer to agree to cease contracting out work or to agree to arbitrate the "grievance," the union brought this action in the District Court, under para. 301 of the Labor Management Relations Act for a decree compelling the employer to submit the "grievance" to arbitration. The District Court, holding that the contracting out of work was, and over a long course of dealings had been interpreted and understood by the parties to be "strictly a function of management," and was therefore specifically excluded from arbitration by the terms of the contract, denied the relief prayed. The Court of Appeals affirmed, and we granted certiorari.

The Court now reverses the judgment of the Court of Appeals. It holds that the arbitrator's source of law is "not confined to the express provisions of the contract," that arbitration should be ordered "unless it may be said with positive assurance that the arbitration clause is not susceptible to an interpretation that covers the asserted dispute," that "(d)oubts (of arbitrability) should be resolved in favor of coverage," and that when as here, "a no-strike clause is included in the agreement, then . . . everything that management does is subject to (arbitration)." I understand the Court thus to hold that the arbitrators are not confined to the express provisions of the contract, that arbitration is to be ordered unless it may be said with positive assurance that arbitration of a particular dispute is excluded by the contract, that doubts of arbitrability are to be resolved in favor of arbitration, and that when as here the contract contains a no-strike clause, everything that management does is subject to arbitration.

This is an entirely new and strange doctrine to me. I suggest, with deference, that it departs both the contract of the parties and the controlling decisions of this Court. I find nothing in the contract that purports to confer upon arbitrators any such general breadth of private judicial power. The Court cites no legislative or judicial authority that creates for or gives to arbitrators such broad general powers. . . .

With respect, I submit that there is nothing in the contract here to indicate that the employer "signified (its) willingness" to submit to arbitrators whether it must cease contracting our work. Certainly no such intention is "made manifest by plain language," as the law "requires," because such consent "is not to be implied." To the contrary, the parties by their conduct over many years interpreted the contracting out of major repair work to be "strictly a function of management," and if, as the concurring opinion suggests, the words of the contract can "be understood only by reference to the background which gave rise to their inclusion," then the interpretation given by the parties over 19 years to the phrase "matters which are strictly a function of management" should logically have some significance here. By their contract, the parties agreed that "matters which are strictly a function of management shall not be subject to arbitration." The union over the course of many years repeatedly tried to induce the employer to agree to a covenant prohibiting the contracting out of work, but was never successful. The union again made such an effort in negotiating the very contract involved here, and, failing of success, signed the contract, knowing, of course, that it did not contain any such covenant, but that, to the contrary, it contained, just as had the former contracts, a covenant that "matters which are strictly a function of management shall not be subject to arbitration." Does not this show that instead of signifying a willingness to submit to arbitration the matter of whether the employer might continue to contract out work, the parties fairly agreed to exclude at least that matter from arbitration? Surely it cannot be said that the parties agreed to such a submission by any "plain language." Does not then the Court's opinion compel the employer "to submit to arbitration (a) question which (it) has not agreed so to submit"?

. . .

I agree with the Court that courts have no proper concern with the "merits" of claims which by contract the parties have agreed to submit to the exclusive jurisdiction of arbitrators. But the question is one of jurisdiction. Neither may entrench upon the jurisdiction of the other. The test is: Did the parties in their contract "manifest by plain language" their willingness to submit the issue in controversy to arbitrators? If they did, then the arbitrators have exclusive jurisdiction of it, and the courts, absent fraud or the like, must respect that exclusive jurisdiction and cannot interfere. But if they did not, then the courts must exercise their jurisdiction, when properly invoked, to protect the citizen against the attempted use by arbitrators of pretended powers actually never conferred. That question always is, and from its very nature must be, a judicial one. Such was the question presented to the District Court and the Court of Appeals here. They found the jurisdictional facts, properly applied the settled law to those facts, and correctly decided the case. I would therefore affirm the judgment.

Supreme Court of the United States
United Steelworkers of America v. *Enterprise Wheel and Car Corporation*
June 20, 1960, 363 U.S. 593

Mr. Justice Douglas delivered the opinion of the Court.

Petitioner union and respondent during the period relevant here had a collective bargaining agreement which provided that any differences "as to the meaning and application" of the agreement should be submitted to arbitration and that the arbitrator's decision "shall be final and binding on the parties." Special provisions were included concerning the suspension and discharge of employees. The agreement stated:

Should it be determined by the Company or by an arbitrator in accordance with the grievance procedure that the employee has been suspended unjustly or discharged in violation of the provisions of this Agreement, the Company shall reinstate the employee and pay full compensation at the employee's regular rate of pay for the time lost.

The agreement also provided:

. . . It is understood and agreed that neither party will institute *civil suits or legal proceedings* against the other for alleged violation of any of the provisions of this labor contract; instead all disputes will be settled in the manner outlined in this Article III—Adjustment of Grievance.

A group of employees left their jobs in protest against the discharge of one employee. A union official advised them at once to return to work. An official of respondent at their request gave them permission and then rescinded it. The next day they were told they did not have a job any more "until this thing was settled one way or the other."

A grievance was filed; and when respondent finally refused to arbitrate, this suit was brought for specific enforcement of the arbitration provisions of the agreement. The District Court ordered arbitration. The arbitrator found that the discharge of the men was not justified, though their conduct, he said, was improper. In his view the facts warranted at most a suspension of the men for 10 days each. After their discharge and before the arbitration award, the collective bargaining agreement had expired. The union, however, continued to represent the workers at the plant. The arbitrator rejected the contention that expiration of the agreement barred reinstatement of the employees. He held that the provision of the agreement above quoted imposed an unconditional obligation on the employer. He awarded reinstatement with back pay, minus pay for a 10-day suspension and such sums as these employees received from other employment.

Respondent refused to comply with the award. Petitioner moved the District Court for enforcement. The District Court directed respondent to comply. The Court of Appeals, while agreeing that the District Court had jurisdiction to enforce an arbitration award under a collective bargaining agreement, held that the failure of the award to specify the amounts to be deducted from the back pay rendered the award unenforceable. That defect, it agreed, could be remedied by requiring the parties to complete the arbitration. It went on to hold, however, that an award for back pay subsequent to the date of termination of the collective bargaining agreement could not been enforced. It also held that the requirement for reinstatement of the discharged employees was likewise unenforceable because the collective agreement had expired.

The refusal of courts to review the merits of an arbitration award is the proper approach to arbitration under collective bargaining agreements. The federal policy of settling labor disputes by arbitration would be undermined if courts had the final say on the merits of the awards. . . .

When an arbitrator is commissioned to interpret and apply the collective bargaining agreement, he is to bring his informed judgment to bear in order to reach a fair solution of a problem. This is especially true when it comes to formulating remedies. There the need is for flexibility in meeting a wide variety of situations. The draftsmen may never have thought of what specific remedy should be awarded to meet a particular contingency. Nevertheless an arbitrator is confined to interpretation and application of the collective bargaining agreement; he does not sit to dispense his own brand of industrial justice. He may of course look for guidance from many sources, yet his award is legitimate only so long as it draws its essence from the collective bargaining agreement. When the arbitrator's words manifest an infidelity to this obligation, courts have no choice but to refuse enforcement of the award.

. . . A mere ambiguity in the opinion accompanying an award, which permits the inference that the arbitrator may have exceeded his authority, is not a reason for refusing to enforce the award. Arbitrators have no obligation to the court to give their reasons for an award. To require opinions free of ambiguity may lead arbitrators to play it safe by writing no supporting opinions. This would be undesirable for a well-reasoned opinion tends to engender confidence in the integrity of the process and aids in clarifying the underlying agreement. Moreover, we see no reason to assume that this arbitrator has abused the trust the parties confided in him and has not stayed within the areas marked out for his consideration. It is not apparent that he went beyond the submission. The Court of Appeals' opinion refusing to enforce the reinstatement and partial back pay portions of the award was not based upon any finding that the arbitrator did not premise his award on his construction of the contract. It merely disagreed with the arbitrator's construction of it.

The collective bargaining agreement could have provided that if any of the employees were wrongfully discharged, the remedy would be reinstatement and back pay up to the date they were returned to work. Respondent's major argument seems to be that by applying correct principles of law to the interpretation of the collective bargaining agreement it can be determined that the agreement did not so provide, and that therefore the arbitrator's decision was not based upon the contract. This plenary review by a court of the merits would make meaningless the provisions that the arbitrator's decision is final, for in reality it would almost never be final. . . . [As we emphasized in American Manufacturing Company] the question of interpretation of the collective bargaining agreement is a question for the arbitrator. It is the arbitrator's construction which was bargained for; and so far as the arbitrator's decision concerns construction of the contract, the courts have no business overruling him because their interpretation of the contract is different from his.

We agree with the Court of Appeals that the judgment of the District Court should be modified so that the amounts due the employees may be definitely determined by arbitration. In all other respects we think the judgment of the District Court should be affirmed. Accordingly, we reverse the judgment of the Court of Appeals except for that modification and remand the case to the District Court for proceedings in conformity with this opinion.

It is so ordered.

Mr. Justice Frankfurter concurs in the result.

Mr. Justice Black took no part in the consideration or decision of this case.

Enterprise Wheel and Car Dissenting Opinion

Mr. Justice Whittaker, dissenting.

Claiming that the employer's discharge on January 18, 1957, of 11 employees violated the provisions of its collective bargaining contract with the employer—covering the period beginning April 5, 1956, and ending April 5, 1957—the union sought and obtained arbitration, under the provisions of the contract, of the issues whether these employees had been discharged in violation of the agreement and, if so, should be ordered reinstated and awarded wages from the time of their wrongful discharge. In August, 1957, more than four months after the collective agreement had expired, these issues were tried before and submitted to a Board of Arbitrators. On April 10, 1958, the arbitrators made their award, finding that the 11 employees had been discharged in violation of the agreement and ordering their reinstatement with back pay at their regular rates from a time 10 days after their discharge to the time of reinstatement. Over the employer's objection that the collective agreement and the submission under it did not authorize nor empower the arbitrators to award reinstatement or wages for any period after the date of expiration of the contract (April 5, 1957), the District Court ordered enforcement of the award. The Court of Appeals modified the judgment by eliminating the requirement that the employer reinstate the employees and pay them wages for the period *after* expiration of the collective agreement, and affirmed it in all other respects, and we granted certiorari.

That the propriety of the discharges, under the collective agreement, was arbitrable under the provisions of that agreement, even after its expiration, is not in issue. Nor is there any issue here as to the power of the arbitrators to award reinstatement status and back pay to the discharged employees to the date of expiration of the collective agreement. It is conceded, too, that the collective agreement expired by its terms on April 5, 1957, and was never extended or renewed.

The sole question here is whether the arbitrators exceeded the submission and their power in awarding reinstatement and back pay for any period after expiration of the collective agreements. Like the Court of Appeals, I think they did. I find nothing in the collective agreement that purports to so authorize. Nor does the Court point to anything in the agreement that purports to do so. Indeed, the union does not contend that there is any such covenant in the contract. Doubtless all rights that accrued to the employees under the collective agreement during its terms, and that were made arbitrable by its provisions, could be awarded to them by the arbitrators, even through the period of the agreement had ended. But surely no rights *accrued* to the employees under the agreement after it had expired. Save for the provisions of the collective agreement, and in the absence, as here, of any applicable rule of law or contrary covenant between the employer and the employees, the employer had the legal right to discharge the employees at will. The collective agreement, however, protected them against discharge, for specified reasons, during its continuation. But when that agreement expired, it did not continue to afford rights *in futuro* to the employees—as though still effective and governing. After the agreement expired the employment status of these 11 employees was terminable at the will of the employer, as the Court of Appeals quite properly held . . . and the announced discharge of these 11 employees then became lawfully effective.

Once the contract expired, no rights continued to accrue under it to the employees. Thereafter they had no contractual right to demand that the employer continue to employ them, and *a fortiori* the arbitrators did not have power to order the employer to do so; nor did the arbitrators have power to order the employer to pay wages to them after the date of termination of the contract, which was also the effective date of their discharge.

The judgment of the Court of Appeals, affirming so much of the award as required reinstatement of the 11 employees to employment status and payment of their wages until expiration of the contract, but not thereafter, seems to me to be indubitably correct, and I would affirm it.

Concurring Opinion to Decisions in:
American Mfg. Co. (360)
Warrior and Gulf Navigation Co. (443)
Enterprise Wheel and Car Corp. (538)

Mr. Justice Brennan, with whom Mr. Justice Harlan joins, concurring.

While I join the Court's opinions in Nos. 443, 360, and 538, I add a word in Nos. 443 and 360.

In each of these cases the issue concerns the enforcement of but one promise—the promise to arbitrate in the context of an agreement dealing with a particular subject matter, the industrial relations between employers and employees. Other promises contained in the collective bargaining agreements are beside the point unless, by the very terms of the arbitration promise, they are made relevant to its interpretation. And I emphasize this, for the arbitration promise is itself a contract. The parties are free to make that promise as broad or as narrow as they wish for there is no compulsion in law requiring them to include any such promise in their agreement. The meaning of the arbitration promise is not to be found simply by reference to the dictionary definitions of the words the parties use, or by reference to the interpretation of commercial arbitration clauses. Words in a collective bargaining agreement, rightly viewed by the Court to be the charter instrument of a system of industrial self-government, like words in a statute, are to be understood only by reference to the background which gave rise to their inclusion. The Court therefore avoids the prescription of inflexible rules for the enforcement of arbitration promises. Guidance is given by identifying the various considerations which a court should take into account when construing a particular clause—considerations of the milieu in which the clause is negotiated and particularly underscored that the arbitral process in collective bargaining presupposes that the parties wanted the informed judgment of an arbitrator, precisely for the reason that judges cannot provide it. Therefore, a court asked to enforce a promise to arbitrate should ordinarily refrain from involving itself in the interpretation of the substantive provisions of the contract.

To be sure, since arbitration is a creature of contract, a court must always inquire, when a party seeks to invoke its aid to force a reluctant party to the arbitration table, whether the parties have agreed to arbitrate the particular dispute. In this sense, the question of whether a dispute is "arbitrable" is inescapably for the court.

On examining the arbitration clause, the court may conclude that it commits to arbitration any "dispute, difference, disagreement, or controversy of any nature or character." With that finding the court will have exhausted its function, except to order the reluctant party to arbitration. Similarly, although the arbitrator may be empowered only to interpret and apply the contract, the parties may have provided that any dispute as to whether a particular claim is within the arbitration clause is itself for the arbitrator. Again the court, without more, must send any dispute to the arbitrator, for the parties have agreed that the construction of the arbitration promise itself is for the arbitrator; and the reluctant party has breached his promise by refusing to submit the dispute to arbitration.

In American, the Court deals with a request to enforce the "standard" form of arbitration clause, one that provides for the arbitration of "any disputes, misunderstandings, differences or grievances, arising between the parties as to the meaning, interpretation and application of this agreement. . . ." Since the arbitration clause itself is part of the agreement, it might be argued that a dispute as to the meaning of that clause is for the arbitrator. But the Court rejects this position, saying that the threshold question, the meaning of the arbitration clause itself, is for the judge unless the parties clearly state to the contrary. However, the Court finds that the meaning of that "standard" clause is simply that the parties have agreed to arbitrate any dispute which the moving party asserts to involve construction of the substantive provisions of the contract, because such a dispute necessarily does involve such a construction.

The issue in the Warrior case is essentially no different from that in American, that is, it is whether the company agreed to arbitrate a particular grievance. In contrast to American, however, the arbitration promise here excludes a particular area from arbitration—"matters which are strictly a function of management." Because the arbitration promise is different, the scope of the court's inquiry may be broader. Here a court may be required to examine the substantive provisions of the contract to ascertain whether the parties have provided that contracting out shall be a "function of management." If a court may delve into the merits to the extent of inquiring whether the parties have expressly agreed whether or not contracting out was a "function of management," why was it error for the lower court here to evaluate the evidence of bargaining history for the same purpose? Neat logical distinctions do not provide the answer. The Court rightly concludes that appropriate regard for the national labor policy and the special factors relevant to the labor arbitral process, admonish that judicial inquiry into the merits of this grievance should be limited to the search for an explicit provision which brings the grievance under the cover of the exclusion clause since "the exclusion clause is vague and arbitration clause quite broad." The hazard of going further into the merits is amply demonstrated by what the courts below did. On the basis of inconclusive evidence, those courts found that Warrior was in no way limited by any implied covenants of good faith and fair dealing from contracting out as it pleased—which would necessarily mean that Warrior was free completely to destroy the collective bargaining agreement by contracting out all the work.

The very ambiguity of the Warrior exclusion clause suggests that the parties were generally more concerned with having an arbitrator render decisions as to the meaning of the contract than they were in restricting the arbitrator's jurisdiction. The case might of course be otherwise were the arbitration clause very narrow, or the exclusion clause quite specific, for the inference might then be permissible that the parties had manifested a greater interest in confining the arbitrator; the presumption of arbitrability would then not have the same force and the Court would be somewhat freer to examine into the merits.

The Court makes reference to an arbitration clause being the *quid pro quo* for a no-strike clause. I do not understand the Court to mean that the application of the principles announced today depends upon the presence of a no-strike clause in the agreements.

Mr. Justice Frankfurter joins these observations.

QUESTIONS

1. Law journals and industrial relations periodicals have published many commentaries on the significance of these court decisions. Special attention is called to the incisive analysis, "The Question of 'Arbitrability'—the Roles of the Arbitrator, the Court and the Parties," by Russell A. Smith, *Southwestern Law Journal*, Vol. XVI (April 1962), pp. 1–42; and the pamphlet *Model Arbitration Clauses to Protect Management Rights*, by the Labor Relations and Legal Department, Chamber of Commerce of the United

States, 1961. In view of the decisions, what phraseology would you suggest for an arbitration clause in an agreement? Would you want to limit the power of the arbitrator and exclude cases from his jurisdiction? What might be the practical labor relations consequences of severely restricting the jurisdiction of the arbitrator?

2. What is the probable effect of the court's comments on the nature of arbitration on arbitrators and the lower courts? As an arbitrator would you interpret the decisions as a new "Bill of Rights" for your profession?

3. Given these decisions, what are the benefits and dangers to unions and management in a loosely drawn collective bargaining agreement? Apart from the arbitration clause, do you think that these decisions will motivate the parties to tighten up the wording of their agreements on such matters as just cause for discipline, definition of the bargaining unit, duration of the agreement, and so on? How would you go about reviewing your agreement for loopholes?

4. "The grievance procedure is . . . a part of the continuous collective bargaining process." Discuss.

5. Contrast and evaluate Justice Whittaker's view, "arbitrators are private judges by the parties to decide particular matters specifically submitted," with Justice Douglas's view that "doubts should be resolved in favor of coverage."

6. Note the differences in the specific issues posed for the Court in these cases: Enterprise involves the enforceability of a faulty award after the fact, while Warrior and Gulf and American involve the coverage of the agreement to arbitrate. What questions about arbitrability and the enforcement of awards do these cases leave unanswered?

CASE 3
Remedies for Breach of Contract

This case consists of abstracts of two Supreme Court decisions dealing with the question of remedies for breach of the collective bargaining agreement.

Supreme Court of the United States
Atkins et al. v. Sinclair Refining Company
June 18, 1962, 370 U.S. 238

Mr. Justice White delivered the opinion of the Court.

The respondent company employs at its refinery in East Chicago, Illinois, approximately 1,700 men, for whom the petitioning international union and its local are bargaining agents, and 24 of whom are also petitioners here. In early February 1959, the respondent company docked three of its employees at the East Chicago refinery a total of $2.19. On February 13 and 14, 999 of the 1,700 employees participated in a strike or work stoppage, or so the complaint alleges. On March 12, the company filed this suit for damages and an injunction, naming the international and its local as defendants, together with 24 individual union member-employees.

Count I of the complaint, which was in three counts, stated a cause of action under Section 301 of the Taft-Hartley Act against the international and its local. It alleged an existing collective bargaining agreement between the international and the company containing, among other matters, a promise by the union not to strike over any cause which could be the subject of a grievance under other provisions of the contract. It was alleged that the international and the local caused the strike or work stoppage occurring on February 13 and 14 and that the strike was over the pay claims of three employees in the amount of $2.19, which claims were properly subject to the grievance procedure provided by the contract. The complaint asked for damages in the amount of $12,500 from the international and the local.

Count II of the complaint purported to invoke the diversity jurisdiction of the District Court. It asked judgment in the same amount against 24 individual employees, each of whom was alleged to be a committeeman of the local union and an agent of the international, and responsible for representing the international, the local, and their members. The complaint asserted that on February 13 and 14, the individuals, "contrary to their duty to plaintiff to abide by such contract, and maliciously confederating and conspiring together to cause the plaintiff expense and damage, and to induce breaches of said contract, and to interfere with performance thereof by the said labor organizations, and the affected employees, and to cause breaches thereof, individually and as officers, committeemen and agents of said labor organizations, fomented, assisted and participated in a strike or work stoppage. . . ."

Count III of the complaint asked for an injunction but that matter need not concern us here since it is disposed of in *Sinclair Refining Co.* v. *Atkinson,* decided this day.

The defendants filed a motion to dismiss the complaint on various grounds and a motion to stay the action for the reasons (1) that all of the issues in the suit were referrable to arbitration under the collective bargaining contract and (2) that important issues in the suit were also involved in certain grievances filed by employees and said to be in arbitration under the contract. The District Court denied the motion to dismiss Count I, dismissed Count II, and denied the motion to stay. The Court of Appeals upheld the refusal to dismiss or stay Count I, but reversed the dismissal of Count II, and this Court granted certiorari. . . .

I. We have concluded that Count I should not be dismissed or stayed. Count I properly states a cause of action under Section 301 and is to be governed by federal law. Under our decisions, whether or not the company was bound to arbitrate, as well as what issues it must arbitrate, is a matter to be determined by the Court on the basis of the contract entered into by the parties. "The Congress . . . has by Section 301 of the Labor Management Relations Act, assigned the courts the duty of determining whether the reluctant party has breached his promise to arbitrate. For arbitration is a matter of contract and a party cannot be required to submit to arbitration any dispute which he has not agreed so to submit." We think it unquestionably clear that the contract here involved is not susceptible to a construction that the company was bound to arbitrate its claim for damages against the union for breach of the undertaking not to strike.

While it is quite obvious from other provisions of the contract that the parties did not intend to commit all of their possible disputes and the whole scope of their relationship to the grievance and arbitration procedures established in Article 26, that article itself is determinative of the issue in this case since it precludes arbitration boards from considering any matters other than employee grievances. . . .

Article 26 then imposes the critical limitation. It is provided that local arbitration boards "shall consider only individual or local employee or local committee grievances arising under the application of the currently existing agreement." There is not a word in the grievance and arbitration article providing for the submission of grievances by the company. Instead, there is the express, flat limitation that arbitration boards should consider only employee grievances. Furthermore, the article expressly provides that arbitration may be invoked only at the option of the union. At no place in the contract does the union agree to arbitrate at the behest of the company. The company is to take its claims elsewhere, which it has now done.

The union makes a further argument for a stay. Following the strike, and both before and after the company filed its suit, 14 of the 24 individual defendants filed grievances claiming reimbursement for pay withheld by the employer. The union argues that even though the company need not arbitrate its claim for damages, it is bound to arbitrate these grievances; and the arbitrator, in the process of determining the grievants' right to reimbursement, will consider and determine issues which also underlie the company's claim for damages. Therefore, it is said that a stay of the court action is appropriate.

We are not satisfied from the record now before us, however, that any significant issue in the damage suit will be presented to and decided by an arbitrator. The grievances filed simply claimed reimbursement for pay due employees for time spent at regular work or processing grievances. Although the record is a good deal less than clear and although no answer had been filed in this case, it would appear from the affidavits of the parties presented in connection with the motion to stay that the grievants claimed to have been disciplined as a result of the work stoppage and that they were challenging this disciplinary action. The company sharply denies in its brief in this Court that any employee was disciplined. In any event, precisely what discipline was imposed, upon what grounds it is being attacked by the grievants, and the circumstances surrounding the withholding of pay from the employees are unexplained in the record. The union's brief here states that the important issue underlying the arbitration and the suit for damages is whether the grievants instigated or participated in a work stoppage contrary to the collective bargaining contract. This the company denies and it asserts that no issue in the damage suit will be settled by arbitrating the grievances.

The District Court must decide whether the company is entitled to damages from the union for breach of contract. The arbitrator, if arbitration occurs, must award on deny reimbursement in whole or in part to all or some of the 14 employees. His award, standing alone, obviously would determine no issue in the damage suit. If he awarded reimbursement to the employees and if it could be ascertained with any assurance that one of his subsidiary findings was that the 14 men had not participated in a forbidden work stoppage—the critical issue according to the union's brief—the company would nevertheless not be foreclosed in court since, even if it were bound by such a subsidiary finding made by the arbitrator, it would be free to prove its case in court through the conduct of other agents of the union. In this state of the record, the union has not made out its case for a stay.

For the foregoing reasons, the lower courts properly denied the union's motion to dismiss Count I or stay it pending arbitration of the employer's damage claim.

II. We turn now to Count II of the complaint, which charged 24 individual officers and agents of the union with breach of the collective bargaining contract and tortious interference with contractual relations. The District Court held that under Section 301 union officers or members cannot be held personally liable for union actions, and that therefore "suits of the nature alleged in Count II are no longer cognizable in state or federal courts." The Court of Appeals reversed, however, ruling that "Count II stated a cause of action cognizable in the courts of Indiana and, by diversity, maintainable in the District Court."

We are unable to agree with the Court of Appeals, for we are convinced that Count II is controlled by federal law and that it must be dismissed on the merits for failure to state a claim upon which relief can be granted.

Under Section 301 a suit for violation of the collective bargaining contract in either a federal or state court is governed by federal law and Count II on its face charges the individual defendants with a violation of the no-strike clause. After quoting verbatim the no-strike clause, Count II alleges that the 24 individual defendants "contrary to their duty to plaintiff to abide by" the contract fomented and participated in a work stoppage in violation of the no-strike clause. The union itself does not quarrel with the proposition that the relationship of the members of the bargaining unit to the employer is "governed by" the bargaining agreement entered into on their behalf by the union. It is universally accepted that the no-strike clause in a collective agreement at the very least establishes a rule of conduct or condition of employment the violation of which by employees justifies discipline or discharge. The conduct charged in Count II is therefore within the scope of a "violation" of the collective agreement.

As well as charging a violation of the no-strike clause by the individual defendants, Count II necessarily charges a violation of the clause by the union itself. The work stoppage alleged is the identical work stoppage for which the union is sued under Count I and the same damage is alleged as is alleged in Count I. Count II states that the individual defendants acted "as officers, committeemen and agents of said labor organizations" in breaching and inducing others to breach the collective bargaining contract. Count I charges the principal, and Count II charges the agents for acting on behalf of the principal. Whatever individual liability Count II alleges for the 24 individual defendants, it necessarily restates the liability of the union which is charged under Count I, since under Section 301(b) the union is liable for the acts of its agents, under familiar principles of the law of agency (see also Section 301(e)). Proof the allegations of Count II in its present form would inevitably prove a violation of the no-strike clause by the union itself. Count II, like Count I, is thus a suit based on the union's breach of its collective bargaining contract with the employer, and therefore comes within Section 301(a). When a union breach of contract is alleged, that the plaintiff seeks to hold the agents liable instead of the principal does not bring the action outside the scope of Section 301.

Under any theory, therefore, the company's action is governed by the national labor relations law which Congress commanded this Court to fashion under Section 301(a). We hold that this law requires the dismissal of Count II for failure to state a claim for which relief can be granted— whether the contract violation charged is that of the union or that of the union plus the union officers and agents.

When Congress passed Section 301, it declared its view that only the union was to be made to respond for union wrongs, and that the union members were not to be subject to levy. . . . In the debates, Senator Ball, one of the Act's sponsors, declared that Section 301, "by providing that the union may sue and be sued as a legal entity, for a violation of contract, and that liability for damages will lie against union assets only, will prevent a repetition of the Danbury Hatters case, in which many members lost their homes."

Consequently, in discharging the duty Congress imposed on us to formulate the federal law to govern Section 301(a) suits, we are strongly guided by and do not give a niggardly reading to Section 301(b). We would undercut the Act and defeat its policy if we read Section 301 narrowly. We have already said in another context that Section 301(b) at least evidences "a congressional intention that the union as an entity, like a corporation, should in the absence of agreement be the sole source of recovery for injury inflicted by it." This policy cannot be evaded or truncated by the simple device of suing union agents or members, whether in contract or tort, or both, in a separate count or in a separate action for damages for violation of a collective bargaining contract for which damages the union itself is liable. The national labor policy requires and we hold that when a union is liable for damages for violation of the no-strike clause, its officers and members are not liable for these damages. Here, Count II, as we have said, necessarily alleges union liability but prays for damages from the union agents. Where the union has inflicted the injury, it alone must pay. Count II must be dismissed.

The case is remanded to the District Court for further proceedings not inconsistent with this opinion.

It is so ordered.

Mr. Justice Frankfurter took no part in the consideration or decision of this case.

Supreme Court of the United States
Sinclair Refining Company v. Atkinson et al.
June 18, 1962, 370 U.S. 195

Mr. Justice Black delivered the opinion of the Court.

The question this case presents is whether Section 301 of the Taft-Hartley Act, in giving federal courts jurisdiction of suits between employers and unions for breach of collective bargaining agreements, impliedly repealed Section 4 of the pre-existing Norris–La Guardia Act, which, with certain exceptions not here material, barred federal courts from issuing injunctions "in any case involving or growing out of any labor dispute."

The complaint here was filed by the petitioner Sinclair Refining Company against the Oil, Chemical and Atomic Workers International Union and Local 7–210 of that union and alleged: that the International Union, acting by and with the authority of the Local Union and its members, signed a written collective bargaining contract with Sinclair which provided for compulsory, final, and binding arbitration of "any difference regarding wages, hours or working conditions between the parties hereto or between the Employer and an employee covered by this working agreement which might arise within any plant or within any region of operations"; that this contract also included express provisions by which the unions agreed that "there shall be no slowdowns for any reason whatsoever" and "no strikes or work stoppages . . . (f) or any cause which is or may be the subject of a grievance;" and that notwithstanding these promises in the collective bargaining contract the members of Local 7–210 had, over a period of some 19 months, engaged in work stoppages and strikes on nine separate occasions. . . . In this situation Sinclair claimed there was no adequate remedy at law which would protect its contractual rights and the court should therefore enter orders enjoining the unions and their agents "preliminary at first, and thereafter permanently, from aiding, abetting, fomenting, advising, participating in, ratifying, or condoning any strike, stoppage of work, slowdown or any other disruption of, or interference with normal employment or normal operation or production by an employee within the bargaining unit at plaintiff's East Chicago, Indiana, refinery covered by the contract between the parties dated August 8, 1957, in support of, or because of, any matter or thing which is, or could be, the subject of a grievance under the grievance procedure of the said contract, or any extension thereof, or any other contract between the parties which shall contain like or similar provisions."

.   .   .

We agree with the courts below that this case does involve a "labor dispute" within the meaning of the Norris–La Guardia Act. Section 13 of that Act expressly defines a labor dispute as including "any controversy concerning terms or conditions of employment, or concerning the association or representation of persons in negotiating, fixing, maintaining, changing, or seeking to arrange terms or conditions of employment, regardless of whether or not the disputants stand in the proximate relation of employer and employee." Sinclair's own complaint shows quite plainly that each of the alleged nine work stoppages and strikes arose out of a controversy which was unquestionably well within this definition.

Nor does the circumstance that the alleged work stoppages and strikes may have constituted a breach of a collective bargaining agreement alter the plain fact that a "labor dispute" within the meaning of the Norris–La Guardia Act is involved. Arguments to the contrary proceed from the premise that Section 2 of that Act, which expresses the public policy upon which the specific anti-injunction provisions of the Act were based, contains language indicating that one primary concern of Congress was to insure workers the right "to exercise actual liberty of contract" and to protect "concerted activities for the purpose of collective bargaining." From that premise, Sinclair argues that an interpretation of the term "labor dispute" so as to include a dispute arising out of a union's refusal to abide by the terms of a collective agreement to which it freely acceded is to apply the Norris–La Guardia Act in a way that defeats one of the purposes for which it was enacted. But this argument, though forcefully urged both here and in much current commentary on this question, rests more upon considerations of what many commentators think would be the more desirable industrial and labor policy in view of their understanding as to the prevailing circumstances of contemporary labor-management relations than upon what is a correct judicial interpretation of the language of the Act as it was written by Congress.

In the first place, even the general policy declarations of Section 2 of the Norris–La Guardia Act, which are the foundation of this whole argument, do not support the conclusion urged. That section does not purport to limit the Act to the protection of collective bargaining but, instead, expressly recognizes the need of the anti-injunction provisions to insure the right of workers to engage in "concerted activities for the purpose of collective bargaining *or other mutual aid or protection.*" Moreover, the language of the specific provisions of the Act is so broad and inclusive that it leaves not the slightest opening for reading in any exceptions beyond those clearly written into it by Congress itself. . . .

Since we hold that the present case does grow out of a "labor dispute," the injunction sought here runs squarely counter to the proscription of injunctions against strikes contained in Section 4(a) of the Norris–La Guardia Act, to the proscription of injunctions against peaceful picketing contained in Section 4(e) and to the proscription of injunctions prohibiting the advising of such activities contained in Section 4(i). For these reasons, the Norris–La Guardia Act deprives the courts of the United States of jurisdiction to enter that injunction unless, as is contended here, the scope of that Act has been so narrowed by the subsequent enactment of Section 301 of the Taft-Hartley Act that it no longer prohibits even the injunctions specifically described in Section 4 where such injunctions are sought as a remedy for breach of a collective bargaining agreement. Upon consideration, we cannot agree with that view. . . .

The language of Section 301 itself seems to us almost if not entirely conclusive of this question. It is especially significant that the section contains no language that could by any stretch of the imagination be interpreted to constitute an explicit repeal of the anti-injunction provisions of the Norris–La Guardia Act in view of the fact that the section does expressly repeal another provision of the Norris–La Guardia Act dealing with union responsibility for the acts of agents. If Congress had intended that Section 301 suits should also not be subject to the anti-injunction provisions of the Norris–La Guardia Act, it certainly seems likely that it would have made its intent known in this same express manner. That is indeed precisely what Congress did do in Sections 101(h) and 208(b) of the Taft-Hartley Act, by permitting injunctions to be obtained, not by private litigants, but only at the instance of the National Labor Relations Board and the Attorney General, and in Section 302(e), by permitting private litigants to obtain injunctions in order to protect the integrity of employees' collective bargaining representatives in carrying out their responsibilities. . . .

When the inquiry is carried beyond the language of Section 301 into its legislative history, whatever small doubts as to the congressional purpose could have survived consideration of the bare language of the section should be wholly dissipated . . . at the conference the provision of the House bill expressly repealing the anti-injunction provisions of the

Norris–La Guardia Act, as well as the provision of the bill passed by the Senate declaring the breach of a collective agreement to be an unfair labor practice, was dropped and never became law. . . .

. . .

We cannot accept the startling argument made here that even though Congress did not itself want to repeal the Norris-La Guardia Act, it was willing to confer a power upon the courts to "accommodate" that Act out of existence whenever they might find it expedient to do so in furtherance of some policy they had fashioned under Section 301. . . .

. . . The question of whether existing statutes should be continued in force or repealed is, under our system of government, one which is wholly within the domain of Congress. . . . .

Nor have we found anything else in the previous decisions of this Court that would indicate that we should disregard all this overwhelming evidence of a congressional intent to retain completely intact the anti-injunction prohibitions of the Norris–La Guardia Act in suits brought under Section 301. *Brotherhood of Railroad Trainmen* v. *Chicago River & Indiana R. Co.*, upon which Sinclair places its primary reliance, is distinguishable on several grounds. There we were dealing with a strike called by the union in defiance of an affirmative duty, imposed upon the union by the Railway Labor Act itself, compelling unions to settle disputes as to the interpretation of an existing collective bargaining agreement, not by collective union pressures on the railroad, but by submitting them to the Railroad Adjustment Board as the exclusive means of final determination of such "minor" disputes. Here, on the other hand, we are dealing with a suit under a quite different law which does not itself compel a particular, exclusive method for settling disputes nor impose any requirement, either upon unions or employers, or upon the courts, that is in any way inconsistent with a continuation of the Norris–La Guardia Act's proscription of federal labor injunctions against strikes and peaceful picketing. . . .

Textile Workers Union v. *Lincoln Mills*, upon which some lesser reliance is placed, is equally distinguishable. There the Court held merely that it did not violate the anti-injunction provisions of the Norris–La Guardia Act to compel the parties to a collective bargaining agreement to submit a dispute which had arisen under that agreement to arbitration where the agreement itself required arbitration of the dispute. In upholding the jurisdiction of the federal courts to issue such an order against a challenge based upon the Norris–La Guardia Act, the Court pointed out that the equitable relief granted in that case—a mandatory injunction to carry out an agreement to arbitrate—did not enjoin any one of the kinds of conduct which the specific prohibitions of the Norris–La Guardia Act withdrew from the injunctive powers of United States courts. An injunction against work stoppages, peaceful picketing, or the nonfraudulent encouraging of those activities would, however, prohibit the precise kinds of conduct which subsections (a), (e), and (i) of Section 4 of the Norris–La Guardia Act unequivocally say cannot be prohibited.

Nor can we agree with the argument made in this Court that the decision in Lincoln Mills, as implemented by the subsequent decisions in *United Steelworkers* v. *American Manufacturing Co.*, *United Steelworkers* v. *Warrior & Gulf Navigation Co.*, and *United Steelworkers* v. *Enterprise Wheel & Car Corp.*, requires us to reconsider and overrule the action of Congress in refusing to repeal or modify the controlling commands of the Norris–La Guardia Act. To the extent that those cases relied upon the proposition that the arbitration process is "a kingpin of federal labor policy," we think that proposition was founded not upon the policy predelictions of this Court but upon what Congress said and did when it enacted Section 301. Certainly we cannot accept any suggestion which would undermine those cases by implying that the Court went beyond its proper power and itself "forged . . . a kingpin of federal labor policy" inconsistent with that section and its purpose. Consequently, we do not see how cases implementing the purpose of Section 301 can be said to have freed this Court from its duty to give effect to the plainly expressed congressional purpose with regard to the continued application of the anti-injunction provisions of the Norris–La Guardia Act. The argument to the contrary seems to rest upon the notion that injunctions against peaceful strikes are necessary to make the arbitration process effective. But whatever might be said about the merits of this argument, Congress itself has rejected it. In doing so, it set the limit to which it was willing to go in permitting courts to effectuate the congressional policy favoring arbitration and it is not this Court's business to review the wisdom of that decision.

The plain fact is that Section 301, as passed by Congress, presents no conflict at all with the anti-injunction provisions of the Norris–La Guardia Act. Obedience to the congressional commands of the Norris–La Guardia Act does not directly affect the "congressional policy in favor of the enforcement of agreements to arbitrate grievance disputes" at all for it does not impair the right of an employer to obtain an order compelling arbitration of any dispute that may have been made arbitrable by the provisions of an effective collective bargaining agreement. At the most, what is involved is the question of whether the employer is to be allowed to enjoy the benefits of an injunction along with the right which Congress gave him in Section 301 to sue for breach of a collective agreement. . . .

It is doubtless true, as argued, that the right to sue which Section 301 gives employers would be worth more to them if they could also get a federal court injunction to bar a breach of their collective bargaining agreements. Strong arguments are made to us that it is highly desirable that the Norris–La Guardia Act be changed in the public interest. If that is so, Congress itself might see fit to change that law and repeal the anti-injunction provisions of the Act insofar as suits for violation of collective bargaining agreements are concerned, as the House bill under consideration originally provided. It might, on the other hand, decide that if injunctions are necessary, the whole idea of enforcement of these agreements by private suits should be discarded in favor of enforcement through the administration machinery of the Labor Board, as Senator Taft provided in his Senate bill. Or it might decide that neither of these methods is entirely satisfactory and turn instead to a completely new approach. The question of what change, if any, should be made in the existing law is one of legislative policy properly within the exclusive domain of Congress—it is a question for law-makers, not law-interpreters. . . .

The District Court was correct in dismissing Count 3 of petitioner's complaint for lack of jurisdiction under the Norris–La Guardia Act. The judgment of the Court of Appeals affirming that order is therefore

Affirmed.

Mr. Justice Frankfurter took no part in the consideration or decision of this case.

Sinclair Refining Dissenting Opinion

Mr. Justice Brennan, with whom Mr. Justice Douglas and Mr. Justice Harlan join, dissenting:

I believe that the Court has reached the wrong result because it has answered only the first of the questions which must be answered to decide this case. Of course Section 301 of the Taft-Hartley Act did not, for purposes of actions brought under it, "repeal" Section 4 of the Norris–La Guardia Act. But two provisions do coexist, and it is clear beyond dispute that they apply to the case before us in apparently conflicting senses. Our duty, therefore, is to seek out that accommodation of the two which will give the fullest possible effect to the central purposes of both. Since such accommodation is possible, the Court's failure to follow that path leads it to a result—not justified by either the language or history of Section 301—which is wholly at odds with our earlier handling of directly analogous situations and which cannot be woven intelligibly into the broader fabric of related decisions.

I. Section 301 of the Taft-Hartley Act, enacted in 1947, authorized Federal District Courts to entertain "(s)uits for violation of contracts between an employer and labor organization. . . ." It does not in terms address itself to the question of remedies. As we have construed Section 301, it casts upon the District Courts a special responsibility to carry out contractual schemes for arbitration, by holding parties to that favored process for settlement when it has been contracted for, and, by then regarding its result as conclusive. At the same time, Section 4 of the Norris–La Guardia Act, enacted in 1932, proscribes the issuance by federal courts of injunctions against various concerted activities "in any case involving or growing out of any labor dispute." But the enjoining of a strike over an arbitrable grievance may be indispensable to the effective enforcement of an arbitration scheme in a collective agreement; thus the power to grant that injunctive remedy may be essential to the uncrippled performance of the Court's function under Section 301. Therefore, to hold that Section 301 did not repeal Section 4 is only a beginning. Having so held, the Court should—but does not—go on to consider how it is to deal with the surface conflict between the two statutory commands.

The Court has long acted upon the premise that the Norris–La Guardia Act does not stand in isolation. It is one of several statutes which, taken together, shape the national labor policy. Accordingly, the Court has recognized that Norris–La Guardia does not invariably bar injunctive relief when necessary to achieve an important objective of some other statute in the pattern of labor laws. . . . In Chicago River we insisted that there "must be an accommodation of (the Norris–La Guardia Act) and the Railway Labor Act so that the obvious purpose in the enactment of each is preserved.". . . I think that there is nothing in either the language of Section 301 or its history to prevent Section 4's here being accommodated with it, just as Section 4 was accommodated with the Railway Labor Act.

II. It cannot be denied that the availability of the injunctive remedy in this setting is far more necessary to the accomplishment of the purposes of Section 301 than it would be detrimental to those of Norris–La Guardia. Chicago River makes this plain. We there held that the federal courts, notwithstanding Norris–La Guardia, may enjoin strikes over disputes as to the interpretation of an existing collective agreement, since such strikes flout the duty imposed on the union by the Railway Labor Act to settle such "minor disputes" by submission to the National Railroad Adjustment Board rather than by concerted economic pressures. We so held, even though the Railway Labor Act contains no express prohibition of strikes over "minor disputes," because we found it essential to the meaningful enforcement of that Act—and because the existence of mandatory arbitration eliminated one of the problems to which Norris–La Guardia was chiefly addressed, namely, that "the injunction strips labor of its primary weapon without substituting any reasonable alternative."

That reasoning is applicable with equal force to an injunction under Section 301 to enforce a union's contractual duty, also binding on the employer, to submit certain disputes to terminal arbitration and to refrain from striking over them. The federal law embodied in Section 301 stresses the effective enforcement of such arbitration agreements. When one of them is about to be sabotaged by a strike, Section 301 has as strong a claim upon an accommodating interpretation of Section 4 as does the compulsory arbitration law of the Railway Labor Act. . . .

In any event, I should have thought that the question was settled by *Textile Workers* v. *Lincoln Mills.* In that case, the Court held that the procedural requirements of Norris–La Guardia's Section 7, although in terms fully applicable, would not apply so as to frustrate a federal court's effective enforcement under Section 301 of an employer's obligation to arbitrate. It is strange, I think, that Section 7 of the Norris–La Guardia Act need not be read, in the face of Section 301, to impose inapt procedural restrictions upon the specific enforcement of an employer's contractual duty to arbitrate; but that Section 4 must be read, despite Section 301, to preclude absolutely the issuance of an injunction against a strike which ignores a union's identical duty.

III.   The legislative history of Section 301 affords the Court no refuge from the compelling effect of our prior decisions. That history shows that Congress considered and rejected "the advisability of repealing the Norris–La Guardia Act insofar as suits based upon breach of collective bargaining agreements are concerned. . . ." But congressional rejection of outright repeal certainly does not imply hostility to an attempt by the courts to accommodate all statutes pertinent to the decision of cases before them. Again, the Court's conclusion stems from putting the wrong question. When it is appreciated that there is no question here of "repeal," but rather one of how the Court is to apply the whole statutory complex to the case before it, it becomes more clear that the legislative history does not support the Court's conclusion. First, however, it seems appropriate to discuss, as the Court has done, the language of Section 301 considered in light of other provisions of the statute.

There is nothing in the words of Section 301 which so much as intimates any limitation to damage remedies when the asserted breach of contract consists of concerted activity. The section simply authorizes the District Courts to entertain and decide suits for violation of collective contract. Taking the language alone, the irresistible implication would be that the District Courts were to employ their regular arsenal of remedies appropriately to the situation. That would mean, of course, that injunctive relief could be afforded when damages would not be an adequate remedy. . . .

Sound reasons explain why repeal of Norris–La Guardia provisions, acceptable in other settings, might have been found ill-suited for the purpose of Section 301. And those reasons fall far short of a design to preclude absolutely the issuance under Section 301 of any injunction against any activity included in Section 4 of Norris–La Guardia. . . .

. . . The Congress understandably may not have felt able to predict what provisions would crop up in collective bargaining agreements, to foresee the settings in which those would become subjects of litigation, or to forecast the rules of law which the courts would apply. The consequences of repealing the anti-injunction provisions in this context would have been completely unknowable, and outright repeal, therefore, might well have seemed unthinkable. Congress, clearly, had no intention of abandoning wholesale the Norris–La Guardia policies in contract suits;

but it does not follow that Section 301 is not the equal of Section 4 in cases which implicate both provisions.

. . .

The statutory language thus fails to support the Court's position. The inference is at least as strong that Congress was content to rely upon the courts to resolve any seeming conflicts between Section 301 and Section 4 as they arose in the relatively manageable setting of particular cases, as that Congress intended to limit to damages the remedies courts could afford against concerted activities under Section 301. The Court then should so exercise its judgment as best to effect the most important purposes of each statute. It should not be bound by inscrutable congressional silence to a wooden preference for one statute over the other.

Nor does the legislative history of Section 301 suggest any different conclusion. . . .

I emphasize that the question in this case is not whether the basic policy embodied in Norris–La Guardia against the injunction of activities of labor unions has been abandoned in actions under Section 301; the question is simply whether injunctions are barred against strikes over grievances which have been routed to arbitration by a contract specifically enforceable against both the union and the employer. Enforced adherence to such arbitration commitments has emerged as a dominant motif in the developing federal law of collective bargaining agreements. But there is no general federal antistrike policy; and although a suit may be brought under Section 301 against strikes which, while they are breaches of private contracts, do not threaten an additional public policy, in such cases the anti-injunction policy of Norris–La Guardia should prevail. Insistence upon strict application of Norris–La Guardia to a strike over a dispute which both parties are bound by contract to arbitrate threatens a leading policy of our labor relations law. But there may be no such threat if the union has made no binding agreement to arbitrate; and if the employer cannot be compelled to arbitrate, restraining the strike would cut deep into the core of Norris–La Guardia. Therefore, unless both parties are so bound, limiting an employer's remedy to damages might well be appropriate. The susceptibility of particular concrete situations to this sort of analysis shows that rejection of an outright repeal of Section 4 was wholly consistent with acceptance of a technique of accommodation which would lead, in some cases, to the granting of injunctions against concerted activity. Accommodation requires only that the anti-injunction policy of Norris–La Guardia not intrude into areas, not vital to its ends, where injunctive relief is vital to a purpose of Section 301; it does not require unconditional surrender.

IV. Today's decision cannot be fitted harmoniously into the pattern of prior decisions on analogous and related matters. Considered in their light, the decision leads inescapably to results consistent neither with any imaginable legislative purpose nor with sound judicial administration.

. . .

The question arises whether today's prohibition of injunctive relief is to be carried over to state courts as a part of the federal law governing collective agreements. If so, Section 301, a provision plainly designed to enhance the responsibility of unions to their contracts, will have had opposite effect of depriving employers of a state remedy they enjoyed prior to its enactment.

On the other hand, if, as today's literal reading suggests and as a leading state decision holds, states remain free to apply their injunctive remedies against concerted activities in breach of contract, the development of a uniform body of federal contract law is in for hard times. So long as state courts remain free to grant the injunctions unavailable in federal courts, suits seeking relief against concerted activities in breach of contract will be channeled to the states whenever possible. Ironically, state rather than federal courts will be the preferred instruments to protect the integrity of the arbitration process, which Lincoln Mills and the Steelworkers decisions forced into a kingpin of federal labor policy. Enunciation of uniform doctrines applicable in such cases will be severely impeded. Moreover, the type of relief available in a particular instance will turn on fortuities of locale and susceptibility to process—depending upon which States have anti-injunction statutes and how they construe them.

. . .

V. The decision deals a crippling blow to the cause of grievance arbitration itself. Arbitration is so highly regarded as a proved technique for industrial peace that even the Norris–La Guardia Act fosters its use. But since unions cannot be enjoined by a federal court from striking in open defiance of their undertakings to arbitrate, employers will pause long before committing themselves to obligations enforceable against them but not against their unions. The Court does not deny the desirability, indeed, necessity, for injunctive relief against a strike over an arbitrable grievance. The Court says only that federal courts may not grant such relief, that Congress must amend Section 4 if those courts are to give substance to the congressional plan of encouraging peaceful settlements of grievances through arbitration.

. . .

In the case before us, the union enjoys the contractual right to make the employer submit to final and binding arbitration of any employee grievance. At the same time, the union agrees that "There shall be no strikes . . . for any cause which is or may be the subject of a grievance." The complaint alleged that the union had, over the past several months, repeatedly engaged in "quickie" strikes over arbitrable grievances. Under the contract and the complaint, then the District Court might conclude that there have occurred and will continue to occur breaches of contract of a type to which the principle of accommodation applies. It follows that rather than dismissing the complaint's request for an injunction, the Court should remand the case to the District Court with directions to consider whether to grant the relief sought—an injunction against future repetitions. This would entail a weighing of the employer's need for such an injunction against the harm that might be inflicted upon legitimate employee activity. It would call into question the feasibility of setting up *in futuro* contempt sanctions against the union (for striking) and against the employer (for refusing to arbitrate) in regard to prospective disputes which might fall more or less clearly into the adjudicated category of arbitrable grievances. In short, the District Court will have to consider with great care whether it is possible to draft a decree which would deal equitably with all the interests at stake.

I would reverse the Court of Appeals and remand to the District Court for further proceedings consistent with this dissenting opinion.

QUESTIONS

1. The majority opinion suggests that Congress might (*a*) repeal the anti-injunction provisions of the Norris–La Guardia Act insofar as violations of collective bargaining agreements are concerned, or (*b*) give the NLRB power to enforce collective bargaining agreements, or (*c*) take an entirely new approach in regard to agreement enforcement. Discuss the desirability of each of these alternatives.

2. "This decision deals a crippling blow to the cause of grievance arbitration." Discuss.

3. Discuss the relationship between the Sinclair, Lincoln Mills, Warrior and Gulf Navigation, American Manufacturing, and Enterprise Wheel and Car cases.

4. Before the Sinclair cases, texts on collective bargaining usually said that an employer confronted with a wildcat strike in breach of an agreement had the following remedies available to him: (*a*) cancellation of the whole agreement, (*b*) discharge or other discipline for the strikers, (*c*) suits for damages, and (*d*) injunction against the strike or picketing. How do the Sinclair cases change these remedies? If you were an employer confronted with a wildcat strike over a grievance subject to arbitration how would you go about getting the strikers back to work? Justify your proposed course of action.

CASE 4
Who Speaks for the Union?

Company: Midwest Manufacturing Corporation
Galesburg, Illinois

Union: International Association of Machinists
            Midwest Lodge No. 2063
Arbitrator: Charles N. Anrod

This case involves the authority of representatives and the procedures for amending an agreement during its term.

The following discussion of the issue and the facts in this case was prepared by Charles W. Anrod, the arbitrator.

The Corporation, a wholly owned subsidiary of Admiral Corporation, is engaged in the manufacture of refrigerators, freezers, air conditioners, and electric ranges at Galesburg, Illinois. It employs about 1,750 persons of whom approximately 1,400 are in the bargaining unit represented by the Union.

For many years, the employees in said bargaining unit were represented by Federal Labor Union No. 22,278 which entered into successive collective bargaining agreements with the Corporation. In February 1956, the employees decided, however, to affiliate with the International Association of Machinists (AFL-CIO) and received a charter therefrom for the Union. Since the transfer occurred during the period of the 1955–56 collective bargaining agreement between the Federal Labor Union and the Corporation, the Union became a party to that agreement in lieu of the Federal Labor Union until it expired at about the end of October 1956. Thereafter, the Union negotiated with the Corporation a collective bargaining agreement which was signed on November 26, 1956, and which became effective for the period from November 1956, to November 1957 (hereinafter referred to as the "1956–57 Agreement"). It was signed on behalf of the Corporation by L. H. Moos, vice president and general manager, and on behalf of the Union by the members of a committee consisting of five Union representatives, among them William E. Boen, its president. The signature of William Hammond, special representative of the International Association of Machinists, AFL-CIO, was also affixed to it.

The grievances of three employees in the press room, namely, Virgil F. Odean, Ira D. Luallen, and Howard Hook, which are the subject of this arbitration arose out of the following facts:

The 1955–56 collective bargaining agreement provided initially for strict departmental seniority in the event of temporary layoffs. The application of that rule had, however, caused some dissatisfaction among the employees. As a result, the Federal Labor Union and the Corporation entered into a written agreement, dated June 16, 1955, which modified the pertinent provision of the 1955–56 collective bargaining agreement as follows:

It is agreed between the Company and the Union that when it is necessary to reduce the working force the least senior employee in the classification in the department and on the shift in which the reduction is necessary shall be laid off (Company Exh. No. 4).

This agreement was signed by Harley Morss, then president of the Federal Labor Union, and by Don E. Johnson, director of personnel of the Corporation.

During the negotiations preceding the 1956–57 Agreement, the matter of a satisfactory seniority rule in case of temporary layoff was again discussed between the parties. The Corporation pointed out that, if strict departmental seniority should be applied (as was originally provided in the 1955–56 collective bargaining agreement), it could happen that the youngest employees in a department who had to be laid off temporarily were on the night shift and that their positions had then to be filled by employees from the day shift. This, the Corporation stated, had, in the past, created certain difficulties because some employees so transferred had contended they had been on specific shifts by their choice and felt that they should stay there. Accordingly, the Corporation proposed the following provision for the 1956–57 Agreement:

In applying departmental seniority in temporary layoffs, the least senior employees in the classification and on the shift in which the surplus occurs shall be the first to be laid off . . . (Company Exh. No. 5).

The Union rejected, however, the Corporation's proposal. Its spokesman asserted that, if classification and shift were determining in applying departmental seniority, employees with greater seniority could conceivably be laid off while employees with less seniority remained at work.

The parties finally agreed to restore strict departmental seniority in case of temporary layoffs (as was originally provided in the 1955–56 collective bargaining agreement) and, thereby, rescinded the agreement, dated June 16, 1955 (quoted above).

Their understanding was incorporated into Article VI, Section 6, of the 1956–57 Agreement which provides, so far as pertinent, the following:

In case of a temporary layoff departmental seniority shall prevail (joint Exh. No. 1, P. 8).

Yet, the matter did not come to rest. Shortly after the signing of the 1956–57 Agreement, a temporary layoff occurred. In accordance with the departmental seniority rule as stipulated in said Article VI, Section 6, some employees who happened to be on the night shift were laid off and other employees were then transferred from the day shift to the night shift. This procedure caused unrest among the transferees. They did not want to go on the night shift and also raised the question of overtime premium contending they were working outside their regularly scheduled shifts.

In an effort to find a satisfactory solution, the parties again discussed the question as to which seniority rule should be applied in case of temporary layoffs. They reached a tentative agreement under which seniority in the department and on the shift should govern in such instances. This understanding was submitted to a regular meeting of the Union by William Boen, its president, and approved in said meeting. The parties then entered into the following written agreement:

It is agreed by the parties hereto that the provisions of Article VI Section 6 shall be amended as follows: In case of a temporary layoff the least senior employee in the department and on the shift where such surplus exist shall be first laid off.

> (*signed*)   Don E. Johnson
>   Director of Personnel
> (*signed*)   William Boen, President
>   Midwest Lodge #2063

January 31st, 1957 (Union Exh. No. 1)

Thereafter, the Corporation followed the seniority rule as agreed upon in the above agreement of January 31, 1957. About three months later, the membership of the Union voted, however, to rescind said agreement and sent the following letter dated April 23, 1957, to the Company:

Re: Agreement signed 1–31–57
This will inform you that the membership of Lodge 2063, at their last regular meeting, voted to return to the provisions of the current contract, and to declare the agreement made and signed by the Management and the Union Representatives on the 31st day of the first month in 1957 void. This agreement will have to do with Article VI, Section 6, . . . on the subject of Seniority.
> (*signed*) Roy E. Routt, Rec. Sec'y.
>   Midwest Lodge # 2063

The Corporation took the position that the Union could not unilaterally rescind the written agreement of January 31, 1957. It disregarded, therefore, the Union's letter of April 23, 1957, and continued to make temporary layoffs in accordance with the January 31, 1957, agreement.

On May 16 or 17, 1957, the three grievants were temporarily laid off in conformity with the seniority rule stipulated in said agreement. They then filed the instant grievances (Union Exh. Nos. 3, 4 and 5). The Corporation denied the grievances which are now before the Board of Arbitration for decision.

At the same time these layoffs occurred, John R. Healey, an employee in the inspection department, was also temporarily laid off. His foreman made that layoff in accordance with the original wording of Article VI, Section 6, of the 1956–57 Agreement, i.e., on the basis of strict departmental seniority. Healey filed a grievance which was submitted to the Corporation by John J. Cox, a Union steward. On or about June 4, 1957, the Corporation paid an amount equal to 16 hours' straight time to Healey in settlement of his grievance.

UNION'S POSITION

The Union does not dispute the above-related facts. But it contends that the agreement of January 31, 1957, which amended Article VI, Section 6, of the 1956–57 Agreement regarding the seniority rule in case of temporary layoffs was void.

In support of such contention, the Union asserts the correct procedures as prescribed by the constitution and bylaws of the International Association of Machinists (IAM) were not followed. It particularly states that the agreements of January 31, 1957, was not signed by an international representative of the IAM and, therefore, did not become effective.

It also states that, while said agreement was approved in a regular union meeting, the subject was not posted in advance on the bulletin board as required under the rules of the IAM.

The Union concedes that the letter of April 23, 1957, was afflicted with the same defects and, therefore, regards it void, too.

As a result, the Union concludes that the strict departmental seniority rule as originally contained in Article VI, Section 6, of the 1956–57 Agreement was still in effect when the three grievants were laid off. Since the Corporation followed the terms of the agreement of January 31, 1957, the Union argues that the Corporation violated said Article VI, Section 6.

With respect to the grievance filed by John R. Healey, the Union claims that the Corporation made the payment to Healey for the sole reason that it (the Corporation) was in default of the time limits prescribed for the handling of grievances in the 1956–57 Agreement but not in recognition of the substantive merits of that grievance.

For the above mentioned reasons, the Union seeks an award which would require the Corporation to reimburse the three grievants for the time lost on May 16 and/or 17, 1957.

CORPORATION'S POSITION

The Corporation points out that, while the immediate issue before the Board of Arbitration is whether or not the grievants were properly laid off, there is implicitly a broader question of considerable interest to it involved in this case, namely, whether the Union must live up to and be bound by an agreement made by its duly authorized officers.

The Corporation submits that it had in the past entered into a number of supplementary agreements with the president of the Federal Labor Union during the period of a collective bargaining agreement and that such supplementary agreements had always been carried out by both parties.

Moreover, the Corporation states that, prior to the grievances under consideration, it had no knowledge or notice of any restrictions on the authority of the Union's president to enter into such a supplementary agreement. It specifically emphasizes that it was not aware of any rules or regulations of the IAM requiring the signature of an international representative or the posting of a subject on the bulletin board prior to its discussion in a Union meeting.

The Corporation argues that it acted in good faith when it entered into the January 31, 1957, agreement with the Union and is of the opinion that both parties were bound thereby.

It asserts that, when it was informed of the proper steps as outlined in the rules and regulations of the IAM after the instant grievances had arisen, it readily agreed to respect the requirement of a signature or approval of an international representative in the future and also to adhere no longer to the January 31, 1957, agreement. At the same time, the Corporation contends, it was, however, made clear to the representative of the Union that its (the Corporation's) concessions would not apply retroactively to actions taken in accordance with said agreement in the past.

As to the grievance of John R. Healey, the Corporation contends that it immediately recognized the foreman had made a mistake and informed the Union's representative over the telephone on or about the day of the filing of the grievance that payment would be made.

For the above-mentioned reasons, the Corporation asks that the three grievances here involved be denied.

QUESTIONS

1. Precisely state the issue to be decided by the Board of Arbitration.
2. What "lessons" does this kind of a situation contain for both union and management about (*a*) the nature of the agreement, (*b*) the credentials and authority of representatives, and (*c*) seniority provisions.

CASE 5
Union Security and the Bargaining Unit

Company: Kimball Tire Company, Inc.
         San Luis Obispo, California
Union: International Brotherhood of Teamsters
         Truck Drivers and Helpers Local Union No. 381
Arbitrator: Grady L. Mullenix

This case involves the obligation of two employees to join the union under a union shop agreement. Although this case is not an NLRB dispute over the appropriate unit for collective bargaining, it illustrates some of the criteria which the NLRB often considers.

The following discussion of the issue and facts in this case was prepared by Grady L. Mullenix, the arbitrator.

The question submitted for arbitration, as set forth in the "Agreement to Arbitrate," is as follows:

"Shall William Wall and Ree Anderson become members of Teamsters Union Local 381?"

FACTS

The Kimball Tire Company is a corporation owned and controlled by two men.

The Company is engaged in the retail and wholesale tire business which includes sales and service of new and used tires and tubes and retreading. It also handles batteries. There are 13 employees, including 2 owners, who work at the one place of business at 252 Higuera Street, San Luis Obispo. However, two of the employees travel throughout a designated area contacting customers and potential customers doing sales and customer relations work.

On August 5, 1960, the Company filed a Petition with the National Labor Relations Board requesting a representation election to determine whether or not its employees wished to be represented by the Union. The NLRB conducted the election on August 19, 1960, and the Union was officially certified on August 29, 1960, as the exclusive bargaining agent for the employees in the appropriate bargaining unit agreed upon in the Consent Agreement which was the same as that petitioned for by the Company, as follows:

Included: Production and maintenance employees, including vulcanizers, tire changers and salesmen.

Excluding: Office clericals and supervisors within the meaning of the Act.

A collective bargaining agreement was eventually reached and was signed on March 6, 1961. Section 2 of that agreement is especially pertinent to this arbitration: It reads as follows:

Membership in good standing in the Union (as provided by law) on or after the 30th day following the beginning of employment or the effective date of this agreement, whichever is later, shall be a condition of employment.

The employer shall discharge an employee within seven (7) days after receipt of written notice from the Union that said employee has not become or remained a member in good standing.

In a letter dated April 7, 1961, addressed to Mr. Robenstine of the Company and signed by Mr. Earing for the Union, the following message was delivered:

This is to inform you that William Wall and Ree Anderson, having been in your employ in excess of 30 days, have not become members in good standing with Truck Drivers and Helpers Union, Local No. 381 as provided in Section 2 of our agreement. We therefore request they be discharged.

Anderson was an employee of the Company at the time of the NLRB election and voted in the election. Wall was employed later but was on the payroll prior to the date of the collective bargaining agreement.

CONTENTIONS OF THE PARTIES

The Union contends that Section 2 of the agreement requires that Wall and Anderson, as well as other employees, become members of the Union as a condition of employment. They have not done so, and the Company has refused to discharge them as required by the agreement. The Union does not seek their discharge if it can be avoided, but instead requests that the two men be required to join the Union and that dues be paid by or for them retroactively to 30 days following the date of the agreement.

The Company's position is that Wall and Anderson are not in the bargaining unit and therefore are not required to join the Union. It is contended that Wall was hired as the service manager and that Anderson is now the commercial sales manager. Both are paid on a monthly salary basis, while the union members are all on hourly rates. The Company also argues that both Wall and Anderson intend to buy into the business and will be owners as well as managers in the near future.

The Union challenges the Company's position and denies that either of the subjects is a supervisor or managerial employee. In the case of Anderson, the Union offers testimony that he actually voted in the NLRB election and therefore was recognized by all concerned as properly within the bargaining unit. It is further stated that Anderson's ballot was at first challenged by the Union on the basis that he was an owner of the Company, but in a conference between the parties and the NLRB agent Mr. Robenstine assured them that Anderson did not own stock in the Company but was merely planning to buy in. The Company argued that he was in the bargaining unit and should be permitted to vote. On the basis of this information, the Union withdrew it challenge and Anderson's ballot was counted along with the others.

During negotiations, a question arose about four employees who were receiving salaries above the scale agreed upon for their classifications and the parties agreed that those employees would not suffer a reduction as a result of the contract. Section 10 of the agreement was adopted to cover this situation. The Union makes the point that Anderson was one of the four men involved and that he was discussed along with the others and that the Company did not at that time contend that he was excluded from the bargaining unit.

According to the Union, after the agreement was signed and approximately 30 days had elapsed, Mr. Earing, business representative, called Mr. Robenstine, president of the Company, and pointed out that Anderson and Wall had not applied for membership in the Union as required by Section 2. Mr. Robenstine replied that he was in the process of selling the business to Anderson, Wall, and one other person but that the sale had not reached the final stages. The Union then sent the letter of April 7 requesting the discharge of the two employees. A few days later a meeting was held between the parties and at that time Mr. Robenstine argued that Wall and Anderson were not in the bargaining unit because Wall was the service manager and Anderson was to be made the commercial sales manager.

The Union contends that Anderson is doing exactly the same work now as at the time of the NLRB election and that another employee, Mr. King, also does sales work identical to that performed by Anderson. King is in the Union; Anderson is not.

Likewise, it is contended that Wall performs the same tasks in the service area as other floormen and is not in fact a supervisor.

The Company asserts that changes have been made in the organizational structure of the business since the NLRB election which have changed the classification of Anderson and resulted in the creation of a new classification and position now occupied by Wall. Prior to the signing of the agreement, the Company did not feel that it was necessary to discuss the details of its plans and activities with the Union, thus the Union's lack of information about the changes. According to Mr. Robenstine the business has grown beyond the scope of his ability to manage it alone, so he has planned for some time to make some changes. In fact, at one time in the past he did hire a service manager who resigned after a short time. Since, no one had been found who was competent to fill the job until Wall came along.

Both Robenstine and Wall testified that Wall was hired with the understanding that he would buy a controlling interest in the business eventually and that in the meantime he would be the service manager. However, in order for him to learn all aspects of the business, it was agreed that he would spend about six months working in all phases of the operation. This, it is argued, accounts for the fact that he has worked along with other men rather than strictly in supervision. On this point it is also emphasized that the erratic nature of the tire business makes it necessary at times for all managerial employees, including the president, to work on the floor.

A few weeks prior to the arbitration hearing Wall was actually put on duty in the role of service manager and worked as such for about two weeks, according to the Company. However, because of an emergency resulting from a breakdown of the boiler, he has since been working on that problem.

The Company's description of the primary job of Wall is:

Meets customers as they come in; determines their needs; assigns the work to the proper employee; makes decisions on pricing, discounting, etc.; responsible for billing, making up invoices for customers and seeing that proper records of all transactions are made and kept; also, plans layout and work procedures.

The Union challenges this description of Wall's duties, contending that this may be his future duties but that in the past he has been doing the same work as others. The Company admits that he has done the other work for purposes of learning the business and contends that if he were in the Union he would have to be in one of the designated classifications and could not be shifted from job to job.

Anderson, according to the Company, calls on wholesalers, ranchers, and commercial customers; picks up and delivers tires; takes orders for sales and service; maintains contact with customers; when not traveling, works on the floor in sales and service.

Anderson does not supervise other employees and does substantially the same work as King, but the Company contends that Anderson is the top salesman and is responsible for the commercial area and, further, that a person can be a manager without supervising anyone.

Anderson is paid a salary of $570 per month; King receives $2.37 per hour as provided by the contract. King was also on a salary basis prior to the collective bargaining agreement.

QUESTIONS

1. How would you rule in this case?
2. What criteria for determining the appropriate unit for collective bargaining are illustrated by the arguments in this case?
3. If Wall and Anderson were ordered to join the Union in this case and later became stockholders in the Corporation or were appointed officers of the Corporation, would they still be required to pay Union dues?
4. Why did this case go to arbitration instead of the National Labor Relations Board or the courts?

CASE 6
Prefabrication of Materials

Company: Safeway Stores, Incorporated
San Diego, California
Union: Amalgamated Meat Cutters and Butcher Workmen of North America Local No. 229
Arbitrator: Thomas T. Roberts
Does an employer undermine the union when he introduces prefabri-

cated materials which change the customary work of union members in a retail store?

Thomas T. Roberts, arbitrator in this case, prepared the following discussion of the issues and facts involved.

ISSUE

The stipulated issues are:

a) Did the employer breach the contract by introducing packaged ground beef in one- and two-pound packages in visking casings for direct sale to consumers in the San Diego markets covered by the Contract?

b) If so, what shall the remedy be?

STATEMENT OF FACTS

This grievance arose under, and is controlled by, the agreement between the parties entered into on November 5, 1962, and by its terms in full force and effect until the first Monday of November, 1964.

The Company operates a national chain of food supermarkets. The Union is the exclusive collective bargaining representative for employees working in the meat departments of the Company's markets located in San Diego, California, and surrounding communities. A collective bargaining relationship has existed between the parties since 1937.

This dispute involves the introduction by the Company, in September of 1963, of prepackaged ground beef sold directly to customers in the San Diego area in one- and two-pound quantities encased within visking wrapping. For many years prior to that time, it was the practice of the Company to prepackage ground beef in visking casings of 15- or 20-pound sizes (known as "catch weights") at a central cutting plant located in Los Angeles, California. Two types of ground beef prepackaged in this manner were then supplied to the retail stores in the San Diego area. The first was a coarse ground product which had to be reground before being offered for sale in the markets. The second was a fine grind which did not have to be reground at the store level, except that if it had been placed on display it was sometimes necessary that it be reground prior to being offered for sale on the succeeding day.

The coarse grind ground beef, after its receipt at the market, was recoved from its visking casing, reground, packaged, priced, and displayed for sale. The fine grind ground beef, with the exception noted above, required no regrinding at the store. It was simply sliced, packaged, priced, and then displayed for sale. As to both the coarse and find grinds, all of the above operations conducted at the store level were performed by employees within the jurisdiction of the Union.

In September of 1963, the Company discontinued the shipment to the San Diego area of fine grind beef in the larger catch-weight quantities. In its stead, one- and two-pound "chubs" of prepackaged ground beef in visking casings were introduced. Upon their receipt at the markets, the chubs are simply priced and then displayed for sale in their original package. As was formerly the case with catch-weight quantities, the grinding and packaging of the chubs is accomplished in Los Angeles.

The Union learned of the pending introduction of these chubs and on August 30, 1963, sent the Company two telegrams and a letter protesting that the use of chubs would be a violation of that portion of the collective bargaining agreement which is set forth hereinafter. The Company has nevertheless continued the sale of chubs in the San Diego area and the parties, being unable to resolve their differences, have submitted the matter to arbitration.

CONTROLLING CONTRACT PROVISIONS

Section III
Jurisdiction of Merchandise
Displayed and Sold

a) All fish, poultry, rabbits, meat and/or kindred products, fresh or frozen, cooked or uncooked except as hereinafter provided shall be displayed, handled, and sold under the jurisdiction of Local #229 by journeymen meat cutters under the terms and conditions contained in this Agreement. Wherever any of the above described products and merchandise is being offered for sale at least one (1) employee classified as a head meat cutter or journeyman meat cutter, an employee covered by this Contract, shall be on duty, except during the lunch hour in markets manned by one employee. All sales of products enumerated immediately above shall be credited to the meat department and/or division of the undersigned Employer. All meat products enumerated immediately above shall be cut, prepared, and fabricated on the Employer's premises or immediately adjacent thereto so as to enable said Employer to effectively supervise such operation and conduct the same under sanitary conditions. With regard to beef, veal, lamb and/or pork in carcass form, it is agreed that an exception will be made and the same may be broken down into primal cuts such as rounds, ribs, chucks, plates and loins off the premises, but said primal cuts shall be fabricated on the premises by employees covered by this Contract, and all sales shall be credited to the meat department and/or division of the undersigned Employer. With regard to luncheon meats, presliced bacon, dissected and prefabricated fowls, ground beef and pork sausage in visking casings, fish, rabbits and/or frozen packaged meat, which pursuant to current custom and practices are presently prefabricated, predissected and precut, said products not be cut on the premises, but all of the above products will likewise be handled and sold by employees covered by this Contract, and the sales thereof shall likewise be credited to the meat department and/or the division of the undersigned Employer.

POSITION OF THE UNION

It is the position of the Union that the introduction of chubs to the San Diego area was a violation of Section III of the agreement between the parties. It asks that the sale of such chubs be prohibited in those markets within the jurisdiction.

The Union argues that Section III prohibits the handling, displaying, and selling of ground beef by its members unless such meat is cut, prepared, and fabricated at the markets. It is contended that the new chubs do not qualify as an exception to this mandate because the merchandising of such items is not pursuant to the custom and practice existing at the time the present Agreement was executed in November 1962.

The Union points out that prior to the introduction of the chubs, the sole use of visking casing as a method of packaging ground beef was the transportation of catchweight quantities from Los Angeles to the San Diego markets. Ground beef was never sold directly to the customer in its original visking casing.

At the hearing, the Union introduced an interoffice memo directed to the Company's store managers in San Diego and announcing the pending introduction of the chubs. It is argued that the statements contained therein acknowledge that the new product dispenses with the cutting, packaging, and weighing of fine grind ground beef, all of which were formerly done in the markets.

The alleged failure of the Company to respond to the letter and telegrams from the Union protesting the chubs is cited as an admission on the part of management that the introduction of the new items did in fact involve a violation of the agreement.

The Union draws the attention of the arbitrator to the fact that the agreement does not contain a so-called Management Prerogatives clause and states that the unilateral introduction of the chubs by the Company amounts to "contracting out" bargaining unit work to the derogation of the rights of members of the Union. It is contended that the reduction of work operations here involved constitutes a threat to job security of affected employees and has resulted in layoffs within the meat departments.

POSITION OF THE COMPANY

It is the position of the Company that the introduction of chubs to the San Diego area was not a violation of Section III of the agreement because that provision expressly recites that ground beef in visking casings need not be fabricated in the markets.

The Company contends that in any event Section III restricts the fabrication of meat products only to the "employer's premises" and asserts that the preparation of chubs at its Los Angeles facility falls within the purview of that language. In this regard, it is noted that the employees in the Los Angeles central cutting plant of the Company are represented by the Amalgamated Meat Cutters and Butcher Workmen of North America.

Finally, the Company states that the "existing practice and custom" referred to in the agreement means the packaging of prefabricated ground beef in visking casings of whatever form or weight and the chubs are therefore in conformance with the language of Section III.

QUESTIONS

1. Is the Los Angeles cutting plant part of "the employer's premises" as contemplated by Section III of the agreement?
2. To what does the "current custom and practices" phrase of Section III refer? cutting? grinding? visking casings? or the quantities encased in visking casings?
3. Why is the union grieving in this case?

CASE 7

Assignment of an Employee to Work Outside His Job Classification

Company: Phillips Petroleum Company
Kansas City, Missouri
Union: Oil Chemical and Atomic Workers International Union
Local 5–64
Arbitrator: Marion Beatty

This case involves the performance of work outside of an employee's job description.

The following discussion of the issue and facts in this case was prepared by Marion Beatty, the arbitrator.

The issue is "whether or not the work assignment given to S. Hachinsky on December 25, 1956, pertaining to lineups to tanks on vacuum flasher stream and lube asphalt stream was a violation of the working agreement, particularly Exhibit A thereof."

The Union seeks an award ordering the Company to cease such assignments and allowing the low man in the "asphalt blender loader/senior loader group" on December 25, 1956, to work four hours at overtime rate to correct the alleged violation.

The Company denies that the work assignment in question violated any part of the contract and takes the further position that the arbitrator has no authority to issue any injunctive type of relief applying to the future conduct of the Company.

CONTRACT PROVISIONS

Contract provisions cited by the parties as relevant to the issues in dispute include the Management Prerogatives clause, the Arbitration clause defining the authority and jurisdiction of the arbitrator, a provision for four hours' call-in pay, Article VII, Section 6, entitled "Procedure for Filling Temporary Shift Vacancies," and an Appendix A to the contract which is a chart entitled "Employment, Progression, Regression and Classification Chart." This chart shows three job classifications in the asphalt and loading section and they are, from high to low, "Asphalt blender loader/senior loader," "Loader A," and "Loader-operating helper." It also shows three pumper classifications in a separate section known as the transfer section or pumper section. They are from high to low, "senior pumper," "special pumper," and "pumper."

All of these were considered.

STATEMENT OF FACTS

On December 25, 1956, when many employees in the refinery were off with a paid holiday, S. Hachinsky was employed as a pumper on the 8 A.M. to 4 P.M. shift. His job is in the transfer section. Ordinarily he does not work in the asphalt plant. The asphalt plant was down for the holiday, but several valves had to be turned to make changes in lineups and tanks on the vacuum flasher stream and lube asphalt stream. A supervisor requested Hachinsky to come a short distance from his regular station in the pumping section to the asphalt plant to turn the necessary valves as directed by the supervisor. The turning of such valves is a type of work regularly performed by Hachinsky, but he does not work at the asphalt plant. The work involved required approximately 10 minutes. Hachinsky had ample leisure time to perform the work and did perform the work promptly as directed, but under protest.

These duties ordinarily are performed and are the responsibility of the "asphalt blender loader/senior loader," the title given to the employee who is stationed at the asphalt plant and whose duties embrace, among other things, the turning of such valves for making lineups of charge and yield streams to and from the vacuum flasher and lineups for loading of trucks and tank cars with asphalt.

The Company knew in advance of December 25 that these valves would have to be turned. It could have called in a regular employee in the asphalt plant and paid him four hours at premium rate. It chose to use Hachinsky, a pumper who ordinarily did the same kind of valve turning at a nearby section.

POSITION OF THE UNION

The Union contends that the above-described assignment to Hachinsky violated the working agreement and particularly Article VII, Section 6c and Appendices A and B. The Union states that this work was the duty and responsibility of an "asphalt blender loader/senior loader" and that in his absence it should have been assigned to another employee in the asphalt and loading section in accordance with Article VII, Section 6c of Appendix A, the "Employment Progression, Regression and Classification Chart." It maintained that Hachinsky was regularly employed in the pumper section, not a part of the asphalt and loading section, and that even though he might have known how to turn valves under supervision, he was not familiar with these valves in the asphalt loading section and should not have been called to do any work in another section either permanent or temporary and that an employee in the asphalt section was entitled to the work.

The Union maintains that one of the purposes of the "Progression, Regression and Classification Chart" is to give "organizational status" to the many job classifications shown thereon, not only for the purpose of progression and regression, but also for the filling of vacancies, both temporary and permanent, and for the assignment of work in each basic classification, and that the Company could not cross the definite classification, and for the assignment of work from one to another.

It maintains that the Company violated the contract for the purpose of saving four hours of premium pay which otherwise would have gone to an employee in the asphalt loader section.

POSITION OF THE COMPANY

The Company states that the turning of these valves in making these lineups is the sort of work normally done by pumpers, that all Hachinsky had to do was to turn several valves as directed by the supervisor, the same kind of work which he did normally and regularly, and that it was no violation of any part of the contract, and was proper and reasonable under the circumstances. It states that the work in question is identical in job content and skill required to that work which is performed by him and other pumpers every day.

The Company admits that if it had called in an employee especially for this assignment it would have called someone regularly employed within the asphalt and loading section, but points out that it was not necessary to call one for 10 minutes on a Christmas holiday, and that therefore Article VII, Section 6c, and Appendix A do not apply for they provide a procedure for filling temporary shift vacancy and that no shift vacancy was involved.

The Company contends that there is nothing in the contract which prohibits it from assigning the work in question to pumper Hackinsky who was on duty, qualified and available, doing the same kind of work elsewhere, and in the absence of restriction has the right to exercise its managerial prerogatives.

The Company further contends that the Union is attempting to read jurisdictional lines into the contract where none are provided, and that the contract as well as the progression chart attached thereto is not an outline of job jurisdiction and that jurisdictional lines were never discussed in negotiation.

Lastly the Company points out that it has on 14 previous occasions made similar assignments of pumpers to perform jobs in the asphalt plant when the regular staff was off on holidays.

QUESTIONS

1. The contract and exhibits do not clearly prohibit the Company from assigning Hachinsky to this fill-in job. What sorts of inferential material could be introduced by the Union to support its claim?
2. If the arbitrator upheld this grievance, what effect would his ruling have on plant operations?
3. This dispute appears to be over a very minor issue: "ten minutes" versus "four hours' pay." What are its deeper implications for workers, the Company, and the Union?

CASE 8
"Tandem" Compensation Adjustments for Nonunion Personnel

Names and places in this case are fictitious. The case involves the determination of a policy on salary adjustments for both nonunion and unionized employees. "Mr. Allen" employed one of the authors of this book as a consultant on this problem.

BACKGROUND

The Ralta Company is engaged in the manufacture and distribution of products in an expanding industry. At the present time, it is about midway in a 15-year program of product and process diversification. Profits of both Ralta and its principal competitors reflect the general prosperity and expansion of the industry. In this industry labor costs equal between 15 percent and 20 percent of total costs of production. Ralta sells its products in a somewhat restricted geographic area and could be seriously hurt by geographic price wars which sometimes plague the industry.

In his annual report to stockholders, the president of Ralta said, "With regard to the outlook for next year, we anticipate that demand for our products will average 4 percent to 5 percent higher than this year. Ordinarily we would expect such an increase to result in moderate gain in profits. While management seeks this result, it cannot now be assumed with any assurance because our industry faces more than the usual number of uncertainties." Over the past 5 years, industry estimates of increased volume have leveled off at the 4 percent to 5 percent figure from a higher estimate of progress in the previous decade. Actual progress in the industry has fallen somewhat short of these estimates. However, Ralta has expanded each year approximately at the 4 percent to 5 percent industry estimated rate.

The Ralta Company employs 12,000 wage and salary workers. They are engaged in diverse operations geographically spread over the eastern seaboard and southeastern states. Five thousand hourly employees are concentrated in two plants: one in Pennsylvania employing 4,500 and one in Texas employing 500. Hourly employees are represented by one union in Pennsylvania and by a rival union in Texas. Another 5,000 employees work for a commission or in isolated locations and are not related to the present problem. The direct concern of this case is with 2,310 salaried employees, about 700 of whom are represented by the Pennsylvania union.

The salaried employees of the Ralta Company can be classified into three groups:

A) Earning between $25,000 and $100,000 per year—55 employees—not represented by a union.
B) Earning between $15,000 and $25,000 per year—155 employees—not represented by a union.
C) Earning less than $15,000 per year—2,100 employees—this group includes middle-management people, production supervisors, engineers, and staff personnel (about 1,400 people) earning more than the top rate paid to union represented workers and about 700 employees earning less than the top rate paid to union represented workers. The latter 700 employees include secretarial, clerical, and custodial personnel, some of whom are represented by the union.

Union-negotiated wage increases over the last 15 years have been substantial and frequent (almost annually). The Company and Union have never agreed on basic principles which should be uniformly applied in wage determination. However, changes in the cost of living, Company profitability, wage increases and wage levels paid by the Company's competitors, and changes in productivity have been discussed in negotiations and probably exerted an influence on what was finally agreed to.

For the last 15 years, the Ralta Company has followed the practice of granting salary increases approximately equal to the negotiated wage increases immediately upon the conclusion of negotiations with the union. On several occasions the Company bypassed the A Group positions or gave a fixed dollar increase which was less than the full percentage increase to Group A positions. All employees in Groups A, B, and C may receive annual *merit* increases until they reach the maximum of their salary classification. These merit increases have been awarded apart from and *in addition to* the general "tandem" adjustments for salaried employees.

THE PROBLEM

Members of the top management of the Ralta Company became concerned over the prospect that salaried employees might feel that the unions were negotiating for the salaried people. Management did not want the salaried people to have this sympathetic interest in the success of the unions. When this matter was discussed in the operating executives' meeting, the president of Ralta directed Mr. Allen, the industrial relations director, to look into the situation and recommend a solution.

GATHERING THE FACTS

Mr. Allen started his analysis by stating the following Company objectives:

1. To provide fair and equitable compensation for salaried employees.
2. To retain and attract competent salaried employees at all salary levels.
3. To build management morale and loyalty to the company.
4. To pay salaries which have an incentive value.
5. To provide flexibility in salary administration.
6. Not to prejudice the company's position in collective bargaining.
7. To minimize the belief among salaried employees that their pay is determined by union negotiations.

This listing of objectives by Mr. Allen represented his beliefs concerning the relative priority of each goal. He realized that the goals were not mutually exclusive. He recognized that salary increases had closely paralleled wage increases negotiated with the unions. However, he insisted that this is "natural" since the same economic forces which generated wage increases are responsible for salary increases. Announcement of general salary increases before reaching agreements with rival unions would seriously prejudice the company's position in collective bargaining.

In wage negotiations, Ralta had openly accepted only two criteria for wage increases: (a) practice of industry competitors—"meeting the average" and (b) rapid and substantial increases in the cost of living. However, it was obvious that competitors' concessions and Ralta's willingness to "meet the average" were strongly influenced by the high profits of the industry and the firm. This in turn could be related to rapid technological progress and increasing man-hour productivity.

Mr. Allen wrote to other companies in his industry about how they handled this problem. The responses indicated that every major company in the industry followed Ralta's practice and that they were equally disturbed about its bad psychological effect. No one in the industry proposed a more satisfactory way of handling the problem.

Not satisfied with these responses, Mr. Allen broadened his inquiry to other industries. Some dozen industrial relations directors responded to Allen's inquiry. They added the following possibilities as methods for handling the salary problem:

1. Grant a percentage increase equal to the union-negotiated increase but announce it at times so that it will not be associated with collective bargaining negotiations. "When adjustments were made considerably after union negotiations, it usually became a question in management personnel's minds whether the adjustments granted were related to the last increase given to the union or were a forecast of the next increase to be negotiated. We are not sure that all of the confusion so generated has been to the advantage of the Company."

2. Award all salary increases exclusively on a "merit" basis. Prepare an annual forecast of total salary adjustments and budget funds to each department on the basis of this forecast. Allow each department head to award salary increases to approximately one twelfth of his employees each month. Each meritorious employee receives his salary increase on a strictly personal and confidential basis. "We have encountered two problems with this system. First, if we overestimate or underestimate the forecast in one year, we try to compensate for this error the next year. Although we have been generally successful in providing equity *over a number of years*, inequities have arisen in some individual years. The other problem is the timing of the increases. An employee receiving his increase in January may receive a greater annual increase than a more meritorious employee who receives his increase in November."

3. Announce general adjustments at a predetermined annual date. The amount of the annual adjustment will be determined by an analysis of economic conditions at the time of the announcement.

4. Adopt a fixed formula for general adjustments to be made at a predetermined annual date. One such formula might consider changes in the Consumers' Price Index plus a fixed percentage increase to reflect increases in general "productivity."

5. Provide for salaried employees to participate in a stock-purchase or profit-sharing plan.

RECOMMENDATIONS

You are Mr. Allen. Next week you must present your recommendations to the operating executives' committee.

Prepare your recommendations on the basis of the alternatives developed in your research. Weigh each of the alternatives against the objectives outlined above.

Precisely state the problems surrounding the application of your recommendations.

CASE 9
Arbitration of a General Wage Adjustment

Company: Remco Industries
Union: International Brotherhood of Teamsters
Teamsters Industrial and Allied Workers, Local No. 97
Arbitrator: Daniel House

Cases of this type are rarities. Only in very exceptional cases will a management and a union entrust to an arbitrator the question of general wage adjustments which is vital to both management and the union.

What criteria should an arbitrator use in making or refusing to make a general wage adjustment?

The following discussion of the issue and facts in this case was prepared by Daniel House, the arbitrator.

ISSUE

"Should an increase be granted under Article XXI, Section 2, of the Agreement between the parties; if the answer is in the affirmative, how much shall the increase be?"

The parties agreed that if an increase was granted, it was to be made retroactive to December 23, 1963, and paid to all employees with seniority on that date.

CONTRACT PROVISIONS

Article XXI, Section 2, of the agreement is as follows:

Effective thirty (30) days before December 23, 1963, the Company and the Union shall negotiate wages; failure to agree, the matter shall be submitted to arbitration in accordance with Article VIII, Section 1(d) of this Agreement.

Article VII, Section 1(d), provides for the selection of an arbitrator by the New Jersey State Board of Mediation.

THE CONTROVERSY

Following a strike by the Union, the parties entered into a three-year agreement, effective December 23, 1962, providing, among other things, a general increase of seven cents per hour effective December 23, 1962, and wage negotiations in each of the following two years, subject to arbitration in the event of failure to come to agreement. The parties failed to agree on the wage question in the December, 1963, negotiations. The Union requested a general wage increase of fifteen cents per hour; the Company refused to concede any wage increase.

THE COMPANY'S ARGUMENT

The Company is engaged in the manufacture and sale of toys. The industry is a highly competitive and volatile one, differences of a fraction of a cent an item often making the difference between a sale and no sale, a "fad item" catching on (but with an indeterminate life) suddenly lifting employment in the manufacturing end and, as suddenly, dropping it.

Employment in this Company ranges from 200 to 2,000 employees in production during a year.

The Company argues that its business has been off since 1961; that from an annual net profit ranging, for all the years up to 1961, from 7 to 9 percent, it has reduced each year since, and for the calendar year 1963 was just over 4 percent; that its stock, as a result, is now reduced to about one-half its 1959 value; that it entered into the agreement with the Union in 1962 with misgivings about the wisdom of the seven-cent general increase provided therein but agreed to it as "a token of confidence," hoping that a new item it was about to introduce would go well; that the new item was a disappointment and 1963 a worse year even than 1962; that the Company had ceased to pay cash dividends in 1962 as a result of the declining profit picture; that the financial problems of the successive poor seasons had been compounded by the costs of financing of the new plant they had built to try to keep competitive in manufacturing operations; and that the wage rates paid were in line with those of the major competitors in the area.

The Company stated that the average base rate (before piecework earnings) is about $1.40 per hour. A Union witness thought that the average would be closer to $1.30 per hour. By agreement of the parties, the arbitrator examined payrolls at the Company plant; the data was duplicated and copies submitted to the arbitrator and to the Union by mail. The arbitrator's examination of the records showed that the average base hourly rate for the "basic crew" is $1.38 per hour. The parties agreed that the "basic crew" consisted of about 400 employees who were laid off for only brief periods between seasons; they further agreed that the crew employed at the time of the hearing would be representative of the "basic crew."

In summary, the Company took the position that since its pay rates were not out of line with the competition in the area, since its profit picture was poor, and since the seven-cent wage increase in 1962 had been unwarranted, and the anticipated good season to justify it had not materialized, the 1962 error should not be repeated; the Company urged, therefore, that no wage increase be awarded.

THE UNION'S ARGUMENT

The Union did not contest that the industry is highly competitive and volatile, nor that the Company's wage rates were in line with the area competition. However, the Union argued that the Company was not losing money; that the reduction in profits for the last few years had been more than offset by the continued adequate rate of profits for all the many years prior to 1962; that the Company should have had the foresight to set aside from the profits of the fat years enough to take care of the employees' legitimate desires for improvements in the lean years; further, the Union claimed that the effect of the seven-cent increase in 1962 was in part negated by the operation of the federal law establishing $1.25 minimum wage rate in 1963. For these reasons the Union requested an award of 15 cents per hour general increase.

QUESTIONS

1. If you disregard the actual wage levels in effect at the time this case reached arbitration, what *criteria* for general wage adjustments are argued by the parties? Do the criteria argued by the parties exhaust a list of conceivably valid criteria? As an arbitrator would you feel obligated to consider only the criteria argued by the parties?

2. As representative of the union, how would you justify your demand for a 15 cents per hour general wage increase?

3. Why did the parties in this case sign a reasonably common three-year agreement with annual reopeners? Why did the parties sign an agreement with the *very unusual* provision for arbitration of the general wage adjustment disputes arising at reopening dates?

CASE 10
Discontinuance of Free Meals

Company: Lutheran Medical Center
Union: Retail, Wholesale and Department Store Union, Drug and Hospital Employees Union
Local 1199
Arbitrator: Benjamin H. Wolf

Can an employer practice of providing free meals be discontinued without bargaining with the union? Does the fact that the employer "bought back" the free meals from the union in previous negotiations justify the discontinuance of the meals a long time after the employer bargained the meals away?

The following discussion of the issues and facts in this case was prepared by Benjamin H. Wolf, the arbitrator.

BACKGROUND

This arbitration is concerned with a protest made by the Union against the decision by the Employer to discontinue the practice of supplying meals to its employees in the dietary department.

The parties are in substantial agreement on the facts. Prior to 1951, the employees ate their meals family style at a big table and received their meals without charge. That year a change was made. A cafeteria was established and the hospital announced that employees eating in the cafeteria would be required to pay for whatever food they ate. To compensate for the loss of three meals a day, the employees were given wage increases ranging from $10 to $20 per month.

In 1953 Mrs. Fevang became personnel director of the hospital. At that time all the employees were paying for their meals. Some time between 1953 and 1956 the employees of the dietary department stopped paying for their food. No one seems to know when and how this happened but there is no denial that some of the lower echelon supervisory employees knew about it. When the administrator learned of it, he issued a memorandum directing that dietary employees should no longer receive their meals free and again, in order to compensate them, he announced that they would be paid $10 a month in addition to their regular wage. Sometime between July, 1956, when the memorandum was issued and June, 1963, when the Union agreement was signed, the dietary employees again began eating their meals without paying for them.

Mr. Johnson, the present administrator, came to the hospital in August, 1962. It is conceded by the Employer that Mr. Johnson, who headed the management team in the negotiation of the Union agreement, was aware that the employees in the dietary department were eating meals in the cafeteria and not paying for them. He was not aware, however, of the history of this problem, and that on two occasions the Employer had "brought back" the practice of furnishing free meals to the employees for substantial wage increases.

In November, 1963, the hospital engaged an independent contractor to manage the dietary department. He informed Mr. Johnson that the dietary employees were not paying for their meals. On July 1, 1964, the Hospital notified the dietary employees that from July 15, 1964, on they would have to pay for their meals.

It was stipulated that Marshall Dubin telephoned Mrs. Fevang shortly after July 1, 1964, and told her that the employees were dissatisfied with the notice. He requested a meeting, which was held on July 22.

POSITIONS OF THE PARTIES

On the merits of the controversy, the Union argued that a practice which had existed for a long period of time and which had not been changed by the contract should be left undisturbed by the parties until they jointly agreed to alter it. The Union urged that the granting of a meal to an employee is not only a condition of employment but a method of compensation and that by taking the meal away the Employer reduced the wages of these employees. Thus, it was a basic change not only in the working conditions which existed at the time the bargain was entered into but also in the compensation they had received for more than a year since the contract was signed.

Although there is no provision in the contract which covers the granting of free meals to these employees, the Union urged that the myriad of conditions which exist outside of the contract are part of the collective bargaining relationship and hence, part of the agreement between the parties.

The position of the Employer is that the free meals were not an existing benefit or a past practice in the conventional sense of the word. It urged that the Employer, having already twice bought itself out of this practice, should not be required to negotiate itself out a third time. It stated that the hospital never deemed the free meals as compensation to the employees and, therefore, never reported them on the W-2 tax forms. Under the Internal Revenue Code, therefore, the meals were deemed to have been furnished as a convenience to the hospital, not as compensation to the employees.

The Employer argued that the problem was analogous to the discontinuance of a Christmas bonus when parties made no reference to the bonus and cited two New York Supreme Court cases in support of its position.

QUESTIONS

1. Were the meals for dietary employees "wages" or a "bonus"?
2. What weight should be given to a practice that apparently arose by mistake?
3. How many times must the hospital "buy back" the meals?
4. How would you rule in this case?

CASE 11
Elimination of a Job by the Company

Company: Potter and Brumfield, Inc.
Princeton, Indiana
Union: International Association of Machinists
Local Lodge No. 1459
Arbitrator: Carl A. Warns, Jr.

The case involves the right of the Company to eliminate a job.

The following discussion of the issue and the facts in this case was prepared by Carl A. Warns, Jr., the arbitrator.

The question before the arbitrator is whether or not the Company has violated the contract by eliminating the job of group leader in Department 41.

The Company manufactures electrical relays. Actual production takes place on production lines of varying sizes dependent upon the type of work of each line. Prior to the strike, Line 41, in addition to the usual complement of employees actually servicing the line, contained a "group leader" whose duties are set forth in a job description and whose job title and rate are listed in Appendix A ("a part" of the contract). The group leader on Line 41 did not return to the employ of the Company after the strike and the Company did not replace him. The Union asserts in this grievance that this failure to assign another group leader to the line violates the collective agreement between the parties. The Company explains that time did not justify the training of a new group leader since the line would be moved to another plant within a short time. The group leader's supervisory duties were assigned to the foreman and the remainder of his work to a material handler. The Company states in their post-hearing brief that subsequent to the hearing on this case the line has been in fact moved and that the relays previously produced on Line 41 are manufactured elsewhere. Regardless of this factor, however, it is the position of the Company that they retain the right under the current agreement to eliminate jobs and that there is no contractual basis for this grievance challenging the failure to fill the job of group leader on Line 41 after the strike.

CONTRACT PROVISIONS INVOLVED

Article X—Wages

Section 1: Effective the first pay period after this contract is signed, the Company will grant a general wage increase of five (5) cents per hour and include such increase in Exhibit "A" attached hereto and made a part hereof. On February 4, 1957 all employees shall receive a wage increase of five (5) cents per hour which increase shall be added to the then present rates as shown in Exhibit "A" attached.

. . .

Section 3: Production rates, which serve as the basis of this plan, shall be established by the Company through time study wherein proper allowances are made for unavoidable delays and incentive earnings. These production rates are guaranteed by the Company to remain unchanged except as agreed upon in this contract.

Article XIV—Full Agreement Clause

This Contract represents complete Collective Bargaining and full agreement by the parties in respect to rates of pay, wages, hours of employment or other conditions of employment which shall prevail during the term hereof and neither party may hereafter negotiate on any other matters during the life of this agreement.

POSITION OF THE UNION

The breach of contract by the Company in failing to assign a group leader to Line 41 not only adversely affects the earnings of the employees on that line but establishes a precedent whereby larger lines and more employees are reduced in earning capacity. The employees on Line 41 are compensated on a group incentive basis; the group leader on a full average plant incentive. It is obvious from a reading of the job description of the group leader that he is an essential element in the ability of the individual employee to maintain the rate. It is no answer for the Company to say that the instructional responsibilities of the group leader can be transferred to a foreman; the latter is responsible for several lines and may frequently be absent while the employees are sitting idle on base wages due to lack of parts and instruction. The group leader, on the other hand, is assigned to one line and is therefore constantly available to maintain the flow of materials and to give needed instruction; his importance to the efficient teamwork of the line as reflected in earnings is clear. Nor is it for new classifications such as "material handlers," whose basis of compensation is unknown to the Union, or instructors, to do the work of group leaders at considerably lesser pay. If these "instructors" or "material handlers" are compensated at a straight hourly rate, they lack the incentive of the group leader who had a direct and immediate interest in high production on the line.

This contract contains no management prerogative clause. During the last negotiation the Company wished to have such a provision added but the Union would not agree. Since the contract does not expressly authorize the Company to eliminate the job classification of group leader and in the absence of a management clause which might be argued as permitting this by implication the Company lacks the contractual right to take the action challenged in this grievance. The Union requests the arbitrator to find that the Company violated the contract and the principles of good collective bargaining and to compensate the group leader for all or part of any earnings lost while foremen, material handlers, instructors, or other persons are performing group leader work while such individuals are on layoff and subject to recall.

POSITION OF THE COMPANY

It is well established in industrial relations and confirmed in numerous published arbitration cases that in the absence of a restriction in the collective agreement management has the inherent right to eliminate jobs, classifications, and to combine duties in interest of production. The only limitation is that the admitted right not be exercised in an arbitrary or discriminatory manner. In this case there is no reference to either job descriptions or group leaders in the body of the contract. The only reference to group leaders is in Exhibit "A" which is for the sole purpose of classifying the employees and to designate the rates of pay for each classification. Such classification and rate of pay simply set forth the rate that must be paid to jobholders in particular jobs and does not mean that there must be an employee or employees in each classification at all times. The incumbent group leader on Line 41 resigned from the Company and was not replaced because it was determined that a group leader for so small a group would not make for an efficient operation. In addition, there were no group leaders available with experience on this line. Since it was anticipated that the line would be moved to another plant, it would have been poor management to spend from eight weeks to three months training a group leader for a nonexistent job. Furthermore, group leaders are used as an adjunct in assisting foremen in the operation of the department. Where the department is so small, as here, such a classification is a surplus one. The foreman is fully capable of taking care of all supervisory duties. There is no instructor on Line 41 and the use of a material handler is proper. There is such a classification listed in Appendix A called Material Handler (Machine Shop). The duties of the material handler here are comparable and therefore it was not deemed necessary to add a new job classification or description to be filed with the others.

The Union's position that the absence of a management prerogative clause prevents the Company from exercising traditional prerogatives is untenable. Management has an inherent right to make all essential decisions designed to make the Company competitive. The elimination of jobs and the combination of job duties is one of them. Limitations on this basic right can be granted only at the bargaining table by the Company. Since this contract contains no such limitations, it follows that the Company's decision in this case must be confirmed and the grievance denied.

QUESTIONS

1. The Union argues here that the signing of an agreement without a management's rights clause after negotiations on the inclusion of such a clause means that management has only those rights explicitly stated in the contract. What influence should an unsuccessful management argument for a management's rights clause in negotiations have on this case?

2. What is the significance of Company motivation in a case of this type? The Company here claims that it couldn't fill the job from present employees and that the job was going to be moved to another plant in the near future. Without these special circumstances, could the Company eliminate the job for such a reason as saving money?

3. What kinds of evidence should the Union and Company supply in the controversy over loss of incentive earnings resulting from the elimination of the group leader job? How would you judge the validity of the evidence that might be supplied?

CASE 12
"Banking" of Production by Incentive Workers
as Basis for Discharge

Company: Harnischfeger Corporation
             Milwaukee, Wisconsin

Union: United Steelworkers of America
             Local 1114

Arbitrator: Harold M. Gilden

Can an incentive worker be disciplined for high production which he "banks" and reports in such a way as to stabilize his earnings? What is the impact of such actions on the efficient operation of an enterprise?

Harold M. Gilden, the arbitrator, prepared the following discussion of the issues and facts involved in the case.

ISSUE

Grievance dated April 23, 1964, filed by X——, challenging the propriety of his discharge on April 22, 1964, and requesting reinstatement with full back pay.

NATURE OF CASE

X——, the grievant herein, was hired by the Company as a radial drill press operator on September 9, 1959, and continued to be employed in that classification until April 22, 1964, the date of his discharge.

For April 21, 1964, X—— turned in a work ticket which showed that he had produced 100 pieces of Part No. 15F-427 (order no. 360292) in an elapsed time of six hours. On the following day, April 22, 1964, X——'s work ticket reported that he worked the full eight hours of the shift in running 120 pieces of Part No. 15F-427 (order no. 360292).

It so happened that X——'s immediate supervisor foreman, Frank Wilhelm, sometime during the morning of April 22, 1964, was informed that all 300 pieces of Part No. 15F-427, the total run scheduled to be produced on order no. 360292, were completed. Wilhelm made an on-the-spot inspection of the finished pieces and verified the accuracy of this report. Actually, X—— did not run any pieces of Part No. 15F-427 on April 22, but instead utilized the full eight hours of his shift in working ahead on other jobs that were scheduled to be produced in his department.

On April 22 Wilhelm talked to X——about the apparent discrepancy in the production figures given by X——on his work tickets relating to Part No. 15F-427 and the finished run of 300 pieces already produced and X—— admitted that he had already run all 300 pieces.

Only the week before, around April 14 or 15, Wilhelm had called X——aside and told him that the second-shift radial drill press operators had complained about X——'s "banking" activities and Wilhelm suggested to X——that if X—— was "banking," he should stop it immediately.

After reviewing X——'s employment record with the Company, which revealed four disciplinary suspensions of three days each for various infractions other than banking, a one-day layoff, four written warnings plus the verbal warning given him on "banking," it was decided that he should be discharged and he was terminated on April 22, 1964.

CONTENTIONS

The Union says that special circumstances are present in this case which distinguish it from run-of-the-mill dishonesty situations; that the plant rule relied upon by the Company does not specifically relate to "banking"; that this is the first case in which the rule has been used in this connection; that occasionally employees are directed to rework jobs under circumstances where such performance is absorbed by the employee and not accurately reflected on the work card; that X——had accumulated a bank of 24 standard hours not only to improve his position but, in part, to compensate for the Company's failure to apply the proper rate; that the bank created by X—— simply put him in the same relative position he would have been in had scheduling practices been such as to avoid protracted periods of idle time; that none of the disciplinary penalties assessed against X—— during the approximately five years that X—— had been employed were for "banking," or for any activity reasonably related thereto; that the quality of X——'s work performance was sufficiently high to gain him a merit increase which he held at the time of his discharge; that "banking" had widespread acceptance in the shop and its existence was common knowledge; that X—— had to keep his work cards locked up to prevent employees on other shifts from utilizing his "bank"; that management had no established policy opposed to banking, but in effect winked at the practice and permitted it to exist; that other arbitrators have refused to sustain disciplinary action for employee laxity to which the Company itself was a party; that in resorting to an accepted practice to maintain a favorable earning structure, X——'s actions are readily differentiated from cases involving employee attempts to obtain pay for work not performed; that in discharging X——, the Company departed from a long existing practice of toleration, acquiescence, and even permissive participation in the practice of "banking"; that X—— should not be the first scapegoat of a new policy which the Company desires to put into effect; that "banking" exists at this plant and if it is a problem it should be met head-on across the bargaining table and not

resolved indirectly through the discharge of a selected victim; that X——
should be reinstated to employment and that if any punishment is merited,
it should be limited to a loss of some back pay.

The Company says that honesty is basic where employees are compensated under an incentive program; that supervisors cannot possibly
count every piece produced so the Company must rely on employee
truthfulness; that reliance on the integrity of the employee is implicit in
the mechanics of any "honor system"; that there is not one scintilla of
evidence that the Company was aware of "banking" or that it ever condoned it; that the Company's standard hours program is based on employee honesty and that X—— knew he was performing dishonestly;
that current correct reporting of time spent on jobs is the heart of the
standard hour program; that if "banking" goes on, the Company doesn't
know its costs, can't properly assign the work load and can't properly
price its product; that each man cannot possibly be watched every moment and it is only feasible to check employees on a spot basis; that the
grievant was specifically warned that "banking" was prohibited; that the
nature and extent of X——'s banking practices warrants his discharge;
that the record is abundantly clear that for a long time X—— was laying
out his own work load and determining the amount of compensation he
should receive per work day; that this was not a one-card inadvertent
type of falsification but a carefully concealed plan of running this radial
drill press for X——'s benefit regardless of the Company's costs, its work
schedules and work allocations; that were this practice to be adopted by
the majority of employees on standard hours, it would completely annihi-
late the Company's costs and production setup; that this is a clear case of
an employee practicing a fraudulent scheme for a period of years and who
continues to engage in it after being warned to stop; that the grievance
should be denied.

APPLICABLE CONTRACT PROVISIONS

Section 7. Discharge Cases. In the event any employee is discharged from
and after the date hereof and he believes that he had been unjustly dealt with,
such discharge shall constitute a case arising under the method of adjusting
grievances herein provided. . . . In the event it should be decided under the
rules of this agreement that an injustice has been dealt the employee with
regard to the discharge, the Company shall reinstate such employee and pay
full compensation at not less than the employee's regular rate for the time lost
less any outside wages accrued during the period. . . .

Section 8. The Management of the plant and the direction of the working
forces and of the affairs of the Company, including the right to hire discipline,
or discharge for proper cause, or to transfer from one job to another except
as limited by Section 3, and the right to layoff because of lack of work or for
other legitimate reasons is vested exclusively in the Company.

Plant Rules

. . . These are the things which can lead to discipline, up to and including discharge:

10. Falsifying records, reports, or applications for employment.

In November, 1963, less than six months before his discharge, X——
was suspended for three days for requesting a down time allowance of 3.2 hours due to no work, when in fact there were jobs waiting to be finished.

QUESTIONS

1. Compare "banking" to "punching another person's time card" and to "theft."
2. From the facts given in the case, is "banking" a widespread practice at this company? If "banking" were a widespread practice and management wanted to stop it, what steps should management take?
3. Why would second-shift employees complain about X——'s "banking"?
4. Assume that "banking" is possible only when production standards are loose. Since management has sole responsibility for establishing production standards, do these loose standards condone the practice of "banking"?

CASE 13
Rate Changes Due to Rate Setting Errors

Company: Orr and Sembower, Inc.
Union: United Steelworkers of America
Arbitrator: Jacob Seidenberg

What constitutes a "clerical error" under an agreement which permits the employer to revise incentive wage rates which contain "clerical errors"?

The following discussion of the issue and facts in this case was prepared by Jacob Seidenberg, the arbitrator.

ISSUE

Whether the Company cut the rates in violation of the "Guarantee of Standard Allowed Time" provision of the 1959 Supplemental Agreement.

FACTS

The Company and the Union, despite objections and protests raised by some employees, instituted by Supplemental Agreement dated May 21, 1959, an individual incentive plan in lieu of an existing production performance bonus with a 50–50 arrangement. The prior plan had been in effect from 1953 until the middle of 1959. The new individual incentive plan was installed in the plant on a departmental basis, one department at a time. Under the plan incentive rates were developed by two methods. One involved the use of time studies, and the other involved the use of standard data developed at other production machine shops. The time study method involved the use of rate sheets and the standard data method used standard data charts.

Most of the rates in the machine shop were established from standard data charts while the other rates were developed from time studies made in the shops. From January until November 1960, the time studies were the sole source for the establishment of incentive rates. But in the summer of 1960 the Company determined that faster and more accurate coverage could be obtained from the use of standard data and consequently switched to this method. In November 1960, the first standard data chart was issued and used to determine the rates in the main gas piping assemblies. Since the incentive plan had been installed in the assembly department in January 1960, the rates which had been developed prior to November by the use of the time study method, under the terms of the Supplemental Agreement, had to be, and were, maintained.

The incentive rates are developed in the plant by a review of the existing standard data or the rate sheets from a study of· the applicable drawings and the present rate structure. This work is performed by a standards setting clerk under proper supervision. This position is considered by the Company to be a training job for time study and data work. Time study work is considered to be more difficult and more responsible and is paid a higher salary than standards setting work.

The provision of the Supplemental Agreement which is relevant to the resolution of the grievance states, in part, as follows:

Guarantee of Allowed Standard Time

The Company agrees not to revise allowed time for any operations, unless there is a clerical error or unless changes are made that justify a restudy. Such changes may be methods, feeds, speeds, mechanical equipment, tools, fixtures, materials and designs. Any such change shall not affect an operator's incentive opportunity, provided that the operator maintains substantially the same efficiency and effort on the changed operations as before such changes were affected.

UNION'S POSITION

The Union maintains that under the "Guarantee of Allowed Standard Time" provision the Company has no right to change, unilaterally and without Union concurrence, the rates in question. The Company is undertaking to revise rates which have been in effect for years, rates which the Company knew about and for which it was willing to pay.

If the Company is permitted to change rates at will, then there is no value in having an established rate, no matter how long it has been in effect. All the Company has to do to change a rate is to declare it a mistake. An employee who has become proficient at his job would have to be careful about his output if his rates could be cut at will. In the Company's action giving rise to this grievance, what the Company is calling mistakes are not clerical errors and therefore are not within contract provision.

The Union has not objected in the past to the Company's making legitimate rate changes as long as they were done in accordance with the terms of the contract. This is evidenced by the fact that this grievance is the first one that has gone to arbitration on the issue of rate changing. Other rate changes were done pursuant to the provisions of the agreement and not arbitrarily.

The Union denies the Company allegations that it has only changed rates for four specified reasons and that it has always changed rates for these reasons without Union protest. This is the first time that the Company has changed rates by departing from the contractually established procedures.

In addition the Union wishes to direct attention to Section 5 of the agreement, "Rate Establishment and Adjustment." That contract provision only allows three months within which to challenge a rate, and after that the rate is fixed. The Union disagrees with the Company's contention that Section 5 does not apply to incentive rates. The Union believes that the section applies both to hourly rated and incentive jobs.

The Union also cites an award rendered by the umpire in a Bethlehem Steel case which held that the Company may not correct a long-standing error in the administration of an incentive plan when the agreement provided that rates in effect shall remain in effect unless changed with the consent of the Union.

COMPANY'S POSITION

The Company maintains that it has not improperly changed any rates in violation of the agreement. It has not even changed rates which were improperly set by time study methods. It has classified these improper rates as "red circle" rates and honored them even though it knows full well these rates are incorrect.

The only rates which the Company has corrected are those which are permissible under the Supplemental Agreement, are the result of mistakes made by the employees working in the "standards setting" category, and are of the following nature:

1. Use of a rate sheet when standard data chart should have been used.
2. Use of standard data chart when rate sheet should have been used.

3. Application of data on rate sheet or standard data chart.
4. Arithmetical mistakes.

The Company has consistently made revisions in mistakes resulting from these four types of mistakes. The Company has furnished the Union since August 1961, with copies of all wage changes made. The figures show the following:

1. Over 60,000 rates have been issued since the individual incentive system was initiated.
2. The Company has made 588 corrections in the 60,000 rates due to mistakes in the 4 mentioned categories.
3. Of these 588 corrections, 76 were arithmetical errors and 512 were improper establishment of rates from available data.
4. Of the 588 corrections, 376 increased the rates and 212 decreased the rates.

The Company's action in correcting those rates, which have come within the four mentioned categories, are "clerical errors" and are within the terms of the "Guarantee of Standard Time Allowance" provision of the Supplemental Agreement of 1959. The Company's evidence, in the form of the exhibits it introduced, clearly demonstrates that the types of errors which have been corrected in the past without Union objection fall within the four specified kinds of mistakes. As far as the Company knows, all the rate changes involved in this grievance come within the four categories of mistakes cited here.

The Company also denies that Section 5 of the contract has any applicability to this dispute. Preliminarily, the Company wishes to state that this Section was never mentioned at any stage of the grievance procedure. But in any event, the parties executed a supplemental agreement on October 2, 1959, which specifically governs the method for adjusting incentive rates, including the procedure for investigating incentive rate grievances. It is this supplemental agreement, and not the Section 5 of the contract, which governs.

QUESTIONS

1. Are the four categories of mistakes listed by the Company all of the same character?
2. What weight should be given to the Bethlehem Steel case cited by the Union?
3. The written grievance in this case demanded that the Company cease the practice of cutting rates, but contained no request for damages. In the hearing, the union asked for monetary relief for the aggrieved employees. If you were to uphold the Union's argument, what relief would you grant?

CASE 14
Participation in Political Demonstration

Company: Pleasant Valley Fruitgrowers Association
Union: Cannery Workers, Food Processors Union
                Western Federation of Teamsters
Arbitrator: Eaton H. Conant, Chairman of the Board of Arbitration

The following discussion was prepared by Eaton H. Conant, chairman of the Board of Arbitration.

BRIEF STATEMENT OF THE FACTS

On Thursday, November 13, 1969, a day observed by some persons of the community as "Moratorium Day," employee Edgar brought two black armbands to work at the Association plant. Shortly after work began he offered one band to co-worker Bradley and both men wore the bands on their arms.

Some days earlier Edgar and Bradley had asked the Association, through their supervisor, if they could have November 13 off from work. The general superintendent had replied through the supervisor in words to the effect that if the men could be spared for the 13th, they could be spared generally.

Shortly after the two men donned the armbands, a woman worker in the same department expressed displeasure about the bands to Inspector LaVoice. Inspector LaVoice interpreted this worker to be a spokesman for other women workers who she believed were upset by the bands and not doing their work properly.

Almost immediately after the worker complained, Forelady Jones came to the scene, having been summoned by a worker. Mrs. Jones observed that some of the female workers at the carrot belts were "bunched up," which their work did not require. The belts were conveyors for carrots and the women workers on the belts were grading and sorting the vegetables prior to canning.

Mrs. Jones observed the women, who resumed work, and she immediately left the scene to summon the general superintendent, who went to the area and spoke to Mr. Edgar and Mr. Bradley. The superintendent told the two men that the association had a standing rule against employee political and religious activities during working hours, that the armbands were upsetting some of the women on the crew, and that the bands would have to come off or the two men would be subject to dismissal.

The superintendent then left the scene and returned a few minutes later. On his second visit the two employees were given five more minutes to think the matter over. The two did not take the bands off but Mr. Edgar took the band from his arm and looped it through his belt. The superintendent returned for the third time in about five minutes and gave the two employees a direct order to remove the bands. When the men did not remove the bands, he fired them for insubordination.

On their way out of the plant the employees saw Mr. Samuels and Mr. Raymond, two employees who worked elsewhere in the plant. Mr. Samuels and Mr. Raymond heard details concerning the discharges from Edgar and Bradley. Mr. Samuels and Mr. Raymond then voluntarily quit their employment because of the sympathy they felt with the values expressed by Edgar and Bradley and because they considered this to be a moral protest of the Association's discharge of the two men.

That same day, November 13, 1969, all four men filed grievances under provisions of the labor agreement. In the evening of that day a conference was held where all four workers and the company's superintendent, personnel director, and general manager discussed the events of the day. W. A. Bundy, the union secretary-treasurer, was not able to attend, but the conference was held with his approval.

The grievants contended, first, that there was nothing in the labor agreement or the company rules that pertained to wearing an armband, and second, if the women in their department had walked off the job in protesting the bands, the women and not the grievants would have been the contract and rule violators. The company representatives present offered to return the four men to their jobs as of Monday, November 17, 1969, without loss of seniority, but with loss of pay for November 13, 14, and 15, if the men would indicate they would not wear armbands or engage in political or religious demonstrations on the job. Management also indicated that the grievants should understand they would not be excused from work for a December moratorium, and that they would be replaced and considered to have quit if they did not work on a moratorium day. This was not acceptable to the four men.

On Monday evening, November 17, the union executive committee, acting as shop committee, considered the grievances and requested that labor agreement provision Section V (b) providing for an arbitration committee be implemented. The company subsequently appointed Mr. Norman and Mr. Alton and the union appointed Mr. Friend and Mr. Bundy to the committee.

The arbitration committee met on November 24, 1969, considered the grievances, but was not able to arrive at a majority vote on their disposition. At the meeting the members agreed that the following is a true statement of the points of disagreement and positions of the arbitrators at the close of that meeting:

Points of Disagreement
1. Whether the Association working rule number 4 which says "interfering with workers will not be permitted" is definite enough to have any meaning.
2. Whether the employees were given adequate notice of the Association rules.

3. Whether rule number 4 applied to the situation in this case.

Position of Arbitrators at Adjournment

1. The Union representatives' position was that the two employees discharged should be returned to their former positions without loss of pay or seniority; that the two employees who quit should be returned to their former positions without loss of seniority but with loss of pay.
2. Association representatives felt that all four employees had failed to properly abide by the grievance procedures specified in the labor agreement (specifically the clause which says, "but in no instance shall there be a cessation of work"); that the Association offer to return the employees to their jobs without loss of seniority was a fair compromise of the situation and that it was unreasonable to ask for more than this compromise.

The committee then agreed to secure a list of qualified arbitrators from the Federal Mediation Service and select a fifth member for the committee from the list, as provided for in the labor agreement. Professor Eaton H. Conant of the Industrial Relations Institute of the University of Oregon was subsequently nominated as the fifth member.

POSITION OF THE ASSOCIATION

The Association argues that the labor agreement provides procedures for grievance resolution and the four grievants failed to abide by requirements of the procedures; specifically, that language of Section V (a) that specifies, "In case agreement is not reached, the grievance shall be settled in accordance with Section V (b) hereof, but in no instance shall there be a cessation of work."

It is the position of the Association, therefore, that all four grievants failed to honor the grievance procedure requirements. Two of them, Mr. Edgar and Mr. Bradley, did not obey a legitimate order but persisted in violation of Association rules to ultimate discharge and cessation of their work. Their obligation at the least was to obey the legitimate order of the superintendent and, if that order offended them, to file a grievance under the labor agreement.

Concerning Mr. Raymond and Mr. Samuels, management points out that both men quit voluntarily and ceased work because of their sympathy with Mr. Edgar and Mr. Bradley. At the time these men quit they had only received brief reports of events surrounding the discharges from the men who were discharged. They knew nothing directly from the Association about reasons for the discharges or about circumstances surrounding events. They had an obligation to file grievances without ceasing work. A primary purpose of a grievance procedure is to provide means for peaceful resolution of disputes and avoid work disruptions.

None of the four grievants abided by this purpose and the purpose was specifically stated in the agreement.

The Association argues that the evidence clearly establishes that Mr. Bradley wore the armband for political reasons and that the armbands had the effect of interfering with work of co-workers in their department. At the arbitration hearing Mr. Bradley testified that he wore the armband for purposes that were "broadly political." Mr. Edgar stated at the hearing that he is not a political person and wore the band only to "mourn the dead in Vietnam." Given the entire context of events in the nation on November 13, Moratorium Day, it is difficult not to conclude that a person who wore an armband on that day would be perceived by some others as a person who was making a political expression even if he did not believe he was doing so.

The evidence certainly indicates co-workers of these two grievants interpreted the armbands to be a political expression. Inspector LaVoice and Supervisor Jones both observed that workers were upset and not doing their work properly. Several workers complained to the inspector and supervisor about the armbands. When the superintendent spoke to the grievants some of their co-workers had already briefly ceased working once and he was apprehensive that a general walkout might occur because of the armbands.

The Association concludes its arguments pertaining to the Edgar and Bradley grievances by noting that the discharges were not invoked in a hasty or arbitrary way. The superintendent spoke to the grievants on two occasions before he took final action. He explained to the men that their co-workers were upset and had complained. He stated the company rule he was acting upon and warned Mr. Edgar and Mr. Bradley that discharge could result from failure to remove the bands. He only then fired them for insubordination because of their failure to obey his legitimate request that was based on established rules.

The Association submits that management acted legitimately, in good faith, and without discrimination in discharging Mr. Edgar and Mr. Bradley for cause on November 13, 1969. The substantive bases for the superintendent's decision to discharge the men are the Association rules banning political and religious demonstrations during work time and Association working rule number 4 that states "interfering with workers will not be permitted."

The organization's rule banning political and religious demonstrations has existed for many years. It has been impartially applied in the past to prohibit employees or persons from without the plant from disrupting work by passing out literature, soliciting or arguing for a cause, or otherwise interrupting work with partisan activities. The rule applies to activities on scheduled work time. It has not been the Association's intent to forbid political or religious discussions that may occur informally between employees during nonwork periods.

Association working rule number 4 has been in effect for years for the purpose it directly states. It has the same general objectives as the political and religious rule where it seeks to avoid interference with work. But it is broader in the scope of activities proscribed because the sources of interference that may occur at work obviously are more than political and religious. The rule has a long history. It has been widely promulgated and consistently applied. Each employee at time of hire is required to read the Association working rules and sign to indicate the rules are understood. All four of the grievants read and signed a copy of these rules when they were hired.

Concerning the grievances of Mr. Raymond and Mr. Samuels, the position of the Association is that the grievances are without merit because the two men voluntarily quit their employment. They only belatedly used the grievance procedure after they quit and left the workplace. They made a "cessation of work" such as is prohibited by the grievance section of the labor agreement. They quit after hearing only the most limited statement of the facts of the discharge situation from the two grievants only. Finally, the two men have asked that their grievances be resolved by having them "reinstated" by an employing organization that did not release them.

Given all the facts stated above, the Association believes that the actions of management were justifiable and that the Association offer to return all four employees to their jobs without loss of seniority was a fair settlement of the grievances.

POSITION OF THE UNION

The position argued by the Union may be summarized in the following points. First, the Association's rule against political and religious expressions is not a rule that has been publicized or applied consistently enough so employees are aware of the rule and its implications. Second, rule number 4 is so indefinite that its meaning is completely obscure. Third, all four grievants were not informed or aware of any political-religious activity rule; they could not have been given adequate notice of rules and their implications. They should not be placed in jeopardy, therefore, when they had inadequate foreknowledge of rules and possible sanctions. Finally, rule number 4, by any interpretation of its vague content, could not be interpreted as having application for circumstances of these grievances.

Concerning the rule against political expressions at work, the union points out that the rule is one management invokes infrequently and inconsistently. The rule does not appear on any written document employees see. It specifically is not carried on the list of working rules employees read and sign when they first take employment. In fact, by all criteria that arbitrators use when judging the efficacy of disciplinary rules, it is doubtful one could establish that a bona fide rule does exist.

There are standards for judging the fairness of workplace rules that dictate rules should be "widely promulgated, made known, and consistently applied." The reasons for these standards are well known: An employee should not be disciplined for violations of rules that are obscure or so little publicized that the employee cannot anticipate potential disciplinary consequences of his behavior.

The union respectfully suggests that the arbitrator heard no evidence in the hearing that would indicate that administration of the political rule, and rule number 4 also, met the criteria just stated. Company witnesses responded to a question from Arbitrator Conant by noting that the political-religious rule had been invoked only a few times in four or five years. Very few employees could learn of the existence of the unwritten rule because it is so seldom invoked and it is not publicized.

The union believes rule number 4 is so void of specifics that no neutral person would find it has significant meaning. A rule so vague also places employees in jeopardy. More important, it is difficult to determine how this vague rule could have application in this case.

Mr. Edgar and Mr. Bradley in no way "interfered" with their co-workers. They worked in a normal manner and they were in close proximity to fellow employees. They did not urge other employees to acknowledge the armbands in any way. No unfriendly verbal exchanges occurred concerning the armbands and their significance. The testimony of the grievants at the hearing was that all persons in the department worked normally that morning. Their testimony is a direct challenge to testimony of company witnesses who stated that work was interrupted.

The union does not concede that any significant interruption of work happened. But because the company claims it did happen, the point should be made that Edgar and Bradley could not have deliberately provoked an interruption. Only other employees, by their own choice and with their own interpretation of the symbolism of the bands could have interrupted their own work.

Finally, the union believes it should be pointed out that Edgar and Bradley were told by the superintendent that they were being discharged for "insubordination" and not for violation of rule number 4 at the time they were discharged. The only rule he mentioned at that time was the avowed rule against "political and religious demonstrations"; a rule the men did not know about. They also did not conceive that they were, in fact, "demonstrating."

The union submits, therefore, that Mr. Edgar and Mr. Bradley were discharged for alleged violation of rules that were so vague, unknown, and arbitrary as to be unenforceable. The response of Mr. Raymond and Mr. Samuels was not without justification in the context of the arbitrary nature of management's action against their friends. The union requests that the two discharged employees be returned to their former positions without loss of pay or seniority. It is requested that Mr. Raymond and Mr. Samuels be returned to their positions without loss of seniority, but with loss of pay for November 13, 14, and 15, 1969.

QUESTIONS

1. Does the Company's rule number 4 against "interfering with workers" imply that there must be actual physical interference? Exchange of words? Gestures? What would constitute interference?

2. Would you consider it a political demonstration if you saw someone wearing a U.S. flag in his buttonhole? What if it were a Viet Cong flag? Or a black armband on a day *not* set aside for a national demonstration? How about the same armband on Moratorium Day?

3. Does a company have the right to forbid workers to wear outward signs of political or religious affiliation on company property during working hours—a cross, for example; or a peace symbol; or the symbol of Women's Liberation? How about campaign buttons for political candidates? If the company forbade any one of these, would it have to forbid them all?

4. In this case the company offered to reinstate not only the two men it had fired, but the two who quit in sympathy with them, on certain conditions. Were the conditions reasonable? Should the men have accepted? If not, why not? If so, why should the union have taken their cases to arbitration?

5. How would you rule in this case? Could you make a ruling that might not be considered "political"?

CASE 15
Eligibility for Holiday Pay and Layoffs

Company: Metropolitan Body Company
Union: United Automobile, Aerospace and Agricultural
   Implement Workers of America
   Local 505
Arbitrator: Connecticut State Board of Mediation and Arbitration:
   Joseph F. Donnelly, Vincent J. Sirabella, and
   George H. Reama.

When does a layoff begin in connection with eligibility for holiday pay which excludes "those on layoff"?

The following discussion of the issue and facts in this case was prepared by Joseph F. Donnelly and Vincent J. Sirabella, two of three arbitrators in this case. George H. Reama dissented.

MATTER FOR ARBITRATION

In a signed stipulation the parties submitted the following question: Were the employees who were laid off on May 29, 1964, entitled to holiday pay for Memorial Day?

CONTRACT CLAUSE INVOLVED

Article VIII, Hours of Work and Holidays
Section 4.

(*a*) The Plant will close for New Year's Day, Good Friday, Memorial Day, Independence Day, Labor Day, Thanksgiving Day, Christmas Day, and the half day before Christmas and New Years (it is agreed that the half day before Christmas and the half day before New Years may be redesignated by joint agreement between the Union and the Company three (3) months prior to the holiday to be designated). The Company agrees to pay eight (8) hours pay at the employee's current straight time average hourly rate to all employees except those on Layoff or absent without a reasonable excuse on the work day before or the work day after the holiday. Employees who are absent the day before or the day after the designated holiday due to authenticated injury or illness, but who work at least one (1) day during the week in which the holiday falls shall be eligible for the holiday pay.

(*b*) When one of the holidays designated herein falls within the employee's scheduled vacation, he will be granted an additional day off with pay to be taken either immediately preceding or immediately following his scheduled vacation.

(*c*) In the event that one of the above mentioned holidays falls on Saturday or Sunday, the Company agrees that pay for such holidays will be in accordance with the provisions of this section.

(*d*) With respect to the holidays referred to it in the above section hereof, employees who work on such days shall receive pay of double time of their regular rate of pay for the time actually worked in addition to the regular holiday pay for which they may be eligible.

AGREED-ON FACTS

On May 27, 1964, the Company notified 21 employees that they would be laid off on May 29. Saturday, May 30, was a scheduled holiday, which by agreement of the parties was to be observed on Monday, June 1. Claiming that the employees in question were on layoff, the Company did not pay them for the holiday.

UNION POSITION

The union claims that the language of Article VIII, Section 4, obliges an employee to work either the day before or the day after a holiday. The employees in question are entitled to holiday pay because they worked the day before the holiday.

Moreover, holiday pay is part of an employee's total earnings. It is part of his negotiated benefits. He cannot be deprived of this benefit by the unilateral action of the Company in invoking a layoff.

The Union rejects the claim of the Company that the employees were on layoff. They had been notified of a layoff but the layoff did not begin until they began to lose time. This means that they were not on layoff until the following Tuesday and on this basis they have a claim to holiday pay.

COMPANY POSITION

The company states that under the agreement employees must work both the day before the holiday and the day after the holiday unless excused in accord with Article VIII, Section 4. However, it is not on this basis that the employees were denied holiday pay. On May 27, these employees were notified that they would be laid off effective at 3:30 P.M. on May 29. They were so laid off. Clearly under Article VIII, Section 4, they are not entitled to holiday pay.

QUESTIONS

1. Evaluate the Union's claim that the agreement obligates an employee to work only either the day before or the day after a holiday to be eligible for holiday pay.

2. Is holiday pay a negotiated benefit earned by past service or is it an investment by the Company in *future* employee productivity? What is the purpose of the agreement language requiring the employees' presence on the workday immediately preceding and/or immediately following the holiday?

3. For the 21 employees, did the layoff start on May 27 (date of notification), or May 29 (last day worked), or June 2 (first day of lost pay)?

CASE 16
The Year-End Bonus

Company: Tonawanda Publishing Company
Union: Newspaper Guild of Buffalo
             Local 26
Arbitrator: Peter Seitz

This case deals with a year-end bonus. The following discussion of the issue and facts in this case was prepared by Peter Seitz, the arbitrator.

ISSUE

The issue presented for decision is whether the Employer has violated Article VI, Paragraph 7, of the collective bargaining agreement by refusing and failing to pay the Christmas bonus in 1962, and if it has, the appropriate relief to be directed.

Paragraph 7 reads:

7. There shall be no reduction in salaries during the life of this agreement except as may occur in Section 2b and 2c of this article. (The exceptions have no direct relationship to this case.)

BACKGROUND

In the briefest compass, the relevant and significant facts are as follows:

From at least 1947 (and prior to the recognition of the Guild) through 1961, the publisher, each year, made a Christmas payment to employees. Until 1960 the payment was in an amount equal to one-half the gross weekly salary of the recipient excepting that employees who had less than one year of service received a prorated payment. Employees not on the payroll at the time received no Christmas payment. In 1960 and 1961 the Company departed from this procedure and practice to this extent: The Company in those years deducted the appropriate withholding taxes from the moneys paid. Accordingly, there was a reduction in the amounts of the payments on a given salary. Employees were given stubs reflecting the accounting procedures involved somewhat similar to stubs received by employees generally when deductions are made from their paychecks. No complaint was voiced or grievance filed with respect to this variance from past usage.

The money was paid by check handed to each employee by Mrs. Ruth L. Hewitt, general manager of the publisher, a few days before each Christmas, and the giving was accompanied by a handshake and Christmas greetings and an expression of "appreciation for a good job done."

This Christmas payment had been made to all employees in all departments of the Employer excepting the publisher and the assistant publisher. So far as the record reveals, there were no employees on the active payroll at the time of giving who failed to receive a check or who received a check in a lesser amount than would result from the formula referred to above.

None of the several labor agreements entered into by the parties refer to a Christmas bonus or gift. The only discussions between the parties with reference to such a payment took place in 1954—10 years ago. According to my notes taken at the hearing, Mrs. Hewitt testified:

The Guild wanted inclusion of the bonus as part of the contract. The Company said because it was a gift it should not be part of the contract. The Union felt if the paper should be sold, it needed assurances that the bonus would be paid in the contract year. The Company agreed to include a statement in a supplement to the 1954 contract.

Louis Simon, a Guild witness who was present when the request was made for a writing with respect to the payment, testified:

> Management said this was not necessary—it was not necessary to add language to the contract that was already practice.

Harvey Hough, managing editor, also testified that the Guild representative said the Guild wanted the bonus written into the contract "because Mrs. Hewitt could die or the paper be sold."

Thus, in a document signed by both parties dated September 9, 1954, among other things, it is stated:

> This letter confirms the agreement to pay members of the Editorial department who have been employed by The News for the entire year of 1954 a Christmas gift in the amount of one half week's salary at Christmas 1954, and to those with less than one year's employment a proportionate amount based on length of service during 1954.

In 1961 the parties were bargaining with respect to a new agreement. In July, 1962, Mrs. Hewitt, on behalf of the publisher, gave the Guild some data in writing reflecting unfavorable advertising receipts. She testified:

> At about the time of the exhibit I spoke to Carl Rothfuse, a member of the Board of Directors and an officer of the Corporation, and discussed the economic problems of the paper with him and said I felt it was necessary to discontinue the bonus. He advised to wait until later. I made a decision around Thanksgiving when I had 11 months [advertising] figures.

The record of testimony is in some confusion as to the dates of events occurring in late November 1961, and early December. Mrs. Hewitt was of the opinion that the terms of the agreement were finally agreed upon in late November, when she said she made her decision to discontinue the Christmas payment. The weight of the evidence, however, persuades me that negotiations were not completed before December 3, 1961. At any rate, in the 1961 negotiations there was no reference made to the Christmas payment.

Apparently, it took some time to reduce the new agreement to writing for signature. Earle Y. Hannel, one of the two signatories for the Guild, placed his signature on the document, he says, on December 18, 1962. (This is the date written in, apparently in Hannel's handwriting, above the typed names of the signatories.) Then, according to his testimony at 7 A.M. the next day, December 19, he saw a notice on the bulletin board. The notice stated that the Christmas bonus would be discontinued because of a decrease in advertising linage in 1962. No copy of the notice is available as an exhibit. Mrs. Hewitt testified that her decision to discontinue the bonus was made in late November, but she posted the notice on December 19 "because this was the period of the year when the bonus was to be paid."

QUESTIONS

1. Should the bonus be considered as a gift or as salary?
2. Did the decline of advertising revenues create a situation which would free the company from the bonus obligation?
3. Did the Company violate the contract?

CASE 17
Company Practice versus Agreement Language in Recall from Layoff

Company: Seymour Manufacturing Company
Union: United Automobile, Aircraft and Agricultural Implement Workers of America
Local 1827
Arbitrator: Sidney L. Cahn

Does the long continuance of a practice clearly contrary to the wording of the agreement take precedence over the agreement?

The following discussion of the issue and facts in this case was prepared by Sidney L. Cahn, the arbitrator.

THE ISSUE

"Did the Company violate the Collective Bargaining Agreement, Article VIII, Sections 1, 2(a), 2(c), 5, 6, and 15, governing seniority for the purposes of recall when it recalled employees L—— and M—— instead of employees X——, Y——, and Z——? If so what should be the remedy?"

THE FACTS

In June 1963, the Company laid off a number of its employees predicated upon its shutdown of the rolling mills. Among the employees laid off at that time were the three grievants, X——, Y——, and Z——. X—— was then a roller in the rolling mill with a plantwide seniority date of November 7, 1949; Y—— was then a jitney driver in the rolling mill with a plantwide seniority date of October 26, 1949; and Z—— was then a pickler in the wire mill with a plantwide seniority date of February 14, 1950. Other employees laid off included L—— and M——, fine wire drawers in the wire mill, with plantwide seniority dates of July 31, 1961, and August 4, 1961, respectively.

In the Spring of 1964 two jobs of fine wire drawer in the wire mill became open, one on April 20 and the other on April 27. The Company recalled L—— and M—— to the jobs. None of the grievants (all of whom had greater plantwide seniority than L—— or M——, but none of whom had ever worked the jobs in question) were recalled to work until a later date.

The Union filed the instant grievance claiming that plantwide length of service should have been the sole criterion employed in determining which employees should be first recalled. Under this criterion, concededly all of the grievants would have been entitled to have been recalled prior to either L—— or M——.

OPINION

Article VIII of the parties' collective bargaining agreement dated November 15, 1961, deals with the question of seniority. This article *inter alia* sets forth general policy in Section 1 (i.e., "to provide maximum job security and opportunity based upon—continuous service"); it defines "seniority" as "total length of unbroken service" in (Section 2); it provides for departmental seniority to govern in the case of layoff from a department (Section 3) with the right of a laid-off employee to exercise plant seniority to replace an employee in another department with less plant seniority (Section 5); and it considers the questions, among others, of recalls to work (Section 6); bidding for open jobs (Section 7); promotions (Section 8); and retention of certain employees by the Company regardless of seniority (Section 15).

Section 6 of this article is the section dealing with the immediate problem before me. This section provides as follows:

Rehiring in all mills except the Laboratory Department shall be on the basis of plantwide seniority, *governed by the nature of the job to be filled, with due consideration being given to the necessary skill and ability to do the* required work. (emphasis supplied).

This section then goes on to deal with the exception pertaining to the laboratory department, not here relevant.

The grievants in the instant case all had greater plantwide seniority than both L—— and M——. Although Section 15 of this article gives the Company the right with certain limitations "to retain seven employees, irrespective of seniority, who possess value to the operation of the Company" it is conceded that neither L—— nor M—— were recalled pursuant to this section, and accordingly it need not concern me any further. The sole question, therefore, is whether the above-emphasized language found in Section 6 applies to the instant case and justifies the Company's recall of L—— and M——.

The Union has not attempted to show that at the time L—— and M—— were recalled any of the grievants possessed "the necessary skill and ability to do the required work" as contemplated by the emphasized language. It argues instead that the Company has at least, since 1946, totally disregarded contractual references in this and prior agreements as to skill and ability in recalling employees; that it has been solely governed by length of continuous service in recalling employees whether employees were recalled to jobs previously held or to jobs never held by them; and that by reason of this fact the Company has in effect waived any rights it may have had to rely upon the emphasized language and to question a senior employee's skill and ability in recalling him from layoff.

The testimony introduced was impressive and convincing on this score. It appears without contradiction and in fact was admitted that since at least 1946, until the instant situation, the Company consistently recalled its employees based solely upon plantwide seniority, and without reference to skill and ability. Only three alleged "exceptions" to this practice were shown.

a) One alleged exception dealt with employees recalled to jobs in the laboratory department; this, however, is clearly made an exception to Section 6 by the express language of that section and accordingly is not a relevant exception to the practice claimed by the Union;

b) Another exception occurred in 1949 when the Company recalled a junior employee to a wire drawer job in preference to a utility man on layoff; this exception resulted in a grievance which was settled to the satisfaction of the Union by calling in additional help;

c) The third and only relevant exception involved the recall in October, 1963, without objection by the Union, of a junior employee to the job of machinist third class. However, even as to this exception the Union took the position that this was consistent with the practice, claiming that this recall was made pursuant to Section 15 referred to above, and was not made pursuant to Section 6; the Company took issue with this claim and this is the only factual matter in dispute.

Under Article X, Section 5, of the collective bargaining agreement, the arbitrator has no authority to "add to, subtract from or in any way modify" the terms of the parties' collective bargaining agreement.

QUESTIONS

1. The arbitrator here is confronted with a choice between agreement language and the existence of a well-established practice. What factors should he consider in making his choice?
2. How would you rule in this case? Why?

CASE 18
"Marked Differences" in Performance as a Basis for Layoff

Company: McEvoy Company
Houston, Texas
Union: International Association of Machinists
Lodge 12, District 37
Arbitrator: R. H. Morvant

How are "marked differences" in performance measured? What problems arise in applying these marked differences as a criterion in layoffs?

The following discussion of the issue and facts in this case was prepared by R. H. Morvant, the arbitrator.

THE QUESTION

From the contentions of the parties and from the evidence and testimony presented, the following questions developed to be answered by the arbitrator:

1. Did the Company violate the collective bargaining agreement and in particular Article VI of said agreement when they laid off X—— on or about August 21, 1963?
2. If answer to question No. 1 above is affirmative, what remedy is ordered?

THE FACTS

The grievant, X——, was employed by the Company on January 5, 1955, as an engine lathe operator. In August of 1963 the Company found it necessary to lay off a number of employees. On August 12, 1963, Gordon Gibson, general shop superintendent, drafted a list of employees to be laid off based on a list of machines which were to be shut down rather than on the employees' seniority status. When this list was submitted to the shop committee they protested that it was not in accordance with the plant seniority provisions of the labor agreement. The list was withdrawn and a new list submitted by W. C. Uhl, shop superintendent, based upon plant seniority, except that the grievant, X——, was now marked for layoff where in the previous list X—— had not been mentioned. Further, the seniority list of the lathe operators indicates that there were three operators junior to X—— at the time of his layoff.

From the testimony of the Company, which was unrefuted by the Union, it is gathered that while the first list was being discussed by the men in the shop and before it was withdrawn, several junior lathe operators approached the Company requesting that the "marked difference" provision of Article VI be utilized in their behalf in the engine lathe department. Further, it is to be gathered that the Company did use a relative efficiency report of the lathe operators to determine "marked differences" between the operators and thus determined that X—— should be laid off even though he was senior to others in the department.

When the Company submitted the layoff list dated August 21, 1963, to the Union, some of the men on the list chose to bump into their classifications which they had the right to do by virtue of their seniority and Article VI. X——, however, chose not to bump but elected layoff status from which, on August 23, 1963, he filed a grievance protesting his layoff out of line of his seniority.

The grievance was processed through the various steps of the grievance procedure of the collective bargaining agreement without arriving at a settlement satisfactory to the parties; hence, the grievance was processed to arbitration.

The following excerpts from the collective bargaining agreement existing between the parties are pertinent to this case:

Article I—Preamble

The intent and purpose of the parties hereto is that this agreement will promote, improve and maintain industrial, economic, and harmonious relations between the Union and the Company, and to set forth herein the basic agreement covering the rates of pay, hours of work, and conditions of employment to be observed by the Union and the Company.

The Union agrees to cooperate with the Company to increase productivity. The Union will urge its members to produce more and will work with the Company to eliminate other causes for inefficiency.

Article IV—Management's Rights

The Management of the plant and of the work and direction and classification of the working forces, including the right to hire, suspend, or discharge for proper cause, or transfer, and the right to relieve employees from duty because of lack of work or for any other legitimate reason shall be vested in the Company. This authority will not and cannot be used for the purpose of discrimination.

The Company reserves the right to adopt, establish, submit, revise, and enforce reasonable factory and safety rules. Such rules shall not be used for the purpose of unlawful discrimination or to violate the express provisions of this agreement.

Article VI—Seniority

Section 1. In promotion, demotion, layoff, and restoration to service, plant seniority shall prevail unless there is a marked difference in ability. In this connection Management and the Shop Committee shall confer prior to promotion, layoff, or restoration of service, and in the event Management and the Shop Committee are unable to agree, Management shall have the right to make the determination, subject to the grievance procedure provided in the contract.

The "marked difference" between the lathe operators was established by efficiency reports of the employees during the 18-month period between January 1, 1962, and July 1, 1963. The records of the men employed as lathe operators are as follows:

Employee	Seniority Date	Relative Efficiency
Baker	3–24–41	76
Parker	8–8–49	68
Storey	8–29–51	71
Rich	1–5–55	61
X——	1–5–55	52
Vaughn	8–18–56	78
Stewart	12–1–56	75
Bridwell	1–14–57	77

The efficiency of an employee is based upon amount of pieces produced times the "job standard" divided by actual time devoted. In other words a "job standard" is previously established by time and motion study. Employee assigned to manufacture these pieces is graded in efficiency by the number of pieces he runs divided by the time devoted and the result compared to the standard. The result is shown in percentages of the previously set standard. The standard, however, does not apply to all of the work assigned to the operator. Hence, as it is possible for an operator to be assigned work not "standardized" or not subject to "standardization," the Company established codes to distinguish the various means of accomplishing the work under the various conditions to be encountered.

1. Code 1—Work performed on the same kind of machine and with the same kind of machine and with the same kind of material under which the standard is set. Presumably ideal as to both machine and material. Standard applies.
2. Code 2—Pieces made with the same material but on a different machine. No standard applies.
3. Code 3—Pieces made on the same machine but with substitute material. No standard applies.
4. Code 4—Pieces made with both material and machine substituted. No standard applies.
5. Rush Work—No standard applies.
6. Rework—Errors in pieces corrected. No standard applies.
7. Repair Work—Used pieces sent in by customer repaired. 100 percent efficiency credit allowed.

THE ISSUE

The Union contended that for the past 20 years layoffs have been made under the seniority rule in spite of the exceptions offered by the

Company. Thus, the Union argued, the basic contractual provisions here involved must mean what the parties have interpreted them to mean in 20 years of contractual relations. In the past, when layoffs were necessary, the Company selected the classification and number of employees to be reduced and submitted the list of names to the Union, the Union argued. Further, the Union stated, such a list was composed of the junior employees in the classification to be reduced. These junior employees from a department forced to reduce manpower were then permitted to bump into lower or parallel classifications where their plant seniority and qualifications permitted such bumping. In such instances, the Union argued, qualifications meant only "if the employee could perform the work," he could bump. In any event, the Union concluded, the circumstances giving rise to the instant grievance is a radical departure from a tried and tested system which has worked best over the years.

Concerning the six examples of departure from strict seniority which the Company cited, the Union argued there is not enough similarity between them and this instant case to prove a precedent of sufficient weight to permit a departure from well-established past practice. Continuing, the Union pointed out that only two of the cases cited were arbitrated, and of the remaining four either no grievance was filed, or the grievance was dropped at the grievant's request after being filed.

After briefly discussing the two arbitration cases which upheld the "marked difference" argument of the Company, the Union stated:

So, each of the cases litigated reveal that the employee senior in the plant who was attempting to prevail on the strength of his seniority was a mere novice on the job in comparison to the junior employee retained. It is questionable in each case whether or not it could be said that the senior employee was actually qualified to perform the work. In all things said in the case it has never been maintained by the Union that any employee could prevail on seniority alone. An employee could not retain a job on his seniority unless he had substantial qualifications to perform the work in question, and he had to have more than just an orientation period on the work.

Concerning the three cases cited in which no grievance was filed and the one case in which a grievance was filed and later dropped, the Union takes the position that such incidents should not be considered as precedents. Under the agreement the right to file a grievance rests only with the employee affected, the Union argued. Arguing further, the Union stated, "By clear contract language the Union has bargained away its right to file grievances; by practice, it has been the employee who has the right either to drop or pursue a grievance once entered. Hence, an incident which could have been the basis of a grievance, or an incident under which a grievance was filed and dropped prior to final litigation, should not be considered as precedent."

In comparing the six cases cited by the Company to this instant case the Union pointed out that production efficiency was not used in the previous cases as it was in this instant case. Further the Union argued that the efficiency reports were unilaterally established by the Company without the acquiescence or cooperation of the Union. Thus, the Company violated Article VI in that they failed to confer with the Union as to who is to be laid off and how "marked difference" is to be determined.

The Union contends it is their belief that the efficiency reports devised by the Company are not competent to measure "marked difference." In the Union's opinion the standards are inaccurate and the manner in which they are kept bespeaks of haphazardness. The Union also argued that the use of efficiency reports was a departure from past practice in that the grievant survived at least three layoffs during his tenure of employment and that on one such occasion Bridwell, the junior in the department, was laid off but allowed to bump. At that time, the Union argued, it is evident from the Company testimony that the efficiency records were neither known nor used in the layoff.

In conclusion, the Union requested that the grievance of X—— be sustained and that he be reinstated to his former position without loss of pay or other rights or benefits.

COMPANY'S POSITION

The Company argued strongly and repeatedly that Article VI gives them the right to lay off out of line of seniority where there is a "marked difference in ability." In this instant case the Company contends the efficiency difference between X—— and Bridwell ranges between 24 percent to 37 percent, thus eliminating any doubt that a "marked difference existed" between the men regardless of their seniority status.

Concerning their past practice, the Company argued that from the evidence and testimony it is clear that the "marked difference" language of the agreement has been used where applicable. In such instances in the past, the Company pointed out, the Union at times grieved or failed to grieve and on two occasions went to arbitration and was denied. Thus, the Company argues, there can be no doubt that the "marked difference" provision has been used in the past and that the evidence does not support the Union's contentions regarding past practice.

Concerning the Union's attack on the Company's efficiency standards, the Company argued that regardless of their attempt to discredit, the fact remains that both X—— and Bridwell were measured against the same yardstick. In discussing their standards the Company pointed out that approximately 50 percent of a man's work would be performed under Code 1, which is work that is performed by an employee when circumstances are as nearly correct as possible. Using only Code 1 work, the Company made the following comparison between Bridwell and X——. During the 18-month period which was used, X—— performed 1,297 hours of Code 1 work, while Bridwell's total was 1,093 hours. The production efficiency difference between the men in this period was 25 percent. Using the same period but comparing work involving the same operations, number of parts, etc., the difference between the two men was 23 percent. The hours involved in this latter comparison were Bridwell 293 and X—— 400. From this comparison the "marked difference" in the production efficiency of the two men is clearly demonstrated, the Company argued.

When questioned by the arbiter as to whether the Company was misusing and misinterpreting the seniority and layoff provision of the agreement, by confusing their right to discipline for inefficiency with their right to layoff out of line of seniority, the Company answered:

The Employer submits that it has not misapplied the provision of this agreement. The express language of the agreement contemplates that the 'marked difference' is applicable to the layoff situation. At no time has the Employer taken the position that X——'s layoff was disciplinary. To the contrary, the layoff was occasioned solely by forces outside the production department. It was inventory control which designated the machines and shifts which were to be discontinued. This was an economic decision which resulted in an economic layoff to a number of men. If this layoff had not come along, X—— would probably still be working at McEvoy and his supervisors would probably still be discussing his production efficiency with him on a weekly basis.

In conclusion, the Company submitted that the layoff of X—— was made in full compliance with the labor agreement and that the grievance should therefore be denied.

THE OPINION

From the facts, evidence, and testimony presented in this case one could quite readily reach the hasty conclusion that this case is concerned with simple contract interpretation. But unfortunately such a conclusion would be in error and an oversimplification of a very complex problem. In truth the parties in this case are not apart or in dispute as to the correct interpretation of Article VI. The Company stoutly maintains that contractually they have the right to lay off out of the line of seniority where there is a "marked difference of ability." The Union confirms this interpretation and in point of fact concurs in the Company position when they stated in their post-hearing brief:

. . . In all the things said in this case it has never been maintained by the Union that any employee could prevail on seniority alone. An employee could not retain a job on his seniority unless he had substantial qualifications to perform the work in question, and he had to have more than just an orientation period on the work.

Under these circumstances, it is safe to conclude that both parties agree that seniority alone is not absolute in layoffs where a substantially marked difference of ability exists between employees in a department. In other words, as there is no evident dispute between the parties as to the correct interpretation of the contract, the difference between the parties must lie in other areas.

While there seems to be agreement between the parties as to the correct contract interpretation, conversely there is sharp conflict between the parties as to past practice involving layoff. The Company maintains that it has been their practice to use the "marked difference" provisions whenever applicable and thus lay off out of line of seniority. The Company also argues that the Union did not always protest such a procedure, and that in the two cases that went to arbitration the arbiter upheld the Company. The Union, however, strongly argues that production efficiency reports were new and had never been used before in deciding "marked difference" between employees. In this instant case, the Union claims that, by using efficiency reports to determine "marked differences" between employees, the Company violated the contract as well as established past practice.

At this point the dispute between the parties becomes clear, and it best can be described by asking: (1) Is the use of efficiency reports a new method established by the Company to determine marked differences between employees for purposes of layoff; (2) does the use of efficiency reports conflict with past practice to the point that it may not now be used; and (3) are the present efficiency reports used by the Company a good measurement capable of truly determining "marked differences" between employees for purposes of layoff? In the opinion of this arbiter the answers to these questions are the crux of the differences between the parties, and the heart of their dispute.

QUESTIONS

1. Do you agree with Arbitrator Morvant's opinion that this case is not "concerned with simple contract interpretation" but involves the more complex issue of past practice? Why?

2. Referring to the negotiation of Article VI, Section 1, did the Union consciously agree to layoffs based on ability? Would this be a wise decision on the part of the Union? What conditions would make such an agreement necessary from the viewpoint of the Union?

3. From the facts presented in the case, discuss the validity of the Company's "relative efficiency" measure. In general practice, layoffs based on "relative efficiency" are very uncommon. Why?

4. Is an employer forever bound to continuing past practice? Is the only way that an employer can break from past practice to negotiate a new clause specifying exactly what new method he intends to use?

5. How would you rule in this case? Justify your award.

CASE 19
Discharge of a Senior Employee for
"Failure to Perform Work as Required"

Company: Hawaiian Telephone Company
Union: International Brotherhood of Electrical Workers
              Local 1260
Arbitrator: Ted T. Tsukiyama

What obligation does an employer have to an employee 48 years old with 26 years of seniority who appears to be incapable of doing the job she has filled for this long time?
The following discussion of the issue and facts in this case was prepared by Ted T. Tsukiyama, the arbitrator.

ISSUE

Was the Company's action on July 20, 1964, in discharging the grievant on ground of "failure to perform work as required" undertaken with just cause in accordance with the terms of the collective bargaining agreement in effect between the parties?

CONTRACT CLAUSE

Section 6 of the agreement covering discipline applicable in this grievance is quoted in part as follows:

Supervision and Discipline
6.1 The supervision and control of all operations and the direction of all working forces, which shall include, but not be limited to, the right to hire, to establish work schedules, to suspend or discharge for proper cause, to promote or transfer employees, to relieve employees from duty because of lack of work, or for other legitimate reasons, shall be vested exclusively in the Company, except as otherwise covered in this Agreement.
6.2 Proper causes for suspension or discharges shall include, but not be limited to, insubordination, pilferage, use of intoxicants during working hours, incompetence, failure to perform work as required, falsification of reports, violation of the terms of this Agreement, violation of the secrecy of communications, failure to observe safety rules and regulations, failure to observe the Company's House Rules, which shall be conspicuously posted.

BACKGROUND FACTS

Up to the time of her discharge, grievant was employed as a toll operator in the traffic department of the Company. Grievant is 48 years old and had started working with the Company on another island in 1936. After nine years she began working for the Company in its Honolulu office where, after a maternity leave in 1947, she worked up to the date of discharge—a total period of 26 years' employment with the Company. The toll operator's job duties generally involve the placing and maintaining of long-distance calls for customers on the switchboard, servicing such calls to the extent necessary, and registering certain pertinent information concerning each call on an IBM mark sense card to be used by the Company for billing purposes.

About August 5, 1963, it came to the attention of the general traffic manager that the grievant was committing a significant number of "ticket errors" and "irregularities" in the performance of her duties as toll operator. Grievant's work record was reviewed by the manager at that time upon discovery of an erasure on one of her ticket entries, which is considered a serious "irregularity" on the toll board operations. The "irregularities" noted on her record included tardiness, talking at the switchboard, monitoring (listening) of calls, dozing off at the board, failure to give notifications, and low board loads and failure to collect on toll calls. The Company found grievant particularly weak in "ticket errors" which consisted of errors made on the mark sense cards, which were rejected by the IBM machines or which were otherwise not acceptable for billing purposes. Such errors included failure to mark certain capsules (spaces), marking the wrong capsule, or failing to note necessary data on the cards. The chief operator recommended dismissal of grievant but the traffic manager, considering grievant's long seniority with the Company, sent grievant a written reprimand and warning on August 26, 1963 (Company's Exhibit "A"), which listed all of her job weaknesses, required at least average job performance in the future, and exhorted her to do better.

On or about April 19, 1964, grievant failed to collect a $109.75 charge from a coin station call. Another review of her work record subsequent to August, 1963, revealed a high average of ticket errors committed by grievant, which convinced her superiors that the warning had not been effective, and grievant was consequently suspended for two weeks following this incident. The evidence shows that from the August, 1963, warning letter to the suspension in April, 1964, grievant's work record indicated at least seven failures to notify, four late notifications, several failures to collect, poor timing (failure to record correct time on each call), and numerous ticket errors (e.g., 156 errors for December, January, February, 1964). When notified of her suspension, grievant requested her chief operator to be transferred to the auxiliary operators' group in the department, but this was denied on the basis of a department policy prohibiting transfers between the toll and auxiliary work groups. The letter of suspension (Company's Exhibit "B") sent to her on April 23, 1964, listed all of her recent failures and insisted that her future performance (1) must abide by all work rules, (2) must show a 65 percent improvement in ticket errors, failure to notify, etc., (3) must not fail to collect on pay station calls, and (4) show good attendance and punctuality. Otherwise discipline, including dismissal, would follow.

Although the chief operator again recommended discharge on April 23, 1964, the traffic manager recommended against grievant's dismissal at this point because of her long years of service and because he thought the Company should make further attempt to rehabilitate grievant's work performance. Thus when grievant returned from her suspension, two service assistants were assigned to give special supervision, attention, and training to the grievant on her mark sensing work at the switchboard. During the remainder of the month of May, 1964, grievant received special supervision from Pauline Nakamori up to 1½ hours per day and about six 15–20 minute special training sessions from Irene Iseri until the first part of June, when the special assignments were terminated. Both service assistants testified that grievant showed improvement in her mark sensing work during the limited periods they supervised grievant.

During May, June, and July of 1964, an unexpected heavy load of long-distance traffic calls occurred, resulting in a six-day workweek with considerable overtime for the toll operators group. In the middle of July, 1964, a compilation sheet of operators' ticket errors revealed that grievant had committed 121 ticket errors during the month of June, which called for another review of her record by the traffic manager. The traffic manager and chief operator found that grievant had the highest number of ticket errors among the operators (29.38 error average) for that month and concluded that she had made no improvement in failures to notify, timing, and mark sensing; thus they found no alternative but to dismiss the grievant. Grievant was dismissed on July 20, 1964, on grounds of "failure to perform work as required" under Section 6 of the agreement.

DISCUSSION

There is no evidence in the record that grievant consciously or knowingly or deliberately committed the shortcomings and errors noted in her performance record. There is not even a suggestion of any evidence that she wilfully "laid down" on the job or wantonly committed irregularities and errors to spite the Company or her superiors. The evidence does reveal that grievant often tried to alibi or offer excuses, such as personal or domestic problems, when confronted with her poor performance, that she has a crusty temperament and is probably not easy to work with or over, that she felt the Company should be more tolerant of the job weaknesses of "old-timers" like herself. It is also easily inferable from her statements that she chaffed at finding herself, a veteran of many years' service, taking direction from employees much younger than herself who had ascended into "supervisory" positions over her. On one occasion, she argued with a service assistant about the length of a coffee break and signing out (7/11/64—charged with "uncooperative attitude").

She may have been unfit, unable, or incapable of meeting certain job standards, but this is not to say she was unwilling or refused to do what she was physically and mentally able to perform. There was no instance shown where she balked at carrying out any order or instruction of her superiors or was otherwise guilty of insubordination. When her superiors asked her to try to improve her work, the evidence shows that she did make a genuine and bona fide attempt (albeit the results were not satisfactory to the Company).

WORK RECORD

Grievant regularly committed a high, if not one of the highest, number of mark sense ticket errors compared to the other toll operators. In addition there were at least four failures to collect on toll calls involving sums of $55 and $25.30 besides the 4/19/64 incident, customer complaints for eight failures to give three-minute notification and for four late notifications, and poor timing and overlapping operations, contributing to her ticket and billing errors. She was also tardy to work a dozen times. In view of this type of performance record, I find the Company's action in reprimanding grievant on her 7/18/63 ticket erasure and suspending her for two weeks on her 4/19/64 failure to collect to be fully warranted. And the Company's efforts toward corrective discipline in lieu of discharge on these occasions, as reflected by the traffic manager's recommendation that she be given another chance and more rehabilitation was most considerate and commendable.

In the 2½-month period following her return from suspension on May 5, 1964, the evidence shows that Grievant had three complaints for failure to notify and one late notification, two failures to collect, 26 ticket errors for April (3 weeks), 42 ticket errors for May (27 days) and 121 ticket errors for June. Bearing in mind the four minimum conditions set forth in the Company's suspension letter of 4/19/64, grievant fell down in two areas (ticket errors and failure to collect) and the promised disciplinary action was forthcoming.

Against this record several counterconsiderations should be weighed. The two service assistants who gave grievant direct and personal supervision testified that grievant's mark sensing and board work was improving during the limited time they were assigned to her. (Note that grievant's ticket error average for May (27 days) while under special training was roughly 70 percent of her monthly average up to that time.) Why, then, should grievant's ticket errors suddenly jump more than 200 percent over her usual average in the very next month? There is no indication that the Company attempted to look into the reasons for this unusual phenomenon, an astoundingly dramatic and high error level even for this subject. Nothing in the record explains why those working around and over grievant had not been aware that her ticket errors during

June had become alarmingly frequent and high, a fact not discovered until two weeks passed in July. It was made clear that neither the traffic manager nor the chief operator interviewed or obtained an evaluation report from the two employees who were specially assigned to help grievant and upgrade her work, which raises another question as to the seriousness or bona fides of the attempted rehabilitation. In explaining why the two service assistants were not consulted, the traffic manager stated they were not supervisory employees and were not in a position to judge "over-all performance" of an operator, but further went on to state that errors were the heavyweight item in over-all job performance—the very item these two employees were instructed to correct and improve. Further, the traffic manager repeatedly emphasized grievant failed to improve in "over-all performance," yet it is clear that it must have been only the 121 ticket errors in June that precipitated her downfall, since other aspects of her performance did not appear noticeably bad in comparison with her prior record. Also, there was no evidence to show how the Company determined that grievant had failed to make a 65 percent improvement in her performance as laid down in the April 23, 1964, "ultimatum." Finally, consideration must be given to the unexpected peak traffic that hit the Company during this exact period from May to July, which caught it short staffed, required a heavier workweek and overtime schedule for all operators, and which, incidentally, raised the ticket error average for all operators during this period. In short, this exact period when grievant's job was put at stake was a highly abnormal period for all concerned. Suffice it to surmise that grievant probably "got lost in the shuffle" during this rush period and was forgotten until those 121 errors came to light.

QUESTIONS

1. Is there a difference between "incompetence," "failure to perform work as required," and "falsification of records"? Is the grievant guilty of each of these offenses?
2. Evaluate the Company's efforts at constructive discipline as applied to the grievant.
3. What weight should be given to the grievant's "attitude" and long service record in this discharge proceeding?

CASE 20
Voluntary or Forced Retirement?

Company: Louisville Public Warehouse
Louisville, Kentucky
Union: International Brotherhood of Teamsters
General Drivers, Warehousemen and Helpers, Local 89
Arbitrator: Louis C. Kesselman

Is old age a justifiable cause for discharge or forced resignation? This is one of several questions raised by this case.

The following discussion of the issue and facts in this case was prepared by Louis C. Kesselman, the arbitrator.

The issue is "Whether or not the discharge of William Wilding on July 5, 1957 and the alleged forced resignation of Edward Roehr on June 28, 1957, were in accordance with Article V and Article VII, paragraphs (a) and (b) of the existing agreement between the parties?"

CONTRACT PROVISIONS INVOLVED

Article V. Extra Contract Agreements

The Company shall not ask employees who are members of the Union to enter into any agreement in conflict with this agreement . . .
Article VII. Discharge or Suspension

(a) The Employer shall not discharge or suspend any employee without just cause, but in respect to discharge must give at least one (1) warning notice of the complaint against such employee to the employee, in writing, with a copy to the Union, except that no warning notice need be given to an employee before he is discharged or suspended for dishonesty, drunkenness, use of alcoholic beverages while on duty, keeping intoxicating liquor on Company premises, smoking where smoking is not allowed, disobedience of posted Company rules or participation in a strike or slow down, or refusal to perform his usual normal duties as directed by management.

(b) Discharge must be by proper written notice to the employee and the Union. Warning notices shall have no force or effect after nine (9) months from the date thereof. Any employee may request an investigation as to his warning notice, discharge or suspension and such request shall be handled as provided for in Article XIV of this Agreement.
Article VIII. Sickness or Injury.

In case of sickness and inability to work, the employee shall receive his former position and seniority upon recovery within six (6) months but only if he is physically fit and able to perform his regular work satisfactorily. In case of injury on the job the six (6) months limit shall not apply.
Article XIII. Classifications and Hourly Rates
   Warehouseman . . . . $1.95.

BACKGROUND

In June, 1957, Edward Roehr, 67-year-old warehouseman employed since October 5, 1937, was told by company president W. H. Kinnaird that he was not physically able to perform the normal work required of a warehouseman and that his services would have to be terminated. Kinnaird told Roehr that if he would resign without waiting for discharge, he would be given $750 in severance pay. Roehr accepted the offer as of June 28, 1957, and was given a check for $560.12 for terminal pay minus deductions.

A similar conference was held with William Wilding, 64-year-old warehouseman, employed since May 13, 1936. On June 27, 1957, Wilding was sent a letter with a copy to the Union, in which he was told, "In our opinion, your age and physical condition make it impossible for you to do the full work required of a warehouseman." He was offered $1,000 in a lump sum or in installments if he would retire voluntarily by July 5, 1957. If the offer were not accepted by that date, stated the letter, "it will be withdrawn and we will proceed to exercise our legal rights as we see fit." Wilding was discharged on July 5, 1957, when the Company's deadline for voluntary retirement passed. He received no severance pay.

On July 9, 1957, Wilding and Roehr filed grievances protesting their dismissals. Failure of the parties to resolve the grievances satisfactorily resulted in their submission to arbitration in accordance with Article XIV of the agreement.

UNION'S CONTENTIONS

1. The Company is not justified in discharging Wilding and Roehr for old age under the discharge for "just cause" provision in Article VII (a) of the agreement.

2. The Company failed to give Wilding and Roehr "at least one (1) warning notice of the complaint . . . in writing, with a copy to the Union" as required by Article VII (a). Roehr received no notice in writing. Wilding received a letter dated June 27, 1957, which was not a warning notice but rather a "proposition and a threat that if he does not accept the Company's proposition, he would be discharged." Roehr's resignation was forced, not voluntary.

3. The Company violated Article V of the agreement and Section 9 of the Labor Relations Act by bargaining with the employees individually in conflict with the agreement.

4. The Company's charge that the two men had worked approximately 18½ years in the bottling house and had not been hired to do warehouse work is ill-founded because bottling house work is comparable to warehouse work. In any case, if their warehouse work had not been satisfactory, the Company should have put them on notice before 18 months had elapsed.

5. Medical certificates bear out the contention that the two men are in excellent physical condition for their ages and "are perfectly capable to continue to perform, as required by management."

6. The Company admits that the two men were willing employees and had never refused to perform any work assigned to them. Therefore, the Company "had no right whatsoever to complain about the quantity or quality of work done by these two men, let alone discharging them for something that they had no right to complain about in the first place."

7. The Company is "asking the arbitrator to permit them to discharge an employee or to make a deal with an employee in the form of severance pay, because of their old age, and the Union's argument is, that this is not grounds for discharge . . . this problem should be decided by contract negotiations in form of severance pay, pension plans, or retirement plans on a collective bargaining basis for all employees. Union offered to negotiate such a plan when the question of retiring Wilding, and Roehr first arose.

8. If the Company is permitted to discharge employees for old age it will make it difficult to negotiate a pension plan with this and other companies signatory to the agreement.

9. Union did not agree to Company's right to retire men but indicated willingness to withdraw objection if the separation pay was equivalent to the proposed Union pension plan and the men involved were willing to go along.

10. Fellow employees did not object to working with Wilding and Roehr.

11. The Company has always taken care of older employees until recently by finding lighter work for them to do.

COMPANY'S CONTENTIONS

1. Wilding was discharged and Roehr resigned not because they had reached a specific retirement age but rather because of their inability to perform the work. "Inability of an employee to perform the duties for which he was employed is 'just cause' for discharge under the opening clause of Article VII."

2. Management has the sole prerogative to determine whether an employee is physically able to perform his normal duties, so long as Management acts in good faith. No charge of ulterior motive or lack of good faith has been made.

3. The Company's officers and supervisors are unanimous in their judgments that these men were physically unable to do the work required of them as warehousemen.

4. Fellow employees had freely criticized the inability of the two men to do their share of the work in the warehouse.

5. Wilding is unable to operate a fork-lift truck, pull tags off appliances, serve as an efficient checker, or do general warehouse duties without danger to himself. Wilding is unable to raise his arms above his shoulders although the stacking of various commodities requires higher lifting. Roehr is similarly unable to do the work of a warehouseman. At the hearing Roehr refused to say whether he wanted his job back if it involved performing exactly the same type and amount of heavy labor performed by the other warehousemen.

6. Article VIII by requiring reemployment of a sick or injured employee "only if he is physically fit and able to perform his regular work satisfactorily" shows that both parties agreed that inability to do the work is "just cause" for discharge.

7. The medical statements in behalf of Wilding and Roehr were solicited and were not based upon observation of the jobs which the men were expected to do.

8. It is neither feasible nor practical in the Company's operation to put some warehousemen on light work exclusively and leave the heavy work for others. There is no differentiation in the wage classifications for warehousemen performing light duties and those performing heavy work. The Company has had no past practice of putting men suffering from physical disability on lighter work in the warehouse which is the Company's only operation at present.

9. The Company attempted to work out the problem with the Union's Business Agent who refused to discuss the cases of the two men unless the Company would adopt the Union's pension plan. The Union by implication recognized the Company's right to discharge physically unfit employees by stating its willingness to accept $5,000 to $5,400 each for the men, rather than the sum proposed by the Company. In effect, the Company followed the procedure for separating physically unfit older workers suggested by Joe Burrell, union vice president at the time the contract was negotiated.

10. The Company complied with Article VII (a) by providing a warning notice to Wilding and a copy to the Union. Notice did not say that the employee was doing something wrong and that he had to correct it "because Wilding's physical condition was something which was beyond his power to correct." No warning notice was necessary in the case of Roehr because he voluntarily chose to resign. Roehr was not threatened or coerced to resign; to the contrary, he was happy to resign and receive a gratuity.

11. The Company did not violate Article V by asking employees to enter into any agreement in conflict with the contract. Company did not discuss "rates of pay, wages, and hours of employment or conditions of employment" with the men without Union representatives being present.

QUESTIONS

1. Was Roehr discharged or did he voluntarily resign?
2. Does a belief on the part of the Company that an employee is unable to correct his alleged inability to perform work free the Company of the obligation to warn an employee before discharge?
3. What bearing does the Business Agent's refusal to discuss the Roehr and Wilding cases unless the Company adopted the Union's pension plan have

on the issues in these cases? Had the employer given $5,000 and $5,400 each for the men, could the Union still argue that the Company had violated the agreement?

4. Did the Company conferences with Wilding and Roehr violate the agreement? Why or why not?

5. Are Wilding and Roehr entitled to light work or special treatment in deference to their age and long service to the Company?

6. Does this situation suggest any principles that might be applied to such matters as work assignments, severance pay, and pension plans? Prepare a check list of collective bargaining issues raised by this case which should be considered in the next union-management negotiations.

CASE 21
Tests as Measures of Ability in Job Bidding

Company: National Seal Company
              Van Wert, Ohio
Union: United Rubber Workers of America
              Local 426
Arbitrator: Harry J. Dworkin

Can the employer eliminate a senior employee from consideration for a new job on the basis of test scores? This case involves the interpretation of an agreement on promotion and transfers.

The following discussion of the issue and facts in this case was prepared by Harry J. Dworkin, the arbitrator.

The issue submitted for arbitration and developed during the course of the hearing concerns itself with the application of the contract provisions pertaining to seniority and the qualifications and "job requirements" of employees who bid for a job opening in a particular classification.

The grievant, Frances Brotherwood, bid for the job of packer and machine operator which had been duly posted by management. In accordance with the established procedure, the company gave a test to the job applicants in order to determine whether they met the job requirements with particular reference to aptitude for simple mathematics. On the basis of the results of the examination, the grievant was given a failing score and was adjudged by the company to lack the job requirements insofar as they concerned proficiency in simple mathematics. The grievant, although having greater seniority, was bypassed and the job was given to an applicant who was successful in the examination, even though she had less seniority than the grievant.

The union thereupon processed a grievance on behalf of Frances

Brotherwood, claiming that she was entitled to the job vacancy. The grievance is as follows:

STATEMENT OF GRIEVANCE

I signed a job posting for the job of packer in the packing department on the 2nd shift. The job was given to a employee who has less seniority than I do. The Co. made a mistake in giving the job to the less senior employee. I am asking to be given the job & back pay up to the time the less senior employee was transferred to that job.

P.S. I have done the job several times before the job posting was put up.

(Signed) Frances Brotherwood
Signature of Employee

COMPANY RESPONSE

The company's answer was based on the fact that she failed to attain the minimum requirements necessary to qualify:

Performance on numbers test fell considerably below the minimum requirements necessary to qualify for the job. The position was filled by a person meeting minimum qualifications.

The company further explained its position in a subsequent step of the grievance procedure:

The contract provides that selection of employees to fill this job will be made on the basis of seniority and job requirements.

Because employees performing this job are required to calculate, from the number of shipping cases and seals per case, the seals packed, and are responsible for making the final report of transfer to the shipping department, the requirements of this job include reasonable proficiency at simple arithmetic.

The aggrieved states that she has done this job. It is true that she has done *a part* of this job. But obviously she is not qualified to do *all* the job.

The job was given to the most senior employee who met the minimum job requirements.

In an explanatory letter to the union dated December 21, 1956, the company pointed out that this is the only female job in the plant except department clerks on which written tests are used to determine whether or not the employee meets the job requirments. Since this job involves the computation of seals packed for delivery to the customer, this requirement along with legibility of writing is critical on the job. The math requirements can be determined objectively by tests which have been standardized for industry and such tests have been used for at least the past four years for that purpose.

The test that was used for the purpose of determining mathematical proficiency is prepared by the Industrial Psychology Corporation and its use is explained by the company as follows:

The test used is standardized on a percentile basis. The lowest 1% of scores are in the 1st percentile group and the highest 1% in the 100th percentile group, etc. The minimum acceptable on the job is a score in the 25th percentile group. (Far below average but acceptable as a minimum.) This is consistent with the requirement for successful bidding on the job for at least the past 4 years, and has been required of other employees bidding on this job. Frances' score was in the 8th percentile group. To award her the job when in the past other bidders who came closer to meeting the job requirement were denied the job would not only be hazardous as far as computing seals packed is concerned but would also be discriminatory. There were no grievances filed in the other cases.

As was previously suggested, if Frances believes there were any circumstances at the time she took the test which did not permit her to work on it effectively, we were and are willing for her to take another form of the same test.

The examination paper itself was introduced in evidence and the following portion is indicative of the nature of the test given:

	1	2	3	4	Answer
4 plus 7 plus 3 equals:	12	13	14	15	( )
24 divided by 6 plus 3 equals:	7	8	6	10	( )
5 times 9 plus 4 equals:	45	49	51	54	( )

The job description for the packer and machine operator (female) includes the following duties:

What duties does the incumbent personally perform in the usual course of work?

Duties include operations related to packaging of seals and preparation of cartons and cases. These operations involve packing finished seals in rolls, cartons, or envelopes; operating equipment such as multigraph, printing press, box opener, box closer, and stapler; and preparing shipping cases for packing.

Must be able to read and interpret Production Orders, count production, make out stock receipts, etc.

Performs other duties as directed.

Specific education requirements: High school graduation or equivalent.

The job of packer and machine operator was created in November 1954, resulting from an amalgamation of two then existing separate jobs, and since that time the posting of the job indicated a requirement of proficiency in simple arithmetic and "all of the employees have taken the test." The company has consistently utilized the test as a means for determining whether the employee met the job requirements with reference to proficiency in simple mathematics, and the union has consistently opposed the use of the test, and has refused during the course of prior contract negotiations to acknowledge the propriety of the test by way of contract language. However, no prior grievance has been filed by any employee although successful applicants for jobs have been rated in part by the results of the examination.

In accordance with the terms of the current contract, the issue was developed by the parties during the course of the oral hearing, at which time the parties submitted oral testimony and documentary evidence in support of their respective positions. An opportunity was given the parties to file a brief by way of summation, the union indicating that it preferred to submit the case on basis of the evidence adduced, whereas the company has filed a post-hearing brief. In addition, all of the proceedings before the arbitrator were embodied in transcript of the evidence which has been considered in the preparation of this opinion and award.

PROVISIONS OF CONTRACT

The collective bargaining agreement between the company and the union, effective November 1, 1956, provides as follows with reference to the filling of vacancies:

Section 3. Job Bidding and Shift Preference.
. . . Selection of employees to fill such jobs shall be made on the basis of seniority and job requirements for all jobs except machine set up classifications. . . .

A trial period is given to employees who have successfully bid for a job opening:

Section 4. General Provisions.
B. An employee transferred to a job as a result of job bidding will have a reasonable trial period not exceeding thirty (30) calendar days. If he fails to qualify for the job during this period he will return to the job from which he transferred and all other employees affected by the return of this employee will be moved back to their former jobs also.

The contract further contains the customary management prerogative clause:

Article I. Statement of Policy.
The right to hire, promote, discharge or discipline for just cause and to maintain discipline and efficiency of employees is solely the responsibility of the Company, subject to the terms of this Agreement.

POSITION OF THE UNION

The Union bases its grievance upon the charge that the Company violated the collective bargaining agreement and the provisions relating to the filling of vacancies, and contends that the grievant had greater seniority than the employee who was assigned to the job. Accordingly, the

Union claims that the grievant was bypassed in violation of her rights under the contract.

It is the Union's position that on the basis of seniority, prior job experience, and familiarity with the duties required, the grievant was entitled to the opportunity to bid for the job and that she should have been permitted to fill the job on a trial basis since she, in fact, possessed the job requirements and had the ability to do the work required. The Union points to her background and experience, including the fact that she had performed the job on a temporary basis for a total period of thirty-three (33) days, and that her work generally was satisfactory.

The Union contends that the examination used by the company in determining an employee's aptitude is unjust and beyond the scope of the contract. The Union states that the examination is "an added burden on the part of an employee who bids on a job."

The Union further points out that in the contract negotiations it informed the Company that it would not accept or recognize written tests on job bidding, and that the language in the present contract governing selection of employees to fill job vacancies omits any reference to written examinations and requires that selection be made on the basis of "seniority and job requirements."

In the course of the contract negotiations, the Union represents that the Company had consistently endeavored to phrase the contract in such a manner as to put job requirements ahead of seniority, while the Union has maintained the position that seniority should be the determining factor in job promotion with the ability to meet the job requirements a matter of secondary significance. In any event, written tests were at no time agreed to by the Union as the means for determining whether an employee was possessed of the required aptitude and qualifications.

Furthermore, as evidence that the grievant had the qualifications for the job, the Union established that previously she had been assigned to this classification on a temporary basis and had performed the work satisfactorily and without complaint.

The Union reasons that under Section 3 of the contract seniority is the determining factor in the designation of the applicant for an available position where such applicant has the ability to perform the work and is possessed of the necessary physical qualifications: that in the event there is any question or doubt concerning such applicant's ability or fitness she should be accorded a qualifying trial period of thirty (30) days; that in this instance the grievant was denied the right to qualify for the job as specified in Section 4(B) of Article VIII of the agreement. While the Union acknowledges that the contract language requires that vacancies be filled on the basis of both seniority and job requirements, it points out that the contract language does not include the testing procedure adopted by the Company, and that this is, therefore, an "added burden" not within the scope of the contract.

With reference to the uncontroverted evidence on behalf of the Company that the Company had consistently since November 1, 1956, when the job as presently described came into existence, required that all of the employees who bid on the job vacancies in the classification take the test, and that no prior grievances had been filed in similar situations, the Union representative states as follows:

I might say this, that some of the tests that the company referred to that they had been denied jobs, the Union was aware of some of those. They were protected. Because of individual circumstances or feelings, the employees did not wish to protest and file a grievance and process it on through. We do not consider, because one employee does not consider it important enough to process a grievance—that it does not relinquish the rights of another employee to protest and file a grievance.

The Union asserts that it has never orally or in writing acknowledged the validity or propriety of the tests used by the Company, and that, in fact, it has orally protested their use on a number of occasions. The Union therefore states that although the contract required that when a vacancy occurred in a classification, the employee with the highest seniority was entitled to first preference provided he met the job requirements, this procedure was not followed or adhered to by the Company.

The employee who was awarded the position had less seniority than the grievant, and, in the event there remained any doubt or question as to the ability of the grievant to do the job required, she should have been given a thirty (30) day qualifying trial. Accordingly, the Union states that the Company violated the contract with reference to seniority and requests that the arbitrator rule that she be assigned to the job, together with an award of compensation of any lost wages.

POSITION OF THE COMPANY

The Company contends that the Union's claims are unfounded and that its action with respect to the assignment of an employee to the classification of packer and machine operator was fully justified and warranted by the evidence and was consistent with the terms of the collective bargaining agreement, and in accordance with established past practice. The Company's position is that its action was not the result of any arbitrary, capricious, or discriminatory conduct or bias toward the grievant, and points out that the contract does not provide for filling a vacancy on the basis of seniority alone; that the express language of the contract requires that that the employee's rights to the job in question must be determined on whether the applicant can fulfill the job requirements.

Furthermore, the procedure which was followed in this instance has been consistently adhered to since November 1, 1954, in the filling of approximately eighteen (18) vacancies in which each applicant was required to take a test to determine mathematical proficiency, and that no prior grievance has been filed. The Company vigorously contends that the testing method is the only known means for objectively determining the proficiency of the applicant for the job, and whether she is possessed of the job requirements involved in the job description.

The examination which the grievant failed to pass by the required minimum grade is prepared by the Industrial Psychology Corporation and is a type of test used widely in industry. The test is standardized on a percentile basis and, to determine average proficiency in simple arithmetic, anyone whose score is twenty-five (25) percentile or above meets the requirements and is considered as having demonstrated the minimum mathematical proficiency required. On the basis of the results of the examination, the Company gave the job to the employee who met the minimum posted job requirements in preference to the grievant who claimed the job on the basis of her seniority plus job experience.

Since the time this job was classified, all persons who have made application for existing vacancies have been required to meet the job requirements, one of which being "average proficiency in simple arithmetic." The Company has uniformly insisted that all applicants for these jobs pass a test to establish the necessary knowledge and has consistently refused the job to senior applicants who did not meet the requirements. At least eighteen (18) employees were denied jobs during 1955 and 1956 for failure to pass the same test which was given to the grievant without any formal grievance having been filed. The test itself is reasonable and was properly administered.

The Company points out that it is a standard test, widely used and accepted in industry generally. There is no recognized means for objectively and fairly determining an employee's proficiency in simple arithmetic except through a test in the subject matter. Since the job description and evaluation plan require that the applicant be either a high school graduate or have the equivalent educational background, and since the applicant was not a high school graduate, the test was a reasonable requirement in order to determine whether she had the "equivalent" requirement.

In the interpretation of the contract language pertaining to job bidding, the Company points out that under the express language of the agreement, the job must be given to the senior employee who meets the job requirements "not to some employee who has temporarily worked on the job or who claims to be qualified by ability or who thinks he can learn the job in a reasonable time. *The employee must meet the job requirements.*"

Thus, the Company urges that there is an apparent difference between the phrases, "meeting job requirements" and "ability to qualify or perform a job." The successful bidder for a vacancy must *first* meet the job requirements and *then* qualify on the job within a reasonable time. To grant the grievance in this case would have the effect of leaving the Company completely without any objective standard to apply in filling job vacancies and would result in interminable grievances on the part of senior employees whose claims to the vacancies would be based solely upon their length of service in disregard of their lack of ability to meet the requirements of the job.

Furthermore, the Company represents that the practice of requiring the job applicants to submit to a reasonable examination has been followed for almost three years and it would be unfair to both the Company and the employees to upset the established procedure, and would render the contract terms meaningless; this would be tantamount to reading into the contract language limitations that are not therein expressed.

By way of summary of its position, the Company states that the test and the manner in which it is given are both fair and reasonable and is within the inherent right of the Company in light of the pertinent contract language referred to:

> This right rests not only upon past practice, but upon the contractual power to fix job requirements and require some proof that they are met. Without objective means of measuring the meeting of job requirement, they are meaningless. A requirement of a certain height is nonsense if the man's height cannot be measured. A job requirement of average proficiency in simple arithmetic is nonsense if the employee's proficiency cannot be measured. There is absolutely no way to measure objectively and impartially the physical or mental attainments of an applicant other than by a test. The Union has not and cannot suggest any alternative.

Accordingly, the Company alleges that it has faithfully followed the clear language of the contract in the awarding of the job; that the test was voluntarily taken by the applicant and was fairly administered; that she failed to demonstrate the minimum requirement of mathematical proficiency; and that, therefore, the job was properly assigned to the employee with less seniority who qualified under the testing procedure. The Company urges that, for the aforesaid reasons, the union's grievance be denied.

QUESTIONS

1. Does the Union's repeated refusal to accept tests or an agreement upgrading the ability criterion in negotiations deny management the right to use nondiscriminatory testing methods in determining ability?
2. Does the wording of the agreement clearly define the relative emphasis which will be given to ability and seniority?
3. On what basis did the Company justify its promotion of a junior employee?
4. Under this agreement, who is the final judge of ability? Who determines the criteria for this judgment?
5. The Union argues that the grievant's past temporary placement on the job

is substantiation for her ability. The Company later attempted to rebut this argument by introducing evidence of errors in the grievant's work. What is the relevancy of the Union's contention and the Company's rebuttal to the issue in this case?

CASE 22
Mechanical Aptitude Tests for Filling New Jobs

Company: Pretty Products, Incorporated
Union: United Rubber, Cork, Linoleum and Plastic Workers of America
Local 50
Arbitrator: Maurice E. Nichols

Are mechanical aptitude tests the same as a "trial" on a new job? Does a union's past failure to challenge tests commit the union to their use in the future?

The following discussion of the issues and facts in this case was prepared by Maurice E. Nichols, the arbitrator.

BACKGROUND

The Company is a producer of rubber products, many of which are sold to automobile companies and accessories dealers. The business is highly competitive, and frequent model and style changes necessitate changes in and modifications of equipment, tools, and fixtures. The effectiveness of the maintenance department materially influences and controls the productivity of the producing department. For some period of time prior to the events resulting in this dispute the job titled Maintenance Helper had not been filled, although it is listed (with stipulated rates of pay) in the rate schedule attached to and made a part of the collective bargaining agreement.

The Company had experienced an acute shortage of capable maintenance personnel. The department has operated six and seven days per week (most men averaging 55 hours per week), and it was still necessary to contract out some maintenance work. On January 2, 1964, the Company posted a job opening for Maintenance Man B, indicating on the posted notice that tests would be used in determining the successful bidder. The Union grieved (Union Ex. 1), stating:

Grievance No. 10

We feel that the wording used by the Company in the job posting for Maintenance Man-B dated Jan. 2 indicates the Company's intention to violate paragraph 60 and/or provisions or the Union-Company Agreement. It appears as though it may have been designed to discourage prospective bidders. We ask that said job posting be voided and the Maintenance Man-B job be posted and filled in the same manner as any other vacancy, in accordance with the Agreement.

> The Union
> S/SIMON CHENEY, Pres.
> WILLIAM A. NOON

The Company replied:

Management does not believe that the Union ever intended that any part of the Union-Management Agreement should support an unworkable situation. The job posting in question could not possibly be satisfactorily filled by open bidding as requested above. Any employee who thinks he could do the work required by this classification has a perfect right to sign the posting and demonstrate his ability in a practical test. Management has no intention of discouraging any employee who has the ability and skills to fill this job.

> S/H.D. ROBSON
> Personnel Department 1/3/64

Following further discussion of this dispute and the problem of obtaining maintenance personnel, the Company postponed activation of this posting by submitting the following letter:

> January 9, 1964

U.R.C., & P.W.A.
LOCAL 50
Coshocton, Ohio
Gentlemen:

This letter is in answer to your grievance #10 dated January 3, 1964, and signed by Simon Cheney and William Noon.

The company will take no action on the job posting which you have objected to and will in the near future present a plan for your consideration on establishing an apprentice program and a method to improve the language in the contract and our over-all maintenance situation.

> Yours truly,
> S/EARL RICHARD
> Plant Superintendent

The parties then proceeded to negotiate, attempting to reach a mutually acceptable maintenance apprentice program. They arrived at a program which was accepted by the Union committee but rejected by the Union membership. At this point, the Company issued the following letters—both dated April 9, 1964 (three months after postponement):

Gentlemen:

This is in reference to our letter dated January 9, 1964, pertaining to your grievance #10 dated January 3, 1964, and signed by Simon Cheney and William Noon.

In our letter we stated that we would take no action on the job posting which was posted on January 3, 1964, for Maintenance Man "B" and signed by G. Robinson and Cecil E. Johnson and that we would present a plan for your consideration on our over-all maintenance situation.

Since no agreement has been reached on this situation we are advising you that this job posting is being voided as of this date.

Yours truly,
S/Earl Richard
Plant Superintendent

The second letter (April 9, 1964):

Gentlemen:

Since the Union has seen fit to reject all proposals made by the Company on a very serious situation in our Maintenance Department, this letter is to advise you that any and all proposals made by the Company to the Union regarding the Maintenance Program have been withdrawn as of this date.

Yours truly,
Earl Richard
Plant Superintendent

The Company then proceeded to post the following:

Date: May 25, 1964
Opening: Maintenance Helpers
Base Rate: $1.96

(Job Description)

_____

_____

_____

Passing a mechanical aptitude test will be a necessary qualification.

All things being equal, the one having the most seniority and the necessary qualifications will be accepted.

Eight employees bid on the job. All were given aptitude tests covering three areas: (1) Mechanical Knowledge; (2) Space Relations; (3) Shop Arithmetic. These were standard tests used extensively in measuring mechanical aptitude. Of the eight employees bidding (and subsequently tested) three were selected. The grievant, who had the greatest length of service, was not one of the three. As a result, he filed the grievance:

June 11, 1964

Grievance No. 22

I feel that I should have the job as maintenance helper. Men with less seniority than I were put on the job.

The Company has violated Paragraph 60 of the contract.

S/P.M.

This protest was processed through the steps of the grievance procedure and, not being resolved, is the Issue to be resolved in these proceedings.

CONTENTIONS OF THE UNION

The Union bases its position on the specific language of Paragraph 60:

60. When vacancies occur, or new jobs are created, such vacancies or jobs shall be posted for bids, concurrently in the department and plantwide for forty-eight (48) hours, and senior regular employees (as defined in Paragraph 49) *shall be given the opportunity to trial on such jobs as per classification* (male or female) if the employee so desires. Jobs will be filled in the following manner: (Emphasis added.)
   1. Senior employees within the department.
   2. Senior employees, plantwide.
   3. After the application of Paragraph 66, new hires.

It is the contention of the Union that the senior bidder on any job is entitled (by the language of this paragraph 60) to a trial period on the job. There are no exceptions. Until and/or unless these provisions of the agreement are changed by negotiations between the parties, they must be complied with. To do otherwise would render seniority useless and of no purpose to secure a better or more satisfactory job.

The Union asks that the grievance be sustained and the grievant made whole for any loss of earnings sustained since the date of the grievance.

CONTENTIONS OF THE COMPANY

The Company disagrees with the Union premise that isolates Paragraph 60 and thereby disregards all other paragraphs having to do with job placement and further contends that the language of the agreement should be interpreted with due consideration given to practice which has been in effect for an appreciable period of time without protest.

The Company submits that it has, for many years past, included tests as a part of the trial for maintenance jobs. Company Exhibit No. 1 (May 15, 1962) was submitted as an example and is shown on the following page.

Date—MAY 15, 1962
Opening—DEPARTMENT "Z"
Maintenance Men—"B"
Basic Rate—$2.25 PER HOUR

Men must be qualified to weld without instruction, as no supervision will be on the night shifts, qualified to do electrical wiring, steam piping, machine and equipment repairs.

Examinations will be given to applicants after the postings are down.

All things being equal and conditions remaining the same, the person most qualified and having the most seniority will be selected for the job.

The Union had cooperated in giving these tests—assigning observers to be present when tests were given. Those observers were supplied information about the tests and their influence on determination of the successful bidder. There have been two labor agreements (each of three-years' duration) negotiated since the testing program was installed, and at no time has the use of tests been challenged during these negotiations. The Company contends, therefore, that there is an established practice of using tests in selecting maintenance personnel.

The Company points to the fact that no objection was raised when the job of maintenance helper was posted on May 25, 1964. In fact, no protest was filed when the tests were administered to the eight applicants. It was only when the jobs were awarded and the grievant was not included that any dissenting opinion was voiced.

With respect to the influence of test scores on selection, the Company points out that the three selected were not the highest on tests but were the longest service employees among those that achieved *satisfactory scores* on the tests. The grievant was seventh—scoring 21 points out of a total of 109. Six of the eight scored over 50. In checking answers to questions (applicants were not required to write answers), the grievant was the only one of the eight who failed to follow the simple instructions (he checked 2 or 3 of the multiple choice answers to certain questions). Had this been charged against him, his score would have been 17 instead of 21. It is obvious, the Company states, that this applicant could not have performed maintenance work—particularly since it was contemplated that the helper would, as soon as feasible, be upgraded to Maintenance B status, and the agreement (Par. 60 quoted earlier) gives preference to applicants "within the department."

The Company rejects the interpretation of agreement language which recognizes only length of service in determining one's right to a job. It cites:

Par. 53—Which requires previous experience in order to exercise plant-wide bumping privileges.

Par. 59—Senior employees must be qualified operators in order to exercise shift preference.

Par's. 62 & 63—emphasize ability and management judgment.

Par. 64—Seniority plays a minor part in selection of inspectors.

Par's. 75 & 76—benefit certain unfortunate employees, but only if they have proper qualifications and ability.

Thus, the Company submits, the over-all language of the agreement indicates an awareness of the parties which negotiated it of the importance of qualifications for assignment to critical jobs. Maintenance jobs are most critical—particularly under present conditions where the shortage of personnel is so acute. It is unreasonable to presume that the Company ever agreed to terms which would require it knowingly to assign incompetent personnel to such vital work.

The Company cites the strong management rights clause:

Par. 88—The right to hire, promote, discharge, or discipline for just cause and to maintain discipline and efficiency of employees, is recognized as the responsibility of the Company except that the Union members shall not be discriminated against as such. The Union recognizes that the Company has the exclusive right to manage plant and direct its affairs and working forces, so long as it does not conflict with this Agreement. . . ."

Since nothing in the agreement prohibits the use of tests as part of the "trial" called for in Paragraph 60, it is the contention of the Company that this Paragraph 88, coupled with the clearly established past practice, gives it the unquestioned right to use such tests so long as it does so in a purely nondiscriminatory manner.

The Union withdrew from consideration under these proceedings any question of grievant's qualifications for the work in the maintenance department. It limited the discussion and argument (no witnesses were questioned) to the allegedly "clear and unambiguous" language of Paragraph 60 which requires that *"senior regular employees shall be given the opportunity to trial on such jobs . . . if the employee so desires."* It holds that no consideration may be given to any factor other than seniority when considering bids for job openings.

QUESTIONS

1. Does the Union failure to contest the Company's claim that tests have been used to fill maintenance jobs in the past dilute the clear wording of Paragraph 60?
2. What is a "trial"?
3. Is the issue here limited to Paragraph 60 or should paragraphs 53, 59, 62 & 63, 64, and 75 & 76 be "read into" Paragraph 60? Why?
4. Do you think that the Union's decision to argue this case solely on Paragraph 60 and not to challenge the tests used or to assert the competence of the grievant was in the best interest of the grievant and the Union? Why?

CASE 23
"Skill and Ability" Requirements for Promotion

Company: Emhart Manufacturing Company
Union: United Automobile Workers
                Local 462
Arbitrator: Burton B. Turkus

Is an employee's record of absenteeism evidence of lack of "skill and ability" and therefore grounds for disqualification for promotion?

The following discussion of the issue and facts in this case was prepared by Burton B. Turkus, the arbitrator.

ISSUE

"Under the provisions of the contract, is the Company required to promote X—— to the job of Tool Crib Lead Man? If yes, what shall the remedy be?"

RELEVANT CONTRACT PROVISIONS

Article IX, Vacancies and Promotions, in pertinent part, provides:

Section 4. When permanent vacancies exist to which no employee has recall rights, and which offer an opportunity for promotion or advancement to employees, such vacancy will be posted by the Company on the bulletin board for not less than three (3) working days. Employees interested in the vacancy shall make such application for the opening by personally signing the bulletin board notice. Employees who make application will be advised of the outcome by his supervisor. Employees on recall status interested in the vacancy will notify their foreman or the Personnel Department.

Section 5. The Company will fill such vacancies from employees who make application *on the basis of seniority provided such employees have the skill and ability to meet the requirements of the job classification.* (Emphasis added.)

. . .

Section 7. If no qualified employees bid for the vacancy, the Company may select candidates from any source to fill such vacancy.

BACKGROUND OF THE DISPUTE

The job involved is a newly created one—a direct result of the Company's reorganization of the tool room system and function. Prior to reorganization, the only job classification applicable to the tool room was "Tool Room Attendant" carrying a Labor Grade H 6 classification. After reorganization, the new position of "Tool Crib Lead Man" was created and after negotiation with the Union was assigned Labor Grade No. 10, the highest in the plant.

The function of the tool room is to provide the entire shop with adequate tools. The tool room system prior to reorganization was antiquated—and the service provided had been unsatisfactory and inadequate. There were constant, frequently justified complaints by the Union and employees of delays encountered in locating tools and of the inadequacy (poor working condition) of the tools supplied to the men in the plant. In short, the tool room situation had become a potent source of discussion, irritation, and dissatisfaction.

As a consequence, the Company, based on a study by its industrial engineers, reorganized the tool room system and function. At a substantial cost, changes in location or ordering points were made to bring the tool crib into close proximity to the cutter grinders for efficiency and better liaison. Newly designed cabinets and bins were fabricated and an improved and modernized record keeping and reordering system was installed to expedite the finding of needed tools and to assure that the tools supplied were in proper working condition. To secure adequate management and function of the tool crib as reorganized, the new position and job description of tool crib lead man resulted.

The tool crib lead man, as provided in the job description, is responsible for the effective operation of the tool crib. He is required to have a good working knowledge of machine-shop practice and machine cutting tools and accessory equipment; to assist with the guide tool and cutter grinding operations; and to check tools and cutters for proper grinding. He must maintain, in accordance with established procedures, all inventory records, and all records required for receipt, storage, issuance and transfer of tools, jigs and fixtures. He assigns work to other employees and instructs and checks the quality of work of the other tool crib employees. The tool crib lead man carries out these responsibilities with a minimum of detailed supervision and reports directly to the plant superintendent rather than to the foreman or general foreman.

On October 4, 1963, the Company, in accordance with the provisions of Article IX of the labor agreement of the parties, posted the job of tool crib lead man for bidding. The job description was attached to the posting. Along with several others, grievant, X——, bid for the job. At the time of his bid, X—— had 14 years seniority with the Company, was a tool and cutter grinder (A) on the night shift, and held a red circle rate of Labor Grade 10, the highest labor grade under the contract.

The Company determined that none of the applicants were qualified to meet the requirements of the job of tool crib lead man and on October 9, 1963, assigned the job to another (who had not bid for the job) under the provision of Article IX of the contract.

At this point all other applicants (bidders for the job) then had their names withdrawn and the Union on October 15, 1963, filed a formal grievance in behalf of X——, asserting that the Company had violated the contract by reason of its failure to promote him to the tool crib lead man job for which he was fully qualified. The grievance was processed through the various steps of the grievance procedures and submitted to arbitration under the stipulated issue aforesaid.

THE FACTS

The proof in the instant case was concentrated on the issue of "skill and ability to meet the requirements of the job classification"—the matter of grievant's seniority was not in the area of controversy.

The regularly scheduled work within the plant contemplates 2,000 hours per year. The average number of hours during which employees were absent is 80 hours per year.

In 1961, the grievant was absent for various reasons a total of 192 hours. In 1962, he was absent a total of 674 hours. In 1963, from January to October (October 9, 1963, being the date of the Company's decision not to promote him), he was absent a total of 285 hours.

The preponderant bulk of these absences was due to a variety of illnesses but also included absences for other reasons. In 1961 he was absent and away from work for personal or tardiness reasons a total of 30 hours; in 1962, a total of 122 hours and in 1963, a total of 39 hours.

While amassing this absentee record, which "the Union readily concedes was top-heavy," the grievant during the three-year period preceding his bid for promotion was engaged in a series of outside business activities alien to his regular employment. In 1961 and 1962 he had an orange juice business; in 1960 and 1961 he had a TV repair business; and in 1962 and 1963 he had a gasoline station business (which he sold in March, 1963), admittedly devoting an average of between four to five hours a day thereto.

The grievant's excessive absenteeism and simultaneous devotion to outside business ventures was a matter of serious concern and Company action for a substantial period of time prior to his bid for promotion. In a series of discussions in which he pointed up the impact upon the Company of the unpredictable excessive lost time and the contributory nature of grievant's outside business thereto, the plant manager personally "tried everything that was published on the subject," including two visits to grievant's gasoline station for discussion designed to have grievant improve his attendance record, but to no avail.

Preparatory, then, to ultimate termination if the procedure proved ineffective, the grievant was given an oral warning on October 1, 1962, that his lost time record must be improved. On November 5, 1962, he was given a written warning that "unless your lost time record shows a definite improvement disciplinary action will be taken." On February 1, 1963, the grievant was given another written warning, to wit:

Your excessive absence during the past year has placed a hardship on the company. We have had an off-balanced condition because of your unpredictable excessive lost time. We can no longer tolerate this condition and hereby offer you a six-month leave of absence, or as an alternative, work your scheduled hours for a year, or the company suggests you resign. If none of these suggestions results in correction of this condition, the company must take appropriate action.

At or about the time of that written warning, the plant manager found the grievant at his gasoline station directing his 14-year-old son "how to change a tire." Father and son were the only individuals at the station and grievant's hands as well as his clothes indicated that he had been performing some labor at the very time that he was absent from work on account of sickness.

The job to which the grievant sought to be promoted by his bid constitutes the only tool crib lead man in the plant. The entire shop, moreover, is dependent upon the tool room. Regular attendance on the part of the tool crib lead man, responsible for the effective operation of the tool room, is an essential requirement of the job.

QUESTIONS

1. Is a good attendance record a part of "the skill and ability to meet the requirements of the job classification"?
2. What consideration should be given to the series of warnings given to X——in view of the fact that no formal disciplinary action had been taken against him?
3. How would you rule in this case?

CASE 24
Conflict of Loyalty to the Company and the Union

Company: Contra Costa Readymix and Building Materials, Inc.
Union: International Brotherhood of Teamsters
Local No. 70
Arbitrator: Adolph M. Koven

This case involves the dual loyalty of a worker to his employer and to his union.
The following discussion of the issue and facts in this case was prepared by Adolph M. Koven, the arbitrator.

THE ISSUE

Was J— P— discharged for just cause under Article X of the Contract? If not, what is the appropriate remedy under Article X?

RELEVANT SECTIONS OF THE CONTRACT

Article X. Union Activity
No employee shall suffer discharge without just cause. In the event of discharge without just cause the employee may be reinstated with payment for time lost. In the event of a dispute, the existence of "just cause" shall be determined as provided in Article IX, "Adjustment of Grievances."
Article IX. Adjustment of Grievances
The Umpire shall have only that limited jurisdiction and authority necessary to interpret, apply, or ascertain compliance with the provisions of this Agreement, insofar as shall be necessary for the determination of grievances appealed to the Umpire. Among those subjects the Umpire shall have neither jurisdiction nor authority to consider or decide shall be those subjects although

not limited thereto, involving . . . the assignment of work duties . . . the scheduling of work, and working conditions not otherwise agreed to within the Agreement. The Umpire shall not have jurisdiction or authority to add to, detract from, or alter in any way, the provisions of this Agreement.

Article XVII. Prior Agreements and/or Practices

All written and/or oral agreements, all past practices, including agreements resulting from grievance settlements not specifically contained or referred to in this Contract shall become null and void as of the effective date of this Agreement.

On December 21, 1961, the grievant was directed to make piers. When asked by the dispatcher to do this work, the grievant replied, "I can't," and stated that the Union had told him he was not to do yard work. After the dispatcher had pointed out the consequences of a refusal, the grievant was directed to get his timecard and report to the general manager. To the general manager, the grievant still insisted, "I can't," when asked to give his reason for refusing to pour piers. The grievant was thereupon discharged.

Two sister locals of the Teamsters, Warehouse Local No. 853 and Auto Truck Drivers Local No. 70, each have contracts with the Company. Though making piers is covered in its contract by Local No. 853, there is no jurisdictional dispute between the two sister locals. Prior to two years ago when Local No. 853 signed its first contract with the Company, Local No. 70 performed yard work. Currently Local 70 also performs similar work in other plants in the industry.

The problem of doing such work was first raised when employees returned to work on December 1, right after their four-month strike ended. On December 4, the dispatcher was approached by two employees who raised the question of making piers and stated they had been instructed by the Union not to do such work. The dispatcher told them they would be well off to follow work orders until the matter was straightened out between the parties. During that day following that discussion, one of these two employees was assigned to make piers and did the work without refusal.

On December 6, two employees refused to set up screens because they had been told not to do this work by their Union. They are still in the employ of the Company despite this refusal. As a result of this incident, the president of the Company directed his management staff to warn the employees that any refusal from then on would result in disciplinary consequences.

Accordingly, on the next day, December 7, the employees were put on notice by both the general manager and the dispatcher, who each contacted different employees. The general manager stated he personally warned the grievant on this day, which the grievant denies.

A major incident next occurred on December 15. Edwards, a Local No. 70 member, when asked to do yard work stated that "I am sorry but

I can't" because he could not afford a $50 fine. Edwards was then sent to see the general manager and while discussing his dilemma, the work in the meantime was completed by a Local 853 man, so that the issue of refusing to do the work was never sharply joined. The Company views the difference between the Edwards's incident and the grievant's situation as a matter of lucky circumstances for Edwards and in the difference of attitude of both men. Earlier that day, another Local No. 70 employee had been asked to do yard work and followed the order without refusal.

The next and last incident, of course, occurred on December 21, and involved the grievant's refusal to pour piers and his subsequent discharge.

On the grievant's background and the facts of his discharge, there was considerable testimony. He had been an employee since June 1955, and was characterized by the Company as an average driver with a fair work history. The grievant described himself as one who had always tried to do a good job. The Company stated that he had never before refused to do work assigned to him and that his discharge was related only to this one event of December 21, and not to any previous history.

The general manager, president of the Company, and dispatcher each testified that on December 7, 14, and 21, respectively, they personally either warned the grievant of the consequences of a refusal or put him on notice that he would have to carry out any order given him by a supervisor. The grievant denies that management ever talked with him until the day of discharge about the problem of not doing the work.

In his testimony, the general manager stated that the grievant refused to disclose his reason to him for refusing to make piers, and it was his feeling that the grievant was daring the Company to do something about his refusal. Yet, he would not characterize the grievant's manner as belligerent and stated that the grievant would not, in his opinion, have refused to do any other work in Local No. 70's jurisdiction if given such an assignment. Perhaps if there had been a long discussion of the problem, as there had been with Edwards, the Company might have relented in its decision to discharge.

According to the grievant, on December 21, when the dispatcher told him he was supposed to do the work and if he had any objections to file a grievance afterward, he replied that if he would do that, he would be "scabbing" on the warehouse Union. When the dispatcher insisted, the grievant stated he wasn't refusing, but he just couldn't make piers. Furthermore when he was called into the general manager's office he wasn't testing the Company, but was just "scared" because he didn't want to get fired.

There have been a considerable number of times when the grievant was instructed by the Union that he should not do Local No. 853 work, and that he would be "scabbing" on the warehouse Union if he did. The reason he did not tell the general manager the basis for his refusal is that he was directed by the Union not to give the reason. He has also been directed by the Union not to file a grievance, first, because he was not supposed to do such work in the first instance, and second, because filing a grievance would be a useless act since the umpire under the contract does not have the authority to decide grievances involving questions of work assignments. Apparently the Company also holds the same view that an arbitrator would not have such authority.

Both parties stated for the record that they have not submitted the issue of deciding work jurisdiction to this arbitrator in the instant case and that he is precluded from making an award which affects the work jurisdiction of the two Unions with whom the Company has collective bargaining agreements.

POSITION OF THE COMPANY

The grievant was discharged for refusing to do work under a proper work order. He had ample warning of the consequences of any refusal, for he was warned in some fashion on December 4, and specifically on December 7, 14, and 21, by the general manager, president of the Company, and dispatcher, respectively.

If it is correct to say that the blame for generating the situation falls upon the Union, then the equities may suggest that the Union has been unfair to the grievant. However, this was a situation where the Company had to act, and if the grievant willingly or unwillingly became the foil of the Union, then it also became the grievant's problem and not the Company's. The Company could no nothing other than what it did do. It had no other alternative.

But the grievant had a choice. He could have done the work, he could have discussed his situation with management, and he could have resorted to the grievance procedure. The grievant had the time from December 4 until December 21, a period of 17 days, to think through his situation. Instead he made a deliberate intentional attack upon the authority of the Company.

The only question before the arbitrator is not whether disciplinary action was proper but only whether discharge was the proper penalty for this industrial offense. Discharge was a proper penalty because the question of work jurisdiction never serves as a ground for mitigation. The grievant cannot look to misunderstanding as a mitigating factor, for he knew exactly where he stood, and instead of taking on the Union and the $50 fine, he chose to take on the Company. He did so at his peril.

The only other possible point in the grievant's favor is the alleged discrimination in favor of Edwards. But the cases differ on the facts. Edwards was never faced with the ultimate order to do the work and so did not have the opportunity to refuse. The grievant, however, was given an order. He refused to carry it out. It was for this refusal that he was discharged.

Since this is the type of offense which warrants discharge and one which has been consistently upheld by arbitrators, the discharge of this grievant should be sustained.

POSITION OF THE UNION

This is a case involving the broad terms of just cause and involves a claim by the Company against the grievant of insubordination where he declines to perform certain work.

No one has claimed that the grievant was defiant or recalcitrant, but rather that his attitude was one of peaceful resistance to an order. The compliance with that order would have subjected him to sanctions from another source. And since his attitude cannot be said to have been malicious, certainly the Company should not have insisted on being so retaliatory and so bent on recrimination as to treat this grievant, an employee of seven years' standing, as if it were dealing with a man who had repeatedly refused to perform work.

A discharge must be examined in the light of the sociological questions involved, because discharge is a punishment. More and more in our modern time, punishment is exacted only where it serves some valuable social or industrial purpose. The Union believes that retaliation, although that might be the momentary instinct which all of us sometimes give in to and which could have been involved in the case, cannot be advanced as a justification for the discharge.

At the time of the discharge, the grievant did not have the full opportunity to consult with someone with a little more expert knowledge on such a complicated question of resolving the dilemma of a choice between loyalties. Subsequent to his discharge he has had time to think it over and has come to a different conclusion. The grievant has now come to a clearer understanding as to what he must now do and that is to follow Company orders as given until the parties resolve their difficulties on the larger issue.

What purpose is served by holding that the grievant cannot go back to work where the only complaint the Company has is that on one day he declined to do work which he now says he will do? It cannot serve any valuable purpose at all. And this is particularly true because there is no damage to the Company resulting from that particular incident on that one day.

Thus, the Union urges that the grievant be reinstated and that he be compensated for time lost, with restoration of seniority and other rights.

QUESTIONS

1. What rights on the part of J—— P——, the Company, and the Union are involved here?

2. Both the Company and the Union reminded the arbitrator that he is *not* authorized to settle the jurisdictional dispute involved in this case. How would the arbitrator's ruling on J—— P——'s discharge influence the outcome of the jurisdictional dispute?

3. Both the Company and the Union admit that J—— P—— is the unfortunate victim of circumstances beyond his control. Is this a fair conclusion or did J—— P—— have control over his own fate?

4. How would you rule in this case? Why?

CASE 25
An Accident Record as a Basis for Discharge

Company: Our Own Bakeries, Inc.
Union: Retail, Wholesale and Department Store Union
             Local No. 655
Arbitrator: Robert S. Thompson

This case involves the discharge of a truck driver for a second serious accident in six months. This case requires not only a definition of just cause but also consideration of the standards of discipline which are appropriate to employees who work without direct supervision and have individual responsibility for very expensive equipment.

The following discussion of the issue and facts in the case was prepared by Robert S. Thompson, the arbitrator.

Our Own Bakeries is a large and well-known wholesale bakery which distributes its products throughout the Upper Peninsula of Michigan and parts of Wisconsin. Robert Carlton, the grievant, was a transport driver, one of six such who drove large tractor-trailer equipment. The route covered by Mr. Carlton was from Marquette to Ironwood, a round distance of about 310 miles. His schedule called for leaving Marquette about 1 A.M. and returning about 11 A.M. He had been employed with the Company about nine years, the last four years as a transport driver. On October 29, 1960, he had an accident which resulted in the total loss of his tractor-trailer and merchandise. The next day, October 30, he was discharged because of a poor driving and accident record.

ACCIDENT RECORD

From testimony at the hearing and various accident reports entered into evidence by the Company, a summary of Mr. Carlton's record is presented below:

October 29, 1960, 5. A.M. heavy fog, poor visibility, vehicle left the road on the left side of highway. Tractor-trailer and merchandise nearly a total loss. Mr. Carlton had cut on temple and a bruised leg, but walked mile to phone police. Officer did not reach scene until about two and a half hours later. Sales manager, Mr. Roberts, in charge of transport drivers, came out from Marquette. Accident report stated: "It is the opinion of the officer that the driver fell asleep causing him to drive to the left side of the road." Mr. Carlton stated he did not know what happened. Testified that it had taken him from 30–45 minutes to drive 18 miles; that poor visibility made it impossible to follow the center line; also suggested that trailer might have turned over because of imbalance in loading. Estimated damages about $4,100. Not ticketed.

March 22, 1960, 12:45 A.M. Struck private automobile parked or stalled on highway. Impact pushed car into driver who was standing near. Severe blizzard conditions with low visibility. No police report in evidence. Not ticketed. Insurance carrier paid claims in amount of $937.60.

November 6, 1959, 1:30 A.M. Mr. Carlton's trailer was struck from behind by tractor-trailer driven by Mr. Bengry, another transport driver employed by the Company. Heavy snow storm. Grievant was to make left turn from Highway 41 into Highway 95. Snow plow at the intersection and to left of grievant's truck. Grievant stopped when hit. Company alleged that grievant was in conversation with snow plow operator. Grievant claims snow plow was blocking intersection. Snow so thick rear lights probably obscured. Extensive damage to both units. Tractor of other truck was total loss. Not ticketed.

April 17, 1956, 9:10 A.M. Slippery conditions. Grievant started to slow down as a private automobile approached from other direction. Double tracks slipped off right side of pavement; his truck started to skid; touched brake and went into a jackknife to the left side of road. Approaching car hit grievant's truck toward right rear. Driver of car seriously injured and passenger (wife) killed. State trooper who investigated checked these items on report: Vision *not* obscured; excessive speed; snowing; no improper driving by second driver. Not ticketed. Insurance carrier paid in total of $12,969 in claims.

In addition to the accidents listed above, the record of Mr. Carlton on file with Michigan Secretary of State shows the following:

November 21, 1956. Closed without action.
January 21, 1959. Drove left of center line. Improper left turn.
July 13, 1960. Driving 80 miles in 65 mph zone.

Before his employment by the Company, when 17 years old, Mr. Carlton was involved in a fatal accident. This was in 1945. In a suit for $25,000 damages the judge directed a verdict in favor of the defendant, Mr. Carlton.

Complete data as to the accident records of the other transport drivers was not available. Ray Trevillion, driver with highest seniority, has had one accident in the last five or six years (due to falling asleep). John Stone, sales route driver for four years, and transport driver for last six months, has had two nonticketed accidents in that period.

PUBLISHED AWARDS

An examination of a number of published arbitration awards (several cited by Mr. Kirkwood plus others) turns up little of assistance in the instant matter. In contrast to the law, precedent is generally considered to have little weight in arbitration. The situation in each arbitration tends to be unique, and part of the usefulness and vitality of arbitration inheres in its rejection of legalisms. However, published awards are sometimes helpful in being suggestive. With respect to discharge of truck and bus drivers for highway accidents, the decisions show wide diversity.

In Hudson County Bus Owners Association, 3 LA 786, the discharge of a bus driver was upheld on the ground of a bad record of minor accidents and one serious accident; in Schreiber Trucking Company, 5 LA 430, a discharge following a third accident was sustained, mainly on the basis that the "driver habitually drove at excessive speed"; in Ward Baking Co., 8 LA 837, discharge of a driver-salesman was affirmed after his sixth accident within three years (average rate of other company drivers within same three-year period was one accident); in Chestnut Farms, Chevy Chase Dairy, 8 LA 897, a driver with five accidents within a period of less than a year was held to be properly discharged. In Kroger Co., 24 LA 48, a seventh accident within five years, with the last four of the seven occurring within a three-month period, plus a warning that the next accident would bring discharge, was considered to justify discharge.

On the other hand, discharges were voided and reinstatements directed in the following: In Boston & Maine Transportation Co., 5 LA 3, a driver involved in an accident resulting in several deaths was reinstated even though there was evidence of violation of safety rules; in Mason & Dixon Lines, 9 LA 775, a trailer truck driver who lost control and collided with a gasoline truck causing a loss of $30,000 was reinstated even though he had failed to take action which might have kept his truck on the road; in Safe Bus Co., 21 LA 456, a bus driver who had had two accidents within six months and who was at fault in the second was reinstated even though the damages exceeded $1,000; in Pacific Greyhound Lines, 30 LA 830, reinstatement without back pay was ordered of a driver responsible for a serious accident in which his bus struck a truck in the rear on a highway.

• • •

This arbitration is based upon a contractual agreement between the parties. Article VII acknowledges the power to discharge, but it also requires that "this power be exercised with justice with regard for the reasonable rights of the Employees."

QUESTIONS

1. Do the cited cases suggest standards for an award in this dispute?
2. In assessing Carlton's accident record, what weight should be given to negligence, extent of damage resulting, driving conditions, the obligation to meet a delivery schedule, the elapsed time between accidents?
3. How would you rule in this case? Why?

CASE 26
Falsification of Medical History as a Basis for Discharge

Company: Rexall Drug Company
         Columbus, Ohio
Union: Retail, Wholesale, and Department Store Union
         Local 379
Arbitrator: Harry J. Dworkin

This case involves the issue of falsification of medical records in an application for employment.

The following discussion of the issue and facts in the case was prepared by Harry J. Dworkin, the arbitrator.

THE ISSUE

The grievant was hired on July 30, 1957. She was in the employ of the Company for approximately five years, classified as an inventory clerk in the warehouse. On January 17, 1962, she was discharged on four counts of alleged employee misconduct; (1) willful falsification of her application for employment form and physical examination record in failing to disclose prior injuries and disabilities, (2) chronic absenteeism, (3) uncooperative attitude in failing to properly carry out her assigned duties and instructions of supervision, and (4) false filing of claim for nonindustrial sick benefits.

The evidence established that on July 2, 1957 the grievant completed her application for employment, and was thereafter hired on July 30, 1957. One part of the application signed by the grievant included the following question: "Have you ever received compensation for injury? When?" These questions were left unanswered. Another portion of the application, entitled "Physical Examination Record," required answers as to whether the applicant had ever been treated for any of 38 listed conditions, including "backache" and "back injury." The grievant signed the application leaving all of the spaces opposite the columns of physical conditions unanswered. The form required a checkmark in the event the applicant had ever had any of the enumerated conditions, or received treatment for such.

The record evidence submitted to the hearing established that in 1953 the grievant had sustained an industrial injury to her back while employed at Albers Supermarket. This prior employment, as well as the injury, came to light when she filed an application with the Bureau of Workman's Compensation of Ohio for a back injury sustained on June 25, 1958, while in the employ of Rexall. The June 25 injury resulted when a forklift truck struck a pallet on which she was seated, throwing her to the cement floor and injuring her back. Her supporting affidavit was filed on January 11, 1960, approximately 18 months after the accident. She claimed that the pain radiated from her lower back into her left leg.

A record of the emergency room of Mt. Carmel Hospital also established that on May 16, 1956, the grievant had been involved in an auto accident while leaving the Westinghouse plant, where she was then employed. The diagnosis was "possible back injury." A claim was asserted against the driver of the automobile, which was later settled through the assistance of her attorney.

On March 10, 1959, while employed by Rexall, the grievant was confined in St. Anthony's Hospital with an admission diagnosis of "low back pains." The personal history related that approximately five years earlier, she had developed a pain in her back which was recurrent, "sharp and of constant severity," and that for the past two years she had "a continued ache in her entire back area—it would vary in intensity but was always present," with occasional sharp pains in the upper back which radiated the inguinal area.

On January 5, 1954, the grievant was admitted to White Cross Hospital with a diagnosis of "herniated nuclear pulposis," and complaints of "backache." This history as given by the patient disclosed that while lifting a case of canned beans, she felt a sharp pain in her back. This occurred while employed at Albers. She had experienced frequent attacks of pain in her back, "two to three times a week." Her treatment consisted of traction to both legs.

The information as regards the grievant's prior back injury, and her previous employment with Albers, was disclosed when the grievant processed her application for additional compensation, relating to her injury on June 25, 1958, while employed by Rexall. A Company representative attended the hearing during which her prior back injury was discussed with the hearing officer. In her application the grievant stated that the disability resulting from the Rexall injury consisted of "pain all over my back and my left leg." The affidavit of her attending physician, dated January 14, 1960, disclosed that he first treated the claimant on approximately May 16, 1956, because of a "compression fracture T 10," which injury she sustained in the auto accident while employed at Westinghouse. Her physician fitted her with a Taylor brace as part of his treatment.

DISABILITY AWARD

As a result of the Rexall accident, she was awarded permanent partial disability of 10 percent. The award was apparently on the basis that the Rexall accident aggravated her preexisting back disability. The records revealed that she had been awarded permanent partial disability to the extent of 40 percent of 1956 resulting from the Albers accident in 1954, and a 10 percent increase in disability due to the Rexall occurrence, making a total over-all disability of 50 percent. The medical department recommended the additional 10 percent disability on the basis that her Rexall accident "aggravated her preexisting back disability."

Other record evidence related to the grievant's application for surgical and hospital benefits under a plan maintained by the Company with the John Hancock Life Insurance Company. Under this plan employees are entitled to make application for benefits for sick leave compensation and medical expense when due to nonindustrial sickness or accidental injury. The claimant filed an application for benefits for the period March 10 to April 27, 1959, in which she stated that her disability was not due to injury. She was paid $153.45 for medical benefits, and $520 in sick leave compensation or a total of $673.45. The claim for sick leave benefits included charges incurred at St. Anthony's Hospital and medical fees for treatment of her back injury on June 19, 1958, while working at Rexall. In support of her claim for sick leave benefits, the grievant wrote to the Company on April 16, 1959, that "my back sprain wasn't due to an accident. I don't know what caused it, and the doctor doesn't either." This letter was written during the pendency of the grievant's claim for workmen's compensation. At least one of her physicians whose charges were included in the nonindustrial claim for medical payment was also compensated by the Commission, as evidenced by his fee statement submitted to the Bureau for treatment of her back on April 2, 1959. The Company claims that the grievant deliberately made application under the medical plan for a nonindustrial condition, and collected on her claim, knowing that her back condition for which she was disabled was caused in part by her 1958 accident at Rexall, as evidenced by her claim for workmen's compensation, and the proof on file in connection with her claim.

In addition to the foregoing, the Company asserted that termination was justified on the basis of her chronic absentee record. The grievant's supervisor testified that she had the poorest attendance record in the Columbus operation; that since her employment, she had been absent 223 full days and 28 half days out of a possible 700 workdays; that if the two 13-week sick leave absences were to be disregarded, the grievant lost 93 full days and 28 half days out of a possible 570 workdays. The record further indicated that out of 41 scheduled workweeks, the grievant had missed work in 21 separate weeks, and that she had been warned that her attendance record had to show substantial improvement.

Finally, the Company represented that the grievant manifested an uncooperative work attitude and failed to carry out the instructions of management. Specifically, the Company claimed that the grievant did not adhere to the order-filling procedure with reference to the selection of stock, which was required to be on a first-in first-out basis. The Company states that the grievant disregarded instructions in filling orders, and that on the basis of her unsatisfactory work attitude, together with the other acts of employee misconduct, termination was justified.

PERTINENT PROVISIONS OF CONTRACT

The Union claims that the discharge was unjust and that the Company's action was discriminatory in violation of Article III, Section 1 of the labor agreement:

The Union agrees that its members will individually and collectively perform loyal and efficient work in service and that they will use their influence and best efforts to protect the property of the Company and its interests and that they will cooperate with the Company and the employees of all departments in promoting efficient operations and advancing the welfare of the Company and services at all times. The Union further agrees that its members will cooperate with and assist the Company in simplifying and improving job methods and performance. The Company agrees that it will cooperate with the Union in a mutual effort to promote harmony and efficiency among all the Company's employees. The Company further agrees that it will not discriminate against Union Members in any way whatsoever.

Article II, Section 7, makes reference to the Company booklet furnished to all employees, entitled "Welcome to Rexall":

Getting Hired. It is Rexall policy to hire only the men and women best able to perform the work on the jobs available. Therefore, you are hired *only after a careful review of your work history* and qualifications and after you have been interviewed by your prospective supervisor. (Emphasis added.)

The Company relies upon Article III, quoted above, directing attention to the contractual obligations of employees to perform loyal and efficient work, and to cooperate in promoting efficient operation. The Company also relies on Article XV, Management Rights:

The direction of working forces, including but not limited to the right to plan and control operations, hire, promote, determine ability, suspend or discharge for proper cause, to enforce established rules of conduct, to relieve employees from duty because of lack of work, or for other legitimate reasons, and to introduce new and improved methods or facilities of operation is hereby vested exclusively in the management of the Company; and it is the *responsibility and the right of the Company to maintain discipline and efficiency*, but the Company shall be the sole judge of the quality of work required and shall have that freedom of action necessary to discharge its responsibilities for the successful operation of the Company, and all other functions of management not expressly limited by this Agreement, provided nothing contained herein shall be used for the purpose of discriminating against any employees. Rights not expressly waived by this Agreement shall be retained by the Company. The listing of specified rights in this Agreement is not intended to be nor shall be considered restrictive of, or a waiver of any rights of the Company not listed herein whether or not such rights have been exercised by the Company in the past. (Emphasis added.)

POSITION OF UNION

The Union maintains that a reasonable appraisal of all of the evidence and background giving rise to this grievance fails to establish the existence of just cause, and that the discharge was unwarranted. The Union maintains that the Company acted in a discriminatory manner in terminating the grievant's employment, in disregard of the express prohibition of the labor agreement. The Union feels that the Company was motivated in this case by ulterior considerations and that its decision to discharge the grievant was prompted by the fact that she had filed a claim for workmen's compensation, which after being denied twice, was allowed on appeal. The Union claims that the Company was apprised of her 1954 injury during the initial hearing with reference to her claim, the first hearing being on February 16, 1960, and that she was allowed to continue on her job without any action being taken until the Commission ruled in favor of the claimant early in January, 1962. Accordingly, the Union reasons that the claim that the grievant had falsified her work record was advanced only after she had prevailed with reference to her Rexall accident; that if the reasons advanced by the Company had in fact been the true basis for her discharge, the Company would have taken action after it became aware of her prior accident, in February, 1960.

As regards the failure to disclose her prior back injury, the grievant stated at the hearing that she was not specifically questioned concerning this, and that she did not read all of the employment application, and therefore was not fully aware of its contents. The grievant acknowledged that she had completed other applications including those relating to her employment at Westinghouse, General Motors, and Sylvania Electric, all of which information was omitted in her Rexall application. She acknowledged that she had an auto accident in 1956 while leaving the Westinghouse plant, that she was off work due to her disability, and that she was required to wear a back brace for approximately one month.

The Union maintains that the Company was neglectful of its own responsibility in failing to make a careful review of her work history and qualifications in accordance with the policy expressed in "Welcome to Rexall." Under all of the circumstances, the Union reasons that the omission on the grievant's application form was not of sufficient and serious import to warrant termination of employment, particularly where the Company became aware of the omission sometime prior to her termination. Similarly, the Union claims that the omissions in the grievant's applications were not of major significance, that the Company's decision to terminate her employment resulted from the fact that management was irked when her appeal was allowed for compensation resulting from her

Rexall accident, and that her five-year employment record precludes her discharge. In view of the circumstances, the Union urges that the arbitrator rule that the Company has failed to support its position, that her discharge was discriminatory and in violation of the labor agreement.

POSITION OF COMPANY

The Company denies that its decision to discharge the grievant was motivated by a discriminatory attitude, or that her discharge was in any way related to the fact that she prevailed in her workmen's compensation claim. The Company's grounds for the discharge are predicated upon the evidence relating to the five counts of employee misconduct, and particularly that she deliberately withheld information as regards her prior injuries, accidents, and places of employment, when completing her application. The company states that the required information was of major importance in order to enable management to determine whether the applicant is eligible for employment in the type of work which was available. Particularly, the Company points to the fact that she had been declared to be 40 percent disabled on a permanent partial basis as a result of her back injury while employed at Albers, and that she withheld the name of this employer, as well as others.

The Company claims that it was not aware of the "deliberate falsifications" of her employment application until some time in 1960, and was not aware of the "degree of deception" until 1962. The Company stated that it would have been improper to have acted prior to the final notice by the Industrial Commission as regards her 50 percent back disability, which included 10 percent aggravation due to the industrial accident at Rexall in 1958. The Company reasons that a decision prior to the final ruling by the Commission would have been premature and that it withheld final action until management had "complete proof of the falsification of (the) employment application."

The Company reasons that the deliberate withholding of pertinent information on the employment application, the failure to complete the physical examination record, the false claims for medical benefits and sick leave benefits under the insurance plan, together with her poor work attitude and job performance, and her chronic absenteeism, cumulatively presented a case which precluded her continued employment with the Company. For the foregoing reasons, the Company maintains that just cause has been amply established, and that the discharge should be upheld.

OPINION OF ARBITRATOR

The principal issue before the arbitrator is whether the grievant's discharge was for just cause, and consistent with the facts disclosed by the evidence, and the terms of the labor agreement.

QUESTIONS

1. How would you rule in this case?
2. What is the significance of the fact that this report is silent on whether the Physical Examination Record contained a statement that falsification of this report was a grounds for discharge?
3. What is the significance of the fact that the Union did not argue that the grievant had overlooked the back injury question on the Physical Examination Record?

CASE 27
Sleeping on the Job as a Basis for Discharge

Company: Rockwell-Standard Corporation, Transmission and Axle Division
          Kenton, Ohio
Union: Allied Industrial Workers
          Local 109
Arbitrator: Edwin R. Teple

Under what conditions is sleeping on the job grounds for discharge? The following discussion of the issue and facts in this case was prepared by Edwin R. Teple, the arbitrator.

THE ISSUE

The only question in this case is whether the Company's action discharging the grievant, E—— C——, for sleeping on the job was for just cause as required by the terms of Article IV, Section 1, of the collective bargaining agreement between these parties.

THE CIRCUMSTANCES

The grievant had been employed by the Company for a period of 13½ years, first as a machine operator for about 1½ years and 12 years as an inspector. His work record was without blemish, the grievant having had no warnings or prior penalties of any kind. On August 17, 1962, however, he was found sleeping on the job and was discharged immediately. Thereafter, under date of August 20, 1962, the following grievance report was filed by the Union Committee.

We the bargaining committee believe the penalty imposed on Mr. E—— C—— to be much too strong. We are requesting the plant mgr. to reconsider and restore Mr. C—— to working status. On the basis of his 13 years of service with no previous record of disciplinary action of a serious nature.

The parties stipulated that the grievant was found asleep at approximately 5:30 A.M. on the third shift (11:30 P.M to 7:30 A.M.) on the day in question. It was also agreed that he was found in a position back in the stock room which amounted to concealment.

According to the grievant, he had his lunch at the usual time between 3:30 and 4 A.M., and then went back to work and made his rounds. He testified that he saw the foreman at approximately 5:10 A.M. over in heat treat, but the foreman did not see the grievant at that time. The grievant testified that he went out to the stockroom at about 5:20 A.M.

The foreman testified that he had heard that the grievant had been doing some sleeping. Several "boys," according to the Company witness, had noticed grievant was away "an awful lot." According to the foreman, a guard had told him that he found the grievant asleep on one previous occasion, but the guard did not testify and apparently no official action was taken. On the night in question, the foreman testified, he needed the grievant in the department, and began looking for him sometime after lunch—he didn't know just what time it was when he started looking. He also said that some of the men started kidding him about hunting for someone sleeping. He finally found an opening back in the stock room and when he crawled up in there he found the grievant.

The testimony of the Union witnesses was concerned largely with the Company's disciplinary policy when other workmen had been found sleeping. According to them, sleeping on the midnight shift was not uncommon, although it developed on cross-examination that most of this occurred during the lunch period. In the case of a cutter-grinder who was found sleeping on the job, it was said, the employee was sent home for the balance of the shift and was given a three-day suspension. This was the most severe penalty previously imposed for this infraction that the Union witnesses could recall.

The Company witnesses testified that sleeping definitely was not condoned and was considered a serious infraction. It was admitted, however, that there was no posted rule on the subject and no prescribed penalty.

In the case of the cutter-grinder, his foreman testified that when he found the employee he was already up but he had a pillow and it clearly appeared that he had been sleeping. On the basis of the circumstantial evidence, he was given an "abnormal" for sleeping. In the Company's vernacular, an "abnormal" is a written warning or other penalty for some infraction which the Company feels should warrant discipline. As this witness recalled, he was given a week off without pay.

The same foreman testified that he had issued "abnormals" to another employee for sleeping. He did not know, however, if the employee's eventual discharge was for this or some other reason. This particular employee was issued two abnormal reports for too much time off in 1951. In 1953 he was discharged for his third abnormal, which was issued when he was found sleeping.

Another employee, working in quality control, was discharged early in 1959 for failure to report for work. This man was subsequently reinstated under a special agreement between the parties and placed on probation for two years, subject to immediate discharge for any major violation of factory rules or practices. Thereafter, he was discharged in October, 1960, for sleeping on the job.

The grievant admitted that he could have asked for a pass-out to go home if he got sleepy on the job. On the date of the incident in question, he testified that he had a headache and his back had been bothering him. He said he had been working in the drum department and had been doing quite a bit of heavy lifting. However, he lives 15 miles from the plant and was riding with someone else on August 17 so did not consider requesting a pass-out.

COMPANY'S POSITION

The Company takes the position that just cause has been admitted by the Union and that the grievance amounts merely to a plea for clemency. According to the Company, it is a generally accepted rule that once just cause has been established the arbitrator should not substitute his judgment for that of management. Arbitrators have universally held, the Company maintains, that discharge is an appropriate penalty for sleeping on the job.

UNION'S POSITION

The Union contends that in previous cases of discharge at this plant the employees had poor work records of one kind or another. The Union also claims that in these other cases the employees were put back to work pursuant to special agreements between the Company and the Union. In contrast, the Union points out, the grievant had a good prior work record. The Company had no fixed rule, it is said, for the penalty to be imposed for sleeping on the job.

The Union contends that in this case it is simply seeking equal justice for the grievant and on this basis requests reinstatement of the grievant without back pay, and loss of one year's seniority.

QUESTIONS

1. Sleeping on the job is a serious offense. However, arbitration awards have been widely divided on: (*a*) proof of sleeping, (*b*) the consequences and causes of sleeping, and (*c*) proper penalties. In this case, what were the consequences of E—— C——'s sleeping? What is the significance of the fact that E—— C—— was asleep in a concealed place?
2. What weight should be given to the fact that E—— C——'s 13½ year employment record is without blemish?

3. What is the disciplinary policy of Rockwell-Standard in regard to sleeping on the job?
4. How would you rule in this case?

CASE 28
Creating a Disturbance as a Basis for Discharge

Company: F. H. Lawson Company
           Cincinnati, Ohio
Union: International Association of Machinists
           District 34, Local Lodge 1089
Arbitrator: Samuel S. Kates

When two employees are engaged in a fight, or "horseplay," should the disciplinary penalty be the same for both?

The following discussion of the issue and facts in this case was prepared by Samuel S. Kates, the arbitrator.

ISSUE

As stipulated by the parties at the arbitration hearing, the issue to be determined is whether the grievant under Grievance No. 278 was discharged for just cause on October 5, 1964, and if not, what remedy should be awarded.

The grievant was hired in November 1959, and was discharged October 5, 1964. The Company's termination sheet states that he was "dismissed" for "creating a disturbance." A second man (hereinafter called Jerry) who was dismissed at the same time as the grievant in connection with the same incident is shown in the latter's termination sheet as having been dismissed for "fighting."

Each of these dismissed employees filed grievances in connection with such dismissal, but Jerry's grievance was not carried to arbitration and his dismissal now stands unchallenged. The grievant's challenge to his dismissal for "creating a disturbance" is the one involved in the present arbitration.

The incident directly resulting in both dismissals and the events leading to it are shown by the evidence to have been substantially as follows:

Several weeks before October 5, 1964, the grievant borrowed from Jerry a pair of tinsnips owned by Jerry, worth about $6 when new, for use in connection with the grievant's work in the plant. That same day they were missed by the grievant after he had been away from his work station for a short time. He promised Jerry that he would get him another pair.

The grievant, who had a second job in an automobile service station immediately after ending each day's work for the Company, found it inconvenient to shop for another pair of tinsnips. When urged by Jerry to buy them, the grievant became annoyed, told Jerry he was "getting too smart," and raised a doubt as to whether he would actually replace the tinsnips. Jerry reported this to his own supervisor. That supervisor reported it to the grievant's supervisor, who talked with the grievant about it. Thereafter, the grievant's supervisor reported the matter to the personnel director, after additional time had passed without replacement of the tinsnips.

The personnel director talked with the grievant about this, who asked whether he was being ordered by the Company to replace the tinsnips. The personnel director told the grievant that he was not being ordered to replace the tinsnips, but that the matter ought to be resolved. In the meantime, in an atmosphere of oral horseplay, apparently continuously prevalent in the area where the grievant was working, others in the area were teasing both Jerry and the grievant about the matter, seeking to arouse each against the other.

In any event, the grievant did buy another pair of tinsnips during the week end preceding October 5, and brought them to the plant on the 5th. That same morning the grievant sent word to Jerry through another employee that he had brought the replacement tinsnips to the plant and would give them to Jerry after the end of the shift at 3:30 that day.

At about 2 o'clock, Jerry was returning from the washroom near the grievant's work station. The grievant called him over, and in effect said that he had bought a pair of tinsnips but because Jerry had been "too smart" he wasn't sure he would give them to him. This, coupled with teasing remarks and laughter by others working nearby, resulted in heated words between Jerry and the grievant. Without adequate provocation, Jerry struck the grievant with his fist. The grievant thereupon reached for the tinsnips. Jerry pulled a knife from his pocket, opened it, and through the threat of the knife forced the grievant to drop the tinsnips. Jerry turned to leave. The grievant reached to pick up the tinsnips. Others nearby shouted to Jerry that the grievant was reaching for the tinsnips. Jerry promptly turned and kicked the grievant while he was reaching for the tinsnips. Jerry then left.

The evidence did not show that the grievant at any time struck Jerry, or that he did more than undertake to defend himself.

The grievant promptly reported the incident to the Company's executive vice president. Both men were dismissed shortly thereafter on the same day.

The next day, the Company's senior vice president of manufacturing made an investigation of the matter. On the basis of this investigation he affirmed the discharges. In this investigation he learned of incidents involving the grievant of which he had no prior knowledge, but most of which had been known to his subordinates in supervision, as mentioned below.

The grievant's personnel file disclosed only three writings involving any alleged previous breaches of duty by the grievant, one in December 1961, asking the grievant to "please be more careful' about ringing out his time card; the second in September, 1962, warning the grievant of his "slipshod method of ringing in and out" and indicating that he would "on the next occasion be reprimanded, plus a layoff of two or three days to jog your memory," and the third showing that the grievant had been transferred from his towmotor job in June, 1963, because of carelessness and property damage. No disciplinary suspension was ever imposed against the grievant.

The evidence indicates that previously, in the course of the grievant's employment, he had at various times been guilty of idling and spending excessive working time in talking with other employees, but apparently no special point of this was made to him by management at any of these times; he had said to a certain supervisor of another department who had criticized him, "You can't talk that way to me," and had been called to the office about it but nothing was done there beyond a general discussion; he had at times argued with other employees—but oral spats among employees in this plant were not uncommon and no special point of this was made by management; he had boasted of his fighting abilities—but there was no evidence of any actual fighting by him in the plant or relating to his work (except the shaking incident mentioned below); he would at times playfully punch others in the plant on the arm or shoulder, but no special point of this was made to him by management; at times he was such a good worker that he was complimented by supervision, while at other times his work was not good; he was absent for illness, but the frequency of these absences or how they compared with the absences of other employees was not shown.

Within a couple of months before the October 5 discharge, the grievant had told a woman employee to kiss his a——when she upbraided him for not bringing her enough material of the proper kind. She also saw him shaking an older man who had inadvertently removed the grievant's coffee from a truck which such older man had to move. These incidents were reported to management by this woman, but nothing was said to the grievant by management about them, and no reprimand or warning was given him and no discipline was imposed.

There was also some secondary hearsay testimony about the grievant having pushed a truck out of his way in anger and bumping another employee. This was apparently not known to management until after the grievant's discharge.

Evidence was also presented, which was received conditionally, over objection, that the grievant had been court-martialed while in the military service some years before for being absent from duty without leave (AWOL); that in the summer of 1963 he had been convicted of assault and battery in connection with an altercation originating outside a bar-room after working hours, and that he had been sentenced to pay court costs and to serve five days, with the days suspended; that he had a military service-connected disability involving a back ailment and related nervous condition for which he had been awarded a 10 percent disability allowance by the government; that his wife, in connection with her own nervous breakdown, had had the grievant committed to a hospital for examination for 30 days for an alleged nervous condition, although he was released within 11 days. The Company did nothing by way of complaint, reprimand, warning, or attempted discipline about these matters.

The Company sought to show certain other occurrences outside the plant involving the grievant, which I held and still hold to be irrelevant to the present case.

The Company sought to suggest, at least by inference, that the grievant was subject to a persecution complex and to delusions of being spied upon, but in my opinion the evidence failed to support these suggestions. The evidence showed that the grievant had been examined by VA doctors in January 1964, without any finding of mental, emotional, or physical disability, and that after his dismissal from his job the grievant sought another examination because of comments as to his emotional state made by a Company official, but was unable to have it made before the date of the arbitration hearing.

The grievant had been a Union official before his discharge but was so no longer at that time.

A company booklet pertaining to employee conduct was received in evidence. This booklet refers to the Company's more than 140 years of continuous existence, and specifies close to 50 different offenses for which warning or punishment might be expected. In one place the booklet states as follows:

Listed here are the actions or types of conduct which we consider undesirable and for which the employee will be dismissed without warning. In general, these cover practices involving—dishonesty, insubordination, destructiveness, carelessness, creating a disturbance, or contributing to improper working atmosphere.

Then follow a list of 23 offenses which are included within the above-quoted general statement, including among these specific offenses: "Fighting or wrestling in the plant."

There is no evidence to show whether the Union had or had not agreed to the enforceability of these rules of conduct and the indicated penalties as written.

The booklet goes on to state that:

Certain other objectionable actions or tendencies will result in a verbal or written warning for the first offense, a reprimand including restriction of privileges and/or layoff for a second offense, and dismissal without further warning for any additional violation.

Among these "other objectionable actions or tendencies" are "tardiness, poor attendance, horseplay . . . carelessness . . . inefficiency, inability to to do the work . . . violating any established procedure."

Except for very serious first offenses in themselves warranting dismissal the Company has subscribed to the principle of progressive corrective discipline.

QUESTIONS

1. What weight should be given to the company booklet in view of the fact that there were no negotiated rules?
2. The arbitrator received conditionally, over objection, evidence on the grievant's court-martial, marital relationship, and off-duty personal conduct. What weight should be given to such evidence in a ruling?
3. What is progressive corrective discipline? Does the Company practice of this principle have an influence on this case?
4. Fighting on the job is considered to be a most grave offense. Was the grievant guilty of this or of provoking this "fight"?

CASE 29
Authority of Union Committee to Make Final Disposition of a Grievance

Company: Marathon Millwork Corporation
Union: Midwestern Millmen District Council
       Local Union 1451
Arbitrator: Robert J. Mueller

This case involves the right of a grievance committee to make a final disposition of a grievance and the right of a grievant to due process.

The following discussion of the issue and facts involved in the case was prepared by Robert J. Mueller, the arbitrator.

The Marathon Millwork Corporation is engaged in the business of manufacturing wood and building products in Wausau, Wisconsin. During the course of its business, an employee, who also happened to be the president of the Local Union, was discharged from his employment. Pursuant to the provisions of the collective bargaining agreement existing between them, the employee submitted a grievance to the Employer disputing his discharge. No satisfactory adjustment was made in step one, and the grievance was then submitted to the shop committee composed of the vice president of the Union and three stewards. A meeting was held between said shop committee and the Employer, at which time the shop committee signed the following document:

Oct. 22, 1960

As members of the Union Shop Committee, we as individual members unanimously agreed that the Company was justified in its action by discharging Leonard Habeck on October 10, 1960.

Marvin Roepke
Theodore J. Blue
Laurence Van Densen
Courtney Hoyt

Upon being advised of this action, the grievant took up the matter with the business representative of the Union, Mr. Robert Warosh. Warosh contacted the Employer and attempted to resolve the matter and upon being unable to do so, requested the Wisconsin Employment Relations Board to appoint an arbitrator to determine the dispute, the Employer concurring therein. On November 8, 1960, the Board appointed the undersigned as arbitrator. A hearing was held in Wausau, Wisconsin, on December 8, 1960, wherein the parties, including the grievant, were given full opportunity to offer oral and written evidence, and to make such arguments as they deemed pertinent.

EMPLOYER'S POSITION

At the outset of the hearing, the Employer contended that the only issue before the arbitrator was the question of the procedural finality of the settlement between the shop committee and the Employer. The Employer asserted that the merits of the discharge were not arbitrable on the basis that the grievance had been disposed of in a final and binding manner pursuant to the second step of the contract.

UNION'S POSITION

The Union contended that the grievant was deprived of his rights of due process inasmuch as he was not present at the final disposition of his case, nor was he consulted by the shop committee at any time during the meeting of step two and the rendering of the decision.

ISSUE

Does the agreed settlement between the Employer and the Union shop committee, which was executed in writing, constitute a final disposition of the grievance of Lenard Habeck?

PERTINENT CONTRACT PROVISIONS

Article XII—Grievances
A. The Union may as it desires select one (1) Shop Steward and a Shop Committee from its members working in the Plant. There is, however, to be no

Union activity of any kind on Company time or on Company property except that a representative of the Union shall be privileged to confer with the steward in the office during working hours at reasonable times, but must first apply to the office. There shall be no responsibility on the part of the Company to compensate the steward or shop committee for conferences or meetings unless such conferences or meetings are requested by the Company.

B. Both the Company and the Union shall have the right to submit grievances which shall be submitted to the other party in writing within one (1) week after the cause of the grievance first arose. If no satisfactory adjustment is made within (1) working day, the Shop Committee shall take up the matter with the Company and if no adjustment is made within one (1) working day, a Union Representative shall take up the matter with the Company within two (2) working days thereafter. Should such representative and Company still be unable to agree, the matter may be referred to Arbitration in the following manner.

DISCUSSION

The Union contends that Habeck was deprived of his due process when he was not present at the disposition of his grievance. The Employer on the other hand asserts that he was afforded due process in accordance with the terms of the collective bargaining agreement.

QUESTIONS

1. Under what authority did Mr. Warosh intervene?
2. Why did the employer agree to arbitration on this case?

CASE 30
Job Changes and Superseniority for Stewards

Company: Duro Company
              Dayton, Ohio
Union: United Automobile Workers
              Local Union No. 888
Arbitrator: Walter G. Seinsheimer

This case involves the impact of a substantial change in business on superseniority for stewards.

The following discussion of the issue and facts in the case was prepared by Walter G. Seinsheimer, the arbitrator.

The grievance is:

Failure on the Company's behalf to recognize Committeeman's top seniority rights as stated in the Agreement.[1]

Remedy requested was:

---

[1] It was indicated on the grievance form that "This is a Policy Grievance."

Give the Committeeman top seniority rights due him, and also pay Committeeman all money lost while waiting for these rights to be established.

Foreman's answer:

The Company laid off according to the Seniority provisions of Article VII. Regular members of the shop committee head the seniority list in their own department and areas. The departments with which these two committeemen are concerned are being discontinued, as explained to the committee and the International Representative, in our meeting of 1/12/62.

PERTINENT CONTRACT PROVISIONS

The Union claimed in the grievance that Article VII, Section 2, and Article IV, Section 1, had been violated; these, and others cited during the hearing, are as follows:

Article VII, Section 2:
Regular members of the Shop Committee shall head the seniority lists in their own department and areas as provided in the Representation Section of this Agreement during their term of office and shall revert to their regular places on the seniority lists at the end of their services in such capacity.

Article VII, Section 4: Lay-off and Rehire Procedures:
For extended periods of lay-off the work force will be reduced according to the following procedure:

(a) For the purpose of applying this procedure the work force has been divided into Job Classification Groups according to the Flow Chart, Appendix B.

(b) When a lay-off is scheduled the Chairman of the Shop Committee will be advised so that the seniority list can be examined and the rights of any employees affected can be explained.

(c) When there are employees in the Job Classification Group affected who will remain after the lay-off and who are capable of performing the jobs which remain, the employees with the least seniority will be laid off first from that Job Classification Group. When an employee or employees are displaced from a Job Classification Group by reason of seniority, they will move into the next Job Classification Group according to the Flow Chart. They will be assigned jobs in that Job Classification Group, which they are qualified to perform, if such jobs are held by employees of lesser seniority. When these changes are made, the employee or employees with the least seniority will move into the next Job Classification Group according to the Flow Chart, where the same procedure will be followed. Capable of performing the job shall mean, for the purpose of this Article, that the employee possesses the physical and mental ability to perform the job in a workmanlike manner. If there is a disagreement as to whether an employee is capable of performing the job, the matter will be discussed between the Company and the Shop Committee. Factors to be considered will include the nature of the work to be done, whether or not the particular employee has had satisfactory experience on that job or a similar job and whether or not any special skills or knowledge not readily acquired are necessary for proper performance of the job. If the

Company and the Shop Committee agree, the affected employee may be given a trial period on the job. If the matter cannot be satisfactorily settled in this manner it may be submitted through the grievance procedure.

(d) An employee displaced from Group 5 will be allowed to exercise his seniority in any other Job Classification Group (except Groups 1 and 2) displacing an employee in that Job Classification Group with lesser seniority provided he is capable of performing the job and has demonstrated that capability either at The Duro Co. or with some other company. An employee will not be allowed to exercise his seniority from any Job Classification Group into Groups 1 or 2 unless he has had prior satisfactory experience on that job with the Company.

Article VII, Section 8:

The Chairmen of the Shop Committee will be given notice of all lay-offs at or before the time such notice is given to the employee, so that the Chairman of the Shop Committee will be able to check the seniority lists as to the employee affected.

Article VII, Section 9:

When deemed by it necessary, the Company shall have the right to retain or recall any employee, irrespective of seniority, who by reason of special knowledge, training or skill, has special value to the Company. The Company agrees not to abuse this right, and further agrees to explain fully to the Shop Committee the reasons for exercising this right.

Article IV, Union Representation:

Section 1. The employees of the bargaining unit shall be represented by Shop Committee of not more than 3 regular members, to be elected in any manner determined by the Union. All members of the Shop Committee must be employed by the Company. The Union shall elect three alternate members to the Shop Committee but only when a regular member of the Shop Committee is not at work shall his alternate be recognized by the Company. The Union will give written notice to the Company showing the names and terms of office of the three regular members of the Shop Committee, and also the three alternate members.

Section 2. The Company agrees to recognize all committeemen designated by the Union, for the purpose of discussing and adjusting grievances. The Union will notify the Company in writing of any changes made in the committeemen.

Section 3. For the purposes of the grievance procedure hereinafter provided, the bargaining unit will be divided into three areas as follows:

AREA I. Machine Shop, Tool Room, and Sub Assembly.

AREA II. Assembly Department, Shipping Department, Stock and Material Handling, and Service Department.

AREA III. Tank Shop, Inspection, Janitors and Maintenance.

The Union will designate and furnish the Company in writing the name of one regular member and one alternate member of the Shop Committee to represent the Union as to each of the three areas. The Union shall also designate one of the members of the Shop Committee to act as Chairman.

Section 4. The Company shall negotiate with the Shop Committee as representatives of the Bargaining Unit, and will discuss and attempt to adjust all grievances with this Committee.

BACKGROUND AND POSITION OF THE PARTIES

The situation arose out of the fact that the Company substantially reduced its scope and volume of operations. Late in the year of 1961 the Company disposed of its domestic water pump, tank and hot dip galvanizing operations and moved from a three-story building with 90,000 square feet to a one-floor building with slightly over 13,000 square feet. It reduced its work force from 60 to 65 employees, to 6 employees.

Prior to the contraction, the operations were divided up as indicated in Section 3 of Article IV above, with:

AREA I. Including the Machine Shop, Tool Room, and Sub Assembly.
AREA II. Assembly Department, Shipping Department, Stock and Material Handling, and Service Department.
AREA III. Tank Shop, Inspection, Janitors and Maintenance.

As provided in this section, a committeeman was assigned to represent the Union in each of these three areas.

According to the Company, all the former operations were discontinued except for assembly of water softening and filtering equipment, plus certain other auxiliary operations, such as final inspection, clean up, and maintenance. This last was mostly involved with the moving from the large building to the smaller, and according to management, would probably also be eliminated in the very near future.

Since the biggest bulk of the work fell in the assembly category, the Company decided that the top seniority of Dewey Watkin, committeeman for Area II, should be recognized, and he was retained. Further, the Company reasoned that the contract Article VII, Section 2, provides that a committeeman head the list only in his own department, and since these other departments to all intent and purpose were eliminated, jobs as well as physical area, then no superseniority could be considered for Roll and Bilbey, who were committeemen for Areas I and III.

The Company maintained that the reason for superseniority for committeemen "was to insure that so long as there were employees in the particular departments and areas, there would be a committeeman available to represent them." With the elimination of the departments as well as jobs, and the reduction of large areas on multiple floors to a simple one-floor setup with six persons, the reasons for the superseniority for more than one committeeman no longer existed. Furthermore, it was pointed out that it "would be an injustice to two other employees with much greater seniority who would have to be displaced."

Believing that it had handled the matter in the proper way with a reasonable interpretation of the literal language of the contract, and consistent with the whole seniority principle, the Company concluded its arguments by pointing out that when the parties signed the contract earlier in the year there was no contemplation of the tremendous change, and that the agreement was made for an entirely different setup than what is now in existence; that the employees when they ratified the contract with superseniority for their committeemen did not intend to abandon "their seniority status to provide jobs for committeemen, when there was no useful purpose to be served."

The Union maintained that some work that had been done in all three areas was still being performed, such as subassembly from Area I and inspection, which was included in Area III. This, added to the fact that the contract makes no mention of plant size or number of persons to be represented by committeemen, indicates all three committeemen should have been retained.

It was pointed out that the parties in this situation were not dealing with "what is morally right, only with what the Contract says."

The Union stated that it understood there were mitigating circumstances that caused management to do what it did; it also pointed out that the Company could have discussed the matter with the representatives and that probably an agreement could have been reached that would have alleviated the situation. However, it was claimed that the Company did not see fit to do this, and the Union feels duty bound to insist that management abide by the contract, even though the Union finds it distasteful to displace persons with much longer service than the committeemen.

During the hearing the parties indicated that they were negotiating a new contract and in its post-hearing brief the Union called attention to the changes in the representation section of the agreement, a copy of which was sent to me. It was also pointed out by the Union that during the hearing they indicated they "would have been agreeable to modifying the Representation Section of the Agreement when Management reduced the employment, but Management indicated no desire to do so and simply stated that under the terms of the Agreement they were right, and that the Union should pursue the issue to arbitration.

The Union concluded its arguments by stating that the representation section of the old contract clearly calls for superseniority for committeemen, and that there is no alternative but for it to demand that the two committeemen be returned to work and be reimbursed for all time lost.

QUESTIONS

1. What is the purpose of superseniority for stewards? Does superseniority for stewards attach to the person of the steward or to the job of the steward?

2. What intraunion problems develop as a result of this case going to arbitration?

3. If the union finds it "distasteful to displace persons with much longer service than the committeemen," why did the Union take this case to arbitration?

4. How would you rule in this case? Why?

CASE 31
Payment for Stewards' Time on Grievance Processing

Company: Gross Company, A Division of Miehle-Gross-Dexter, Inc.
Union: International Association of Machinists
              District 8
Arbitrator: William H. Pedrick

Did the employer have a right to unilaterally promulgate a rule specifying the maximum amount of time union officers would be compensated for in handling grievances?

The following discussion of the issue and facts in the case was prepared by Willard H. Pedrick, the arbitrator.

ISSUE

Did the Company have authority under the contract to issue a rule limiting the amount of grievance time for shop chairman, co-chairmen, and committeemen to be paid for by the Company?

EXTRACTS FROM THE RULE IN QUESTION

Grievance Time for Goss Employees Representing
The International Association of Machinists,
District #8—Effective July 13, 1964

The following rule defines the maximum amount of grievance time for which the shop Chairman, Co-Chairmen and Committeemen will receive their regular hourly rate of pay from the Goss Company. No payment shall be made by the Goss Company for any grievance time charged by the shop Chairman, Co-Chairmen or Committeemen beyond the limits of this rule.

This rule is instituted to define the limits to which the Goss Company will allow payment for grievance time, and is not to be construed as a rule that sets a limit on the amount of time that the shop Chairman, Co-Chairmen or Committeemen may spend on grievance activity.

For purposes of this rule, grievance time is defined as the time required to investigate and process grievances or other matters arising under the contract and applies only to the time spent in the Goss plant during the regular shift of the shop Chairman, Co-Chairman or Committeeman charging such time.

The shop Chairman will be allowed a maximum of forty (40) hours of paid grievance time per each four week period.

The shop Co-Chairmen will each be allowed a maximum of twenty-four (24) hours of paid grievance time per each four week period.

. . .

The shop Committeemen will each be allowed a maximum of four (4) hours of paid grievance time per each four week period.

Prior to engaging in any grievance activity or any other activity arising under the contract during working hours of their shift, union representatives must notify their foreman and must also notify the foreman of the department to be visited in accordance with the terms of the contract.

The Pertinent Provisions of the Contract:

Article 1—Recognition:

Section D—There shall be no discrimination against any employee because of his acting as an officer or committeeman or any other lawful and proper activities in the interest of the Union.

Article II—Management

Section A—The Management of the plant, and the direction of the working force, including the right to continue and to adopt such rules and regulations and institute such methods as the Company may from time to time deem necessary and proper to carry on its business . . . is vested solely in the Company, provided that any action taken hereunder shall not conflict with any of the express terms of the Agreement.

Article X—Grievances

Section D—No shop Chairman or Committeeman shall leave his job or department for the purpose of handling grievances or for any other purpose under this Agreement without first notifying his foreman. Should the Foreman be unavailable, the Chairman or the Committeeman shall leave a note at the Foreman's desk establishing the location of this visit. Such Shop Chairman or Committeeman also shall notify the Foreman of the Department to be visited by him that the purpose of his visit is to discuss with an employee in said department a matter arising under this Agreement.

Section A—Should any employee or employees believe the Company has violated any of the provisions of this Agreement, he may initiate a grievance which shall be processed in the following order:

1. Between the aggrieved employee or employees together with the Department Committeeman and the Foreman of the department or departments involved; if not settled, then,
2. Between the Shop Committee Chairman, Department Committeeman and the Shop Superintendent; if not settled, then,
3. Between the Shop Committee Chairman, Co-Chairman and the Personnel Director.

SUMMARY STATEMENT OF FACTS

For a very long time, said by the Union to be as long as 50 years, the Company has paid employees without deduction for time spent by the employees as Union representatives in adjusting grievances. The Company agrees that it has for a very long period paid for such "grievance time." Against the background of this settled practice the present contract confirms this practice in its provision in Article X governing the procedure to be followed when a shop chairman or committeeman leaves his duty post "for the purpose of handling grievances" or other "matters arising under this Agreement."

Over a period of several years the Company has kept records, not challenged as to accuracy, on the average hours per week spent on "labor relations time" by shop chairman, co-chairmen and committeemen. These records indicate that whereas an average of 15 to 30 hours per week was charged as "labor relations time" in the period 1959 to 1962 inclusive, in the years 1963 and 1964 the figure jumped to 52 and 79 hours per week respectively. The Company undertook to deal with the matter by the rule in question issued under an effective date of July 13, 1964. Under the prescribed rule the Company announced that it would continue to pay for "grievance time" only within the limits of 10 hours per week for shop chairman, 6 hours per week for co-chairman and 1 hour per week for shop committeemen. Depending on the number of co-chairmen and shop committeemen this time allowance is in line with the 1959–62 experience.

The Company has made no charge of malingering on the part of the chairman and committeemen and apart from the very substantial increase in the over-all amount of time spent on labor relations matters the Company has not charged that any particular amount of time expended was unwarranted. It is fair to say that the Company attitude is one of skepticism as to whether the grievance work really required the expenditure of time in fact charged to that activity.

There has been a modest increase in the number of employees in the plant with 918 in 1958, a drop to 786 and 880 in 1959 and 1960 respectively, with increases since that date bringing the number to 1,072 for 1964. There is some evidence that in the past two years the Company has been endeavoring to regularize its procedures with employees, or as it is sometimes said, "To go by the book," with the generation of some friction in the process.

Prior to the issuance of the rule of July 13, 1964, the Company did not consult with the Union and in fact the rule was issued unilaterally by the Company on its own authority.

Since the promulgation of the rule of July 13, 1964, there has been no instance of an employee's actually suffering a wage deduction on account of time spent on grievance matters beyond that specified by the rule.

THE UNION'S CONTENTIONS

The Union contends that the Company has no authority unilaterally to prescribe a limit for the "labor relations time" to be paid for by the Company in the face of an established practice of many years' duration of paying for all "labor relations time."

THE COMPANY'S CONTENTIONS

The Company contends that it has authority to correct abuses in expenditure of excessive time on labor relations matters by employees serving as chairman and co-chairman. The Company further contends that the established practice of payment for "labor relations time" relates to a period during which the amounts of such time were reasonable and that the rule issued by the Company really returns to the settled practice. The Company's position is that the rule in question was within the authority of the Company as a reasonable measure intended to restore the former practice and accordingly was not a matter requiring negotiation or evidencing any anti-Union discrimination.

QUESTIONS

1. "Labor relations time" can be an expensive item. How could the Company bring it under control?
2. What is the significance of past practice in this case?
3. How would you rule in this case? Why?

CASE 32
Union Representation during Overtime Work

Company: Lionel Pacific, Inc.
Union: International Association of Machinists
             Aeronautical Lodge 720
Arbitrator: Thomas T. Roberts

Under a clause providing for union representation during overtime work, what is the responsibility of the Union to assure that a committee-man is available for such work?

The following discussion of the issue and facts in this case was prepared by Thomas T. Roberts, the arbitrator.

ISSUES

A hearing in this matter was conducted on October 15, 1964, in the offices of the Company located at Gardena, California. At the time of the hearing, the parties orally stipulated to the following statement of the issues herein submitted:

1. Did the Company violate Article XV, Section 5 of the existing Company-Union agreement on August 26, 1964?
2. If so, what is the appropriate remedy, if any?

STATEMENT OF FACTS

This grievance arose under, and is controlled by, the agreement between the parties effective from Novmber 11, 1963, through November 10, 1964.

The Company is engaged primarily as a subcontractor to the aerospace industry. The Union is the exclusive collective bargaining representative for production, maintenance, shipping and receiving employees, and truck drivers at its Gardena, California, facility.

The instant dispute involves two hours of overtime worked beyond the 3:30 P.M. termination of the day shift on August 26, 1964. It was originally agreed that three employees were then designated as "chairmen" for the purpose of in-plant Union representation and that none worked beyond the end of the shift, so that no such representation was available during the period from 3:30 P.M. to 5:30 P.M. Later, the Company asserted, one of the employees who did work overtime was also a duly appointed chairman.

At approximately 2:10 P.M. on the day in question, Mr. John Wilson, a chairman, was asked if the job to which he was then assigned could be finished that day on an overtime basis. He replied that it could. Sometime later in the afternoon, a decision was made to retain 19 bargaining unit employees to work a total of two hours beyond the end of the shift.

At 3:25 P.M., Mr. Wilson was asked to work the indicated overtime. He declined because of prior personal commitments. No effort was then made to contact the remaining chairmen in order to offer them an opportunity to work the overtime.

On August 28, 1964, a grievance was filed by the Union on behalf of X——, one of the chairmen on the day shift, which alleges that the Company violated the agreement by not arranging for the presence of a chairman during the overtime hours worked on August 26, 1964. The grievance (which asks that X—— be paid as though he had so worked) was denied by the Company and the matter has ultimately come to arbitration.

CONTROLLING CONTRACT PROVISIONS

Article XV. Overtime
5. In the event scheduled overtime requires ten (10) employees or more, a Chairman or Chairmen will be part of the overtime work force.

POSITION OF THE UNION

It is the position of the Union that the failure of the Company to solicit all three chairmen for the overtime work in question was a violation of the agreement between the parties.

The Union argues Article XV, Section 5, requires the Company to arrange for the presence of a chairman when 10 or more employees work overtime and that obligation is excused only in a situation where all of the duly appointed chairmen decline such work.

In conclusion, the Union asks that the grievant, Chairman X——, be awarded two hours of overtime wages to compensate for his not having been asked to so work on August 26, 1964.

POSITION OF THE COMPANY

It is the position of the Company that it fully complied with its commitment under Article XV, Section 5, when Chairman Wilson was offered and declined the opportunity to work overtime.

The Company states that after the processing of the instant grievance, but prior to arbitration, it discovered that Roger Spradlin worked the overtime here in dispute and, further, that he was a duly appointed chairman on August 26, 1964.

The Company argues that it was the responsibility of Mr. Wilson, as a chairman, to work the overtime when he was asked to do so and the Union is therefore estopped from requesting that the grievant be paid for hours not worked.

Finally, the Company contends that when Mr. Wilson, at 3:25 P.M., was asked and declined to work overtime, sufficient time did not remain before the end of the shift to seek out the remaining chairmen in order to ascertain whether or not they would be available for such work.

Under the agreement, "all overtime is understood to be on a voluntary basis."

QUESTIONS

1. To what extent is the Union responsible for providing a chairman to work overtime under Article XV, Section 5?
2. Did the presence of Roger Spradlin on August 26 overtime fulfill the obligation of the agreement?
3. How much time did the Company have to arrange for the presence of a chairman? Did it use this time wisely? If all chairmen had refused overtime could the Company schedule overtime on August 26?

CASE 33
Sex Discrimination in a Layoff

Company: International Paper Company, Southern Craft Division
           (Springhill, La.)
Union: United Papermakers and Paper Workers
           Local 398
Arbitrator: Ralph Roger Williams

Under a contract providing that no opportunity could be closed to any employee because of sex, was the company justified in laying off five senior female employees rather than five male employees with less seniority when the jobs in question required physical ability and "muscle power?"

The following discussion of the issue and facts in this case was prepared by Ralph Roger Williams, the arbitrator.

This case requires an interpretation of the antidiscrimination clause of the Agreement, on the basis of sex. It involves the layoff of five female grievants who were senior to five male employees who were retained. All the employees involved worked in the Company's Finishing Department, but regularly performed different jobs. While the five grievants and the five junior male employees all performed base-rated jobs, they did not regularly perform the same jobs. The issue may be stated to be:

"Did the Company violate the Agreement, and Section V(C) thereof, by laying off senior female employees and retaining junior male employees in base-rated jobs?"

"Base-rated jobs" are jobs for which no lines of progression are established.

The hearing was duly held at Springhill, Louisiana, on October 21, 1966, and the parties filed post-hearing briefs with the arbitrator on November 30, 1966.

The grievants are five female employees classified as "Finishing Room Girls," their names and Company seniority dates being:

Ruth Thomas—July 8, 1953
Dorothy Dennis—August 6, 1951
Vera Riggs—July 13, 1948
Hettie Dean—August 8, 1947
Modie Crye—October 23, 1946.

On September 27, 1965 (the date here involved), all the above-named grievants were working on base-rated jobs. They were laid off for lack of work for a period of more than seven days, and five male employees (all of whom also worked on base-rated jobs) were retained. Each of the retained male employees had less seniority than the least senior of the laid-off female employees.

The Agreement provides:

"The parties signatory to this Agreement shall not discriminate against any Employee because of race, color, sex, religion, or national origin."
(Section V-C)
"Base-rated Employees will be laid off according to Paragraph (E) (6) below."
(Section VI-2 E-2)
"For layoffs of seven days or more, base-rated Employees will be laid off according to Company seniority."
(Section V-E-6)

Prior to 1963, female work in the Finishing Department had always been confined to sorting and counting cut sheets. In 1963, when a grievance was filed on the matter, it was suggested by the Union that the Company try females on three base-rated jobs where they had not previously worked. The Company subsequently made a study to determine whether or not three jobs suggested by the Union (carton filling, carton stitching, and unstacker) could be performed by women. After the study, the Company placed these jobs—as well as the job of "Stenciller"—in the category which it considered women could perform. Women were placed in these jobs, and have performed satisfactorily in them.

Prior to the 1963 grievance and subsequent study, the jobs referred to had traditionally not been considered female jobs, and the parties had apparently recognized that women had been hired to do only counting and sorting.

The Company now contends that its 1963 study revealed that the nature of the other Finishing Room jobs contained required tasks which involved physical demands "that would put an unfair physical burden on women, and even contained physical lifting in tasks that women could not do." It contends that, in assigning women to the additional four jobs in 1963, "the Company proved to the Union that the other jobs could not be performed by women."

During the hearing on the instant grievance, the Company contended that the jobs now being performed by men could not be performed completely by women. Certain jobs were suggested by the Union at the hearing as being within the physical capabilities of women. Job summaries were placed in evidence.

CONTENTIONS

The Union contends the Company violated the Agreement and discriminated against the female grievants because of their sex, by laying them off while retaining junior male employees. It alleges that the Company failed to consider each female employee based on her ability and capacity to perform a specific job, with respect to layoffs and promotions, and contends the Company only considers its female employees as a group rather than as individuals.

The Company contends that the female grievants were laid off because there were no jobs which they could physically perform, and that therefore they were not discriminated against because of their sex. It contends the grievants were denied the assignments because of their lack of qualifications, and that physical ability to perform all aspects of a job falls within the category of qualifications. It also contends that no requirements were added to the existing jobs. The Company contends that Section VI(E)6, (a) of the Agreement must be interpreted within the conditions that exist in a specific case and under the actual circumstances, and that the judgment which the Company made was fair, reasonable, and based upon sufficient data and job information, and that the Agreement was not violated.

QUESTIONS

1. Title VII, Section 703, of the 1963 Civil Rights Act contains an exception allowing the limitation of equal employment opportunities on the basis of sex, when sex is a bona-fide qualification reasonably necessary to the normal operation of the business. Although the company did not cite this law to justify its position, would its provisions apply in this case?
2. When the company opened four base-rated jobs to women in 1963 that were previously performed by men, and the union accepted the changes, did this exclude women from other base-rated jobs that had not been opened up?
3. Who is to determine whether a job cannot be performed by a woman? How would such a determination be made?

CASE 34
Discharge for Falsification of Time Records and Insubordination

Company: Boyce Machinery Corporation (Reserve, La.)
Union: United Steelworkers of America,
Local 6841
Arbitrator: Leonard Oppenheim

May a company truck driver take an unauthorized route to his destination and make unauthorized stops on the way? Does such behavior constitute insubordination?

The following discussion of the issues and facts in this case was prepared by Leonard Oppenheim, the arbitrator.

This arbitration involving the discharge of the Grievant is full of the usual contradictions and discrepancies of testimony offered in such cases. The Company's version of the events which led to the discharge is as follows:

Although the Company presented a large number of witnesses, the principal witness was Mr. Billy M. Bishop, the assistant Parts Manager on the date of the discharge. According to Mr. Bishop, the Grievant, who had been assigned to warehouseman-truck driver duties prior to July, 5 1966, was relieved of truck driver duties in December, 1965 because he was not following instructions as to using the most direct route on trips and was taking longer than other drivers on like or similar trips. Because of a scheduling problem, and at the request of the Grievant, on or before July 5, 1966 the Company reassigned the Grievant to his truck driver duties.

The Grievant drove the truck on July 5, 6, 7, 8 and 11. On July 11, Mr. Bishop noticed at about 5:00 P.M. that the Grievant had not returned from a trip to New Orleans, and having learned that the Grievant had again been using the River Road and was taking excessive time to make trips, decided to look for him. Mr. Bishop then asked Mr. Ratcliff, the Parts and Service Sales Manager, who was assigned a Company automobile, to accompany him in his attempt to find the Grievant.

Mr. Bishop and Mr. Ratcliff, with the latter operating the automobile, drove from the Company Plant to the River Road, and turning south on that road, proceeded on toward LaPlace and slightly beyond Reserve, Louisiana, when having failed to locate X— or the truck which he was driving, they agreed to return to the plant. As he was turning and while Mr. Bishop was adjusting the two-way radio, Mr. Ratcliff noticed a truck pass on the River Road with the Grievant at the wheel. As the Company car completed the turn, the truck driven by the Grievant proceeded ahead on the River Road and when the company car passed the New Rhythm Club, Mr. Bishop noticed the company's truck parked behind the club. Mr. Ratcliff then parked in front of the club and since no one was in the truck, Mr. Bishop and Mr. Ratcliff entered the front door of the club. On not discovering the Grievant in the club, the two men started to leave and at that point saw the Grievant driving the truck at a rapid rate toward the plant along the River Road. They then returned to the plant, Mr. Ratcliff driving on away after having left Mr. Bishop out at the front door.

Mr. Bishop, on entering the building, went into an office to make a phone call to his home. The Grievant entered the office and Mr. Bishop and the Grievant walked together to the parts area. The Grievant then asked Mr. Bishop why he was being followed and Mr. Bishop stated that they would talk about it later. The Grievant said that he preferred to speak about it immediately but Mr. Bishop ordered him back to work in the warehouse. The Grievant pulled out his wallet and threw it in front of Mr. Bishop. The wallet had a badge in it and the Grievant stated that he did not want to be followed and that he did not have to drive that truck. The Grievant then went into the warehouse mumbling something. Mr. Bishop testified that he told the Grievant three times to go into the warehouse before he complied and that the Grievant appeared irritated and very angry.

Since it was Company policy that one superior could not on his own discharge an employee, Mr. Bishop telephoned Mr. Conner, the General Manager, and was told to go home and that the matter would be discussed the next day. At 9:00 A.M. the morning of July 12, Mr. Bishop, Mr. White and Mr. Conner met to discuss the incident of the previous day and the Grievant generally. Mr. Skelton, the Grievant's direct supervisor, was called in and the matter was reviewed with him. The decision was then made to discharge the Grievant. Mr. Skelton went into the warehouse and brought the Grievant back with him. Mr. Conner informed the Grievant of the discussion and the decision. The Grievant said nothing and Mr. Conner gave him his pay check and discharge slip. Mr. Conner asked the Grievant if he had anything to say but there was no reply. When he started out the door, the Grievant turned and started to say something, then changed his mind and left. The reasons for discharge given on the separation slip were, "Falsification of time records and insubordination."

Two of the other witnesses who testified on behalf of the Company stated that they overhead Mr. Bishop telling the Grievant to go back to the warehouse after his return from the River Road incident, telling him that he did not wish to discuss the matter, and the Grievant replying that he did not want to be followed. The remainder of the Company witnesses testified as to their knowledge of the direct route rules, that the Grievant took excessive time to make trips, that the Grievant was not a cooperative or eager employee, that he had received a written warning for leaving work without permission to attend a Union meeting, and that an incident wherein he had refused by his actions to pick up an order had been written up and put into his file but not disclosed to the Grievant or the Union.

The sole witness for the Union was the Grievant himself. His version of what took place is as follows:

He was employed on May 28, 1964 as a truck driver for the "hot-shot truck route." However, the proposed system of using a "hot-shot truck route" was never adopted by the Company and the Grievant worked as a warehouseman. At various times he drove a truck but in the latter part of 1965 the Grievant was taken off truck driving and was told to remain in the warehouse. According to the Grievant's testimony, he was never told why he was removed from truck driving although Mr. Benie Jones, the Shipping Clerk in charge of the warehouse, testified to the effect that he had told the Grievant the reasons why this had been done. On July 5, 1965, the Grievant was put back on the truck at his request because he believed he could be of greater service to the Company in that capacity, but again no explanation was offered as to why he had previously been removed from truck driving. He stated that on the day in question he made a delivery to Kenner and then went to the airport to check for a package. After he left the airport he went to the drop off point in New Orleans and then back to the airport. When he reached the lights at LaPlace he turned off to the River Road, but before he did so, he saw Mr. Ratcliff on the Airline Highway at the Conoco Station in an automobile with someone else, who was fooling with the two-way radio. The Grievant then stopped at the New Rhythm Club to get a drink of water, parking the truck behind the club near the kitchen. His mother, who owned the club, came into the kitchen and told him that some men with Boyce emblems were in the bar but he did not see them until he had returned to the plant. Upon returning to the plant, he sought Mr. Bishop and, finding him at the telephone, waited until he came out of the office.

Mr. Bishop started walking and the Grievant walked along with him. Mr. Bishop did not want to talk to him but told him to get back to the warehouse. The Grievant then told Mr. Bishop his part time job as deputy sheriff in Jefferson Parish was being jeopardized by his having been followed, showing him his deputy's badge in his wallet. Since Mr. Bishop did not want to talk to him, he then went into the warehouse. The Grievant also stated that Mr. Bishop told him that anything he said would be held against him. As to the discharge, the Grievant stated that he did not say anything, even though he had had a half-hour legitimate delay on the trip, because the decision had been made and his check and separation slip had been thrown at him. As to the other statements, Grievant testified that he believed he was a willing and cooperative employee and that he did not understand why complaints had been made against him.

After his discharge, the Grievant filed a grievance protesting the discharge and asking that he be reinstated with full pay for all time lost. The parties decided to handle the grievance in the first step and then to by-pass the second step. Not having settled the grievance, the matter was brought to arbitration.

ISSUE

The issue in this arbitration is whether the Grievant was discharged for just cause under the Agreement between the Parties.

DISCUSSION

Since the following provisions of the Agreement between the Parties are pertinent in this Arbitration, they are set forth below:

Article IV. Management

Section 1. The Union recognizes that the Company possesses, except to the extent that they are specifically relinquished or modified by this Agreement, all the rights, powers and privileges or authority that it had prior to the signature of this Agreement. These rights shall include but not be limited to the management of the plant, the direction of the working force, the sole right to hire, discipline, discharge, lay-off, assign, promote and transfer employees within the bargaining unit, and to determine the starting and quitting time and the number of hours to be worked. These rights shall also include but not be limited to the right to fix standards of quality and quantity of work; to transfer men from one shift to another in accordance with seniority; to control the type of work, volume of production and scheduling of operations; to designate the place of work; to limit union activities on company property and on company time; to install new machines and to change methods of operations; to have the exclusive right to contract outside of the bargaining unit for the maintenance and repair of the Company's facilities insofar as such activity does not replace any of the bargaining unit employees of the Company; to contract outside of the bargaining unit for the construction of new facilities: to contract for office and plant services including but not limited to waste disposal services, guard or watchmen services, yard services, timekeeping services, pest control and maintenance and repair of communication equipment services, maintenance of vehicle (Company automobiles and trucks) services and other maintenance and repair of company facilities services and janitorial services provided such contract for janitorial services and maintenance and repair of Company facilities services does not replace any bargaining unit employee in the bargaining unit who performs such services, all of the above subject only to the restrictions and regulations governing the exercise of these rights as are expressly provided in this contract.

Article V. Discipline and Discharge

The Company retains the sole right to discipline and discharge employees for just cause.

Disciplinary Rules

GROUP 1. Commission of the following acts shall constitute just cause for immediate discharge:

1. Dishonesty, such as—but not limited to—stealing from the Company or other employees, falsification of time records, punching time cards of other employees, or furnishing false information for personnel records.

3. Insubordination, including refusal or deliberate failure to perform work assignments or instructions given by supervisors.

In the summary in its Brief (page 21), the Company argues as follows:

1. X— falsified his time records by claiming pay for time not worked;
2. X— was clearly insubordinate in willfully using a route he was ordered not to use;
3. X— was clearly insubordinate in stopping for his own purposes when he knew he was not to do this;
4. X— was insubordinate by not obeying the orders of Mr. Bishop to return to work;
5. X— was insubordinate in the presence of other employees by using and directing loud, unruly and contemptuous language and actions toward Mr. Bishop;
6. The eleven witnesses presented by the Company presented uncontradicted facts concerning all phases of the matter as to X's— violations of standards, and rules of conduct;
7. The testimony of X— is self serving and manifestly full of contradictions, errors, and in most pertinent matters contrary to sworn statements presented by numerous other witnesses and is not to be believed;
8. X's— past record and attitude justified the penalty imposed.

For all the above reasons, the Company contends that the Grievant's discharge was for just cause.

QUESTIONS

1. Does failure to "clock out" while engaged without permission on personal business during working hours constitute falsification of time records?

2. Do the grievant's actions as recounted in the arbitration proceedings constitute insubordination? If not, what would you consider to be insubordination?

3. How would you rule in this case? Why?

CASE 35
Bumping after Layoff when Superseniority Lapsed

Company: Otis Elevator Company, Harrison Works
Union: International Union of Electrical, Radio and Machine Workers, Local 490
Arbitrator: Benjamin C. Roberts.

Does an employee who was forced to change job classifications during layoff have the right to bump a former shop steward with less seniority who was retained during layoff by his superseniority but was subsequently not reelected?

The following discussion of the issues and facts in this case was prepared by Benjamin C. Roberts, the arbitrator.

The proceedings were initiated by Grievance No. 4596 dated January 12, 1966 protesting the Company's failure to reinstate George Russomanno to his former occupational classification of CKA-7 (Checker-Receiving) in the Shipping and Receiving Department as of January 1, 1966 to replace Robert Weingardner whose superseniority as a Steward of the department terminated on December 31, 1965 when he failed to be reelected. The latter had less actual seniority than Russomanno. There had been a reduction of forces in that classification on or about September 13, 1965 when Weingardner was retained over Russomanno who was excessed, based upon his stewardship under Article IV, Section 6 of the contract.

The Company rejected the grievance, claiming that there had been no violation of the collective bargaining agreement and that it had followed the established and accepted practice since the inception of the Union.

ISSUE

The issue as stipulated by the parties was the following:

"Has the Company violated Article IV of the collective bargaining agreement by failing to return George Russomanno to his former job of CKA-7 (Checker-Receiving) in the Shipping and Receiving Department? If so, what shall the remedy be?"

Article IV, Section 1(a) provides, ". . . that when making layoffs and when rehiring seniority shall govern." Article IV, Section 6(a) provides that "Notwithstanding the other provisions of this Article, the Stewards shall, among the employees in the department, be the last to be laid off and the first to be rehired, provided they have the ability to handle the work . . ."

The layoff procedure is implemented by the Seniority Agreement attached as Exhibit "B" to the collective bargaining agreement. It provides, in pertinent part, as follows.

Exhibit B

1. If there are no realistic objections, when it is necessary to lay off personnel the following procedure shall be observed:

A. The employee with the least seniority in the occupational classification where the lay off is to occur shall be removed from that classification.

. . .

It then proceeds to detail the multiple step procedure to be followed by excessed personnel, including bumping options, both laterally and vertically. Russomanno, upon his removal from classification CKA-7 selected to bump into classification WEE-7 (Welder-Spot), and when he did not qualify in two (2) weeks, he chose the classification COR-8 (Crane Operator-Receiving). Although there has been no permanent opening in classification CKA-7 from September 13, 1965, Russomanno has been assigned to it temporarily from time to time at the rate of pay of the classification.

Appendix "B" of the contract grants severance pay upon permanent layoff, as defined. It provides in Section 4 that upon acceptance of a lump sum payment, employment is terminated and recall rights are surrendered. However, for those receiving weekly payments, the recall rights are retained in accordance with the collective bargaining agreement.

ARGUMENT BY THE UNION

The Union argued that the superseniority right of the Shop Steward as against those of rank and file members occasionally was an intra-Union matter and of little consequence to the interest of management; that its purpose was to insure Union representation within the area served even though a reduction in forces might otherwise result in his leaving; that it followed that upon expiration of the Union official's term of office, his superseniority terminated simultaneously and the seniority of older members came into play. It maintained that otherwise, the older members would be deprived of this most valued privilege without any reason other than some slight inconvenience to the Company.

In response to the Company's assertion that to restore Russomanno and others similarly situated to their former jobs would involve a certain amount of clerical work, the Union pointed out that the Company was unable to say how this would differ either in kind or degree from that in any reduction in force.

The holding of the arbitrator in the matter of Rockwell Spring and

Axle Co. (25 LA 175; 1965) was cited as applicable. It reinstated an employee displaced by superseniority under a finding that the superseniority provision had to be construed in conformity with its limited and special purposes, and that the privileges and rights it conferred were temporary and ceased with the term of the office, while seniority was a continuing thing. The Union concluded that the instant grievance should be granted upon general seniority and labor relations principles and in the light of the language and practices under the present collective bargaining agreement.

ARGUMENT BY THE COMPANY

The Company noted that concededly when the Grievant was bumped from his classification CKA-7 job there was no violation of the contract, and argued that none occurred in January 1966 when Weingardner lost his Steward's badge and the Company did not automatically remove him from the classification when he became subject to removal from his classification just as any other least senior man; that under the contract the removal of employees from their classifications occurred only when the Company laid off or discharged an employee or a position was otherwise opened by Company action; that the Union would automatically create an opening upon a loss of a Union election and which had no basis in the contract.

The Company maintained that Exhibit "B" implementing Article IV, Section 1 established that the least senior man in the classification could only be removed upon a surplus or layoff in the classification or by being displaced by a surplused employee of greater seniority due to the operation of the bumping procedure; that under Article IV, Section 1(a), and under Exhibit "B", Sections 4 and 6 there were "recall rights" upon an opening in a higher classification previously worked by an employee displaced from a lower classification; that Exhibit "B" presupposed the displacement of an employee who seeks to displace the least senior employee from his classification.

The Company contended that there was no language in the contract, either expressed or implied, to indicate that seniority rights of ex-Stewards were different or inferior to those of any other employee not enjoying superseniority, and that neither the Union nor the Company ever intended such a result; that the Union's position would mean that every Union official who lost his office in the last election immediately would be displaced by the more senior man whom he last bumped irrespective of the date of the bumping; that this would be contrary to the language of Article IV and Exhibit "B" and the consistent practice of the Company; that it would be demoralizing to low seniority Union officials who periodically stand for reelection.

The Company pointed out that upon such immediate displacement, openings would be created in the existing classification of the more senior man and which in turn would have to be filled by the the employee who had been displaced by him, and that the chain reaction would continue until someone laid off would have to be recalled, and discriminated against anyone who accepted the lump sum severance payment; that the back pay demand would similarly require adjustments, and that this process would have to be repeated for all senior employees affected by all Union officials' loss of offices after every second election held by the Union up to the present time, causing administrative chaos, as well as hereafter. The Company emphasized that if this procedure had been intended by the parties, it would have been followed from the time of the second election held by the Union, or else a grievance would have been filed a long time ago. Other provisions said to support the Company's position included those on loss of seniority, promotion and discharge.

With respect to the Rockwell case, the Company noted that the contract there specifically provided that members of the Bargaining Committee were to be transferred to the first shift "for the time they hold office," and that when a less senior employee on the first shift lost his Bargaining Committee membership, the Grievant who had previously been displaced was held by the arbitrator to be justified in seeking reinstatement. The Company submitted that this award had no bearing on the instant case.

Under contract and past practice, seniority can be used to bump another employee only when layoff results in more senior employee being forced from his existing job; this has not occurred since time former steward lost his special seniority status.

QUESTIONS

1. What is the purpose of superseniority for stewards? Does superseniority attach to the person of the steward, or to the job?
2. Superseniority arrangements take effect from the provisions of the labor agreement, but the union elects the stewards. Does this make questions of seniority as between stewards and rank-and-file members, as the union contends, an "intra-union matter"?
3. Did the lapse of Weingartner's superseniority when he failed to be re-elected steward have the effect of creating a vacancy to be filled by straight seniority?
4. In the Rockwell case cited by the union, the agreement contained the following wording: "The members of the Bargaining Committee shall be transferred to the first shift *for the time they hold office*." (Emphasis added.) Are the contract provisions in the present case parallel in meaning and intent?
5. Could the arbitrator in this case deny the grievance without denying the principle of superseniority for stewards?

CASE 36
Union "Self-Help" to Enforce Agreement Terms

Agency: Board of Junior College District No. 508
               Cook County, Ill.
Union: Cook County College Teachers Union
               American Federation of Teachers, AFL-CIO, Local 1600
Arbitrator: Arthur A. Malinowski

In the conduct of its affairs a public agency often issues rules and regulations that touch on issues the same agency has negotiated in collective bargaining with a union. When the rules seem to conflict with the agreement, and the agreement provides a grievance procedure ending in arbitration, can the union engage in "self-help" to enforce its interpretation of the terms of the agreement?

An unusual feature of this case is that the employer filed the grievance against the union.

Arthur A. Malinowski, the arbitrator, prepared the following statement of the facts and issues in the case.

THE ISSUE

Based upon the evidence and arguments presented, the Arbitrator finds the issue to be as follows:

Did the Union violate the Labor Agreement when it directed the membership to disregard the Board's Rules?
If yes, what shall the remedy be?

DISCUSSION

Essentially, the subject matter of this Arbitration concerned the propriety of portions of a letter which was sent by the Union's President to the membership and which related to a controversy then pending before another Arbitrator.

The applicable provisions of the Labor Agreement are set out below and read in part as follows:

Article XV—Grievance Procedure
It is the declared objective of the Union and the Board to encourage the prompt and informal resolution of complaints of faculty members as they arise and to provide recourse to orderly procedures for the satisfactory adjustment of complaints.

. . .

Section B. General Procedures

. . .

3. Arbitration (Step 3).
    g. The Arbitrator shall limit his decision strictly to the application and

interpretation of the provisions of this Agreement and he shall be without power or authority to make any decision:

(1) Contrary to, or inconsistent with, or modifying or varying in any way, the terms of this Agreement; or

(2) Limiting or interfering in any way with the powers, duties, and responsibilities of the Board under applicable law.

. . .

Section F. General Provisions as to Grievance and Arbitration

1. The filing or pendency of any grievance under the provisions of this Article shall not prevent the Board and its representatives from taking the action complained of, subject, however, to the final decision on the grievance.

In addition, the Parties in Appendix E of the Labor Agreement set out the historical background relating to its execution on May 8, 1967. Similarly, the Arbitrator finds that for the purposes of this Opinion and Award, some further background material must be set out so as to place the act complained of into proper perspective.

The record showed that, shortly after the execution of the Labor Agreement, the Board, on July 13, 1967, adopted and promulgated its "Rules . . . for the management and government of the Chicago City College."

These Rules principally dealt with the following: (1) Organization of the Board; (2) Administrative Organization and Personnel Policies; (3) Students, and (4) Business and Financial Policies.

Almost immediately, the Union objected to these rules and regulations and asserted that a number of variations existed between the Board rules and the terms of the Labor Agreement, and that the Board could not unilaterally change the provisions of the Parties' Labor Agreement.

Accordingly, on August 14, 1967, the Union filed a grievance with the Chancellor and alleged the Board rules represented a major breach of the Labor Agreement.

The Chancellor denied the Union's grievance and after having failed to resolve the dispute in the grievance procedure, the matter was submitted to Arbitration pursuant to the terms of Article XV, Section B, Part 3 of the basic Agreement.

During the pendency of the dispute before another Arbitrator, the Union President on September 29, 1967, sent a letter to all the members of the Union and wrote in part as follows:

This letter is to report that on Tuesday, September 26, 1967, we held a meeting with Mr. Shabat regarding the Board's wholesale violation of our Contract by the unilateral passage of new Board Rules on July 13, 1967. . . .

Since Mr. Shabat was in no position to make a commitment for the Board which would guarantee the rescission of the new Board Rules, the Union has taken this major breach of our Contract to arbitration. In the meantime, however, it has come to our attention that the new Board Rule Book, the "Blue Book," has been distributed at many campuses of the Chicago City College.

Let me caution every Union member that these new "Board Rules" contain 27 violations of our Collective Bargaining Contract. The new "Rules" are replete with insertions and deletions changing many important aspects of our Agreement. If you have already received a copy of the new "Rules" please disregard them and, instead, follow the original wording of our Contract. This matter has already been taken to arbitration, and we are confident that the arbitrator will order the Board to rescind the new "Rules" wherever they violate our Contract.

Thereafter, on October 13, 1967, the Board filed a grievance against the Union, and asserted the President's letter violated the Labor Agreement. Failing settlement in the subsequent steps of the grievance procedure, the matter was submitted to this Arbitrator for a final Award.

The Board basically contended that the Union's act of instructing its members to disregard the "Rules" was a violation of the Labor Agreement; that said letter was a bad-faith attempt to undermine and usurp the powers and prerogative of the Board; that the Board had the right to govern and manage the colleges involved; that the Board had the right to supervise and direct the faculty; and that the Union should be ordered to countermand and rescind its instructions to the members.

The Union, on the other hand, contended that the disputed letter was not meant to usurp the prerogatives of the Board; that it simply advised the faculty members of the existence of discrepancies between the Labor Agreement and the Board's Rules; that said members were merely advised that contract benefits might be lost if the Rules and not the Labor Agreement were followed and that the letter was not intended to have the members violate the Board Rules pending the Arbitrator's decision.

The Union further asserted that while the Parties were trying to settle the Rules dispute, the fall semester opened; that the basic Agreement had not been applied during a regular school semester; that many faculty members were not completely familiar with the terms of the Labor Agreement; that said members were probably not aware of the differences between the Agreement and the Rules; that it was the Union's duty to so inform the members; that the Board disciplined no faculty member for having violated any of its Rules and that the Union did not violate the Labor Agreement. Accordingly, the Union claimed that the grievance should be denied.

QUESTIONS

1. How persuasive do you find the Association's disclaimer of intent to instruct its members to disregard the Board's rules?
2. Does the Board's failure to discipline Association members who disregarded the rules commit the Board to accept the Association's interpretation of the rules?
3. Many industrial firms follow the policy expressed in the rather cynical

maxim: management acts, the union grieves; and it is true that management usually takes the initiative in operations while the union initiates grievance actions. In this case the Board seems to have followed the maxim in the first arbitration case (referred to in the case, and still pending at the time). Why do you think the Board reversed its approach this time, to press a grievance against the union?

4. If you were the arbitrator in this case, would you want to wait and see how the other case came out before rendering your opinion? Would an award upholding the Association in the other case be consistent with a decision to uphold the Board in this one; or vice versa?

CASE 37
Subcontracting

Agency: City of Alpena, Mich.
Union: United Stone and Allied Products Workers of America,
              AFL-CIO, Local 203
Arbitrator: Alan Walt

Unions usually object when an employer subcontracts work which union members could do, because this deprives them of possible earnings. Employers in the public sector sometimes turn to contracting to keep down costs as collective bargaining raises wages. In this case, which came up in the first year of the first agreement between the contracting parties, the arbitrator has to consider a union grievance directed against subcontracting by the employing City.

The arbitrator, Mr. Alan Walt, prepared the following statement of facts and issues in the case.

NATURE OF DISPUTE

On May 1, 1967 a Demand For Arbitration was filed on behalf of the Union against the City of Alpena stating:

The Union protests the City's hiring of privately owned equipment and personnel for snow removal on Sunday January 29th while City employees were available and City's snow removal equipment was lying idle in the garage. This has never been a past practice of the City.

At its remedy, the Union seeks that 12 men be paid for "this time lost."

STATEMENT OF CASE

In July of 1966 the City entered into its first collective bargaining agreement with its employees, represented by Local No. 203 of the United Stone and Allied Products Workers of America, International Union, AFL-CIO. The happenings which give rise to this arbitration occurred

Sunday, January 29, 1967; however, events on Friday, January 27, and Saturday, January 28, 1967 are also directly related.

Over 11 inches of snow fell in the city on Friday, January 27, and the following day an additional 2-2/10 inches of snow was added. Wind velocities reached 21.6 miles per hour on Friday and over 11 miles per hour on Saturday with the result that the snow accumulated into high drifts.

It has always been the City's practice to clear its streets of snow as soon as possible with special emphasis being placed on the downtown area. Of approximately 30 employees in the highway department, at least 18 were engaged in snow removal operations during the period here involved. The regularly scheduled work week for these employees commences and ends at 7 A.M. on Monday, with each regular eight hour day shift beginning at 7 A.M. With the onset of heavy snows on Friday, 16 employees worked between 7½ and 12 hours overtime following completion of the regular work shift. All of Saturday was an overtime day with 15 employees accepting overtime calls and working between 7½ and 16 hours solely in snow removal operations. City crews were at work on snow removal until 7–8 o'clock on Sunday morning, January 29.

At approximately 8 o'clock Sunday morning, the City engaged the services of a private contractor to continue snow removal operations in the downtown area. This individual employed his own workers, utilizing his own equipment consisting of nine 10-yard trucks and three 2½ yard front-end loaders, was paid a fixed rate per hour for men and equipment, and worked for more than eight hours that day.

While the outside contractor was so engaged, no City equipment or City employees were utilized in snow removal, nor was any City employee offered the opportunity to work. However, upon completion of operations by the independent contractor that Sunday, 8 City employees were then called for snow removal work, 7 accepting the call and working between 8 and 13½ hours per man. However, 10 City employees who normally engage in snow removal were not called to work that day.

The City acknowledges that no special equipment was necessary for Sunday's snow removal operations and also that it possessed sufficient employees and equipment to do the job for which the private contractor was hired. It readily admits that its own employees were perfectly capable of doing the job and that no time deadline was involved.

The reason given by the City for engaging the services of a private contractor was its concern that, in the event of continued heavy snows during the following week, its own work force might not be "in shape" to function at full strength. Because of the substantial amount of overtime already worked by its employees on Friday and Saturday, January 27 and 28, there was concern that the work force might drop below its normal size if the heavy snowfalls were to continue. The City denies that its purpose in contracting out snow removal operations was to deprive its employees of additional premium pay, pointing out that employees engaged in snow removal operations worked a considerable amount of overtime both before and after the events here involved.

There had been other occasions following adoption of the collective bargaining agreement when the City engaged the services of an outside contractor for snow removal, but at such times its own employees were removing snow as well. This is the first instance of contracting out snow removal operations when City employees were not working in the same operation.

CONTRACTUAL PROVISIONS

Article II of the Agreement between the parties entitled "Management" reads:

The management of the City and the direction of the working forces, including the right to plan, direct and control City operations, to hire, suspend or discharge for cause, or transfer, to relieve employees from duty because of lack of work or for other legitimate reasons, and the right to introduce new or improved working methods or facilities, are vested exclusively in the City, provided that, in the exercise of these prerogatives the City shall not violate the provisions of this Agreement.

The subject of hours and overtime is dealt with in Article V of the contract. Section A states that the "regularly scheduled work week shall begin and end at 7 A.M. Monday," with §A2 thereof providing:

For the purpose of computing overtime, eight (8) hours shall constitute a day's work. All time over eight (8) hours in any twenty-four (24) hour period, and all time worked over forty (40) hours in any one workweek shall be paid at the rate of time and one-half; provided that overtime rates shall not be paid when more than eight (8) hours in twenty-four (24) are worked as a result of regular shift changes or as a result of employees trading shifts for their own convenience.

The City may not change work schedules or work days to avoid the payment of overtime. *Article V. §B, 2.*

Nothing is contained in the contract concerning the matter of subcontracting or contracting out work, and it is agreed by the parties that the negotiations instituted in the fall of 1965 and culminating in the first contract between the City and its employees in July of 1966 did not touch on this area.

Grievance procedures are delineated in Article IX of the contract. §C thereof defines a grievance as "any controversy between the parties . . . or between the City and any employee . . . which relates to:

1. Working conditions in the City not specifically *covered by the Agreement*, or

2. Interpretation or violation of any provision of this Agreement. (Emphasis supplied.)

§D,5a of Article IX sets forth the arbitrator's jurisdiction and authority in the following terms:

The Arbitrator shall have the jurisdiction and authority to interpret and apply the provisions of this Agreement insofar as it shall be necessary to the determination of the grievance before him, but he shall have no jurisdiction or authority to alter or amend in any way the provisions of this Agreement.

THE UNION'S POSITION

The Union argues that in hiring a private concern on Sunday, January 29, 1967, the City was in violation of the collective bargaining agreement. Acknowledging that the contract is silent in this area, the Union nevertheless contends that to permit the City to contract out work regularly done by its own employees would result in the utter frustration of the terms of the contract by depriving City employees of the fruits of the agreement as it was negotiated.

It is further pointed out that no special or unusual skills were necessitated not already possessed by City employees, nor were any items of specialized equipment required not already owned by the City. Not only were City employees available but 10 regularly assigned to snow removal operations were not even offered the opportunity to work.

Furthermore, while it is the City's policy to remove snow in the downtown area as quickly as possible, there exists no time limitation for such operations, and the City cannot justify hiring outside help to the exclusion of its own employees merely because it anticipates additional acts of God, i.e., the continuation of abnormally heavy snowfalls. Even had heavy snows continued, it is pure speculation to argue that City employees would not have been available or "in shape" to undertake the continued removal of snow in their regular employment.

Since at least 12 City employees would have been required to operate the same amount of City equipment as utilized by the outside contractor, the Union asks that the 12 men with the lowest overtime during the pay period here involved be compensated at premium rates for time worked Sunday, January 29, 1967 by the independent contractor.

THE CITY'S POSITION

Noting that the collective bargaining agreement is silent on the question of contracting out work or outside hiring, the City argues that it is not prohibited from doing so and further, that the management provision of the contract—Article II—clearly reserves such decisions to the City.

Furthermore, it points out that prior to adoption of the collective bargaining agreement, many forms of work regularly performed by City employees had been contracted out. These have included sewer main, sidewalk, water main, curb and gutter, and street construction, tree cutting and stump removal, street base stabilization, building construction and repairs, plumbing, painting and automotive repair. Since adoption of the contract in July of 1966, the City has contracted out sidewalk and street construction, tree stump removal, street base stabilization and repairs, plumbing, painting and automotive repair. Furthermore, it has contracted out street base stabilization work even though it had the manpower and equipment available to do the work. Its decision to contract out the work here under discussion, therefore, is not only within the sole authority of the City under Article II of the contract but is also firmly established as a permissible past practice on the part of the City.

The City contends that its action in contracting out snow removal was taken for the sole purpose of insuring the availability of its regular work force in the ensuing week, and that in so doing, no change was made in the work schedules of any of its employees. It denies any intent to deprive City employees of premium pay, showing that those regularly engaged in snow removal operations earned substantial amounts of overtime both before and after January 29.

QUESTIONS

1. When a labor agreement is silent on the point at issue in an arbitration case, where can the arbitrator turn for guidance in making his decision? Does past practice rule? Similar, but not identical, practices? Bargaining history? Other guides? To the extent that any of these appear in evidence in this case, what do they indicate that would help him reach a decision?

2. The Union seems not to have protested the City's subcontracting other kinds of work; why should it do so over snow removal? Does the Union's apparent acquiescence in these other instances mean it may not object in this one?

3. Does the matter of overtime pay have any bearing on the subcontracting issue?

CASE 38
Ability to Pay—Defeat of a School Millage Levy

Agency: Wayne (Michigan) Community School District
Union: Wayne Education Association
Arbitrator: Robert G. Howlett

A School Board, operating on a fixed budget subject to the will of the voters, is more likely than a private enterprise to plead inability to pay in responding to union demands. This case deals with measures taken by the

Board to cut the budget after a millage measure was defeated at the polls, by adjustment of "normal teaching loads" written into a collective bargaining agreement.

The arbitrator in this case chooses to argue the various points as he presents the facts, and the positions of the parties. It is therefore appropriate to precede the text of the opinion and award with a summary, prepared by Estelle R. Tracy for the American Arbitration Association.

SUMMARY

Working Conditions—"Normal Weekly Teaching Load"—Effect of Failure of Electorate to Approve Funds Requested by School Administrators

A contractual statement that "the normal weekly teaching load in the elementary schools will be 25 teaching hours" was held to be subject to an introductory statement that "the Board shall make a continuous effort to comply" with this and other requirements contained in the same article. It was therefore neither a violation of the contract nor evidence of bad-faith bargaining that the school administrators, following rejection by the electorate of a financial proposal, assigned four art teachers to general duties and terminated teachers with temporary certificates, thereby causing the teaching load to be increased above the indicated level.

The National Education Association was not upheld in its view that the contract must be construed to mean that the "normal weekly teaching load" may not exceed 25 hours.

IMPLICATIONS OF "NORMAL"

"It is doubtful that hours of work for teachers can be strictly limited to a specified number of hours. The evidence disclosed, for example, that students start arriving in the classroom at 8:20 A.M. and that some students are transported by school buses at the end of the day, and that these buses do not always leave at exactly the same time each day. If pupils in a schoolroom prior to 8:30 A.M. is considered as part of a 'teaching load,' it is impossible to fix the teacher's load with complete exactitude. As the exact time at which a bus may depart cannot be determined, a teacher must supervise her students until they are on the bus. Thus, 'normal' seems to recognize the impracticability, and probably the impossibility, of defining precisely the number of hours which a teacher will work. A teacher's duties cannot start and stop with timeclock accuracy as in a manufacturing plant."

Although there was disagreement between the parties as to whether periods of recess were to be counted as teaching hours, the evidence "tends to prove" that "teaching load" was meant to include "all time during which teachers have supervision of their students."

"CONTINUOUS EFFORT TO COMPLY"

The Association was not persuasive in its contention that the introductory phrase ("The Board shall make a continuous effort to comply with the following provisions for making assignments:") applies only to the paragraph immediately following, and not to the third following paragraph, which deals with the "normal weekly teaching load" of 25 hours.

Rebutting this contention are the facts that (1) "provisions" was used in the plural, not singular; (2) the numbering system shows that all paragraphs following the quoted sentence are subordinate to the paragraph in which the sentence appears; and (3) the logic of all the paragraphs supports the school administrator's view.

The Education Association representative may have understood that the "continuous effort" phrase applied to only one paragraph, but "there was no evidence to establish that this was a mutual agreement of the board and association during the bargaining," and a board representative testified that he understood the clause in the manner now urged.

"During the bargaining sessions the association committee sought to secure a decrease in the number of hours during which teachers supervised students. [A board spokesman] testified that the understanding was that the teaching load was to be firmly fixed at twenty-five hours, the language of the contract . . . supports the testimony of [the board's representative]."

THE QUESTION OF GOOD FAITH

The evidence leads to the conclusion that the board made the good-faith continuous effort required by the contract. When the electorate turned down a financial proposal, the board planned a new proposal, which was again rejected. Later, when state aid became available, the board was able to apply the funds, but some reductions still became necessary, and these reductions were not made solely at the expense of teachers. Reductions included foreign language summer sessions, supplies, text books, conferences, assistant principals, clerical workers, hot lunches, and other budgetary items.

"The total reductions voted by the board were $558,100, of which the reduction in music and physical education teachers is a total of $49,500. Four art teachers were assigned to classroom duties, as teachers with temporary certificates were terminated. It was this reassignment of art teachers which resulted in the longer hours of which the grievants complain."

"In summary, the evidence establishes that the board did all that was feasible to lessen the impact of the voters' refusal" to vote funds.

ASSOCIATION'S FAILURE TO BARGAIN

It is "evident" from the association president's reply to a letter from the board asking for suggestions on dealing with the situation created by the electorate that "any failure to bargain rests with the Association. . . ."

"While the refusal of a labor organization to bargain in good faith is not, under the Public Employment Relations Act, an unfair labor practice, the obligation to bargain in good faith is mutual. As the Michigan Labor Mediation Board held, if a labor organization is unwilling to bargain it is not in a position to complain that an employer should have done better at bargaining."

What follows is the opinion of the arbitrator, Robert G. Howlett.

This arbitration involves the interpretation of a collective bargaining contract effective from June 1, 1966 to June 30, 1968, between the Board of Education of the Wayne Community School District, of Wayne, Michigan, and the Wayne Education Association, which was certified as collective bargaining representative for the certified teachers in the Wayne school system in October, 1965.

At issue is interpretation of Article IV of the Agreement, entitled "Teaching loads and Assignments":

4. 1   The teaching profession is unique in many aspects. Educators perform their responsibilities in a variety of settings and conditions other than those of the classroom. The Board shall make a continuous effort to comply with the following provisions for making assignments:

4. 1. 1   Pupils are entitled to be taught by teachers who are working within their area of competence. Teachers shall not be assigned except temporarily, without their consent, outside the scope of their teaching certificate or their major or minor field of study. The Superintendent of schools shall be prepared to give the Association a list of such persons and their areas of competence upon request by the Association.

4. 1. 2   The normal weekly teaching load in the secondary schools will be 25 teaching periods and five unassigned preparation periods; or 20 teaching periods, five study hall periods, and five unassigned preparation periods. Every effort shall be made to assign no more than two preparations wherever possible.

4. 1. 3   The normal weekly teaching load in the elementary schools will be 25 teaching hours. The elementary classroom teachers shall have planning, preparation, and relief time while their classes are receiving instruction in music, art, and physical education. They shall not be required to grade students in these areas.

4. 1. 4   Teachers shall not be required to report for duty earlier than 15 minutes before the opening of the pupils' school day and shall not be required

to remain longer than 30 minutes after the close of the pupils' school day, except when required for necessary staff meetings.

4. 1. 5 All teachers shall continue to have a duty-free lunch period except for the present policy of being periodically available on a scheduled basis for emergency consultation if one of the parent supervisors needs assistance. It is further agreed that this responsibility is supplementary to the principal in his role in the building. It is further agreed that the Board will not shorten the present lunch hour in the elementary schools, and will guarantee a minimum of a one-half hour lunch period at the secondary schools.

Also cited by the Association in support of its position is Article X, entitled "Additional Compensation for Extra Duty":

10. 1 The salary schedule attached as Schedule A is based upon a normal weekly teaching load as hereinbefore designated. . . .

The issue involves a contention by the Association that the "normal weekly teaching load" as specified in Paragraph 4. 1. 3 may not be more than "25 teaching hours," and that the Board by requiring more than "25 teaching hours" has breached the agreement. The primary contention of the Board is that the "25 teaching hours" limitation in Paragraph 4. 1. 3 is subject to the last sentence of the first paragraph of Article IV, hence is not a fixed or absolute requirement, but is a "goal."

A grievance dated November 27, 1966, was filed by the Association, which Superintendent of Schools Harry Howard refused to "accept" on the ground that it did not "state what the alleged violation is."[1] The Association therefore submitted a more detailed grievance:

Your letter of December 7 reveals misunderstandings with both the grievances submitted on November 27 and our telephone conversation of December 6.

1. The Association did not allege violations of the contract in two areas as stated in your letter of December 7. The November 27 letter introduces Grievance One, a violation of Section 4. 1. 3 of the Master Contract, and Grievance Two, a misinterpretation of Section 4. 1. 4.

2. Your letter states that "the grievance" was insufficiently detailed. The Association believes that each grievance submitted was properly and adequately identified by Section number in the Master Contract. No provision in the Contract requires more detail than was provided in the November 27 letter.

3. Further, at no point does the Contract allow the superintendent, or any other recipient of a grievance, to refuse acceptance of a grievance for alleged lack of information.

4. During our December 6 telephone conversation, it was not agreed that the Association would "resubmit its grievance" concerning Sections 4. 1. 3 and 4. 1. 4. I did agree to furnish some additional information for your convenience.

---

[1] The Association is correct in its contention that the Superintendent had no right or power to refuse to "accept" the grievance.

I further suggested that even though the grievance time limit as outlined in Section 8. 3. 4 would expire on December 16, the Association would agree to extend this deadline.

The following information is submitted for your convenience:

Grievance I—Section 4. 1. 3 of the Contract states, "the normal weekly teaching load in the elementary schools will be 25 teaching hours . . ."

It has come to our attention that many elementary teachers are teaching in excess of these maxima per week.

The Association believes this is in violation of Section 4. 1. 3 of the Master Contract.

The Association's letter continued with "Grievance II" which was not submitted to me.

Grievance II—Section 4. 1. 4 of the Contract states that, "Teachers shall not be required to report for duty earlier than 15 minutes before the opening of the pupils' school day and shall not be required to remain longer than 30 minutes after the close of the pupils' school day, except when required for necessary staff meetings."

In your communication of November 2, 1966, you indicate that your interpretation of this is that teachers must be in school 15 minutes before the beginning of the pupils' school day and must remain 30 minutes after the close of the pupils' school day.

The Association believes this is a misinterpretation of the Master Contract.

There are two principal issues before me:

(1) Does Article IV require that the "normal weekly teaching load" is limited to "25 teaching hours"?

(2) If the answer to Question 1 is in the negative, has the Board made a "continuous effort" to comply with the "goal" in Paragraph 4. 1. 3 that the "normal weekly teaching load" shall be not more than "25 teaching hours"?

Another possible issue is whether "normal weekly teaching load" means that teachers shall supervise students for not more than, or exactly, twenty-five hours, or whether the adjective "normal" allows some flexibility in the teaching load assignments. The evidence in this case makes unnecessary the determination of this issue, although "(the) express use of the word 'normal' implies occasional resort to the 'abnormal.' "[2] It is doubtful that hours of work for teachers can be strictly limited to a specified number of hours. The evidence disclosed, for example, that students start arriving in the classroom at 8:20 A.M. and that some students are transported by school buses at the end of the day, and that these buses do not always leave at exactly the same time each day. If the presence of pupils in a schoolroom prior to 8:30 A.M. is considered as part of a "teaching load," it is impossible to fix the teacher's load with complete exactitude. As the exact time at which a bus may depart cannot be determined, a teacher must supervise her students until they are on the bus.

---

[2] *Carnegie-Illinois Steel Corp.,* 12 LA 810 (Ralph T. Seward, 1949).

Thus, "normal" seems to recognize the impracticability, and probably the impossibility, of defining precisely the number of hours which a teacher will work. A teacher's duties cannot start and stop with time-clock accuracy as in a manufacturing plant.

There was disagreement between the Association and the Board as to whether recess is included in the "teaching hours." While unnecessary to the decision, the evidence tends to prove that by use of the phrase "teaching load" the parties did mean to include all time during which teachers have supervision of their students. Marjorie Frazier, Chairman of the Professional Rights and Responsibilities Committee, who participated in the bargaining sessions, testified that "recess was considered by both parties as part of teaching time." Superintendent Harry Howard did not directly deny this testimony, but on cross-examination, when referring to charts offered in evidence by the Association, suggested that reference to the charts showed that recess was not part of the school day.

It was also disclosed by the evidence that at some of the schools there is a practice among teachers, approved by the school administrators, to share recess supervision, although partial responsibility remains with the teacher who has turned over her students to another teacher.[3]

Decision depends upon the interpretation of the last sentence, or phrase, of Paragraph 4.1 as applicable to the remaining paragraphs of Article IV.

The Association, in support of its position, urges that the phrase which ends with a colon is applicable only to Paragraph 4. 1. 1.[4] In support of this contention, the Association urges that (1) it is "hardly to be presumed that the parties intended to take away in one section of Article IV what they conferred in another section," (2) Marjorie Frazier testified that "her understanding" from the discussions at the bargaining sessions was that the phrase referred exclusively to Paragraph 4. 1. 1, and (3) only Paragraph 4. 1. 1 of "the following provisions" deals with "making assignments," the remaining section dealing with teaching loads, which the Association urges is "hardly a matter of assignments."

I shall discuss each of these contentions:

1. The contract does not "take away" in Paragraph 4. 1 any benefit provided for the teachers in Paragraph 4. 1. 3. The placing of the "continuous effort" phrase at the end of the first paragraph of Article IV and its conclusion with a colon persuades me that it was intended to apply to all paragraphs listed below, not solely to Paragraph 4. 1. 1. This is further supported by the use of "following provisions." Had it been intended to apply the phrase to only one paragraph of Article IV, the word "provision," rather than "provisions," would have been used. Had the parties

---

[3] It was testified, for example, that if there is an injury during recess, the report is filled out by the teacher whose student was hurt, even though another teacher is in attendance during the recess period.

[4] I shall use the work "phrase" rather than "sentence" because the determinative language does not end with a period.

intended to limit the phrase to Paragraph 4. 1. 1, the logical place to have placed it would have been inside of, and as the first sentence of, Paragraph 4. 1. 1, rather than in the general paragraph which preceded the five following paragraphs. The numbering system, i.e., the use of 4. 1 for the first paragraph and subnumberings of 1 through 5, inclusive, also supports the Board's thesis that the phrase was intended to apply to all subsidiary paragraphs of Article IV.

2. While Marjorie Frazier may have understood that the "continuous effort" phrase was applicable only to Paragraph 4. 1. 1, there was no evidence to establish that this was a *mutual* agreement of the Board and Association during the bargaining. No record of the negotiations was kept, and Superintendent Howard testified that the understanding of the Board representatives was that the phrase applied to all of the paragraphs in Article IV, and that to limit the teaching load to twenty-five teaching hours was a "goal." The interpretation of Superintendent Howard is consistent with the grammatical structure of Article 5; the interpretation of Chairman Frazier is not.

3. A reading of Paragraphs 4. 1. 2, to 4. 1. 5, inclusive, discloses that all of them are concerned with "making assignments," as well as with "teaching loads" if, indeed, the two concepts can be separated.

4. 1. 2, for example, refers to the teachers' assignment for teaching periods and preparation periods. This involves both teaching loads and assignments.

4. 1. 3 must of necessity involve assignments because teachers are *assigned* to their teaching hours.

4. 1. 4 affects assignments because it requires teachers to report at least fifteen minutes before the opening of the "pupils' school day," which is an assignment of a teacher to her classroom.

4. 1. 5 provides for duty-free lunch periods, except under certain emergency conditions when teachers may be *assigned* to assist a parent supervisor.

The Association cites Article X, urging that the salary schedule is "based on a normal weekly teaching load" of twenty-five hours. But Paragraph 10. 1 refers, not to twenty-five hours as such, but to a "normal weekly teaching load *as hereinbefore designated*." The "normal weekly teaching load" which is designated is that teaching load specified in paragraph 4. 1. 3, for which the Board "shall make a continuous effort," limited by the other exceptions in Article IV, such as possible assignments to lunch duty as in the case of emergencies, and supervision of students because the school bus is late in arriving.

Decision, then, depends on whether the Board has made a "continuous effort" to provide a "normal weekly teaching load (of) 25 teaching hours."

During 1965–66 the "normal teaching load" for elementary teachers was twenty-seven and one-half hours. This schedule included hours when students were receiving instruction in music, art, and physical education, as the classroom teachers were required to remain in their rooms during these instruction periods.

During the bargaining sessions the Association Committee sought to secure a decrease in the number of hours during which teachers supervised students. Superintendent Howard agreed to the desirability of reducing supervision hours. The Board negotiators, he testified, concluded that a teaching load of twenty-five hours was not only desirable, but possible, if it were a "goal." While Association witness Frazier testified that her understanding was that the teaching load was to be firmly fixed at twenty-five hours, the language of the contract, as discussed above, supports the testimony of Superintendent Howard.

Remaining is the question whether the Board has made a good faith continuous effort to comply with paragraph 4. 1. 3. The evidence leads to the conclusion that it has complied with this covenant. This conclusion follows whether recess is, or is not, considered as part of the "teaching load."

The contract was dated on June 17, 1966 following negotiations over an extended period. There is nothing in the record to suggest that the Board did not enter into this contract in good faith, and with the intention of reducing the teaching load to a "normal . . . load" of twenty-five hours.

While the voters of the Wayne Community School District defeated a millage proposal on June 13, 1966, the Board planned a new vote on millage, which was held September 12, 1966. Again the voters defeated a proposal for additional millage. An increase in state aid made possible the increase which had been placed in effect in spite of the June 13 millage defeat, but the result of the September election required the reductions discussed below.

The Board started the 1966–67 school year believing that the needed millage would be approved at the September 12 election. When the voters rejected the millage the Board was faced with the necessity of reducing its budget by approximately $600,000.

The Board did not make the reduction solely from teachers' salaries or in reduction of the number of teachers, but studied the proposed budget of $11,540,745 and made specific cuts of $602,100 in the following items: text books ($30,000), teaching supplies ($50,000), conferences and mileage ($10,800), foreign language summer seminars ($10,000), one sabbatical leave ($4,500), continuing education ($30,000), assistant elementary principals ($60,000), merging classrooms ($52,000), reduction in art staff ($26,000), nonemployment of three vocal music teachers ($20,000), nonemployment of two visiting teachers ($13,000), nonemployment of one instrument music teacher ($6,500), counseling account ($20,000), physical education ($13,000), overtime in custodial and clerical accounts ($18,000), discontinuance of hot lunch program in secondary schools ($34,000), elimination of one teacher aide ($4,500), reduction in transportation budget ($76,300), reduction in the central office staff ($24,300), custodian budget ($25,000), interest on loan ($4,600), contract services for special service $3,900), contract guard services ($3,000), equipment repair man ($3,700), one delivery position ($4,000), replacement of equipment $10,000), new furniture and equipment ($20,000), and athletic budget ($15,000).

The total reductions voted by the Board were $558,100, of which the reduction in music and physical education teachers is a total of $49,500. Four art teachers were assigned to classroom duties, as teachers with temporary certificates were terminated. It was this reassignment of art teachers which resulted in the longer hours of which the grievants complain.

The Board's action was patiently and carefully considered and executed with the best interests of the educational needs of the students in mind.

The Board of Education did not take the September 12, 1966 defeat "lying down," but again submitted to the voters a millage proposal consisting of the 4 new mills together with 4 mills which were expiring. This time the campaign was successful as the voters approved both the expiring 4 mills and the additional 4 mills, the latter, however, not collectible until December 1967.

Superintendent Howard testified that efforts were made to find music teachers and visiting teachers but they were not available.

In summary, the evidence establishes that the Board did all that was feasible to lessen the impact of the voters' refusal to vote the millage necessary to continue in effect the provisions of Article IV.

The Association urges that the Board made the changes unilaterally, contrary to the bargaining requirements in Section 10 (e) of the Public Employment Relations Act. The evidence does not sustain this contention.

On September 23, 1967, Board officials met with the Association committee to discuss the future in light of the rejection of the millage on September 12, 1966. Superintendent Howard requested the Association committee to offer suggestions concerning the necessary budget reduction.

No proposals or suggestions were forthcoming.

On October 6, 1966, Superintendent Howard addressed a letter to the Association President calling his attention to the meeting of September 23 and noting that the Board had solicited and received suggestions from the public and the staff, but none from the Association.

In a reply dated October 9, 1966, the Association President stated, in part: ". . . We agree that cuts must be made, but we must also submit that the responsibility for financing the educational program rests with electors of the district. Therefore, we shall also resist any efforts to have teachers subsidize that program."

It is evident from this reply and the testimony that any failure to bargain rests with the Association, not the Board. While the refusal of a labor organization to bargain in good faith is not, under the Public Employment Relations Act, an unfair labor practice, the obligation to bargain in good faith is *mutual.* As the Michigan Labor Mediation Board had held, if a labor organization is unwilling to bargain it is not in a position to complain that an employer should have done better at bargaining.[5]

The Association noted in its brief a finding by a fact-finder who said, "it is as much a part of the (public employer's) responsibility to pay reasonable and fair wages as it is to provide reasonable and fair services and capital improvement. The employees should not be required to bear a disproportionate burden of the (employer's) present inability to secure sources of revenue."[6] The evidence established that the Board made an effort to avoid having the teachers "bear a disproportionate burden" of the reduction required by the failure of the voters of the Wayne Community School District to recognize their civic responsibility; and indeed, the Board appears to have succeeded in its endeavor.

The Association brief avers that "illegal activities plainly cannot fulfill the duties of a public employer under a contract." There was nothing about the Board's activities which are in any way illegal. On the contrary, the evidence establishes that members of the Board acted with objectivity and mature consideration of the problems facing them.

AWARD

The grievance filed by the Wayne Education Association dated November 27, 1966, and supplemented December 11, 1966 is denied.

QUESTIONS

1. Does the arbitrator's manner of arguing this case, point by point, rather than presenting (as is usually done) each side's arguments in turn before making the analysis and coming to a decision, detract from the objectivity of his opinion and award?
2. What are some of the arguments in favor of a "normal teaching load" expressed in hours per week for professional employees? What are some of the arguments against?
3. Suppose the Board had not succeeded (in the second special election and from other sources) in getting money enough to run the schools, what would have been its alternatives with respect to the normal teaching load? The Association's alternatives?

---

[5] *Detroit Downtown Travel Lodge and Hotel, Motel and Restaurant Workers,* Local 705, No. C 66F-60, 1967 Labor Opinions.

[6] *Matter of City of Grand Rapids,* SLMB Case No. 63 K-15 (Hyman Parker, 1964).

CASE 39
Authority of the Arbitrator in Public Sector Cases

Agency: Lincoln Park Board of Education, Lincoln Park, Mich.
Union: Lincoln Park Education Association
Arbitrator: David G. Heilbrun

Like craft unions, which demand that jobs go only to journeymen who have "served their time" as apprentices, professional associations of certificated teachers insist that advancement on the job go only to those who possess professional qualifications; and further, that when assignments require special abilities, only fellow-professionals can properly evaluate the abilities. Thus teachers demand a voice in selecting colleagues for promotion. In the case that follows, a branch of the National Education Association accuses its School Board of violating the terms of a collective agreement providing for teacher participation in promotion procedures. It also raises, in the public sector, the question of an arbitrator's authority. For background on this aspect of the case, see the Enterprise Wheel decision of the U.S. Supreme Court, presented as part of Case 2 in this book.

INTRODUCTION

This arbitration concerns the manner of selecting individuals to serve as teachers for the Project H.E.L.P. program as such was to function during the current school year.

The original grievance reads:

Failure of the Board of Education to follow the promotional procedure as defined in Article VII—Promotions of the Master Agreement between the Board of Ed. and the LPEA. No screening committee was established to consider the applicants. Some teachers were dropped from the application list arbitrarily.

By resolution of November 6, 1967, the Board denied this grievance. Underlying this denial was an earlier written response of Deputy Superintendent Campbell, dated September 28, 1967, to the following effect:

In accordance with Article VII, the H.E.L.P. program is not considered an extra compensable job. This grievance is denied.

FACTS

In September, 1966, certain persons employed by this school district, both as teachers and among the administration, determined to reactivate an attempt to secure federal funding for an educational concept directed at the problem of school dropouts. This concept had previously been reduced to a twenty-nine page educational proposal and forwarded to federal officials administering the federal aid to education program popularly known as "Title III." This original proposal was not granted federal funding.

Ronald Militello, an English teacher in the school system and an individual who had participated in the earlier effort, was asked to serve as chairman of the Project H.E.L.P. committee. Militello and others so functioned during the 1966–1967 school year with Board approval and completed a comprehensive, 97-page presentation of the proposed Project H.E.L.P.

This document, describing the Project H.E.L.P. program as "An exemplary and innovative program to help and advise potential dropouts to complete their high school education," was completed January 14, 1967, and forwarded for funding consideration under Title III. A funding grant was awarded in spring 1967, to be effective June 19, 1967.

Screening procedures under the promotional provisions of the collective bargaining agreement between the parties were undertaken for the Project Director and Militello was approved by the Board for this position.

Project H.E.L.P. contemplated a teaching staff of thirty to thirty-five individuals who would be excused from one of their academic periods per day in order to work closely with the identified potential dropout or group of dropouts. A main theme of the program, traced from its earliest conception, was that the teachers who would participate in it would be of a type possessing an especially refined sense of empathy with students who for various reasons were disadvantaged or otherwise inadequately motivated to complete an amount of education necessary to their future well being and development.

Aside from the daily educational and motivational contact with students, the persons of the Project H.E.L.P. program, aided by outside consultants, were to attend a pre-school year seminar of 10 days duration and approximately 18 staff meetings during the school year.

The Project H.E.L.P. presentation, at page 63, recited:

Teachers involved in the Project on a part-time basis will be paid $6.00 an hour which is the expected hourly rate for those teachers in the Lincoln Park School District who work beyond their contracted time in September, 1967.

The $6.00 hourly rate figure was entered after Militello consulted with Executive Secretary Kersul of the Association. At the time of this inquiry the parties were still engaged in negotiations for the basic salary schedule to cover school year 1966–1967, then half-way through completion. It was Kersul's estimate that the direction of the negotiations was tending to lead to an ultimate agreement in which the professional hourly rate (also termed "the night school rate") would turn out to be $6.00 per hour.

One of Militello's first acts as Project Director (the duties of which he commenced about June 1, 1967) was the distribution of an informational sheet soliciting teachers for the program. This sheet reads:

Project H.E.L.P.

Lincoln Park having received $119,476 to assist potential dropouts, we are now in search of teachers willing to undertake the demanding tasks of educational innovation.

Project H.E.L.P. is of national concern. Its very center is the dynamic teacher, the teacher who can practice what he preaches in educational philosophy, upon whom students can depend.

Project H.E.L.P. is idealism practiced realistically.

Lincoln Park High School has professional personnel capable of working in this program. If you are interested, complete information is available by notifying Ron Militello.

Proposed Schedule of a
Project H.E.L.P. Teacher

10-day seminar August 21 to September 1 from 9 A.M. to 12 A.M. and from 1 P.M. to 4 P.M.

4 classes and conference period plus one hour daily to counsel for Project H.E.L.P.

18 semi-monthly conferences to discuss techniques, methods, and progress of students involved, plus a convention, the costs of which will be paid by Project H.E.L.P.

All teachers will be paid $6.00 an hour for attending the ten-day seminar, August 21 to September 1 and for attending 18 staff meetings.

Experience and research data will be made available to staff members for pertinent Master's studies.

Availability of three consultants:

Dr. Ronald Esposito
Dr. Donald Hamecheck
Dr. Morrell Clute.

By late June the various applicants had been considered and an initial list of proposed teachers was formulated. This list was, in turn, revised by a committee consisting of Militello, Superintendent for Personnel Archie Cairns, High School Principal Thomas Cuozzo and Deputy Superintendent Campbell. On August 7, 1967, the Board gave its approval for twenty-six persons spread among various departments. Certain teachers of the school system who had not been selected filed grievances and were added to the program, "if and when needed," by Board action of September 11, 1967.

A total of approximately 25 persons attended the ten-day seminar of late August, 1967, and this total included those who were later officially added to the program by Board action on their pending grievances.

A collective bargaining Agreement had been entered into by the parties February 27, 1967. The term of the Agreement was July 1, 1966—

June 30,1968, having the practical effect of covering school years 1966–1967 and 1967–1968. This was the first comprehensive collective bargaining contract between the parties pursuant to Act 379 of 1965. A reopener clause as to "the salary schedule or other economic matters" was operative upon written notice during the 60-day period prior to May 1, 1967. In fact, such reopener notification occurred and in the course of negotiations pursuant to such reopener the parties reached a new basic salary schedule for the current school year as well as other economic changes in the Agreement. The negotiations did not result in any change in the positions listed in the "Schedule 'A,' continued" containing a listing of the various positions paid at $5.00 per hour and the various sports and activities coaches, coordinators and directors receiving additional fixed annual compensation for such activities.

Included in the language of Article III—*Professional Compensation* of the Agreement is the following language:

For extra work of a professional nature which is not voluntary, and for certain specified extra duties, the teacher shall be entitled to appropriate additional professional compensation, at an established professional hourly rate or at the specified rates provided in Schedule A, as applicable. The professional hourly rate shall be the night school rate. The teacher shall be paid such established hourly rate or specified rate, as applicable, in addition to his base salary, for all time spent before and after the regular school day in such activities as parent-teacher conferences. PTA meetings, supervision of extra-curricular activities of students, teacher meetings after established school hours of any day or on Saturdays, Sundays or holidays, and attendance at any educational or civic functions, but only where participation is not voluntary but required, or where extra compensation is otherwise prescribed herein, . . .

The language of Article VII—Promotions, begins:

All positions in the school system carrying contractual compensation, and providing that such compensation is not considered a part of the teachers' salary schedule, shall be listed in the School Policies and considered as promotional positions in this school district.

CONTENTIONS

The Association contends that the teaching positions of the Project H.E.L.P. program are of a promotional nature by reason of the definition contained in Article VII. The Association reasons that since the positions have been compensated at a salary other than that listed in the teachers salary schedule, namely, at $6.00 hourly rate which at no place appears in the salary schedule or the Schedule "A" continuation, they are, therefore, by definition, promotional and must be filled by the meticulous screening procedures of Article VII. Included in these procedures are the appointment of an evaluation committee of five persons, two of whom have been selected by the Superintendent from a panel of seven named teachers provided by the Association without regard to organizational affiliation. The Association seeks no retroactive effect to any arbitration decision nor does it seek any change in the Project H.E.L.P. program for the balance of the current school year. Its position is that with the program already five months under way it would be educationally prejudicial to disrupt existing relationships that have been established through the efforts and ingenuity of Project H.E.L.P. teachers. It contends instead that the Arbitrator direct that future staffing of the Project H.E.L.P. program, for subsequent school years, beginning with such seminar as may be comparably scheduled just before the opening of the next school year, be in perfect compliance with the screening provisions of Article VII of the Agreement. The Association contends that positions such as those with Project H.E.L.P. are of the very type contemplated by the parties in reaching the language of Article VII, by which thorough and evenhanded consideration would be given to all applicants for promotional positions, as such would be properly recognized. The Association seeks a declaration that Project H.E.L.P. utilizes extra compensable positions necessitating the selection procedures of Article VII.

The Board contends that a proper reading of Article III of the Agreement, in conjunction with Article VII, necessitates the conclusion that Project H.E.L.P. positions, other than the Director, are not promotional. The reasoning here is that Project H.E.L.P. is essentially a program in which the teacher substitutes this specialized activity for one of the academic periods he would otherwise be assigned and in this sense he is earning "contractual compensation" already part of the salary schedule. The Board asserts that since this is the case, a promotional position is not cognizable under the definition of Article VII and, therefore, the entire screening procedures are inapplicable. The Board notes that positions already on "Schedule 'A,' continued," as such has been effective both for the past and the current school year, namely, at least those for the summer school program, and the adult education program, bear extra compensation at a $5.00 hourly rate and yet are not considered promotional as seen from the manner of selection in which interested faculty members merely apply for such additional duty and are selected by the Program Director. Closely related to this is another program of the school district called the "learning Improvement Center" in which currently a position is in the process of being filled by the more informal manner of direct approval by the Program Director from among applicants.

The Board also contends that Project H.E.L.P. was not in contemplation of the parties in reaching their Agreement and also that it would have been highly impractical, if not impossible, to have attempted to staff the program under Article VII because time did not permit such a formalized procedure.

QUESTIONS

1. In what way does the Supreme Court's decision in the Enterprise Wheel case apply to the powers of the arbitrator in this case? (See Case 2.)
2. Can the H.E.L.P. project positions be called promotions under the wording of the agreement?
3. If the arbitrator gave an advisory opinion in this case, without binding effect, what influence might it have? Would it seem worthwhile to do so?

CASE 40
Learning to Live with a Union of Policemen

Agency: The City of Port Huron, Mich.
Union: American Federation of State, County and Municipal Employees, AFL-CIO, Local No. 1518, Council No. 55
Arbitrator: M. David Keefe

Adjusting to the presence of a union in day-to-day work relations is not easy for public administrators used to having their own way and dealing directly with individual employees. This adjustment is all the more difficult for police patrolmen and officers accustomed to the procedures of a paramilitary type of organization. This case deals with the problems of both parties in disciplinary cases for which the collective agreement provides due process through a grievance procedure.

Mr. David Keefe, the arbitrator, prepared the statement of facts and issues in the case that follows.

The hearing took place on July 29, 1968, in conference quarters of the City-County Building located in Port Huron, Michigan. The parties stipulated that the single grievance scheduled for hearing was free from procedural defects under the Agreement between the parties dated July 1, 1967 (Joint Ex. #1) and was properly before the arbitrator for final and binding decision.

STATEMENT OF THE CASE

On January 5, 1968, the grievant, Patrolman N., reported as scheduled on the second shift. He immediately approached Lt. Lewis (who at the time was Sergeant on the desk) to straighten out an overtime pay problem which affected the Grievant. After a short discussion, Lt. C. (who was in charge of the shift) entered the conversation but was rudely rebuffed by Patrolman N. Lt. C. invited the Grievant into the Captain's office for a private talk. Patrolman N. demanded Union representation. Lt. C. thereupon asked Lt. Cole (then Sergeant Cole) to be present as his witness. At the time, no Union representative was there. Lt. C. demanded that the Grievant come into the office. Patrolman N. refused to do so unrepresented. The Lieutenant then ordered him to comply or go home. The Grievant persisted in his refusal. He was thereupon suspended, with the penalty being later fixed at thirty (30) days off without pay.

PERTINENT CONTRACT PROVISIONS CITED BY THE PARTIES

Item 1: Section 1–3. *Management Clause*
   The Union recognizes fully all rights and prerogatives of the Employer to operate and manage its affairs in all respects in accordance with the Employer's responsibilities, and all rights, powers, and authority which the Employer has not officially abridged, delegated or modified by the agreement are retained by the Employer.

Item 2: Section 3–13. *Use of Past Records*
   The employer agrees that for the purposes of promotion and in matters of discipline, the employees' performance records covering incidents of minor infractions shall not be used beyond the time period of four (4) years. This is in no way to be interpreted that the Employer does not have the right to retain on file the complete personnel records of the employees from the initial hire date.

Item 3: Section 4–1.1. *Notice of Discharge or Discipline*
   The Employer agrees promptly upon the discharge or discipline of an employee to notify in writing the Steward of the discharge or discipline.

Item 4: Section 4–1.2.
   The discharged or disciplined employee will be allowed to discuss his discharge or discipline with the Steward of the shift. Upon request, the Employer or his designated representative will discuss the discharge or discipline with the employee and the Steward.

STIPULATIONS BY THE PARTIES

   The parties stipulated that the grievant's past performance record, as submitted to the arbitrator, was accurate. These documents consist of both commendations and disciplinary notices, which latter include three (3) time-off suspensions. The most recent of these occurred more than four (4) years prior to the incident in this case. The parties, having failed to establish criteria for differentiating between minor and major offenses, empowered the arbitrator to evaluate each of these previous infractions for purposes of making such a determination. Finally, inasmuch as the current contract is the initial Agreement and AFSCME did not previously enjoy representation rights, protests against these disciplinary actions could not follow contract grievance procedure but, rather, were restricted to the civil service appeals system which was not utilized.

SUMMARY OF THE GRIEVANT'S PAST PERFORMANCE RECORD

Patrolman N. has been a member of the Port Huron Police Department for a period in excess of twelve years. His record, compiled during that span, shows the following:

Item 1   4–18–56:   Police Chief's Commendation; job well done, alert to duty

Item 2   8–10–56:   Police Chief's Commendation; job well done—citation

Item 3   2–14–57:   Police Chief's Commendation; job well done—splendid

Item 4   7– 2–57:   Police Chief's Commendation; polite, courteous, considerate

Item 5   8–20–57:   Reassignment from patrol car; near accident

Item 6   2– 4–58:   Police Chief's Commendation; alert, attentive to duty

Item 7   4–20–59:   Employee Performance Report—rated satisfactory

Item 8   8– 3–61:   15 day Suspension—"conduct unbecoming officer"

Item 9   6– 2–62:   Police Chief's Commendation; diligence and follow-up

Item 10   10–31–62:   10 day Suspension—"conduct unbecoming officer"

Item 11   11–15–62:   County Sheriff's Commendation; assistance and cooperation

Item 12   1– 3–64:   20 day Suspension—"conduct unbecoming officer"

Item 13   10– 8–64:   U.S. Immigration Service Commendation—efficient, prompt action

Item 14   3–29–65:   Record Notation: attended FBI classes on own time

Item 15   7–22–65:   Police Captain Notation: keen observation, quick action

Item 16   8–27–65:   Citizen's Commendation; credit to force

Item 17   3–10–67:   Police Captain Commendation; keen observation, fine police work

Item 18   8– 8–67:   Record Notation; failure to respond to direct order

Item 19   5–12–68:   Citizen's Commendation; prompt action saved 2 fingers

THE CITY OF PORT HURON'S POSITION

The City pointed out that a police force is a semi-military organization which functions through compliance with orders. Unless self-discipline is ingrained as an employee attitude toward his vocation, it must be imposed by the Employer or the effectiveness of and purpose for the organization's existence will be undermined from within itself. It is not only the City's inherent right to maintain discipline among and require respect from the members of this employee group; it is, in fact, an absolute responsibility. In this case, the City contends that the Grievant was guilty of flagrant public insubordination to a superior officer.

Lieutenant C., who had overheard the overtime pay discussion between the Grievant and then Sergeant Lewis, testified that, with constructive intent, he interposed with a remark that the payroll records were unavailable at that hour. The Grievant turned to him and, in substance, retorted that the witness should keep his nose out of the matter; that it was none of his business and that he (the Grievant) was tired

of "this shit." The witness, who averred that he had not been antagonistic, described Patrolman N.'s attitude as hostile, in the manner of an
offended person. His comments had been expressed quite loudly. The
witness, who considered the matter trivial at that stage, felt that he
should talk privately on the matter with the grievant and asked him
into the Captain's office, which was vacant. Patrolman N. thereupon
declared that he wanted Union representation. Lt. C. countered that, in
such case, he, in turn, wanted then Sergeant Cole with him as a witness.
The Grievant, continuing to demand representation, went to the Squad
Room and talked to Officer Bowns, Unit President. The witness fol-
lowed-up with Patrolman N. and told him to come into the office. The
Grievant said he wanted Officer Klaus, the Union Steward, to be present.
Patrolman Klaus was out on call. Lt. C. then ordered the Grievant to
come into the office or put his gear away and go home. Officer N. persisted in his refusal, putting his gear away—but not leaving. He never
went to the Captain's office.

Steward Klaus returned within five minutes of the Grievant's suspension and asked Lt. C. about the incident. The witness told him that he
would have discussed the matter before Patrolman N. was suspended
but refused to meet on the matter at that point. The Lieutenant told the
Steward that the Grievant was dismissed to return at the pleasure of the
Chief of Police. There was no further discussion until a later grievance
meeting was called by the Union.

Lt. C. admitted, under cross examination, that he had raised his voice
during the development of the difference. He was loud but hesitated to
describe his tone as "yelling." At any rate, neither man used out-and-out
profanity in their exchange, according to the witness.

Lieutenants Lewis and Cole (then Sergeants) confirmed the general
account given by Lt. C. They both testified that the Grievant and Lieutenant were loud—but not yelling or screaming. The altercation was overheard by other officers (the shifts were just changing and many were in
the vicinity) and, also, by certain prisoners who were in the process of
being booked.

Police Chief Falk testified that he was told of the incident on the following day. He asked Lt. C. for a written report. Personnel Director
Provost was then informed and, together with the Chief, investigated
the incident through interviews with Lts. C. and Cole. Lt. Lewis was
talked to on the phone. The Grievant was unavailable. However, Steward
Klaus asked for a meeting which took place on January 6, 1968. This
meeting was followed by a further session in which the incident was
fully explored. At that time, the penalty had not been fixed. The grievant
was asked if he had made the initial remark about "none of your business,
etc." and admitted that he might have used words to that effect. He was
also asked if he had refused to go into the Captain's office and affirmed
that he had refused unless and until he had representation. As far as the

Lieutenant's alleged abuse of him, the Grievant reported that it was not what was said that was improper but rather how it was said, with sarcasm. At the end of the session, the Chief felt that he had the facts and, based on the seriousness of the insubordination, the aggravating circumstances of the public display and the past record of three (3) suspensions, recommended a thirty (30) day suspension as the penalty in this case.

Personnel Director Provost corroborated the account given by Chief Falk as to the meetings and method for evaluation of the penalty.

The City argued that the image, public acceptance of and respect for the Police Department was damaged to the extent that citizens, in the process of being booked, overheard what transpired. Internally, organizational morale and decorum was dealt a blow due to the presence during the incident of many officers in the building because of shift change. These aggravating circumstances, when considered as the background to the outright and persistent refusal of the Grievant to comply with a direct order, added up to a most serious infraction. When considered in the light of the three (3) previous suspensions, discharge was deemed merited but was not imposed out of recognition of the commendations in the Grievant's record.

The City asked that the grievance be denied.

THE UNION'S POSITION

Grievant N. related that, when he approached Lt. Lewis on his overtime pay problem, he observed Lt. C. nearby, who seemed upset. At any rate, in the course of his conversation with Lt. Lewis, Lt. C. rudely interrupted and was very sarcastic in giving his advice. The Grievant told him to keep his nose out of the conversation. The Lieutenant then began to yell, calling for Lt. Cole and telling the Grievant to get his ass into the Captain's office for a talk. The witness felt that he was in a tenuous position, with Lt. C. acting extremely excited. He stated that he wanted Union representation in any projected interviews. Lt. C. reminded him that he was, actually, the Union President and asked why he needed representation. The Grievant went to the Squad Room, looking for Steward Klaus. There, he met Unit President Bowns who was about to leave and who advised him Officer Klaus was working the shift. He could not be found at the time. It developed that he was out on a call right then. Lt. C., meanwhile, continued yelling. He threatened to send the Grievant home. Patrolman N. explained that he was waiting for the return of Steward Klaus before entering into the interview. At that point, Lt. C. ordered him to go home. The Steward came in almost immediately after that. The Grievant informed him of the incident. When the pair approached the Lieutenant to discuss the problem, Lt. C. refused and "ranted" at the Grievant that: "Ever since this God damned Union came in you've been pretty cocky and stuck your nose into everything around here. You think this is your Union and the word is out that it's N.'s Union." The grievant added that, in the January 6 meeting, he had been cut short from presenting his side in full.

Officer Klaus was absent on vacation and, therefore, did not testify. However, *Officer Everitt* appeared in behalf of the grievant. He stated that, as the incident began, he was in the hall, outside the office where the altercation first took place. He heard Lt. C. speaking in a loud voice, although he could not make out what was said. The Grievant came out of the office. Lt. C. followed, calling for Lt. Cole. He called to the Grievant to go to the Captain's office. Patrolman N. said he wanted a Union representative before he went in. Lt. C. then loudly told him to go to the office or put his gear away and go home. At that stage, Patrolman Everitt, who was finishing his shift, went home. He added that the exchange which he witnessed was marked by yelling on the part of Lt. C. but not by the Grievant.

The Union argued that Lt. C. was motivated by bias against the Grievant due to his Union activity and that this incited him to lay down the ultimatum which precipitated the suspension. When Steward Klaus appeared, almost on the heels of this overt decision, he was rebuffed, in spite of his contract right to meet with the Lieutenant on the matter. Furthermore, the required written notice to the Steward was not rendered until some days later. All this, in the Union's view, adds up to intemperate and improper management action. The initial exchange had been described by Lt. C. as trivial. Obviously, then, it was blown up to federal-case proportions by the Lieutenant, inspired by his animosity against the Grievant.

The Union asked that the grievance be upheld.

QUESTIONS

1. What allowance, if any, should an arbitrator make for the inexperience of career police officers in the new relationship with subordinates brought on by a first collective bargaining agreement? Does this apply both ways: to the union and its members as well as management?

2. Under the terms of the agreement, what weight would you give to Patrolman N's past performance record? Would you count it in his favor or against him? Does it apply at all? Do you think his superiors gave it proper consideration in coming to their disciplinary decision? Why, or why not?

3. Should Patrolman N's past performance record count at all in the disposition of this case?

4. Did the police lieutenant and the Department follow the grievance procedures set down in the agreement? Did the grievant? The union? What weight should this have in the arbitrator's award? Does the stipulation that the grievance was "free from procedural defects" prevent the arbitrator from considering this?

APPENDIXES

Federal Statutory and Administrative Laws
on Collective Bargaining

APPENDIX I

Norris–La Guardia Act

Taft-Hartley Act as Amended

Landrum-Griffin Act as Amended

APPENDIX II

Executive Order 11491

APPENDIX I

The major federal laws on collective bargaining in effect at the close of 1966 were the Railway Labor Act of 1926 as amended; the Norris–La Guardia Act of 1932; the Labor-Management Relations Act of 1947 (Taft-Hartley Act) as amended by Public Law 86–257, 1959 (Landrum-Griffin Act); and the Labor-Management Reporting and Disclosure Act of 1959 (Landrum-Griffin Act) as amended. The Railway Labor Act of 1926 will not be covered in this appendix because of its limited application.

This appendix is designed as a ready reference to the *major* elements of national labor relations law. This appendix excludes the rich interpretations of the statutes cited which have been developed by the National Labor Relations Board and the courts.

THE NORRIS–LA GUARDIA ANTI-INJUNCTION ACT OF MARCH 23, 1932

This law was passed for the purpose of eliminating certain abuses of the injunction in labor disputes. It severely restricts the authority of federal courts to issue injunctions in labor disputes. The full text of the original law is reproduced below. The Norris–La Guardia Act was amended by the Labor Management Relations Act of 1947 (the Taft-Hartley law).

NORRIS–LA GUARDIA ANTI-INJUNCTION ACT
OF MARCH 23, 1932

(Public—No. 65—72d Congress)
(H.R. 5315)

AN ACT

To amend the Judicial Code and to define and limit the jurisdiction of courts sitting in equity, and for other purposes.

Be it enacted by the Senate and House of Representatives of the United States of America in Congress assembled, that no court of the United States, as herein defined shall have jurisdiction to issue any restraining order or temporary or permanent injunction in a case involving or growing out of a labor dispute, except in a strict conformity with the provisions of this Act; nor shall any such restraining order or temporary or permanent injunction be issued contrary to the public policy declared in this Act.

Sec. 2. In the interpretation of this Act and in determining the jurisdiction and authority of the courts of the United States, as such jurisdiction and authority are herein defined and limited, the public policy of the United States is hereby declared as follows:

Whereas under prevailing economic conditions, developed with the aid of governmental authority for owners of property to organize in the corporate and other form of ownership association, the individual unorganized worker is commonly helpless to exercise actual liberty of contract and to protect his freedom of labor, and thereby to obtain acceptable terms and conditions of employment, therefore, though he should be free to decline to associate with his fellows, it is necessary that he have full freedom of association, self-organization, and designation of representatives of his own choosing, to negotiate the terms and conditions of his employment, and that he shall be free from the interference, restraint, or coercion of employers of labor, or their agents, in the designation of such representatives or in self-organization or in other concerted activities for the purpose of collective bargaining or other mutual aid or protection; therefore, the following definitions of, and limitations upon, the jurisdiction and authority of the courts of the United States are hereby enacted.

SEC. 3. Any undertaking or promise, such as is described in this section, or any other undertaking or promise in conflict with the public policy declared in section 2 of this Act, is hereby declared to be contrary to the public policy of the United States, shall not be enforceable in any court of the United States and shall not afford any basis for the granting of legal or equitable relief by any such court, including specifically the following:

Every undertaking or promise hereafter made, whether written or oral, express or implied, constituting or contained in any contract or agreement of hiring or employment between any individual, firm, company, association, or corporation, and any employee or prospective employee of the same, whereby

(a) Either party to such contract or agreement undertakes or promises not to join, become, or remain a member of any labor organization or of any employer organization; or

(b) Either party to such contract or agreement undertakes or promises that he will withdraw from an employment relation in the event that he joins, becomes, or remains a member of any labor organization or of any employer organization.

SEC. 4. No court of the United States shall have jurisdiction to issue any restraining order or temporary or permanent injunction in any case involving or growing out of any labor dispute to prohibit any person or persons participating or interested in such dispute (as these terms are herein defined) from doing, whether singly or in concert, any of the following acts:

(a) Ceasing or refusing to perform any work or to remain in any relation of employment;

(b) Becoming or remaining a member of any labor organization or of any employer organization, regardless of any such undertaking or promise as is described in section 3 of this Act;

(c) Paying or giving to, or withholding from, any person participating or interested in such labor dispute, any strike or unemployment benefits or insurance, or other moneys or things of value;

(d) By all lawful means aiding any person participating or interested in any labor dispute who is being proceeded against in, or is prosecuting, any action or suit in any court of the United States or of any State;

(e) Giving publicity to the existence of, or the facts involved in, any labor dispute, whether by advertising, speaking, patrolling, or by any other method not involving fraud or violence;

(f) Assembling peaceably to act or to organize to act in promotion of their interests in a labor dispute;

(g) Advising or notifying any person of an intention to do any of the acts heretofore specified;

(h) Agreeing with other persons to do or not to do any of the acts heretofore specified; and

(i) Advising, urging, or otherwise causing or inducing without fraud or violence the acts heretofore specified, regardless of any such undertaking or promise as is described in section 3 of this Act.

Sec. 5. No court of the United States shall have jurisdiction to issue a restraining order or temporary or permanent injunction upon the ground that any of the persons participating or interested in a labor dispute constitute or are engaged in an unlawful combination or conspiracy because of the doing in concert of the acts enumerated in section 4 of this Act.

Sec. 6. No officer or member of any association or organization, and no association or organization participating or interested in a labor dispute, shall be held responsible or liable in any court of the United States for the unlawful acts of individual officers, members, or agents, except upon clear proof of actual participation in, or actual authorization of, such acts, or of ratification of such acts after actual knowledge thereof.

Sec. 7. No court of the United States shall have jurisdiction to issue a temporary or permanent injunction in any case involving or growing out of a labor dispute as herein defined, except after hearing the testimony of witnesses in open court (with opportunity for cross-examination) in support of the allegations of a complaint made under oath, and testimony in opposition thereto, if offered, and except after findings of fact by the court, to the effect—

(a) That unlawful acts have been threatened and will be committed unless restrained or have been committed and will be continued unless restrained, but no injunction or temporary restraining order shall be issued on account of any threat or unlawful act excepting against the person or persons, association, or organization making the threat or committing the unlawful act or actually authorizing or ratifying the same after actual knowledge thereof;

(b) That substantial and irreparable injury to complainant's property will follow;

(c) That as to each item of relief granted greater injury will be inflicted upon complainant by the denial of relief than will be inflicted upon defendants by the granting of relief;

(d) That complainant has no adequate remedy at law; and

(e) That the public officers charged with the duty to protect complainant's property are unable or unwilling to furnish adequate protection.

Such hearing shall be held after due and personal notice thereof has been given, in such manner as the court shall direct, to all known persons against whom relief is sought, and also to the chief of those public officials of the county and city within which the unlawful acts have been threatened or committed charged with the duty to protect complainant's property: *Provided, however,* That if a complainant shall also allege that, unless a temporary restraining order shall be issued without notice, a substantial and irreparable injury to complainant's property will be unavoidable, such a temporary restraining order may be issued upon testimony under oath, sufficient, if sustained, to justify the court in issuing a temporary injunction upon a hearing after notice. Such a temporary restraining order shall be effective for no longer than five days and shall become void at the expiration of said five days. No temporary restraining order or temporary injunction shall be issued except on condition that complainant shall first file an undertaking with adequate security in an amount to be fixed by the court sufficient to recompense those enjoined for any loss, expense, or damage caused by the improvident or erroneous issuance of such order or injunction, including all reasonable costs (together with a reasonable attorney's fee) and expense of defense against the order or against the granting of any injunctive relief sought in the same proceeding and subsequently denied by the court.

The undertaking herein mentioned shall be understood to signify an agreement entered into by the complainant and the surety upon which a decree may be rendered in the same suit or proceeding against said complainant and surety, upon a hearing to assess damages of which hearing complainant and surety shall have reasonable notice, the said complainant and surety submitting themselves to the jurisdiction of the court for that purpose. But nothing herein contained shall deprive any party having a claim or cause of action under or upon such undertaking from electing to pursue his ordinary remedy by suit at law or in equity.

Sec. 8. No restraining order or injunctive relief shall be granted to any complainant who has failed to comply with any obligation imposed by law which is involved in the labor dispute in question, or who has failed to make every reasonable effort to settle such dispute either by negotiation or with the aid of any available governmental machinery of mediation or voluntary arbitration.

Sec. 9. No restraining order or temporary or permanent injunction shall be granted in a case involving or growing out of a labor dispute, except on the basis of findings of fact made and filed by the court in the record of the case prior to the issuance of such restraining order or injunction; and every restraining order or injunction granted in a case involving or growing out of a labor dispute shall include only a prohibition of such specific act or acts as may be expressly complained of in the bill of complaint or petition filed in such case and as shall be expressly included in said findings of fact made and filed by the court as provided herein.

Sec. 10. Whenever any court of the United States shall issue or deny any temporary injunction in a case involving or growing out of a labor dispute, the court shall, upon the request of any party to the proceedings and on his filing the usual bond for costs, forthwith certify as in ordinary cases the record of the case to the circuit court of appeals for its review. Upon the filing of such record in the circuit court of appeals, the appeal shall be heard and the temporary injunctive order affirmed, modified, or set aside with the greatest possible expedition, giving the proceedings precedence over all other matters except older matters of the same character.

Sec. 11. In all cases arising under this Act in which a person shall be charged with contempt in a court of the United States (as herein defined), the accused shall enjoy the right to a speedy and public trial by an impartial jury of the State and district wherein the contempt shall have been committed: *Provided,* That this right shall not apply to contempts committed in the presence of the court or so near thereto as to interfere directly with the administration of justice or to apply to the misbehavior, misconduct, or disobedience of any officer of the court in respect to the writs, orders, or process of the court.

Sec. 12. The defendant in any proceeding for contempt of court may file with the court a demand for the retirement of the judge sitting in the proceeding, if the contempt arises from an attack upon the character or conduct of such judge and if the attack occurred elsewhere than in the presence of the court or so near thereto as to interfere directly with the administration of justice. Upon the filing of any such demand the judge shall thereupon proceed no further, but another judge shall be designated in the same manner as is provided by law. The demand shall be filed prior to the hearing in the contempt proceeding.

SEC. 13. When used in this Act, and for the purposes of this Act—

(a) A case shall be held to involve or to grow out of a labor dispute when the case involves persons who are engaged in the same industry, trade, craft, or occupation; or have direct or indirect interests therein; or who are employees of the same employer; or who are members of the same or an affiliated organization of employers or employees; whether such dispute is (1) between one or more employers or associations of employers and one or more employees or associations of employees; (2) between one or more employers or associations of employers and one or more employers or associations of employers; or (3) between one or more employees or associations of employees and one or more employees or associations of employees; or when the case involves any conflicting or competing interests in a "labor dispute" (as hereinafter defined) of "persons participating or interested" (as hereinafter defined).

(b) A person or association shall be held to be a person participating or interested in a labor dispute if relief is sought against him or it, and if he or it is engaged in the same industry, trade, craft, or occupation in which such dispute occurs, or has a direct or indirect interest therein, or is a member, officer, or agent of any association composed in whole or in part of employers or employees engaged in such industry, trade, craft, or occupation.

(c) The term "labor dispute" includes any controversy concerning terms or conditions of employment, or concerning the association or representation of persons in negotiating, fixing, maintaining, changing, or seeking to arrange terms or conditions of employment, regardless of whether or not the disputants stand in the proximate relation of employer and employee.

(d) The term "court of the United States" means any court of the United States whose jurisdiction has been or may be conferred or defined or limited by Act of Congress, including the courts of the District of Columbia.

SEC. 14. If any provision of this Act or the application thereof to any person or circumstance is held unconstitutional or otherwise invalid, the remaining provisions of the Act and the application of such provisions to other persons or circumstances shall not be affected thereby.

SEC. 15. All Acts and parts of Acts in conflict with the provisions of this Act are hereby repealed.

Approved, March 23, 1932.

The National Labor Relations Act of 1935 (Wagner Act)

From 1935 to 1947, the Wagner Act was the major federal law regulating collective bargaining. This law provided for the establishment of the National Labor Relations Board to certify employee representatives for collective bargaining and to prevent five "unfair labor practices" *by management*. These management unfair labor practices were essentially unchanged by the Labor Management Relations Act of 1947.

THE LABOR MANAGEMENT RELATIONS ACT OF 1947 (TAFT-HARTLEY LAW AS AMENDED)

Title I of the Labor Management Relations Act was entitled Amendments to the National Labor Relations Act. The major change was the addition of Section 8(b), unfair labor practices by labor organizations. The Taft-Hartley law also made major procedural changes in National

Labor Relations Board operations and added four entirely new titles to collective bargaining law. The Taft-Hartley law has been amended by Public Law 189, 82d Congress, and the Landrum-Griffin law (the Labor Management Reporting and Disclosure Law of 1959). The Taft-Hartley law and its amendments are shown in the text below:

TEXT OF LABOR MANAGEMENT RELATIONS ACT, 1947, AS AMENDED BY PUBLIC LAW 86–257, 1959*

[PUBLIC LAW 101—80TH CONGRESS]

AN ACT

To amend the National Labor Relations Act, to provide additional facilities for the mediation of labor disputes affecting commerce, to equalize legal responsibilities of labor organizations and employers, and for other purposes.

Be it enacted by the Senate and House of Representatives of the United States of America in Congress assembled,

SHORT TITLE AND DECLARATION OF POLICY

SECTION 1. (a) This Act may be cited as the "Labor Management Relations Act, 1947."

(b) Industrial strife which interferes with the normal flow of commerce and with the full production of articles and commodities for commerce, can be avoided or substantially minimized if employers, employees, and labor organizations each recognize under law one another's legitimate rights in their relations with each other, and above all recognize under law that neither party has any right in its relations with any other to engage in acts or practices which jeopardize the public health, safety, or interest.

It is the purpose and policy of this Act, in order to promote the full flow of commerce, to prescribe the legitimate rights of both employees and employers in their relations affecting commerce, to provide orderly and peaceful procedures for preventing the interference by either with the legitimate rights of the other, to protect the rights of individual employees in their relations with labor organizations whose activities affect commerce, to define and proscribe practices on the part of labor and management which affect commerce and are inimical to the general welfare, and to protect the rights of the public in connection with labor disputes affecting commerce.

TITLE I—AMENDMENT OF NATIONAL LABOR RELATIONS ACT

SEC. 101. The National Labor Relations Act is hereby amended to read as follows:

FINDINGS AND POLICIES

SECTION 1. The denial by some employers of the right of employees to organize and the refusal by some employers to accept the procedure of

---

* Section 201(d) and (e) of the Labor-Management Reporting and Disclosure Act of 1959 which repealed Section 9(f), (g), and (h) of the Labor Management Relations Act, 1947, and Section 505 amending Section 302(a), (b), and (c) of the Labor Management Relations Act, 1947, took effect upon enactment of Public Law 86–257, September 14, 1959. As to the other amendments of the Labor Management Relations Act, 1947, Section 707 of the Labor-Management Reporting and Disclosure Act provides:

The amendments made by this title shall take effect sixty days after the date of the enactment of this Act and no provision of this title shall be deemed to make collective bargaining lead to strikes and other forms of industrial strife or unrest, which have the intent or the necessary effect of burdening or obstructing commerce by (a) impairing the efficiency, safety, or operation of the instrumentalities of commerce; (b) occurring in the current of commerce; (c) materially affecting, restraining, or controlling the flow of raw materials or manufactured or processed goods from or into the channels of commerce, or the prices of such materials or goods in commerce; or (d) causing diminution of employment and wages in such volume as substantially to impair or disrupt the market for goods flowing from or into the channels of commerce.

The inequality of bargaining power between employees who do not possess full freedom of association or actual liberty of contract, and employers who are organized in the corporate or other forms of ownership association substantially burdens and affects the flow of commerce, and tends to aggravate recurrent business depressions, by depressing wage rates and the purchasing power of wage earners in industry and by preventing the stabilization of competitive wage rates and working conditions within and between industries.

Experience has proved that protection by law of the right of employees to organize and bargain collectively safeguards commerce from injury, impairment, or interruption, and promotes the flow of commerce by removing certain recognized sources of industrial strife and unrest, by encouraging practices fundamental to the friendly adjustment of industrial disputes arising out of differences as to wages, hours, or other working conditions, and by restoring equality of bargaining power between employers and employees.

Experience has further demonstrated that certain practices by some labor organizations, their officers, and members have the intent or the necessary effect of burdening or obstructing commerce by preventing the free flow of goods in such commerce through strikes and other forms of industrial unrest or through concerted activities which impair the interest of the public in the free flow of such commerce. The elimination of such practices is a necessary condition to the assurance of the rights herein guaranteed.

It is hereby declared to be the policy of the United States to eliminate the causes of certain substantial obstructions to the free flow of commerce and to mitigate and eliminate these obstructions when they have occurred by encouraging the practice and procedure of collective bargaining and by protecting the exercise by workers of full freedom of association, self-organization, and designation of representatives of their own choosing, for the purpose of negotiating the terms and conditions of their employment or other mutual aid or protection.

DEFINITIONS

SEC. 2. When used in this Act—

(1) The term "person" includes one or more individuals, labor organizations, partnerships, associations, corporations, legal representatives, trustees, trustees in bankruptcy, or receivers.

(2) The term "employer" includes any person acting as an agent of an employer, directly or indirectly, but shall not include the United States or any wholly owned Government corporation, or any Federal Reserve Bank, or any State or political subdivision thereof, or any corporation or association operating a hospital, if no part of the net earnings inures to the benefit of any private shareholder or individual, or any person subject to the Railway Labor Act, as amended from time to time, or any labor organization (other than when acting as an employer), or anyone acting in the capacity of officer or agent of such labor organization.

---

an unfair labor practice, any act which is performed prior to such effective date which did not constitute an unfair labor practice prior thereto.

(3) The term "employee" shall include any employee, and shall not be limited to the employees of a particular employer, unless the Act explicitly states otherwise, and shall include any individual whose work has ceased as a consequence of, or in connection with, any current labor dispute or because of any unfair labor practice, and who has not obtained any other regular and substantially equivalent employment, but shall not include any individual employed as an agricultural laborer, or in the domestic service of any family or person at his home, or any individual employed by his parent or spouse, or any individual having the status of an independent contractor, or any individual employed as a supervisor, or any individual employed by an employer subject to the Railway Labor Act, as amended from time to time, or by any other person who is not an employer as herein defined.

(4) The term "representatives" includes any individual or labor organization.

(5) The term "labor organization" means any organization of any kind, or any agency or employee representation committee or plan, in which employees participate and which exists for the purpose, in whole or in part, of dealing with employers concerning grievances, labor disputes, wages, rates of pay, hours of employment, or conditions of work.

(6) The term "commerce" means trade, traffic, commerce, transportation, or communication among the several States, or between the District of Columbia or any Territory of the United States and any State or other Territory, or between any foreign country and any State, Territory, or the District of Columbia, or within the District of Columbia or any Territory, or between points in the same State but through any other State or any Territory or the District of Columbia or any foreign country.

(7) The term "affecting commerce" means in commerce, or burdening or obstructing commerce or the free flow of commerce, or having led or tending to lead to a labor dispute burdening or obstructing commerce or the free flow of commerce.

(8) The term "unfair labor practice" means any unfair labor practice listed in section 8.

(9) The term "labor dispute" includes any controversy concerning terms, tenure or conditions of employment, or concerning the association or representation of persons in negotiating, fixing, maintaining, changing, or seeking to arrange terms or conditions of employment, regardless of whether the disputants stand in the proximate relation of employer and employee.

(10) The term "National Labor Relations Board" means the National Labor Relations Board provided for in section 3 of this Act.

(11) The term "supervisor" means any individual having authority, in the interest of the employer, to hire, transfer, suspend, lay off, recall, promote, discharge, assign, reward, or discipline other employees, or responsibly to direct them, or to adjust their grievances, or effectively to recommend such action, if in connection with the foregoing the exercise of such authority is not of a merely routine or clerical nature, but requires the use of independent judgment.

(12) The term "professional employee" means—

(a) any employee engaged in work (i) predominantly intellectual and varied in character as opposed to routine mental, manual, mechanical, or physical work; (ii) involving the consistent exercise of discretion and judgment in its performance; (iii) of such a character that the output produced or the result accomplished cannot be standardized in relation to a given period of time; (iv) requiring knowledge of an advanced type in a field of science or learning customarily acquired by a prolonged course of specialized intellectual instruction and study in an institution of higher learning or a hospital, as distinguished from a general academic education or from an apprenticeship or from training in the performance of routine mental, manual, or physical processes; or

(b) any employee, who (i) has completed the courses of specialized intellectual instruction and study described in clause (iv) of paragraph (a), and (ii) is performing related work under the supervision of a professional person to qualify himself to become a professional employee as defined in paragraph (a).

(13) In determining whether any person is acting as an "agent" of another person so as to make such other person responsible for his acts, the question of whether the specific acts performed were actually authorized or subsequently ratified shall not be controlling.

NATIONAL LABOR RELATIONS BOARD

SEC. 3. (a) The National Labor Relations Board (hereinafter called the "Board") created by this Act prior to its amendment by the Labor Management Relations Act, 1947, is hereby continued as an agency of the United States, except that the Board shall consist of five instead of three members, appointed by the President by and with the advice and consent of the Senate. Of the two additional members so provided for, one shall be appointed for a term of five years and the other for a term of two years. Their successors, and the successors of the other members, shall be appointed for terms of five years each, excepting that any individual chosen to fill a vacancy shall be appointed only for the unexpired term of the member whom he shall succeed. The President shall designate one member to serve as Chairman of the Board. Any member of the Board may be removed by the President, upon notice and hearing, for neglect of duty or malfeasance in office, but for no other cause.

(b) The Board is authorized to delegate to any group of three of more members any or all of the powers which it may itself exercise. The Board is also authorized to delegate to its regional directors its powers under section 9 to determine the unit appropriate for the purpose of collective bargaining, to investigate and provide for hearings, and determine whether a question of representation exists, and to direct an election or take a secret ballot under subsection (c) or (e) of section 9 and certify the results thereof, except that upon the filing of a request therefor with the Board by any interested person, the Board may review any action of a regional director delegated to him under this paragraph, but such a review shall not, unless specifically ordered by the Board, operate as a stay of any action taken by the regional director. A vacancy in the Board shall not impair the right of the remaining members to exercise all of the powers of the Board, and three members of the Board shall, at all times, constitute a quorum of the Board, except that two members shall constitute a quorum of any group designated pursuant to the first sentence hereof. The Board shall have an official seal which shall be judicially noticed.

(c) The Board shall at the close of each fiscal year make a report in writing to Congress and to the President stating in detail the cases it has heard, the decisions it has rendered, the names, salaries, and duties of all employees and officers in the employ or under the supervision of the Board, and an account of all moneys it has disbursed.

(d) There shall be a General Counsel of the Board who shall be appointed by the President, by and with the advice and consent of the Senate, for a term of four years. The General Counsel of the Board shall exercise general supervision over all attorneys employed by the Board (other than trial examiners and legal assistants to Board members) and over the officers and employees in the regional offices. He shall have final authority, on behalf of the Board, in respect of the investigation of charges and issuance of complaints under section

10, and in respect of the prosecution of such complaints before the Board, and shall have such other duties as the Board may prescribe or as may be provided by law. In case of a vacancy in the office of the General Counsel the President is authorized to designate the officer or employee who shall act as General Counsel during such vacancy, but no person or persons so designated shall so act (1) for more than forty days when the Congress is in session unless a nomination to fill such vacancy shall have been submitted to the Senate, or (2) after the adjournment *sine die* of the session of the Senate in which such nomination was submitted.

SEC. 4. (a) Each member of the Board and the General Counsel of the Board shall receive a salary of $12,000* a year, shall be eligible for reappointment, and shall not engage in any other business, vocation, or employment. The Board shall appoint an executive secretary, and such attorneys, examiners, and regional directors, and such other employees as it may from time to time find necessary for the proper performance of its duties. The Board may not employ any attorneys for the purpose of reviewing transcripts of hearings or preparing drafts of opinions except that any attorney employed for assignment as a legal assistant to any Board member may for such Board member review such transcripts and prepare such drafts. No trial examiner's report shall be reviewed, either before or after its publication, by any person other than a member of the Board or his legal assistant, and no trial examiner shall advise or consult with the Board with respect to exceptions taken to his findings, rulings, or recommendations. The Board may establish or utilize such regional, local, or other agencies, and utilize such voluntary and uncompensated services, as may from time to time be needed. Attorneys appointed under this section may, at the direction of the Board, appear for and represent the Board in any case in court. Nothing in this Act shall be construed to authorize the Board to appoint individuals for the purpose of conciliation or mediation, or for economic analysis.

(b) All of the expenses of the Board, including all necessary traveling and subsistence expenses outside the District of Columbia incurred by the members or employees of the Board under its orders, shall be allowed and paid on the presentation of itemized vouchers therefor approved by the Board or by any individual it designates for that purpose.

SEC. 5. The principal office of the Board shall be in the District of Columbia, but it may meet and exercise any or all of its powers at any other place. The Board may, by one or more of its members or by such agents or agencies as it may designate, prosecute any inquiry necessary to its functions in any part of the United States. A member who participates in such an inquiry shall not be disqualified from subsequently participating in a decision of the Board in the same case.

SEC. 6. The Board shall have authority from time to time to make, amend, and rescind, in the manner prescribed by the Administrative Procedure Act, such rules and regulations as may be necessary to carry out the provisions of this Act.

RIGHTS OF EMPLOYEES

SEC. 7. Employees shall have the right to self-organization, to form, join, or assist labor organizations, to bargain collectively through representatives of their own choosing, and to engage in other concerted activities for the purpose

* Pursuant to Public Law 88–426, 88th Congress, 2d Session, Title III, approved August 14, 1964, the salary of the Chairman of the Board shall be $28,500 per year and the salaries of the General Counsel and each Board member shall be $27,000 per year.

of collective bargaining or other mutual aid or protection, and shall also have the right to refrain from any or all of such activities except to the extent that such right may be affected by an agreement requiring membership in a labor organization as a condition of employment as authorized in section 8(a) (3).

UNFAIR LABOR PRACTICES

Sec. 8. (a) It shall be an unfair labor practice for an employer—

(1) to interfere with, restrain, or coerce employees in the exercise of the rights guaranteed in section 7;

(2) to dominate or interfere with the formation or administration of any labor organization or contribute financial or other support to it: *Provided,* That subject to rules and regulations made and published by the Board pursuant to section 6, an employer shall not be prohibited from permitting employees to confer with him during working hours without loss of time or pay;

(3) by discrimination in regard to hire or tenure of employment or any term or condition of employment to encourage or discourage membership in any labor organization: *Provided,* That nothing in this Act, or in any other statute of the United States, shall preclude an employer from making an agreement with a labor organization (not established, maintained, or assisted by any action defined in section 8(a) of this Act as an unfair labor practice) to require as a condition of employment membership therein on or after the thirtieth day following the beginning of such employment or the effective date of such agreement, whichever is the later, (i) if such labor organization is the representative of the employees as provided in section 9(a), in the appropriate collective-bargaining unit covered by such agreement when made, and (ii) unless following an election held as provided in section 9(e) within one year preceding the effective date of such agreement, the Board shall have certified that at least a majority of the employees eligible to vote in such election have voted to rescind the authority of such labor organization to make such an agreement: *Provided further,* That no employer shall justify any discrimination against an employee for nonmembership in a labor organization (A) if he has reasonable grounds for believing that such membership was not available to the employee on the same terms and conditions generally applicable to other members, or (B) if he has reasonable grounds for believing that membership was denied or terminated for reasons other than the failure of the employee to tender the periodic dues and the initiation fees uniformly required as a condition of acquiring or retaining membership;

(4) to discharge or otherwise discriminate against an employee because he has filed charges or given testimony under this Act;

(5) to refuse to bargain collectively with the representatives of his employees, subject to the provisions of section 9(a).

(b) It shall be an unfair labor practice for a labor organization or its agents—

(1) to restrain or coerce (A) employees in the exercise of the rights guaranteed in section 7: *Provided,* That this paragraph shall not impair the right of a labor organization to prescribe its own rules with respect to the acquisition or retention of membership therein; or (B) an employer in the selection of his representatives for the purposes of collective bargaining or the adjustment of grievances;

(2) to cause or attempt to cause an employer to discriminate against an employee in violation of subsection (a)(3) or to discriminate

against an employee with respect to whom membership in such organization has been denied or terminated on some ground other than his failure to tender the periodic dues and the initiation fees uniformly required as a condition of acquiring or retaining membership;

(3) to refuse to bargain collectively with an employer, provided it is the representative of his employees subject to the provisions of section 9(a);

(4) (i) to engage in, or to induce or encourage any individual employed by any person engaged in commerce or in an industry affecting commerce to engage in, a strike or a refusal in the course of his employment to use, manufacture, process, transport, or otherwise handle or work on any goods, articles, materials, or commodities or to perform any services; or (ii) to threaten, coerce, or restrain any person engaged in commerce or in an industry affecting commerce, where in either case an object thereof is:

(A) forcing or requiring any employer or self-employed person to join any labor or employer organization or to enter into an agreement which is prohibited by section 8(e);

(B) forcing or requiring any person to cease using, selling, handling, transporting, or otherwise dealing in the products of any other producer, processor, or manufacturer, or to cease doing business with any other person, or forcing or requiring any other employer to recognize or bargain with a labor organization as the representative of his employees unless such labor organization has been certified as the representative of such employees under the provisions of section 9: *Provided,* That nothing contained in this clause (B) shall be construed to make unlawful, where not otherwise unlawful, any primary strike or primary picketing;

(C) forcing or requiring any employer to recognize or bargain with a particular labor organization as the representative of his employees if another labor organization has been certified as the representative of such employees under the provisions of section 9;

(D) forcing or requiring any employer to assign particular work to employees in a particular labor organization or in a particular trade, craft, or class rather than to employees in another labor organization or in another trade, craft, or class, unless such employer is failing to conform to an order or certification of the Board determining the bargaining representative for employees performing such work:

Provided, That nothing contained in this subsection (b) shall be construed to make unlawful a refusal by any person to enter upon the premises of any employer (other than his own employer), if the employees of such employer are engaged in a strike ratified or approved by a representative of such employees whom such employer is required to recognize under this Act: *Provided further,* That for the purposes of this paragraph (4) only, nothing contained in such paragraph shall be construed to prohibit publicity, other than picketing, for the purpose of truthfully advising the public, including consumers and members of a labor organization, that a product or products are produced by an employer with whom the labor organization has a primary dispute and are distributed by another employer, as long as such publicity does not have an effect of inducing any individual employed by any person other than the primary employer in the course of his employment to refuse to pick up, deliver, or transport any goods, or not to perform any services, at the establishment of the employer engaged in such distribution;

(5) to require of employees covered by an agreement authorized under subsection (a)(3) the payment, as a condition precedent to becoming a member of such organization, of a fee in an amount which the Board finds excessive or discriminatory under all the circumstances. In making such a finding, the Board shall consider, among other relevant factors, the practices and customs of labor organizations in the particular industry, and the wages currently paid to the employees affected;

(6) to cause or attempt to cause an employer to pay or deliver or agree to pay or deliver any money or other thing of value, in the nature of an exaction, for services which are not performed or not to be performed; and

(7) to picket or cause to be picketed, or threaten to picket or cause to be picketed, any employer where an object thereof is forcing or requiring an employer to recognize or bargain with a labor organization as the representative of his employees, or forcing or requiring the employees of an employer to accept or select such labor organization as their collective bargaining representative, unless such labor organization is currently certified as the representative of such employees:

(A) where the employer has lawfully recognized in accordance with this Act any other labor organization and a question concerning representation may not appropriately be raised under section 9(c) of this Act,

(B) where within the preceding twelve months a valid election under section 9(c) of this Act has been conducted, or

(C) where such picketing has been conducted without a petition under section 9(c) being filed within a reasonable period of time not to exceed thirty days from the commencement of such picketing: *Provided,* That when such a petition has been filed the Board shall forthwith, without regard to the provisions of section 9(c)(1) or the absence of a showing of a substantial interest on the part of the labor organization, direct an election in such unit as the Board finds to be appropriate and shall certify the results thereof: *Provided further,* That nothing in this subparagraph (C) shall be construed to prohibit any picketing or other publicity for the purpose of truthfully advising the public (including consumers) that an employer does not employ members of, or have a contract with, a labor organization, unless an effect of such picketing is to induce any individual employed by any other person in the course of his employment, not to pick up, deliver or transport any goods or not to perform any services.

Nothing in this paragraph (7) shall be construed to permit any act which would otherwise be an unfair labor practice under this section 8(b).

(c) The expressing of any views, argument, or opinion, or the dissemination thereof, whether in written, printed, graphic, or visual form, shall not constitute or be evidence of an unfair labor practice under any of the provisions of this Act, if such expression contains no threat of reprisal or force or promise of benefit.

(d) For the purposes of this section, to bargain collectively is the performance of the mutual obligation of the employer and the representative of the employees to meet at reasonable times and confer in good faith with respect to wages, hours, and other terms and conditions of employment, or the negotiation of an agreement, or any question arising thereunder, and the execution of a written contract incorporating any agreement reached if requested by either party, but such obligation does not compel either party to agree to a proposal or require the making of a concession: *Provided,* That where there is in effect a collective-bargaining contract covering employees in an industry affecting commerce, the duty to bargain collectively shall also mean that no party to such contract shall terminate or modify such contract, unless the party desiring such termination or modification—

(1) serves a written notice upon the other party to the contract of the proposed termination or modification sixty days prior to the expiration date thereof, or in the event such contract contains no expiration date, sixty days prior to the time it is proposed to make such termination or modification;

(2) offers to meet and confer with the other party for the purpose of negotiating a new contract or a contract containing the proposed modifications;

(3) notifies the Federal Mediation and Conciliation Service within thirty days after such notice of the existence of a dispute, and simultaneously therewith notifies any State or Territorial agency established to mediate and conciliate disputes within the State or Territory where the dispute occurred, provided no agreement has been reached by that time; and

(4) continues in full force and effect, without resorting to strike or lockout, all the terms and conditions of the existing contract for a period of sixty days after such notice is given or until the expiration date of such contract, whichever occurs later:

The duties imposed upon employers, employees, and labor organizations by paragraphs (2), (3), and (4) shall become inapplicable upon an intervening certification of the Board, under which the labor organization or individual, which is a party to the contract, has been superseded as or ceased to be the representative of the employees subject to the provisions of section 9(a), and the duties so imposed shall not be construed as requiring either party to discuss or agree to any modification of the terms and conditions contained in a contract for a fixed period, if such modification is to become effective before such terms and conditions can be reopened under the provisions of the contract. Any employee who engages in a strike within the sixty-day period specified in this subsection shall lose his status as an employee of the employer engaged in the particular labor dispute, for the purposes of sections 8, 9, and 10 of this Act, as amended, but such loss of status for such employee shall terminate if and when he is reemployed by such employer.

(e) It shall be an unfair labor practice for any labor organization and any employer to enter into any contract or agreement, express or implied, whereby such employer ceases or refrains or agrees to cease or refrain from handling, using, selling, transporting or otherwise dealing in any of the products of any other employer, or to cease doing business with any other person, and any contract or agreement entered into heretofore or hereafter containing such an agreement shall be to such extent unenforceable and void: *Provided,* That nothing in this subsection (e) shall apply to an agreement between a labor organization and an employer in the construction industry relating to the contracting or subcontracting of work to be done at the site of the construction, alteration, painting, or repair of a building, structure, or other work: *Provided further,* That for the purposes of this subsection (e) and section 8(b)(4)(B) the terms "any employer," "any person engaged in commerce or in industry affecting commerce," and "any person" when used in relation to the terms "any other producer, processor, or manufacturer," "any other employer," or "any other person" shall not include persons in the relation of a jobber, manufacturer, contractor, or subcontractor working on the goods or premises of the jobber or manufacturer or performing parts of an integrated process of production in the apparel and clothing industry: *Provided further,* That nothing in this Act shall prohibit the enforcement of any agreement which is within the foregoing exception.

(f) It shall not be an unfair labor practice under subsections (a) and (b) of this section for an employer engaged primarily in the building and construction industry to make an agreement covering employees engaged (or who, upon their employment, will be engaged) in the building and construction industry with a labor organization of which building and construction employees are members (not established, maintained, or assisted by any action defined in section 8(a) of this Act as an unfair labor practice) because (1) the majority status of such labor organization has not been established under the provisions of section 9 of this Act prior to the making of such agreement, or (2) such agreement requires as a condition of employment, membership in such labor organization after the seventh day following the beginning of such employment or the effective date of the agreement, whichever is later, or (3) such agreement requires the employer to notify such labor organization of opportunities for employment with such employer, or gives such labor organization an opportunity to refer qualified applicants for such employment, or (4) such agreement specifies minimum training or experience qualifications for employment or provides for priority in opportunities for employment based upon length of service with such employer, in the industry or in the particular geographical area: *Provided,* That nothing in this subsection shall set aside the final proviso to section 8(a)(3) of this Act: *Provided further,* That any agreement which would be invalid, but for clause (1) of this subsection, shall not be a bar to a petition filed pursuant to section 9(c) or 9(e).*

REPRESENTATIVES AND ELECTIONS

SEC. 9. (a) Representatives designated or selected for the purposes of collective bargaining by the majority of the employees in a unit appropriate for such purposes, shall be the exclusive representatives of all the employees in such unit for the purposes of collective bargaining in respect to rates of pay, wages, hours of employment, or other conditions of employment: *Provided,* That any individual employee or a group of employees shall have the right at any time to present grievances to their employer and to have such grievances adjusted, without the intervention of the bargaining representative, as long as the adjustment is not inconsistent with the terms of a collective-bargaining contract or agreement then in effect: *Provided further,* That the bargaining representative has been given opportunity to be present at such adjustment.

(b) The Board shall decide in each case whether, in order to assure to employees the fullest freedom in exercising the rights guaranteed by this Act, the unit appropriate for the purposes of collective bargaining shall be the employer unit, craft unit, plant unit, or subdivision thereof: *Provided,* That the Board shall not (1) decide that any unit is appropriate for such purposes if

* Section 8(f) is inserted in the Act by subsection (a) of Section 705 of Public Law 86–257. Section 705(b) provides:

Nothing contained in the amendment made by subsection (a) shall be construed as authorizing the execution or application of agreements requiring membership in a labor organization as a condition of employment in any State or Territory in which such execution or application is prohibited by State or Territorial law.

such unit includes both professional employees and employees who are not professional employees unless a majority of such professional employees vote for inclusion in such unit; or (2) decide that any craft unit is inappropriate for such purposes on the ground that a different unit has been established by a prior Board determination, unless a majority of the employees in the proposed craft unit vote against separate representations or (3) decide that any unit is appropriate for such purposes if it includes, together with other employees, any individual employed as a guard to enforce against employees and other persons rules to protect property of the employer or to protect the safety of persons on the employer's premises; but no labor organization shall be certified as the representative of employees in a bargaining unit of guards if such organization admits to membership, or is affiliated directly or indirectly with an organization which admits to membership, employees other than guards.

(c)(1) Wherever a petition shall have been filed, in accordance with such regulations as may be prescribed by the Board—

(A) by an employee or group of employees or any individual or labor organization acting in their behalf alleging that a substantial number of employees (i) wish to be represented for collective bargaining and that their employer declines to recognize their representative as the representative defined in section 9(a), or (ii) assert that the individual or labor organization, which has been certified or is being currently recognized by their employer as the bargaining representative, is no longer a representative as defined in section 9(a); or

(B) by an employer, alleging that one or more individuals or labor organizations have presented to him a claim to be recognized as the representative defined in section 9(a);

the Board shall investigate such petition and if it has reasonable cause to believe that a question of representation affecting commerce exists shall provide for an appropriate hearing upon due notice. Such hearing may be conducted by an officer or employee of the regional office, who shall not make any recommendations with respect thereto. If the Board finds upon the record of such hearing that such a question of representation exists, it shall direct an election by secret ballot and shall certify the results thereof.

(2) In determining whether or not a question of representation affecting commerce exists, the same regulations and rules of decision shall apply irrespective of the identity of the persons filing the petition or the kind of relief sought and in no case shall the Board deny a labor organization a place on the ballot by reason of an order with respect to such labor organization or its predecessor not issued in conformity with section 10(c).

(3) No election shall be directed in any bargaining unit or any subdivision within which, in the preceding twelve-month period, a valid election shall have been held. Employees engaged in an economic strike who are not entitled to reinstatement shall be eligible to vote under such regulations as the Board shall find are consistent with the purposes and provisions of this Act in any election conducted within twelve months after the commencement of the strike. In any election where none of the choices on the ballot receives a majority, a run-off shall be conducted, the ballot providing for a selection between the two choices receiving the largest and second largest number of valid votes cast in the election.

(4) Nothing in this section shall be construed to prohibit the waiving of hearings by stipulation for the purpose of a consent election in conformity with regulations and rules of decision of the Board.

(5) In determining whether a unit is appropriate for the purposes specified in subsection (b) the extent to which the employees have organized shall not be controlling.

(d) Whenever an order of the Board made pursuant to section 10(c) is based in whole or in part upon facts certified following an investigation pursuant to subsection (c) of this section and there is a petition for the enforcement or review of such order, such certification and the record of such investigation shall be included in the transcript of the entire record required to be filed under section 10(e) or 10(f), and thereupon the decree of the court enforcing, modifying, or setting aside in whole or in part the order of the Board shall be made and entered upon the pleadings, testimony, and proceedings set forth in such transcript.

(e)(1) Upon the filing with the Board, by 30 per centum or more of the employees in a bargaining unit covered by an agreement between their employer and a labor organization made pursuant to section 8(a)(3), of a petition alleging they desire that such authority be rescinded, the Board shall take a secret ballot of the employees in such unit and certify the results thereof to such labor organization and to the employer.

(2) No election shall be conducted pursuant to this subsection in any bargaining unit or any subdivision within which, in the preceding twelve-month period, a valid election shall have been held.

PREVENTION OF UNFAIR LABOR PRACTICES

Sec. 10. (a) The Board is empowered, as hereinafter provided, to prevent any person from engaging in any unfair labor practice (listed in section 8) affecting commerce. This power shall not be affected by any other means of adjustment or prevention that has been or may be established by agreement, law, or otherwise: *Provided,* That the Board is empowered by agreement with any agency of any State or Territory to cede to such agency jurisdiction over any cases in any industry (other than mining, manufacturing, communications, and transportation except where predominantly local in character) even though such cases may involve labor disputes affecting commerce, unless the provision of the State or Territorial statute applicable to the determination of such cases by such agency is inconsistent with the corresponding provision of this Act or has received a construction inconsistent therewith.

(b) Whenever it is charged that any person has engaged in or is engaging in any such unfair labor practice, the Board, or any agent or agency designated by the Board for such purposes, shall have power to issue and cause to be served upon such person a complaint stating the charges in that respect, and containing a notice of hearing before the Board or a member thereof, or before a designated agent or agency, at a place therein fixed, not less than five days after the serving of said complaint: *Provided,* That no complaint shall issue based upon any unfair labor practice occurring more than six months prior to the filing of the charge with the Board and the service of a copy thereof upon the person against whom such charge is made, unless the person aggrieved thereby was prevented from filing such charge by reason of service in the armed forces, in which event the six-month period shall be computed from the day of his discharge. Any such complaint may be amended by the member, agent, or agency conducting the hearing or the Board in its discretion at any time prior to the issuance of an order based thereon. The person so complained of shall have the right to file an answer to the original or amended complaint and to appear in person or otherwise and give testimony at the place and time fixed in the complaint. In the discretion of the member, agent, or agency conducting the hearing or the Board, any other person may be allowed to intervene in the said proceeding and to present testimony. Any such proceeding shall, so far as practicable, be conducted in accordance with the rules of evidence applicable in the district courts of the United States under the rules of civil procedure for the district courts of the United States, adopted by the Supreme Court of the United States pursuant to the Act of June 19, 1934 (U.S.C., title 28, secs. 723-B, 723-C).

(c) The testimony taken by such member, agent, or agency or the Board shall be reduced to writing and filed with the Board. Thereafter, in its discretion, the Board upon notice may take further testimony or hear argument. If upon the preponderance of the testimony taken the Board shall be of the opinion that any person named in the complaint has engaged in or is engaging in any such unfair labor practice, then the Board shall state its findings of fact and shall issue and cause to be served on such person an order requiring such person to cease and desist from such unfair labor practice, and to take such affirmative action including reinstatement of employees with or without back pay, as will effectuate the policies of this Act: *Provided,* That where an order directs reinstatement of an employee, back pay may be required of the employer or labor organization, as the case may be, responsible for the discrimination suffered by him: *And provided further,* That in determining whether a complaint shall issue alleging a violation of section 8(a)(1) or section 8(a)(2), and in deciding such cases, the same regulations and rules of decision shall apply irrespective of whether or not the labor organization affected is affiliated with a labor organization national or international in scope. Such order may further require such person to make reports from time to time showing the extent to which it has complied with the order. If upon the preponderance of the testimony taken the Board shall not be of the opinion that the person named in the complaint has engaged in or is engaging in any such unfair labor practice, then the Board shall state its findings of fact and shall issue an order dismissing the said complaint. No order of the Board shall require the reinstatement of any individual as an employee who has been suspended or discharged, or the payment to him of any back pay, if such individual was suspended or discharged for cause. In case the evidence is presented before a member of the Board, or before an examiner or examiners thereof, such member, or such examiner or examiners, as the case may be, shall issue and cause to be served on the parties to the proceeding a proposed report, together with a recommended order, which shall be filed with the Board, and if no exceptions are filed within twenty days after service thereof upon such parties, or within such further period as the Board may authorize, such recommended order shall become the order of the Board and become effective as therein prescribed.

(d) Until the record in a case shall have been filed in a court, as hereinafter provided, the Board may at any time, upon reasonable notice and in such manner as it shall deem proper, modify or set aside, in whole or in part, any finding or order made or issued by it.

(e) The Board shall have power to petition any court of appeals of the United States, or if all the courts of appeals to which application may be made are in vacation, any district court of the United States, within any circuit or district, respectively, wherein the unfair labor practice in question occurred or wherein such person resides or transacts business, for the enforcement of such order and for appropriate temporary relief or restraining order, and shall file in the court the record in the proceedings, as provided in section 2112 of title 28, United States Code. Upon the filing of such petition, the court shall cause notice thereof to be served upon such person, and thereupon shall have jurisdiction of the proceeding and of the question determined therein, and shall have power to grant such temporary relief or restraining order as it deems just and proper, and to make and enter a decree enforcing, modifying, and enforcing as so modified, or setting aside in whole or in part the order of the Board. No objection that has not been urged before the Board, its member, agent, or agency, shall be considered by the court, unless the failure or neglect to urge such objection shall be excused because of extraordinary circumstances. The findings of the Board with respect to questions of fact if supported by substantial evidence on the record considered as a whole shall be conclusive. If either party shall apply to the court for leave to adduce additional evidence and shall show to the satisfaction of the court that such additional evidence is material and that there were reasonable grounds for the failure to adduce such evidence in the hearing before the Board, its member, agent, or agency, the court may order such additional evidence to be taken before the Board, its member, agent, or agency, and to be made a part of the record. The Board may modify its findings as to the facts, or make new findings, by reason of additional evidence so taken and filed, and it shall file such modified or new findings, which findings with respect to questions of fact if supported by substantial evidence on the record considered as a whole shall be conclusive, and shall file its recommendations, if any, for the modification or setting aside of its original order. Upon the filing of the record with it the jurisdiction of the court shall be exclusive and its judgment and decree shall be final, except that the same shall be subject to review by the appropriate United States court of appeals if application was made to the district court as hereinabove provided, and by the Supreme Court of the United States upon writ of certiorari or certification as provided in section 1254 of title 28.

(f) Any person aggrieved by a final order of the Board granting or denying in whole or in part the relief sought may obtain a review of such order in any circuit court of appeals of the United States in the circuit wherein the unfair labor practice in question was alleged to have been engaged in or wherein such person resides or transacts business, or in the United States Court of Appeals for the District of Columbia, by filing in such court a written petition praying that the order of the Board be modified or set aside. A copy of such petition shall be forthwith transmitted by the clerk of the court to the Board, and thereupon the aggrieved party shall file in the court the record in the proceeding, certified by the Board, as provided in section 2112 of title 28, United States Code. Upon the filing of such petition, the court shall proceed in the same manner as in the case of an application by the Board under subsection (e) of this section, and shall have the same jurisdiction to grant to the Board such temporary relief or restraining order as it deems just and proper, and in like manner to make and enter a decree enforcing, modifying, and enforcing as so modified, or setting aside in whole or in part the order of the Board; the findings of the Board with respect to questions of fact if supported by substantial evidence on the record considered as a whole shall in like manner be conclusive.

(g) The commencement of proceedings under subsection (e) or (f) of this section shall not, unless specifically ordered by the court, operate as a stay of the Board's order.

(h) When granting appropriate temporary relief or a restraining order, or making and entering a decree enforcing, modifying, and enforcing as so modified, or setting aside in whole or in part an order of the Board, as provided in this section, the jurisdiction of courts sitting in equity shall not be limited by the Act entitled "An Act to amend the Judicial Code and to define and limit the jurisdiction of courts sitting in equity, and for other purposes," approved March 23, 1932 (U.S.C., Supp. VII, title 29, secs. 101–115).

(i) Petitions filed under this Act shall be heard expeditiously, and if possible within ten days after they have been docketed.

(j) The Board shall have power, upon issuance of a complaint as provided in subsection (b) charging that any person has engaged in or is engaging in an unfair labor practice, to petition any district court of the United States (including the District Court of the United States for the District of Columbia), within any district wherein the unfair labor practice in question is alleged to have occurred or wherein such person resides or transacts business, for appropriate temporary relief or restraining order. Upon the filing of any such petition the court shall cause notice thereof to be served upon such person, and thereupon shall have jurisdiction to grant to the Board such temporary relief or restraining order as it deems just and proper.

(k) Whenever it is charged that any person has engaged in an unfair labor practice within the meaning of paragraph (4)(D) of section 8(b), the Board is empowered and directed to hear and determine the dispute out of which such unfair labor practice shall have arisen, unless, within ten days after notice that such charge has been filed, the parties to such dispute submit to the Board satisfactory evidence that they have adjusted, or agreed upon methods for the voluntary adjustment of, the dispute. Upon compliance by the parties to the dispute with the decision of the Board or upon such voluntary adjustment of the dispute, such charge shall be dismissed.

(l) Whenever it is charged that any person has engaged in an unfair labor practice within the meaning of paragraph (4) (A), (B), or (C) of section 8(b), or section 8(e) or section 8(b)(7), the preliminary investigation of such charge shall be made forthwith and given priority over all other cases except cases of like character in the office where it is filed or to which it is referred. If, after such investigation, the officer or regional attorney to whom the matter may be referred has reasonable cause to believe such charge is true and that a complaint should issue, he shall, on behalf of the Board, petition any district court of the United States (including the District Court of the United States for the District of Columbia) within any district where the unfair labor practice in question has occurred, is alleged to have occurred, or wherein such person resides or transacts business, for appropriate injunctive relief pending the final adjudication of the Board with respect to such matter. Upon the filing of any such petition the district court shall have jurisdiction to grant such injunctive relief or temporary restraining order as it deems just and proper, notwithstanding any other provision of law: *Provided further,* That no temporary restraining order shall be issued without notice unless a petition alleges that substantial and irreparable injury to the charging party will be unavoidable and such temporary restraining order shall be effective for no longer than five days and will become void at the expiration of such period: *Provided further,* That such officer or regional attorney shall not apply for any restraining order under section 8(b)(7) if a charge against the employer under section 8(a)(2) has been filed and after the preliminary investigation, he has reasonable cause to believe that such charge is true and that a complaint should issue. Upon filing of any such petition the courts shall cause notice thereof to be served upon any person involved in the charge and such person, including the charging party, shall be given an opportunity to appear by counsel and present any relevant testimony: *Provided further,* That for the purposes of this subsection district courts shall be deemed to have jurisdiction of a labor organization (1) in the district in which such organization maintains its principal office, or (2) in any district in which its duly authorized officers or agents are engaged in promoting or protecting the interests of employee members. The service of legal process upon such officer or agent shall constitute service upon the labor organization and make such organizations a party to the suit. In situations where such relief is appropriate the procedure specified herein shall apply to charges with respect to section 8(b)(4)(D).

(m) Whenever it is charged that any person has engaged in an unfair labor practice within the meaning of subsection (a)(3) or (b)(2) of section 8, such charge shall be given priority over all other cases except cases of like character in the office where it is filed or to which it is referred and cases given priority under subsection (1).

INVESTIGATORY POWERS

SEC. 11. For the purpose of all hearings and investigations, which, in the opinion of the Board, are necessary and proper for the exercise of the powers vested in it by section 9 and section 10—

(1) The Board, or its duly authorized agents or agencies, shall at all reasonable times have access to, for the purpose of examination, and the right to copy any evidence of any person being investigated or proceeded against that relates to any matter under investigation or in question. The Board, or any member thereof, shall upon application of any party to such proceedings, forthwith issue to such party subpenas requiring the attendance and testimony of witnesses or the production of any evidence in such proceeding or investigation requested in such application. Within five days after the service of a subpena on any person requiring the production of any evidence in his possession or under his control, such person may petition the Board to revoke, and the Board shall revoke, such subpena if in its opinion the evidence whose production is required does not relate to any matter under investigation, or any matter in question in such proceedings, or if in its opinion such subpena does not describe with sufficient particularity the evidence whose production is required. Any member of the Board, or any agent or agency designated by the Board for such purposes, may administer oaths and affirmations, examine witnesses, and receive evidence. Such attendance of witnesses and the production of such evidence may be required from any place in the United States or any Territory or possession thereof, at any designated place of hearing.

(2) In case of contumacy or refusal to obey a subpena issued to any person, any district court of the United States or the United States courts of any Territory or possession, or the District Court of the United States for the District of Columbia, within the jurisdiction of which the inquiry is carried on or within the jurisdiction of which said person guilty of contumacy or refusal to obey is found or resides or transacts business, upon application by the Board shall have jurisdiction to issue to such person an order requiring such person to appear before the Board, its member, agent, or agency, there to produce evidence if so ordered, or there to give testimony touching the matter under investigation or in question; and any failure to obey such order of the court may be punished by said court as a contempt thereof.

(3) No person shall be excused from attending and testifying or from producing books, records, correspondence, documents, or other evidence in obedience to the subpena of the Board, on the ground that the testimony or evidence required of him may tend to incriminate him or subject him to a penalty or forfeiture; but no individual shall be prosecuted or subjected to any penalty or forfeiture for or on account of any transaction, matter, or thing

concerning which he is compelled, after having claimed his privilege against self-incrimination, to testify or produce evidence, except that such individual so testifying shall not be exempt from prosecution and punishment for perjury committed in so testifying.

(4) Complaints, orders, and other process and papers of the Board, its member, agent, or agency, may be served either personally or by registered mail or by telegraph or by leaving a copy thereof at the principal office or place of business of the person required to be served. The verified return by the individual so serving the same setting forth the manner of such service shall be proof of the same, and the return post office receipt or telegraph receipt therefor when registered and mailed or telegraphed as aforesaid shall be proof of service of the same. Witnesses summoned before the Board, its member, agent, or agency, shall be paid the same fees and mileage that are paid witnesses in the courts of the United States, and witnesses whose depositions are taken and the persons taking the same shall severally be entitled to the same fees as are paid for like services in the courts of the United States.

(5) All process of any court to which application may be made under this Act may be served in the judicial district wherein the defendant or other person required to be served resides or may be found.

(6) The several departments and agencies of the Government, when directed by the President, shall furnish the Board, upon its request, all records, papers, and information in their possession relating to any matter before the Board.

SEC. 12. Any person who shall willfully resist, prevent, impede, or interfere with any member of the Board or any of its agents or agencies in the performance of duties pursuant to this Act shall be punished by a fine of not more than $5,000 or by imprisonment for not more than one year, or both.

LIMITATIONS

SEC. 13. Nothing in this Act, except as specifically provided for herein, shall be construed so as either to interfere with or impede or diminish in any way the right to strike, or to affect the limitations or qualifications on that right.

SEC. 14. (a) Nothing herein shall prohibit any individual employed as a supervisor from becoming or remaining a member of a labor organization, but no employer subject to this Act shall be compelled to deem individuals defined herein as supervisors as employees for the purpose of any law, either national or local, relating to collective bargaining.

(b) Nothing in this Act shall be construed as authorizing the execution or application of agreements requiring membership in a labor organization as a condition of employment in any State or Territory in which such execution or application is prohibited by State or Territorial law.

(c)(1) The Board, in its discretion, may, by rule of decision or by published rules adopted pursuant to the Administrative Procedure Act, decline to assert jurisdiction over any labor dispute involving any class or category of employees, where, in the opinion of the Board, the effect of such labor dispute on commerce is not sufficiently substantial to warrant the exercise of its jurisdiction: *Provided,* That the Board shall not decline to assert jurisdiction over any labor dispute over which it would assert jurisdiction under the standards prevailing upon August 1, 1959.

(2) Nothing in this Act shall be deemed to prevent or bar any agency or the courts of any State or Territory (including the Commonwealth of Puerto Rico, Guam, and the Virgin Islands), from assuming and asserting jurisdiction over labor disputes over which the Board declines, pursuant to paragraph (1) of this subsection, to assert jurisdiction.

SEC. 15. Wherever the application of the provisions of section 272 of chapter 10 of the Act entitled "An Act to establish a uniform system of bankruptcy throughout the United States," approved July 1, 1898, and Acts amendatory thereof and supplementary thereto (U.S.C., title 11, sec. 672), conflicts with the application of the provisions of this Act, this Act shall prevail: *Provided*, That in any situation where the provisions of this Act cannot be validly enforced, the provisions of such other Acts shall remain in full force and effect.

SEC. 16. If any provision of this Act, or the application of such provision to any person or circumstances, shall be held invalid, the remainder of this Act, or the application of such provision to persons or circumstances other than those as to which it is held invalid, shall not be affected thereby.

SEC. 17. This Act may be cited as the "National Labor Relations Act."

SEC. 18. No petition entertained, no investigation made, no election held, and no certification issued by the National Labor Relations Board, under any of the provisions of section 9 of the National Labor Relations Act, as amended, shall be invalid by reason of the failure of the Congress of Industrial Organizations to have complied with the requirements of section 9(f), (g), or (h) of the aforesaid Act prior to December 22, 1949, or by reason of the failure of the American Federation of Labor to have complied with the provisions of section 9(f), (g), or (h) of the aforesaid Act prior to November 7, 1947: *Provided*, That no liability shall be imposed under any provision of this Act upon any person for failure to honor any election or certificate referred to above, prior to the effective date of this amendment: *Provided, however,* That this proviso shall not have the effect of setting aside or in any way affecting judgments or decrees heretofore entered under section 10(e) or (f) and which have become final.

EFFECTIVE DATE OF CERTAIN CHANGES*

SEC. 102. No provision of this title shall be deemed to make an unfair labor practice any act which was performed prior to the date of the enactment of this Act which did not constitute an unfair labor practice prior thereto, and the provisions of section 8(a)(3) and section 8(b)(2) of the National Labor Relations Act as amended by this title shall not make an unfair labor practice the performance of any obligation under a collective-bargaining agreement entered into prior to the date of the enactment of this Act, or (in the case of an agreement for a period of not more than one year) entered into on or after such date of enactment, but prior to the effective date of this title, if the performance of such obligation would not have constituted an unfair labor practice under section 8(3) of the National Labor Relations Act prior to the effective date of this title, unless such agreement was renewed or extended subsequent thereto.

SEC. 103. No provisions of this title shall affect any certification of representatives or any determination as to the appropriate collective-bargaining unit, which was made under section 9 of the National Labor Relations Act prior to the effective date of this title until one year after the date of such certification or if, in respect of any such certification, a collective-bargaining contract was entered into prior to the effective date of this title, until the end of the contract period or until one year after such date, whichever first occurs.

SEC. 104. The amendments made by this title shall take effect sixty days after the date of the enactment of this Act, except that the authority of the

---

* The effective date referred to in Sections 102, 103, and 104 is August 22, 1947. For effective dates of 1959 amendments, see footnote on first page of this text.

President to appoint certain officers conferred upon him by section 3 of the National Labor Relations Act as amended by this title may be exercised forthwith.

TITLE II—
CONCILIATION OF LABOR DISPUTES IN INDUSTRIES AFFECTING COMMERCE; NATIONAL EMERGENCIES

SEC. 201. That it is the policy of the United States that—

(a) sound and stable industrial peace and the advancement of the general welfare, health, and safety of the Nation and of the best interest of employers and employees can most satisfactorily be secured by the settlement of issues between employers and employees through the processes of conference and collective bargaining between employers and the representatives of their employees;

(b) the settlement of issues between employers and employees through collective bargaining may be advanced by making available full and adequate governmental facilities for conciliation, mediation, and voluntary arbitration to aid and encourage employers and the representatives of their employees to reach and maintain agreements concerning rates of pay, hours, and working conditions, and to make all reasonable efforts to settle their differences by mutual agreement reached through conferences and collective bargaining or by such methods as may be provided for in any applicable agreement for the settlement of disputes; and

(c) certain controversies which arise between parties to collective-bargaining agreements may be avoided or minimized by making available full and adequate governmental facilities for furnishing assistance to employers and the representatives of their employees in formulating for inclusion within such agreements provision for adequate notice of any proposed changes in the terms of such agreements, for the final adjustment of grievances or questions regarding the application or interpretation of such agreements, and other provisions designed to prevent the subsequent arising of such controversies.

SEC. 202. (a) There is hereby created an independent agency to be known as the Federal Mediation and Conciliation Service (herein referred to as the "service," except that for sixty days after the date of the enactment of this Act such term shall refer to the Conciliation Service of the Department of Labor). The Service shall be under the direction of a Federal Mediation and Conciliation Director (hereinafter referred to as the "Director"), who shall be appointed by the President by and with the advice and consent of the Senate. The Director shall receive compensation at the rate of $12,000* per annum. The Director shall not engage in any other business, vocation, or employment.

(b) The Director is authorized, subject to the civil-service laws, to appoint such clerical and other personnel as may be necessary for the execution of the functions of the Service, and shall fix their compensation in accordance with the Classification Act of 1923, as amended, and may, without regard to the provisions of the civil-service laws and the Classification Act of 1923, as amended, appoint and fix the compensation of such conciliators and mediators as may be necessary to carry out the functions of the Service. The Director is authorized to make such expenditures for supplies, facilities, and services as he deems necessary. Such expenditures shall be allowed and paid upon presenta-

---

* Pursuant to Public Law 88–426, 88th Congress, 2d Session, Title III, approved August 14, 1964, the salary of the Director shall be $27,000 per year.

tion of itemized vouchers therefor approved by the Director or by any employee designated by him for that purpose.

(c) The principal office of the Service shall be in the District of Columbia, but the Director may establish regional offices convenient to localities in which labor controversies are likely to arise. The Director may by order, subject to revocation at any time, delegate any authority and discretion conferred upon him by this Act to any regional director, or other officer or employee of the Service. The Director may establish suitable procedures for cooperation with State and local mediation agencies. The Director shall make an annual report in writing to Congress at the end of the fiscal year.

(d) All mediation and conciliation functions of the Secretary of Labor or the United States Conciliation Service under section 8 of the Act entitled "An Act to create a Department of Labor," approved March 4, 1913 (U.S.C., title 29, sec. 51), and all functions of the United States Conciliation Service under any other law are hereby transferred to the Federal Mediation and Conciliation Service, together with the personnel and records of the United States Conciliation Service. Such transfer shall take effect upon the sixtieth day after the date of enactment of this Act. Such transfer shall not affect any proceedings pending before the United States Conciliation Service or any certification, order, rule, or regulation theretofore made by it or by the Secretary of Labor. The Director and the Service shall not be subject in any way to the jurisdiction or authority of the Secretary of labor or any official or division of the Department of Labor.

FUNCTIONS OF THE SERVICE

SEC. 203. (a) It shall be the duty of the Service, in order to prevent or minimize interruptions of the free flow of commerce growing out of labor disputes, to assist parties to labor disputes in industries affecting commerce to settle such disputes through conciliation and mediation.

(b) The Service may proffer its services in any labor dispute in any industry affecting commerce, either upon its own motion or upon the request of one or more of the parties to the dispute, whenever in its judgment such dispute threatens to cause a substantial interruption of commerce. The Director and the Service are directed to avoid attempting to mediate disputes which would have only a minor effect on interstate commerce if State or other conciliation services are available to the parties. Whenever the Service does proffer its services in any dispute, it shall be the duty of the Service promptly to put itself in communication with the parties and to use its best efforts, by mediation and conciliation, to bring them to agreement.

(c) If the Director is not able to bring the parties to agreement by conciliation within a reasonable time, he shall seek to induce the parties voluntarily to seek other means of settling the dispute without resort to strike, lockout, or other coercion, including submission to the employees in the bargaining unit of the employer's last offer of settlement for approval or rejection in a secret ballot. The failure or refusal of either party to agree to any procedure suggested by the Director shall not be deemed a violation of any duty or obligation imposed by this Act.

(d) Final adjustment by a method agreed upon by the parties is hereby declared to be the desirable method for settlement of grievance disputes arising over the application or interpretation of an existing collective-bargaining agreement. The Service is directed to make its conciliation and mediation services available in the settlement of such grievance disputes only as a last resort and in exceptional cases.

SEC. 204. (a) In order to prevent or minimize interruptions of the free flow of commerce growing out of labor disputes, employers and employees and their representatives, in any industry affecting commerce, shall—

(1) exert every reasonable effort to make and maintain agreements concerning rates of pay, hours, and working conditions, including provision for adequate notice of any proposed change in the terms of such agreements;

(2) whenever a dispute arises over the terms or application of a collective-bargaining agreement and a conference is requested by a party or prospective party thereto, arrange promptly for such a conference to be held and endeavor in such conference to settle such dispute expeditiously; and

(3) in case such dispute is not settled by conference, participate fully and promptly in such meetings as may be undertaken by the Service under this Act for the purpose of aiding in a settlement of the dispute.

SEC. 205. (a) There is hereby created a National Labor-Management Panel which shall be composed of twelve members appointed by the President, six of whom shall be selected from among persons outstanding in the field of management and six of whom shall be selected from among persons outstanding in the field of labor. Each member shall hold office for a term of three years, except that any member appointed to fill a vacancy occurring prior to the expiration of the term for which his predecessor was appointed shall be appointed for the remainder of such term, and the terms of office of the members first taking office shall expire, as designated by the President at the time of appointment, four at the end of the first year, four at the end of the second year, and four at the end of the third year after the date of appointment. Members of the panel, when serving on business of the panel, shall be paid compensation at the rate of $25 per day, and shall also be entitled to receive an allowance for actual and necessary travel and subsistence expenses while so serving away from their places of residence.

(b) It shall be the duty of the panel, at the request of the Director, to advise in the avoidance of industrial controversies and the manner in which mediation and voluntary adjustment shall be administered, particularly with reference to controversies affecting the general welfare of the country.

NATIONAL EMERGENCIES

SEC. 206. Whenever in the opinion of the President of the United States, a threatened or actual strike or lock-out affecting an entire industry or a substantial part thereof engaged in trade, commerce, transportation, transmission, or communication among the several States or with foreign nations, or engaged in the production of goods for commerce, will, if permitted to occur or to continue, imperil the national health or safety, he may appoint a board of inquiry to inquire into the issues involved in the dispute and to make a written report to him within such time as he shall prescribe. Such report shall include a statement of the facts with respect to the dispute, including each party's statement of its position but shall not contain any recommendations. The President shall file a copy of such report with the Service and shall make its contents available to the public.

SEC. 207. (a) A board of inquiry shall be composed of a chairman and such other members as the President shall determine, and shall have power to sit and act in any place within the United States and to conduct such hearings either in public or in private, as it may deem necessary or proper, to ascertain the facts with respect to the causes and circumstances of the dispute.

(b) Members of a board of inquiry shall receive compensation at the rate of $50 for each day actually spent by them in the work of the board, together with necessary travel and subsistence expenses.

(c) For the purpose of any hearing or inquiry conducted by any board appointed under this title, the provisions of sections 9 and 10 (relating to the attendance of witnesses and the production of books, papers, and documents) of the Federal Trade Commission Act of September 16, 1914, as amended (U.S.C. 19, title 15, secs. 49 and 50, as amended), are hereby made applicable to the powers and duties of such board.

SEC. 208. (a) Upon receiving a report from a board of inquiry the President may direct the Attorney General to petition any district court of the United States having jurisdiction of the parties to enjoin such strike or lock-out or the continuing thereof, and if the court finds that such threatened or actual strike or lock-out—

(i) affects an entire industry or a substantial part thereof engaged in trade, commerce, transportation, transmission, or communication among the several States or with foreign nations, or engaged in the production of goods for commerce; and

(ii) if permitted to occur or to continue, will imperil the national health or safety, it shall have jurisdiction to enjoin any such strike or lock-out, or the continuing thereof, and to make such other orders as may be appropriate.

(b) In any case, the provisions of the Act of March 23, 1932, entitled "An Act to amend the Judicial Code and to define and limit the jurisdiction of courts sitting in equity, and for other purposes," shall not be applicable.

(c) The order or orders of the court shall be subject to review by the appropriate circuit court of appeals and by the Supreme Court upon writ of certiorari or certification as provided in sections 239 and 240 of the Judicial Code, as amended (U.S.C., title 29, secs. 346 and 347).

SEC. 209. (a) Whenever a district court has issued an order under section 208 enjoining acts or practices which imperil or threaten to imperil the national health or safety, it shall be the duty of the parties to the labor dispute giving rise to such order to make every effort to adjust and settle their differences, with the assistance of the Service created by this Act. Neither party shall be under any duty to accept, in whole or in part, any proposal of settlement made by the Service.

(b) Upon the issuance of such order, the President shall reconvene the board of inquiry which has previously reported with respect to the dispute. At the end of a sixty-day period (unless the dispute has been settled by that time), the board of inquiry shall report to the President the current position of the parties and the efforts which have been made for settlement, and shall include a statement by each party of its position and a statement of the employer's last offer of settlement. The President shall make such report available to the public. The National Labor Relations Board, within the succeeding fifteen days, shall take a secret ballot of the employees of each employer involved in the dispute on the question of whether they wish to accept the final offer of settlement made by their employer as stated by him and shall certify the results thereof to the Attorney General within five days thereafter.

SEC. 210. Upon the certification of the results of such ballot or upon a settlement being reached, whichever happens sooner, the Attorney General shall move the court to discharge the injunction, which motion shall then be granted and the injunction discharged. When such motion is granted, the

President shall submit to the Congress a full and comprehensive report of the proceedings, including the findings of the board of inquiry and the ballot taken by the National Labor Relations Board, together with such recommendations as he may see fit to make for consideration and appropriate action.

COMPILATION OF COLLECTIVE-BARGAINING AGREEMENTS, ETC.

Sec. 211. (a) For the guidance and information of interested representatives of employers, employees, and the general public, the Bureau of Labor Statistics of the Department of Labor shall maintain a file of copies of all available collective-bargaining agreements and other available agreements and actions thereunder settling or adjusting labor disputes. Such file shall be open to inspection under appropriate conditions prescribed by the Secretary of Labor, except that no specific information submitted in confidence shall be disclosed.

(b) The Bureau of Labor Statistics in the Department of Labor is authorized to furnish upon request of the Service, or employers, employees, or their representatives, all available data and factual information which may aid in the settlement of any labor dispute, except that no specific information submitted in confidence shall be disclosed.

EXEMPTION OF RAILWAY LABOR ACT

Sec. 212. The provisions of this title shall not be applicable with respect to any matter which is subject to the provisions of the Railway Labor Act, as amended from time to time.

TITLE III

SUITS BY AND AGAINST LABOR ORGANIZATIONS

Sec. 301. (a) Suits for violation of contracts between an employer and a labor organization representing employees in an industry affecting commerce as defined in this Act, or between any such labor organizations, may be brought in any district court of the United States having jurisdiction of the parties, without respect to the amount in controversy or without regard to the citizenship of the parties.

(b) Any labor organization which represents employees in an industry affecting commerce as defined in this Act and any employer whose activities affect commerce as defined in this Act shall be bound by the acts of its agents. Any such labor organization may sue or be sued as an entity and in behalf of the employees whom it represents in the courts of the United States. Any money judgment against a labor organization in a district court of the United States shall be enforceable only against the organization as an entity and against its assets, and shall not be enforceable against any individual member or his assets.

(c) For the purposes of actions and proceedings by or against labor organizations in the district courts of the United States, district courts shall be deemed to have jurisdiction of a labor organization (1) in the district in which such organization maintains its principal offices, or (2) in any district in which its duly authorized officers or agents are engaged in representing or acting for employee members.

(d) The service of summons, subpena, or other legal process of any court of the United States upon an officer or agent of a labor organization, in his capacity as such, shall constitute service upon the labor organization.

(e) For the purposes of this section, in determining whether any person is acting as an "agent" of another person so as to make such other person responsible for his acts, the question of whether the specific acts performed were actually authorized or subsequently ratified shall not be controlling.

RESTRICTIONS ON PAYMENTS TO EMPLOYEE REPRESENTATIVES

Sec. 302. (a) It shall be unlawful for any employer or association of employers or any person who acts as a labor relations expert, adviser, or consultant to an employer or who acts in the interest of an employer to pay, lend, or deliver, or agree to pay, lend, or deliver, any money or other thing of value—

(1) to any representative of any of his employees who are employed in an industry affecting commerce; or

(2) to any labor organization, or any officer or employee thereof, which represents, seeks to represent, or would admit to membership, any of the employees of such employer who are employed in an industry affecting commerce; or

(3) to any employee or group or committee of employees of such employer employed in an industry affecting commerce in excess of their normal compensation for the purpose of causing such employee or group or committee directly or indirectly to influence any other employees in the exercise of the right to organize and bargain collectively through representatives of their own choosing; or

(4) to any officer or employee of a labor organization engaged in an industry affecting commerce with intent to influence him in respect to any of his actions, decisions, or duties as a representative of employees or as such officer or employee of such labor organization.

(b)(1) It shall be unlawful for any person to request, demand, receive, or accept, or agree to receive or accept, any payment, loan, or delivery of any money or other thing of value prohibited by subsection (a).

(2) It shall be unlawful for any labor organization, or for any person acting as an officer, agent, representative, or employee of such labor organization, to demand or accept from the operator of any motor vehicle (as defined in part II of the Interstate Commerce Act) employed in the transportation of property in commerce, or the employer of any such operator, any money or other thing of value payable to such organization or to an officer, agent, representative or employee thereof as a fee or charge for the unloading, or the connection with the unloading, of the cargo of such vehicle: *Provided,* That nothing in this paragraph shall be construed to make unlawful any payment by an employer to any of his employees as compensation for their services as employees.

(c) The provisions of this section shall not be applicable (1) in respect to any money or other thing of value payable by an employer to any of his employees whose established duties include acting openly for such employer in matters of labor relations or personnel administration or to any representative of his employees, or to any officer or employee of a labor organization, who is also an employee or former employee of such employer, as compensation for, or by reason of, his service as an employee of such employer; (2) with respect to the payment or delivery of any money or other thing of value in satisfaction of a judgment of any court or a decision or award of an arbitrator or impartial chairman or in compromise, adjustment, settlement, or release of any claim, complaint, grievance, or dispute in the absence of fraud or duress; (3) with respect to the sale or purchase of an article or commodity at the prevailing market price in the regular course of business; (4) with respect to money deducted from the wages of employees in payment of membership dues in a labor organization: *Provided,* That the employer has received from each employee, on whose account such deductions are made, a written assignment which shall not be irrevocable for a period of more than one year, or beyond the termination date of the applicable collective agreement, whichever occurs sooner; (5) with respect to money or other thing of value paid to a trust fund established by such representative, for the sole and exclusive benefit of the employees of such employer, and their families and dependents (or of such employees, families, and dependents jointly with the employees of other employers making similar payments, and their families and dependents): *Provided*, That (A) such payments are held in trust for the purpose of paying, either from principal or income or both, for the benefit of employees, their families and dependents, for medical or hospital care, pensions on retirement or death of employees, compensation for injuries or illness resulting from occupational activity or insurance to provide any of the foregoing, or unemployment benefits or life insurance, disability and sickness insurance, or accident insurance; (B) the detailed basis on which such payments are to be made is specified in a written agreement with the employer, and employees and employers are equally represented in the administration of such fund, together with such neutral persons as the representatives of the employers and the representatives of employees may agree upon and in the event the employer and employee groups deadlock on the administration of such fund and there are no neutral persons empowered to break such deadlock, such agreement provides that the two groups shall agree on an impartial umpire to decide such dispute, or in event of their failure to agree within a reasonable length of time, an impartial umpire to decide such dispute shall, on petition of either group, be appointed by the district court of the United States for the district where the trust fund has its principal office, and shall also contain provisions for an annual audit of the trust fund, a statement of the results of which shall be available for inspection by interested persons at the principal office of the trust fund and at such other places as may be designated in such written agreement; and (C) such payments as are intended to be used for the purpose of providing pension or annuities for employees are made to a separate trust which provides that the funds held therein cannot be used for any purpose other than paying such pensions or annuities; or (6) with respect to money or other thing of value paid by any employer to a trust fund established by such representative for the purpose of pooled vacation, holiday, severance or similar benefits, or defraying costs of apprenticeship or other training program: *Provided*, That the requirements of clause (B) of the proviso to clause (5) of this subsection shall apply to such trust funds.

(d) Any person who willfully violates any of the provisions of this section shall, upon conviction thereof, be guilty of a misdemeanor and be subject to a fine of not more than $10,000 or to imprisonment for not more than one year, or both.

(e) The district courts of the United States and the United States courts of the Territories and possessions shall have jurisdiction, for cause shown, and subject to the provisions of section 17 (relating to notice to opposite party) of the Act entitled "An Act to supplement existing laws against unlawful restraints and monopolies, and for other purposes," approved October 15, 1914, as amended (U.S.C., title 28, sec. 381), to restrain violations of this section, without regard to the provisions of sections 6 and 20 of such Act of October 15, 1914, as amended (U.S.C., title 15, sec. 17, and title 29, sec. 52), and the provisions of the Act entitled "An Act to amend the Judicial Code and to define and limit the jurisdiction of courts sitting in equity, and for other purposes," approved March 23, 1932 (U.S.C., title 29, secs. 101–115).

(f) This section shall not apply to any contract in force on the date of enactment of this Act, until the expiration of such contract, or until July 1, 1948, whichever first occurs.

(g) Compliance with the restrictions contained in subsection (c)(5)(B) upon contributions to trust funds, otherwise lawful, shall not be applicable to contributions to such trust funds established by collective agreement prior to January 1, 1946, nor shall subsection (c)(5)(A) be construed as prohibiting contributions to such trust funds if prior to January 1, 1947, such funds contained provisions for pooled vacation benefits.

BOYCOTTS AND OTHER UNLAWFUL COMBINATIONS

SEC. 303. (a) It shall be unlawful, for the purpose of this section only, in an industry or activity affecting commerce, for any labor organization to engage in any activity or conduct defined as an unfair labor practice in section 8(b)(4) of the National Labor Relations Act, as amended.

(b) Whoever shall be injured in his business or property by reason of any violation of subsection (a) may sue therefore in any district court of the United States subject to the limitations and provisions of section 301 hereof without respect to the amount in controversy, or in any other court having jurisdiction of the parties, and shall recover the damages by him sustained and the cost of the suit.

RESTRICTION ON POLITICAL CONTRIBUTIONS

SEC. 304. Section 313 of the Federal Corrupt Practices Act, 1925 (U.S.C., 1940 edition, title 2, sec. 251; Supp. V, title 50, App., sec. 1509), as amended, is amended to read as follows:

SEC. 313. It is unlawful for any national bank, or any corporation organized by authority of any law of Congress to make a contribution or expenditure in connection with any election to any political office, or in connection with any primary election or political convention or caucus held to select candidates for any political office, or for any corporation whatever, or any labor organization to make a contribution or expenditure in connection with any election at which Presidential and Vice Presidential electors or a Senator or Representative in, or a Delegate or Resident Commissioner to Congress are to be voted for, or in connection with any primary election or political convention or caucus held to select candidates for any of the foregoing offices, or for any candidate, political committee, or other person to accept or receive any contribution prohibited by this section. Every corporation or labor organization which makes any contribution or expenditure in violation of this section shall be fined not more than $5,000; and every officer or director of any corporation, or officer of any labor organization, who consents to any contribution or expenditure by the corporation or labor organization, as the case may be, in violation of this section shall be fined not more than $1,000 or imprisoned for not more than one year, or both. For the purposes of this section "labor organization" means any organization of any kind, or any agency or employee representation committee or plan, in which employees participate and which exists for the purpose, in whole or in part, of dealing with employers concerning grievances, labor disputes, wages, rates of pay, hours of employment, or conditions of work.

TITLE IV

CREATION OF JOINT COMMITTEE TO STUDY AND REPORT ON BASIC PROBLEMS AFFECTING FRIENDLY LABOR RELATIONS AND PRODUCTIVITY

* * * * * * *

TITLE V

DEFINITIONS

SEC. 501. When used in this Act—

(1) The term "industry affecting commerce" means any industry or activity in commerce or in which a labor dispute would burden or obstruct commerce or tend to burden or obstruct commerce or the free flow of commerce.

(2) The term "strike" includes any strike or other concerted stoppage of work by employees (including a stoppage by reason of the expiration of a collective-bargaining agreement) and any concerted slow-down or other concerted interruption of operations by employees.

(3) The terms "commerce," "labor disputes," "employer," "employee," "labor organization," "representative," "person," and "supervisor" shall have the same meaning as when used in the National Labor Relations Act as amended by this Act.

SAVING PROVISION

SEC. 502. Nothing in this Act shall be construed to require an individual employee to render labor or service without his consent, nor shall anything in this Act be construed to make the quitting of his labor by an individual employee an illegal act; nor shall any court issue any process to compel the performance by an individual employee of such labor or service, without his consent; nor shall the quitting of labor by an employee or employees in good faith because of abnormally dangerous conditions for work at the place of employment of such employee or employees be deemed a strike under this Act.

SEPARABILITY

SEC. 503. If any provision of this Act, or the application of such provision to any person or circumstance, shall be held invalid, the remainder of this Act, or the application of such provision to persons or circumstances other than those as to which it is held invalid, shall not be affected thereby.

THE LANDRUM-GRIFFIN ACT OF 1959 AS AMENDED

Popularly known as the "union reform law," the Landrum-Griffin Act contains seven titles, the first six regulating the internal affairs of unions and employers and the seventh amending the Taft-Hartley Act. Landrum-Griffin Title VII amendments to the Taft-Hartley Act are shown in that act above. What follows is the first six titles of the Landrum-Griffin Act.

LABOR-MANAGEMENT REPORTING AND DISCLOSURE ACT OF 1959, AS AMENDED[1]

[Revised text showing in bold face new or amended language provided by Public Law 89—216, as enacted September 29, 1965, 79 Stat. 888]

AN ACT

To provide for the reporting and disclosure of certain financial transactions and administrative practices of labor organizations and employers, to prevent

---

[1] Public Law 257, 86th Congress (73 Stat. 519–546), as amended by Public Law 216, 89th Congress (79 Stat. 888). This revised text has been prepared by the U.S. Department of Labor.

abuses in the administration of trusteeships by labor organizations, to provide standards with respect to the election of officers of labor organizations, and for other purposes.

Be it enacted by the Senate and House of Representatives of the United States of America in Congress assembled, That this Act may be cited as the "Labor-Management Reporting and Disclosure Act of 1959."

Declaration of Findings, Purposes, and Policy
(29 U.S.C. 401)

SEC. 2. (a) The Congress finds that, in the public interest, it continues to be the responsibility of the Federal Government to protect employees' rights to organize, choose their own representatives, bargain collectively, and otherwise engage in concerted activities for their mutual aid or protection; that the relations between employers and labor organizations and the millions of workers they represent have a substantial impact on the commerce of the Nation; and that in order to accomplish the objective of a free flow of commerce it is essential that labor organizations, employers, and their officials adhere to the highest standards of responsibility and ethical conduct in administering the affairs of their organizations, particularly as they affect labor-management relations.

(b) The Congress further finds, from recent investigations in the labor and management fields, that there have been a number of instances of breach of trust, corruption, disregard of the rights of individual employees, and other failures to observe high standards of responsibility and ethical conduct which require further and supplementary legislation that will afford necessary protection of the rights and interests of employees and the public generally as they relate to the activities of labor organizations, employers, labor relations consultants, and their officers and representatives.

(c) The Congress, therefore, further finds and declares that the enactment of this Act is necessary to eliminate or prevent improper practices on the part of labor organizations, employers, labor relations consultants, and their officers and representatives which distort and defeat the policies of the Labor Management Relations Act, 1947, as amended, and the Railway Labor Act, as amended, and have the tendency or necessary effect of burdening or obstructing commerce by (1) impairing the efficiency, safety, or operation of the instrumentalities of commerce; (2) occurring in the current of commerce; (3) materially affecting, restraining, or controlling the flow of raw materials or manufactured or processed goods into or from the channels of commerce, or the prices of such materials or goods in commerce; or (4) causing diminution of employment and wages in such volume as substantially to impair or disrupt the market for goods flowing into or from the channels of commerce.

Definitions
(29 U.S.C. 402)

SEC. 3. For the purposes of titles I, II, III, IV, V (except section 505), and VI of this Act—

(a) "Commerce" means trade, traffic, commerce, transportation, transmission, or communication among the several States or between any State and any place outside thereof.

(b) "State" includes any State of the United States, the District of Columbia, Puerto Rico, the Virgin Islands, American Samoa, Guam, Wake Island, the Canal Zone, and Outer Continental Shelf lands defined in the Outer Continental Shelf Lands Act (43 U.S.C. 1331–1343).

(c) "Industry affecting commerce" means any activity, business, or industry in commerce or in which a labor dispute would hinder or obstruct commerce or the free flow of commerce and includes any activity or industry "affecting commerce" within the meaning of the Labor Management Relations Act, 1947, as amended, or the Railway Labor Act, as amended.

(d) "Person" includes one or more individuals, labor organizations, partnerships, associations, corporations, legal representatives, mutual companies, joint-stock companies, trusts, unincorporated organizations, trustees, trustees in bankruptcy, or receivers.

(e) "Employer" means any employer or any group or association of employers engaged in an industry affecting commerce (1) which is, with respect to employees engaged in an industry affecting commerce, an employer within the meaning of any law of the United States relating to the employment of any employees or (2) which may deal with any labor organization concerning grievances, labor disputes, wages, rates of pay, hours of employment, or conditions of work, and includes any person acting directly or indirectly as an employer or as an agent of an employer in relation to an employee but does not include the United States or any corporation wholly owned by the Government of the United States or any State or political subdivision thereof.

(f) "Employee" means any individual employed by an employer, and includes any individual whose work has ceased as a consequence of, or in connection with, any current labor dispute or because of any unfair labor practice or because of exclusion or expulsion from a labor organization in any manner or for any reason inconsistent with the requirements of this Act.

(g) "Labor dispute" includes any controversy concerning terms, tenure, or conditions of employment, or concerning the association or representation of persons in negotiating, fixing, maintaining, changing, or seeking to arrange terms or conditions of employment, regardless of whether the disputants stand in the proximate relation of employer and employee.

(h) "Trusteeship" means any receivership, trusteeship, or other method of supervision or control whereby a labor organization suspends the autonomy otherwise available to a subordinate body under its constitution or bylaws.

(i) "Labor organization" means a labor organization engaged in an industry affecting commerce and includes any organization of any kind, any agency, or employee representation committee, group, association, or plan so engaged in which employees participate and which exists for the purpose, in whole or in part, of dealing with employers concerning grievances, labor disputes, wages, rates of pay, hours, or other terms or conditions of employment, and any conference, general committee, joint or system board, or joint council so engaged which is subordinate to a national or international labor organization, other than a State or local central body.

(j) A labor organization shall be deemed to be engaged in an industry affecting commerce if it—

(1) is the certified representative of employees under the provisions of the National Labor Relations Act, as amended, or the Railway Labor Act, as amended; or

(2) although not certified, is a national or international labor organization or a local labor organization recognized or acting as the representative of employees or an employer or employers engaged in an industry affecting commerce; or

(3) has chartered a local labor organization or subsidiary body which is representing or actively seeking to represent employees of employers within the meaning of paragraph (1) or (2); or

(4) has been chartered by a labor organization representing or actively seeking to represent employees within the meaning of paragraph (1) or (2) as the local or subordinate body through which such employees may enjoy membership or become affiliated with such labor organization; or

(5) is a conference, general committee, joint or system board, or joint council, subordinate to a national or international labor organization, which includes a labor organization engaged in an industry affecting commerce within the meaning of any of the preceding paragraphs of this subsection, other than a State or local central body.

(k) "Secret ballot" means the expression by ballot, voting machine, or otherwise, but in no event by proxy, of a choice with respect to any election or vote taken upon any matter, which is cast in such a manner that the person expressing such choice cannot be identified with the choice expressed.

(1) "Trust in which a labor organization is interested" means a trust or other fund or organization (1) which was created or established by a labor organization, or one or more of the trustees or one or more members of the governing body of which is selected or appointed by a labor organization, and (2) a primary purpose of which is to provide benefits for the members of such labor organization or their beneficiaries.

(m) "Labor relations consultant" means any person who, for compensation, advises or represents an employer, employer organization, or labor organization concerning employee organizing, concerted activities, or collective bargaining activities.

(n) "Officer" means any constitutional officer, any person authorized to perform the functions of president, vice president, secretary, treasurer, or other executive functions of a labor organization, and any member of its executive board or similar governing body.

(o) "Member" or "member in good standing," when used in reference to a labor organization, includes any person who has fulfilled the requirements for membership in such organization, and who neither has voluntarily withdrawn from membership nor has been expelled or suspended from membership after appropriate proceedings consistent with lawful provisions of the constitution and bylaws of such organization.

(p) "Secretary" means the Secretary of Labor.

(q) "Officer, agent, shop steward, or other representative," when used with respect to a labor organization, includes elected officials and key administrative personnel, whether elected or appointed (such as business agents, heads of departments or major units, and organizers who exercise substantial independent authority), but does not include salaried nonsupervisory professional staff, stenographic, and service personnel.

(r) "District court of the United States" means a United States district court and a United States court of any place subject to the jurisdiction of the United States.

TITLE 1—BILL OF RIGHTS OF MEMBERS OF LABOR ORGANIZATIONS

Bill of Rights

(29 U.S.C. 411)

SEC. 101. (a)(1) EQUAL RIGHTS.—Every member of a labor organization shall have equal rights and privileges within such organization to nominate candidates, to vote in elections or referendums of the labor organization, to attend membership meetings and to participate in the deliberations and voting upon the business of such meetings, subject to reasonable rules and regulations in such organization's constitution and bylaws.

(2) Freedom of Speech and Assembly.—Every member of any labor organization shall have the right to meet and assemble freely with other members; and to express any views, arguments, or opinions; and to express at meetings of the labor organization his views, upon candidates in an election of the labor organization or upon any business properly before the meeting, subject to the organization's established and reasonable rules pertaining to the conduct of meetings: *Provided,* That nothing herein shall be construed to impair the right of a labor organization to adopt and enforce reasonable rules as to the responsibility of every member toward the organization as an institution and to his refraining from conduct that would interfere with its performance of its legal or contractual obligations.

(3) Dues, Initiation Fees, and Assessments.—Except in the case of a federation of national or international labor organizations, the rates of dues and initiation fees payable by members of any labor organization in effect on the date of enactment of this Act shall not be increased, and no general or special assessment shall be levied upon such members, except—

(A) in the case of a local organization, (i) by majority vote by secret ballot of the members in good standing voting at a general or special membership meeting, after reasonable notice of the intention to vote upon such question, or (ii) by majority vote of the members in good standing voting in a membership referendum conducted by secret ballot; or

(B) in the case of a labor organization, other than a local labor organization or a federation of national or international labor organizations, (i) by majority vote of the delegates voting at a regular convention, or at a special convention of such labor organization held upon not less than thirty days' written notice to the principal office of each local or constituent labor organization entitled to such notice, or (ii) by majority vote of the members in good standing of such labor organization voting in a membership referendum conducted by secret ballot, or (iii) by majority vote of the members of the executive board or similar governing body of such labor organization, pursuant to express authority contained in the constitution and bylaws of such labor organization: *Provided,* That such action on the part of the executive board or similar governing body shall be effective only until the next regular convention of such labor organization.

(4) Protection of the Right To Sue.—No labor organization shall limit the right of any member thereof to institute an action in any court, or in a proceeding before any administrative agency, irrespective of whether or not the labor organization or its officers are named as defendants or respondents in such action or proceeding, or the right of any member of a labor organization to appear as a witness in any judicial, administrative, or legislative proceeding, or to petition any legislature or to communicate with any legislator: *Provided,* That any such member may be required to exhaust reasonable hearing procedures (but not to exceed a four-month lapse of time) within such organization, before instituting legal or administrative proceedings against such organizations or any officer thereof: *And provided further,* That no interested employer or employer association shall directly or indirectly finance, encourage, or participate in, except as a party, any such action, proceeding, appearance, or petition.

(5) Safeguards Against Improper Disciplinary Action.—No member of any labor organization may be fined, suspended, expelled, or otherwise disciplined except for nonpayment of dues by such organization or by any officer thereof unless such member has been (A) served with written specific

charges; (B) given a reasonable time to prepare his defense; (C) afforded a full and fair hearing.

(b) Any provision of the constitution and bylaws of any labor organization which is inconsistent with the provisions of this section shall be of no force or effect.

Civil Enforcement
(29 U.S.C. 412)

SEC. 102. Any person whose rights secured by the provisions of this title have been infringed by any violation of this title may bring a civil action in a district court of the United States for such relief (including injunctions) as may be appropriate. Any such action against a labor organization shall be brought in the district court of the United States for the district where the alleged violation occurred, or where the principal office of such labor organization is located.

Retention of Existing Rights
(29 U.S.C. 413)

SEC. 103. Nothing contained in this title shall limit the rights and remedies of any member of a labor organization under any State or Federal law before any court or other tribunal, or under the constitution and bylaws of any labor organization.

Right to Copies of Collective Bargaining Agreements
(29 U.S.C. 414)

SEC. 104. It shall be the duty of the secretary or corresponding principal officer of each labor organization, in the case of a local labor organization, to forward a copy of each collective bargaining agreement made by such labor organization with any employer to any employee who requests such a copy and whose rights as such employee are directly affected by such agreement, and in the case of a labor organization other than a local labor organization, to forward a copy of any such agreement to each constituent unit which has members directly affected by such agreement; and such officer shall maintain at the principal office of the labor organization of which he is an officer copies of any such agreement made or received by such labor organization, which copies shall be available for inspection by any member or by any employee whose rights are affected by such agreement. The provisions of section 210 shall be applicable in the enforcement of this section.

Information as to Act
(29 U.S.C. 415)

SEC. 105. Every labor organization shall inform its members concerning the provisions of this Act.

TITLE II—REPORTING BY LABOR ORGANIZATIONS, OFFICERS AND EMPLOYEES OF LABOR ORGANIZATIONS, AND EMPLOYERS

Report of Labor Organizations
(29 U.S.C. 431)

SEC. 201. (a) Every labor organization shall adopt a constitution and bylaws and shall file a copy thereof with the Secretary, together with a report, signed by its president and secretary or corresponding principal officers, containing the following information—

(1) the name of the labor organization, its mailing address, and any other address at which it maintains its principal office or at which it keeps the records referred to in this title;

(2) the name and title of each of its officers;

(3) the initiation fee or fees required from a new or transferred member and fees for work permits required by the reporting labor organization;

(4) the regular dues or fees of other periodic payments required to remain a member of the reporting labor organization; and

(5) detailed statements, or references to specific provisions of documents filed under this subsection which contain such statements, showing the provisions made and procedures followed with respect to each of the following: (A) qualifications for or restrictions on membership, (B) levying of assessments, (C) participation in insurance or other benefit plans, (D) authorization for disbursement of funds of the labor organization, (E) audit of financial transactions of the labor organization, (F) the calling of regular and special meetings, (G) the selection of officers and stewards and of any representatives to other bodies composed of labor organizations' representatives, with a specific statement of the manner in which each officer was elected, appointed, or otherwise selected, (H) discipline or removal of officers or agents for breaches of their trust, (I) imposition of fines, suspensions, and expulsions of members, including the grounds for such action and any provision made for notice, hearing, judgment on the evidence, and appeal procedures, (J) authorization for bargaining demands, (K) ratification of contract terms, (L) authorization for strikes, and (M) issuance of work permits. Any change in the information required by this subsection shall be reported to the Secretary at the time the reporting labor organization files with the Secretary the annual financial report required by subsection (b).

(b) Every labor organization shall file annually with the Secretary a financial report signed by its president and treasurer or corresponding principal officers containing the following information in such detail as may be necessary accurately to disclose its financial condition and operations for its preceding fiscal year—

(1) assets and liabilities at the beginning and end of the fiscal year;

(2) receipts of any kind and the sources thereof;

(3) salary, allowances, and other direct or indirect disbursements (including reimbursed expenses) to each officer and also to each employee who, during such fiscal year, received more than $10,000 in the aggregate from such labor organization and any other labor organization affiliated with it or with which it is affiliated, or which is affiliated with the same national or international labor organization;

(4) direct and indirect loans made to any officer, employee, or member, which aggregated more than $250 during the fiscal year, together with a statement of the purpose, security, if any, and arrangements for repayment;

(5) direct and indirect loans to any business enterprise, together with a statement of the purpose, security, if any, and arrangements for repayment; and

(6) other disbursements made by it including the purposes thereof; all in such categories as the Secretary may prescribe.

(c) Every labor organization required to submit a report under this title shall make available the information required to be contained in such report to all of its members, and every such labor organization and its officers shall be under a duty enforceable at the suit of any member of such organization in any State court of competent jurisdiction or in the district court of the United States for the district in which such labor organization maintains its principal office, to permit such member for just cause to examine any books, records, and accounts necessary to verify such report. The court in such action may, in its discretion, in addition to any judgment awarded to the plaintiff or plaintiffs, allow a reasonable attorney's fee to be paid by the defendant, and costs of the action.

(d) Subsections (f), (g), and (h) of section 9 of the National Labor Relations Act, as amended, are hereby repealed.

(e) Clause (i) of section 8(a) (3) of the National Labor Relations Act, as amended, is amended by striking out the following: "and has at the time the agreement was made or within the preceding twelve months received from the Board a notice of compliance with sections 9 (f), (g), (h)."

Report of Officers and Employees of Labor Organizations
(29 U.S.C. 432)

SEC. 202. (a) Every officer of a labor organization and every employee of a labor organization (other than an employee performing exclusively clerical or custodial services) shall file with the Secretary a signed report listing and describing for his preceding fiscal year—

(1) any stock, bond, security, or other interest, legal or equitable, which he or his spouse or minor child directly or indirectly held in, and any income or any other benefit with monetary value (including reimbursed expenses) which he or his spouse or minor child derived directly or indirectly from, an employer whose employees such labor organization represents or is actively seeking to represent, except payments and other benefits received as a bona fide employee of such employer;

(2) any transaction in which he or his spouse or minor child engaged, directly or indirectly, involving any stock, bond, security, or loan to or from other legal or equitable interest in the business of an employer whose employees such labor organization represents or is actively seeking to represent;

(3) any stock, bond, security, or other interest, legal or equitable, which he or his spouse or minor child directly or indirectly held in, and any income or any other benefit with monetary value (including reimbursed expenses) which he or his spouse or minor child directly or indirectly derived from, any business a substantial part of which consists of buying from, selling or leasing to, or otherwise dealing with, the business of an employer whose employees such labor organization represents or is actively seeking to represent;

(4) any stock, bond, security, or other interest, legal or equitable, which he or his spouse or minor child directly or indirectly held in, and any income or any other benefit with monetary value (including reimbursed expenses) which he or his spouse or minor child directly or indirectly derived from, a business any part of which consists of buying from, or selling or leasing directly or indirectly to, or otherwise dealing with such labor organization;

(5) any direct or indirect business transaction or arrangement between him or his spouse or minor child and any employer whose employees his organization represents or is actively seeking to represent, except work performed and payments and benefits received as a bona fide employee of such employer and except purchases and sales of goods or services in the

regular course of business at prices generally available to any employee of such employer; and

(6) any payment of money or other thing of value (including reimbursed expenses) which he or his spouse or minor child received directly or indirectly from any employer or any person who acts as a labor relations consultant to an employer, except payments of the kinds referred to in section 302(c) of the Labor Management Relations Act, 1947, as amended.

(b) The provisions of paragraphs (1), (2), (3), (4), and (5) of subsection (a) shall not be construed to require any such officer or employee to report his bona fide investments in securities traded on a securities exchange registered as a national securities exchange under the Securities Exchange Act of 1934, in shares in an investment company registered under the Investment Company Act of 1940, or in securities of a public utility holding company registered under the Public Utility Holding Company Act of 1935, or to report any income derived therefrom.

(c) Nothing contained in this section shall be construed to require any officer or employee of a labor organization to file a report under subsection (a) unless he or his spouse or minor child holds or has held an interest, has received income or any other benefit with monetary value or a loan, or has engaged in a transaction described therein.

Report of Employers
(29 U.S.C. 433)

Sec. 203. (a) Every employer who in any fiscal year made—

(1) any payment or loan, direct or indirect, of money or other thing of value (including reimbursed expenses), or any promise or agreement therefor, to any labor organization or officer, agent, shop steward, or other representative of a labor organization, or employee of any labor organization, except (A) payments or loans made by any national or State bank, credit union, insurance company, savings and loan association or other credit institution and (B) payments of the kind referred to in section 302(c) of the Labor Management Relations Act, 1947, as amended;

(2) any payment (including reimbursed expenses) to any of his employees, or any group or committee of such employees, for the purpose of causing such employee or group or committee of employees to persuade other employees to exercise or not to exercise, or as to the manner of exercising, the right to organize and bargain collectively through representatives of their own choosing unless such payments were contemporaneously or previously disclosed to such other employees;

(3) any expenditure, during the fiscal year, where an object thereof, directly or indirectly, is to interfere with, restrain, or coerce employees in the exercise of the right to organize and bargain collectively through representatives of their own choosing, or is to obtain information concerning the activities of employees or a labor organization in connection with a labor dispute involving such employer, except for use solely in conjunction with an administrative or arbitral proceeding or a criminal or civil judicial proceeding;

(4) any agreement or arrangement with a labor relations consultant or other independent contractor or organization pursuant to which such person undertakes activities where an object thereof, directly or indirectly, is to persuade employees to exercise or not to exercise, or persuade employees as to the manner of exercising, the right to organize and bargain collectively through representatives of their own choosing, or undertakes to supply such employer with information concerning the activities of employees or a labor organization in connection with a labor dispute involving such employer,

except information for use solely in conjunction with an administrative or arbitral proceeding or a criminal or civil judicial proceeding; or

(5) any payment (including reimbursed expenses) pursuant to an agreement or arrangement described in subdivision (4);

shall file with the Secretary a report, in a form prescribed by him, signed by its president and treasurer or corresponding principal officers showing in detail the date and amount of each such payment, loan, promise, agreement, or arrangement and the name, address, and position, if any, in any firm or labor organization of the person to whom it was made and a full explanation of the circumstances of all such payments, including the terms of any agreement or understanding pursuant to which they were made.

(b) Every person who pursuant to any agreement or arrangement with an employer undertakes activities where an object thereof is, directly or indirectly—

(1) to persuade employees to exercise or not to exercise, or persuade employees as to the manner of exercising, the right to organize and bargain collectively through representatives of their own choosing; or

(2) to supply an employer with information concerning the activities of employees or a labor organization in connection with a labor dispute involving such employer, except information for use solely in conjunction with an administrative or arbitral proceeding or a criminal or civil judicial proceeding;

shall file within thirty days after entering into such agreement or arrangement a report with the Secretary, signed by its president and treasurer or corresponding principal officers, containing the name under which such person is engaged in doing business and the address of its principal office, and a detailed statement of the terms and conditions of such agreement or arrangement. Every such person shall file annually, with respect to each fiscal year during which payments were made as a result of such an agreement or arrangement, a report with the Secretary, signed by its president and treasurer or corresponding principal officers, containing a statement (A) of its receipts of any kind from employers on account of labor relations advice or services, designating the sources thereof, and (B) of its disbursements of any kind, in connection with such services and the purposes thereof. In each such case such information shall be set forth in such categories as the Secretary may prescribe.

(c) Nothing in this section shall be construed to require any employer or other person to file a report covering the services of such person by reason of his giving or agreeing to give advice to such employer or representing or agreeing to represent such employer before any court, administrative agency, or tribunal of arbitration or engaging or agreeing to engage in collective bargaining on behalf of such employer with respect to wages, hours, or other terms or conditions of employment or the negotiation of an agreement or any question arising thereunder.

(d) Nothing contained in this section shall be construed to require an employer to file a report under subsection (a) unless he has made an expenditure, payment, loan, agreement, or arrangement of the kind described therein. Nothing contained in this section shall be construed to require any other person to file a report under subsection (b) unless he was a party to an agreement or arrangement of the kind described therein.

(e) Nothing contained in this section shall be construed to require any regular officer, supervisor, or employee of an employer to file a report in connection with services rendered to such employer nor shall any employer be required to file a report covering expenditures made to any regular officer, supervisor, or employee of an employer as compensation for service as a regular officer, supervisor, or employee of such employer.

(f) Nothing contained in this section shall be construed as an amendment to, or modification of the rights protected by, section 8(c) of the National Labor Relations Act, as amended.

(g) The term "interfere with, restrain, or coerce" as used in this section means interference, restraint, and coercion which, if done with respect to the exercise of rights guaranteed in section 7 of the National Labor Relations Act, as amended, would, under section 8(a) of such Act, constitute an unfair labor practice.

Attorney-Client Communications Exempted
(29 U.S.C. 434)

SEC. 204. Nothing contained in this Act shall be construed to require an attorney who is a member in good standing of the bar of any State, to include in any report required to be filed pursuant to the provisions of this Act any information which was lawfully communicated to such attorney by any of his clients in the course of a legitimate attorney-client relationship.

Reports Made Public Information
(29 U.S.C. 435)

SEC. 205. (a)[2] The contents of the reports and documents filed with the Secretary pursuant to sections 201, 202, **203, and 211** shall be public information, and the Secretary may publish any information and data which he obtains pursuant to the provisions of this title. The Secretary may use the information and data for statistical and research purposes, and compile and publish such studies, analyses, reports, and surveys based thereon as he may deem appropriate.

(b)[3] The Secretary shall by regulation make reasonable provision for the inspection and examination, on the request of any person, of the information and data contained in any report or other document filed with him pursuant to section 201, 202, **203, or 211.**

(c)[4] The Secretary shall by regulation provide for the furnishing by the Department of Labor of copies of reports or other documents filed with the Secretary pursuant to this title, upon payment of a charge based upon the cost of the service. The Secretary shall make available without payment of a charge, or require any person to furnish, to such State agency as is designated by law or by the Governor of the State in which such person has his principal place of business or headquarters, upon request of the Governor of such State, copies of any reports and documents filed by such person with the Secretary pursuant to

[2] Prior to amendment by section 2(a) of Public Law 89–216, the first sentence of section 205(a) read as follows: "Sec. 205. (a) The contents of the reports and documents filed with the Secretary pursuant to sections 201, 202, and 203 shall be public information, and the Secretary may publish any information and data which he obtains pursuant to the provisions of this title."

[3] Prior to amendment by section 2(b) of Public Law 89–216, section 205(b) read as follows: "(b) The Secretary shall by regulation make reasonable provision for the inspection and examination, on the request of any person, of the information and data contained in any report or other document filed with him pursuant to section 201, 202, or 203."

[4] Prior to amendment by section 2(c) of Public Law 89–216, the second sentence of section 205(c) read as follows: "The Secretary shall make available without payment of a charge, or require any person to furnish, to such State agency as is designated by law or by the Governor of the State in which such person has his principal place of business or headquarters, upon request of the Governor of such State, copies of any reports and documents filed by such person with the Secretary pursuant to section 201, 202, or 203, or of information and data contained therein."

section 201, 202, **203, or 211,** or of information and data contained therein. No person shall be required by reason of any law of any State to furnish to any officer or agency of such State any information included in a report filed by such person with the Secretary pursuant to the provisions of this title, if a copy of such report, or of the portion thereof containing such information, is furnished to such officer or agency. All moneys received in payment of such charges fixed by the Secretary pursuant to this subsection shall be deposited in the general fund of the Treasury.

Retention of Records
   (29 U.S.C. 436)

   Sec. 206. Every person required to file any report under this title shall maintain records on the matters required to be reported which will provide in sufficient detail the necessary basic information and data from which the documents filed with the Secretary may be verified, explained or clarified, and checked for accuracy and completeness, and shall include vouchers, work-sheets, receipts, and applicable resolutions, and shall keep such records available for examination for a period of not less than five years after the filing of the documents based on the information which they contain.

Effective Date
   (29 U.S.C. 437)

   Sec. 207. (a) Each labor organization shall file the initial report required under section 201(a) within ninety days after the date on which it first becomes subject to this Act.

   (b)[5] Each person required to file a report under section 201(b), 202, 203(a), **the second sentence of section 203(b), or section 211** shall file such report within ninety days after the end of each of its fiscal years; except that where such person is subject to section 201(b), 202, 203(a), **the second sentence of section 203(b), or section 211,** as the case may be, for only a portion of such a fiscal year (because the date of enactment of this Act occurs during such person's fiscal year or such person becomes subject to this Act during its fiscal year) such person may consider that portion as the entire fiscal year in making such report.

Rules and Regulations
   (29 U.S.C. 438)

   Sec. 208. The Secretary shall have authority to issue, amend, and rescind rules and regulations prescribing the form and publication of reports required to be filed under this title and such other reasonable rules and regulations (including rules prescribing reports concerning trusts in which a labor organization is interested) as he may find necessary to prevent the circumvention or evasion of such reporting requirements. In exercising his power under this section the Secretary shall prescribe by general rule simplified reports for labor organizations or employers for whom he finds that by virtue of their size a detailed report would be unduly burdensome, but the Secretary may revoke

---

   [5] Prior to amendment by section 2(d) of Public Law 89–216, section 207(b) read as follows: "(b) Each person required to file a report under section 201(b), 202, 203(a), or the second sentence of 203(b) shall file such report within ninety days after the end of each of its fiscal years; except that where such person is subject to section 201(b), 202, 203(a), or the second sentence of 203(b), as the case may be, for only a portion of such a fiscal year (because the date of enactment of this Act occurs during such person's fiscal year or such person becomes subject to this Act during its fiscal year) such person may consider that portion as the entire fiscal year in making such report."

such provision for simplified forms of any labor organization or employer if he determines, after such investigation as he deems proper and due notice and opportunity for a hearing, that the purposes of this section would be served thereby.

Criminal Provisions
(29 U.S.C. 439)

SEC. 209. (a) Any person who willfully violates this title shall be fined not more than $10,000 or imprisoned for not more than one year, or both.

(b) Any person who makes a false statement or representation of a material fact, knowing it to be false, or who knowingly fails to disclose a material fact, in any document, report, or other information required under the provisions of this title shall be fined not more than $10,000 or imprisoned for not more than one year, or both.

(c) Any person who willfully makes a false entry in or willfully conceals, withholds, or destroys any books, records, reports, or statements required to be kept by any provision of this title shall be fined not more than $10,000 or imprisoned for not more than one year, or both.

(d) Each individual required to sign reports under sections 201 and 203 shall be personally responsible for the filing of such reports and for any statement contained therein which he knows to be false.

Civil Enforcement
(29 U.S.C. 440)

SEC. 210. Whenever it shall appear that any person has violated or is about to violate any of the provisions of this title, the Secretary may bring a civil action for such relief (including injunctions) as may be appropriate. Any such action may be brought in the district court of the United States where the violation occurred or, at the option of the parties, in the United States District Court for the District of Columbia.

Surety Company Reports[6]
(29 U.S.C. 441)

Sec. 211. Each surety company which issues any bond required by this Act or the Welfare and Pension Plans Disclosure Act shall file annually with the Secretary, with respect to each fiscal year during which any such bond was in force, a report, in such form and detail as he may prescribe by regulation, filed by the president and treasurer or corresponding principal officers of the surety company, describing its bond experience under each such Act, including information as to the premiums received, total claims paid, amounts recovered by way of subrogation, administrative and legal expenses and such related data and information as the Secretary shall determine to be necessary in the public interest and to carry out the policy of the Act. Notwithstanding the foregoing, if the Secretary finds that any such specific information cannot be practicably ascertained or would be uninformative, the Secretary may modify or waive the requirement for such information.

TITLE III—TRUSTEESHIPS

Reports
(29 U.S.C. 461)

SEC. 301. (a) Every labor organization which has or assumes trusteeship over any subordinate labor organization shall file with the Secretary within

[6] Section 211 was added by section 3 of Public Law 89-216 (79 Stat. 888).

thirty days after the date of the enactment of this Act or the imposition of any such trusteeship, and semiannually thereafter, a report, signed by its president and treasurer or corresponding principal officers, as well as by the trustees of such subordinate labor organization, containing the following information: (1) the name and address of the subordinate organization; (2) the date of establishing the trusteeship; (3) a detailed statement of the reason or reasons for establishing or continuing the trusteeship; and (4) the nature and extent of participation by the membership of the subordinate organization in the selection of delegates to represent such organization in regular or special conventions or other policy-determining bodies and in the election of officers of the labor organization which has assumed trusteeship over such subordinate organization. The initial report shall also include a full and complete account of the financial condition of such subordinate organization as of the time trusteeship was assumed over it. During the continuance of a trusteeship the labor organization which has assumed trusteeship over a subordinate labor organization shall file on behalf of the subordinate labor organization the annual financial report required by section 201(b) signed by the president and treasurer or corresponding principal officers of the labor organization which has assumed such trusteeship and the trustees of the subordinate labor organization.

(b) The provisions of section 201(c), 205, 206, 208, and 210 shall be applicable to reports filed under this title.

(c) Any person who willfully violates this section shall be fined not more than $10,000 or imprisoned for not more than one year, or both.

(d) Any person who makes a false statement or representation of a material fact, knowing it to be false, or who knowingly fails to disclose a material fact, in any report required under the provisions of this section or willfully makes any false entry in or willfully withholds, conceals, or destroys any documents, books, records, reports, or statements upon which such report is based, shall be fined not more than $10,000 or imprisoned for not more than one year, or both.

(e) Each individual required to sign a report under this section shall be personally responsible for the filing of such report and for any statement contained therein which he knows to be false.

Purposes for Which a Trusteeship May Be Established
(29 U.S.C. 462)

Sec. 302. Trusteeships shall be established and administered by a labor organization over a subordinate body only in accordance with the constitution and bylaws of the organization which has assumed trusteeship over the subordinate body and for the purpose of correcting corruption or financial malpractice, assuring the performance of collective bargaining agreements or other duties of a bargaining representative, restoring democratic procedures, or otherwise carrying out the legitimate objects of such labor organization.

Unlawful Acts Relating to Labor Organization Under Trusteeship
(29 U.S.C. 463)

Sec. 303. (a) During any period when a subordinate body of a labor organization is in trusteeship, it shall be unlawful (1) to count the vote of delegates from such body in any convention or election of officers of the labor organization unless the delegates have been chosen by secret ballot in an election in which all the members in good standing of such subordinate body were eligible to participate or (2) to transfer to such organization any current receipts or other funds of the subordinate body except the normal per capita tax and assessments payable by subordinate bodies not in trusteeship: *Provided,*

That nothing herein contained shall prevent the distribution of the assets of a labor organization in accordance with its constitution and bylaws upon the bona fide dissolution thereof.

(b) Any person who willfully violates this section shall be fined not more than $10,000 or imprisoned for not more than one year, or both.

Enforcement
(29 U.S.C. 464)

SEC. 304. (a) Upon the written complaint of any member or subordinate body of a labor organization alleging that such organization has violated the provisions of this title (except section 301) the Secretary shall investigate the complaint and if the Secretary finds probable cause to believe that such violation has occurred and has not been remedied he shall, without disclosing the identity of the complainant, bring a civil action in any district court of the United States having jurisdiction of the labor organization for such relief (including injunctions) as may be appropriate. Any member or subordinate body of a labor organization affected by any violation of this title (except section 301) may bring a civil action in any district court of the United States having jurisdiction of the labor organization for such relief (including injunctions) as may be appropriate.

(b) For the purpose of actions under this section, district courts of the United States shall be deemed to have jurisdiction of a labor organization (1) in the district in which the principal office of such labor organization is located, or (2) in any district in which its duly authorized officers or agents are engaged in conducting the affairs of the trusteeship.

(c) In any proceeding pursuant to this section a trusteeship established by a labor organization in conformity with the procedural requirements of its constitution and bylaws and authorized or ratified after a fair hearing either before the executive board or before such other body as may be provided in accordance with its constitution or bylaws shall be presumed valid for a period of eighteen months from the date of its establishment and shall not be subject to attack during such period except upon clear and convincing proof that the trusteeship was not established or maintained in good faith for a purpose allowable under section 302. After the expiration of eighteen months the trusteeship shall be presumed invalid in any such proceeding and its discontinuance shall be decreed unless the labor organization shall show by clear and convincing proof that the continuation of the trusteeship is necessary for a purpose allowable under section 302. In the latter event the court may dismiss the complaint or retain jurisdiction of the cause on such conditions and for such period as it deems appropriate.

Report to Congress
(29 U.S.C. 465)

SEC. 305. The Secretary shall submit to the Congress at the expiration of three years from the date of enactment of this Act a report upon the operation of this title.

Complaint by Secretary
(29 U.S.C. 466)

SEC. 306. The rights and remedies provided by this title shall be in addition to any and all other rights and remedies at law or in equity: *Provided,* That upon the filing of a complaint by the Secretary the jurisdiction of the district court over such trusteeship shall be exclusive and the final judgment shall be res judicata.

TITLE IV—ELECTIONS

Terms of Office; Election Procedures

(29 U.S.C. 481)

SEC. 401. (a) Every national or international labor organization, except a federation of national or international labor organizations, shall elect its officers not less often than once every five years either by secret ballot among the members in good standing or at a convention of delegates chosen by secret ballot.

(b) Every local labor organization shall elect its officers not less often than once every three years by secret ballot among the members in good standing.

(c) Every national or international labor organization, except a federation of national or international labor organizations, and every local labor organization, and its officers, shall be under a duty, enforceable at the suit of any bona fide candidate for office in such labor organization in the district court of the United States in which such labor organization maintains its principal office, to comply with all reasonable requests of any candidate to distribute by mail or otherwise at the candidate's expense campaign literature in aid of such person's candidacy to all members in good standing of such labor organization and to refrain from discrimination in favor of or against any candidate with respect to the use of lists of members, and whenever such labor organizations or its officers authorize the distribution by mail or otherwise to members of campaign literature on behalf of any candidate or of the labor organization itself with reference to such election, similar distribution at the request of any other bona fide candidate shall be made by such labor organization and its officers, with equal treatment as to the expense of such distribution. Every bona fide candidate shall have the right, once within 30 days prior to an election of a labor organization in which he is a candidate, to inspect a list containing the names and last known addresses of all members of the labor organization who are subject to a collective bargaining agreement requiring membership therein as a condition of employment, which list shall be maintained and kept at the principal office of such labor organization by a designated official thereof. Adequate safeguards to insure a fair election shall be provided, including the right of any candidate to have an observer at the polls and at the counting of the ballots.

(d) Officers of intermediate bodies, such as general committees, system boards, joint boards, or joint councils, shall be elected not less often than once every four years by secret ballot among the members in good standing or by labor organization officers representative of such members who have been elected by secret ballot.

(e) In any election required by this section which is to be held by secret ballot a reasonable opportunity shall be given for the nomination of candidates and every member in good standing shall be eligible to be a candidate and to hold office (subject to section 504 and to reasonable qualifications uniformly imposed) and shall have the right to vote for or otherwise support the candidate or candidates of his choice, without being subject to penalty, discipline, or improper interference or reprisal of any kind by such organization or any member thereof. Not less than fifteen days prior to the election notice thereof shall be mailed to each member at his last known home address. Each member in good standing shall be entitled to one vote. No member whose dues have been withheld by his employer for payment to such organization pursuant to his voluntary authorization provided for in a collective bargaining agreement shall be declared ineligible to vote or be a candidate for office in such organization by reason of alleged delay or default in the payment of dues. The votes cast by members of each local labor organization shall be counted, and the results published, separately. The election officials designated in the constitution and bylaws or the secretary, if no other official is designated, shall preserve for one year the ballots and all other records pertaining to the election. The election shall be conducted in accordance with the constitution and bylaws of such organization insofar as they are not inconsistent with the provisions of this title.

(f) When officers are chosen by a convention of delegates elected by secret ballot, the convention shall be conducted in accordance with the constitution and bylaws of the labor organization insofar as they are not inconsistent with the provisions of this title. The officials designated in the constitution and bylaws or the secretary, if no other is designated, shall preserve for one year the credentials of the delegates and all minutes and other records of the convention pertaining to the election of officers.

(g) No moneys received by any labor organization by way of dues, assessment, or similar levy, and no moneys of an employer shall be contributed or applied to promote the candidacy of any person in an election subject to the provisions of this title. Such moneys of a labor organization may be utilized for notices, factual statements of issues not involving candidates, and other expenses necessary for the holding of an election.

(h) If the Secretary, upon application of any member of a local labor organization, finds after hearing in accordance with the Administrative Procedure Act that the constitution and bylaws of such labor organization do not provide an adequate procedure for the removal of an elected officer guilty of serious misconduct, such officer may be removed, for cause shown and after notice and hearing, by the members in good standing voting in a secret ballot conducted by the officers of such labor organization in accordance with its constitution and bylaws insofar as they are not inconsistent with the provisions of this title.

(i) The Secretary shall promulgate rules and regulations prescribing mimimum standards and procedures for determining the adequacy of the removal procedures to which reference is made in subsection (h).

Enforcement
(29 U.S.C. 482)

Sec. 402. (a) A member of a labor organization—
(1) who has exhausted the remedies available under the constitution and bylaws of such organization and of any parent body, or
(2) who has invoked such available remedies without obtaining a final decision within three calendar months after their invocation,
may file a complaint with the Secretary within one calendar month thereafter alleging the violation of any provision of section 401 (including violation of the constitution and bylaws of the labor organization pertaining to the election and removal of officers). The challenged election shall be presumed valid pending a final decision theron (as hereinafter provided) and in the interim the affairs of the organization shall be conducted by the officers elected or in such other manner as its constitution and bylaws may provide.

(b) The Secretary shall investigate such complaint and, if he finds probable cause to believe that a violation of this title has occurred and has not been remedied, he shall, within sixty days after the filing of such complaint, bring a civil action against the labor organization as an entity in the district court of the the United States in which such labor organization maintains its principal office to set aside the invalid election, if any, and to direct the conduct of an election or hearing and vote upon the removal of officers under the supervision of the Secretary and in accordance with the provisions of this title and such rules and regulations as the Secretary may prescribe. The court shall have power to take such action as it deems proper to preserve the assets of the labor organization.

(c) If, upon a preponderance of the evidence after a trial upon the merits, the court finds—

(1) that an election has not been held within the time prescribed by section 401, or

(2) that the violation of section 401 may have affected the outcome of an election,

the court shall declare the election, if any, to be void and direct the conduct of a new election under supervision of the Secretary and, so far as lawful and practicable, in conformity with the constitution and bylaws of the labor organization. The Secretary shall promptly certify to the court the names of the persons elected, and the court shall thereupon enter a decree declaring such persons to be the officers of the labor organization. If the proceeding is for the removal of officers pursuant to subsection (h) of section 401, the Secretary shall certify the results of the vote and the court shall enter a decree declaring whether such persons have been removed as officers of the labor organization.

(d) An order directing an election, dismissing a complaint, or designating elected officers of a labor organization shall be appealable in the same manner as the final judgment in a civil action, but an order directing an election shall not be stayed pending appeal.

Application of Other Laws
(29 U.S.C. 483)

SEC. 403. No labor organization shall be required by law to conduct elections of officers with greater frequency or in a different form or manner than is required by its own constitution or bylaws, except as otherwise provided by this title. Existing rights and remedies to enforce the constitution and bylaws of a labor organization with respect to elections prior to the conduct thereof shall not be affected by the provisions of this title. The remedy provided by this title for challenging an election already conducted shall be exclusive.

Effective Date
(29 U.S.C. 484)

SEC. 404. The provisions of this title shall become applicable—

(1) ninety days after the date of enactment of this Act in the case of a labor organization whose constitution and bylaws can lawfully be modified or amended by action of its constitutional officers or governing body, or

(2) where such modification can only be made by a constitutional convention of the labor organization, not later than the next constitutional convention of such labor organization after the date of enactment of this Act, or one year after such date, whichever is sooner. If no such convention is held within such one-year period, the executive board or similar governing body empowered to act for such labor organization between conventions is empowered to make such interim constitutional changes as are necessary to carry out the provisions of this title.

TITLE V—SAFEGUARDS FOR LABOR ORGANIZATIONS

Fiduciary Responsibility of Officers of Labor Organizations
(29 U.S.C. 501)

Sec. 501. (a) The officers, agents, shop stewards, and other representatives of a labor organization occupy positions of trust in relation to such organization and its members as a group. It is, therefore, the duty of each such person, taking into account the special problems and functions of a labor organization, to hold its money and property solely for the benefit of the organization and its members and to manage, invest, and expend the same in accordance with its constitution and bylaws and any resolutions of the governing bodies adopted thereunder, to refrain from dealing with such organization as an adverse party or in behalf of an adverse party in any matter connected with his duties and from holding or acquiring any pecuniary or personal interest which conflicts with the interests of such organization, and to account to the organization for any profit received by him in whatever capacity in connection with transactions conducted by him or under his direction on behalf of the organization. A general exculpatory provision in the constitution and bylaws of such a labor organization or a general exculpatory resolution of a governing body purporting to relieve any such person of liability for breach of the duties declared by this section shall be void as against public policy.

(b) When any officer, agent, shop steward, or representative of any labor organization is alleged to have violated the duties declared in subsection (a) and the labor organization or its governing board or officers refuse or fail to sue or recover damages or secure an accounting or other appropriate relief within a reasonable time after being requested to do so by any member of the labor organization, such member may sue such officer, agent, shop steward, or representative in any district court of the United States or in any State court of competent jurisdiction to recover damages or secure an accounting or other appropriate relief for the benefit of the labor organization. No such proceeding shall be brought except upon leave of the court obtained upon verified application and for good cause shown which application may be made ex parte. The trial judge may allot a reasonable part of the recovery in any action under this subsection to pay the fees of counsel prosecuting the suit at the instance of the member of the labor organization and to compensate such member for any expenses necessarily paid or incurred by him in connection with the litigation.

(c) Any person who embezzles, steals, or unlawfully and willfully abstracts or converts to his own use, or the use of another, any of the moneys, funds, securities, property, or other assets of a labor organization of which he is an officer, or by which he is employed, directly or indirectly, shall be fined not more than $10,000 or imprisoned for not more than five years, or both.

Bonding
(29 U.S.C. 502)

Sec. 502. (a)[7] Every officer, agent, shop steward, or other representative or employee of any labor organization (other than a labor organization whose

---

[7] Prior to amendment by section 1 of Public Law 89–216, the first sentence of section 502(a) read as follows: "Sec. 502.(a) Every officer, agent, shop steward, or other representative or employee of any labor organization (other than a labor organization whose property and annual financial receipts do not exceed $5,000 in value), or of a trust in which a labor organization is interested, who handles funds or other property thereof shall be bonded for the faithful discharge of his duties." Section 1 of Public Law 89–216 also added the proviso at the end of section 502(a).

property and annual financial receipts do not exceed $5,000 in value), or of a trust in which a labor organization is interested, who handles funds or other property thereof shall be bonded **to provide protection against loss by reason of acts of fraud or dishonesty on his part directly or through connivance with others.** The bond of each such person shall be fixed at the beginning of the organization's fiscal year and shall be in an amount not less than 10 per centum of the funds handled by him and his predecessor or predecessors, if any, during the preceding fiscal year, but in no case more than $500,000. If the labor organization or the trust in which a labor organization is interested does not have a preceding fiscal year, the amount of the bond shall be, in the case of a local labor organization, not less than $1,000, and in the case of any other labor organization or of a trust in which a labor organization is interested, not less than $10,000. Such bonds shall be individual or schedule in form, and shall have a corporate surety company as surety thereon. Any person who is not covered by such bonds shall not be permitted to receive, handle, disburse, or otherwise exercise custody or control of the funds or other property of a labor organization or of a trust in which a labor organization is interested. No such bond shall be placed through an agent or broker or with a surety company in which any labor organization or any officer, agent, shop steward, or other representative of a labor organization has any direct or indirect interest. Such surety company shall be a corporate surety which holds a grant of authority from the Secretary of the Treasury under the Act of July 30, 1947 (6 U.S.C. 6–13), as an acceptable surety on Federal bonds: *Provided,* **That when in the opinion of the Secretary a labor organization has made other bonding arrangements which would provide the protection required by this section at comparable cost or less, he may exempt such labor organization from placing a bond through a surety company holding such grant of authority.**

(b) Any person who willfully violates this section shall be fined not more than $10,000 or imprisoned for not more than one year, or both.

Making of Loans; Payment of Fines
(29 U.S.C. 503)

Sec. 503. (a) No labor organization shall make directly or indirectly any loan or loans to any officer or employee of such organization which results in a total indebtedness on the part of such officer or employee to the labor organization in excess of $2,000.

(b) No labor organization or employer shall directly or indirectly pay the fine of any officer or employee convicted of any willful violation of this Act.

(c) Any person who willfully violates this section shall be fined not more than $5,000 or imprisoned for not more than one year, or both.

Prohibition Against Certain Persons Holding Office
(29 U.S.C. 504)

Sec. 504. (a) No person who is or has been a member of the Communist Party[8] or who has been convicted of, or served any part of a prison term resulting from his conviction of, robbery, bribery, extortion, embezzlement, grand larceny, burglary, arson, violation of narcotics laws, murder, rape,

---

[8] The U.S. Supreme Court, on June 7, 1965, held unconstitutional as a bill of attainder the section 504 provision which imposes criminal sanctions on Communist party members for holding union office (*U.S.* v. *Brown,* 381 U.S. 437, 85 S. Ct. 1707).

assault with intent to kill, assault which inflicts grievous bodily injury, or a violation of title II or III of this Act, or conspiracy to commit any such crimes shall serve—

(1) as an officer, director, trustee, member of any executive board or similar governing body, business agent, manager, organizer, or other employee (other than as an employee performing exclusively clerical or custodial duties) or any labor organization, or

(2) as a labor relations consultant to a person engaged in an industry or activity affecting commerce, or as an officer, director, agent, or employee (other than as an employee performing exclusively clerical or custodial duties) of any group or association of employers dealing with any labor organization,

during or for five years after the termination of his membership in the Communist Party, or for five years after such conviction or after the end of such imprisonment, unless prior to the end of such five-year period, in the case of a person so convicted or imprisoned, (A) his citizenship rights, having been revoked as a results of such conviction, have been fully restored, or (B) the Board of Parole of the United States Department of Justice determines that such person's service in any capacity referred to in clause (1) or (2) would not be contrary to the purposes of this Act. Prior to making any such determination the Board shall hold an administrative hearing and shall give notice of such proceeding by certified mail to the State, county, and Federal prosecuting officials in the jurisdiction or jurisdictions in which such person was convicted. The Board's determination in any such proceeding shall be final. No labor organization or officer thereof shall knowingly permit any person to assume or hold any office or paid position in violation of this subsection.

(b) Any person who willfully violates this section shall be fined not more than $10,000 or imprisoned for not more than one year, or both.

(c) For the purposes of this section, any person shall be deemed to have been "convicted" and under the disability of "conviction" from the date of the judgment of the trial court or the date of the final sustaining of such judgment on appeal, whichever is the later event, regardless of whether such conviction occurred before or after the date of enactment of this Act.

Amendment to Section 302, Labor Management Relations Act, 1947

SEC. 505. Subsections (a), (b), and (c) of section 302 of the Labor Management Relations Act, 1947, as amended, are amended to read as follows:

"SEC. 302. (a) It shall be unlawful for any employer or association of employers or any person who acts as a labor relations expert, adviser, or consultant to an employer or who acts in the interest of an employer to pay, lend, or deliver, or agree to pay, lend, or deliver, any money or other thing of value—

"(1) to any representative of any of his employees who are employed in an industry affecting commerce; or

"(2) to any labor organization, or any officer or employee thereof, which represents, seeks to represent, or would admit to membership, any of the employees of such employer who are employed in an industry affecting commerce; or

"(3) to any employee or group or committee of employees of such employer employed in an industry affecting commerce in excess of their normal compensation for the purpose of causing such employee or group or committee directly or indirectly to influence any other employees in the exercise of the right to organize and bargain collectively through representatives of their own choosing; or

"(4) to any officer or employee of a labor organization engaged in an industry affecting commerce with intent to influence him in respect to any of his actions, decisions, or duties as a representative of employees or as such officer or employee of such labor organization.

"(b)(1) It shall be unlawful for any person to request, demand, receive, or accept, or agree to receive or accept, any payment, loan, or delivery of any money or other thing of value prohibited by subsection (a).

"(2) It shall be unlawful for any labor organization, or for any person acting as an officer, agent, representative, or employee of such labor organization, to demand or accept from the operator of any motor vehicle (as defined in part II of the Interstate Commerce Act) employed in the transportation of property in commerce, or the employer of any such operator, any money or other thing of value payable to such organization or to an officer, agent, representative or employee thereof as a fee or charge for the unloading; or in connection with the unloading, of the cargo of such vehicle: *Provided*, That nothing in this paragraph shall be construed to make unlawful any payment by an employer to any of his employees as compensation for their services as employees.

"(c) The provisions of this section shall not be applicable (1) in respect to any money or other thing of value payable by an employer to any of his employees whose established duties include acting openly for such employer in matters of labor relations or personnel administration or to any representative of his employees, or to any officer or employee of a labor organization, who is also an employee or former employee of such employer, as compensation for, or by reason of, his service as an employee of such employer; (2) with respect to the payment or delivery of any money or other thing of value in satisfaction of a judgment of any court or a decision or award of an arbitrator or impartial chairman or in compromise, adjustment, settlement, or release of any claim, complaint, grievance, or dispute in the absence of fraud or duress; (3) with respect to the sale or purchase of an article or commodity at the prevailing market price in the regular course of business; (4) with respect to money deducted from the wages of employees in payment of membership dues in a labor organization: *Provided*, That the employer has received from each employee, on whose account such deductions are made, a written assignment which shall not be irrevocable for a period of more than one year, or beyond the termination date of the applicable collective agreement, whichever occurs sooner; (5) with respect to money or other thing of value paid to a trust fund established by such representative, for the sole and exclusive benefit of the employees of such employer, and their families and dependents (or of such employees, families, and dependents jointly with the employees of other employers making similar payments, and their families and dependents): *Provided*, That (A) such payments are held in trust for the purpose of paying, either from principal or income or both, for the benefit of employees, their families and dependents, for medical or hospital care, pensions on retirement or death of employees, compensation for injuries or illness resulting from occupational activity or insurance to provide any of the foregoing, or unemployment benefits or life insurance, disability and sickness insurance, or accident insurance; (B) the detailed basis on which such payments are to be made is specified in a written agreement with the employer, and employees and employers are equally represented in the administration of such fund together with such neutral persons as the representatives of the employers and the representatives of employees may agree upon and in the event of the employer and employee groups deadlock on the administration of such fund and there are no neutral persons empowered to break such deadlock, such agreement provides that the two groups shall agree on an impartial umpire to decide such dispute, or in event of their failure to agree within a reasonable length of time, an impartial umpire to decide such dispute shall, on petition of either group, be appointed by the district court of the United States for the district where the trust fund has its principal office, and shall also contain provisions for an annual audit of the trust fund, a statement of the results of which shall be available for inspection by interested persons at the principal office of the trust fund and at such other places as may be designated in such written agreement; and (C) such payments as are intended to be used for the purpose of providing pensions or annuities for employees are made to a separate trust which provides that the funds held therein cannot be used for any purpose other than paying such pensions or annuities; or (6) with respect to money or other thing of value paid by any employer to a trust fund established by such representative for the purpose of pooled vacation, holiday, severance or similar benefits, or defraying costs of apprenticeship or other training programs: *Provided,* That the requirements of clause (B) of the proviso to clause (5) of this subsection shall apply to such trust funds."

TITLE VI—MISCELLANEOUS PROVISIONS

Investigations
(29 U.S.C. 521)

Sec. 601. (a) The Secretary shall have power when he believes it necessary in order to determine whether any person has violated or is about to violate any provision of this Act (except title I or amendments made by this Act to other statutes) to make an investigation and in connection therewith he may enter such places and inspect such records and accounts and question such persons as he may deem necessary to enable him to determine the facts relative thereto. The Secretary may report to interested persons or officials concerning the facts required to be shown in any report required by this Act and concerning the reasons for failure or refusal to file such a report or any other matter which he deems to be appropriate as a result of such an investigation.

(b) For the purpose of any investigation provided for in this Act, the provisions of sections 9 and 10 (relating to the attendance of witnesses and the production of books, papers, and documents) of the Federal Trade Commission Act of September 16, 1914, as amended (15 U.S.C. 49, 50), are hereby made applicable to the jurisdiction, powers, and duties of the Secretary or any officers designated by him.

Extortionate Picketing
(29 U.S.C. 522)

Sec. 602. (a) It shall be unlawful to carry on picketing on or about the premises of any employer for the purpose of, or as part of any conspiracy or in furtherance of any plan or purpose for, the personal profit or enrichment of any individual (except a bona fide increase in wages or other employee benefits) by taking or obtaining any money or other thing of value from such employer against his will or with his consent.

(b) Any person who willfully violates this section shall be fined not more than $10,000 or imprisoned not more than twenty years, or both.

Retention of Rights Under Other Federal and State Laws
(29 U.S.C. 523)

SEC. 603. (a) Except as explicitly provided to the contrary, nothing in this Act shall reduce or limit the responsibilities of any labor organization or any officer, agent, shop steward, or other representative of a labor organization, or of any trust in which a labor organization is interested, under any other Federal law or under the laws of any State, and, except as explicitly provided to the contrary, nothing in this Act shall take away any right or bar any remedy to which members of a labor organization are entitled under such other Federal law or law of any State.

(b) Nothing contained in titles I, II, III, IV, V, or VI of this Act shall be construed to supersede or impair or otherwise affect the provisions of the Railway Labor Act, as amended, or any of the obligations, rights, benefits, privileges, or immunities of any carrier, employee, organization, representative, or person subject thereto; nor shall anything contained in said titles (except section 505) of this Act be construed to confer any rights, privileges, immunities, or defenses upon employers, or to impair or otherwise affect the rights of any person under the National Labor Relations Act, as amended.

Effect on State Laws
(29 U.S.C. 524)

SEC. 604. Nothing in this Act shall be construed to impair or diminish the authority of any State to enact and enforce general criminal laws with respect to robbery, bribery, extortion, embezzlement, grand larceny, burglary, arson, violation of narcotics laws, murder, rape, assault with intent to kill, or assault which inflicts grievous bodily injury, or conspiracy to commit any of such crimes.

Service of Process
(29 U.S.C. 525)

SEC. 605. For the purposes of this Act, service of summons, subpena, or other legal process of a court of the United States upon an officer or agent of a labor organization in his capacity as such shall constitute service upon the labor organization.

Administrative Procedure Act
(29 U.S.C. 526)

SEC. 606. The provisions of the Administrative Procedure Act shall be applicable to the issuance, amendment, or rescission of any rules or regulations, or any adjudication, authorized or required pursuant to the provisions of this Act.

Other Agencies and Departments
(29 U.S.C. 527)

SEC. 607. In order to avoid unnecessary expense and duplication of functions among Government agencies, the Secretary may make such arrangements or agreements for cooperation or mutual assistance in the performance of his functions under this Act and the functions of any such agency as he may find to be practicable and consistent with law. The Secretary may utilize the facilities or services of any department, agency, or establishment of the United States or of any State or political subdivision of a State, including the services of any of its employees, with the lawful consent of such department, agency, or establishment; and each department, agency, or establishment of the United

States is authorized and directed to cooperate with the Secretary and, to the extent permitted by law, to provide such information and facilities as he may request for his assistance in the performance of his functions under this Act. The Attorney General or his representative shall receive from the Secretary for appropriate action such evidence developed in the performance of his functions under this Act as may be found to warrant consideration for criminal prosecution under the provisions of this Act or other Federal law.

Criminal Contempt
(29 U.S.C. 528)

SEC. 608. No person shall be punished for any criminal contempt allegedly committed outside the immediate presence of the court in connection with any civil action prosecuted by the Secretary or any other person in any court of the United States under the provisions of this Act unless the facts constituting such criminal contempt are established by the verdict of the jury in a proceeding in the district court of the United States, which jury shall be chosen and empaneled in the manner prescribed by the law governing trial juries in criminal prosecutions in the district courts of the United States.

Prohibition on Certain Discipline by Labor Organization
(29 U.S.C. 529)

SEC. 609. It shall be unlawful for any labor organization, or any officer, agent, shop steward, or other representative of a labor organization, or any employee thereof to fine, suspend, expel, or otherwise discipline any of its members for exercising any right to which he is entitled under the provisions of this Act. The provisions of section 102 shall be applicable in the enforcement of this section.

Deprivation of Rights Under Act by Violence
(29 U.S.C. 530)

SEC. 610. It shall be unlawful for any person through the use of force or violence, or threat of the use of force or violence, to restrain, coerce, or intimidate, or attempt to restrain, coerce, or intimidate any member of a labor organization for the purpose of interfering with or preventing the exercise of any right to which he is entitled under the provisions of this Act. Any person who willfully violates this section shall be fined not more than $1,000 or imprisoned for not more than one year, or both.

Separability Provisions
(29 U.S.C. 531)

SEC. 611. If any provision of this Act, or the application of such provision to any person or circumstances, shall be held invalid, the remainder of this Act or the application of such provision to persons or circumstances other than those as to which it is held invalid, shall not be affected thereby.

TITLE VII—AMENDMENTS TO THE LABOR MANAGEMENT RELATIONS ACT, 1947, AS AMENDED

(The Title VII amendments to the Labor Management Relations Act, 1947, as amended, have been incorporated into the text of the latter act as presented above.)

APPENDIX II

President John F. Kennedy's Executive Order 10988 authorized collective bargaining in the federal service in 1962. President Richard M. Nixon replaced and superseded it with EO 11491, the text of which appears below.

EXECUTIVE ORDER 11491
LABOR-MANAGEMENT RELATIONS IN THE FEDERAL SERVICE

WHEREAS the public interest requires high standards of employee performance and the continual development and implementation of modern and progressive work practices to facilitate improved employee performance and efficiency; and

WHEREAS the well-being of employees and efficient administration of the Government are benefited by providing employees an opportunity to participate in the formulation and implementation of personnel policies and practices affecting the conditions of their employment; and

WHEREAS the participation of employees should be improved through the maintenance of constructive and cooperative relationships between labor organizations and management officials; and

WHEREAS subject to law and the paramount requirements of public service, effective labor-management relations within the Federal service require a clear statement of the respective rights and obligations of labor organizations and agency management:

NOW, THEREFORE, by virtue of the authority vested in me by the Constitution and statutes of the United States, including sections 3301 and 7301 of title 5 of the United States Code, and as President of the United States, I hereby direct that the following policies shall govern officers and agencies of the executive branch of the Government in all dealings with Federal employees and organizations representing such employees.

GENERAL PROVISIONS

SECTION 1. *Policy.* (a) Each employee of the executive branch of the Federal Government has the right, freely and without fear of penalty or reprisal, to form, join, and assist a labor organization or to refrain from any such activity, and each employee shall be protected in the exercise of this right. Except as otherwise expressly provided in this Order, the right to assist a labor organization extends to participation in the management of the organization and acting for the organization in the capacity of an organization representative, including presentation of its views to officials of the executive branch, the

761

Congress, or other appropriate authority. The head of each agency shall take the action required to assure that employees in the agency are apprised of their rights under this section and that no interference, restraint, coercion, or discrimination is practiced within his agency to encourage or discourage membership in a labor organization.

(b) Paragraph (a) of this section does not authorize participation in the management of a labor organization or acting as a representative of such an organization by a supervisor, except as provided in section 24 of this Order, or by an employee when the participation or activity would result in a conflict or apparent conflict of interest or otherwise be incompatible with law or with the official duties of the employee.

SEC. 2. *Definitions.*   When used in this Order, the term—

(a) "Agency" means an executive department, a Government corporation, and an independent establishment as defined in section 104 or title 5, United States Code, except the General Accounting Office;

(b) "Employee" means an employee of an agency and an employee of a nonappropriated fund instrumentality of the United States but does not include, for the purpose of formal or exclusive recognition or national consultation rights, a supervisor, except as provided in section 24 of this Order;

(c) "Supervisor" means an employee having authority, in the interest of an agency, to hire, transfer, suspend, lay off, recall, promote, discharge, assign, reward, or discipline other employees, or responsibly to direct them, or to evaluate their performance, or to adjust their grievances, or effectively to recommend such action, if in connection with the foregoing the exercise of authority is not of a merely routine or clerical nature, but requires the use of independent judgment;

(d) "Guard" means an employee assigned to enforce against employees and other persons rules to protect agency property or the safety of persons on agency premises, or to maintain law and order in areas or facilities under Government control;

(e) "Labor organization" means a lawful organization of any kind in which employees participate and which exists for the purpose, in whole or in part, of dealing with agencies concerning grievances, personnel policies and practices, or other matters affecting the working conditions of their employees; but does not include an organization which—

(1) consists of management officials or supervisors, except as provided in section 24 of this Order;

(2) asserts the right to strike against the Government of the United States or any agency thereof, or to assist or participate in such a strike, or imposes a duty or obligation to conduct, assist or participate in such a strike;

(3) advocates the overthrow of the constitutional form of government in the United States; or

(4) discriminates with regard to the terms or conditions of membership because of race, color, creed, sex, age, or national origin;

(f) "Agency management" means the agency head and all management officials, supervisors, and other representatives of management having authority to act for the agency on any matters relating to the implementation of the agency labor-management relations program established under this Order;

(g) "Council" means the Federal Labor Relations Council established by this Order;

(h) "Panel" means the Federal Service Impasses Panel established by this Order; and

(i) "Assistant Secretary" means the Assistant Secretary of Labor for Labor-Management Relations.

SEC. 3. *Application.* (a) This Order applies to all employees and agencies in the executive branch, except as provided in paragraphs (b), (c) and (d) of this section.

(b) This Order (except section 22) does not apply to—

(1) the Federal Bureau of Investigation;

(2) the Central Intelligence Agency;

(3) any other agency, or office, bureau, or entity within an agency, which has as a primary function intelligence, investigative, or security work, when the head of the agency determines, in his sole judgment, that the Order cannot be applied in a manner consistent with national security requirements and considerations; or

(4) any office, bureau or entity within an agency which has as a primary function investigation or audit of the conduct or work of officials or employees of the agency for the purpose of ensuring honesty and integrity in the discharge of their official duties, when the head of the agency determines, in his sole judgment, that the Order cannot be applied in a manner consistent with the internal security of the agency.

(c) The head of an agency may, in his sole judgment, suspend any provision of this Order (except section 22) with respect to any agency installation or activity located outside the United States, when he determines that this is necessary in the national interest, subject to the conditions he prescribes.

(d) Employees engaged in administering a labor-management relations law or this Order shall not be represented by a labor organization which also represents other groups of employees under the law or this Order, or which is affiliated directly or indirectly with an organization which represents such a group of employees.

ADMINISTRATION

SEC. 4. *Federal Labor Relations Council.* (a) There is hereby established the Federal Labor Relations Council, which consists of the Chairman of the Civil Service Commission, who shall be chairman of the Council, the Secretary of Labor, an official of the Executive Office of the President, and such other officials of the Executive branch as the President may designate from time to time. The Civil Service Commission shall provide services and staff assistance to the Council to the extent authorized by law.

(b) The Council shall administer and interpret this Order, decide major policy issues, prescribe regulations, and from time to time, report and make recommendations to the President.

(c) The Council may consider, subject to its regulations—

(1) appeals from decisions of the Assistant Secretary issued pursuant to section 6 of this Order;

(2) appeals on negotiability issues as provided in section 11(c) of this Order;

(3) exceptions to arbitration awards; and

(4) other matters it deems appropriate to assure the effectuation of the purposes of this Order.

SEC. 5. *Federal Service Impasses Panel.* (a) There is hereby established the Federal Service Impasses Panel as an agency within the Council. The Panel consists of at least three members appointed by the President, one of whom he designates as chairman. The Council shall provide the services and staff assistance needed by the Panel.

(b) The Panel may consider negotiation impasses as provided in section 17 of this Order and may take any action it considers necessary to settle an impasse.

(c) The Panel shall prescribe regulations needed to administer its function under this Order.

SEC. 6. *Assistant Secretary of Labor for Labor-Management Relations.* (a) The Assistant Secretary shall—

(1) decide questions as to the appropriate unit for the purpose of exclusive recognition and related issues submitted for his consideration;

(2) supervise elections to determine whether a labor organization is the choice of a majority of the employees in an appropriate unit as their exclusive representative, and certify the results;

(3) decide questions as to the eligibility of labor organizations for national consultation rights under criteria prescribed by the Council; and

(4) except as provided in section 19(d) of this Order, decide complaints of alleged unfair labor practices and alleged violations of the standards of conduct for labor organizations.

(b) In any matters arising under paragraph (a) of this section, the Assistant Secretary may require an agency or a labor organization to cease and desist from violations of this Order and require it to take such affirmative action as he considers appropriate to effectuate the policies of this Order.

(c) In performing the duties imposed on him by this section, the Assistant Secretary may request and use the services and assistance of employees of other agencies in accordance with section 1 of the Act of March 4, 1915, (38 Stat. 1084, as amended; 31 U.S.C. § 686).

(d) The Assistant Secretary shall prescribe regulations needed to administer his functions under this Order.

(e) If any matters arising under paragraph (a) of this section involve the Department of Labor, the duties of the Assistant Secretary described in paragraphs (a) and (b) of this section shall be performed by a member of the Civil Service Commission designated by the Chairman of the Commission.

RECOGNITION

SEC. 7. *Recognition in General.* (a) An agency shall accord exclusive recognition or national consultation rights at the request of a labor organization which meets the requirements for the recognition or consultation rights under this Order.

(b) A labor organization seeking recognition shall submit to the agency a roster of its officers and representatives, a copy of its constitution and by-laws, and a statement of its objectives.

(c) When recognition of a labor organization has been accorded, the recognition continues as long as the organization continues to meet the requirements of this Order applicable to that recognition, except that this section does not require an election to determine whether an organization should become, or continue to be recognized as, exclusive representative of the employees in any unit or subdivision thereof within 12 months after a prior valid election with respect to such unit.

(d) Recognition, in whatever form accorded, does not—

(1) preclude an employee, regardless of whether he is a member of a labor organization, from bringing matters of personal concern to the attention of appropriate officials under applicable law, rule, regulation, or established agency policy; or from choosing his own representative in a grievance or appellate action;

(2) preclude or restrict consultations and dealings between an agency and a veterans organization with respect to matters of particular interest to employees with veterans preference; or

(3) preclude an agency from consulting or dealing with a religious, social, fraternal, or other lawful association, not qualified as a labor organization, with respect to matters or policies which involve individual members of the association or are of particular applicability to it or its members. Consultations and dealings under subparagraph (3) of this paragraph shall be so limited that they do not assume the character of formal consultation on matters of general employee-management policy, except as provided in paragraph (e) of this section, or extend to areas where recognition of the interests of one employee group may result in discrimination against or injury to the interests of other employees.

(e) An agency shall establish a system for intra-management communication and consultation with its supervisors or associations of supervisors. These communications and consultations shall have as their purposes the improvement of agency operations, the improvement of working conditions of supervisors, the exchange of information, the improvement of managerial effectiveness, and the establishment of policies that best serve the public interest in accomplishing the mission of the agency.

(f) Informal recognition shall not be accorded after the date of this Order.

SEC. 8. *Formal Recognition.* (a) Formal recognition, including formal recognition at the national level, shall not be accorded after the date of this Order.

(b) An agency shall continue any formal recognition, including formal recognition at the national level, accorded a labor organization before the date of this Order until—

(1) the labor organization ceases to be eligible under this Order for formal recognition so accorded;

(2) a labor organization is accorded exclusive recognition as representative of employees in the unit to which the formal recognition applies; or

(3) the formal recognition is terminated under regulations prescribed by the Federal Labor Relations Council.

(c) When a labor organization holds formal recognition, it is the representative of its members in a unit as defined by the agency when recognition was accorded. The agency, through appropriate officials, shall consult with representatives of the organization from time to time in the formulation and implementation of personnel policies and practices, and matters affecting working conditions that affect members of the organization in the unit to which the formal recognition applies. The organization is entitled from time to time to raise such matters for discussion with appropriate officials and at all times to present its views thereon in writing. The agency is not required to consult with the labor organization on any matter on which it would not be required to meet and confer if the labor organization were entitled to exclusive recognition.

SEC. 9. *National Consultation Rights.* (a) An agency shall accord national consultation rights to a labor organization which qualifies under criteria established by the Federal Labor Relations Council as the representative of a substantial number of employees of the agency. National consultation rights shall not be accorded for any unit where a labor organization already holds exclusive recognition at the national level for that unit. The granting of national consultation rights does not preclude an agency from appropriate dealings at the national level with other organizations on matters affecting their members. An agency shall terminate national consultation rights when the labor organization ceases to qualify under the established criteria.

(b) When a labor organization has been accorded national consultation rights, the agency, through appropriate officials, shall notify representatives of the organization of proposed substantive changes in personnel policies that affect employees it represents and provide an opportunity for the organization to comment on the proposed changes. The labor organization may suggest changes in the agency's personnel policies and have its views carefully considered. It may confer in person at reasonable times, on request, with appropriate officials on personnel policy matters, and at all times present its views thereon in writing. An agency is not required to consult with a labor organization on any matter on which it would not be required to meet and confer if the organization were entitled to exclusive recognition.

(c) Questions as to the eligibility of labor organizations for national consultation rights may be referred to the Assistant Secretary for decision.

SEC. 10. *Exclusive Recognition.* (a) An agency shall accord exclusive recognition to a labor organization when the organization has been selected, in a secret ballot election, by a majority of the employees in an appropriate unit as their representative.

(b) A unit may be established on a plant or installation, craft, functional, or other basis which will ensure a clear and identifiable community of interest among the employees concerned and will promote effective dealings and efficiency of agency operations. A unit shall not be established solely on the basis of the extent to which employees in the proposed unit have organized, nor shall a unit be established if it includes—

(1) any management official or supervisor, except as provided in section 24;

(2) an employee engaged in Federal personnel work in other than a purely clerical capacity;

(3) any guard together with other employees; or

(4) both professional and nonprofessional employees, unless a majority of the professional employees vote for inclusion in the unit.

Questions as to the appropriate unit and related issues may be referred to the Assistant Secretary for decision.

(c) An agency shall not accord exclusive recognition to a labor organization as the representative of employees in a unit of guards if the organization admits to membership, or is affiliated directly or indirectly with an organization which admits to membership, employees other than guards.

(d) All elections shall be conducted under the supervision of the Assistant Secretary, or persons designated by him, and shall be by secret ballot. Each employee eligible to vote shall be provided the opportunity to choose the labor organization he wishes to represent him, from among those on the ballot, or "no union." Elections may be held to determine whether—

(1) a labor organization should be recognized as the exclusive representative of employees in a unit;

(2) a labor organization should replace another labor organization as the exclusive representative; or

(3) a labor organization should cease to be the exclusive representative.

(e) When a labor organization has been accorded exclusive recognition, it is the exclusive representative of employees in the unit and is entitled to act for and to negotiate agreements covering all employees in the unit. It is responsible for representing the interests of all employees in the unit without discrimination and without regard to labor organization membership. The labor organization shall be given the opportunity to be represented at formal discussions between management and employees or employee representatives concerning grievances, personnel policies and practices, or other matters affecting general working conditions of employees in the unit.

Agreements

Sec. 11. *Negotiation of Agreements.* (a) An agency and a labor organization that has been accorded exclusive recognition, through appropriate representatives, shall meet at reasonable times and confer in good faith with respect to personnel policies and practices and matters affecting working conditions, so far as may be appropriate under applicable laws and regulations, including policies set forth in the Federal Personnel Manual, published agency policies and regulations, a national or other controlling agreement at a higher level in the agency, and this Order. They may negotiate an agreement, or any question arising thereunder; determine appropriate techniques, consistent with section 17 of this Order, to assist in such negotiation; and execute a written agreement or memorandum of understanding.

(b) In prescribing regulations relating to personnel policies and practices and working conditions, an agency shall have due regard for the obligation imposed by paragraph (a) of this section. However, the obligation to meet and confer does not include matters with respect to the mission of an agency; its budget; its organization; the number of employees; and the numbers, types, and grades of positions or employees assigned to an organizational unit, work project or tour of duty; the technology of performing its work; or its internal security practices. This does not preclude the parties from negotiating agreements providing appropriate arrangements for employees adversely affected by the impact of realignment of work forces or technological change.

(c) If, in connection with negotiations, an issue develops as to whether a proposal is contrary to law, regulation, controlling agreement, or this Order and therefore not negotiable, it shall be resolved as follows:

(1) An issue which involves interpretation of a controlling agreement at a higher agency level is resolved under the procedures of the controlling agreement, or, if none, under agency regulations;

(2) An issue other than as described in subparagraph (1) of this paragraph

which arises at a local level may be referred by either party to the head of the agency for determination;

(3) An agency head's determination as to the interpretation of the agency's regulations with respect to a proposal is final;

(4) A labor organization may appeal to the Council for a decision when—

(i) it disagrees with an agency head's determination that a proposal would violate applicable law, regulation of appropriate authority outside the agency, or this Order, or

(ii) it believes that an agency's regulations, as interpreted by the agency head, violate applicable law, regulation of appropriate authority outside the agency, or this Order.

Sec. 12. *Basic Provisions of Agreements.* Each agreement between an agency and a labor organization is subject to the following requirements—

(a) in the administration of all matters covered by the agreement, officials and employees are governed by existing or future laws and the regulations of appropriate authorities, including policies set forth in the Federal Personnel Manual; by published agency policies and regulations in existence at the time the agreement was approved; and by subsequently published agency policies and regulations required by law or by the regulations of appropriate authorities, or authorized by the terms of a controlling agreement at a higher agency level;

(b) management officials of the agency retain the right, in accordance with applicable laws and regulations—

(1) to direct employees of the agency;

(2) to hire, promote, transfer, assign, and retain employees in positions within the agency, and to suspend, demote, discharge, or take other disciplinary action against employees;

(3) to relieve employees from duties because of lack of work or for other legitimate reasons;

(4) to maintain the efficiency of the Government operations entrusted to them;

(5) to determine the methods, means, and personnel by which such operations are to be conducted; and

(6) to take whatever actions may be necessary to carry out the mission of the agency in situations of emergency; and

(c) nothing in the agreement shall require an employee to become or to remain a member of a labor organization, or to pay money to the organization except pursuant to a voluntary, written authorization by a member for the payment of dues through payroll deductions.

The requirements of this section shall be expressly stated in the initial or basic agreement and apply to all supplemental, implementing, subsidiary, or informal agreements between the agency and the organization.

Sec. 13. *Grievance procedures.* An agreement with a labor organization which is the exclusive representative of employees in an appropriate unit may provide procedures, applicable only to employees in the unit, for the consideration of employee grievances and of disputes over the interpretation and application of agreements. The procedure for consideration of employee grievances shall meet the requirements for negotiated grievance procedures established by the Civil Service Commission. A negotiated employee grievance procedure which conforms to this section, to applicable laws, and to regulations of the Civil Service Commission and the agency is the exclusive procedure available to employees in the unit when the agreement so provides.

SEC. 14. *Arbitration of Grievances.* (a) Negotiated procedures may provide for the arbitration of employee grievances and of disputes over the interpretation or application of existing agreements. Negotiated procedures may not extend arbitration to changes or proposed changes in agreements or agency policy. Such procedures shall provide for the invoking of arbitration only with the approval of the labor organization that has exclusive recognition and, in the case of an employee grievance, only with the approval of the employee. The costs of the arbitrator shall be shared equally by the parties.

(b) Either party may file exceptions to an arbitrator's award with the Council, under regulations prescribed by the Council.

SEC. 15. *Approval of Agreements.* An agreement with a labor organization as the exclusive representative of employees in a unit is subject to the approval of the head of the agency or an official designated by him. An agreement shall be approved if it conforms to applicable laws, existing published agency policies and regulations (unless the agency has granted an exception to a policy or regulation) and regulations of other appropriate authorities. A local agreement subject to a national or other controlling agreement at a higher level shall be approved under the procedures of the controlling agreement, or, if none, under agency regulations.

NEGOTIATION DISPUTES AND IMPASSES

SEC. 16. *Negotiation Disputes.* The Federal Mediation and Conciliation Service shall provide services and assistance to Federal agencies and labor organizations in the resolution of negotiation disputes. The Service shall determine under what circumstances and in what manner it shall proffer its services.

SEC. 17. *Negotiation Impasses.* When voluntary arrangements, including the services of the Federal Mediation and Conciliation Service or other third-party mediation, fail to resolve a negotiation impasse, either party may request the Federal Service Impasses Panel to consider the matter. The Panel, in its discretion and under the regulations it prescribes, may consider the matter and may recommend procedures to the parties for the resolution of the impasse or may settle the impasse by appropriate action. Arbitration or third-party fact finding with recommendations to assist in the resolution of an impasse may be used by the parties only when authorized or directed by the Panel.

CONDUCT OF LABOR ORGANIZATIONS AND MANAGEMENT

SEC. 18. *Standards of Conduct for Labor Organizations.* (a) An agency shall accord recognition only to a labor organization that is free from corrupt influences and influences oppposed to basic democratic principles. Except as provided in paragraph (b) of this section, an organization is not required to prove that it has the required freedom when it is subject to governing requirements adopted by the organization or by a national or international labor organization or federation of labor organizations with which it is affiliated or in which it participates, containing explicit and detailed provisions to which it subscribes calling for—

(1) the maintenance of democratic procedures and practices, including provisions for periodic elections to be conducted subject to recognized safeguards and provisions defining and securing the right of individual members to participation in the affairs of the organization, to fair and equal treatment under the governing rules of the organization, and to fair process in disciplinary proceedings;

(2) the exclusion from office in the organization of persons affiliated with Communist or other totalitarian movements and persons identified with corrupt influences;

(3) the prohibition of business or financial interests on the part of organization officers and agents which conflict with their duty to the organization and its members; and

(4) the maintenance of fiscal integrity in the conduct of the affairs of the organization, including provision for accounting and financial controls and regular financial reports or summaries to be made available to members.

(b) Notwithstanding the fact that a labor organization has adopted or subscribed to standards of conduct as provided in paragraph (a) of this section, the organization is required to furnish evidence of its freedom from corrupt influences or influences opposed to basic democratic principles when there is reasonable cause to believe that—

(1) the organization has been suspended or expelled from or is subject to other sanction by a parent labor organization or federation of organizations with which it had been affiliated because it has demonstrated an unwillingness or inability to comply with governing requirements comparable in purpose to those required by paragraph (a) of this section; or

(2) the organization is in fact subject to influences that would preclude recognition under this Order.

(c) A labor organization which has or seeks recognition as a representative of employees under this Order shall file financial and other reports, provide for bonding of officials and employees of the organization, and comply with trusteeship and election standards.

(d) The Assistant Secretary shall prescribe the regulations needed to effectuate this section. These regulations shall conform generally to the principles applied to unions in the private sector. Complaints of violations of this section shall be filed with the Assistant Secretary.

SEC. 19. *Unfair Labor Practices.* (a) Agency management shall not—

(1) interfere with, restrain, or coerce an employee in the exercise of the rights assured by this Order;

(2) encourage or discourage membership in a labor organization by discrimination in regard to hiring, tenure, promotion, or other conditions of employment;

(3) sponsor, control, or otherwise assist a labor organization, except that an agency may furnish customary and routine services and facilities under section 23 of this Order when consistent with the best interests of the agency, its employees, and the organization, and when the services and facilities are furnished, if requested, on an impartial basis to organizations having equivalent status;

(4) discipline or otherwise discriminate against an employee because he has filed a complaint or given testimony under this Order;

(5) refuse to accord appropriate recognition to a labor organization qualified for such recognition; or

(6) refuse to consult, confer, or negotiate with a labor organization as required by this Order.

(b) A labor organization shall not—

(1) interfere with, restrain, or coerce an employee in the exercise of his rights assured by this Order;

(2) attempt to induce agency management to coerce an employee in the exercise of his rights under this Order;

(3) coerce, attempt to coerce, or discipline, fine, or take other economic sanction against a member of the organization as punishment or reprisal for, or for the purpose of hindering or impeding his work performance, his productivity, or the discharge of his duties owed as an officer or employee of the United States;

(4) call or engage in a strike, work stoppage, or slowdown; picket an agency in a labor-management dispute; or condone any such activity by failing to take affirmative action to prevent or stop it;

(5) discriminate against an employee with regard to the terms or conditions of membership because of race, color, creed, sex, age, or national origin; or

(6) refuse to consult, confer, or negotiate with an agency as required by this Order.

(c) A labor organization which is accorded exclusive recognition shall not deny membership to any employee in the appropriate unit except for failure to meet reasonable occupational standards uniformly required for admission, or for failure to tender initiation fees and dues uniformly required as a condition of acquiring and retaining membership. This paragraph does not preclude a labor organization from enforcing discipline in accordance with procedures under its constitution or by-laws which conform to the requirements of this Order.

(d) When the issue in a complaint of an alleged violation of paragraph (a) (1), (2), or (4) of this section is subject to an established grievance or appeals procedure, that procedure is the exclusive procedure for resolving the complaint. All other complaints of alleged violations of this section initiated by an employee, an agency, or a labor organization, that connot be resolved by the parties, shall be filed with the Assistant Secretary.

MISCELLANEOUS PROVISIONS

SEC. 20 *Use of Official Time.* Solicitation of membership or dues, and other internal business of a labor organization, shall be conducted during the non-duty hours of the employees concerned. Employees who represent a recognized labor organization shall not be on official time when negotiating an agreement with agency management.

SEC. 21. *Allotment of Dues.* (a) When a labor organization holds formal or exclusive recognition, and the agency and the organization agree in writing to this course of action, an agency may deduct the regular and periodic dues of the organization from the pay of members of the organization in the unit of recognition who make a voluntary allotment for that purpose, and shall recover the costs of making the deductions. Such an allotment is subject to the regulations of the Civil Service Commission, which shall include provision for the employee to revoke his authorization at stated six-month intervals. Such an allotment terminates when—

(1) the dues withholding agreement between the agency and the labor organization is terminated or ceases to be applicable to the employee; or

(2) the employee has been suspended or expelled from the labor organization.

(b) An agency may deduct the regular and periodic dues of an association of management officials or supervisors from the pay of members of the association who make a voluntary allotment for that purpose, and shall recover the costs of making the deductions, when the agency and the association agree in writing to this course of action. Such an allotment is subject to the regulations of the Civil Service Commission.

SEC. 22. *Adverse Action Appeals.*   The head of each agency, in accordance with the provisions of this Order and regulations prescribed by the Civil Service Commission, shall extend to all employees in the competitive civil service rights identical in adverse action cases to those provided preference eligibles under sections 7511–7512 of title 5 of the United States Code. Each employee in the competitive service shall have the right to appeal to the Civil Service Commission from an adverse decision of the administrative officer so acting, such appeal to be processed in an identical manner to that provided for appeals under section 7701 of title 5 of the United States Code. Any recommendation by the Civil Service Commission submitted to the head of an agency on the basis of an appeal by an employee in the competitive service shall be complied with by the head of the agency.

SEC. 23. *Agency Implementation.*   No later than April 1, 1970, each agency shall issue appropriate policies and regulations consistent with this Order for its implementation. This includes but is not limited to a clear statement of the rights of its employees under this Order; procedures with respect to recognition of labor organizations, determination of appropriate units, consultation and negotiation with labor organizations, approval of agreements, mediation, and impasse resolution; policies with respect to the use of agency facilities by labor organizations; and policies and practices regarding consultation with other organizations and associations and individual employees. Insofar as practicable, agencies shall consult with representatives of labor organizations in the formulation of these policies and regulations, other than those for the implementation of section 7(e) of this Order.

SEC. 24. *Savings Clauses.*   (a) This Order does not preclude—

(1) the renewal or continuation of a lawful agreement between an agency and a representative of its employees entered into before the effective date of Executive Order No. 10988 (January 17, 1962); or

(2) the renewal, continuation, or initial according of recognition for units of management officials or supervisors represented by labor organizations which historically or traditionally represent the management officials or supervisors in private industry and which hold exclusive recognition for units of such officials or supervisors in any agency on the date of this Order.

(b) All grants of informal recognition under Executive Order No. 10988 terminate on July 1, 1970.

(c) All grants of formal recognition under Executive Order No. 10988 terminate under regulations which the Federal Labor Relations Council shall issue before October 1, 1970.

(d) By not later than December 31, 1970, all supervisors shall be excluded from units of formal and exclusive recognition and from coverage by negotiated agreements, except as provided in paragraph (a) of this section.

SEC. 25. *Guidance, Training, Review and Information.* (a) The Civil Service Commission shall establish and maintain a program for the guidance of agencies on labor-management relations in the Federal service; provide technical advice and information to agencies; assist in the development of programs for training agency personnel and management officials in labor-management relations; continuously review the operation of the Federal labor-management relations program to assist in assuring adherence to its provisions and merit system requirements; and, from time to time, report to the Council on the state of the program with any recommendations for its improvement.

(b) The Department of Labor and the Civil Service Commission shall develop programs for the collection and dissemination of information appropriate to the needs of agencies, organizations and the public.

SEC. 26. *Effective Date.* This Order is effective on January 1, 1970 except sections 7(f) and 8 which are effective immediately. Effective January 1, 1970, Executive Order No. 10988 and the President's Memorandum of May 21, 1963, entitled Standards of Conduct for Employee Organizations and Code of Fair Labor Practices, are revoked.

(Signed) Richard Nixon

THE WHITE HOUSE,
October 29, 1969.
[F.R. Doc. 69–13052; Filed, Oct. 29, 1969; 1:49 P.M.]

Indexes

INDEX OF AUTHORITIES CITED

INDEX